James B. Cunnam III
Christmas 2000

D0850422

TERRY SANFORD

TERRY SANFORD

Politics, Progress, and Outrageous Ambitions

Howard E. Covington Jr. and Marion A. Ellis

DUKE UNIVERSITY PRESS   Durham and London, 1999

© 1999 Duke University Press
All rights reserved
Printed in the United States of America
on acid-free paper ♾
Typeset in Quadraat by Tseng
Information Systems, Inc.
Library of Congress Cataloging-
in-Publication Data appear on the
last printed page of this book.

Contents

Foreword

DAVID GERGEN

WHAT MAKES A GREAT LEADER? Examining the lives of American presidents, Henry Adams once observed that "he must have a helm to grasp, a course to steer, a port to seek." Throughout a half century of service to his beloved state of North Carolina, Terry Sanford had all of these—and by the time of his death in 1998 he had brought countless numbers of his fellow citizens within sight of port.

Terry never had any trouble finding a helm. He was a born leader and responsibilities naturally flowed in his direction. From his teenage years on, others sought him out to run for office, to seek the governorship, to take charge of a major university, to gain a place in the U.S. Senate, and to lend his time and imagination to innumerable projects that would strengthen civic life. He was a pre-eminent member of the World War II generation that rebuilt the country in the closing half of the twentieth century.

What truly distinguished Terry Sanford, however, was not just the number of posts he held, rather it was the unquenchable spirit that he brought to every one of them. In his soul he believed that people could shape their own futures, that men and women weren't just flotsam and jetsam floating on the tides of history but rather could choose their own destiny. Even toward the end, as Howard Covington and Marion Ellis write in this warm, engaging story of his life, Terry was in character. When doctors told him cancer would take his life within six months, he cheerfully told the press, "They said it was inoperable, but they didn't say it was incurable." That was one of the few campaigns he ever lost.

His was a moral leadership. He never thought of himself as perfect, but he thought that people working together could create a more perfect world. Nowhere did Terry put that idea to work with more imagination and courage than in advancing civil rights. Long before almost every other political figure in the South, he insisted that blacks, women, and the dispossessed should have an honorable seat at the table, too. It wasn't a popular stand—indeed, he suffered at the polls—yet he never flinched. Ultimately, he was vindicated by the enormous progress that liberation brought to his own people, white and black alike.

Each of us who was touched by Terry Sanford has a story to tell. I was in college when he was in the governor's chair, and one of his prized assistants, Joel Fleishman, came to campus to recruit interns. Those were the years when John F. Kennedy was firing up the idealism of young people nationwide, and a young governor of North Carolina was electrifying the native sons and daughters in much the same way. I signed up on the Sanford team and was promptly assigned to the Department of Commerce in Raleigh, where I was asked to write a market report for a company that made retreads for car tires and was thinking of settling in the state. My boss ordered me to visit a couple of existing companies and count how many tires they had in their lots. After a boiling day on a company lot in Cary, carefully counting a gazillion tires, I called Joel Fleishman to ask if there might be room for a restless intern on a new commission the governor was creating, the North Carolina Good Neighbor Council. Joel gave his blessing, and I was off to one of the most satisfying experiences in public service I have ever been privileged to enjoy.

At that time, David Coltrane was, for the most part, the entire Council. Terry had persuaded him to serve as chairman, and when I joined him as an intern he had only a bare office and a secretary. Coltrane was a no-nonsense fellow who had once been a farmer but went on to serve in several state posts, notably as budget director. For most of his sixty-plus years he had been a conservative Democrat who accepted segregation as a southern way of life. But he had a heart of 14-karat gold, and Terry helped to convince him that segregation was wrong and had to end. Later, because Coltrane carried so much weight among local townsfolk, Terry wanted him to run the statewide Council.

The governor was a shrewd judge of people, and in Coltrane he once again found just the right person for the job. With demonstrators engaged in sit-ins from Greensboro to Greenville and a murderous look coming into the eyes of local toughs, David's job was to criss-cross the state, carrying the governor's message and setting up local good neighbor councils that would bring together leading whites and blacks. Ostensibly, the councils were to focus on jobs and education for black citizens, but the more immediate purpose was to keep racial peace until changes could come. I spent three summers with David, often traveling with him to little places I never knew existed. "Driving Mr. Dave," as I recall it these days.

What I saw in those early 1960s was not only the effectiveness of a convert like Coltrane, whose memory I still cherish, but the good that a singular political leader like Terry Sanford can do when he holds the highest office in the state and appeals to the best instincts of his people. Despite a sizable presence of the Klan—its North Carolina membership swelled to the largest in the South in the mid-1960s—North Carolina mostly kept the peace. The local councils turned confrontation into conciliation. Best of all, the state began to turn the corner, heading into a new day of racial liberation. That was one of Terry's greatest gifts to North Carolina and to the South. As much as the coming of technology and dynamos like the Research Triangle, the civil rights era was a springboard toward the economic and social advances that transformed the state. Putting an end to the separation between black and white was not only the right thing to do but also broke down the separation between the South and the rest of the country. By law he could serve only a single, four-year term, but in that brief moment a Harvard survey found that Sanford had earned his way into history as one of the ten best governors of the century.

Joel Fleishman, who assisted Terry Sanford in so many ways through life and now has his own army of admirers, put it well at Terry's funeral in Duke Chapel. His dear friend, he said, was "a great-spirited, great-souled man, a man of passion, a man with a conscience that had real bite, a man of loyalty. But most of all Terry Sanford was a creative genius, but a thoroughly practical one who transformed everything he touched into something finer, better, worthier, and more useful to the world. If I had to describe him with a single phrase, it would be the 'great transformer.' " That phrase rang true with everyone who has studied leadership and knows the distinction that the scholar James MacGregor Burns draws between typical politicians— the "transactive"—and those rare sorts, the "transformational."

Instinctively, Sanford knew something else about leaders: that the best are teachers. A century and a half ago, John Stuart Mill defined leadership in a democracy as "a rostra or teacher's chair for instructing and impelling the public mind." In our own land, James Madison argued that in a democracy the role of the leader is "to refine and enlarge the public views." Soon after he was inaugurated, Franklin Roosevelt declared that his was pre-eminently an office of moral leadership, and that one entrusted with high office must clearly define for people the moral issues of their time, as Jefferson defined freedom in the Declaration and Lincoln defined a new birth of freedom at Gettysburg.

Sanford loved to teach, whether in the governor's chair or in the classrooms at Duke. As proud as he was in his accomplishments as president of the university, which he propelled into the highest ranks of the nation, one had a sense as he grew older that nothing gave him more pleasure than talking with undergraduates about their dreams. He might look solemn for a moment, but as soon as a student spoke to him his eyes twinkled, a dimply smile lit up his face, and he was off and running in conversation.

Where does a man get these values? In his case, they sprang first from North Carolina clay, the small town, the loving family. And then from people and challenges along the way. I was among those who crowded his doorstep to pay final tribute as he was dying. Over coffee at his home, his thoughts turned time and again to his youth and experiences in World War II. He talked of his roots in a rural town and his continuing pride in having become an Eagle Scout. "That probably saved my life in the war," he said. "Boys who had been scouts or had been in the CCC (the Civilian Conservation Corps of Franklin Roosevelt) knew how to look after themselves in the woods."

As with many of this century's leaders—Harry Truman was one, John Kennedy another, George Bush still another—Sanford discovered his own personal bravery in combat. He had to talk his way into uniform ("they rejected me the first time because of flat feet") and wound up a paratrooper. He jumped into southern France, survived the horrendous winter of 1944–45, fought in the Battle of the Bulge, and came home a decorated hero. "We become brave by doing brave acts," Aristotle wrote, and so it was with Sanford.

There was another strong, equally important influence in his life, and that was his wife, Margaret Rose, and their two children. Theirs was an admirable partnership, as anyone could tell who came to know them. In my last visit with him, she was suffering from a fall, and it was inspiring to watch how each tried to comfort the other. If Harvard were to take another survey, Margaret Rose Sanford would surely take her place as one of the best First Ladies of the century.

Howard Covington asked me what kind of president Terry Sanford would have made. We'll never know for certain, of course; his heart failed him in his one serious attempt at that office and he never had a chance to run the gamut of primaries. I imagine he would have been a crackerjack. He had old-fashioned values but a progressive spirit, a combination that would have held the country together even as he spurred us forward toward the ideals of the Declaration. Certainly, it would have been an adventure worth taking. Yet, even if great men are often the ones who never make it to the White House, as Lord Bryce told us years ago, we should not be saddened that Terry didn't. He had a very full life and would have been the first to say that his cup always ranneth over. As for us, we can be grateful that so many of us tasted its sweetness.

The historian Oswald Spengler has written that the first task of a statesman is to make himself somebody. The "second—less obvious, but harder and greater in its ultimate effect—is to create a tradition, to bring on others so that one's work may be continued with one's own pulse and spirit, to release a current of like activity that does not need the original leader to maintain it in form." It is this higher form of statesmanship that attracts talent from all quarters, imbues those successors with that same vision, and then creates a tradition of service and striving in others.

Gathering in Duke Chapel for the final farewell, one sensed among the throng how many people—women and men, blacks and whites, the lowly and the elite, activists and scholars—had become part of a tradition created by Terry Sanford. There in the chapel and out across the state and nation, the thousands who learned to follow him now seek his same vision. In the end, he had a firm grasp of the helm; he steered a true course and, because of him, all of us are closer to port.

Acknowledgments

❈

A DUKE UNIVERSITY SENIOR midway through a semester in Terry Sanford's course on creativity in state government was asked to explain what he and his fellow students were really studying. Without hesitation, the young man replied, "I'm studying him."

Indeed, during the course of his more than forty years in public life, Sanford had seen more, done more, and appeared in public print more than any of his contemporaries. He had been a World War II paratrooper, lawyer and magistrate, state legislator, governor, presidential candidate, university president, and U.S. Senator. He had written four books on topics ranging from the presidential nominating process to aging, and he was working on a novel when he died.

He could have been describing himself when he characterized the vision of Duke's early leaders as "outrageous ambitions." Rather than honor tradition and wait for his "time" to run for governor, he broke in line and won a historic race in 1960. A decade later, when college administrators were huddled in "war rooms" to defend their campuses against student protest, Sanford walked into crowds of students and talked with earnest young people who believed they could change the world. He carried some of these same new voters with him into two presidential campaigns, an ambition for national office that most of his old friends never really understood. And he won election to the U.S. Senate at an age when his contemporaries were shifting comfortably into retirement.

Outrageous ambitions. That was why the authors approached Sanford late in 1992 and asked if he would cooperate in the writing of this biography. He considered the request and agreed, with two conditions: that all material gathered in the course of the research be deposited at Duke University and that he be permitted to read the manuscript for factual errors.

Sanford offered complete assistance. He provided unlimited access to personal files, journals, scrapbooks, and unpublished manuscripts as well as a vast collection of material archived at Duke University and the Southern Historical Collection at the University of North Carolina Library at Chapel Hill. Dr. William King, the Duke University archivist, and David Moltke-Hansen and Tim Cagle of the Southern Historical Collection provided valuable assistance in the use of these papers, some of which had never been inventoried.

From January 1993 until as late as three weeks before his death in April 1998, Sanford made himself available for interviews and questions. As a writer himself, he appreciated the detail and cadence of a good story, and he enhanced accounts of his experiences with attention to the sound and feel of life. He responded to every question, although some he answered more candidly than others. He was most guarded in talking about life-shaping events—his experiences in combat, his grief over the death of a president, and personal disappointments—though he never simply refused to comment. But revealing personal fears and emotions was something he just did not do.

In December 1997, just prior to the diagnosis of his illness, Sanford reviewed all but the final three chapters of the manuscript. He offered a few additions and questioned certain dates and spellings of names. He was uncomfortable with references to his occasional use of alcohol, just as he was when he was governor and newspapers reported that guests might enjoy a drink in the private quarters of the governor's mansion. He noted sections that might prove awkward for him, but he made no request of the authors to change a word.

The writers found a man with common human foibles. His vanity was such that he carried his eyeglasses in his coat pocket even when he could not make out a face in a crowd. He became so accustomed to traveling with an entourage that in his later years he wanted a companion along even when out on a simple errand. He could rationalize defeat into victory and possessed a certain stubbornness that on occasion left him on the embarrassing side of losing business deals and political contests. He was a man of unfailing devotion to friends and political allies, sometimes past believing. Loyalty was expected in return, and if it wasn't forthcoming, Sanford did not forget.

Some portions of this book are told through Sanford's words, found in the journal he kept during his years in the Senate and in the early months of his years at Duke. Some of his reflections on his governorship are taken from an unpublished manuscript that he began writing as his term came to a close. Portions of that manuscript also became part of his book But What About the People? The authors made liberal use of Sanford's memoirs, particularly when these offered the insight into people and events that Sanford himself was reluctant to talk about. Thus, in a sense, this is Sanford's story, but it also is the authors' story of Terry Sanford and the transition of a state during a difficult period in the Southern experience. Sanford was a member of what one historian described as the last generation of the Civil War. He lived through a social revolution and played a major role in its outcome.

In addition, more than seventy-five persons consented to be interviewed to help the authors understand that relationship. The authors drew on first-person accounts found in the oral history collections at Duke, the University of North Carolina Library, the John F. Kennedy Library, and the Lyndon B. Johnson Library. Early support for this book came from Dr. and Mrs. James Semans of Durham, and the authors are indebted to the Mary Duke Biddle Foundation, which provided an initial research grant. Additional underwriting was provided by J. B. Fuqua Foundation Inc., Felix Harvey Foundation, Harry L. Dalton Foundation Inc., NationsBank, J. B. Pritzker, Walter Davis, Frank Kenan, Charles Sanders, Julia Morton, Hugh Morton, John Hoving, Jennifer Hillman, Wallace Hyde, Anthony Harrington, John L. Atkins III, Robert L. Jones, SEHED II Ltd., and Tom Drew. Funding for the project was supervised by MDC Inc., a nonprofit agency that traces its lineage to the North Carolina Fund. George Autry and the MDC staff were patient and understanding throughout and the authors appreciate their support. The authors also appreciate the comments on the manuscript provided by John Ehle and Eli Evans, two writers of accomplishment, who reviewed early drafts and made suggestions.

The visual story of Terry Sanford that accompanies the text was enhanced greatly by the generosity of Hugh Morton of Grandfather Mountain, whose camera has captured more of the life and times of North Carolina than any other's. He searched his considerable collection on behalf of this book to recover some photographs that have never before been published.

If Sanford had had his way, there would have been more pictures for Morton's archive, for Sanford fully expected to equal his mother's one hundred years. He faced his last challenge with uncommon optimism and determination. A few weeks before his death, he pulled out his ubiquitous legal pad and listed the things he planned to do when he got well. At the top of the list was the fulfillment of his vision for a $100 million performing arts center for North Carolina that would equal New York's Lincoln Center and Washington's Kennedy Center.

As his strength faded, he encouraged others to work all the harder. Indeed, he was a man of outrageous ambitions.

CHAPTER ONE

Double Moons over Laurinburg

THE THREE SIMPLE FRAME HOUSES standing side by side along Caledonia Road on the eastern edge of tiny Laurinburg, North Carolina, had once been the classrooms and dormitory of Laurinburg High School. A private institution, the school was presided over for twenty-one years by William Graham Quackenbush, an orphaned and crippled Virginian who had opened the doors to as many as a hundred students a little more than a dozen years after the end of the Civil War and taught them Latin, Greek, geography, history, math, spelling, English grammar, and music.

Until the school closed in 1901, a year after Laurinburg became the county seat of the newly created Scotland County, Quackenbush and his school had been a source of intense pride for the independent Scots who had settled the lands between the Yadkin and Cape Fear Rivers more than a hundred years before. Indeed, Laurinburg thought so highly of their professor that after his death in 1903 a monument was raised in his honor and placed in front of the courthouse on Main Street. Virtually every county seat across the South had a monument in the square, usually one topped by a musket-toting soldier facing north. Few, if any, memorialized an educator. "Christian, Scholar, Philanthropist," the chiseled inscription read. "His life was gentle and the elements so mixed in him that nature might stand up and say to all the world this was a man."

Nearly two decades after Quackenbush's school gave way to classrooms operated at public expense, the buildings were still in use. The largest of the three, the two-story with dormers on the front that had housed boarding students and Quackenbush's office, was the home of the Butler family. Next door, in a smaller, story-and-a-half version with a plain front and a broad front porch, the King family lived in what had once been classrooms. Just beyond, where the dusty road sloped to meet the crossing of the Seaboard Air Line Railway, the Sanfords—Cecil and Betsy and their three children—lived in an identical classroom turned residence.

The Sanfords had moved to Caledonia Road not long after their second child, James Terry, was born on August 20, 1917. Along with their eldest son, Cecil Leroy Jr., who had been born the year before, and their daughter, Elizabeth Martin, who arrived in 1919, the Sanfords found life on Caledonia Road to be comfortable and adequate. It would do nicely until Cecil Sanford saved enough to afford the new house he planned to build on a lot he owned closer to the center of town. In the meantime, the Sanfords warmed to their neighbors, the Butlers and the Kings, as well as the Ropers, whose house sat under huge oaks on a slight rise beyond the railroad tracks, and the Fairleys, who lived in a big white house directly across Caledonia Road.

A. M. Fairley was superintendent of the Dickson, Prince, and Scotland cotton mills and a man of considerable importance in Laurinburg. From his front porch, he could hear the hum of the spindles in the mills that spun yarn from cotton grown on Scotland County farms. The first of the low, one-story factory buildings was less than a hundred yards behind the Sanfords' house; the rest anchored the southern shoulder of the railroad tracks, one mill building after another down the right-of-way for a quarter of a mile or more. Adjacent to the mills and spread out over a dozen streets from First to Twelfth was the company's mill village, an orderly collection of more than a hundred small, white, frame houses and privies that offered little more than basic shelter for many of the company's eight hundred workers. The first blast of the company's morning whistle awoke those inside, and the second called them to their labor.

This section of Caledonia Road reflected life in Laurinburg in the 1920s as well as any other. The town was small, about twenty-six hundred residents at the 1920 census, which meant that rich and poor, powerful and powerless, merchant and farmer, all lived in close proximity. The proud local gentry said that what really mattered in Laurinburg, and throughout Scotland County, was not wealth or power, but industry and personal responsibility. "Scotch blood runs strong in the veins of these people," a writer would later describe them. "They know that work is not only practical, it is proper. It is the rock of character, the mother of discipline and the conqueror of handicap."[1]

The people were Baptists and Presbyterians mostly, clean, steadfast, and sober. The nation's first temperance society had been organized at nearby Wagram in 1855 in a white hectagonal building that stood for years. Violators of the temperance pledge paid a fine of five dollars for the first violation; members were expelled after a second. When the Civil War broke out, members resolved that "each man return as sober, moral and upright as he is now." With names like McCall, McKinnon, McDuffie, McLean, McLaurin, McNair, and Evans, the Laurinburg families traced their lineage to the Highland Scots who had followed the Cape Fear River up to Fayetteville and then kept going. During the Revolution, some had fought for the Crown and formed a Tory resistance that had been put down at the battle of Moore's Creek Bridge. Flora MacDonald, a heroine of the Loyalists, was remembered by Presbyterians, who named a small Presbyterian college located at Red Springs, about twenty miles northeast of Laurinburg, in her honor.

This was flat country, save for the rolling pine lands of the Sandhills in the northeastern corner of the county, and well watered. In this corner of North Carolina the plain was crossed by streams with names like Shoe Heel, Juniper, and Gum Swamp. Drowning Creek, which formed the headwaters of the Lumber River, crossed to the north. The rise from the coast was so gentle that folks took pride in the nearby village of Old Hundred, which was said to be at the end of the longest stretch of arrow-straight rail line in the Western Hemisphere.

For such a tranquil land, where on a late afternoon the only sound came from circling crows and the wind in the pines, Scotland County was the product of turbulent times. The white supremacy movement of 1898, led by the Democratic Party, had sounded its opening call in Laurinburg at a public meeting on Confederate Memorial Day, May 10, that was attended by nearly every white man in the county, according to one who was there. That fall, armed and mounted men, wearing symbolic red shirts, demonstrated sufficiently to keep most African Americans from polls and discourage support for a ticket of Populists and Republicans. There was no physical violence, at least not in Laurinburg, but at nearby Mason's Crossroads an angry mob of three hundred white citizens forced a Republican who had expressed his affection for African Americans to stand in a buggy and apologize to one and all. "He was then told to hit the grit, which he did," wrote Josephus Daniels, whose newspaper, the *News & Observer* of Raleigh, fanned the opposition to the Republican-Fusionist government. Daniels witnessed one political meeting featuring South Carolina's most rousing and vitriolic spokesman for the white race, "Pitchfork" Ben Tillman, who arrived in Lumberton, just east of Laurinburg, with an escort of mounted armed guards.

> He had spoken violently . . . saying that the white folks of South Carolina would chunk enough Negroes in the river before they would permit their domination.
>
> If you have never seen three hundred red-shirted men towards sunset with the sky red and the red shirts seeming to blend with the sky, you can conceive the impression it makes. It looked like the whole

world was carmine. I then understood why red-shirted men riding through the country, even if they said nothing and shot off no pistols, could carry terror to the Negroes in their quarters.

[W]hen the red shirts marched, . . . their appearance was the signal for the Negroes to get out of the way, so that when the red shirt brigade passed through the Negro end of town, it was as uninhabited to all appearances as if it had been a graveyard.[2]

Laurinburg's reward for loyalty to the resurgent Democrats, who reclaimed control of the state legislature, was delivered in the 1899 session. At the insistence of Representative Hector McLean of Lumberton, the legislators separated the southeastern corner of Richmond County and drew a line to the South Carolina border to create Scotland County. In 1900, Laurinburg welcomed not only a new century but a new level of local control that was vested mainly in the hands of the plantation owners and businessmen of the town. A majority of the population was black, but it was a white man's land.

By the 1920s, much of Scotland County's 317 square miles was the private domain of the McNairs. Laurinburg's first family carefully managed textile mills, cotton gins, fertilizer plants, flour mills, and a bank that had grown from the enterprise of John F. McNair, a four-year veteran of the Civil War who returned to the family homestead and began putting together his empire based in the fertile farms across three counties. Most of the McNair lands were tended by black tenant farmers, many of whom had migrated to the cotton fields of the Carolina coastal plains after the boll weevil devastated crops in the Deep South. Between 1910 and 1925, North Carolina had the largest increase in black farmers in the nation, many of them in Scotland County. Yet only one in ten of the black farmers around Laurinburg owned the soil they worked from dawn to dusk.

Terry Sanford's father had come of age with Scotland County. The elder Sanford was born in 1877, nine years after Laurinburg was incorporated as a town, and was not quite a teenager when the Red Shirts gained control in the 1898 elections. He had received his early education under Professor Quackenbush, and his only absence from the sandy streets of Laurinburg had been a stint at business school in Nashville, Tennessee, where he was sent to sharpen his skill with numbers. He returned to work with his father in the J. D. Sanford & Son hardware store on Main Street in Laurinburg not far from his aunt's millinery shop, which was successful enough to rate a listing in Dun & Bradstreet.

Terry's grandfather had been a cabinetmaker before he turned merchant. Grandfather Sanford was the son of a Richmond County farmer who had died for the Confederacy at Bristoe Station, Virginia, in October 1863, the victim of his commander's miscalculation of the strength of a retreating Union force. James Kendrick Sanford had enrolled as a private at age forty-one in the 44th North Carolina Regiment, known as the Montgomery Guards, when the regiment were mustered in at Camp Mangum near Raleigh in April 1862. Following the war, his son, James D., left the farm for Laurinburg and worked in the railroad shops. He had stayed on in 1894 when the shops were moved to Hamlet, seventeen miles to the west, when the Seaboard consolidated its works at the intersection of the main north-south line out of Raleigh.

J. D. Sanford raised his family in Laurinburg, making his home in a house set on a rise north of the railroad tracks in a perfect line of sight to his store on Main Street. His wife was the daughter of a planter from nearby Sampson County, who in later years would tell her grandchildren about life before her father's slaves were freed by invading Yankee soldiers. Sherman's troops had ridden through the Carolinas in March 1865, stopping long enough at nearby Laurel Hill Presbyterian Church to destroy the rail lines and set fire to the shops at Laurinburg before moving on to join the main force at Goldsboro.

Like most of the South, Laurinburg had recovered slowly in the years following the war. The railroad had been reopened to Wilmington and extended farther west to Rutherfordton in the foothills of the western Carolina mountains, which helped turn the town into something more than an isolated outpost a hundred miles from Charlotte, Greensboro, Wilmington, Raleigh, or any city of significant size or reputation.

The size of the cotton crop remained the principal measure of the local economy, but in the years following World War I, some farmers were beginning to develop markets in fruit and melons. In 1920, the county reached a peak in cotton production with more than forty-five thousand bales processed at the local gins. The success at the gin meant business for the Sanfords, whose hardware store enjoyed a prime location midway along Main Street. Packed into this busy collection of storefronts between the railroad tracks and the Methodist Church three blocks south were grocers and clothing stores, three banks, restaurants—including two run by Greeks—a Chinese laundry, a jewelry store, MacDougald's furniture store and funeral parlor, the Scotland County courthouse, and the Chetwyn Hotel with its white-tiled lobby floors. Banquets were held on the second floor of the Belk department store, and the Argyle Club, whose members were prominent men of the community, occupied rooms in the State Bank Building. Main Street continued south to pass in front of the large homes of Laurinburg's wealthy families in the blocks immediately beyond the town square, whose southern corners were guarded by two large churches, one for the Presbyterians and the other for the Methodists.

On the northern fringe of the business district were the railway offices, the depot, cotton gins, and the Goose Girl flour mill, which, at six stories, was the tallest structure in the county. Across the tracks was New Town, where Laurinburg's African Americans lived a separate and unequal existence. Yet, in a community that had witnessed some of the meanest racial intimidation at the turn of the century, there existed a private school called the Laurinburg Institute, which had been founded in 1904 by the E. M. and T. M. McDuffie families and recruited paying students from black families all across the South.

Terry's father, Cecil, was a quiet man of medium height and sturdy build, with a keen wit and comfortable personality, strong features, and a steady countenance. His education had not been extensive, but he maintained a keen interest in public affairs and for three years, before World War I, was town clerk. His window on the world was the Raleigh *News & Observer* that arrived a day late by mail. The brand of Southern Democratic liberalism preached by Josephus Daniels suited him just fine. He took his religion seriously and found a solid spiritual base at the Methodist Church.

When he spotted Elizabeth Martin, or Betsy as she was called, on the town's tennis courts, he was twenty-eight years old and a most eligible bachelor. She was two years younger and had been in Laurinburg less than a year, having arrived in the summer of 1913 to teach in Laurinburg schools. She was a spunky young woman who first thought that Cecil's attentions were directed at one of the other single teachers who lived with her at the teacherage, a boarding house for the school staff. Besides, her mind was not on romance. She nurtured a dream of becoming a missionary in South America or China.[3]

Laurinburg was a long way from Betsy's home in the Shenandoah Valley town of Salem, Virginia, where she had grown up with a house full of sisters and brothers. Her father, David Terry Martin, called the family home Beaconsfield, after British Prime Minister Benjamin Disraeli's English estate. He owned a feed store and coal business in Salem and did well; his barns at Beaconsfield stabled some of the finest horses in the county, including a particularly striking black stallion named Prince. Oats, wheat, and rye—feeds that he sold in town—were harvested off his farm of nearly a thousand acres. Large orchards of apple and pear trees and vegetables from a large garden filled the family larder. There were always hogs for slaughter in the fall and nobody went hungry. An educated man, he had finished three years of study at Emory and Henry College and was well read. The *Roanoke Times* came daily to his office.

Beaconsfield was a busy place, full of children and visiting relatives. Betsy was bright, active, athletic, and something of a tomboy. A lasting childhood memory was the year she pitched the girls' baseball team to victory over the boys. She adored her father and often stopped for a treat at his office in Salem on her way home from school. On occasion, when she would see him approaching the house at the end of the day, she would run down the hill to meet him and he would sweep her onto the back of his horse and gallop home. Once, after hearing the minister at the Presbyterian Church preach that only the righteous would enter heaven, she became inconsolable that she would be eternally separated from her father, who did not join his family in the pew on Sunday.

She excelled in the Salem schools, losing by a fraction of a point the award for excellence in mathematics. In 1906, her father enrolled her at Randolph-Macon Woman's College in Lynchburg, Virginia, where she registered for a double load of mathematics, taking the freshman and sophomore courses simultaneously. In addition, she studied French, English, and science. College life introduced her to a new world of acquaintances, including a Chinese student who arrived on campus virtually destitute. Her wardrobe consisted of the long, high-collared jacket of her native land that she had on her back. Betsy and other girls helped her pick out her first Western dress.

As Betsy's first year was coming to a close, her father died at the age of fifty-four, the victim of a heart attack and subsequent stroke. His death left the family in total confusion. David Martin had made no plans for his estate nor had he confided his business affairs to anyone in the family. There were debts to be paid and his widow was left at the mercy of her husband's business partner. When his affairs finally were settled, the family had little money and Betsy was able to return to Randolph-Macon for her sophomore year thanks only to the $1,000 her mother received for selling her husband's prize stallion, Prince.

In her second year, she again doubled her math studies, taking the junior and senior courses together. It was a struggle; her other courses included chemistry and Spanish. Her math professor worked with her to help her finish with better than a C average so she could qualify for a teaching certificate, as this was to be her last year in college. Meanwhile, she did better in her other courses, particularly English, and cultivated a growing ambition to become a published writer.

She returned to Salem and took a teaching assignment in a two-room school in the Blue Ridge Mountains not far from her home, where she taught grades five through seven and prepared two young men for college. The next year, she moved to Lincolnton, North Carolina, after answering a magazine ad soliciting teachers for the town. At the end of the school year, she went back to Salem to be with her mother. In the late summer of 1913, she arrived in Laurinburg to teach for the former principal at her Lincolnton school, who had been named Laurinburg's superintendent of schools and had invited her to join the faculty.

Cecil and Betsy's courtship was a lengthy one. He proposed during her first year in town, but she returned to Salem the following year while her mother made elaborate preparations for a June wedding at Beaconsfield in 1915. The separation was not of Betsy's choosing, but rather at the insistence of her mother, who wanted to be sure the relationship was sound. Betsy and Cecil corresponded almost daily in chatty letters that Betsy stored carefully in a chest. Just before Cecil left Laurinburg for Salem and the wedding, he was sworn in as a deputy clerk of court, a step up from his town clerk's position. He was twenty-nine years old.

The young couple moved into the old Methodist parsonage just off Laurinburg's Main Street where their son Cecil was born, then moved within the year to Church Street, where Terry was born in a small frame house across from the Methodist Church, where Cecil and Betsy had become active members. Betsy had come to Laurinburg a Presbyterian, but the local pastor urged her not to raise a family with split allegiance and insisted she join her husband in the Methodist church. When the Sanfords moved to Caledonia Road, they found a bigger house to better accommodate a growing family. A daughter they named Betsy was born in 1920.

In March 1923, Terry was six when his father reorganized the family business and incorporated the Sanford Hardware Company in hope of recovering from a period of some economic distress. Laurinburg and Scotland County had not enjoyed continued success with the cotton crops that had filled bank accounts in the years immediately after the end of the Great War. From time to time, Cecil Sanford had borrowed money on various pieces of property he owned, including the lot on Church Street near the school where he hoped to build a home.

The family had its share of personal setbacks. Terry was five years old when his mother was diagnosed with tuberculosis. She became easily fatigued, and Dr. Peter John, who had delivered all the Sanford children, arranged for Betsy to be admitted to a sanatorium run by Dr. John McCain near Aberdeen, a quiet village twenty-eight miles north of Laurinburg set amid the tall pines and restful resort atmosphere of the North Carolina Sandhills. At the time, the world's medical community was virtually overwhelmed with this disease that reduced normally healthy people to wheezing, debilitated invalids who would eventually drown in their own blood. The public responded with fear and shunned "consumptives," who were denied admission to public places and refused service at hotels. Even their children were ostracized. The disease spread across the nation, and by the end of the decade there were more than three million American citizens suffering from tuberculosis.

For five months while his wife underwent treatment at Aberdeen, Cecil Sanford lived at home with his eldest son, who had just entered the first grade, while the young ones, Terry and his sister, were sent to Wilmington, where each was placed with one of Betsy's sisters. Terry's custodians were Helen and Bill Shaw, who later moved to Fayetteville. Cecil tended the store and traveled to and from the sanatorium on the Old Wire Road, a dusty rolling trail between Laurinburg and Aberdeen. Finally, his wife was released and returned home. She would continue to test positive for tuberculosis for years, but her robust lifestyle would be a marvel to friends and family. Almost as if to emphasize her recovery, Betsy Sanford gave birth to a fourth child and second daughter in January 1924. Mary Glenn was followed in May 1925 by Helen. She called the two girls her "second batch." [4]

The economy of small farm communities improved slightly in the mid-1920s, but then slumped again as one year fell a little behind the one before. The signs that the nation was sliding toward economic disaster were apparent in Laurinburg long before the Wall Street crash in 1929. The Sanford Hardware business slid into bankruptcy and had closed by the early part of that year, following a disastrous yield from the 1928 cotton crop. Not only had the cotton crop been reduced by heavy rains, but local farmers were making little from crops of cantaloupes and watermelons that had offered some promise as an alternative to the uncertainties of cotton.

A second tragedy devastated the Sanford family. Just after school was dismissed for the summer in 1929, nine-year-old Betsy fell ill. Dr. John, the family's physician, could not diagnose her illness; neither could two other doctors in town. Terry would never forget the somber looks on the faces of adults who huddled with one another and spoke in muffled tones. One night he retreated to the back porch, where he closed his eyes and wagered with himself that Betsy would live if he opened his eyes and saw only one moon. He opened his eyes and looked to the sky, but his tears doubled his vision. Later, talking with his brother, he told him their sister would die. [5]

Finally, an ambulance was called and Betsy was carried a hundred miles to Dr. J. B. Sidbury's children's hospital at Wrightsville Beach, North Carolina, where the family learned she suffered from spinal meningitis that had progressed beyond the point of effective treatment. Betsy died June 14, 1929.

Cecil Sanford brought his daughter's body home in a small coffin and placed it in the front room of his house. Terry didn't know how to understand such a loss and refused to set foot in the room. Late one night before the burial, he crawled from bed and peeped into the room, where he saw his parents standing together, holding each other tight and looking down into the small coffin.

The Sanfords buried Betsy in Laurinburg Memorial Cemetery. After the service, they returned home to find that the house had been quarantined. Health officials were not quite sure how the disease was transmitted, and in a curious mix of courtesy and callousness, had waited until after the funeral was over to close the house and order it fumigated. Family members and townspeople had streamed in and out of the place for days after Betsy had fallen ill. They filled the house with fried chicken, cakes and pies and vegetables during the period of mourning. A black woman who lived nearby, someone Mrs. Sanford had helped years earlier recover from an injury, also came to pay her respects. "Mrs. Sanford, I can't bring nothing. But I do love you," she told her friend. "Can I mop up the kitchen floor for you?"[6]

The loss of a child was too much for Mrs. Sanford. Normally strong, resilient, and optimistic, her grief and tears surprised her children. Young Mary Glenn never spoke of death for years thereafter for fear of upsetting her mother; mere mention of her dead sister's name would cause her mother to break down. Betsy Sanford blamed her loss on the family's long-time friend and medical attendant, Dr. John, and never called on him again.

Terry was not quite twelve years old when the family's idyllic life was thus shattered and he was made aware that the world could produce fierce consequences. He already had begun to wonder why families in the mill village just beyond the back fence had no indoor plumbing and so hauled water to their homes from a communal spigot. He didn't understand why other neighbors were losing their farms to foreclosure. And he saw how financial loss had attacked his father's spirit. No one had a name for it yet, but the Great Depression had arrived in Laurinburg.

CHAPTER TWO

Runnin' on Rims

WHEN TERRY SANFORD WAS ONLY thirteen he paid a dollar for an old Model T Ford that had no tires and a front seat fashioned from a board laid across the gasoline tank. In time, he and Jimmy Hollis, the Hunter boys, and the Beverly brothers from next door replaced the missing parts with junkyard purchases and got the motor running. After Betsy Sanford taught Terry how to drive, he chased over the dusty Scotland County roads, running on rims and burning up gasoline he and his buddies collected from the overflow catch basins on the tank cars parked overnight on the Seaboard rail sidings.

The car added one more level of freedom for youngsters such as Terry who turned Laurinburg and the surrounding rural countryside into their personal playground. The nearby fields and forests were for hikes and over-night camping with pan-fried chicken cooked over an open fire. The creeks that meandered across the flat countryside were for swimming and frog gigging. Terry once spent the night in the swamp just to catch butterflies. The boys hitched rides on the cotton wagons, falling back into the cushion of white fluff speckled with the broken bits of cotton boll. In town, they climbed atop the huge bales stacked at the cotton gin and tested their nerve by vaulting from one to another. No one seemed to make much over this or the fact that boys barely into their teens were bumping down the roads in an automobile that was no better prepared for public roadways than were the drivers.

Terry was a lively, adventuresome youngster, somewhat mischievous and pugnacious. He was prone to get himself in minor scrapes and depended on his brother, Cecil, for his rescue. There were the annual Halloween pranks on Mr. Billy Cox, the only known Republican in town, who had once hauled the Sanford boys' father into court for shooting his rooster. (The elder Sanford said the bird was ravaging his garden. He was ordered to pay

$15 in damages.) Terry and his buddies climbed the town's water tower, and from time to time, Cecil and Terry would bound out of their bedroom window at night and beat the fire engines to a call, counting the blasts of the alarm horn along the way to determine the corner of town that faced an emergency.

There were never any serious incidents; the boys didn't step across the line of normally accepted behavior. They all knew that the familiarity of small-town life harbored no secrets of those guilty of misdeeds. The closely bonded mothers of the Sanford brothers and their mates meant that discipline was maintained no matter whose offspring were in the house. All the parents had "spanking privileges." [1]

Betsy Sanford usually handled problems with finesse and seldom resorted to corporal punishment. Once, she drove up in front of the Blue's Drug Store on Main Street to find Terry perched on a crate and puffing on a cheap cigar. He escaped around the corner, but when he arrived home he was met by her laughter at such wholly pretentious behavior. That hurt as much as a switching.

Betsy Sanford would much rather brag on her children, building their confidence and encouraging them to experiment and explore. She introduced them to ideas and challenged their imagination to roam beyond the bounds of little Laurinburg and use books in the home as their ticket to the world. She created a game called Geography in which the children answered questions about strange and faraway places. She also entertained them with her own stories, which she later submitted to popular magazines for publication; one or two were accepted.

Cecil Sanford also wished to bring the world into their home. He loved history and closely followed reports on state affairs carried in the newspaper. Often, he would take his children along to Democratic Party rallies and town meetings. In 1928, when many Southern Democrats deserted their party's presidential nominee, Alfred Smith, largely because he was a Roman Catholic, eleven-year-old Terry marched in a parade carrying a banner made by Scotland County Sheriff F. C. McCormick that read, "Me and Ma is for Al." That same year, Terry attended a political rally with his father and shook hands with O. Max Gardner, the Democrat's candidate for governor, when he campaigned in Laurinburg. Gardner had upset some members of his own party when he too stood up with Smith, declaring in his speech opening the fall campaign, "I won't desert the captain of the ship." Some opposed Smith because of his religion and others for his support of a repeal of Prohibition. Certainly, there was never a drop of liquor in the Sanford home and its use elsewhere was frowned upon, but the Sanfords voted for Gardner, Smith, and the straight Democratic ticket as they always had.

Music, too, was part of life in the Sanfords' home. The children listened to symphony concerts when their parents tuned the radio to the Sunday afternoon broadcasts. In addition, Betsy Sanford played the piano and saw to it there was enough money left at the end of the week to pay for music lessons for all. Cecil played trumpet and Terry took up the saxophone, playing from time to time in a small band that his music teacher organized for performances in a tiny community building in the East Laurinburg mill village. As they grew older, daughters Helen on the violin and Mary Glenn on the piano joined the family ensemble.

Betsy Sanford wanted her children to dream, and Terry's ambitions were as boundless as the horizon on a clear summer day. He saw himself exploring the poles with Admiral Byrd, becoming a doctor and finding a cure for cancer, going west and staking a homestead, being governor, a general in the army, or even president. "I was a genuine Walter Mitty, and upon reflection I must have spent far more time dreaming than working," he later wrote in a recollection of his youth.[2] He believed anything was possible. His parents assured him it was and that every day was a chance to do something worthwhile.

Politics was not necessarily at the top of Terry's list, but once, after a passing car had left him covered with dust as he walked along a county road, he resolved that when he ran for office he would mount a water sprayer on the back of his car to settle the dust so pedestrians could see his sign, "Sanford for General Assembly." He was sure that appreciative voters would remember him on election day.

Frankly, dreams of any sort were in short supply in Laurinburg. The South was on the leading edge of the Great Depression in the late 1920s when agricultural prices plunged and destroyed local economies. Cecil Sanford had plenty of company after his business went under. By 1930, the reality of hard times was firmly fixed; the recent economic troubles were more than just another bump in the road. Some wondered if they weren't at the end of the road. Terry's Model T could just as easily have ended up as a "Hoover cart" carrying yet another family away from a foreclosed farm or tenant house, leaving behind crops that had been sorry and prices that had been worse. From time to time these overburdened travelers passed along Laurinburg's Main Street headed somewhere else. Terry was standing on the corner one day and saw his family's former cook riding atop a pile of furniture on the rear of a battered old pickup, waving and calling out, "Bye, bye Terry boy."

The Sanfords had never been wealthy by any stretch, but income from Cecil Sanford's retail business had provided some middle-class comforts. Their house was rented, but it had indoor plumbing and was reasonably furnished. Unlike mothers in some of the mill houses along the streets beyond the back fence, Betsy Sanford could remain home with her children and pay for help. The family took summer vacations, often by train to Virginia, where they enjoyed visits with Betsy's family amid the cool breezes of the Blue Ridge Mountains. From time to time, Cecil Sanford would crank up his 1924 Studebaker touring car for the eight-hour drive over plank roads to Wilmington to visit Betsy's sister, who lived in a fine home on the edge of Masonboro Sound.

It was on one of these trips to Wilmington, in the summer after their daughter Betsy died, that the Sanfords almost lost their two sons. The family was returning to Laurinburg late at night when the couple heard a thumping noise from the trunk compartment of their Model T. The boys were in the back because the space behind the one bench seat was taken up by their sisters and the family dog, a bulldog named Buck. Cecil Sanford pulled to the side of the road—the thumping was a prearranged signal for him to stop—and before he could get out Terry appeared at the window, muttered something about a sore throat and fell over. The elder Sanford opened the door and tended to Terry while his wife rushed to the rear, where she found young Cecil overcome by carbon monoxide fumes.

Sanford left his wife with the boys and drove into Maxton to fetch a doctor. After he had gone, John R. Lowry, who was on his way to Laurinburg, stopped when he saw Mrs. Sanford and her sons beside the road. After he learned what had happened, he put them all in his car, drove on into Maxton to meet Cecil, and then later drove the boys home after they were found to have suffered no lasting effects from the experience.

The near disaster came at a very low point in the Sanfords' life. Cecil had not only seen his business close, but one of his close friends, the cashier at the State Bank, was forced to call a note after he discovered the hardware business was insolvent. Cecil Sanford's ambitions, such as those for a new house, evaporated and the Church Street lot was sold to pay bills. The family fell several hundred dollars in arrears on rent on the house on Caledonia Road. The McNair Investment Company, which owned the house, let the Sanfords remain on with the rent unpaid, as they did with other tenants.

Steady work was elusive. In the spring after the business failed, Cecil represented the T. W. Woods Seed Company; farmers stopped by the house to draw their purchases from great bags of seed that were stacked on the front porch and throughout the inside rooms. For a time he sold industrial insurance, which required weekly visits to customers to collect the twenty-five-cent premiums due on these modest life policies. And, later, he went "on the road" selling calendars for the Brown & Bigelow Company. His children would help him carry his heavy sample cases to the bus stop at the Chetwyn Hotel where he left for Charlotte or Wilmington. From those cities he would make his way back to Laurinburg, stopping at smaller towns such as Wadesboro and Fayetteville.

One Christmas season he and the boys ran Aubrey Hammond's fire-cracker stand on Bloodfield Street, a dirt alley off Main Street so named because it was often the scene of weekend fights. Father and sons worked from a crude shed with a dirt floor with the fireworks arrayed on shelves across the back. A kerosene stove provided heat. Hammond was well pleased with the results; his profits were higher than previous years because Sanford, a meticulous bookkeeper and thoroughly honest, had turned in every penny of the receipts, unlike some of Hammond's previous managers.

The family's money went mostly for necessities. Terry later recalled that his parents didn't have a real solid connection with Santa Claus, who "was not an equal-opportunity giver." The highlight of the Christmas season was always a huge bonfire that was lighted early Christmas morning behind the Sanford house. The boys collected empty boxes for a week, arranging them in a pile fifteen feet high to produce a spectacular blaze.

There had been no steady income for the family for more than a year when Betsy Sanford returned to teaching in the fall of 1930 after a fifteen-year absence from the classroom. There simply was no escaping the fact that her husband couldn't find steady work, but at least she could provide the family with an income of about a hundred dollars a month. She arranged early enrollment in first grade for her youngest, Helen, and took over the fifth grade at Central Elementary School.

The setbacks for the Sanfords were traumatic and life shaping, but not unusual for the times. All across North Carolina, in small towns like Laurinburg and cities like Charlotte and Wilmington, neighbors found they were all in the same situation. Being woefully short of cash to meet daily needs and late on the rent was simply a fact of life. Yet, years later, Terry recalled, as did many who lived through the Depression, that he never thought of his family as being poor. There was always food on the table, and regardless of circumstances, the Sanfords maintained their social standing in the community. "The trouble is, we didn't have any money to go with it," he later joked.[3]

After O. Max Gardner took office as North Carolina's governor in January 1929, he immediately began to marshal the state's resources and attempt to build the morale of its people against considerable odds. Cotton, which a decade earlier had sold for a dollar a pound, was down to nine cents. Tobacco farmers were struggling and he called on growers to voluntarily reduce their acreage by 25 percent in an effort to stabilize prices. In December, he launched the "Live-at-Home" campaign and used state home demonstration agents to show people how to live off meat and vegetables raised and grown by North Carolina farmers, who had seen prices drop to their lowest levels in a decade.

These measures couldn't stop the slide, of course. Overproduction of cotton drove prices even lower, to the point it was hardly worth picking. During his second year in office, Gardner watched as nearly one hundred of the state's banks, about 20 percent of the total, closed with depositors forfeiting $56 million. Laurinburg lost two institutions, the First National Bank and Scotland County Savings Bank, and scandal ensued when the top executives at Scotland Savings were prosecuted for violating banking laws.[4] During the resulting trial, Terry visited the courtroom with his father, who was the last man to see the bank's cashier before he disappeared. Cecil Sanford had passed the man walking near the edge of town on the bank's final day of business.

Even municipal governments defaulted on their obligations, and North Carolina's credit on Wall Street was in jeopardy until textile baron Charles A. Cannon told New York bankers he would put the resources of Cannon Mills behind his state. In Asheville, where real estate speculation had been rampant, the prices of overrated resort property plummeted and the city found itself in overwhelming debt with a depressed tax base. Local officials were left with huge, ornate office buildings as monuments to the folly of a real estate market driven by unchecked speculation.

Laurinburg met the Depression with classic Scottish independence, steadiness, self-reliance, and a gospel that hard work conquered all. The community's newspaper, the Laurinburg Exchange, even discounted the severity of the plight of most of its readers despite a report from Raleigh showing that one-fourth of the county's population was destitute or dependent on charity. "There are too many who will not work as long as the government will feed them," the paper said in a March 16, 1933, editorial. "Conditions are almost unbelievably bad but maybe not altogether as bad as figures would have us believe sometimes." The community responded with modest local remedies. Red Cross volunteers such as Mrs. A. M. Fairley, the mill superintendent's wife, and Mrs. M. J. Maguire gathered food and clothing to distribute to those in need.

The community's reputation for thriftiness was enhanced by the strength, physical and financial, of the State Bank, which was owned by the McNair family. In March 1933, just as President Franklin D. Roosevelt was taking office, work was completed on the bank's new concrete and steel vault with walls a foot thick. The bank survived the bank holiday that

Roosevelt declared for March 15 without touching a dollar of the new currency that James L. McNair had personally carried in from Charlotte in the trunk of his Buick with an armed escort provided by the sheriff, the Laurinburg chief of police, and a highway patrolman. "The story is that he piled it in the middle of the lobby and said 'If you want it, come and get it,'" McNair's son, John, later recalled. "And everybody said 'If it is there, I don't really want it.'" The bank reopened without shorting a single depositor.[5]

Terry never heard a word of complaint from his father, who struggled to improve the family's situation. The difficulty of the long trips peddling calendars that separated him from his family was eased by the warm welcome he received from adoring daughters who clung to his long legs when he returned home. He never spoke a harsh word against the bank when it foreclosed on his loan and caused his business to fail. Cecil Sanford may have found his situation difficult, but there was nothing to do except work his way out of it and even share a joke or two along the way.

In spite of his own troubles, he found a way to set aside a little for his mother and father, whose condition was no better than his own. He took up his duty as the eldest son to provide what he could and saw that his brother and sister did likewise. For a time, he and Betsy also looked after his Aunt Middie, who moved in with the family despite the fact that she had never spoken kindly of her nephew's wife. Terry's chores increased when he had to draw water daily from an artesian well located near the edge of town because Aunt Middie would die of dehydration before she would let the "city water" in the Sanfords' home pass her lips.

Terry saw what the Depression was doing to people around him and he never forgot the hardships his neighbors endured. The Ropers, who lived just beyond the Sanfords on Caledonia Road, were forced off their farm by foreclosure. He saw legal notices appear in store windows on Main Street, testimony to businesses sent into receivership. He and his brother discovered crude campsites along the railroad tracks where hoboes camped, often after they had visited the back door of the Sanford home for a handout. Before she and her family left town, Mary, a black woman who had worked for the Sanfords in better days, approached Terry one day and asked if his family had any food to spare. He proceeded to gather okra, tomatoes, and corn from the family garden and "instruct" Mary on how to cook a vegetable stew.

The failure of the First National Bank put a serious scare into the youngster. The Laurinburg Rotary Club had loaned Terry twelve dollars to purchase a Boy Scout uniform, but before the uniform arrived, the bank failed and the check was worthless. He worried about having to repay the loan for cash he never received.

Nothing seemed to focus Terry's attention like the Boy Scouts of America. He had little interest in organized sports such as football, which his brother Cecil played with determination. He liked music, and for a time, he and Cecil and two others formed a small dance band. "In the Gloaming" was one of Terry's specialties on the saxophone; his rendition of "When Old Laurinburg Falls in Line" played to the tune of Sousa's "Washington & Lee March" was good enough to get the twelve dollars out of the Rotarians. He liked baseball, but he found he wasn't much of a hitter. Instead, he preferred swimming, hiking, and walking the roads of Scotland County. "Every Saturday we walked," Sanford recalled some years later. "We would walk to Maxton, or Laurel Hill, or to the Lumber River, or to Gibson's Store beyond Sneed's Crossroads. Hiking beat working in the garden."[6] For several years running, he led a ritual hike each Easter Monday, which was a state holiday. He and his friends kicked the shoes from their feet and headed off to the Lumber River as if they had made a barefoot declaration of freedom.

Scout Troop 20 had been formed just as school was closing in June 1930. Terry, Cecil, and their friend Reginald F. "Mutt" McCoy, who was Cecil's age, prevailed on J. H. Fleming, the city's school superintendent, to organize the troop and serve as scoutmaster. Fleming, in turn, named these three and one other boy as patrol leaders for the dozen or so others who joined. An old Navy man, Fleming taught close-order drill, marching his Scouts back and forth across the school grounds, and coached them through their achievement awards. Terry moved quickly up the ranks. He earned his second-class rating by the end of his first month and first class by the end of October. A little more than a year later he was a Star Scout and in July 1932, two years and one month after he raised his first Scout salute, he received his Eagle award.[7]

Each year the Laurinburg troop traveled to Wilmington to compete with other Scouts from around the region. The Laurinburg boys did not earn any special distinction by their presentations, although one year Edmund Baddour, whose father ran a clothing store on Main Street, attracted attention with the nonregulation brown-and-white wing tip oxfords he wore when the troop marched down Wilmington's Princess Street in a grand parade.

Life wasn't entirely carefree. There was no spare cash for allowances from their parents, so Terry and his brother always looked for ways to make a little money. One year they raised pigs, another it was chickens, and from time to time they loaded their Red Flyer wagon with vegetables from the family garden and pulled the produce across the tracks to New Town, where collards brought a nickel and "roastin' ears" ten cents a dozen. Cecil kept a cow that produced milk for sale. Both took Saturday jobs on the surrounding farms, picking cotton and suckering tobacco in the hot summer sun. Cropping tobacco left dark stains on their hands that didn't disappear until Christmas.

Terry delivered telegrams for Postal Telegraph, priding himself on his knowledge of Laurinburg streets and who lived where, and worked as an usher at the Scotland Theater. The brothers also developed a steady income from magazine and newspaper sales; their offerings included the *Saturday Evening Post*, *Ladies' Home Journal*, and *Country Gentleman*. They picked up the magazines at the Railway Express office and loaded them onto their wagon, which they parked in front of Fields' Drugstore while they made deliveries to their regular customers up and down Main Street, peddling single copies to the traveling men in the lobby at the Chetwyn Hotel.

Terry finally landed a job delivering the *Fayetteville Observer*. Some of his best days were the occasions when the *Observer*, an afternoon daily, published extra editions, such as when the kidnapped child of Charles Lindbergh was found and flyer Wiley Post set the record for a round-the-world trip. If extras were on the way, the newspaper alerted him at school, and when the final bell rang, he rushed to meet the truck and quickly sold his one hundred copies.

Working various jobs offered Terry an insight into people and the human condition that escaped the notice of some his age. One magazine customer was a black woman named Stella, who ran a lively and raucous café on Bloodfield and supplied Terry with fish sandwiches. She convinced the boy that an elderly man lived in a large packing crate that was part of the trashy landscape behind the stores on Main Street. Terry also called on the deputy at the county jail, who once told him about a prisoner who said, shortly before he died behind bars, "It has all come to an end, and it is nothing." This depressing epitaph weighed on Terry, who later wrote, "The leading citizens of Laurinburg would have been dismayed to have known that the little *Saturday Evening Post* boy was walking around looking at them, pondering in each case whether the same could be said at the end of their lives."[8]

By November 1933, the Sanford family's financial condition had improved sufficiently to afford a home of their own. Cecil Sanford had a steady job at a building supply company that paid fifteen dollars a week; with Betsy's salary, the couple now had money for the down payment on a one-story, three-bedroom frame house on the corner of McLaurin Avenue and Cronley Street, just three blocks off Main. The house had large rooms with high ceilings and a broad central hallway. It cost just over $2,000 and the Sanfords arranged a ten-year note and monthly payments of $23.50. It was not much larger than the house on Caledonia Road—for which they still owed back rent—but it was their own. On one of his first evenings in the new house, Cecil Sanford planted two pecan trees in the backyard that sixty years later had grown tall and remained bountiful.

Terry was in his last year in high school when the family moved. As he prepared to finish the year, his school record offered no more promise for the future than that of any other of the forty-four students in the class of 1934. His grades had been good, but not spectacular, with math and science his favorite subjects. Cecil had been the more serious student, and Terry watched as other students captured the class offices and athletic honors.

He was a handsome lad, with a pleasing face, blond hair, an athletic build, and features that favored his father. His mother tried to keep him presentable, but usually his shirttail was hanging from his jeans. Though girls outnumbered the boys in the class by better than two to one, Terry's painful shyness and a closely chaperoned social life discouraged anything more serious than flirtation. For a time he was sweet on Helen Kirkpatrick, a Presbyterian minister's daughter who lived five miles out in the country at the historic Laurel Hill Church. One Saturday he made five round trips to Helen's house so she could certify he had ridden the required fifty miles for his bicycling merit badge.

The world was in transition in the spring of 1934 as Terry's class prepared for graduation. Laurinburg was the epitome of a small Southern town, where the established social order was in place and the locals were protected from the intrusion of corrupting influences. Only recently, a *Laurinburg Exchange* editorial had applauded the town council's decision to ban pool halls: "[The pool hall] is the traditional sink of iniquity where Satan finds all the idle hands that he needs. The local minister preaches against it, and the school principal threatens periodically to do something about closing it. Almost always it is controlled by or subservient to the local political boss." Life was simple in the confines of the mile-square town, and the old values held sway. On Confederate Memorial Day, May 10, the Scout troop led a procession from the Confederate monument on the square out to the cemetery to honor those who had served the Lost Cause.

North Carolina remained in the control of a conservative political establishment that reinforced the Scots' credo of self-reliance and community. In Raleigh, Governor J. C. B. Ehringhaus told a gathering of Rotarians from North Carolina cities, "I like to think of the state as a great Rotary club, or an organization of that sort. After all is said and done, governmental activity is simply an effort to put into practical effect the highest service and sentiment of altruism for the group rather than for the individual."[9]

Yet, serious problems at home and abroad lay ahead for Terry and his classmates. As Ehringhaus made the baccalaureate circuit, he had on his desk execution orders for eight men awaiting their turn in the state's electric chair. For the first time since 1925, two white men were scheduled to die on the same day. Violence filled the newspapers. A month before graduation day, the FBI's Public Enemy No. 1, John Dillinger, shot his way out of a ring of police who had surrounded his hideaway in the Wisconsin woods, escaping lawmen for the sixth time. Two days after Terry and his classmates received their diplomas, Bonnie Parker and Clyde Barrow, America's most famous outlaw duo, were killed in an ambush set by lawmen in Louisiana. In New York City, more than twenty thousand persons were preparing to gather at Madison Square Garden to praise the leader of the new Germany, Adolf Hitler. In the Midwest, some farm leaders were predicting that revolution was inevitable if the government was unable to help farmers whose land was literally being blown away in the worst drought the region had ever seen.

On May 16, five days before graduation exercises got underway at Laurinburg High, about three hundred workers — nearly half the workforce — walked off their jobs at the textile mills in East Laurinburg to protest what they claimed were intolerable conditions inside the mills and in the rental houses of the mill village. They called for a strike at all four of the Waverly Mills plants to begin May 21. Soon the number of striking workers swelled to five hundred.

At first, the walkout had a festive air. On the second day of picketing, workers held a wiener roast in the streets beside the mills and, despite their estrangement from management, defended the honor of the company in a baseball game with workers from a Bladenboro mill, which the Waverly players won nine to five. A few days later, they had a fish fry with fish supplied by a local market. The party atmosphere evaporated, however, on the evening of May 27, when a riot broke out between strikers and company loyalists, some of whom fired guns from inside one of the plants. Nine people were injured, one seriously.

News of the Laurinburg strike jumped to the front page of the *News & Observer* and remained there for days. Textile strikes were common in the Carolinas, but violence had not accompanied the walkouts since the bitter disputes of 1929 in Marion and Gastonia. The newspaper sent a reporter to Laurinburg, and his reports aired the workers' complaints about their living conditions.

The Waverly management refused to meet with strike leaders and remained stone silent. Unlike other communities where owners had settled the issue with the help of the National Guard, who restrained strikers while replacements took their jobs, this time there was no intervention from Raleigh. At the same time, however, when the workers called on Ehringhaus for protection, he feigned ignorance of any such requests.

Strike leaders maintained discipline among the picketers and said the shotguns and other weapons they had stacked close by were necessary as long as the governor refused protection. The strikers camped on the streets and maintained checkpoints into the mill village around the clock despite the cold and rainy weather. Laurinburg police maintained their distance. Sheriff McCormick demanded that the strikers disarm, but he made no move to take their weapons. Eventually, local authorities arrested the non-striking workers who had fired on the picketers.

The strikers insisted that their cause was based not on demands for higher pay but for better conditions inside the mills and in the houses they rented from the company for $1.50 a week. They claimed that management had imposed a "stretch out," requiring fewer workers to process more goods. That, along with shorter hours and less pay, had left many with little income. One strike leader said only five dollars remained from his paycheck for two weeks' work and with that he was expected to feed and clothe his family. Even before the strike, about 130 families in the mill village were on relief; as it continued, that number increased.

Health officials soon became concerned about conditions in the mill village, and a team of inspectors was dispatched from Raleigh. A *News & Observer* reporter accompanied them on a tour and reported that "many of [the houses] have leaky roofs, and others have large holes in the plastering. All the plumbing is on the outside, and in most cases the privies are in dilapidated condition. Water spigots are in the yards, each faucet being used by several families. Improvements of the houses is one of the main demands of the strikers. In some instances, paper has been stuck over bare laths in order to keep out wind and rain." In a subsequent report, officials said conditions had deteriorated to the point that they feared a typhoid epidemic.[10]

The strike coincided with other labor unrest elsewhere in the nation. Two days before the shootings at the Waverly mills, National Guard troops fired on more than two thousand rioting workers in Toledo, Ohio, killing two. Union leaders subsequently threatened to call a national strike. The walkout was averted for the time being, but the Laurinburg strike continued for forty-four days before both sides agreed to arbitration. The workers won some concessions: the company agreed to install a water and sewer system in the mill village, but only when emergency federal aid became available to pay for it.

The strike and resulting violence had generated more attention for Laurinburg than anything since the Red Shirt campaign of 1898. However, it left little impression on teenager Terry Sanford and some of his classmates, who in later years could recall few details of the standoff on the streets of East Laurinburg. Despite the proximity to their homes, life in the mill village was separate and apart from that of families "in town." In the local social order, mill families were regarded as second-class citizens, much the same as the African Americans who lived north of the railroad tracks in New Town. A few years before the strike, the town had resisted the enrollment of East Laurinburg children in Laurinburg city schools with as much determination as would meet the enrollment of black students half a century later.[11]

The Waverly strike occurred as Terry was preparing for a great summer adventure. Mrs. Maguire, the American Red Cross leader, had arranged for him to attend a summer camp where he was to qualify as a life-saving instructor. The woman had taken a keen interest in Terry, and she was eager to train lifeguards for an organized swimming program in Laurinburg. Eagle Scout Terry Sanford was a willing and able candidate.

Swimming was as natural as walking for Terry. He had learned on a church outing when the preacher had tossed him into the Lumber River and told him to catch the next cable downstream. In time, he knew all the public swimming areas along the Lumber River's cold dark waters, but his favorite spot was on Leith Creek, which ran beside his house on Caledonia Road. When he returned from the Red Cross camp he scheduled swim classes at Lee's Mill Pond for Laurinburg boys and girls.

At the same time, Terry was absorbed in plans for his future. College had always been a possibility. When the Sanford boys were teenagers, the family had traveled home from their summer trips to Virginia by way of Durham and Chapel Hill to look at the campuses of the universities there. Cecil Sanford was an active and enthusiastic Methodist, and he would have liked for his children to be educated at Duke University. The state university at Chapel Hill, however, with a tuition of $75, better suited the family's financial condition, though even that modest amount was hard to gather. Throughout Terry's last year in high school, his brother had remained at home working at the drugstore to save enough to enter Chapel Hill in the fall of 1934.

Terry's options were limited. He didn't have the money to join his brother and knew that he too would need to work and save if he was ever to get to college. Finally, he decided to enroll at Presbyterian Junior College, whose campus was seven miles away in Maxton. His friend James Fenegan, who was Cecil's age, had just finished his first year at PJC with good grades and he helped arrange part-time work for Terry—mowing grass and washing windows—to earn money toward a semester's tuition. Terry had come to know James after the boy's family had moved to Laurinburg when they lost their farm in South Carolina. Mr. Fenegan took over the tobacco operation on the Roper farm out on the Caledonia Road while his wife maintained a tourist home in a large frame house just beyond the Methodist Church on South Main Street. James was known as "Runt" because of his slight physique, the result of a faulty heart valve that had inhibited his growth.

After classes began that fall, Terry lived at home and caught rides on cars and freight trains to and from Maxton. The arrangement saved him money, but PJC turned out to be a disappointment. He felt the level of instruction was less than what he had received in high school and he resisted being drawn into the college life because he had no plans to stay. He passed on an offer to join the football team, telling the coach he had to keep his job at the A&P grocery store in Laurinburg. The highlight of that first semester was a protest that Terry and James organized in support of a student they believed was unjustly accused of stealing an apple.[12]

Terry was convinced that PJC was not a proper launching pad for his ambitions—which remained undefined—and he began looking for a way to move on to greater opportunities. First, he had to convince his parents that he shouldn't return to the Maxton campus. Finally arriving at a plausible story, he told his parents he wanted to be a doctor and that continuing at PJC was a waste of time because his course credits would not transfer to an institution that could lead to a medical degree. They agreed to his plans not to enroll at PJC for the spring term while he took a job to save money to enter Chapel Hill in the fall of 1935.

Terry's declaration for medical school was not a total dodge. When he was younger, he had considered becoming a doctor and modeling a career on that of old Dr. Hunter, who had once stitched him up after he tripped while trying to leap the front steps of the house next door and opened a wide cut across his nose. The injury had left a bit of a scar but the doctor feared sewing too tight would stretch the skin and later obstruct the tear ducts in Terry's eye. He admired the doctor's bedside manner and dedication, which often drew him out at night to tend to the sick and injured.

Terry took a job at Pender's grocery store and pumped gas at a service station. At one point he went to work in a textile mill but had to quit after two weeks. The foreman, who was a friend, said he couldn't keep him on after receiving complaints from other workers that a "rich town boy" was on the payroll. He found it tough to build any savings.

His hopes for enrolling at the university improved after a Laurinburg boy named Jesse Lewis convinced him there were jobs available at Chapel Hill for students who really wanted to attend. In later years, Terry wrote that without his friend's encouragement, he might have discounted his chances to attend the university. Ironically, Betsy Sanford had been advised by other mothers to discourage Terry from spending time with Jesse, whose family was held in low regard in the community.

In the fall of 1935, Terry and Runt Fenegan, who had finished his second year at PJC, headed to Chapel Hill. Terry had less than $50 to his name when he arrived in what he soon found to be the "promised land."

CHAPTER THREE

The "Promised Land"

TERRY SANFORD AND JAMES FENEGAN left Laurinburg for Chapel Hill in September 1935, riding their thumbs. Borrowed rides from seven separate drivers—interrupted by one four-hour wait in the hot sun—took them the hundred miles or so from the flat cotton fields of Scotland County to the rolling hills of the Carolina Piedmont and the campus of the University of North Carolina. Terry carried a new suitcase and some new clothes, all purchased on credit at Aubrey Hammond's store, as well as his $75 in savings to pay tuition for his first quarter.

Terry had not rushed his decision to apply to the university, but with the confidence of Jesse Lewis's claim, plus what he had banked during his spring and summer jobs, he believed he could safely enroll. James was in a better position; he had won an academic scholarship based on his record at Presbyterian Junior College and he drew a modest state disability check because of his heart condition. But both boys knew they would need jobs almost from the moment they arrived.

Their applications for admission had arrived too late for them to secure a dorm room, so Terry's brother, Cecil, now a sophomore, had found them quarters in a rooming house on Franklin Street, the town's main thoroughfare. It proved to be a disappointment, even if the rate of $4 a month did fit their budget. The room was small and the bathroom and shower were in a room at the end of a long, open porch. They signed in, left their bags in the room, then went in search of something better. They secured more comfortable lodgings with Mrs. R. B. Finch on nearby Rosemary Street, returned for their bags and made their apologies, but forfeited a $2 deposit.

All in all, the University of North Carolina was as financially strapped as many of the 2,765 students that fall. The strain on the university budget had increased from year to year under repeated cuts by the state legislature. Neglect was beginning to show. No new buildings had been constructed on campus since the 1931 completion of the Graham Memorial Student Union, named for former President Edward Kidder Graham. The school's basketball team, the White Phantoms, played in the "Tin Can," a long barn of a wooden frame building covered with tin sheeting that also was a favorite for dances and social events. It was in use despite the fact that it was condemned; decorations and additional wiring were prohibited and no more than two hundred people could enter without violating the orders of the state insurance inspector. Elsewhere on campus, if a building leaked, a makeshift patch was applied. Scaffolding stood unused around buildings where renovations had stopped when the money ran out. Construction of any kind in the entire Chapel Hill community was at a virtual standstill. During the previous year, only $50,000 in new work had begun.[1]

Not only was available student housing spoken for by the time Terry arrived, there was no place on campus for any student to eat. The main dining facility, Swain Hall, had not reopened for the first time in twenty-two years because the university could not afford needed repairs. Students were left to commercial eateries where prices had jumped by five to ten dollars a month for basic meal plans. Chandler's Cafeteria was offering a meal ticket for twenty-one meals at six dollars a month. Breakfast was another forty cents a day.

In some respects, Terry had simply left one North Carolina town suffering through the Depression for another. Poor crop prices had reduced many in Laurinburg to subsistence level while Chapel Hill, whose main industry was education, wasted away under the state budget cuts. The two towns were similar in other respects. They were about the same size and, like all small towns, commerce was limited to shops and stores along one street. On the outskirts of Chapel Hill, in adjacent Carrboro, was a textile mill and nearby its own version of New Town. No direct rail service was available; most long-distance travelers caught the Southern Railway trains in Raleigh, twenty-five miles to the east.

Terry had seen Chapel Hill on drive-through visits returning from family vacations in Virginia. He had not remembered much about the place except the large fraternity houses that lined Columbia Street at the western edge of the campus. He knew he wasn't going to be staying in one of them any time soon as he and Fenegan settled into their boarding house on the eve of freshman orientation.

Yet, despite meager circumstances, Chapel Hill offered eager young men far more opportunity than anywhere else in North Carolina, or the South as a whole. Once Terry stepped beyond the low stone wall at the sidewalk on the south side of Franklin Street and onto the paths across the lawn of McCorkle Place, once he passed the honored founding spot at the Davie Poplar and caught sight of the weathered brick of South Building at the center of the campus, he found people who were in the business of expanding the horizons of all the Terry Sanfords. The life of this cautious eighteen-year-old began to change the Saturday before the first classes on Monday, September 23. At a freshman smoker, the venerable mathematician-philosopher Dr. Archibald Henderson told the university's class of 1939 "they were as fortunate as if an angel from heaven came down and, touching here and there, brought you each the greatest opportunity of your life." The same orientation included a welcome from the university's president, Dr. Frank Porter Graham, Edward Kidder Graham's cousin, who told the freshmen, "You have come to a place free, but you come with a responsibility, and you come to a place with traditions and honor." [2]

Freedom. Graham always talked persuasively, even passionately about freedom. At his inauguration in 1931 he spent seventy-eight minutes meticulously outlining the university's responsibility to open inquiry, unfettered discourse, and tolerance of free expression. He had called the university a "stronghold of learning and an outpost of light and liberty." [3] A balding, stocky man just five-and-a-half-feet tall, Graham was friendly and generous as well as a visionary who took the words of the American creed literally. The door to his office in South Building was always open, usually with a line of visitors waiting outside. Students and trustees waited alike; no one got favored treatment. When Graham was at home on Sunday evenings and the front porch light was lit, students knew they were welcome to step into the spacious front room of the stately home with large columns and a broad front porch for several hours of lively discussion. From his office he could look out over Polk Place, a quadrangle anchored on the south by the university library with its massive domed top and flanked on the east by buildings erected in the expansive 1920s under President Harry Chase.

Graham could just as easily be found striding across the campus calling students by name as he passed. Upon introduction, Graham would draw on his encyclopedic knowledge of the state and its families and recall a student's cousin, aunt, or uncle whom he knew; he would share a recollection or two and then he was off. He never forgot a name. Newspaper editor Jonathan Daniels once described him as looking "like Molly Cottontail as he goes scurrying by on his short legs." More important, Daniels wrote, Graham "had an honest passion for the welfare of the people." [4]

Journalist Gerald W. Johnson observed that Graham "is reputed to be the friendliest soul in the three and a half millions between Murphy and Manteo, yet he has started more fights than ever were precipitated by Blackbeard, the pirate, who, I suppose, was the unfriendliest of all North Carolinians." Graham, Johnson wrote, "does harbor one idea that is radical in the extreme, so radical that it would make him conspicuous in Moscow, not to mention North Carolina. This is the idea that the Sermon on the Mount is sound social and economic doctrine." [5]

Governor O. Max Gardner had conscripted Graham into the presidency in 1931 despite Graham's insistence that another was better suited for the job. Some of Graham's critics agreed. As a faculty member, Graham's controversial declarations on some of the hottest issues of the day, particularly his support of textile workers to organize labor unions, had infuriated many in the state's industrial and political elite. Graham's new position didn't still his fervor. In the fall of 1935, this same crowd was seething over Graham's defense the year before of a former student and socialist leader caught up in a strike in Thomasville, North Carolina. Before that, in 1932, Graham defended faculty members who had invited black poet Langston Hughes, who was a communist, and socialist philosopher Bertrand Russell to speak on campus. In yet another episode a year later, New York newspapers commended Graham for removing a quota on Jews admitted to the university's medical school, but at home the state's medical community resented his decisions that led ultimately to the resignation of the dean.

As Terry Sanford prepared for his first classes, Graham was sorting out a reorganization of the state's university campuses in Raleigh, Chapel Hill, and Greensboro that had been ordered by the legislature. Changes promoted by Graham had unsettled some of his own supporters on the board of trustees. Beginning that September, all engineering students were assigned to North Carolina State College in Raleigh, not the university at Chapel Hill, whose engineering program had been shut down. Alumni were not happy.

Despite the swirl of controversy, Graham successfully navigated storms using his persuasive personal charm to wheedle a few more dollars out of legislators who were wholly unsympathetic with his politics but whose loyalty to the campus was undeniable, no matter who was in charge. Members slow to fund the university got what was called the "Graham treatment," a close encounter with the man whose ambitions for their alma mater would not be denied.

Graham's appeal was for support of education at all levels, from the primary grades to the university. He believed the state's education program was one big system, one extended campus. By pleading the cause for education, he further expanded his universe of supporters and left his detractors appearing callous and insensitive to the needs of the state's future generations. Graham was, Gerald Johnson wrote, "a champion who could plead [education's] cause effectively with people distracted by fearful catastrophe." [6]

Terry Sanford's view of the world was less cosmic. While Fenegan enrolled in a concentrated study of French — he was determined to be Phi Beta Kappa and teach in college — Terry signed up for the regular freshman regimen and added a double load of chemistry. He might become Dr. Hunter or perhaps a healer whose research would do far more than carefully repair a bloody seven-year-old. And the two young men went looking for work to see if Jesse Lewis was as good as his word.

Lewis had one of the best-paying student jobs on campus as head of the circulation department of the *Daily Tar Heel*. Although the paper was student-run and focused mostly on campus affairs, it served as the newspaper for the village of Chapel Hill. More than three thousand copies were delivered five days a week in time for breakfast in the dorms and in homes in town. Terry and James signed up for routes and rose at daybreak to meet the delivery truck. Terry headed off campus on foot on a route that covered the hills and valleys on the western side of town. Fenegan also got a job washing dishes; Terry signed up for a "self-help" campus job and a student loan at the YMCA.

Terry had had litle personal acquaintance with folks who loaned money. Considering the prevailing attitude toward bankers, he approached the student loan office with some trepidation. "Jimmy Williams was the loan officer and I was scared to death when I went in there," Sanford later recalled. "I thought I was going to see a banker. He made me feel like I was doing him a favor."[7] The young man's signature, along with an endorsement from his parents, was enough to satisfy Williams, who that year approved student loans of nearly $50,000 to students, of which $50 a month went to the young man from Laurinburg.

The course work suited Terry fine. He did well in his classes and focused his energy on them and on his job carrying papers. Though he would hold many jobs while a student, nothing compared to the challenges of the unusual winter of 1936 when, in late January, Terry and James slogged through repeated snowstorms, including a seven-inch accumulation in early February. Yet the *Daily Tar Heel* arrived on time.

When classes resumed in January after the holidays, each issue of the newspaper brought more distressing news. Student leaders rallied support for Graham, who once again was the target of a movement to replace him with someone, virtually anyone, who would be more acceptable to the state's conservative power structure. Graham was too radical, his opponents said, and he was mishandling the affairs of the multicampus system. Chapel Hill loyalists were still offended that the engineering program had been shifted to that "cow college" at State, a land-grant school held in low regard by the elite. Moreover, Graham was actively pursuing a program with other colleges in the South to overhaul campus athletics and outlaw financial support for galloping halfbacks.

Responding to this latest attack on their president, campus leaders published an open letter to the trustees:

> Dr. Graham has insisted on intellectual freedom and the university has become famous through the world for its liberalism. But opposition in the state has defamed it as the "hot-bed of radicalism."
>
> Dr. Graham has seen his task, as president of the state university, to lead the people in raising the standards of living of our laborers and our farmers. Yet business interests have called him "Communist" and his policies "radical."

These students believed in their president, who stood "for the integrity and freedom of the three institutions of one university and the right of teachers to think out loud, to exercise the same constitutional rights as other citizens, self-government capacity of students, the organization of working people in collective bargaining for the necessities of a fair living, the cooperative organization of farmers for a better rural life and the human and civil rights of all citizens, including unpopular minorities."

A month later, in March, the trustees gave Graham a vote of confidence while he rested in Florida, recovering from a chronic respiratory ailment. Though Gardner was no longer governor, his handpicked successor, J. C. B. Ehringhaus, remained steadfast in his support of Graham.

Other disturbing news that winter would strongly affect freshman Terry Sanford when a cheating ring was discovered on campus. Reports of widespread violations of the honor code filled the columns of the *Daily Tar Heel*, and the state's daily newspapers carried stories about the growing scandal. The undoing of the violators was the work of one of Terry's classmates, who returned from the Christmas holiday after promising his father to do something about the cheating he had discovered. He took what he knew to Jack Pool, the student body president, who in turn set up a conference with Graham. The president reminded the two young men of the university's system of student governance and told them that it was up to the students to deal with assaults on the school's integrity. He gave them his full support in their investigation, and they left to build their case against the guilty.

Initial accounts of the scandal appeared in the January 30 edition of the *Daily Tar Heel*. A week later the paper published an exhaustive report detailing how copies of quizzes had been stolen from Bingham Hall and sold, some with answers and some without. The account also described a system where substitutes had been hired to take the exams of slackers, and that the ringleader confessed to completing themes and other work for students on campus or taking correspondence courses from out of town. Altogether, ninety-eight students were brought before the honor council on charges;

fifty-one students were dismissed. Caught up in the affair were members of Phi Beta Kappa and the Golden Fleece, a campus honor society.

Terry never forgot the example set by Pool, who was a well-regarded senior and leader in campus affairs. As the honor council disposed of charges against those caught up in the affair, Pool reported himself to the student council for cheating in a French class when he was a freshman. Pool's transgressions had nothing to do with the latest allegations; in fact, he had disclosed the infraction two years earlier when nothing was said about his violation of the honor code. Nonetheless, he resigned his office and moved his own suspension from the university.

At the height of the furor, Graham gathered the freshman class for a special assembly, where the young men stood and repeated the pledge to uphold the honor system. "The fact that Pool himself exposed a five-year-old episode," Graham told the freshmen on a cold February morning, "is proof that the honor system is working here." He expressed hope that the class of 1939 would graduate "without a blot on its record."

"We become a part of what we tolerate," Graham said, "and if we tolerate what has been going on, we are cheating. We can't live and grow while such a situation exists."[8]

Terry finished his freshman year with good grades, including an A in qualitative analysis. He enjoyed his English courses; one of the themes he wrote was a short story based on the cashier at the failed Laurinburg bank who had disappeared the day it closed. It had been a stimulating year and the beginning of an experience he later would call "an opening up of a world that I didn't know anything about."[9] He enjoyed the competition with able students who were more challenging than any he had known before. He had listened to his first symphony concert and seen art hanging in a gallery. He had come under the influence of Frank Porter Graham.

As challenging as the work were the new ideas that he encountered in Chapel Hill. Reflecting on this introduction to the world some years later, Sanford said:

> I would say that I probably would have followed a different path and probably been a different kind of person if I hadn't gone to Chapel Hill.
>
> I always saw [Graham] as the kind of person not that I would like to be, because there were a lot of things about him that I thought were weaknesses that he didn't really need to have, but I saw him as representing the ideals that I thought were proper and I would like to have as my ideals.
>
> I think Frank Graham woke people up to the fact that we could do

something about some of our problems. He woke them up to the fact that it wasn't so bad to champion the cause of the sharecropper and the black and the working man that wasn't unionized and was being pretty much treated as chattel.[10]

This was treacherous stuff in many quarters of the state and among those in the Chapel Hill student body, which some have called the last post–Civil War generation. Not all on campus agreed with their president. "They weren't necessarily hostile, but had a little skepticism here and there, or they just weren't on his band wagon," recalled Alexander Heard, then a campus leader and later president of Vanderbilt University.[11] But the attacks on Graham worked a curious chemistry within the student body. His supporters were vigorous in their defense and constantly rallied to his support.

Whenever Terry returned home, he faced questions at the barber shop or on Main Street from his elders who called the campus a "cesspool of communism." What else would you call it when one of Graham's sociology professors, Guy B. Johnson, had been quoted as saying that the South's segregated world of "separate-but-equal" was a failure and the only economical answer was integration? Recalling the attacks, the grilling he would endure from skeptics, Sanford later said, "That was the old reactionary crowd. But that was good for us as students. Frank Graham said the best way to fight communism was to let people see a communist. You had to defend Frank Graham and it solidified your views."[12]

As his first year at Chapel Hill drew to a close, Terry thought ahead to the summer. Jobs were still tough to find; his choices, based on past experience, included pumping gas or working at the grocery store. Finally, he decided to expand on the summer swimming program he had run for the American Red Cross out at Lee's Mill Pond and began making plans to open a boys' camp.

He called it Camp Pawnee for no better reason than he liked the sound and the romance of American Indian names. The camp was little more than a rustic cabin on the edge of Pine Lake outside Marston near the Scotland and Rockingham county line about twenty miles outside of Laurinburg. Terry had approached the cabin's owner in the spring and convinced him to let him use his place without charge. With the help of some friends, he installed bunks and cots and began taking applications from youngsters around town. The fee was $4.50 a week and Terry enrolled thirty campers his first season. The camp was well received, in part because Laurinburg mothers believed that if Betsy Sanford would let her son run a camp then it must be all right. At the same time, Terry's reputation as an Eagle Scout and his success with the swimming program were seen as a fair demonstration of his ability to look after those placed in his care.

Terry recruited his friends Albert Phillips and Archie Purcell to work as counselors, paying them each five dollars a week. Archie also doubled as the cook. "The first time he cooked rice he didn't know that rice swelled up so," Sanford recalled. "We had an old oil stove and it spilled out all over it." Dickson Phillips, a Laurinburg lad who was the age of Terry's younger sisters, was one of the campers and found the activities exciting, he later recalled, "but we almost starved to death."[13]

Swimming and canoeing on Pine Lake were a big part of the campers' day, but the boys also played baseball and learned how to wrestle and box. Terry led hikes through the woods where he taught nature lore and the basics of outdoor life. The first season of Camp Pawnee resulted in a modest financial success and Terry made plans for a second season the following summer.

By the time Terry returned to Chapel Hill that fall, he had reconsidered his career plans. The life of a country doctor held less appeal than it had the year before and faded completely from the picture of his future when he learned that a full medical education might require as much as $15,000. He skimmed the university catalogue and signed up for a variety of courses, supplementing his math and science with economics and philosophy.

At the start of his sophomore year, Terry was determined to get a job better than hauling newspapers around before dawn in the snow. He went to see Edwin S. Lanier, who ran the National Youth Administration program for students through the YMCA, and was assigned to work in Swain Hall, which had reopened after $60,000 in renovations. The dining hall job came with an extra benefit. He was allowed to room in the basement without charge along with another self-help student, a junior from Monroe named John Bowles. John and Terry rose early and put in most of their required three hours a day before leaving for class. One of Terry's chores was to prepare ten dozen eggs, breaking them into cups for the cooks to fry or scramble on the serving line—"You got a rotten one about every twenty-fifth one," he later recalled—and then he bussed tables in the main hall.

That fall Terry and Cecil Sanford got an unexpected financial boost after their mother made the winning selections in a football pool and won a new Plymouth automobile. "She didn't know a thing about football," Sanford recalled. "I don't know how she picked the scores, arbitrarily, at random. She might have talked to Daddy a little. They might have known that UCLA was better than Oklahoma."[14] The Sanfords took delivery of the car but soon returned it for a cash award of $500. They passed along part of their windfall to their sons.

Terry had turned in good grades as a freshman, but his marks suffered during his sophomore year after he lost his motivation to be a doctor and drifted from one course of study to another. One classmate recalled at a reunion some years later that Terry was dozing in class one day when the professor called on him with a question. "Terry woke up with a jolt and said, 'Will you repeat the question please?' The professor repeated it and Terry said, 'What would you think is the answer?' 'I don't think,' the professor said, 'I know.' 'I don't think I know either,' Terry replied." [15]

He remained active in the YMCA, but his second year was not one of distinction. Before the final quarter was over, he also lost his good friend, James Fenegan. Fenegan was about to graduate when he suffered a heart attack and died. The doctor at the university infirmary delivered the news to the Fenegan family in Laurinburg.

Terry had spent part of his spring term preparing for another summer camping season. He talked his German professor into helping him prepare a promotional booklet that he reproduced on a Mimeograph machine on campus and circulated throughout Laurinburg. Again parents entrusted their sons to his care; however, one mother did raise a question about some of his declarations in the new promotional literature. When she came to look over the camp, Sanford said she asked, "I thought you said you had an experienced cook? I said, 'No ma'am, I said we had an experienced camp cook.' And that satisfied her." [16]

To boost registrations, Sanford told the Laurinburg Rotary Club about a Fresh Air Camp for underprivileged boys sponsored by the *Charlotte Observer* and he convinced the club to underwrite the fees of boys from the East Laurinburg mill village for a separate session of their own. The experience remained something of a puzzle years later as he questioned whether separating Laurinburg's haves and have-nots was a good idea: "I never was satisfied that we did that the right way because somehow there got to be a certain stigma that we weren't mature enough to figure out. They got as good an outing as the other boys did." [17]

Camping was work that Terry thoroughly enjoyed, and he was good at it. He liked spending time with the younger boys, teaching them about the woods and wildlife. They responded to his attention, and the second year was as successful as the first. Campers suffered the usual scrapes and bruises but no serious injury, and the boys of Camp Pawnee returned to their parents sound and probably a little more fit than when they left home. The only scare came one night as Terry and his counselors led a small group of campers whom they had selected for induction into the Clan of the Tahkadah, a name Terry created to add a little mystery to the honor. Walking to the campfire ceremony, one of the boys slipped and fell from the edge of the dam at the end of the lake. Terry saw the boy totter and jumped at about the same time, landing below and saving him from serious injury.

At the close of the camp season, Terry and his crew of four counselors packed up the camp's lake fleet—a short, canvas-covered canoe and a rowboat they had bought at Sears—and put in the Cape Fear River at Fayetteville determined to make the Atlantic Ocean and Masonboro Beach, about 120 miles away. It was pure adventure and a test of their survival skills.

Below Fayetteville, the Cape Fear was a wandering river that flowed through virtual wilderness, broken by tobacco and cotton fields and an occasional farmhouse. The river's current was fed by hundreds of creeks and smaller rivers upstream that frequently flooded in the springtime, depositing all sorts of debris on the bottom and along the shore. By summer, the river depth was reduced to stump level, which demanded that boaters keep a watchful eye for snags and shoals that could upright small craft; the teenagers navigated around the hazards. When they reached the three locks and dams maintained by the U.S. Army Corps of Engineers, the lock masters extended the small flotilla the same courtesy they did the barges that plied the river.

The second day out, the boys came upon a long log raft made up of eight sections of huge gum trees tied together like cars in a freight train. On the front section, they found the pilot, a man named Butler, who had built a small shack, fashioned a fire pit out of clay, and was traveling with his dog and a small boy. He invited the young adventurers aboard. The boys pulled their canoe and rowboat out of the water and spent the next two days diving, swimming, and fishing from the raft. They listened to the old man's tales of the river and wild animals that lived on the small islands they passed along the way. At night they lay wrapped in their bedrolls cradled between the huge logs. The morning they parted company, eager to complete their journey, they left with the aroma of hoecakes in the air and a glimpse of a way of life that was disappearing with each truck that rolled along the highways headed to the mills at Wilmington.

Recalling the adventure years later, Sanford said he learned a valuable lesson about life from that trip. Good camp sites were few along the river, particularly along the swampy regions closer to the coast where the land is flat: "You had better decide when you went by whether or not you were going to camp because once you went on, you couldn't turn back. Once you pass that opportunity, you can't go back." [18]

When Terry returned to Chapel Hill in September 1937 to begin his junior year, his brother was not with him. Instead, Cecil had joined the merchant marine and was aboard a freighter out of Baltimore bound for the Pacific. Terry was a bit jealous of his older brother at the same time that he admired his courage and adventurous spirit. Meanwhile, Terry had improved on his arrangements and landed a job running a laundry route in the dormitories. The work required him to deliver orders to the dormitories and see that the dorm managers distributed them properly. He also began to pick up other jobs around campus thanks to Bill McCachren, a tall, strong, versatile athlete whom he had met on the Swain Hall detail. They got to know one another better during spring break, when they remained on campus to earn a few extra dollars grading papers for Dr. Guy B. Phillips, a professor in the School of Education, who had a host of student achievement tests from across the state to evaluate.

McCachren was from Charlotte and the third of four McCachren brothers to attend the university. He played basketball and was a high jumper on the track team. He also competed in the shot put after the track-and-field coach, Bob Fetzer, saw him casually toss a stray shot. Basketball was his real love, however, and he would go on to captain the 1939 White Phantom squad. McCachren's ambition was to graduate and become a coach and a teacher.

McCachren and Sanford became good friends, sharing not only jobs but one another's clothes despite a serious disparity in their sizes. McCachren's trousers were far too long for Terry, who was shorter and heavier, but Terry wore a pair of McCachren's shoes until the soles had holes. In time, McCachren and Sanford teamed with Paul Thompson, who hailed from Wadesboro, North Carolina, and was a member of the football team. They all came from similar circumstances and each was a hustler who looked out for his buddies. "Like a lot of us," McCachren recalled, "he didn't have anything when he got here. If one of us had a job, and we needed somebody else, well, that's the ones we'd call." [19]

One source of extra income came from the campus social life. McCachren had followed his brother, David, onto the dance committee and so was well situated to know when extra help was needed to work dances at the Tin Can. McCachren and his crew racked coats at the door, sold soft drinks, and saw that liquor stayed outside.

McCachren and Sanford also controlled the wait staff at Graham Memorial, where faculty members and university officials would arrange for catered meals for special occasions. Once, as the two were preparing the tables for a private party, Graham pulled them aside and asked if they would mind serving African Americans. Both assured Graham they would have no problem treating all the dinner guests alike.

It had been a simple question, but one complicated by time and place. For Terry, it was the first time he had ever been asked to declare himself on the issue that more than any other defined the South and its people. He had not been raised to be a bigot, and he didn't think of himself as such. His parents had instilled an attitude of tolerance and compassion "to those less fortunate," as the elders in Christian homes would have put it. Indeed, his mother had once quietly admonished him after he finished telling the family at supper about the taunts he and his buddies had heaped on a boy they called Stinky because of an "accident" at school. "I thought it was hilarious," Sanford later wrote, "but my mother did not laugh. Instead, she said, 'I was hoping you would be the one that would take up for him.' I found it awfully hard to taunt anybody after that." [20] Terry also had heard his father take late-night phone calls from residents of New Town who had landed in jail and needed a white friend to vouch for them. The elder Sanford had seen the Red Shirts ride through his town in 1898 demonstrating the rawest form of intimidation against African Americans eager to exercise their right to vote, but he was the one at the courthouse in 1928 who registered the first black citizens to vote in Scotland County since those turbulent days.

Terry had seen other crude divisions created by Jim Crow laws and the social and cultural restrictions on the lives of African Americans. When he was working at the grocery store, he listened to the complaints of a black employee who was denied the same rights and privileges as whites. He also was well aware that the desperate conditions of white mill workers in East Laurinburg were exceeded only by what he saw in New Town where he peddled vegetables. Yet, like almost everyone else in town, he accepted the condition of African Americans the same way he accepted his family's own desperate condition. That was just the way things were: "When I came to Chapel Hill I had been brought up in a society that taught that you were decent to blacks but that was the extent of the obligation. You could hardly expect them to want the ordinary benefits of American life," Sanford later recalled. "It took a little bit of shock treatment to shake people out of that mode. Frank Graham furnished that shock treatment in his own modest, direct way. He could bring attention to things that were not right and you thought about it. And when you thought about it, you said, 'Of course, it isn't right.' " [21]

Similar conversions were taking place across a campus that defended an atmosphere of concern and interest in the future of the South and its burden of race. The reputation of Chapel Hill as an island of liberalism had not begun with Graham. Playwright Paul Green, whose In Absalom's Bosom had won the Pulitzer Prize in 1929, bothered those defending the status quo, as did W. T. Couch, director of the University of North Carolina Press, who provided an outlet for black writers and the liberal social philosophy that challenged long-held Southern traditions. Another prominent figure was sociologist Dr. Howard Odum, whose monumental work, Southern Regions *of the United States*, had established him as the authority on the region and its problems. Published in 1936, Odum's study arrived at the same time as Franklin Roosevelt's declaration that the South was America's number one economic problem, a statement that galled North Carolina's conservative leaders who had largely ignored the poverty and desperation that was driving people off the land.

Terry never studied under Odum but he did have classes with Dr. S. Huntington Hobbs, one of Odum's associates, who in 1929 published a study of economic conditions in North Carolina. Hobbs not only detailed the plight of the state's people and institutions, but he provided remedies for uplifting the human condition and dealing with the ravages of the sharecropper system and endemic poverty. One day in his classroom on the ground floor of the library, "Honey" Hobbs, as he was known, challenged his students to do something about getting electricity to the rural farms, improving sanitary conditions in mill villages, and ending the sharecropper system. "He said 'If anybody will adopt my program,'" recalled Sanford, 'I'll support you for governor.' I said, 'I'll adopt it,' and did." 22

One Friday Hobbs announced he was leaving for Washington at two that afternoon and asked if any students wanted to come along. Terry nudged his friend Norman McCullough and said, "Let's go to Washington." They gathered up their bags and headed off for their first trip to the nation's capital. As Hobbs drove through Richmond, Virginia, however, the two took their leave to visit McCullough's cousin who lived there. The overnight stay included a big dance, but they were up early Saturday and hitchhiked to Washington, where they met Hobbs in the offices of Josiah Bailey, North Carolina's senior senator, who, though an austere conservative, had deflected a challenge in his bid for reelection in 1936 by posing as a supporter of Roosevelt and the New Deal. After he won and was secure for another six years, he showed he was no friend of the president. He helped draft the Conservative Manifesto, a statement of Republicans and Southern Democrats who halted expansion of the New Deal in Congress.

On that first trip to Capitol Hill, Sanford was more impressed with the streetcars than he was with important people such as Bailey. It was not that public figures did not leave an impression. He carried the memory of his handshake with O. Max Gardner as a singular childhood event and would never forget the discovery that Franklin Roosevelt was disabled, a fact hid from most of the American public. This he had learned in 1936, when he drove Mrs. Maguire and a group of her friends to Charlotte for the president's appearance there. Terry was standing near enough to the stage to see the Secret Service agents help the president from his wheelchair and carry him up the stairs.

The clash of political ideologies would soon rouse the attention of the class of 1939, who were coming of age in a nation aboil with often desperate designs of economic salvation, from the stiff conservatism of Josiah Bailey, who Jonathan Daniels said "struts even when he sits down,"[23] to the revolutionary proposals of Upton Sinclair of California, the socialist turned Democrat who threw a scare into Republicans and Democrats during his gubernatorial campaign in 1936. The growing threat of war in Europe presented a new set of questions for young men who might have to fight and die abroad. All of this was brought to Terry and his classmates through a new and vigorous campus organization known as the Carolina Political Union.

Formed in the fall of 1936, the CPU provided a political forum for the presidential campaign and candidates like Frank Knox, the Republican vice presidential candidate, and Norman Thomas, the Socialist Party candidate who had campaigned in the South. The following year, senior Alexander Heard became the chairman. He had come to Chapel Hill to study to be an engineer but switched to the "Dean Hobbs curricula," according to the 1938 edition of the UNC yearbook, the *Yackety-Yak*. Heard, who would return to teach at Chapel Hill before moving on to Vanderbilt, issued invitations to a host of controversial speakers, leaving it to Graham to handle the occasional uproar over his choices. Campus visitors included Earl Browder, the chairman of the Communist Party, as well as Hiram Wesley Evans, the Imperial Wizard of the Ku Klux Klan. In time, the ambassadors to the United States from Germany, Japan, and the Soviet Union were given the podium even as their nations prepared for war. A thousand students, more than a quarter of the entire student body, turned out in October 1938 to hear Margaret Sanger, the outspoken proponent of birth control. The next month Dr. George H. Derry of Detroit, a well-known anticommunist, was met with derogatory leaflets from a group of students who objected to his appearance on campus.

In early December 1938, Memorial Auditorium was packed with students and guests awaiting President Roosevelt's arrival. While on a return to Washington from his retreat at Warm Springs, Georgia, he left his train at the town of Sanford and, accompanied by a newsreel truck, rode in a caravan of more than twenty cars the fifty miles to Chapel Hill, where he was to receive an honorary doctor of laws degree in Kenan Stadium. A cold, drizzling Carolina rain forced the program indoors to Memorial Auditorium.

The president's speech was preceded by a concert from a WPA chorus of seventy-five African Americans from Durham and Winston-Salem. Senior Voit Gilmore, the CPU chair who would travel on to Washington with the presidential party, spoke briefly, and then Governor Clyde Hoey welcomed the president, who delivered a speech outlining the development of liberalism from the early days of the Republic. "It is only the unthinking liberals in this world," Roosevelt said, "who see nothing but tragedy in the slowing up and temporary stopping of liberal progress. It is only the unthinking conservatives who rejoice when a social and economic reform fails to be 100 percent successful." [24]

Roosevelt's remarks were probably nettlesome to Hoey. Like Bailey, the governor had only feigned support of the New Deal in his 1936 election campaign after a groundswell of public support for maverick Ralph McDonald and the New Deal scared the state's conservative element.[25] One issue in the campaign was continuation of the state sales tax, which had been imposed by the General Assembly in 1933 to save the state from financial collapse. Hoey defended the tax and in defeating McDonald, who opposed it, settled the matter, at least for the time being.

Hoey was a consummate politician who favored swallow-tailed coats, a fresh carnation in his lapel, and Methodism. He was a walking contradiction. His weekly Sunday school lesson was broadcast by a Raleigh radio station, but out on the stump there were plenty of stories of his fondness for the ladies. His speeches sang with his flowery phrases and pleased his audiences, but he once confessed after an address, "I didn't have anything to say. So I turned it on and let it run until I thought they had enough, and then cut it off." [26]

Although the state's political leaders fought the New Deal, they weren't above accepting their share of money from Washington. Federal funds were changing the face of Chapel Hill. After years of watching scaffolding rust and rot, major construction projects were on the drawing boards. Five million dollars in WPA money was scheduled to pay for new dormitories, a new dining hall, and a $700,000 power plant.

By his senior year, Terry was twenty-one years old and managing Everett Hall, one of the men's dormitories, where he earned a fair living off his share of the profits from the dorm store. In addition to this income, he and McCachren earned money by teaching swimming at the pool in the new Woolen Gymnasium. Some of the beginning swimmers were young victims of polio, then a mysterious disease that crippled communities with fear as easily as it destroyed the muscles of its victims. Terry's life-saving certificate qualified him to teach an advanced Red Cross program as well. He also had become the person to see for freshmen enrolling from Laurinburg. Perhaps Terry saw himself in the young men who arrived on campus without a place to stay or a job; he would help newcomers locate both, and sometimes took younger students under his care for late-night study sessions.

He had begun to dabble in student politics, but with limited success. The previous year he and McCachren had worked to elect Henry Hudson senior class president. The way Terry later recalled it, Hudson casually invited him to attend a meeting of the University Party, and to his surprise Hudson introduced him as his campaign manager. That first campaign turned out to be a loser. Hudson's main stump speech consisted of a tear-jerking account of his own hard-luck life story. The students were not impressed and neither was Terry, who discounted Hudson's chances from that moment.

Terry stayed busy with his odd jobs and classes. He had played intramural football when his team won the championship, but he led a limited social life and as a self-help student was prohibited from joining a fraternity, even if such a thing had appealed to him. Despite his admiration of Graham, the president's Sunday evening sessions had never ignited much of his interest. He went to the president's home a few times but never became part of the regular crowd and mostly listened to the discussions rather than take part. For the most part, he considered the Sunday night regulars to be a supercilious lot.

He had finally settled on a major, in a backhand sort of way. One day, he was walking through Saunders Hall when his friend John Umstead III suggested that Terry take the comprehensive exam in political science that was scheduled for the following Saturday. All students were required to pass a comprehensive in their major before they could graduate. Terry had taken only one political science course, but he agreed to join Umstead at the appointed hour and take the exam, which he passed. "So, that determined my major," he recalled. "I wasn't about to take a comprehensive on something else." [27]

Cecil Sanford had rejoined his brother in Chapel Hill by the fall of 1938, planning to graduate with a degree in English literature the following year. Terry envied Cecil's year of adventure away from campus. Cecil had seen much of the world, but had come close to not living to tell about it. On a return voyage from Australia the crew on his ship became embroiled in a mutiny and he was put ashore in Jamaica. While waiting there for another berth, he was jumped by muggers, knifed, and left for dead. Throughout it all, his family knew nothing, although Betsy Sanford awoke one night and told her husband that she was sure something had happened to her son and that he was lost to them forever. Not long after, she received a letter from a Chinese doctor in Jamaica, who wrote about finding Cecil and nursing him back to health. By the time Cecil arrived in Chapel Hill, his wounds had healed, though he did carry scars on his forehead that gave him an appearance of constant worry.

Terry's own travel adventures paled in comparison. Aside from his trip to Washington, he had seldom strayed far from home. Once, he had set out for Florida with a buddy from Laurinburg. They got as far as St. Augustine and were staying in a dilapidated rooming house when their money ran out. Terry called his friend Donald McCoy back in Laurinburg, who wired him five dollars for bus fare home.

While Cecil made plans for graduate school and a career as a college professor, Terry's ambitions wandered from one thing to another. During his senior year, he applied for a job with Standard Oil Company and hoped for an assignment in South America. The company turned him down. Next, he decided that he wanted a job as a Boy Scout executive and went after the position with enthusiasm. When he failed to get even a suggestion of interest, the disappointment was deep; he was hurt by the rejection of an organization that had been an important part of his life for nearly ten years.

Yet Terry wasn't entirely without prospects. He and McCachren had been talking about running a summer camp for boys. It was not going to be just another camp—there already were several popular locations in the North Carolina mountains—for they believed that in time their camp would become the camp for North Carolina. The opportunity arose through their connections with Dr. Guy Phillips, the education professor. Phillips, his brother Charles W. Phillips, who taught at Woman's College in Greensboro, and seven other school men in the state owned Camp Black Bear, located on 430 acres north of Marion, near the lower end of Linville Gorge. They had run the camp for several years before closing it because none of the investors was in a position to properly manage the place. The facilities included a dozen rough cabins perched on a hillside, a large screened-in dining hall, an open-air gymnasium, tennis courts, ball fields, a private lake fed by two mountain streams, and access to some of the most beautiful and rugged mountain wilderness in the eastern United States.

McCachren and Sanford had plenty of camp experience. While Terry had been running Camp Pawnee, McCachren had spent his summers working as a counselor at a camp near Hendersonville, North Carolina. Yet, they knew their own résumés were not enough. If the camp was to succeed they needed an older person, someone parents would trust, as camp director. That spring they hired G. Flake "Red" Laird, who was coaching football and baseball at Davidson College. Laird not only brought along his wife, who became the camp dietitian, but he also recruited a number of paying campers who had been with him at another camp the year before.

McCachren needed the spring quarter to complete his requirements for graduation, but Terry had enough credits. He left his partner in Chapel Hill and headed to the mountains, where he patched roofs on the cabins and supervised repairs to the dam at Lake Jimmy, the camp's two-and-a-half-acre lake. He also rebuilt a small electrical generator powered by a waterwheel on one of the creeks and ran wires to the single lightbulbs hanging from the rafters in each cabin.

The first season at Camp Black Bear was a success. Sanford and McCachren closed the camp's eight-week season with enough income to pay Laird and the counselors, take care of their bills, and make a token payment to Phillips and the other owners. They began making plans as career camp owners. The arrangement appeared ideal for McCachren; at the end of the summer, he was headed to a job as a coach and director of intramural athletics at Oak Ridge Military Institute, a small college preparatory school located outside of Greensboro. The appointment gave him everything he had wanted plus it left his summers free to run Camp Black Bear. Terry, meanwhile, needed something to tide him over until the next camping season. He was at loose ends when he thought about entering law school. He held no deep-seated ambition to be a lawyer, but he could recall an adolescent urge in that direction after he had witnessed a mock trial in school. For the moment, it offered a way to keep himself occupied until the next summer.

In September he returned to Chapel Hill and walked across the quadrangle to Manning Hall, the home of the law school. "I went into the dean's office," Sanford later recalled, "and I said, 'Miss Lucy'—she was the secretary everybody knew on campus—I said, 'I believe I will go to law school.' And she said, 'Fill out this form.' " [28]

CHAPTER FOUR

Albert's Boys

AMONG THE SEVEN MEMBERS of the law school faculty at the University of North Carolina when Terry Sanford arrived as a first-year student was Albert Coates, a gruff, demanding, sometimes profane, and single-minded man who operated under the curious notion that all of North Carolina was his classroom, not just the space inside the walls of Manning Hall.

Coates had grown up amidst the rural life of eastern North Carolina and graduated from the university in 1919. He remained in Chapel Hill at the request of President Harry Chase to help raise money for construction of a student activities building planned as a memorial to Chase's predecessor, the late Edward Kidder Graham. He finally left to enroll in Harvard Law School in 1920, where he finished his third year with financial support arranged by Chase, who subsequently hired him to teach upon the recommendation of Harvard Dean Roscoe Pound.

Coates nervously approached his first classes in the fall of 1924. He was not only younger than his fellow faculty members, but he was self-conscious about his own lack of experience. Traditionally, faculty members had been called from the ranks of experienced members of the bar, and virtually all of Coates's colleagues brought to the classroom an understanding of the profession shaped by their years in court. Coates had never defended a client, had never tried a case, had not so much as drawn a deed or a will. To compensate for his shortcomings, he proceeded to invite judges and practicing attorneys into his classroom and then, finally, he simply immersed himself in the state's criminal justice system. He traveled at his own expense to towns and counties where he rode with policemen as they made predawn patrols and chased bootleggers at ninety miles an hour. He testified in court as an investigating officer, he worked with prosecutors, he sat on juries, and he went into the prisons to study the penalties meted out in court. He once said he "crawled through the bloodstream" of the state's judicial system.[1]

By the time Terry Sanford, a sandy-haired twenty-two-year-old, took a seat about midway back on the right in Coates's class, Coates had organized a unique enterprise called the Institute of Government. The idea came naturally to Coates from his idol Edward Kidder Graham, who had preached that the university should serve the entire state, not just those seeking degrees. This lesson had been reinforced by law professor Eugene Cunningham Branson, who had made the state's institutions and policies the subject of considerable research and used Coates as a research assistant.[2]

For Coates, his Institute bridged the gap between the law in books and the law in action. Through seminars and short courses at the Institute, he extended the resources of the law school to the very vitals of public life, from the cop walking a beat in Charlotte to the tax collector in Harnett County who came to Chapel Hill for specialized training in classes conducted by law professors, judges, and selected state officials. He had launched the Institute in 1932 and his old Harvard Law dean was on hand to open the first seminar for local government officials. By 1939, Coates's dream of a home for the Institute finally was a reality as he prepared for the dedication of the Institute's own building on Franklin Street.

When he was an undergraduate, Terry had been only vaguely aware of the Institute and its creator. But a relationship that would change his life developed in Coates's classroom, where Terry came to enjoy the professor's lectures and legal sparring. He frequently rose to Coates's badgering on points of law and the two became friends. Just before Thanksgiving, Coates asked Terry to find volunteers in the dormitories who turned over their rooms for use by local officials in Chapel Hill for the dedication of the Institute building.

Organizing such an exchange was an easy chore for Terry, who had developed a network of contacts among the student body due at least in part to his growing interest in campus politics. In the spring of 1939, he had worked from his base in the dorms to elect John McCormick secretary-treasurer of the student council. McCormick was a self-helper whom Terry had assisted over the rough spots in some courses with nightly study sessions he called "the late shift." McCormick was a reluctant political candidate; Terry had drafted him at the last minute when the party came up short of names. He then organized his campaign around a simple campaign slogan: "And John McCormick." Terry didn't care who voters picked at the top of a ticket, just as long as they voted for their candidate "And John McCormick."[3]

In that same election, Terry supported Don Bishop's bid to become editor of the *Daily Tar Heel*. They beat a candidate who had the solid backing of the rest of the newspaper's staff in a campaign that featured what Terry called an "outhouse" poster for Bishop. On the night before the election, Terry arranged for a flyer promoting Bishop's candidacy to be taped to the inside of the toilet stalls in every dormitory. Potential voters were a captive audience the next morning.

Terry got his first semester of law school behind him before he put his own name on a ballot and filed as a candidate for one of the seats in the newly created student legislature. The university had a long history of student government, and there was no greater defender of self-governance than Frank Graham. A new student legislature had grown out of the cheating scandal, when campus leaders undertook a study of the full range of student-run activities. The result was a new constitution that proposed major changes, including a popularly elected legislature thought to provide broader representation. This legislature limped through its first year. It had no budget and no regular meeting time and held only two formal sessions. By the fall of 1939, the *Daily Tar Heel* questioned whether a student legislature whose presiding officer was the vice president of the student council could work effectively. Two things happened to effect major change, and both revolved around the election of William McWhorter Cochrane, an experienced campus politician who found in Terry Sanford an able ally for fine-tuning the system.

Cochrane hailed from Newton, a small town in the mountain foothills of Catawba County. His father had been a merchant until the Depression closed his store; his mother was an accomplished pianist who had once taught at Catawba College before the school was moved to Salisbury. He had arrived in Chapel Hill in 1933 at the age of sixteen with $29. Like Terry, he had parlayed one campus job into another, and in the spring of 1940, he was in his second year in law school and, like Terry, had one of the best jobs on campus, managing a dormitory. Cochrane had sturdy features, unruly dark hair, an easy manner, and the makings of a politician. He already had mastered Frank Graham's facility for matching places and names and making a stranger feel welcome. He saw potential in the proposed changes to the student legislature that created the office of speaker, although when he announced his candidacy he didn't know if it might all be for naught. If he won and students rejected constitutional amendments creating the position, he would have won election to an office that did not exist.[4]

Terry worked on Cochrane's behalf at the same time that he was promoting his own candidacy as the legislative representative from Everett Dormitory, where he was the manager. The political organization he had crafted was simple yet effective, and not unlike the military's chain of command. He enlisted his closest friends as area coordinators; they, in turn, were assigned to find a person on every floor of each dormitory and in every fraternity house to turn out the vote on election day. Sanford called his co-ordinators "keys" and maintained an index card on each person, down to those at the bottom of this far-reaching pyramid structure. Cochrane won and so did Terry, who twenty years later would produce a statewide political organization in exactly the same way.

One of Terry's index cards carried the name of Martha Bryan Clampitt, a tall, pretty blond from St. Petersburg, Florida, who had become one of the leaders of Chapel Hill's small contingent of female students. She wrote a column for the *Daily Tar Heel*, played intramural softball, and was a member of the swim team. She was a sorority girl and by her senior year had sufficiently intimidated the male leadership of the University Party steering committee to secure herself a seat on their council, a place no woman had ever been. When Clampitt told the men she planned to join them, they said no. "I said, 'Well, you don't get our votes then,' and so I went on," she later recalled.[5] In the 1940 elections, she won a legislative seat on the University Party ticket and Cochrane assigned her to the Ways and Means Committee, where he had rewarded Terry with the chairmanship.

Of all the committees, Ways and Means offered Terry the greatest opportunity to consolidate his political base. The committee reviewed the budgets of all campus organizations and could easily produce the next speaker if things went well. Terry's first legislative test found him and Graham's administration on what might later be considered the wrong side of at least one issue. The campus humor magazine, the *Buccaneer*, had been stirring up a storm of controversy with its racy material for some time. Just the previous year, the student council had ordered destruction of one issue "on the ground that it contained immoral and obscene matter." In the fall of 1940, Terry's committee took up a bill supported by the administration that directed the Campus Publications Board to shut down the *Buccaneer*.

Debate raged for a week. The magazine's supporters said campus humor was nobody's business but the students' and claimed that the bill was an attack on free speech. Opponents argued that the magazine was damaging the university and, frankly, was not as good a magazine as students were capable of producing. When Terry counted the votes, the *Buccaneer* lost thirty-four to six. In its place came a less raucous magazine called *Tar 'n' Feathers*.

The *Buccaneer* debate was but a prelude to a power play that Sanford and Cochrane initiated that following spring. In April, Terry backed a bill to create a single student activity fee under the control of the student legislature. The proposed change came in the wake of questions that had been raised as the legislature passed on the budgets of student organizations.

Most of the budget review sessions had gone smoothly, but the $93 that the Debate Council claimed was paid in "tips" during one trip raised questions. Students struggling to live for an entire semester on that amount of money were enraged when they learned how their money had been spent.

Terry's handling of the issue was impressive. Those who watched him liked his steady, unperturbed bearing and skillful management of the floor debate. "He was constant," Martha Clampitt McKay recalled some years later. "Always friendly, always measured, never blowing off, never mean." The Daily Tar Heel said, "In an hour and a half session which heard the fullest and most intelligent discussion shown in the legislature all year, Chairman Terry Sanford of the ways and means committee answered question after question until the bill was fully explained."[6] The bill passed, and in the elections the following spring Terry was elected to succeed Cochrane as speaker of the legislature. He won with support from both political parties.

Sanford's friendship with Cochrane was more than a political alliance. Early in 1941, the two had gone to work for the Institute of Government, replacing older staff members who had been forced to leave when Coates was unable to afford full-time help. The Institute had always struggled for money; often, Coates had paid the Institute's bills from his own paycheck. During lean times, staff lawyers had even pooled their money to at least keep those with larger families fed. Finally, Coates had turned to law students, who worked at a fraction of the cost of professional help.

Coates was particularly eager for Cochrane to edit the Institute's magazine, Popular Government. Cochrane told his professor, whom he called "the captain," that he'd take the job if he would also hire Sanford and another student, George Riddle. Coates agreed and told the three that he would pay the going rate for self-help jobs, about fifty dollars a month. That figure at least matched what they were earning elsewhere and they signed on.

The North Carolina General Assembly was about to open its biennial session in Raleigh when Sanford, Cochrane, and Riddle went to work. They were assigned to help produce one of the Institute's most useful services, a daily bulletin of legislative activity that Coates mailed to subscribers in law offices and courthouses across the state. Each day of the legislative session, Coates gathered details of action on bills in the House and Senate, then hurried back to Chapel Hill where brief, one- or two-sentence descriptions of the daily legislative business were typed, proofed, reproduced, and mailed. Nobody, not even the News & Observer in Raleigh, which was considered the paper of record for state government, provided as detailed or as thorough an account of daily legislative action.[7]

The job at the Institute agreed with Sanford, according to a letter he wrote his parents on Institute stationery bearing his name as a staff member: "It's a good job because I can just about work to suit myself, so long as I get it all done." He enclosed a photograph of Coates taken on the occasion of a reception at the Institute offices for William Bullitt, the U.S. ambassador to France, who had been on campus for a speech to the International Relations Club. And he noted, "The Institute had the honor of being the decent element on campus to welcome the Ambassador." In lieu of a month and date, Sanford noted the day of his writing with "Monday, day of third inaugural of President Roosevelt."[8]

Roosevelt, the threat of the collapse of Britain in the face of Nazi bombing raids, and the fall of Dunkirk were on Sanford's mind. Just a few weeks earlier, Roosevelt had announced his lend-lease plan to shore up the British war effort with destroyers and supplies, drawing criticism from isolationists. Sanford wrote his parents: "Certainly am glad that the President has now everybody but [Senator Burton K.] Wheeler agreeing that England shall not be allowed to lose, no matter what the cost to US. They should have come around to that doctrine several months ago, but it may still be soon enough for us to keep out of war. Funny a gambling nation like America hasn't realized what game they're in and what the stakes are until now. If we follow Wheeler we can't hope to avoid war (that goes for Lindberg [sic] and Anne too) but if we take a gamble now the chances are that we may accomplish what we have eventually got to accomplish without going to war. But it is no use for me to go ahead and develop such an argument, because I know that nobody home is having any truck with the Wheelerites."[9]

Indeed, neither Laurinburg nor any other town in the South gave much support to the isolationists. Even the university's leading pacifist, Dr. E. E. Ericson, had done an about-face after Hitler's attack on Russia. "I think we must now pour all-out aid, even to the extent of convoys to Great Britain and Russia," he told the Daily Tar Heel.[10] However, the outspoken opponents to American involvement in the growing European conflict did include one of North Carolina's senators. Robert "Our Bob" Reynolds from Asheville had won reelection in 1938 in a campaign in which he had declared his steadfast support of the New Deal and Roosevelt. He had voted for wage-hour legislation and told the president the state was solidly behind his expansion of the Supreme Court. But that was all political grandstanding. His promises had as much substance as the notoriety he gained after he kissed Hollywood star Jean Harlow on the Capitol steps, or when he endorsed Lucky Strike cigarettes with the claim they allowed him to enjoy great traditions of Southern life—tobacco and oratory. After his reelection, Reynolds promptly joined the conservatives opposing Roosevelt and became an out-spoken opponent of immigration and defender of Fortress America.[11]

A small isolationist contingent held forth at Chapel Hill, but most of the young men there didn't need the draft registrations that began on October 16, 1940, to stir their patriotic spirit. More than 450,000 men registered in the state on that one day. Many of Terry's classmates had already volunteered. His brother, Cecil, had joined the Navy after finishing one year of graduate school and had shipped out to Annapolis for Officers Candidate School. Cochrane and Bill Dees, a fellow law student, headed for the recruiting office in Raleigh, where they were accepted for Navy commissions.

Terry was set on a commission in the Army's Air Corps. During his second year in law school, he had begun flying lessons available through the Civil Air Patrol at a small dirt strip north of Chapel Hill. Like Scouting, trekking Linville Gorge, and rafting the Cape Fear River, flying offered the adventure and daring he enjoyed. He had quickly learned to pilot the small Piper Cub trainer over the rolling North Carolina landscape, flying to and from towns using his skill with a compass, navigating by landmarks and a map. At one point he was spending so much time in the cockpit that the dean of the law school, the venerable M. S. Van Hecke, called him aside and cautioned him about falling behind in his studies.

As Terry logged hours in the air, he became confident to the point of cocky. He got his comeuppance, however, on a routine turn-around trip to Raleigh. The flight out had been perfect, the landing had been smooth, and he was feeling good about himself when he marched into the office at the air field to get his log book validated. Back in his plane he joined a line of others awaiting takeoff. When it came his turn, he hit the rudder, turning the plane crisply for takeoff, and jammed forward the throttle. Immediately, he discovered his plane was not headed down the runway but toward a line of airplanes on a parallel taxi way. He pulled up quickly and turned in time to avoid a collision but worried through each of the twenty-five miles back to Chapel Hill that someone had called ahead to warn about a crazy student pilot. As he made his way home he replayed the near disaster and realized that the drag on the rear of his small plane skidded more easily on the concrete runway at Raleigh than it did on the dirt strips where he had done most of his flying, causing him to head off course.[12]

Sanford earned his pilot's license but failed to qualify for the Air Corps. When he went for his physical examination, he learned he was nearsighted; the Army accepted only candidates with perfect vision. He decided to try the Marine Corps and went to Raleigh with his friend John Umstead to apply for a commission. The Marines turned him down, too. So did the Navy. That was the cruelest blow; he didn't even like the Navy that much.

As his friends awaited their orders, Sanford found himself with the choice of enlisting as a private or taking a commission in a noncombatant branch. Neither choice held much appeal.

One disappointment simply followed another. Sanford and McCachren learned that it was unlikely they were going to be big-time summer camp owners. The second season at Camp Black Bear had begun with great promise. Using photos snapped during their first year, the two had produced an impressive, thirty-two-page catalogue. "Camp Black Bear is not a summer resort or a boys' country club," they declared. "It was developed with the fundamental idea of keeping it what it now is—a REAL camp." For $200 a camper got an eight-week outdoor adventure and the opportunity, if he excelled, to be elected into the Tahkadah Clan, which was a revival of the elite club Sanford had created at Camp Pawnee. A full contingent of campers enrolled. "Our aspirations were to be the camp in western North Carolina," McCachren recalled some years later. "We thought we could be, because we could have horseback riding, we could have canoeing, we could have overnight hikes. We were right there on the Appalachian Trail. We had the facilities, potential facilities for one of the best camps, and we had Lake James right there with 155 miles of shoreline." [13]

The camp was in good shape when they began the summer. Rural electrification had reached the mountain foothills and the new service relieved the camp of dependence on the water-powered generator. The two had added a chaplain to the staff. They also had "installed" a telephone. Actually, the camp had no phone line; the nearest service was in Marion. But they had a telephone set in the camp office that was used as a decoy to assure campers who longed for contact with home. When homesickness threatened, one of the counselors would take the boy to the camp office, pick up the headset, and "call" home to tell parents he was in good hands.

Just before the end of the camping season, disaster struck. In early August, a hurricane hit the coast between Charleston, South Carolina, and Savannah, Georgia, killing thirty-five people. The storm continued north across the two states before it spent itself against the North Carolina mountains. So much rain fell on the slopes of the Black Mountains east of Asheville that the city's entire water system was disrupted. The French Broad River rose five feet above flood stage at Asheville. In the mountains above Camp Black Bear, five inches of rain fell in one afternoon on Grandfather Mountain and the flood of water turned once-peaceful mountain streams into raging torrents by the time it reached the foothills.

Campers retreated to the safety of their cabins, which sat on a hillside overlooking the ball field and tennis courts that quickly became covered with water. The flooding creeks filled Lake Jimmy, a small lake adjacent to the camp, to a level that threatened the dam that Terry had rebuilt just the summer before. Sanford and McCachren dug furiously to expand the overflow, but their work was in vain. Just before the earthen dam gave way, they retreated to safety. With everyone accounted for, the staff and campers hunkered down in the cabins to ride out the storm.

The next day everyone was safe—the only casualties were the cook's chickens—but the camp was totally isolated. The flooded streams had torn out the bridge on the main road leading to the camp and large trees felled by the storm blocked the way to Marion, where eight inches of rain had fallen in a twenty-four-hour period. Much of western North Carolina lay severely crippled. All roads east and west of Asheville were closed.

The first job was to get the boys to Marion where the camp staff could notify parents their children were safe. Terry and his counselors organized the campers for the hike to town, imitating a trek all had seen the week before when the boys had seen the movie Northwest Passage. When they reached town, the campers settled into the Hotel Marion and awaited their parents, who were sent telegrams notifying them all was well.

As Sanford and McCachren assessed the damage and made plans for rebuilding they found the dam at Lake Jimmy would need repair as well as the roads and bridges. All was not lost. The water had covered the mess hall with mud but otherwise it was sound. Fortunately, the camp's station wagon, a used Plymouth, had been in Marion for repairs and escaped damage. Altogether, Sanford and McCachren figured they needed about $4,000 to put the camp back in shape. That was far more than they had on hand, so they approached the banker who had been very understanding the year before. On this visit, Terry was reminded of the story about the one-eyed banker who was so coldhearted the customers couldn't tell his glass eye from his real one. The banker answered their question about a loan with a single question: "Let me ask you boys, what is your draft number?"

Terry wrote his family that he regretted he wouldn't spend the summer in the mountains but it looked like he might work in the summer of 1941 with Coates in an Institute program planned for a U.S. Coast Guard station at Cape Hatteras. Terry said he preferred the sun and saltwater of the coast to the hills anyhow. At the end of that summer, he returned to Chapel Hill with Coates to help organize the Boys' State, a mock legislative program for high school seniors.[14]

As classes resumed that fall Terry was preparing for his final year in law school as an important student leader. His post as speaker of the student legislature was a job with as much prestige, and considerably more power, than that of student body president. Every student organization was beholden to the legislature, which approved the distribution of student fees.

He had come a long way since arriving as a nervous freshman. He made enough money to pay his bills, and when he picked up the *Daily Tar Heel* now, it was not to deliver it, but to see his name in print. In addition, he was a popular man on campus, someone who had tamed the political system sufficiently to win an endorsement from both parties. Moreover, people liked Terry and his easygoing yet purposeful manner. He also had come to terms with his military situation. With Coates's help, he believed he had found an honorable alternative to the bars of a second lieutenant in the Air Corps. When he finished law school in 1942, he would have a job waiting for him at the Federal Bureau of Investigation; Terry was going to be a G-man for J. Edgar Hoover. The spectacular exploits of the Bureau in capturing John Dillinger and other Public Enemies hyped by Hollywood's cameras made that opportunity look as exciting as being an Army aviator.

Coates had good connections in Washington, where his mission to introduce professionalism to local law enforcement dovetailed nicely with Hoover's desire to create a first-class investigative agency free of corruption and bungling. In 1935 Hoover had assigned Edward Scheidt, the special agent in charge of the Charlotte office and one of Coates's former law students, to help the Institute develop training programs. An initial three-month leave was extended to six months and then to nine. When Scheidt learned of Terry's interest in joining the Bureau he came to Chapel Hill, interviewed him, and then shepherded him through the preliminary stages.

That same fall Terry had begun spending a lot of time with a lively young woman from Hopkinsville, Kentucky, named Margaret Rose Knight. Terry had dated occasionally as an undergraduate, but had never really settled on any one woman. A favorite companion had been Martha Clampitt, and during one period he fancied another coed who joined him for study sessions at the library. Terry had no trouble attracting friends. He was personable, handsome, with a boyish appearance accented by dimples and blond hair he combed casually across the front. But basically, he was shy and busied himself with matters other than an active social life. He had seen Margaret Rose on campus and was attracted to her but it wasn't until the final semester of her senior year that she responded with any interest. Most of her attention had been directed toward her regular companion, a tall, dark-haired senior named Richard "Fish" Worley of Asheville, who was also a big man on campus as director of activities at Graham Memorial, where Margaret Rose worked typing menus at the union soda fountain.[15]

Two things inhibited Terry's social life. One was money; more often than not he was working at campus dances trying to earn a few bucks rather than escorting a date. The other was talent on the dance floor. He wasn't much of a dancer in an era when major social events revolved around a big band

and evenings spent jitterbugging to the latest tunes. Sanford did not dance well, though he did try, but his confidence, which seldom failed him, didn't follow him onto the dance floor. Dating Margaret Rose relieved some of the pressure to perform; she was so popular she never had to wait on a partner.

Margaret Rose had transferred to Chapel Hill from Christian College in Columbia, Missouri, to study drama. Her friend, Molly Albritton, had told her two things about Chapel Hill before she arrived in the fall of 1937: that Frederick Koch's Playmakers was one of the best college companies around, and that the ten-to-one male-female ratio was a girl's dream come true. She changed her major to English and a career as a teacher, however, when she found the reputation of the drama crowd not to her liking. "I remember seeing a girl riding a bicycle with a dog on a chain and somebody pointed to her and said she's a Playmaker," she recalled some years later. "And I thought, Lord have mercy, she had on pants." [16] Margaret Rose's tastes were more conventional. She favored ankle-length dresses, saddle shoes, bobby socks, and Brahma crewneck sweaters. She was an attractive companion, with curls in her shoulder-length brown hair, a full open face, and expressive eyes. In the spring of her senior year, she found herself attracted to a knot of campus politicians that included Sanford, Cochrane, McCachren, and Worley, whom she had taken home to meet her family.

Terry was soon never far from her mind, however. Margaret Rose's Aunt Hettie Dickson, who had been her guardian since her parents died when she was fifteen, was nudging her niece in Terry's direction. After Aunt Hettie met Terry at her niece's graduation, she told her that if Terry Sanford was interested in her then she should show him a little more encouragement. Terry was steady and dependable, she told Margaret Rose, and she fancied herself a good judge of character.

Terry and Margaret Rose were dating regularly in the fall of 1941 but had made no commitments. After she spent the summer at home, she returned to North Carolina for a student teaching assignment in Pittsboro, just south of Chapel Hill, to complete her requirements for a teaching certificate. She spent her weekends in Chapel Hill, where she would date both Sanford and Worley. Terry wasn't pushing her to declare herself, but Coates was growing impatient with the relationship. Once, Coates and his wife, Gladys, drove Margaret Rose back to a rooming house where she was staying for the weekend. Just before she stepped out of the car, Coates turned to her and put the question bluntly: "All right now, which way are you leaning?" [17]

Whatever plans the two had changed on December 7, 1941. They were leaving the Carolina Theater on Franklin Street in Chapel Hill when they learned that Japanese aircraft had attacked Pearl Harbor. The street was full of people, and later about two thousand students, nearly two-thirds of the student body, turned out to listen to Frank Graham tell them "We should have unity in this country, a unity without tyranny, without compulsion, and without jails or concentration camps." The world should know, he said, that "we stand for free discussion and accurate information, even in time of war."[18]

In Laurinburg the Sanford family waited anxiously for word from Cecil, who was an ensign aboard a destroyer anchored at Pearl Harbor. The family had heard from him only a few weeks earlier when a shipment of Christmas presents — mostly island novelties and baskets — had arrived in Laurinburg. Cecil had shipped them early to ensure they arrived by December 25. For all they knew, Cecil was among the more than forty-five hundred casualties. Details were sketchy, partly because of the remoteness of Pearl Harbor and the lid clamped on information that might be considered a threat to security. It was weeks before the family learned that Cecil's ship, the U.S.S. Reid, had been anchored away from the area that received the brunt of the attack and had actually gotten up steam to escape the air raid and set out in vain to find the Japanese fleet.

Terry also awaited word on his friend John Umstead, whose Marine Corps unit was at Pearl Harbor. Ervin Ericson, the son of the outspoken English professor, also was stationed there as a member of the coast artillery. Both survived the attack but neither returned home from war. Umstead died in island fighting later in the war and was buried in Hawaii. Ericson was presumed killed when a Japanese prison transport ship he was aboard was sunk off Luzon with a loss of more than nine hundred men POWs.

On the Monday after the attack, the same day President Roosevelt asked for a declaration of war against Japan, Terry received a telegram from the FBI offering him immediate entrance into the Bureau's training program. Hoover had waived the bureau's requirement of a law degree and notified him his application was accepted. In Sanford he found a willing and ready new agent. After he finished his exams on December 19, Terry prepared to report to the FBI training center at Quantico, Virginia.

The initial phase of training included physical conditioning and weapons orientation. Terry had kept in shape in college and his compact, sturdy, athletic build served him well. So did the time he had spent hunting small game in the woods of Scotland County, although the weapons at the FBI academy were far different from the .22-caliber rifle he carried as a boy; the Bureau's arsenal included everything from pistols to machine guns. By early spring he had finished the field training and moved into a rooming house in Washington, where he lived during a period of classroom instruction on the techniques of modern law enforcement that Hoover had developed.

In May, Terry reported for his first duty assignment in St. Louis, Missouri. The adventure he thought he would find had yet to develop; instead, he was buried in the dull routine of chasing car thieves and draft dodgers and investigating multistate prostitution rings. He did have a part in one national security investigation after German agents were said to be plotting to blow up the bridge across the Mississippi River. The Army sent out an armed guard and Terry followed a few leads but made no arrests and the threat passed.

Margaret Rose had returned that spring to her home in Kentucky to teach school while Terry completed his FBI training. When he got to St. Louis, he asked her to meet him there. They spent a weekend together and when she headed home on Monday she was wearing a diamond engagement ring that Terry had bought on credit. They set their wedding date for July 4, a date of more practical than sentimental significance. The Fourth fell on a Saturday, and Terry reasoned that he could take the preceding Friday as a travel day on the way to the FBI's Cincinnati office, where he was to receive a new assignment, and the following Monday as a holiday, which would give him and Margaret Rose at least a brief honeymoon.

The wedding was a quiet, simple affair in Aunt Hettie's home in Hopkinsville. Terry arrived early on the Fourth on the train from St. Louis, got a shoe shine at the station, and met Margaret Rose's brother, John, a graduate of West Point posted to the Air Corps who had agreed to loan the newlyweds his car for their honeymoon. None of Terry's family could come; gasoline rationing prevented his parents from making the trip, and train fare for them and Terry's sisters was too expensive. Terry had asked Bill McCachren to serve as his best man, but McCachren couldn't leave Chapel Hill, where he was an instructor in the Navy's V-12 program.

The service was brief and the union blessed by a Baptist minister who was called in to replace the pastor of the Christian Church, where Margaret Rose usually attended services, because he didn't pass Aunt Hettie's muster. After the ceremony, the couple left on a brief honeymoon to tourist sites in the area, including the Great Onyx Cave, before they traveled on to Cincinnati. There, Terry completed some paperwork before heading north to Columbus, his new post. The Sanfords took a room in the Deschler-Wallach Hotel, the fanciest in town, and lived off the FBI's per diem expenses while they looked for an apartment.

Terry had not told his bride he was wrestling with what he later would describe as one of the most important decisions in his life: leaving the safety and security of an honorable wartime job in the States for the uncertainty and danger of combat. The routine of FBI duty was beginning to gnaw at him. There were no John Dillingers to hunt now, no spies in Columbus, Ohio, and he knew that the war years were too big an event in his life to spend in the backwater of service in the States. He wanted to be part of the action, yet he didn't want to quit; he had never quit anything in his life. At the same time, he did not want to miss the most important event of his lifetime. As he later recalled, "I just felt like I was being left out of my generation." [19]

His duties often took him to the Army post outside of Columbus, and when he got the chance he talked with an officer there to learn what his choices would be if he enlisted. Terry fancied an armored division where he could ride a motorcycle. He learned, however, that if he enlisted he wouldn't have a choice, and when the Army learned of his FBI training he probably would end up in some sort of investigative service. To Terry that sounded like the FBI in uniform.

Finally, an article in a news magazine caught his eye. It was about a new unit called the parachute infantry. Jumping out of airplanes was the kind of challenge that appealed to Terry, and the hype generated by the Army to boost enlistment found a ready audience. "A parachutist must be tough. Because the job is dangerous, all must volunteer, and entrance requirements are strict. A man must be between 21 and 32, unmarried, athletic, have a high IQ. He must realize that he is likely to get hurt," a May 12 article in *Life* magazine reported. "Long after he makes his first jump, his studying goes on, for a parachutist landing in strange country must be ready to read maps, operate a radio, seize and hold an airfield, blow up a bridge." [20] *Life*'s photo feature showed members of the 501st Parachute Infantry Battalion diving from lumbering Douglas C-39 transports flying at 750 feet above scrub pines in Georgia. Major W. M. Miley, the unit commander, explained that if a trooper's main chute fails, "he pulls the ripcord for the emergency chute to his chest. This should open in two seconds, giving him 2.5 seconds of leeway before death." At the time, there were fewer than a thousand members of the parachute infantry, but by year's end the Army wanted a strength of eight battalions—more than five thousand men.

Terry was intrigued. The paratroopers were going to be frontline units. If he wanted to get in the war, these looked like the wildest cowboys of them all. And, a recruiting officer told him, he would have no trouble getting his choice. "If you volunteer for that, they have to take you and not put you anywhere else," the officer said. "It is an absolute priority." [21] The marriage requirement also would be no problem. It had been dropped.

He said nothing to Margaret Rose about his plans until late in August, when the two were back in Chapel Hill. Coates had arranged with the FBI for Terry to return and help him run another edition of Boys' State. The one-week program was ending and Terry and Margaret Rose were walking out of Gimghoul Hall when he finally told her he was thinking about joining the Army. Margaret Rose took the news with resignation and some concern. She worried that her friends and family back in Hopkinsville would believe that the marriage hadn't worked out. But she understood Terry's desire to be part of the biggest event in their lives. The two remained in Columbus through the fall while Terry lobbied for a military leave of absence from the FBI. He opted for a leave rather than offering a resignation, deciding that if he got shot up in the war, at least the Bureau would pay disability payments. Finally, Hoover approved his application. In early December, Margaret Rose boarded a train for Hopkinsville and Aunt Hettie's.

Terry signed his enlistment papers in Columbus on December 7, 1942, and boarded a train the same night for Fort Thomas, Kentucky, where he was to report for induction. As the train pulled out of Columbus he walked to the rear car and stepped out on the platform to watch the city lights fade in the darkness. He had made what he believed to be the biggest decision of his life. Never before had the future seemed so uncertain. He pulled off the snap-brim hat, his FBI trademark, and sailed it off into the night as a dramatic good-bye gesture to J. Edgar Hoover.[22]

CHAPTER FIVE

The Battling Buzzards

❈

NO ONE WAS MORE APPREHENSIVE about Terry Sanford's decision to enlist in the Army and volunteer for the paratroopers than his mother. Despite her son Cecil's repeated brushes with death, Terry was the son she feared would not return from the war. He had shown he was responsible and had distinguished himself at Chapel Hill, accomplishing more than most young men his age, but she worried that his impetuous streak, the daredevil ambition that led him to learn to fly an airplane, would get him killed.

Terry was having his own second thoughts before he arrived on a cold morning in late November at a former National Guard training post near Toccoa, Georgia, that had been called Camp Toombs before the regular Army took it over. The foreboding of the former name, chosen to honor one of Georgia's Civil War heroes, was only emphasized by the location of the Toccoa rail station next to a casket company.

On the train ride from Kentucky, Terry discovered he was the old man at twenty-five among his eighteen- and nineteen-year-old companions who had signed up to go to war by jumping out of airplanes. Some had come up poor, just as he had, but they had taken turns that had not led to college or the FBI; they had been persuaded to enlist by recruiters who had promised that their criminal records would be expunged if they joined the paratroopers. Sanford had tried to get Bill McCachren to come with him, but McCachren wasn't about to trade the prospects of a Navy commission. As Sanford pondered his choice he had his own doubts about shelving the security and respectability of the FBI to become a slick-sleeve private among what one historian later called "adventurous kids from the wrong side of the tracks."[1]

Fortune did improve shortly after he stepped down from the train in Georgia and heard someone call his name. A young lieutenant ran up and threw his arms around him. Terry was pleased, but confused. Although he didn't let on, he couldn't remember the fellow's name, yet Tom Lytle, an Asheville native who had been a few years behind him at Chapel Hill, treated him like a long-lost brother. Lytle was in charge of moving the recruits to the training site and he offered Terry a ride in his jeep while the others bounced into Camp Toccoa on hard wooden seats in the back of a truck. Later that night Terry finally put the name and face together.

Camp Toccoa was situated in the foothills of the southern Appalachians of northern Georgia. Despite its remote location, it was the primary receiving depot for volunteers for the paratroops from across the United States. The camp had been hastily outfitted as the Army scrambled to increase the ranks of this new service. Only days before Terry enlisted, American paratroopers had seen their first combat action when units dropped ahead of ground troops during the Allies' November push into Tunisia. News magazines had carried reports of the paratroopers that read like promotional releases for the 1941 RKO Radio movie *Parachute Battalion*, a rousing feature-length picture starring Robert Preston, Edmund O'Brien, and Buddy Ebsen that closed with paratroopers marching past the camera singing their new song, "The Parachute Infantry."

The paratroopers diving out of airplanes for Hollywood's benefit were from the 501st Parachute Battalion, the first paratroop outfit. It had been organized in 1940 with fifty volunteers who were sent to practice riding parachutes to the ground from 125-foot towers like those that entertained tourists at the 1939 World's Fair. Previously, the Army had considered parachute jumping little more than a novelty, leaving practical use to the U.S. Forest Service, which had more trained jumpers than the military. Army commanders changed their minds after learning of the success of both German and Russian paratroop units in the early days of the war in Europe.[2]

Now the Army was in a hurry to expand the 501st from five hundred troopers to nearly five thousand, and was forming new battalions from the thousands of volunteers who arrived weekly at Camp Toccoa. This was no movie set, however. Conditions were spartan. Terry spent his first night on the floor because there weren't enough bunks for new arrivals; the mess hall was short of regular rations so breakfast was cold turnip greens and light bread. So much for the recruiter's promise of steak at every meal. Disappointment followed during the day when Terry filed through the medical tent for his initial examination and the physician marked him for requalification because of flat feet. Terry knew his arches were fine and went looking for Lytle, who learned that the doctor had "disqualified" a number of otherwise promising men to keep them from being assigned to a rifle platoon; he planned to use his rejects to staff a medical unit. The following day Terry was "examined" again and assigned to the medical detachment.

The 501st cadre drew on the talents of the recruits to help with the training and Terry was immediately given responsibilities. He had completed just about every course the American Red Cross had to offer and the Boy Scouts had trained him how to live in the field. More important was the FBI weapons training that he had completed less than nine months earlier. He was assigned to teach marksmanship to the medical detachment and became an assistant to the unit's first sergeant. Every prospective trooper was expected to qualify as a sharpshooter on his primary weapon and marksman on a second. The choices included the .45 caliber pistol, the M-1 rifle, and the submachine gun. Terry also studied the Army's Manual of Arms and succeeded in producing troops who could properly shoulder a weapon and march in step.

The first phase of the basic training at Toccoa was to weed out the faint-hearted. Virtually upon arrival, recruits were ordered up a thirty-five-foot tower where they slipped into a parachute harness and were told to ride a cable to the ground. Those who refused to jump and retreated down the ladder were shipped off to the regular infantry. When Terry got to the edge of the platform, he followed the advice to concentrate on the horizon, not the ground below, and sailed safely down the cable to a relatively soft landing in a sand pile.

Physical conditioning was the second measure of whether a man remained with the outfit. The paratroop units were less than two years old, but already a mystique had developed around them. An article in the American Legion's magazine had described them as "the hardest, toughest soldiers in the Army."[3] Troopers and their officers moved everywhere at double-time and began the day with two-mile runs. At least twice a week the men ran the three-and-a-half miles to the fire tower atop Mount Curahee, a promontory that rose above the rolling hills of the Georgia countryside.

Less than half of those who stepped off the train at Toccoa made it through jump training. Terry had arrived more than twenty pounds overweight, but he was strong and in good condition. In a letter home after his first three weeks he was upbeat and enthusiastic. The family had sent along nuts, cakes, tangerines, and a chess set. "It might be some time until I play chess, but that is a neat outfit," he wrote his parents. He spent Christmas day with the family of a doctor in Toccoa and the holiday passed with little excitement and a modest meal. It wasn't home, but "they had rugs on the floor and egg nog, etc.," he wrote his folks.[4]

When the eight weeks of training, most of it conducted outdoors in the mud and cold rain of a Georgia winter, was over Terry was wearing the stripes of a staff sergeant. During the brief interim before his unit was due at Fort Benning near Columbus, Georgia, for jump training, he made plans to meet Margaret Rose in Charlotte. He qualified for a weekend pass but had no dress uniform, only the fatigues he had been issued when he arrived. He wasn't going to miss the trip for the sake of a suit of clothes and borrowed an officer's uniform, sewed on his sergeant's stripes, and headed off to North Carolina for a rendezvous with his bride. He risked court martial if his irregular dress was discovered, so he braced for the consequences when an Army major dining in the same Charlotte restaurant as the young couple called him over and asked what kind of uniform he was wearing. "Paratrooper," Sanford answered smartly. "We're different, you know." The officer seemed to appreciate learning something about the Army's new service and wished him well.

Jump training followed at Fort Benning, where the south Georgia countryside was so flat and dusty that in the summertime the training ground was called "the Frying Pan." There the new men mastered the paratrooper's drop-and-roll, a standard landing technique practiced with jumps from platforms, each one a little higher than the last. Next, they moved to controlled jumps with chutes guided by cables and finally a free fall from a 250-foot tower. Each day's schedule included more physical training, field exercises, and judo. Finally, in their fourth week, the troops double-timed to the airstrip and climbed aboard C-47s for their first real jump.

Americans were fascinated with the new parachute troops, and weekly and monthly periodicals obliged their interest. One publication, *American Magazine*, carried a description of jump school written by a trooper who completed his training about the same time as Terry. "We all sweat out every jump. We get up in the morning thinking of it, and all the time we're waiting to go up, all the time we're in the plane until we jump, we have a million butterflies in our stomachs and are sweating like hell. But after we get out the door, the chute opens and we look up and see that it is all right, with no suspension lines over the canopy, and the tension just drops away. We see we're OK and we look up again and say, 'Oh, you sweet beautiful baby you.' "[5]

Terry's first jump was sheer excitement, another challenge, another adventure. It was the Boy Scouts for grownups. His knees were steady when he stood in the open doorway of the C-47 despite the fact that everything rational told him men don't leap from airplanes. He focused on the horizon and waited for the jump master's instructions. His exit went smoothly and the white nylon opened with a powerful jerk a few seconds after he fell beyond the prop blast of the plane, spreading a thirty-two-foot canopy above him. Altogether, he made his required five jumps without incident, trying at least once to land standing. In mid-April he qualified to sew the blue-and-white paratroop patch on his uniform. Proudly, he tucked his pant legs into his jump boots, a distinctive style that set the troopers apart from the "straight-leg" infantry.

His jump training over, Terry left Fort Benning for Camp Mackall, a paratroop training camp in the North Carolina Sandhills on the edge of Scotland County. Mackall was named for the first trooper killed in action in North Africa and was located at the edge of the huge military reservation at Fort Bragg, where the XVIII Airborne Corps had its headquarters. Bragg had become the training center for the 82nd and 101st as well as the 11th and 13th Airborne Divisions. When Terry arrived at Mackall he was made assistant first sergeant in the 501st's Regimental medical detachment. The new post couldn't have brought him closer to home; Laurinburg was less than thirty miles away. After he was promoted to first sergeant a month later, he would hail a jeep and a driver and make it home to McLaurin Street in time for dinner with his family.

For an isolated farming community, Laurinburg was in the thick of the stateside war effort. Fort Bragg was the largest artillery post in the world. Established in 1918 during World War I, it covered 122,000 acres, much of it empty, cut-over timber land where exploding shells splintered the few remaining pine trees and pounded the sandy soil. In 1940, only fifty-four hundred troops were assigned there, but that changed dramatically in 1942. By the end of the war, more than one hundred thousand would fill the barracks hastily constructed on the post. The Bragg complex also included Pope Air Field, where the transports for the paratroops were based. Another Army air base was just east of Laurinburg at Maxton.

Military men and their families had overwhelmed Fayetteville, an otherwise sleepy eastern North Carolina farming community. Renters spilled over into the nearby towns of Hamlet and Laurinburg, where soldiers and their wives took rooms in private homes. Now that Terry was finished with his initial training, Margaret Rose came south and moved into Betsy and Cecil Sanford's house, where she was welcomed like a daughter.

The Sanford family had joined the war effort. For Terry's father, the war brought steady work at good pay. He signed on at the Wilmington ship-yards and his new paycheck supplied the cash for the last payment on his house. He spent weekdays away from Laurinburg, riding the train home for the weekends. Daughter Mary, who dreamed of becoming an architect, also found work in Wilmington. She had begun studies at Woman's College in Greensboro, planning to transfer to State College in Raleigh to study architecture, but in 1942 she took a job drawing construction plans for troop and cargo ships that her father was helping to build.

Terry was undergoing combat training with the 501st when his application was approved for Officers Candidate School. The Army had revamped its plans to recruit officers for paratroop outfits from the regular infantry after discovering that it was easier to train paratroopers to be officers than to find officers who wanted to be jumpers. The day after his first wedding anniversary, July 5, Terry headed back to Fort Benning as part of the first contingent of paratroopers picked for officer training.

En route to Georgia, Sanford met Dean Swem, a husky, gravel-voiced crane operator from southwestern Michigan who had enlisted in the Army right after Pearl Harbor. He had learned of the paratroops from a platoon sergeant who had been in one of the first test platoons. Swem liked the promise of excitement and better pay and volunteered. He had finished training at Toccoa ahead of Terry and was a first sergeant in the 501st when he signed up for OCS. Swem was all Army, a stickler for details, and proud of his family's military tradition, which included two brothers in other Army units. He took a liking to Sanford and his wry, self-deprecating humor. At Fort Benning, Sanford and Swem often shared rides into Columbus, where their wives had found small apartments. Geneva Swem had followed Dean from camp to camp from the day they were married in Toccoa. Later, when he was transferred to Camp Mackall, the couple had rented rooms in Hamlet in the home of a retired railroad engineer.

Sanford and Swem were nearing graduation from OCS when Swem washed out. He blamed it on another candidate who resented his gung-ho attitude and gave him bad marks in a "buddy system" evaluation. Terry almost jeopardized his own graduation when, in a display of paratrooper bluster, he showed up in formation with his trousers tucked in his boots, paratroop style, rather than loose like the regular infantry. He received his bars, however, and took his commission on November 9, 1943, before heading back to Camp Mackall to become a platoon leader in A Company, First Battalion, 517th Parachute Infantry Regiment.

By the time Terry finished OCS, he was trim, fit, and the image of the perfect paratrooper. He had qualified as an expert with a .45-caliber machine gun, or "grease gun," as it was called, as well as the standard-issue M-1, but he also received training in light and heavy machine guns, mortars, and the M-1 carbine. As a newly minted lieutenant he also was qualified in night infiltration, map reading, close combat, jungle fighting, street fighting, and malaria control.

With Terry again stationed at Camp Mackall, Margaret Rose returned to Laurinburg and found a job as a secretary in the draft board office. The move was only temporary. The 517th, along with every other parachute unit, was being prepared for the invasion of Europe and took part in the so-called Tennessee maneuvers, a massive training exercise that opened in miserable weather in late January 1944. Terry was assigned to the 2nd Army's umpire pool, a job that kept him in the cold and mud for two weeks and landed him in the Camp Campbell, Kentucky, hospital for a week for treatment of a severe case of poison oak on his face and hands.

That spring Margaret Rose prepared to return to Kentucky before the 517th moved out in early May for Camp Patrick Henry near Newport News, Virginia. Rumors said the unit was to sail to England, where the Allies were massing troops for the long-expected cross-channel invasion and that airborne units were sure to participate. The 501st, Terry's old unit, and others already had gone over. In preparation for its first combat assignment, the 517th Infantry Regiment was combined with the 460th Parachute Artillery Battalion and the 596th Parachute Engineer Company to form the 517th Regimental Combat Team. Together the three units were to operate as a highly mobile small division.

Whatever anxiety Terry may have harbored on the train to Camp Toccoa eighteen months earlier had now vanished. He was convinced that joining the paratroopers was the right thing to do, the only thing to do. He had won his bars the hard way, but he had finally accomplished what he had failed to do when he made the rounds of the recruiting offices before the war. And he certainly had a chance to match the tales his brother Cecil might bring home after the war.

Though that would be tough. Cecil had been in virtually every theater of the war. After Pearl Harbor, his ship had seen action at Midway, then sailed into the South Atlantic, passed through the Suez Canal into the Mediterranean, and was then waiting to join the Navy patrols to protect the Allied invasion at Normandy. Even before Pearl Harbor, Cecil had narrowly escaped losing his ship. He had been assigned to the Armed Guard prior to America's entry into the war and was in a convoy delivering materials to Russia when his ship had to drop out because of engine trouble. A few days later, German airplanes discovered the convoy in the North Sea and sank every vessel.

On May 17, the 517th boarded a former luxury liner, the *Santa Rosa*, and joined a convoy sailing east. In addition to a detachment of replacement aviators, the ship also carried two hundred Wacs. Their final destination was unknown until the convoy passed the hulking Rock of Gibraltar in the dead of night and they knew they were headed to Italy, not England. The convoy reached Naples on May 31.[6]

After taking Sicily in a swift invasion, the Allied forces had begun rolling up the Italian peninsula. Naples had been liberated, and when the *Santa Rosa* arrived, Terry's unit was ordered to join the American forces closing in on Rome. The 517th was immediately sidelined, however, because its vehicles and crew-served weapons were aboard another ship which was overdue. Second Lieutenant Sanford was camped with his men in the crater of an extinct volcano when he learned that his old outfit, the 501st, had jumped into France behind the beaches at Normandy as part of the largest invasion force assembled in the war.

Rome fell on June 6, the same day Allied forces landed at Normandy and began pushing inland across France. All attention was focused on operations in France, and the men of the 517th began to think they were going to spend the rest of the war in a nameless lava pit. Terry was not impressed with Italy, at least not at first. He called it a "dirty land of beggars" in a letter home. But in a light tone that would color most of his mail to the states, he put as good a face on the situation as he could: "It is spring and we are living in the crater of an old volcano that was, before the war, reserved for the King's hunting."[7]

In mid-June, with its heavy weapons intact, the 517th waited for landing craft in preparation for a landing farther up the Italian coast at Anzio. By the time their boats arrived they were no longer needed, and the units were dropped at the small fishing village of Civitavecchia north of Rome. They pushed out into the rugged mountains, where two weeks of fighting gave the 517th its first taste of combat against German units retreating northward.

The 517th performed well. Its commander, Lieutenant Colonel Rupert D. Graves, liked what he saw of his officers and men, whom he would later call the 517th buzzards, an image captured in the unit's logo. He had taken command just a few days before they had sailed for Europe, replacing a cocky, aggressive younger commander who had organized the unit and led it through training. The men and officers of his new command were anxious about the change and treated Graves cautiously. He was West Point (class of 1924) and older by a dozen years or more than the officers in his command. He couldn't help but be pleased with the 517th's training record—the unit had broken all manner of records—but the men were untested in battle.

Terry's first taste of combat came in action against German units retreating through the Italian mountains. It gave him an unexpected sense of exhilaration that he kept to himself. In the brief notes he scribbled in pencil on V-mail letters sent back to Laurinburg or Hopkinsville, his messages were breezy and light, more like a travelogue of a vacation than a description of war. "I'm living in a house now," he wrote in mid-July, "and sleeping on an inner-spring mattress—although I have no bed. An old, cross-eyed woman, her 70-year-old father, and a cute little blond bambini—about 4— live with us. The old lady keeps the place clean and we bring her left-over food every few days for rent. Life is simple."[8]

By the first of July, the 517th was pulled off the line and sent into reserve, which offered the men time to look around. Terry went to Rome, which he liked better than Naples, and visited Vatican City, "which was old and not as clean" as he expected but where he found chocolate and vanilla ice cream. "The people differ from Americans in that they have evidently in the past given pedestrians the right of way over automobiles," he observed in one letter. "They walk in the center of the road and make no move when they hear a vehicle, but the boys have introduced the American custom of running over them, so they're learning our ways." [9]

Like England earlier in the year, Italy had become a staging area for invasion and Terry discovered a number of friends from Laurinburg and Chapel Hill among the thousands of Americans stuffed into cantonment areas. He had seen Mutt McCoy shortly after his unit had landed. In July he wrote home to tell about another Carolina chum: "He's been over here two years, but that is easy by the fact that he is in the Air Corps ground service with a house and bed with springs. I'm not envious, of course. (I keep telling myself.)" [10] Another friend from Chapel Hill, Daywell M. Anderson, sent the Sanford family a photograph of Terry standing in the door of his airplane. He also sent one to Margaret Rose, who had found a teaching job for the upcoming school year.

The 517th was to be part of the Allied invasion of southern France. General Dwight D. Eisenhower had continued to push for it although the British command wanted all available units to join the fighting in northern Europe. Eisenhower had his eye on the port of Marseilles and prevailed. First code-named Anvil and later renamed Dragoon, the invasion was set for August 15. The paratroopers would be the first in, jumping behind the German coastal defenses at night to secure key locations before being relieved by a landing force due to land at Toulon on the southern coast.

The mission of the 517th's First Battalion—its part in the last large nighttime airborne invasion of the war—was the capture of a point of high ground overlooking a major highway and railroad overpass about three miles west of Le Muy. The troops were to seize and hold critical junctions and prevent German troops garrisoned there from reinforcing the coast against the Allies' seaborne force. In addition, the 517th was to clear the countryside of obstacles and prepare landing sites for glider troops due at daybreak. In the days leading up to the invasion, platoon leaders such as Terry spent hours around a sand table where the details of the French countryside were replicated in miniature. Roads, streams, even houses, barns, and village streets had been reproduced. Secrecy was paramount and the names of French towns were replaced with Hoboken, Milwaukee, and others. Troopers were not told the exact location until days before the operation was to begin, when French-language phrase books were distributed.

An American paratrooper carried more than one hundred pounds of weapons and equipment when he jumped out of a C-47 flying at about ninety miles an hour fifteen hundred feet up in the sky. In addition to the main and reserve chutes, each trooper was armed with either an M-1 rifle or a submachine gun, eighty rounds of ammunition, three fragmentation grenades, and two knives. He also carried a gas mask, Mae West life preserver, entrenching tool, personal items, and enough food and water to last two days. Some men carried escape kits that included maps and a compass, along with $100 in American currency. Terry also packed fifteen cigars sent by his dad. Because his "stick," or jump unit, included the mortar squad, he had extra rounds stuffed in his pack.[11]

Terry was scheduled to jump with his platoon in A Company, but just hours before the planes were loaded he was ordered to take over as executive officer of B Company after the company commander became ill and B Company's executive officer, First Lieutenant Charles Hillsdale, moved up to replace him. During the two weeks of fighting north of Rome Terry had developed a reputation as a steady leader, someone who, when given a job, would complete it with efficiency and dispatch.

On the evening of August 14, the paratroopers completed the rigging of their packs and smeared greasepaint made by Lily Dache, the cosmetics manufacturer, on their faces and hands as camouflage. They had already been through a spray-paint line, where clothing and equipment had received a dose of varying shades of yellow, green, and black that now was dry and crusty on their jumpsuits. At midnight, the First Battalion marched to waiting planes at the Canino airfield and climbed aboard. At one o'clock, pilots in 396 C-47s cranked their engines and began taking off from ten airfields across northern Italy. By the time the first planes carrying the fifty-six hundred paratroopers of a combined American and British force reached the French coast, the entire formation was nearly a hundred miles long.

Terry was the jump master of plane 36, part of the sixth series of C-47s. With him in his stick were the company first sergeant, company headquarters personnel, a mortar squad, and the battalion aidmen. As his plane headed for the French coast he could see the outline of ships carrying the landing force. He thought about his brother and wondered whether Cecil's destroyer was among those massed in the Mediterranean. Just after five in the morning Terry saw the red light appear overhead and he took his place at the head of the line. He stood in the open doorway intent on the glowing bulb. When the red turned to green he jumped out into the dark night. One by one the others followed until the last man, the first sergeant, cleared the door.

From his time around the sand table Sanford knew what to look for in the terrain where his men were due to land. Moments after he hit the ground, he realized that the pilots had misjudged their location. In fact, Terry and his troopers were about ten miles northeast of the intended drop zone, but in no worse shape than most of the others. Altogether, only 20 percent of the entire unit had landed on target in a wide valley west of Le Muy. The First Battalion had been scattered over thirty-five to forty square miles by anxious pilots who became disoriented by an unexpected fog bank that cut visibility to a half mile. (Later investigation also found gross navigational error and the failure of a lighting system designed to coordinate the release of troops from the planes.)

To make matters worse, the Germans had been expecting the paratroopers, despite Allied attempts at secrecy. The night before the jump, American soldiers listening to propaganda broadcasts from Berlin were told that they wouldn't need their parachutes because they could walk to earth on the flak. Ironically, the Germans believed the invasion force was much larger than it really was and the scattered troops reinforced that notion as the Americans were seen all across the countryside. By daybreak, the hills and pastures were littered with parachutes and German patrols had begun to engage the invaders.

When he landed, Terry found himself on the edge of a patch of woods near a ravine. Nothing looked familiar except the first sergeant, who had landed nearby along with equipment bundles containing mortar shells and other gear that went out the door with the third and fourth man. Using the password and countersign of "Lafayette" and "Democracy," a handful of the fifteen who had left plane 36 found one another. Not all could be accounted for. One man was dead for sure. Uncertain of his location and confident that there were plenty of Germans in the area, Terry waited until daylight to move. He gave orders to leave the equipment bundles after he decided that the bulky containers would slow their movement cross-country. When the first sergeant balked at his order to leave government equipment unguarded, he learned the easygoing Southerner was not to be trifled with, at least not on a battlefield. Lieutenant Sanford raised his machine gun and reminded the sergeant that disobeying a direct order in combat was a serious offense. The equipment remained behind.[12]

As the group was making its way out of the woods, Terry spotted a single C-47 escorted by two fighters fly over and leave two parachutes opening in its wake. When Terry approached the jumpers he saw American flags stitched to their shoulders and found himself standing face-to-face with Major General Robert T. Frederick, the task force commander. Frederick commandeered Terry and his squad and ordered the paratroopers to provide security for his headquarters in a nearby château. As they approached the building, they found a group of British troopers already encamped and brewing tea. The British had been assigned to clear landing areas for the gliders that were expected in the early morning. They had done the best they could, but the Germans had erected all manner of barriers, rock piles, and poles, as well as mined the suspected landing areas. After Terry saw the damage that these obstructions did to the flimsy gliders, he was grateful he had arrived by parachute.

The house Frederick had chosen for his headquarters was occupied by a family that gave the Americans a warm welcome. "The women quickly packed their belongings in baskets," Sanford later wrote home, "covered their heads with shawls, and took to the hills, not knowing whether we had come in strength, not knowing if we could drive the Allemande out." [13] Most of the men remained behind, including one old farmer whose heroism Terry would never forget. Time after time the man led his horse-drawn cart out into the nearby open fields braving sniper fire to retrieve wounded Americans and carry them to the American aidmen.

Terry was eager to be on his way and rejoin his outfit. Shortly after noon, with the arrival of Frederick's security detail, he and a force growing in size with each hour headed south led by one of the farmers who knew the territory. Terry commandeered an old steam-powered truck, and moved along picking up other troopers attempting to find their units. As they moved down country roads, residents who had been hiding in their homes ran out to welcome them. "It was as if they knew we were coming," Terry wrote home, "and had sat up waiting." Some warned of ambush by Germans. Terry's men moved cautiously, but after responding to repeated unfounded warnings finally decided that at least in their immediate area the Germans were otherwise occupied. "We figured they didn't know what they were talking about, so . . . we smiled and said 'No, Allemande kaput,' or smiled and said 'Merci, get the hell out of the way.' But I loved them because they wept at our feet." At one house, Terry stopped to listen to a man's insistent requests that he come in, "and not just for a hospitable bottle of wine. We found in his bedroom one of our men who had been shot through the cheek, cared for by an old solid woman who was bathing his bloody face with warm water. They had found him in the field unconscious and had brought him in before there were any other American troops around. We took him, and by this time our standard exchange was a 'V' with the fingers, and 'Vive la France!' and their answer was, 'No! No! Vive la Amerikan!' " [14]

By late afternoon Terry had reached his objective with an accumulated force of about fifty men. When he arrived, he learned that B Company's commander, Lieutenant Hillsdale, was still unaccounted for, along with the battalion commander, Major William J. Boyle. Hillsdale and his troopers had landed some fifteen miles west of Terry, near the town of Lorgues, and immediately encountered enemy patrols as they made their way cross-country. Boyle and about fifty men were under heavy attack in Les Arcs, a crossroads village. Boyle, a determined West Pointer (class of 1939), refused to give up his position and held off repeated assaults. He and his group at the "Little Alamo," as they called it, remained isolated until reinforcements arrived on the afternoon of the second day, when Boyle pulled out and finally reached his command post on a steep bluff west of Les Arcs called Roque Rousse.

Boyle's headquarters was on the same high ridge as the regimental command post, which was located in an old ivy-covered complex of buildings surrounded by vineyards called Château Saint Rosaline. Some of the château's buildings dated to the medieval period and the remains of fourteenth-century Rosaline de Villeneuve were preserved in a nearby abbey. The château's owner, Baron de Rasque de Laval, welcomed the Americans. His own son, Louis, was a captain in the French II Corps, which was about to disembark as part of the sea invasion. As the fighting continued through the day, a courtyard at the château became the main aid station.[15]

From the heights, Boyle directed the fighting that continued in a large vineyard and along the railroad west of Les Arcs. While artillery pounded the vineyard, B Company, temporarily under Terry's command, held a roadblock on the major roadway into the town near the point of the railroad overpass. Around two o'clock in the afternoon a motorized patrol from the first of the seaborne forces arrived at the roadblock and inquired whether the overpass had been prepared for demolition. Terry didn't know for sure and sent a nine-man squad forward to investigate. Just as the men approached the bridge they were caught in the open by a larger group of Germans moving west toward the roadblock. The squad leader and two privates were killed and a third was seriously wounded. Four others were pinned down and couldn't move. One trooper escaped and returned immediately to warn the others. The Germans engaged B Company in a fight that lasted two hours before they withdrew back toward the bridge.

Another day passed before Hillsdale and the missing men of B Company arrived at the roadblock. While they had waited for Hillsdale, Terry had sent a detail back to the jump site to recover the body of the trooper who had been killed early on D-Day and found that local people had given him a complete Catholic burial service at a village chapel. The young lieutenant from Laurinburg was touched by the warmth of villagers who had cared for his wounded men, buried his dead comrades, and offered food, wine, and kisses. Yet, at the same time, he was angered by the vicious response that he witnessed among Frenchmen who, when certain they would no longer be subject to German reprisals, heaped their own brutality on prisoners taken in the fighting.

Back home, the Sanfords and Margaret Rose waited anxiously for news of the invasion of southern France. "One of my friends out here—Viola, stayed with me Tuesday night," Margaret Rose wrote the Sanfords two weeks after the invasion. "And we talked and talked—Her husband is in the invasion of S. France too. He's on a LST—and so she heard from him the other day." [16] Finally, in a letter dated September 3, the Sanfords got their first letter from their son and immediately wired Margaret Rose that he was safe.

Terry revealed little in his early letters and said nothing about the confusion surrounding the first days of combat. "We had a well-planned jump and it didn't go too badly, according to the newspaper reports I've seen," he wrote in one letter. He said he had heard from friends in the 501st who had been part of the Normandy invasion, including one who was awarded a Silver Star. He did not mention his part in the engagement with the Germans at the roadblock, for which General Frederick would later recommend him for a Bronze Star. Instead, he was cheerful and upbeat: "You don't need to worry about this boy. The life suits me fine. I'm getting plenty of goat's milk from the natives and I'm taking life as easy as it can be taken in combat." [17]

Margaret Rose had received word from Terry at about the same time as the Sanfords. By the time these letters arrived in the States, however, the 517th was moving northeast through France. Before heading out, the unit had been given a few days rest at the château, and a multicolored tent city sprang up in the countryside. Replacements arrived to fill the slots vacated by the killed and wounded, and the troopers shed jumpsuits for clean fatigues. Altogether the regiment had lost 19 killed, 126 wounded, and 137 injured in the jump—about 14 percent, which was higher than the average for the airborne units involved in Dragoon. The impact of the losses was all the greater because they had occurred in just two days of fighting. By the end of August, after traveling northwest on a route parallel to the coast, all the airborne troops had crossed the Var River. Beyond lay the towering peaks of the Maritime Alps and the retreating Germans, who had taken fortified positions along the treacherous, narrow, winding mountain roads.

Sanford's outfit pushed on into the mountains, where fighting was intermittent but fierce in the rugged terrain. During September, the regiment lost more men than it had in August, including a buddy of Terry's, Lieutenant Charles Sadlo, who had rejoined the unit after being wounded on D-Day; he would be killed in combat in October 1944. Sadlo had been responsible for the only nickname that Terry ever answered to. Because their last names could be confused in radio transmissions, radio operators called Sanford "Fat Sam"; Sadlo was "Slim." As a youngster, Terry had fiercely resisted being called anything but his given name.[18]

In mid-September, Terry's thoughts were pulled home when he saw a curé in a mountain village preparing a school for fall classes. "[He] was cleaning our equipment out of the school so he can get started here, and it reminded me of the preparation at home. Don't work too hard," he wrote his mother in one letter. The longer the 517th remained in France, the more Terry saw that both thrilled and disgusted him. "There can be no comparison between these people and the Italians," he wrote his parents. "The French have fought with us; though unorganized and poorly equipped, they led us through German lines, cared for our wounded, buried our dead. They deserve to be free." In one village after another, the paratroopers were cheered as liberators: "As we came to the towns and through the towns on our march after the enemy we met a population of joyously weeping women, old women (and young) who wanted to kiss every soldier, men and women standing in the streets pouring out wine for the passing troops, middle-aged women singing the songs they had learned in 1917 — 'Pack up your troubles . . .' — 'It's a long way . . .' 'America.' Little girls and little boys (who had not yet learned to say: 'Chew gum please') throwing flowers and passing out grapes and fruit." [19]

One day he was on patrol with two other troopers when they reached the top of a mountain and found a small cottage. Inside was an old shepherd. "Bon jour," the man said, "I am glad to see you." He invited the soldiers inside and served them warm goat's milk flavored with sugar and a pinch of coffee. He told them he had not seen any Germans so high in the mountains. "I stay up here with the wind and my goats most of the time, and the Germans have never bothered me. But the people are free now; the Americans want nothing except for the people to be free; and they will leave when the fighting is done." [20]

In the same letter in which he told of the warmth and hospitality of the shepherd, he recounted another incident at a village where he and his men had taken a pounding from German artillery: "We were met by an irate mayor who said: 'We have never had any Germans here before; we have never been shelled before; and now when you come the Germans have almost destroyed our town and one of our babies has been killed.' 'Yes, damn you,' we said, 'and we lost twenty men getting here today. Now take us to a spot where we can see the valley or there will be *two* French dead in this town today.' " He also observed that the towns through which he passed were filled with men wearing the armbands of the FFI (Free French of the Interior):

There were now fifty johnnies-come-lately with the FFI insignia swaggering in the streets and saloons, basking in the glory earned by the fighting spirits and the blood of the men who were not afraid to resist.

They smoked American cigarettes, and many of them wore American clothes, and all of them would privately state that they had liberated France.

And in the windows of their shops, and on their billboards, and in their papers were ten pictures of Stalin to two of Roosevelt to one of Churchill. (I accredit this not to public sentiment, but to the usual efficient organization of The International.)

So there are some of both, and there are some of all kinds. And just as we have many people who dodge the draft, and are afraid War Bonds are a bad investment, and sell defective wire to the Army, and buy black market gas, those people are not America; and these people of France who have placed themselves in the fullest view of the American troops are surely not France.[21]

Such an outpouring of commentary was unusual for Terry, whose letters included mostly details of his diet—fried rabbit and K rations seemed regular items—and grateful thanks for the packages he received from home. Late in September he told his mother he appreciated the soap she sent but said he had nowhere to use it: "We haven't gotten water to waste with washing." He thanked his father for a handful of cigars. The fifteen he carried with him on the jump had been supplemented by an occasional gift from another trooper. He was out of smokes when his father's resupply arrived. "They hit the spot. I am smoking one now."[22] The souvenirs he mailed to Margaret Rose included a piece of his parachute, a gold Cross of Lorraine he said a marquis had given him, and shoulder patches from a German aviator's uniform. Another package included phonograph records and a photograph album with pictures of Rome.

In early October, after fifty days of combat, Terry got his first pass. He and other officers enjoyed the best of the luxury hotels in Nice, where the prices were right but the diet limited; the restaurants, short of regular supplies, served C rations to their guests. He did get his first hot bath since Italy. Terry called Nice "the watering point of millionaires. I paid 75 francs ($1.50) per night at the best, for a room facing the Mediterranean through full glass doors." His time in combat had passed quickly, he said. "Hope the war ends before the snows start."[23]

The regiment's push into the Alps continued until late October, when it reached the town of Sospel near the Italian border. German troops holding the town had been under attack for nearly two months when they suddenly evacuated the town, leaving nothing but destruction behind. Forty-four townspeople had been killed and a hundred lay wounded from the artillery barrages. The hospital and bridges had been demolished. Sospel was the last French town liberated, but there was no cheering or flowing wine when the 517th's F Company patrol arrived. The Americans also were puzzled by the German retreat. They left behind a heavily fortified position. No one in the West was aware of the concentration of German strength that was already underway behind the screen of the dense Ardennes forest farther north.

As winter closed in on the French Alps the 517th was pulled out of southern France and sent to the town of Soissons, located about eighty miles north of Paris, where amidst rain and mud the unit began refitting. Five hundred new men had recently joined the regiment, half to replace combat losses and the others to provide additional firepower for the rifle squads. An eight-week schedule of training had been prescribed for replacements and veterans were told to shape up. The regimental command felt the appearance and tone of the officers had slipped badly during the weeks in the field. Accordingly, the evening meal became a military formation with dress uniforms required. The menu was still C rations, but at least they were served in style. Terry began planning a Christmas party.

He was a first lieutenant now and had been battalion adjutant since October, when he replaced another officer who had requested duty with a rifle platoon. His former company commander, Donald Fraser, now a major and executive officer of the battalion, recommended him for the job. So far he had escaped serious injury, and the assignment to headquarters company allowed for a modest margin of safety, although all the officers of the 517th Infantry Regiment were expected to be where the action was. Battalion commander Boyle, now a lieutenant colonel, believed in commanding from the front; within a few minutes of the first shots fired at his men in Italy, he was with the company that had made contact.

It had been raining when the 517th arrived in Soissons and the bad weather looked like it was going to continue through the holidays. Terry settled in to move a mountain of paperwork and was looking forward to a reunion with some of his buddies in the 501st. He also had spent some time visiting Château-Thierry and other battlefields from the last great war and had found a filling meal of fresh eggs and steak. In anticipation of Margaret Rose's arrival in Laurinburg, where she planned to spend the Christmas holidays, he was posting his letters to North Carolina rather than Kentucky. A package from his mother containing nuts and mints hit the spot. He was wearing the scarf and sweater she had sent him in anticipation of winter while he wrote a letter home on December 11.

The 517th had been pulled north under a hopeful, even expectant, mood that the war would soon be over. The men were issued fresh clothes, new weapons and equipment and finally were sleeping in beds under a roof. The barracks at Soissons were the first they had seen since Italy. Everyone, from the high command on down, believed that their part of the fighting was all but over. Sketchy reports of activity behind the German lines were discounted. Allied leaders believed the German army defense on the western front "is thinner, more brittle and more vulnerable than it appears on G-2 maps or to troops in the line," one top-level intelligence officer reported.[24]

Then, at dawn on December 16, an overwhelming German counterattack crashed out of the Ardennes, catching American commanders by surprise. Led by an astonishing array of armored vehicles, the Germans rolled over the Allied line, manned by unprepared American soldiers who believed the war had passed them by. The objective of the German effort was the port of Antwerp. Adolf Hitler believed that if his troops could reach the port through which valuable supplies were pouring in to support the Allied effort, he could split his enemy's forces and perhaps reach a negotiated settlement.

The 517th was well back from the initial attack, but the unit was immediately put on alert as the Allied command frantically tried to organize a response. Airborne units such as the 517th, which had been performing like firemen and were assigned where most needed, were immediately called and told to be ready to move with two hours' notice. On December 21, Terry finished a letter home in which he told his parents, "Don't worry about this kid—I'm enjoying life," but he already had carried orders to Boyle that the First Battalion would leave at six that night. It was cold and sleet and snow were falling when the first trucks carrying the men of the 517th pulled out heading north toward Belgium.

At Namur the trucks turned southeast and rolled on through the night and into the next day toward Soy, where they arrived at sunset. The village was under attack and the First Battalion suffered immediate casualties. Boyle had arrived ahead of the convoy and convinced Colonel R. L. Howze of the 36th Armored Infantry, who commanded the Soy garrison, that his men would be ready to fight when they arrived. He organized his troops and, though weary from their twenty-four-hour ride to the front, they moved southwest of the town, where enemy forces had taken positions in the hills at Haid Hits. The initial objective was to take this high ground and open the roadway to Hotton, a nearby town where a small isolated unit of American engineers was holding a bridge across the Ourthe River. The initial assault by the First Battalion was repulsed, as were others throughout the evening. The troopers took losses from heavy weapons and machine gun emplacements that controlled the ridges above the narrow valley through which the road passed. Terry felt a sense of doom as the German artillery hammered his unit. He figured he could easily get killed before morning and not even know where he was. Visibility was reduced to grenade range, and the dark forest cast ominous shadows on the deep snow that buried a frozen landscape.

On the morning of the 23rd, Boyle left Major Fraser in command of the force at Haid Hits and with a smaller group swung to the right, bypassing the enemy emplacements. The plan called for him to link up with the forces at Hotton and then turn and advance toward Soy along the highway, where he would meet up with Fraser. Just after noon, Fraser's group, reinforced with nine tanks that had come up from Soy, pushed off again. Fighting continued through the day and into the night, when visibility in the dense underbrush was reduced to just a few feet. Moreover, the region was covered with more than a foot of snow and temperatures were below zero. The bodies of the dead lay where they had fallen, often frozen to the ground. Fraser pressed forward even after German guns knocked out six of the armored vehicles sent to assist his men. The following day, with Boyle moving toward Haid Hits from the opposite direction, Fraser's group pushed the German forces from their position and the First Battalion secured the road.

One of Fraser's men, Pfc Melvin E. Biddle from B Company, was awarded the Congressional Medal of Honor for his part in the fighting at Haid Hits. During the night of the 23rd, he was the lead scout and advanced alone into the woods, where over the next several hours he killed seventeen of the enemy with nineteen shots from his M-1. He also knocked out three machine gun emplacements unassisted and led the advance the following morning. During his night in the woods he moved undetected among the German positions, eluding sentries and patrols. He was so close at one point that a German soldier stepped on his hand. The information he gathered helped Fraser flank the German strong point and reach his objective.

On Christmas Eve, the men of the First Battalion were exhausted. They had been on the move for three straight days, in combat for two. Fighting on the 23rd had claimed more than fifty casualties and about the same number on the 24th. With the Soy-Hotton road secure, the battalion pulled back to Soy. The fight was far from over. Germans still held positions south of the town, and at the command post intelligence reports told of a new wrinkle. Army interrogators found that German soldiers in American uniforms had been assigned to destroy the headquarters and disrupt communications: "They are traveling in American jeeps, four to a jeep, and speak with an American accent." [25]

Christmas Day was bitterly cold and snowing. American soldiers were reminded of the holiday by the German machine gunners, who yelled "Merry Christmas, Merry Christmas" as they held off the attacks. At least the First Battalion had spent a night in bedrolls and took their first hot food in three days, a Christmas meal of roast turkey that the men ate in their positions on the line. At noon, however, units of the First Battalion were rousted to head back into action. The night before, two battalions of the 75th Infantry had passed through to press the attack south of Soy. These were green troops, most of whom had thought they would be an occupation force. They were badly mauled by the Germans, suffering more than two hundred casualties.

Howze called on Boyle to take his men, who were now holding the Soy-Hotton road, and advance. With A Company and a platoon from C Company, plus Terry and men from headquarters company, Boyle's attack force jumped off shortly after 2 P.M. and pushed toward the ridge through heavy woods. The paratroopers had experience advancing behind an artillery barrage and made it to the heights under intense fire. By dusk the ridge was secure at a cost of forty-six casualties. That evening Boyle and his officers organized a defense of the hill using men from the 75th Division.

On the morning of the 26th, Terry was still on the line. During the night he had moved from one location to another, filling in as Boyle had needed his help in organizing a defensive position along the hill with the shaken and battered remainder of the 75th Division units. He was with a line of infantry on the ridge when the Germans mounted a counterattack. He had his men about four feet apart, just inside trees at the top of a hill whose slopes were open to full view. As a regiment of Germans approached, he ordered his men to hold their fire. Finally, with the Germans within about thirty feet of his position, he ordered them to fire. In the confusion, an officer leading the German counterattack ran into the American line, virtually into Terry's arms. He grabbed him by his belt, ordered him to surrender, and relieved him of two pistols. The officer complied and Terry put the man in the front of his jeep, held a weapon at his back, and drove him to the rear for interrogation. Boyle later received the Distinguished Service Cross in recognition of his leadership in this action and the First Battalion was awarded a Presidential Distinguished Unit Citation.

Many years later Terry would continue to wonder about the fate of his captured officer. He feared that the major was shot before he ever made it to a POW collection point. The men of the 517th knew about the German massacre of American POWs at nearby Malmedy, and American soldiers already had begun to seek their revenge. Moreover, those on the line found it difficult to manage prisoners or send them to the rear and shelter when they themselves were deprived of basic necessities.[26]

Terry revealed none of the brutality of what he had seen and experienced in his letters home. "Christmas was cold but the best I ever spent in this country," he said in a one-line V-mail written less than forty-eight hours after the action on the ridge south of Hoy. "Just keeping you informed that things are going well in this country," he wrote in another dated a day later. It continued, "More food than elsewhere and more cooperative. Maybe it's because they've just had another scare." He didn't explain that the extra helpings of the belated though hot Christmas meal were due to the high casualty rate in the 517th—rear-echelon cooks had prepared for the unit's full complement.[27]

On New Year's Day, the 517th moved back into action as the Allies pushed west against steady opposition from the retreating Germans and the worst winter weather Europe had seen in years. At night the temperatures ranged from zero to ten below. Soldiers in foxholes could freeze to death if they fell asleep. Snow was eighteen inches deep and lay on frozen ground virtually impenetrable to the GI's entrenching tool. Visibility was reduced to a few meters, and as Sanford and his troopers moved forward during one night maneuver they had to hold onto the equipment of the man ahead so as not to get lost in the darkness and dense underbrush.

The immediate objective of the First Battalion was the town of Bergeval, which Boyle occupied with two companies before moving on under the cover of darkness to a position on a bluff east of the town. He had been told to expect other Allied units there. When he reached the high ground, his small force was alone and there was evidence of German activity on his flank.

In an effort to better coordinate his position, Boyle, Sanford, and two others headed back to Bergeval. The four were moving across level ground in the darkness when they were challenged in German and dove for cover from machine gun fire, which hit both Boyle and Sanford. At the same time, heavier fire erupted at a point farther away. The group finally made it to Bergeval, but by the time the two wounded men got to an aid tent, the regimental doctor thought Boyle was dead.

Sanford's wounds were less serious. Medics patched up his left hand where he had been hit by a piece of shrapnel and though his injuries were serious enough to warrant a trip to the rear, he remained with Boyle, holding cigarettes for him as he waited to be evacuated. (Boyle recovered after months of treatment and later fought in Korea.) In Terry's next V-mail home, dated less than a week after he was wounded, he wrote: "Just want you to know that everything is moving along well in these parts." He made no mention of his wounds.

On January 21 the Allies captured the Belgian town of St. Vith, effectively bringing an end to the Battle of the Bulge. The 517th had been in continuous action for thirty-seven days and losses had been heavy; the unit had suffered more than seven hundred casualties. The Allied push was unrelenting, however. After a break of about ten days, the 517th continued east and Terry's mail home was soon coming from Germany. As always, the tone was light as he asked Margaret Rose to furnish him with treats. His shopping list included shrimp, tomato soup, anchovies, sliced pineapples, Chinese food, crackers, cigars, fruit cocktail, and marshmallows.

In late February, the 517th was recalled to Joigny, France, where preparations were being made for an airborne assault. For those who fought in Belgium, it was a defining experience. Winston Churchill called it the greatest American battle of the war. Losses included more than sixteen thousand killed and sixty thousand wounded. Like thousands of others, Terry would never forget the stark contrasts of dark forests and white snow, punctuated by the brilliance of shell bursts, that would reappear years later as visions of a scene replayed from deep in his memory. He had survived the worst, he believed, and he had performed well, his superiors said in efficiency reports: "Excellent speaker and organizer"; "Obtains maximum results with minimum of effort"; "He is a creative officer with the ability to see ahead and take corrective action; always one step ahead." [28] In the days after the hardest of the fighting he considered an appointment as an aide to General Matthew Ridgeway, the commander of the XVIII Airborne Corps, but passed on the opportunity.

For his service in the Battle of the Bulge, Sanford received a ribbon for the Bronze Star he had won in France as well as a Purple Heart. The 517th prepared for more combat jumps as part of the 13th Airborne Division, but each time, the missions were scrubbed after the target areas were overrun by the fast-moving Allied advance into Germany.

Duty at Joigny was pleasant enough, particularly as springtime brought color and life back to the gray land. He visited Paris and the Riviera. He also found himself busy with paperwork as his superiors in the new organization demanded to know what had happened to all the equipment the unit had consumed during nine months in the field. Boyle had never been a stickler for such details and excused his staff officers who failed to record whether a machine gun was left behind because there was no one to carry it.

Terry was halfway through his twenty-eighth year. As was true for millions of men in uniform, his personal plans had been set aside for the duration of the war. Now, sitting on a hillside near Joigny, he reflected on questions that carried more significance in the wake of the brutal consequences of life he had just experienced. "What is personal ambition?" he later wrote in a recollection of that time.

> Is it really important to achieve "something of significance" in your life? What about the political life—why get involved?
> Is the kind of commitment that takes your energy off what could

be a futile and fruitless venture of politics something to which you should dedicate yourself?

Isn't winning a rather hollow victory after you get it, anyhow? What have you got?

You are here today and gone tomorrow. Aren't you better off if you give your attention to your personal business, letting someone else handle the politics? Let someone else take the shafts and arrows of criticism. Can't you be a good citizen by simply voting, contributing and working in civic drives? [29]

There were more questions than answers.

A few days later, in mid-April, Terry was awakened by the battalion sergeant major, a man he once described as "a leathery-faced roughneck from the concrete of the Bronx who was about as sentimental as a rifle butt." The sergeant was shaking him by the foot, and through the fog of sleep Terry heard him yelling, "Sir, get up. Get up! Our President is dead." The sergeant's words seared his subconscious. It was "our President," not "the President" or "President Roosevelt." He bounded from bed and stood there in the dark just before dawn and his tears flowed just like those of his sergeant. "Yes, Franklin Delano Roosevelt had suited me fine," he later wrote.

He won the power and he changed things, changed them so that the government, which is all the people, began to get concerned about all the people. Human dignity began to mean more than it had ever meant since a Virginian had written about it, or even since a Galilean had talked about it.

Every individual was important, and this message began to reverberate around the world, and freedom and opportunity began to take on new meaning everywhere. There wasn't any doubt in my mind why in that April we found ourselves on foreign soil, fighting a war. I was proud to be there.[30]

CHAPTER SIX

The Third Primary

DETERMINING WHEN TERRY SANFORD decided he wanted to be governor of North Carolina depends on which political legend people wish to believe. He often said he thought about the job when he was a teenager. Others swear he had made up his mind when he was hip deep in student politics at Chapel Hill. That's not likely, he would later caution, and joke that if he told anyone such a thing it was Margaret Rose and he was just trying to impress her.

Was it when he was sitting on that hillside in France? That's closer. Terry sincerely believed that government could do something about the human condition and Franklin D. Roosevelt had shown what was possible. Yet, just how he might manifest those thoughts remained an open question. He had his misgivings about forsaking a normal life and a career for politics.

There is little doubt that plans for a political career of some sort accompanied him to Chapel Hill in the fall of 1945 as he enrolled for classes to finish law school. He wasn't sure how things would play out, but for the present he was determined to pay more attention to his studies, finish with a respectable ranking in his classes, establish a law practice, and be ready when the opportunity for public office arose.[1]

He had little time for planning anything in the weeks before law school opened in late September. When the war on the European front ended in April, the men of the 517th who didn't have sufficient points for discharge were offered two choices: they could join another outfit for Honor Guard duty in Berlin or head home for thirty days of leave before shipping out for the Pacific Theater, where an invasion of Japan was being planned. Terry favored keeping the 517th intact and became the leading advocate among the officers and men to stay with the outfit, gambling that the Japanese would capitulate and the war truly would be over before the 517th would be needed. On July 20, First Lieutenant Sanford, commander of Headquarters Company, posted embarkation orders for the trip to the States. On his last evening in Joigny, as the small regimental band played retreat and the American flag was lowered from the staff above the town's medieval walls, he thought about friends and relatives who were buried in the cemeteries spread over the green fields of France and Belgium.

Three weeks later, Terry was aboard a troop ship in the middle of the Atlantic Ocean when a buddy interrupted his gin rummy game to tell him that the Japanese had capitulated after atomic bombs had obliterated Hiroshima and Nagasaki. After the ship docked in New York Harbor, the men of the 517th were celebrated with a parade and then boarded troop trains for the ride home, where they awaited final discharge orders. Terry's gamble had paid off. It would be six months or more before those who stayed in Europe would be home. Those in the States with enough points for discharge, including Terry, were released immediately.

Terry met Margaret Rose in Laurinburg on August 22. It was an exhilarating time for this young couple and millions of others like them around the nation. The Great Depression was behind them. The war was behind them. America was the leader of the Free World and their entire lives lay ahead. Anything seemed possible.

In Laurinburg, Cecil and Betsy Sanford's lives had never held more promise. They had their house paid for and both had steady jobs. Cecil was office manager of Domestic Gas Company, a small operation that sold bottled gas and fixtures, and his wife was teaching school. More important, both their sons had returned from the war safe and sound.

Terry and Margaret Rose stayed with the Sanfords while they made preparations to move to Chapel Hill. A few days before classes were to begin on September 24, Terry cranked a 1940 Chevrolet coupe he had bought for $500 and was on his way to Chapel Hill when he stopped for gas at Bill Covington's Esso station on the square. There, he ran into Dickson Phillips, who after graduating from Davidson College in 1943 had enlisted in the Army and, like Sanford, volunteered for the paratroopers.

The last time the two had seen one another was in France in the weeks after the Battle of the Bulge. When Terry had learned Phillips's unit, the 513th Parachute Infantry Regiment, was bivouacked nearby he surprised Phillips one night when he arrived wearing a striking, full-length white leather coat and carrying some "liberated" brandy and cigars. It was quite a reunion. Bunking with Phillips was Dean Swem, Terry's buddy from the 501st who had washed out of OCS. Swem, now a second lieutenant, had received a battlefield commission after the officer ranks of the 513th were decimated in fighting around Bastogne. The 513th subsequently jumped into Holland as part of Operation Varsity, the last large airborne exercise of the war. Phillips survived the jump even though he had landed in a tree, which combat photographer Robert Capa captured on film. A few days later, however, while his company was fighting with the British, he was advancing on a roadblock when an ammunition dump exploded and he was seriously wounded. He spent several months at an Army hospital in Florida and was still recuperating from his wounds when he saw Terry at the filling station.

Phillips was unsure about his future. He had gotten married in July and nurtured some ill-defined plans to go to graduate school and then teach history. When Terry asked him to ride with him to Chapel Hill, he said he had nothing better to do and climbed in the car to spend the day with his friend. That afternoon, he called his wife to tell her he had decided to enroll in law school after a chance meeting with the dean, who told him that if he got his Davidson transcript in quickly he could begin classes immediately. Rather than return to Laurinburg that night as they had planned — Phillips had some details to work out the next day — the two slept in the Institute of Government building, where they found some mattresses stored in the attic.

Reunions like this were commonplace as veterans returned home and then headed to college to take advantage of the free tuition and $100-a-month stipends available under the GI Bill. The university at Chapel Hill was unprepared for the crush of new students, which in a few months would triple the school's enrollment. In fact, the school had not yet been relieved of all its wartime duties; the Navy's V-12 program would continue until October 1. Classes filled to overflowing and housing was in short supply. University President Frank Graham was making plans to ask the state for money to erect 450 prefabricated houses and five new dormitories to accommodate the spiraling student population.

Rental housing was hard to find, but Terry used his connections in town and took a small one-bedroom apartment on the second floor at 111 North Street. Phillips had to take temporary quarters until later in the fall, when he finally found a cottage on the edge of town and his wife, Evelyn, joined him.

Margaret Rose found a job as a counselor in the Dean of Women's Office and began taking organ lessons while Terry buckled down to his studies. Reentry into the academic world did not go as smoothly as he had anticipated. It had been nearly four years since he had opened a textbook or seen the inside of a classroom. And the war had left its mark; he would awake at night with his mind a jumble of legal citations and images of the dark woods and cold, snowy battlefields of Belgium and Germany. Pressing on him most of all was the clear understanding that his future depended on his grades at the end of the semester. As an undergraduate, and even during his first two years in law school, grades had never meant to him as much as they did now.

Yet Terry and the other veterans felt a new spirit, part of an unbounded optimism that invaded every aspect of campus life. The *Tar Heel* (the newspaper did not return to a daily schedule until 1946) greeted students with an editorial that read, "The fact that now is the time for the students to make plans for a great future is everywhere evident. There are some conservatives in student government who will delay our reconversion. We must be on guard against such poisonous statements as 'we are not yet ready to plan for a peacetime campus. There are not enough students here to build a structure like that we had before the war.' "[2]

Classes filled with men who were eager to restart their lives. The law school, which had shut down during the war, had 102 students enrolled in the fall of 1945, more than double the prewar count. It was a serious crowd, older by five or six years than what the professors had seen before. Among Terry's classmates were two Army colonels, a Marine Corps major, and a host of Army lieutenants and Navy ensigns. Coats and ties were the preferred dress among law students, but Terry wore his uniform for the first few weeks until he had the money to afford a civilian wardrobe.

From time to time a group of law students that included William Friday, Sanford, Phillips, and others whose careers would lead them into public life in later years gathered at a filling station on the edge of town, where they talked about common experiences and shared a beer or two. The conversation often drifted into politics, about who would lead their state in the years ahead, about course work, and about readjusting to civilian life. Few, if any, told war stories; those who had experienced combat didn't defame buddies left dead on the battlefield by boasting of their own exploits. Terry thought about his friend, John Umstead, who was buried in Hawaii in the military cemetery called the Punch Bowl, where two other friends were laid to rest.

These survivors were looking to the future, the one they believed they had earned a right to determine for themselves by virtue of their service in Europe and the Pacific. A new age was before them, an old era was passing. If we could lick Hitler, Terry thought, then anything was possible. Writer John Egerton later described the mood this way: "America seemed on the verge of a great renewal, a reinvention of itself. With an air of invincibility, it was facing the future in an expansive, opportunistic, idealistic mood. Implicit in that positive spirit was the admonition that the time to move was at hand, and those who didn't get on board would be left on the dock when the ship sailed."[3]

Change was in the air. A new concept of world federalism excited many students as they watched the formative stages of the organization of the United Nations. In early October, the Campus Religion in Life Committee invited Davidson College professor Dr. Kenneth Foreman to speak on the topic "One World, or None." Terry joined in the chorus of those supporting a new order for an old world.

On college campuses at least, people also were talking about the mammoth study of race in the United States by Swedish sociologist Gunnar Myrdal that had been published in 1944. Myrdal's work, *An American Dilemma*, challenged virtually every popularly held belief on race: that African Americans were happy with their place in society, that they were innately inferior to whites, that whites in the South knew what their African American neighbors wanted, that the race issue was solely a problem for the South to solve. Most troubling of all was the documentation of coast-to-coast racism that revealed the hypocrisy veiled by the democratic ideal of America.

One of the much anticipated speakers on campus in the fall of 1945 was Georgia governor Ellis Gibbs Arnall, who was being touted as the model of progressive leadership in the South. Arnall had been elected in 1942, succeeding Herman Talmadge, who epitomized the race-baiting, wool-hat politics commonly associated with the Deep South. During Arnall's term he had overhauled state government and successfully pushed through legislation to reform the state prison system, eliminate the poll tax, and give the vote to eighteen-year-olds. He even hired an assistant attorney general to do battle with the Ku Klux Klan. Arnall also had led the fight against the practice of discriminatory freight rates, a remnant of Reconstruction, that allowed rail carriers to charge more for shipments going north than those coming south. One of those who had carefully read Arnall's autobiography and treatise on the future of the South, a book he titled *The Shore Dimly Seen*, was Terry Sanford, who treasured his autographed copy.

In Chapel Hill, students may have been encouraged by the movement, however slight, toward more enlightened racial attitudes in the South. But villagers were divided. Forty members of the stately Presbyterian church that President Graham attended on the edge of the campus had walked out after a Navy band that included black members attended services one Sunday. In the aftermath, the minister, Reverend Charles M. Jones, announced that henceforth African Americans would be welcome to attend services any time. A few black worshipers took Jones up on the offer of an integrated church pew, although local ordinances still prohibited them from taking a seat at a diner around the corner and state law prohibited their children from attending a white school.

A delegation met with Governor Gregg Cherry to complain about Graham's support of Jones. Cherry told them, "Gentlemen, I'm a segregation-ist, but I want to say this to you. As president of the university, he obeys the law of this state and this land. As an elder of the Presbyterian Church, backing up Mr. Jones, he obeys the laws of God. Now, what are you gentle-men going to do about it?"[4]

That fall the university's Dialectic Society voted in support of admit-ting black students to white campuses in North Carolina. Graham's most outspoken critic, David Clark, editor of the *Southern Textile Bulletin*, was apo-plectic. Clark, who was a member of the university's board of trustees, challenged the *Tar Heel* to publish the names of those students who had voted to upset generations of segregation: "It might be embarrassing to some very respectable North Carolina families to learn that their sons and daughters were so weak-minded as to have yielded to the influences of professors and instructors who are members of the radical and commu-nistic group at the University of North Carolina." The newspaper accepted his challenge and printed the names along with a letter from the Dialectic Society's president, Douglass Hunt, who wrote:

> To my mind there is one overriding and supremely important fact about men: Whatever their race, nationality, religion or condition they are men. This applies to Negroes; they are men; they are human beings. I cannot conceive that the mere accident of color made me su-perior to them, or to any other racial, national or religious group.
>
> A second compelling fact prompted me to vote to recommend the abolition of Jim Crow laws: This is one world. No matter how many artificial barriers we created, that is the first fact of modern life.
>
> I was born in Winston-Salem; I graduated from the Greensboro public schools; my parents now reside in Rocky Mount. But, if you look for the source of these seditious remarks, turn to that most revo-lutionary of documents, the New Testament.[5]

While this exchange was still fresh, Carolina students further infuriated their elders by pushing the limit on the race issue at the ninth annual State Student Legislature meeting in the house and senate chambers of the state capitol. At a joint session of the mock legislature, a student from Chapel Hill proposed a resolution inviting representatives from the state's black campuses to the 1946 assembly. All in all, the resolution was not nearly as sweeping as one passed earlier in the day, when the student senate adopted a measure urging abolition of Jim Crow laws that had been put forth by Helen Sanford, Terry's sister, who was a student at the Woman's College in Greensboro.

The resolution was unexpected, and after initial debate, a vote was post-poned from Friday until another joint session scheduled for Saturday, when the delegates argued the issue for three hours. Also joining in was North Carolina's Secretary of State Thad Eure, who in his role as an advisor urged caution. "I have no objections if that is the way you want it," he told the delegates, "but I have a feeling that the issue which you have raised here may not be advantageous to them or to you." He told the students that they might find it more beneficial to move "in the direction with a little more care and thoroughness than you appear to have shown" and that "the headlong, headstrong movement" might not be helpful to any group concerned." He suggested that the students let administrators of their institutions explore the idea first.[6]

In the heat of the debate, some opponents of the resolution implied that approval would jeopardize support for the university by the real legislators whose chairs the students had borrowed for the mock session. This infuriated some on the other side, including James Wallace, a first-year law student, who declared that if the cost of doing what was right was a loss of legislative support, then "to hell with the cutting of appropriations for the university." He was quoted as saying that funds for the operation of the school are "at rock bottom now and can't stand very much cutting." The resolution opening the 1946 assembly to all campuses in the state passed by an overwhelming margin of 110 to 48.[7]

Critics howled and charged that the resolution was the work of some out-of-state rabble-rouser after Eure was quoted in one news account as saying the student who proposed the resolution was from the North and studying at Chapel Hill on the GI Bill. President Graham responded in an open letter published in the Tar Heel: "The resolution was introduced by a Carolina student from Cleveland County (Buddy Glenn) who is president of the International Relations Club. It was seconded by a fellow student, a U.S. Marine from south of the Mason and Dixon line and chairman of the Council for Religion in Life (John Lineweaver) which brings to the campus ministers, priests and rabbis for university sermons."[8]

Most galling of all to those in an uproar about a mixed meeting was the Wallace quote that appeared in a Raleigh newspaper account of the meeting and circulated by the wire services. Graham said Wallace's remarks were misunderstood and had been taken out of context: "I personally deplore the language used by a Carolina student in expressing his indignation. In fairness to the young man I must say that he regrets the context of his indignation but has no apologies for his indignation."[9] Wallace's remarks continued to haunt him, however, and he was brought before the Law School honor court, where Terry Sanford handled his defense and efforts to remove Wallace as the law school's representative to the student legislature were denied. The matter soon faded away.

All this excitement changed nothing in everyday life and real politics.

In the early part of 1946, Southern senators, including North Carolina's Clyde Hoey and Josiah Bailey, joined with Republicans to mount a filibuster and defeat President Harry Truman's efforts to extend Franklin Roosevelt's executive order requiring equal opportunity in employment in the federal government and private industry holding government contracts. The segregationists' response was growing in breadth as well as intensity. Any "troublemakers" had to be communists as well, they declared. It was all part of the conspiracy that Congressman Martin Dies had talked about in 1940 when he said, "Moscow has long considered the Negroes of the United States as excellent potential recruits for the Communist Party." [10]

The world was turning upside down to those accustomed to life before the war. Although the Chapel Hill campus retained some of its prewar frivolity (Sadie Hawkins Day went on as scheduled), at the same time, the students had formed a chapter of the Southern Conference on Human Welfare. The SCHW, whose leadership included Frank Graham, had been suspect ever since it conducted integrated meetings in the late 1930s and began addressing problems of social and economic conditions in the South. The first thing on the Chapel Hill chapter's agenda was support of strikers on the picket lines at the Erwin Mills in Durham.

Communists weren't all that hard to find. In 1946, Communist Party organizer Sam J. Hall announced a party recruiting drive in an ad he placed in the *News & Observer.* He claimed to have two hundred members in North and South Carolina. One was Junius Scales, the son of a wealthy Greensboro family, who was a war veteran and an officer on the American Veterans Committee and the campus chapter of the SCHW. The shared goals—avoiding World War III, combating racism, promoting organized labor, raising the standard of living—had enormous appeal to young progressives and liberals on the Chapel Hill campus. Terry attended some of the early meetings of the American Veterans Committee and liked Scales. However, when the organizers began constructing bylaws to expel those who didn't conform to their beliefs, Terry knew there would be problems ahead and departed. [11]

All this activity left Frank Graham forever on the defensive against stronger and stronger attacks from his critics. One university trustee, textile man Thurmond Chatham of Elkin, declared, "Our university is regarded as radical rather than liberal. I don't like the atmosphere and as a trustee I want to protest against it." [12] Chatham and others demanded that Graham do something about the young communists. That raised Graham's hackles. He had never stifled student activity and didn't plan to start now. "I was asked to ship them from the university," Graham later recalled in an interview. "Well, Mr. [Robert] House and I would never have shipped a communist from here. We don't do that way. There were communist cells in some other institutions, but they were underground. They centered on us, because it was open. . . . Give them the air, give them the sunlight and let it be in the open. The students would take care of them. I think in a great many cases, if we'd moved against them, tried to shut them out, we'd have made some communists."[13]

Terry steered clear of most things that did not bear directly on his studies. The attention he paid to his law courses was rewarded with a record of straight As at the end of the fall semester. Toward the end of the spring term, he set about preparing for the bar exam. Because the examination for the North Carolina Bar would be drawn from state cases, he began reading the published reports of the state supreme court, looking first at the head notes, the opening portion where the case is summarized, and then reading the entire case if it looked like it might warrant more attention. By summer, he had covered twenty years of reports. He finished his review at Wrightsville Beach, where he and Margaret Rose went every weekend. He took the bar exam and along with every other member of his class passed. He was admitted to practice on August 9, 1946, after being sworn in by Superior Court Judge Frank Armstrong, whose younger brother, David, had served with Terry in the war.

Though he was now eligible to begin practicing law, Terry and Margaret Rose remained in Chapel Hill. One reason was Albert Coates. Terry and Coates had corresponded during the war, and it was understood there was a place waiting for him at the Institute of Government when he returned. Terry had fended off Coates's repeated requests for one assignment or another during his final year in law school, but in August 1946 he was back in the traces at the Institute running the annual Boys' State program. One of his counselors was his neighbor Bill Friday, a State College graduate who had entered law school in the spring of 1946. When that concluded, Terry signed on as an associate director of the Institute, which included a faculty appointment as an assistant professor in the law school. He joined other returning veterans whom Coates had rehired, such as Bill Cochrane, who was home from his service in the Navy. Because of his FBI experience, Terry's special area of interest was criminal law, which provided a reunion with his old boss, J. Edgar Hoover. Coates took Terry along when he presented Hoover with a copy of the Institute's guide book for traffic laws.

Life looked pretty good in the fall of 1946. Terry and Margaret Rose had more money than they had ever had before. They had moved from the apartment to a comfortable little duplex next door. They were surrounded by an energetic and lively collection of friends. And there was every suggestion from Coates that when he retired Terry would be one of the candidates for leadership of the Institute.

Coates had begun to give Terry more and more responsibilities. He included him in a team he organized to help the city of Charlotte and Mecklenburg County work toward a merger of selected city and county government functions. He also put him in charge of the first comprehensive training program for troopers of the State Highway Patrol, who previously had been taught only how to drive an automobile at high speeds and then were promptly put to work. In early October, the Patrol School opened with 103 recruits. It was Terry's job to winnow the group down to forty-three or forty-four of the best after a course of instruction that included criminal procedure, the law, and how to gather and protect evidence, as well as how to give chase on the open highway.

Terry enjoyed his work and the expanding range of contacts that the Institute offered. Yet, he was bothered that he wasn't doing what he really ought to be doing. Coates's insistence that he remain to help get the Patrol School organized gave him an excuse to delay a decision about moving from Chapel Hill and opening a law practice. More than that, however, he felt a deep sense of duty to Coates, who leaned hard on his young protégés. As Terry struggled with his next step, he was reminded of his decision a few years earlier to forsake the comfort and security of the FBI for the certain danger of combat. His life was not at risk this time, but once again he was giving up a sure thing that had some promise of success for the unknown.

Finally, after more than a year with Coates, Terry told him of his decision to leave. Coates was surprised and warned that he was making a big mistake by throwing away an opportunity that he would find nowhere else. Yet, he didn't try to discourage Terry and Margaret Rose as they began looking for a new home away from Chapel Hill.

Terry immediately ruled out returning to his hometown; everyone in Laurinburg would still see him as Cecil and Betsy's little boy. He believed it would take twenty years to convince anyone there he was really grown. Coates offered to arrange interviews at law firms in Charlotte and Greensboro, but Terry believed it would take too long to make a name for himself in a large city. He had family in Wilmington who could help him get a start there, but that city was too far east and away from the center of activity. The town of Sanford, about fifty miles south of Chapel Hill, ended up on the list, if only by whim. He finally settled on Fayetteville in Cumberland County, an agricultural center turned Army town, despite the admonitions from his former classmate, Hector McGeachy, whose father was sheriff there, that Fayetteville was already overlawyered. In May 1948 the Sanfords packed the Chevy and headed south to Fayetteville.

Fayetteville was appealing for several reasons, including good family connections. A favorite uncle, his mother's brother-in-law, Bill Shaw, was Fayetteville's postmaster; Helen and Bill Shaw had taken Terry in when his mother had been in the sanatorium. Another uncle by marriage, his father's sister's second husband, Tom Hatcher, owned the largest jewelry store in town. In addition, Fayetteville was a town that had enjoyed prosperity during the war, when one hundred thousand soldiers had passed through. Now local boosters were determined their community would not return to its sleepy prewar state. Terry also believed his military record would ride well in a community that included a growing number of retired soldiers as well as active duty members of the XVIII Airborne Corps that called Fort Bragg home. Moreover, newcomers were welcome, and there would be room for one more lawyer, despite McGeachy's warning. Finally, for a young man considering a future in politics, Fayetteville gave Terry a base in eastern North Carolina, the traditional home of the state's Democratic Party.

The Sanfords arrived in Fayetteville with a $500 grubstake from Terry's college buddy, Paul Thompson. Thompson was from Wadesboro and had been part of the self-help student crowd with whom Terry had shared jobs at Chapel Hill before the war. He was back in Chapel Hill working on a master's degree in business when Terry asked him for a loan to keep things together until he could count on some income from his law practice. The young couple rented a duplex on Hillside Street that belonged to Miss Annie Rose, an elder member of a prominent local family. Her cousin had been one of the town's leading attorneys and her nephew, Charles Rose Jr., was carrying on the tradition.

With his Uncle Tom's help, Terry found an office on the third floor of a small building just off Hay Street. He paid a month's rent of $50 but never moved in. Shortly after he arrived in Fayetteville, he was back in Chapel Hill for a gathering of inductees of the Golden Fleece, an honor society at the university, when Rose offered to let him use his office, located on the ninth floor of the First Citizens Bank Building. It was a far more prestigious address, overlooking the square where Fayetteville's historic market building stood in the intersection of the city's main streets.

Terry's first client was Marcus Williams, who ran a grocery store where the Sanfords traded; Terry performed a title search for Williams and was paid $15. He also defended a former student at the Patrol School who had been arrested for drunk driving; Terry convinced a jury that the trooper couldn't be guilty because the car he was "driving" was parked on the street at the time of the arrest. Business improved after another senior member of the Fayetteville legal fraternity, Colonel Terry A. Lyon, who was associated with the Rose firm, took a liking to him. Lyon had a number of companies on retainer and he passed some title work Terry's way. Although clients weren't breaking down the door, Terry was not totally adrift. On his Uncle

Bill's recommendation he was invited to join the Fayetteville Rotary Club as a representative of the city's trial bar.

Fayetteville can be one of the hottest places in North Carolina. It sits on the southeastern edge of the Carolina Sandhills, where the sandy soil absorbs the heat of the summer sun and the landscape never seems to cool until fall. In the summer of 1948, Fayetteville and much of North Carolina, especially east of Raleigh, seemed hotter than usual in the aftermath of Harry Truman's congressional message on civil rights.

Southern Democrats had been on edge ever since Truman's Commission on Civil Rights had issued its report in October 1947 that called for federal action to end racial discrimination. Never before had a federal agency spoken so boldly on the issue. Truman's civil rights message, delivered three weeks after his state of the union address in January, did not endorse all of the commission's recommendations, but one civil rights leader called it "the greatest freedom document since the Emancipation Proclamation." [14] The president called for congressional action to outlaw lynching, to guarantee voting rights and fair employment, to end segregated seating on interstate buses and trains, and to create a civil rights division in the Justice Department to enforce the new laws. Frank Graham had been one of two Southerners on the commission; he did not endorse the final report and instead issued a minority report calling for goodwill and education — not federal law — as the remedy for discrimination.

Six months later, in mid-May 1948, just as Terry and Margaret Rose were preparing to move to Fayetteville, about fifteen hundred delegates from a dozen states gathered in Jackson, Mississippi, to found the States' Rights Party. South Carolina Governor Strom Thurmond told them "all the laws of Washington and all the bayonets of the army cannot force the Negro into our homes, our schools, our churches and our places of recreation." [15] Later in the summer, Thurmond became the new party's candidate for president after delegates from the South bolted from the Democratic Party's convention in Philadelphia. Some North Carolina delegates joined in the walkout, but Governor Gregg Cherry refused to join them, even though his sympathies lay with the states' righters and their defense of segregation. He was seen holding tight to the North Carolina banner to keep it out of the parade of segregationists as they marched from the convention hall.

The North Carolina delegation joined others from the South in support of a rump movement to nominate Senator Richard Russell of Georgia in place of Truman. It had no chance, but it provided the Southerners an opportunity to air their grievances. One who took the podium was a young Alabama state legislator named George Wallace, who seconded Russell's nomination. He told the convention, "[Russell] will see that the South is not crucified on the cross of the so-called civil rights program." [16]

The traditional conservative leadership of the North Carolina Democratic Party was having its own problems. In the spring gubernatorial primaries, W. Kerr Scott had belatedly entered the race for governor and upset the party establishment that had been picking governors for nearly twenty years. Scott was a blunt-spoken dairy farmer from Alamance County, a hefty bull of a man, whose high forehead was crowned with thick brown hair that only enhanced his stature. Called the Squire of Haw River, Scott had announced his plans for reelection as state commissioner of agriculture but then changed his mind and entered the race for governor after a night-long meeting in Burlington, where one man was offered a blank check if he could keep Scott out of the race.[17] Scott conducted a freewheeling campaign with a country-boy manner that belied a shrewd political mind. His victory over the chosen candidate, Charles Johnson, caught virtually everyone by surprise, particularly the so-called Shelby Dynasty, a tight knot of politicians who had controlled the state's top office since O. Max Gardner of Shelby took office in 1929.

Terry did not support Scott in the first primary. His candidate was Mayne Albright, a Raleigh lawyer and World War II veteran who came from the liberal wing of the party. In the first primary, Albright ran a distant third behind Johnson, the leader, and Scott, whose second-place finish qualified him to call for a second primary. Among the tactics that helped Scott defeat Johnson in the second round were leaflets Scott's couriers left behind at country stores across the state that accused Johnson of using his authority as state treasurer to favor certain large banks in North Carolina, particularly Wachovia Bank & Trust Company, with $100 million in deposits of state money they held interest-free. Johnson responded by calling Scott "the wild bull from Alamance who, if we let him, will wreck and bankrupt the state." [18]

Scott's support came from people on the farms and in the rural areas of the state, where the Scott family had been politically active for more than two generations. Charles Brantley Aycock, the state's education governor elected in 1900, and Charles McIver, another turn-of-the century education leader, had taken meals at the Scott table when Kerr was a boy. He was a graduate of State College in Raleigh, where he excelled in track, YMCA work, and debating. According to one of his professors, C. L. Newman, Scott "listened more intently than any student I had." [19] Kerr had succeeded his father as a leader in the state Grange and had been a vigorous proponent of New Deal farm relief programs during the Great Depression. First elected agriculture commissioner in 1936, he beat the son of a man who had defeated his father when the elder Scott campaigned for the same office years before.

Scott called his supporters the Branch-head boys, and the rural leaders who "lived at the head of the branch" turned out voters for him like never before. Some had been followers of Ralph McDonald, the maverick Democrat who had tried to unseat the Shelby crowd in the 1930s and 1940s. But Scott also ran surprisingly well in cities such as Durham, Greensboro (next door to his home in Haw River), Raleigh, and Chapel Hill, where he beat Johnson two to one in the second primary. During his campaign he declared he was going to throw open the windows of state government and let in some fresh air. It was a theme with a strong appeal for an electorate swelled with men impatient with a system that required eager up-and-comers to wait in line before assuming even modest positions of party leadership.

By fall, Democratic leaders in North Carolina were resigned to four years of Kerr Scott, but they were petrified that the party would take a licking with Harry Truman on the ticket. After the tumultuous Philadelphia convention, state party chairman and Truman loyalist Capus Waynick, a former High Point newspaperman who had left his post as U.S. ambassador to Colombia to return home and manage Scott's campaign, called for a strategy session, and members of the congressional delegation and statewide candidates met him at the O. Henry Hotel in Greensboro. Waynick was a skillful negotiator and homegrown diplomat. Nearly twenty years earlier, in 1932, when he was both the editor of the *High Point Enterprise* and a state legislator, he had helped mediate the end to a tense strike when textile and furniture workers closed down plants in High Point and Thomasville.

Before the Greensboro meeting, Waynick had already heard from William Umstead of Durham, his predecessor as party chairman, who had warned him about the depth of the anti-Truman feeling. "Waynick, you can't possibly hope to carry North Carolina for Harry Truman," Umstead said. Waynick asked why and was told, "Well, people around me in Durham say that they'll never vote again for that civil rights s.o.b." [20] When Waynick got everyone together, he heard more of the same. Congressman Robert "Farmer Bob" Doughton, a senior member of the North Carolina delegation who chaired the House Ways and Means Committee, came from the mountains, where he held considerable sway. He declared, "Mr. Chairman, you can't help Harry Truman. If you try, you're going to get us all whipped. He's through and if you try to do anything about him, you'll get the whole ticket defeated. Remember what happened in '28 (when Republican Herbert Hoover carried North Carolina over Democrat Al Smith)." [21]

Even Scott was cautious. He told Waynick he would be too busy with his own campaign to lend Truman much help. Senator Clyde Hoey, who had two more years before he stood for reelection, also offered little more than lame support. Some at the meeting declared they didn't even want posters of Truman and his running mate Alben Barkley of Kentucky put up in party headquarters. Only Representative Charles B. Deane from the Eighth Congressional District in the Sandhills encouraged Waynick to fight boldly for the entire ticket, from the White House to the courthouse. Waynick was as much a maverick as his governor-in-waiting. He ignored all the advice—except Deane's—and scheduled a campaign kickoff in Asheville with Barkley as the keynote speaker.

The fall campaign brought to North Carolina racist rhetoric reminiscent of the Red Shirts campaign that had routed the Populists in 1898. Strom Thurmond kicked off his campaigning with a defiant speech in Cherryville, North Carolina, a textile town near the South Carolina border. His message of resistance continued throughout the fall with advertisements broadcast over the radio and printed in newspapers. The script for one radio spot aired in North Carolina harkened back to the era of Reconstruction, when Union troops were garrisoned in the South to enforce the laws:

> Mill workers and office workers of NC . . . Do you want to work side by side with Negroes, share your rest rooms with Negroes and give up your job to a Negro? Of course, you don't, you are a Southerner . . . but remember. President Truman has boasted he is training a federal police force to make you do just those things. He is trying to stir up trouble in North Carolina. . . . Let's don't let him do it.
>
> A vote for principle is never lost.[22]

Listeners to radio stations in Fayetteville heard a similar refrain in an advertisement that read, in part:

> Farmers of North Carolina . . . Do you want your wives, daughters, sisters and mothers to have to share rest rooms, cafes, beauty shops and picture shows with Negroes? Of course you don't. . . . You are a Southerner, a red-blooded Southerner. . . . But remember, that is just what President Truman has said he is going to make you do. . . . He brags he is now having trained a federal police force to make you do just that thing. Demonstrate your independence as an American citizen on November 2nd by voting for Thurmond and Wright for president and vice president, States' Rights candidates pledged to keep North Carolina just as Southern as your fathers made it.[23]

Sanford wasn't going to stay on the sidelines in a fight like this. Upon his arrival in Fayetteville, he had joined the Young Democratic Club. He believed the YDC could do the same thing it had done in 1928 when it was organized in North Carolina to carry the Democratic Party banner that most party leaders had abandoned when Al Smith led the national ticket.

Terry was determined to do what he could to see that Truman didn't suffer the same fate and offered to debate Franklin Clark of Fayetteville, who was the treasurer of the States' Rights Party. Local party leaders, who knew little about one of the town's newest lawyers, waved him off. Terry continued to rally what support he could for Waynick, who finally prevailed on Scott to make a half-hearted endorsement of the Democratic ticket on the eve of the election. A week before the election, about a hundred thousand people turned out for a campaign appearance Truman made in Raleigh.

The election returns stunned virtually everyone. In the newsroom of the *News & Observer*, editor Jonathan Daniels was preparing the image of the rooster his family had printed in red ink on the front page following every Democratic victory since 1898. Colleagues told him he was crazy; the rooster could stay in the drawer this election year because Truman didn't have a chance. At four in the morning, he got a call from Truman, with whom he had served as press secretary. "Jonathan, we're in," Truman told him.[24] The image of a large rooster, printed in red ink over the front page copy, appeared on more than a hundred thousand copies the morning after the election.

North Carolina gave Truman one of the largest majorities that he enjoyed anywhere in the nation; Thurmond collected less than seventy thousand votes. The Democrats had won, the racist demon was back in the box, and, for the time being at least, North Carolina retained its reputation as the progressive model in the South. Elsewhere in the region, the Democrats appeared to be ready for change. In Arkansas, voters put Sid McMath, an ex-GI and populist reformer, in the governor's office. The Memphis political machine of E. H. "Boss" Crump, which had supported Thurmond, was defeated, and Estes Kefauver, whom Crump had branded a "Communist sympathizer," won election to the U.S. Senate. An optimistic newsman, Harry Ashmore, writing in the *Arkansas Gazette*, declared that racist campaigns were dead. Yet, a troubling atmosphere lingered.

In Fayetteville, Terry was accumulating points from civic organizations of every stripe. Governor Gregg Cherry had given him a state appointment, regional advisory chairman for the North Carolina Book Aid Plan, which collected used books for distribution in Europe. When he attended the September meeting of the American Legion in Charlotte to help an old friend, Joe Grier, get elected state commander, Coy Brewer, another lawyer-vet, suggested that Terry run for judge advocate. He put his name on the ballot and won. It wasn't much of a fluke, as he knew many in the Legion through their support of Boys' State. A photo of Terry wearing his white Legion overseas cap, two-tone wingtips setting off a tan suit and a bow tie, was published in the *Charlotte Observer*.

Shortly after he arrived in town, Terry learned that the army was activating a National Guard infantry unit, Company K of the 119th Infantry Division. He applied to be company commander and was appointed. (Promotion to captain came with the job.) Terry began promoting enlistments through articles in the *Fayetteville Observer*. The National Guard brought in a little extra money and also became another part of an expanding network of comrades. Dickson Phillips took command of a new unit in Laurinburg and another young attorney, Bill Staton, who also had fought at the Bulge, took command of a company organized in nearby Sanford.

Terry joined the Fayetteville Jaycees and in the spring of 1949 succeeded his friend Hector McGeachy as president. A major fund-raising project of the club was the selection of Miss and Mrs. Flame, a beauty contest for redheads only; it was part of the Jaycees' fire prevention awareness program. A year after he had volunteered to work with the American Red Cross, he was elected chapter president. He was a Sunday school teacher at Hay Street Methodist and chairman of a Boy Scout troop committee, and he had been named to the advisory committee of the Leary-Perry Hospital "for the colored." Fayetteville appeared to be just the right spot for a young, ambitious lawyer with a growing family. On February 3, 1949, Terry and Margaret Rose welcomed a daughter they named Elizabeth Knight.

The city was a curious mix of the old South and the new. It sat astride the main north-south route for northern tourists en route to Florida either by car or by train. It touted itself as the inland terminus for barge traffic on the Cape Fear River, which the Corps of Engineers kept clear all the way to Wilmington and the Atlantic. There was a public golf course, a baseball stadium that seated twenty-two hundred fans, and a home for widows and daughters of Confederate veterans in need of a place to spend their final days. The city had a municipal airport, Grannis Field, whose runways were still in grass, but Piedmont Air Lines offered eight flights a day. Downtown, the main thoroughfare, Hay Street, had all the trappings of metropolitan shopping, although the department stores still obliged the small-town custom of closing one afternoon a week during the summer.

Old-timers were proud of the city's history. The charter of the Masonic Lodge had been issued in 1760, nearly thirty years before the North Carolina legislature held sessions in the city before moving to a permanent home in Raleigh. The Fayetteville Independent Light Infantry, organized in 1793, had served as the honor guard for General Lafayette when he visited in 1825 on his farewell tour, lighting his way with candles stuck in the barrels of their muskets. In the center of town stood the old market, whose bells had once called slaves to their quarters at night. Now, one hundred years later, the bells pealed at 7:30 A.M., 1 P.M., and sunset.

But newcomers were changing the face of Fayetteville. Highway planners wanted to reroute U.S. 301 to the edge of town to avoid traffic jams at the intersection with Hay Street and the traffic circle around the historic market building where the North Carolina legislature ratified the U.S. Constitution. Locals were pleased with the new road but it would probably mean the end to the comfortable tourist courts along the old route. Real estate developers were eager to find homes for servicemen who had come south with the Army and remained after their discharge. Yet, the Army brought problems as well. Each time the 82nd Airborne Division, now part of the XVIII Airborne Corps, returned from maneuvers, the soldiers headed to town to party. A few days after the Sanfords arrived, Terry read in the paper about a drunken sergeant who had been arrested after he bit off a policeman's nose; the police report said he believed he was fighting the Japanese.

With the municipal elections in the spring of 1949, city leaders talked about Fayetteville as one of the "New South" communities. The Jaycees and the Veterans of Foreign Wars mounted a vigorous voter registration drive, and their work boosted election day participation to twice the turnout in the previous election. Elected mayor was Joseph O. Talley Jr., a bright young lawyer, a war veteran, and a man of some ambition. Just prior to his election as mayor, he had been named president of the Chamber of Commerce. Elected along with Talley was another young World War II veteran as well as a political newcomer, Dr. W. P. Devane, a black physician. The *Fayetteville Observer* said Devane's success proved that black citizens had full political opportunity in America. "His election in a sense gives the lie to the mouthings of Communists and radicals that the South deliberately opposes and withholds the right of franchise from its colored citizens." (The newspaper apparently had not joined the revolution; the word Negro was still lower-cased, and racial identification was standard in news stories.)

North Carolina as a whole appeared to be living up to its reputation as a progressive, even liberal state, shaking the dust of the past from its overalls and moving forward to prosperity. Governor Scott had challenged the members of the 1949 General Assembly to adopt his "Go Forward" program of road building and improvements to get North Carolina "out of the mud." He championed extending electric power and telephones into the rural areas and gave a sense of participation to a group of voters previously ignored or taken for granted. It was clear he was set on redressing some grievances and tilting the balance of power, shifting influence away from the moneyed interests and lawyers to his supporters who lived on the dirt roads his $200 million bond issue would pave with macadam. In late March he stunned the state's political establishment by naming Frank Graham to succeed U.S. Senator J. Melville Broughton, who had died less than two months after taking office. True to his character, Scott chose the O. Max Gardner Award Dinner in Chapel Hill as the occasion to make his announcement, offering it almost as an afterthought. "While I am on my feet," Scott said after presenting the award, "I want to make the announcement here tonight that your next Senator . . ." he paused and then added, "will be Dr. Frank Graham." [25]

Scott's choice of Graham was not nearly as casual as it appeared. The early speculation was that Scott would name Capus Waynick or L. P. McLendon, a prominent Greensboro attorney and steadfast Scott man. Scott let these options lapse and stalled for time while he and Jonathan Daniels worked to convince Graham to leave Chapel Hill and the university. It was a hard sell, but Graham finally agreed to serve.

That same spring Terry was attending an American Legion meeting when he fell into conversation with David Henderson from Charlotte, who encouraged him to run for president of the state YDC. It was something that Henderson, Bill Friday, and other friends had talked about a few years before at a YDC meeting in Chapel Hill. Terry was interested but he questioned if he could afford the cost or the time necessary to win such a contest. He had few enough law clients and was already taking in laundry, so to speak. To earn some extra income, he was teaching a university extension course on the fundamentals of banking law and planned to go back to Chapel Hill in the summer to help Coates one more time with Boys' State. After he returned home from the Legion meeting, however, Terry pursued the idea with close friends, among them Norman McCullough, who with his mother ran the *Bladen Journal*, a weekly newspaper in nearby Elizabethtown. McCullough liked the idea and called together a group to plan strategy at his family's cottage on White Lake, a popular retreat. He lined up an endorsement from the YDC organization in the southeastern part of the state and Terry called Henderson to say he was in the race.

Two candidates already had declared by the time Terry decided to run. One was George T. Fountain Jr., a lawyer from Tarboro who was a Democratic national committeeman and well-known within the YDC. The other was Eugene Gordon, a Greensboro lawyer who had the endorsement of the governor. Henderson cautioned Sanford about taking on such formidable opposition but agreed to do what he could on his behalf.

The YDC convention opened on September 15, a Friday, as several hundred young politicians—the bylaws restricted membership to those under thirty-five—from all over the state gathered in New Bern. In North Carolina, where the Democratic Party was the only road to statewide elective office, politics was a virtual closed shop and the YDC was an essential entry point and proving ground for future candidates from the courthouse to the state house. Senior party leaders kept tabs on any comers. If a young man, or woman, did well and showed promise he or she was given a place in a long lineup.

The 1949 convention promised to be one to watch. It was the first time since 1941 that the election of the president hadn't been decided beforehand. This year, in addition to the routine politicking, there was a lot of talk about who would challenge Frank Graham in the spring primaries for the special election to fill the remaining four years of Broughton's term. Graham was on a speaking tour of eastern North Carolina when he arrived late Friday afternoon with Scott. The day had been hot, with temperatures well above ninety degrees. But Scott and Graham worked the crowd before the evening barbecue, shaking hands and greeting delegates, many of whom Graham knew from their days at Chapel Hill. This was not a pushover audience, however. Newspaper reporters noted that Graham only drew light applause when he was introduced as "a great Democrat" by Basil Whitener, a Gastonia lawyer later elected to Congress. In his speech, Graham touched on themes that appealed to the progressive and liberal elements of the party and pledged to continue to fight for the rights of minorities. He spoke of North Carolina as the new frontier for the South.[26]

The YDC delegates seemed to have saved their enthusiasm for William Umstead, who had served two years in the U.S. Senate, completing the term of Josiah Bailey, who also had died in office, before losing to Broughton in 1948. Umstead appeared to be the most likely challenger to Graham, and the rousing reception boosted his spirits. Likewise, the lukewarm response to Graham was an early warning of trouble. Scott said later that if he were Graham he would run "like he was being shot at."[27]

Terry avoided getting caught up in the senatorial debate. His supporters concentrated on the task at hand. They were well-organized and drew on connections of various elements that showed an early awareness of political sensitivities. Henderson put Terry's name in nomination and he was followed to the podium for seconding speeches by Dickson Phillips and O. Max Gardner Jr., the son of the former governor. The young Gardner had graduated with honors from the School of Textiles at State College. He was in the Army, serving in Japan, when he learned of the death of a brother who had been running the family's textile mills; in January 1946, he returned home to take his brother's place. But his interests were broader than running a textile mill, and after the Gardner mills were sold in 1948 to J. P. Stevens, he began paying more attention to politics.

Gardner and Sanford found they were kindred spirits. Both admired the new breed of Southern leaders, men like Arkansas's McMath and Georgia's Arnall. They believed that a new day had arrived for their own state and that North Carolina could escape the past that W. J. Cash, another Shelby native, had described in his book, *The Mind of the South*.[28] Gardner had even crossed over to organize Cleveland County for Scott when his father's old political organization had backed Johnson. As the two talked about the future, they seemed to arrive at an understanding that either one of them would make a fine candidate for governor. Gardner had instant name recognition and money, and Sanford had poise and confidence that politics was the most effective means of achieving the vision they shared for North Carolina.

With Gardner guiding the campaign in the west, McCullough in the east, Staton working his connections through the Wake Forest alumni, and Terry's own considerable contacts from Chapel Hill, the YDC contest resulted in a one-on-one showdown with Fountain after Terry agreed to support Gordon for election as national committeeman if he would withdraw as a candidate for president. The Sanford-Gordon coalition was strong enough to give Terry the presidency by a comfortable margin of 470 votes to 200.

Terry's victory accomplished two things: it established him as a new political leader with strong appeal to veterans and others in the postwar crowd who answered to a different call, and it showed that he was willing to take on a challenge. He had campaigned against the governor's candidate, arguing that Scott shouldn't be telling the YDC whom to elect as its president. A few months after his election, Terry was in Chapel Hill for a football game when he saw Scott. He went up to the governor and introduced himself. "Oh yes, oh yes, I know who you are," Scott said. "Congratulations. I'm glad to meet you." He paused, and then added, "It does a fellow good to get beat every now and then." [29]

There was no reason for Sanford and Scott to be on opposite sides. They were from different generations, but Terry liked Scott's programs and the governor's activist approach to government. Scott's mission to "get North Carolina out of the mud" held the same attraction as Roosevelt's New Deal. Moreover, Scott was honest, and his blunt, plain-spoken approach suited Terry. He couldn't help but compare Scott with Ralph McDonald, who had been his father's favorite candidate in 1936. The governor's magnanimous gesture on his YDC victory sealed their relationship.

The YDC presidency offered Terry the perfect platform from which to build a reputation and develop a following among the rising generation of state politicians. Less than a month after he was elected, he made a speech in Chapel Hill in which he challenged the Democratic Party to adapt to a changing world. "The Democratic Party stands a chance of becoming self-satisfied, dictatorial and stagnant in thought," he declared.[30] He said he wanted to expand the YDC, recruit more members, particularly nonlawyers, and men and women who had no particular desire to be candidates but who shared his vision of politics as an agent of change.

The YDC campaign also forged political alliances that would remain together for a generation. Staton had not known Terry well before the campaign, but he emerged as a true believer who understood the kind of political change that Terry represented. "Here was a group of Americans who had served their country, were coming back, establishing homes, getting married, having families, and who were really looking for a better country," Staton later recalled.[31]

Terry's YDC responsibilities carried him all around the state. He traveled whenever and wherever, visiting local clubs and promoting membership drives. He was an appealing leader with enthusiasm and personal charm, augmented by lively wardrobe that included colorful bow ties and two-tone shoes. The constant travel did take its toll on his old Chevy coupe; it finally blew an engine one night as he was returning to Fayetteville. All the while, Terry juggled his political chores with a growing legal practice. After two years of an informal association, he and Rose had decided to create a new firm to be called Rose and Sanford, which they formally announced in February 1950.

It was increasingly apparent to Terry as he listened to Democrats around the state that Frank Graham would not have as easy a time in the spring primary as some had hoped. His liberal views had never been welcome in many corners of North Carolina and had been only tolerated as long as he remained on the campus in Chapel Hill. Now that he had a vote in the U.S. Senate, his support of world federalism, his support of Truman, and his "soft" position on civil rights made him all the more suspect. To make matters worse, the genial Graham seemed to be doing virtually nothing to prepare for what appeared to be the makings of a tough, hard-fought campaign.

As president of the YDC, Terry publicly maintained a position of neutrality in the face of growing division in the upcoming Senate race. Yet he could not remove himself entirely from doing what he could for Graham. Late in 1949, Terry joined Scott and Jonathan Daniels at a fund-raising dinner for Graham in New York City, where Burlington Mills founder Spencer Love, a Graham supporter, had paid for a table for guests from North Carolina. Terry never forgot the exposure to a level of politics he had only imagined, or the stomach-churning experience of traveling with the governor. On the ride to New York, Scott held forth in a National Guard military transport, a C-47, talking politics and filling a cup with juice generated by the wad of tobacco in his mouth. Terry later joked that he had ridden the same kind of plane into combat in France, but Scott's tobacco chewing had upset his stomach more than Nazi flak.[32]

Riding with the governor, Terry urged Scott to find someone to begin putting together a campaign organization for Graham and offered to help find a person to manage the effort. Shortly after his return, Terry, Friday, Gardner, and James Chesnutt, who had been a leader among the returning veterans at Chapel Hill, called on Staton and asked him to take the job. Staton lived close to Raleigh and was well-regarded by the YDC crowd, but more important, he was the youngest member of the board of trustees at Wake Forest College, the academic bastion of the state's conservatives. His participation could broaden Graham's base of support.[33]

Graham announced on January 7, 1950, that Staton would open a campaign headquarters in the Sir Walter Hotel on Raleigh's Fayetteville Street. Graham's announcement came one day after Umstead, who had undergone throat surgery in December, said that he would not be a candidate. Umstead's decision gave a boost to Graham, who some thought now might face only minor opposition from perennial candidate and hog farmer Olla Ray Boyd of Pinetown or former senator Robert "Our Bob" Reynolds of Asheville, who had not decided whether to run against Graham or wait two years and challenge Hoey. Although he was not considered a serious challenger, Reynolds's role as spoiler could make Graham's task all the harder. Those who could not abide Graham in the Senate, nor Scott in the governor's office for that matter, found no comfort in Reynolds, whose isolationist rantings prior to World War II had proved to be an embarrassment. What the anti-Graham element needed was a "conservative" candidate whose stature was sufficient to attract immediate attention and credibility that would overcome a late entry into the race.

In early February the name that surfaced was that of Willis Smith, a Raleigh attorney who recently had ended a term as president of the American Bar Association. Smith was a tall, imposing figure with impeccable civic and professional credentials. His law firm represented some of the state's largest corporations, and he had been a member of the legislature, serving a term in 1931 as speaker of the house. He was a director in the Raleigh YMCA, an active member of the Edenton Street United Methodist Church, supported the Community Chest, had helped organize a local Legal Aid clinic, and was chairman of the Duke University Board of Trustees. Smith told those who urged him to run that he would enter the race if they would put up the money. Three days after Graham's campaign office opened in Raleigh, Smith paid his $125 filing fee and formally declared his candidacy.

Smith's decision left many in uncomfortable situations. Graham was not universally disliked in the high-powered business circles in which Smith moved; some had urged Smith not to challenge Graham and "split the respectable vote." Terry was one of those with split allegiances. He and Smith's son, Willis Jr., were friends, and Terry had come to know the elder Smith through his participation in the young lawyers' section of the ABA. Terry appreciated the time that Smith had devoted to him, including invitations to dinner in Raleigh for young lawyers. Yet, he could not desert Graham. In a meeting with Smith's son, Terry told him, "I have a high regard for your father, but I am all out for Frank Graham. It won't do to have him defeated." Smith responded angrily and tension remained throughout the entire campaign.[34]

Terry took no public position in the campaign. The Smith camp questioned his "neutrality" the following month in Asheville, where the YDC had planned a rally. More than fifteen hundred people turned out for a mountain-style political gathering: square dancing followed by speech making. Speaker of the House Sam Rayburn of Texas was the featured guest and all the candidates were invited. Smith's managers had planned to introduce their candidate to the rousing strains of "Dixie," which they had adopted as their campaign song along with the slogan "Save Our South."[35] As the rally manager and the one who paid the band, Sanford prohibited the Smith crowd from using the tune, fearing its overtones would harken back to the divisive States' Rights campaign two years earlier.

The turnout for the May 27 first primary was overwhelming. The early predictions by experienced newspapermen held that between 425,000 and 475,000 voters would go to the polls. By the end of that hot Saturday, however, nearly 620,000 voters had cast ballots. Graham came in first, only 5,634 votes shy of a clear majority and nearly 53,000 votes ahead of Smith. Graham had survived a blistering campaign mounted in the final two weeks by the Smith camp that Talley, Fayetteville's young mayor, called the most bitter and unethical race ever conducted in the past fifty years. In a speech that carried the earmarks of the Sanford style, Talley said Smith supporters had "whistled for the hounds of hate."[36]

The victory celebration at the Graham headquarters in the Sir Walter was short-lived, however. Smith refused to issue a concession speech and left open the possibility of a second primary. On the Monday following the election, Smith's campaign staff reported to work as usual. The suspense continued throughout the week as the clock ran on Smith's opportunity to declare his intentions. Newspaper reports said Smith's campaign was out of money and that the candidate was tired and unsure whether he and his family could stand the challenge of three more weeks of hard campaigning.

Throughout the day on June 6, two days before the deadline, listeners to Raleigh radio station WRAL began hearing brief advertisements calling on Smith supporters to gather and show their support for a runoff election at Smith's home near the corner of St. Mary's Street and Glenwood Avenue in Raleigh. The appeal was the work of WRAL's young news director, Jesse Helms, who arranged to pay for the time and write the copy for a staff announcer to air eight to ten times an hour throughout the day. Smith had dictated a concession speech to his publicity director, Hoover Adams, but it remained in Adams's pocket as Smith told a modest crowd who trampled the flowers on the well-tended grounds of his home, "Don't be surprised if I go with you." The following day he announced he would call for a second primary.[37]

There was no question what the pivotal issue would be in the second campaign. One day before the rally at Smith's home, the U.S. Supreme Court had ruled on three civil rights cases, and in a clear voice moved another step closer to ending racial segregation. In one case, the Court ordered the admission of a black student to the all-white University of Texas law school even though Texas, like North Carolina and other southern states, had established so-called separate but equal law schools. In a second case, the Court ruled against the University of Oklahoma, which had admitted a black student but devised separate accommodations to isolate her from the white students. And in the third case, the Court ruled against the practice of racially segregated dining cars on the railroads. The headlines about the Court's decisions had greeted readers on the morning of the rally at Smith's home. The accompanying news stories made it clear that it was only a matter of time before black students would be admitted to graduate programs at Chapel Hill or other all-white campuses.

North Carolina voters had not been forced to own up to questions on race in a statewide political campaign for nearly fifty years. This election was emerging as one that would show just how thin a veneer covered deep-seated and fiercely held feelings on the issue. Graham's positions on civil rights and labor had been apparent for years, but now all those questions that before had caused embarrassment and laughter at the barber shop were clearly on the table. Now, Graham's critics were not laughing. In conversation and finally in newspaper ads they asked if Graham was a Red, or just pink? Was he a "nigger-lover"? Was he a true Southerner?

Cumberland County had given Smith a majority of its votes, and Terry resolved to do what he could to improve returns for Graham in the second primary. He asked McGeachy, who was Graham's county manager, to give him a precinct to work and settled on one of the toughest locations, a mill village south of Fayetteville.

The traditional practice of turning out votes in the insulated world of textile mill villages was the same for competing candidates. Each side would hire workers to round up voters and take them to the polls. These "drivers," as they were called, were given money to cover the gas they put in their automobiles as well as something for their time. Aside from money for radio and newspaper advertisements, much of a campaign budget was set aside for this sort of electioneering. Shortly after Smith called for a second primary, Terry found a man who knew the Cumberland Mills precinct like his own front porch, and climbed in his car to go meet voters.

The exercise could convert some votes for Graham, if Sanford was successful. But Terry had other motives as well. As he worked the area, countering the racist pamphlets that appeared on Smith's behalf, he kept a record of his work in a small ring-bound notebook that at night he placed in the drawer of a nightstand by his bed. If he awoke with an idea, he rolled over, pulled out the notebook, and set down his thoughts.

Terry's work in Cumberland Mills was successful. He carried the precinct for Graham, shifting votes from Smith. Statewide, however, Graham lost to Smith, who carried sixty-one of North Carolina's one hundred counties. The final canvas gave Smith 281,000 votes to Graham's 261,000. The Graham campaign had simply been smothered in one racist charge after another. He was accused of passing over a white applicant to appoint a young black man to West Point, of favoring "mingling of the races," of sacrificing white jobs to blacks, and Smith's supporters papered the country stores and mill villages with leaflets as had never been seen before. Graham lost the momentum he had gained in the first primary and never regained it.

Terry's experience in Cumberland Mills filled his notebook with scribbled suggestions, reminders, and ideas, some of them useful and others not. When he weighed his experience and reviewed his notes, two lessons stood out most clearly. A candidate cannot win when constantly on the defensive, as Graham had been day after day, and a candidate should never lose control of his campaign, as he was convinced Smith had done. Terry believed that Smith was not personally responsible for the racist pamphlets that were distributed in his name. He was too ethical to have tolerated such filth, Terry believed, although Smith never attempted to reconcile these differences and remained silent on the question for the remainder of his years.

One other thing was clear. The issue of race was now an open wound in state politics. North Carolina had lost not only Frank Graham in the Senate, but its reputation as a state of moderation and enlightenment as well. The place and time were not set, but when it arrived Terry and others believed they would be prepared for what they would call the "Third Primary."[38]

CHAPTER SEVEN

The Branch-Head Boys

FRANK GRAHAM'S DEFEAT WAS a setback for Governor Kerr Scott, but it would take more than a loss at the polls, even that of his handpicked candidate for the U.S. Senate, to quiet the Squire of Haw River. A few days after the election, while vacationing in the mountains, he showed up in shirt sleeves and told reporters, "I pulled off my coat just to show you that I had not lost my shirt." [1]

Scott plowed on. He showed the same determination after June 1950 that he had during his previous eighteen months in office. He appeared to be having the time of his life, not only opening state government windows "for a little fresh air," but throwing out of those same windows a host of political appointees who didn't suit him.

The housecleaning that followed his inauguration in 1949 had created a backlash that soured some voters and cost Graham votes,[2] but Scott was unconcerned about whose toes got under his brogans. In September 1949 he used the occasion of the formal dedication of a new Carolina Power & Light Company power plant in Lumberton to lecture top CP&L officials and other dignitaries on the failure of public utilities to extend service to farms and houses in remote reaches of the state. The goading followed earlier reports that he had taken to calling CP&L's president, L. V. Sutton, "Low Voltage" Sutton.[3]

Two months after the Graham-Smith campaign, Scott told a state labor gathering in Winston-Salem that white voters should be ashamed of the racist character of the campaign. And after the black delegates finished applauding his remarks, he said, "I notice you colored brethren clapping pretty hard, but you didn't do your part either. You may be another color, but in this election you were just as yellow as the other man." [4]

Scott quickened the pace of change in North Carolina. He had broken the traditional line of succession and his style of politics encouraged younger men like Sanford eager to move the state forward. The Scott tradition shaped Terry's developing ambitions and defined him and his own campaigns a decade later.

Scott thoroughly enjoyed being governor and took pride in being the first farmer elected to that office in more than fifty years. He energetically pushed a liberal agenda that included a referendum on a $200 million bond issue for farm-to-market roads, collective bargaining and repeal of the state's right-to-work laws, equity in funding for black schools and their teachers, and, most especially, expansion of electric power and telephone service to rural areas. He was relentless in his prodding of investor-owned utilities; that day in Lumberton, with Sutton and others of the state's business leadership squirming in their chairs, he said, "[Power companies] have the future before them to justify their existence in the American plan of free enterprise."[5]

Scott was of the populist tradition, clear and simple, and reveled in a humble, plow-boy image. On the day of his inauguration he joked that his formal dress of top hat and tails had cost him his two best cows. But he had a college degree and a keen sense of business and people. He still made an honest claim to his role as spokesman for the families on the farm and those who worked the dusty, dirty jobs in the textile mills that lined the Southern Railway line along the backbone of the Carolina Piedmont crescent. These folks made up two-thirds of the state's population and he made it clear they would now get some attention. He said they suffered under a "mud tax" because of poor roads that isolated them from markets and proper medical care, their churches and schools, and the opportunities of better jobs and a better life. Whatever is bad for two-thirds of the state's people, he said often and loud, was bad for all the people.

He believed in development of rural areas and said the key to that growth was adequate electric power, which he called the cheapest "hired hand" money could buy. Scott had been an early advocate for publicly subsidized electric and telephone service and it galled him that the privately owned utilities had captured the better service areas and left those living in lightly populated regions dependent on kerosene lamps. He said this strategy had turned southeastern North Carolina—the Cape Fear River valley where Terry Sanford made his home at Fayetteville—into the "Sahara of Waters." The region lacked sufficient industry and lagged in development because companies like CP&L had not done their job.

Scott stoutly defended the federally subsidized rural cooperatives, which had been bitterly opposed by the privately owned companies. Speaking at a celebration of rural telephone service one fall afternoon, he told a small-town audience

The utilities trust annually spends millions of its revenue dollars—millions that come from the rates it charges the public—in newspaper, magazine and radio advertisements shouting that the nation is on the verge of socialism because the people, through their legislative bodies, are making it possible for more and more homes to have utility services. The true story is that REA [Rural Electrification Administration] finances have been used only to fill the gaps in imperative public needs which have not been otherwise met.

The wolf cry—paid for by the customers who have to foot the advertising bill—is as phony as a wooden nickel. It is the age-old cry of special interests that arises when the people elect and the legislative officials pledge to give the people what the majority want for themselves and for their children.[6]

His constituents loved it. North Carolina had never seen such a bodacious governor. He won their support in a way that had eluded most Southern populists who usually had resorted to the race issue to warm up a crowd. Scott believed in segregation, but he never leveraged voter appeal to that side of the populist tradition. He refused to play one race against the other, even when cornered. Terry Sanford often heard him tell of a campaign stop at a country store in eastern North Carolina, where he was to meet a local political leader. His appointment was late and Scott said, "I knew I was in trouble. There was this fellow sitting on the counter and he leaned over and said, 'Commissioner, how are you standing on the nigger issue?' I looked right at him and said, 'Mister, I want you to know one thing. I am a white Southern Presbyterian.' The fellow slapped his hand on his leg and said, 'That's all I needed to know.' "[7]

In addition to funding parity for black and white schools and teachers, he also removed salary differences for employees at the state mental hospital for black patients, and he appointed the first African American, Dr. Harold L. Trigg of Raleigh, to the state Board of Education. He said, "I am going to follow through to see that the minority race has a fair opportunity and gets the training to fit into the state's growth."[8] It was the same philosophy that Scott's idol, Governor Charles B. Aycock, had championed earlier in the century. At the time, it was considered a progressive, even bold, attitude.

"He had the instincts of a true liberal," Sanford later said. "He cared about change. He cared about using public policy for improvement of individual opportunities. I suppose that is kind of a definition of a liberal. He was not afraid of new ideas."[9]

Though he had not started out on Scott's side, Terry found the governor to be worthy of his attention. "The war had changed a lot of attitudes," he recalled, "and had given a lot of young people ambitions that something could change, that they didn't have to do like their parents did. He lit a real spark." [10]

In Raleigh, Scott turned the governor's mansion into the people's house. Nearly a quarter million visitors signed the guest books during his term. Charlotte writer Harry Golden, editor of a weekly journal he called *The Carolina Israelite*, wrote that after the Scotts had been in the mansion for a few months, the governor discovered that of all the visitors none were Jewish. " 'Miz Mary,' " Golden quoted Scott saying to his wife, " 'how come no Hebrews have visited the mansion?' And Mrs. Scott said, 'Maybe they're shy.' " Golden said the governor then told his secretary "to call up the Hadassies and have them come on over and visit the mansion so we can have some Hebrews in the books. And, concluded Miz Mary, they were the best behaved bunch of them all." [11]

From the start, Scott was an insult to the state's business establishment, which had worked mightily to defeat him in 1948. He further alienated this crowd with his call to the 1949 General Assembly to eliminate the state's right-to-work law, a major impediment to organized labor's efforts in the state's textile mills. It was a futile gesture; Scott surely knew the conservative members of the legislature would never comply with this radical suggestion when North Carolina didn't even guarantee a minimum wage. He lost the battle, but he did succeed in making good on his campaign promise of requiring banks to pay interest on state money they held on deposit. At the end of his first year in office he announced that North Carolina already had earned more than $2 million in interest.

He kept his opponents on their toes; they never knew when he would next launch a broadside, or at whom. One writer said, "The governor some times spoke Thursday and thought Friday." [12] He chose to review the ills of the legal profession to the state Bar Association meeting; he once told the North Carolina Citizens Association, organized in 1942 by business leaders to foster conservative state government policies, that its magazine *We the People* should be renamed "We the People Against the People." The targets of his verbal jabs fussed and fumed but Scott simply ignored them. When one of his assistants asked what he should do about the reaction to one of the governor's latest attacks, Scott told him to do nothing: he would say something else and simply change the subject. [13]

The state's political establishment had had enough of Scott by the time the General Assembly gathered for business in January 1951. His legislative program was tied up in knots within a few weeks after the session convened. Scott turned to the radio and appealed directly to the people. He said his opponents were simply trying to "hold the line" and accused them of being against better roads, better medical care, better schools, and a better life. The logjam lifted and Scott salvaged at least part of his program.

By the fall of 1951, Scott's opponents had found the man they believed would make a suitable and electable replacement. The crowd that had lost with Charles Johnson in 1948 retrieved a familiar figure from their stable and enrolled William B. Umstead of Durham as their candidate. Umstead was austere and colorless, the teetotaling son of a Methodist preacher, but he had compiled a distinguished and honorable political career. During the Depression, he had served three terms in the U.S. House of Representatives before voluntarily returning home. During the war, he had managed R. Gregg Cherry's successful campaign for governor, chaired the state Democratic Party, and later served the unexpired portion of Josiah Bailey's term after the senator died in December 1946. Umstead lost the Senate nomination to J. Melville Broughton two years later and sat out the 1950 Senate race because of ill health. Now, he said he was ready to serve, even though he often looked wan and sickly.

Scott was not impressed. As his candidate, he recruited an old friend from Lexington, Hubert Olive, a superior court judge who had a booming bass voice, buoyant personality, steady blue eyes, and a full head of white hair. He was a leading Baptist layman and was well-known across the state.

The political atmosphere was highly charged by late May 1952 and the time of the state Democratic Convention, traditionally held about ten days before the first primary election. Scott's own blunt approach to politics had set the pace for this campaign. Neither candidate showed any particular restraint either on the stump or on the radio, where extended public addresses by candidates and public figures had become commonplace. Olive accused Umstead of voting against rural electrification while he was in Congress and cited page and verse of the *Congressional Record* to prove his point. Umstead responded by calling Olive "Governor Scott's crown prince."

Olive said voters were "sick and tired of politicians and lobbyists" (Umstead had been a lobbyist for Duke Power Company). Umstead accused Scott of using the powers of the governor's office to promote Olive: "Despite all the hurried telephone calls from Capitol Hill, all the automobile trips in state cars, all the stakes driven for promised roads, all the propaganda sent out by tipsheets marked 'confidential,' all the whispered insinuations, and all the other evidence of desperation which have been resorted to—it will avail them nothing. The people will not be deceived." [14]

On the eve of the convention, the Democratic faithful began arriving in Raleigh. The headquarters was the Sir Walter Hotel, a four-hundred-room, red brick home away from home for state legislators, lobbyists, politicians, and anyone seeking favors from state government. Some state officials held court in the lobby, where they talked politics, made deals, and waited in overstuffed chairs for the early edition of the *News & Observer* before heading off to bed and a nightcap.

The Sir Walter's location on Fayetteville Street was ideal. Three blocks north was Capitol Square and the state's century-old, copper-domed hall of government. Three blocks south was Raleigh's Memorial Auditorium, a huge cavern of a building designed to accommodate everything from visiting road shows to conventions. A state-run liquor store was conveniently located around the corner. The hotel's mezzanine balcony overlooked the lobby and gave way to rooms around its rim, where candidates for statewide office set up shop for the primary season. On the upper floors, legislators and other regulars from out of town had first call on the hotel's most convenient rooms.

Banners hung from the railing around the mezzanine as Democrats began arriving on Thursday, May 22, prior to the convention on Friday. It was a presidential campaign year and Southern Democrats were rallying behind Senator Richard Russell of Georgia in a futile effort to head off the nomination of Adlai Stevenson. In North Carolina, former governor Cameron Morrison was in charge of Russell's campaign, and Jesse Helms, who had joined Willis Smith's staff after his first year in office, was coordinating Russell's radio and television coverage. Textile executive Everett Jordan from Saxapahaw was party chairman; he held the job by virtue of appointment from Scott, his neighbor from Alamance County. The two were estranged now, however, and a battle was in the making over delegates to the national convention. At the last minute, Scott learned Jordan had changed his selection of at-large delegates, edging Bill Staton, president of the Young Democrats, to an alternate's slot.

Scott was in no mood to be accommodating when he arrived at Memorial Auditorium for the main session. The hall already was stuffy and warm and the backstage maneuvering had wilted any starchy formalities. As one who knew the value of the grand gesture, Scott left his chair on the stage empty as the convention was called to order. He took a seat beside his wife in the audience with the delegation from Alamance County. Jordan, a proper sort, was unnerved by the way events were unfolding and sent J. C. B. Ehringhaus Jr., son of a former governor and now a Raleigh lawyer, to Scott to urge him to a seat on the stage with the rest of the dignitaries. The governor's reply was blunt: "No. I am going to sit out here and you know why." [15]

"To hell with him," Ehringhaus advised Jordan, according to the *News & Observer*'s account. "We've done all we could."

Jordan proceeded with the agenda without taking public notice of Scott's absence. When the chairman called on the governor for his customary remarks, the delegates began looking around for Scott. Finally, the governor stood, almost obscured from his floor position at the back of the hall. According to the *News & Observer* account, "So far as most of them could see, there was no governor around. A few stood up. It is customary for Democrats to stand when the chief executive arises. More got on their feet. Then the whole 3,000 delegates (except possibly a few whose dislike of the governor has improved their sitting ability) were standing."

"I am here," announced Scott, "with the first county of the state, Alamance." Scott's voice was the kind that didn't need amplification, and he addressed the convention from where he stood. His remarks was not controversial and he assured the delegates that Democrats always resolve their differences by the fall.

Indeed, Jordan and Scott crossed paths a week later at Elon College near Greensboro. Jordan told the governor he hoped he wasn't mad. "Mad," Scott was quoted as saying, "Everett, you double-crossed me."

"No, I didn't," Jordan replied.

"Yes, you did," said Scott. "You double-crossed me."

A newspaper reporter said Jordan then told Scott he hoped he would have time to explain things. "Make it some time when you have a lot of time," the governor was quoted in reply. "Because it'll take a lot of explaining why you didn't give me the giant double-cross." [16]

The tangle between Scott and Umstead put Terry Sanford in an awkward position. He was close to Scott, but he had strong ties to the Umstead family as well. William Umstead's nephew was John Umstead III, who had been killed in the Pacific. He liked William's brother, John, who was quite the opposite of his stiff-necked brother. A maverick in the state legislature, John Umstead was loud and unpredictable and liked his bourbon almost as much as his brother abhorred alcohol.

Terry supported Olive in the primary election contest, though he didn't get too far out front. He was involved in his own campaign for a seat in the state senate. It was quite a leap for a newcomer to Cumberland County politics, but the opportunity to run was just too good to let pass. Fayetteville and Cumberland County were part of a three-county district with two seats that rotated around the counties. In 1952, it was Cumberland's time to nominate the Democratic candidate and Terry jumped at the chance. Just like finding a dry campsite along the Cape Fear River, he knew he had to be ready for opportunities when they arrived. Another shot at public office might not be along for a while.

The opportunity to run for the senate arose after a series of events had threatened to sidetrack his plans. In late June 1950, the outbreak of the war in Korea had threatened any long-range plans. As commander of Company K, 119th Infantry, of the North Carolina National Guard, Terry was preparing his men for the annual two weeks of summer training as talk of war began to build. The 30th Division, of which the 119th was a part, was considered one of the likely units to be called, according to the scuttlebutt around Fort Jackson, South Carolina, where the unit was to train in the field. Some of Terry's fellow officers were so certain the unit would be called to active duty in August 1950 that they put down deposits on apartments in nearby Columbia.[17]

Terry resisted the urge to begin house hunting in Columbia, but he was uncertain enough about his own future that he passed on a major legal case that Colonel Terry Lyon had offered him. Terry told his law partner that he couldn't be sure that he would be around to do the necessary work. He also paid a call on the commander of the 82nd Airborne Division headquartered at Fort Bragg. If he went back on active duty, he wanted to return to the Airborne. The 82nd's chief of staff, Colonel William Westmoreland, told him he would be happy to have him back in the silk. The 30th Division was not part of the call-up, however, and Terry never exercised the option.

The talk of war had returned Terry's name to the pages of the *Fayetteville Observer*. During the height of the excitement over activation of the National Guard, Terry took a telephone call from a reporter for the *Observer* who wanted to know if he had heard of any reluctance on the part of his men to go if called. Certainly not, Sanford replied. "We're here to protect the country," he said, and proceeded to deliver a recruiting speech. A few days later, an editorial appeared under the headline "National Guard: Local Unit Shows No White Feather." It read in part: "It is heartening to note that locally there has been no rush of National Guard members to get out of the organization in the face of the danger of war. Our congratulations go to Captain Terry Sanford for having organized in Fayetteville a unit that reflects the highest traditions of the military service." [18] Terry's patriotic fervor apparently had cooled the anger of the paper's editor, who had barred his name from the paper because he had supported Frank Graham.

He had considered running for mayor of Fayetteville in the municipal elections in 1951, succeeding his friend Joe Talley, but he passed. That summer Terry and Margaret Rose did buy their first home, a modest house at 223 Hillside Avenue. The story-and-a-half shingle bungalow had large windows in the front room that opened onto a small porch. In front was a sloping yard that was deeply shaded by a huge oak, whose roots had forced cracks in the sidewalk. They signed a note for $8,800.

His base in the state YDC organization remained strong. Toward the end of the summer of 1951 he attended the YDC's state convention, where delegates adopted a Code of Ethics for Political Campaigns. The drafting of the document had occupied him for the better part of the year following the Smith-Graham contest and was designed to discourage the sort of racist leaflets that had received wide distribution in the closing days of the campaign. The code called for all campaign material to be issued over the name of the candidate and called on candidates to agree that "it shall be deemed unethical to make any appeal of any nature, in any degree, to racial, religious, or other prejudice. It shall be deemed unethical to stir up fear and distrust between the races, or to inject in any manner or degree the question of race relations, since a discussion of race relations during a political campaign can serve no good purpose." [19]

Terry's political stature also increased after Governor Scott appointed him to the State Ports Authority; by the spring of 1952, the senate race seemed to be his best opportunity for moving his political career forward.

Cumberland County had not had a seat in the 1951 senate and there was no incumbent. Sanford heard that the most likely man to run was the last Cumberland County man to serve, an older man named Gilbert Shaw. One day, Sanford saw Shaw on Hay Street, Fayetteville's main street, and asked him if he was going to run. "He said, 'I don't know,' Sanford later recalled. 'I don't much think so.' I said, 'Well, I am if you are not.' He never could recover from that." [20]

Shaw didn't file, but T. C. Bynum, a square-jawed, bespeckled older man with a determined look about him, filed for the seat. He provided only token opposition, and Terry believed the reason Bynum's name was on the ballot at all was to keep Terry from working for Mayor Talley, who was locked in a tight race with Bynum's friend, Ertel Carlyle, the incumbent Seventh District congressman. Bynum had no particular issues other than Sanford's relative youth, his boyish looks, and his rapid rise in politics. "Are you going to vote for this boy?" he asked voters.[21]

Terry was at the height of his campaigning as the Scott-Jordan battle played out in Raleigh. At an appearance the night before he left for the state convention, he told a forum sponsored by the League of Women Voters in Fayetteville that he favored a presidential primary for the state and, if elected, he would see if he could find state money to improve Cape Fear River facilities. No new taxes would be necessary, he claimed, because the revenue picture would improve with new industry moving into the state.

Terry was confident he would win, but he had not taken anything for granted. He organized every precinct with workers he had met through the Jaycees, the American Red Cross, and the National Guard, three organizations that cut across the most important voter segments in the community.

He spent a few dollars to print a nondescript brochure that featured his picture and a reprint of the boilerplate announcement of his candidacy as it was printed—typos and all—in the *Fayetteville Observer*. On the back was his slogan: "For Effective, Conscientious Straightforward Representation in Raleigh Vote for Terry Sanford for State Senate." He also printed some posters that said simply, "Sanford for Senate," leaving off his picture because he believed it took up too much space. A friend, concerned that he had not done enough, paid for one newspaper ad that ran just before election day.

Terry coasted to victory in the June 7 primary, defeating Bynum 5,944 votes to 1,957. The margin in the governor's race was closer, yet decisive; Umstead outdistanced Olive by some thirty thousand votes. The primary results were tantamount to election, although in the fall general election, with Dwight D. Eisenhower leading the Republican ticket, the GOP experienced a revival of sorts in North Carolina. The former general did not carry the state, but Stevenson's vote was nothing like the overwhelming majority given Umstead over Republican H. F. "Chub" Seawell of Carthage. Moreover, for the first time since 1928, voters elected a Republican to Congress. Lincolnton's Charles Jonas carried the state's Tenth District. Terry had no opposition in the fall.

The returns revealed a crack in the solid Democratic foundation in North Carolina politics that would continue to widen in years to come; it was becoming evident that fall as Democrats like Scott campaigned for the entire ticket. Speaking at a rally in Greenville, Scott declared, "I am a Woodrow Wilson, Franklin Roosevelt, Harry Truman, Adlai Stevenson Democrat." [22] He then sat down and glared at the Eisenhower Democrats who shared the podium with him.

On the evening of December 30, 1952, Scott bid farewell in an emotional radio address broadcast from the governor's office in the capitol. He recounted his administration's record, speaking in his strong mellow voice:

> Let us not forget that two-thirds of North Carolina's population is rural, and that one-third live and work in the cities and towns, that another third live in the country and work in the cities and towns and the other third both live and work on the farm.
>
> An impoverished, mud-tax afflicted, rural population makes poor customers for any trading center or metropolitan area. I became a candidate because of these two convictions—that rural North Carolina was a land of forgotten people, and that what is bad for two-thirds of the people is bad for all.

He extended an olive branch to the electric and telephone companies he had battered so relentlessly for four years, thanking them for the new lines they had extended to the homes and farms in the rural precincts of the state. He wasn't saying good-bye, he assured his listeners, and political observers took particular note of his words: "I shall keep current with events to come. My devotion and dedication to North Carolina—our North Carolina ever on the march—will never end. . . . And now my friends, as we approach the end of the row that we have been plowing together for the past four years . . ." Scott's voice broke and he paused before continuing. "I wish for you, for each and every one of you, a happy and prosperous new year, and may the God of us all be with you and with North Carolina forever." [23] Ten days later he delivered the state seal to Umstead's care.

Inauguration Day was January 8, 1953. The air was damp and the sky overcast. A light drizzle had begun to fall when Scott and Umstead arrived at Memorial Auditorium in a yellow Packard convertible. Umstead looked severe and deadly earnest as he took the oath of office. Scott sat through Umstead's hour-long inaugural speech in which the new governor outlined a lengthy legislative agenda that surprised even some of his conservative supporters. He didn't let Scott exit without comment. At one point he noted that the ambitious road building of the previous four years had placed on the state an incalculable burden of maintaining these roads at a cost that depended "in a large measure upon the durability of these roads." [24]

Scott took it all in stride. Asked about Umstead's speech, he said, "He's got a good program. They ought to back him up." [25] He lit a cigar and puffed contentedly while sitting on the reviewing stand for the inaugural parade as some of the first racially integrated Army units passed in review. Shortly after three, Scott and his wife climbed into a new tan Ford sedan that his friends had paid for. Sitting behind the wheel, he was momentarily confused as he studied the gearshift for the car's automatic transmission; after a word of instruction and a handshake from Umstead, he and his wife drove out of town behind a State Highway Patrol escort that led them as far as the Wake County line. When the trooper was gone, Scott pulled the car to the side of the road, where he and Miss Mary enjoyed a picnic of thick meat sandwiches that had been prepared in the mansion kitchen. They waved to passersby as they sat and ate, and then continued on to Hawfields. Twenty minutes after he arrived at the farm he was in the field in his hunting clothes. "I'm on relief now," he told reporters who came to check on him, "and I've got to get us some meat to eat." He bagged eight rabbits.[26]

Umstead had worked on his speech for weeks, and the events of inauguration day were exhausting. After he finished his address he "sank into his chair with relief," a close friend observed.[27] Though he was not feeling well, he still stood for four hours in a receiving line at the mansion before going out that night to an inaugural ball, where he gave in to friends who prevailed upon him to play a few tunes on a harmonica.

He spent the next day in the governor's office, which he found cleaned of both official portraits and other decoration. He arrived to bare walls and the customary office furniture, which he rearranged with the help of his personal secretary, Edwin L. Rankin Jr., a former newsman who had been at Chapel Hill with Terry and Margaret Rose. Before the day was over, however, he had taken another poke at his predecessor by authorizing back pay and allowances to David S. Coltrane, a senior state budget officer. Six months earlier, Scott had accused Coltrane of delaying implementation of his programs and demanded his resignation. Coltrane refused to step down and said Scott was punishing him for supporting Umstead over Olive. Unable to remove him from office, Scott stripped him of his powers. In protest, Coltrane refused to take the pay he was entitled to under his commission. The incident was made all the more curious because Coltrane and Scott had been long-time friends, with Coltrane serving as an assistant to Scott when he was commissioner of agriculture. Umstead's order, reinforced by later legislative action, restored Coltrane's back pay and his authority.

The following day, a Saturday, Umstead worked for a while in his Durham law office and then went to his home near Bahama, north of the city. A doctor was summoned during the night, when the governor had difficulty sleeping because of a persistent cough. He was taken to Watts Hospital in Durham after midnight, where his doctor discovered he had suffered a heart attack and was on the verge of pneumonia. His condition was serious, but the statement from his doctor, Ralph G. Fleming, was that he had a "heavy cold." Later the doctor released a statement saying the governor had experienced "a mild attack of heart trouble." He said he was improving rapidly and would be in bed only twelve to fifteen days.[28]

On Monday, when Senator Terry Sanford arrived in Raleigh for the first working day of the 1953 General Assembly, he found legislative leaders wondering whether to proceed with the governor ill and hospitalized. Umstead insisted the legislature proceed on schedule but gave no instructions to the newly elected lieutenant governor, Luther Hodges, who was a virtual stranger to him and to most in Raleigh. Umstead and Hodges had barely spoken a word to one another since they had won their nominations in separate campaigns in the spring primary. Relations had become strained after Umstead learned Hodges had told an audience that he and Umstead agreed on some issues. Hodges received a telephone call from Umstead, who made it clear "they were not running together."[29]

Lieutenant governors were expected to say little and do less. They presided over the senate but could only vote to break a tie, and they chaired the Board of Education. The lieutenant governor was given a small corner office just off the senate chamber on the second floor of the capitol, but when the legislature wasn't in session—which was about eighteen months out of every twenty-four—he usually returned home until called for. Some legislative officers even drew a higher annual salary than the $1,800 paid the lieutenant governor.

Scott had invited Hodges to sit in on pre-inaugural budget sessions preparing a budget for the next two years, but Umstead had confided none of his legislative plans to his lieutenant governor–elect, which irritated Hodges, who was accustomed to taking charge. Hodges simply proceeded on his own. Between election day and the inauguration, he traveled around the state to meet the members of the senate. When he and Terry chatted in Fayetteville, Hodges made notes on the committees on which Terry said he wished to serve. A few days before the legislature opened, Hodges announced his appointments, releasing them to the members at the same time he gave them to reporters. Hodges named Terry to some of the committees of his choice: conservation and development, education, and one of two judiciary committees that were usually packed with lawyers. He did not put him on the appropriations committee, where Terry had hoped to vote for increased funding for education. Instead, Hodges assigned him to the finance committee, where new tax laws were drafted. It was not an exciting beginning, but a freshman legislator could not expect much.

Hodges's handling of the committee appointments marked him as a newcomer to the cozy nature of legislative politics. In the past, Raleigh insiders and lobbyists had often helped the lieutenant governor make the final assignments. Just prior to the opening of the session, Hodges was in the lobby of the Sir Walter Hotel when a long-time lobbyist approached and said, "Let's you and I take a bottle of Scotch and go up to my room and set up your Senate committees." According to Hodges's biographer, A. G. Ivey:

> The astonished Hodges said, "Will you repeat that?"
> The man said it again. He added, "I've helped before on matters like this."
> "Well, this is where it stops," said Hodges. "No one is going to make my appointments but me."[30]

Hodges was a newcomer to politics. He was a fifty-five-year-old retired executive from Marshall Field and Company when his friend Everett Jordan suggested he file as a candidate for lieutenant governor.[31] He was so nervous on his first outing that he had to brace himself to ask the cashier at a restaurant for her vote when he paid his bill. In the spring primary, he won a plurality in a field of three, and the number two candidate, former state senator Roy Rowe, who had been tapped by the political leadership to serve, chose not to call for a runoff.

On the Monday after Umstead fell ill, Hodges was to make his first appearance as presiding officer of the senate. He left his room at the Sir Walter Hotel and walked alone up Fayetteville Street to the capitol, stopping at a florist shop along the way to pick up a fresh white carnation that he pinned to his lapel.[32] When he arrived at the capitol it was swarming with people. To reach his office he had to cut through the legislators and lobbyists, state officials and other hangers-on whose preferred perch was the rotunda balcony on the second floor just outside the massive wooden doors of the house and senate chambers.

The governor's suite of offices occupied the southwest corner on the first floor. The offices of the state treasurer, the secretary of state, and the state auditor filled the balance of that level. Before the Justice Building had been erected across the street a decade earlier, the state supreme court had met on the third floor, where space also was provided for a law library and balconies for the two chambers. Now legislative committees used these rooms. Otherwise, the place was virtually unchanged in appearance and usage since it was completed in 1840.

Members of the legislature had taken their oath of office a day before the gubernatorial inauguration. Outgoing Lieutenant Governor H. P. Taylor of Wadesboro had sworn in the members of the senate, including Sanford and James A. Bridger of Bladenboro, the other member from the Tenth District. Terry took the seat that Secretary of State Thad Eure had assigned him about three rows from the back near the center aisle. His nearest seatmate was Senator Warren Williams from Sanford.

Margaret Rose watched the ceremonies from the balcony with Betsee, who now was nearly three, and the Sanford's new son, Terry Jr., who was born June 13, 1952, immediately after his father won the Democratic nomination for the state senate. After the inaugural activities, the family returned home and Terry began his routine of spending Mondays in his law office before driving to Raleigh late in the afternoon for the Monday evening legislative session.

Despite Umstead's poor health, he refused to relinquish one whit of control in the days following his collapse. For a time, he even hesitated on sending Hodges to Washington to represent the state at the inauguration of President Eisenhower. Finally, at his urging, the legislature proceeded with its regular business.[33] The doctor's twelve-to-fifteen-days prognosis for recovery proved overly optimistic. The governor remained hospitalized for twenty-seven days and was allowed to return to the mansion only on the condition that he remain in bed and conduct limited business.

In the meantime, Umstead gave direction to his legislative program through his brother, John, who was an influential member of the state house, and his legislative aide W. Frank Taylor of Goldsboro, a former speaker of the house with both a solid reputation and a curious nickname; because of a nervous tick that caused his head to twitch to the side, he had been called "Shaky" since he was a college man. Until Umstead returned to the mansion, Taylor and Ed Rankin ferried between Raleigh and Durham carrying messages and orders for legislative details. After Umstead moved to the mansion, Rankin shepherded legislators in and out of the governor's sick room. With these small groups gathered around his bed, Umstead reviewed the progress of various parts of his program: a boost in teacher pay, more facilities for the mentally ill, more superior court judges, and a bond package to pay for additions to mental hospitals and new buildings at the state's colleges and universities. He even asked for a statewide referendum on alcohol sales, but that bill was never brought to a vote.

The legislative process did little to encourage Terry, who found the General Assembly tedious and confining for a freshman. He had borrowed $2,500 to cover expenses, and he worked weekends and nights at his law practice to pay that back. It was a losing proposition; a legislator's pay was only $1,350 for the session. To save money, Sanford usually shared the weekly commute with Representative Ike O'Hanlon, a big, boisterous fellow from Fayetteville. The two took a room at the Sir Walter, which offered low rates to legislators, who paid for four nights and got the weekends for free. Lobbyists often provided free meals, and the liquor distributors took legislators' orders on Friday and made deliveries to their hotel room door on Monday afternoon. In the evening, many of the senior party leaders would gather in the Sphinx Club, a private retreat just off the hotel lobby, where drinks were mixed from bottles kept in individual lockers. Late in the evening, legislators would snatch up an early edition of the News & Observer to learn where legislative committees were meeting the following day. Because of the cramped quarters of the capitol, committees met in the state government office buildings surrounding Capitol Square.

Terry's legislative record was unremarkable, which was about average for a freshman. He took care of housekeeping matters for his home county and introduced legislation regulating motion picture shows on Sunday, setting the salary of the coroner and jail fees and promoting education on the dangers of alcoholic beverages. He also tinkered with the regulation of taxi cabs and promoted a resolution honoring Cumberland County's bicentennial anniversary. His one dip into the pork barrel was a $2,000 appropriation for the Fayetteville Light Infantry. He also helped O'Hanlon with an appropriation for the Home for Confederate Widows in Fayetteville.

Umstead's friends among the leadership of the legislature allowed for no debate on the governor's program; it was rushed through the legislative process. The restricted debate rankled Terry, who found his picture at the top of the front page of the *News & Observer* the morning after he tried to sideline Umstead's plans for reorganizing the State Highway Commission. The bill had moved swiftly out of committee and was up for a vote in the senate when Terry rose to object to the governor's plan to appoint a five-person committee to determine whether the commission should be increased in size. "Such talk the senators seldom had heard from a freshman," the *News & Observer*'s Woodrow Price reported:

> Especially from a freshman who knew he was bucking a new and potent administration—who knew even before he opened his mouth that the cause was lost.
> But there stood young Terry Sanford, a lawyer serving his first legislative term from the county of Cumberland, saying in candid words just what he thought of the governor's highway reorganization bill.
> "We're abdicating our position.
> "We're passing the buck.
> "It is a mistake in policy. . . . It is setting a bad precedent. It is a bad proposition for the General Assembly to throw down any hot potato.
> "It appears to me to violate the division of authority between the legislative and executive branches." [34]

Terry asked for the bill to be postponed, but he might as well have asked for a commission in the Royal Navy. His motion failed on a voice vote and the bill shuttled on to the house with no recorded opposition. In the house, Terry was joined in his objections by his old history teacher from Laurinburg, Representative Roger Kiser of Scotland County. He also tried to slow the governor's program but was voted down ninety-nine to eight. Three of the eight nay votes came from the few Republicans in the chamber. Terry's dissent earned him a personal visit from Shaky Taylor, who wanted to know what he had against Governor Umstead. Terry allowed as he liked the governor and simply disagreed with the way he was ramming his program through.

If nothing else, the session confirmed Terry's own emerging political plans. He had hoped that a seat on the Senate Education Committee would permit him to do something about improving the condition of schools in the state. Yet, the committee had handled nothing substantive. The items that mattered were in the governor's education budget, and the floor manager for that bill, Senator William Copeland from Murfreesboro, never allowed Terry the floor to even ask a question.

There were others in the 1953 session who chafed at the limits the elders imposed. One was Representative Henry Hall Wilson Jr. from Monroe. Wilson was a few years younger than Terry, but they shared a common background. Wilson had opened a one-man law practice in Monroe the same year Terry had headed to Fayetteville. Both had become active in the YDC; in fact, Wilson had his eye on the presidency of the YDC. Wilson, too, was impatient with the Old Guard. He had first run for the state legislature in 1950 but his opponent tied him to Frank Graham and he lost in a second primary. He succeeded in 1952 and began the first of three terms where, he later wrote, "I couldn't muster more than twenty out of one hundred twenty votes on any showdown, but I could raise hell generally and carry the flag." [35]

One morning, sitting through breakfast long enough to see the restaurant empty of customers, Wilson and Sanford talked of the problems that needed attention in North Carolina. They complained of the resistance to change they found in the state's economic power structure and the restraints imposed by the party leaders who wanted them to wait their turn. They also acknowledged the cold reality of political life and the absurdity of two low-paid, small-town lawyers talking about taking over state government. "We were fed up with the self-righteousness of the second rate," Wilson later noted in a memoir.[36]

Terry needed but one session to learn that the legislature was not the place to effect change. At any rate, because of the rotation agreement, he would not be returning to the senate in 1955, even if he wanted to run again. He considered challenging the process that regulated the change but gave up the idea as a futile effort that wasn't worth the fight. As he headed home at the end of the session, he knew that the next office he campaigned for would be that of governor. "All my remaining doubts were resolved," Sanford wrote in a memoir. "I knew I wanted to be governor and I knew why I wanted to be governor. . . . I remembered that lesson. That convinced me that if I wanted to do anything about education I had better run for governor and make that the issue." [37]

The members of the 1953 General Assembly had been home less than a month when U.S. Senator Willis Smith suffered a heart attack and was taken to Bethesda Naval Hospital in Maryland. He had just finished a grueling three-week schedule making twenty-four speeches in twenty days. Two days after he was admitted, he was stricken again and died on June 26, the third senator from North Carolina to die in office in less than ten years. Vice President Richard Nixon attended Smith's funeral at Edenton Street Methodist Church in Raleigh. Also attending was the man Smith beat in the 1950 race for the Democratic nomination, Frank Graham. Among his pallbearers was his legislative aide, Jesse Helms.

The state's newspapers were filled with speculation about who Umstead would appoint to serve the remaining eighteen months of Smith's term. Umstead said little publicly other than to assure all that he would honor the traditional east-west balance. Because Clyde Hoey was from the western part of the state he was expected to name someone from the east. The list of prospects filled almost an entire column in the *News & Observer.*

A leading contender was John D. Larkins, a forty-four-year-old lawyer from Trenton, a rural hamlet not far from New Bern deep in eastern North Carolina. Reporters pressed Umstead for a decision and began counting the days, comparing Umstead's "delay" with the sixteen days that had elapsed before Scott had appointed Graham. Finally, on a Friday afternoon, July 10, Umstead telephoned Alton Lennon, a tall, lean, redheaded lawyer in Wilmington, and asked him to take the job. Lennon, forty-six, readily agreed.[38]

Umstead's choice was a complete surprise; Lennon's name had never surfaced as one of the top contenders. Some of Umstead's friends said the governor finally tired of all the backroom politicking and made a choice just to be done with it. Aside from the geography, Lennon certainly did not fit Umstead's profile for a replacement. The governor had said he would pick someone close to agriculture. Lennon lived in North Carolina's oldest city and enjoyed relaxing at his beach house at Wrightsville Beach, not the family homestead. But he was close to the governor, having managed Umstead's campaigns in New Hanover County when Umstead ran for the senate in 1948 as well as in 1952 when he ran for governor. His own political portfolio included service in the 1951 General Assembly, where he was one of the "hold-the-liners" Scott had complained about. He had supported Smith in 1950 and was an attractive candidate who was willing to mount a vigorous campaign.

Smith's death guaranteed that the 1954 senatorial primary would be one to watch. Scott, restless back on the farm in Alamance County, had made no formal declarations, but it was no secret he was itching to reclaim the seat lost to Smith in 1950. Some believed that Umstead chose a dark horse like Lennon just because Scott was sure to be a contender in the Democratic primary. The governor believed his own political strength and popularity was sufficient to carry into office someone such as Lennon, who had no scars or political baggage.

One of those who had visited Scott at Haw River to encourage him to run was Terry. During the legislative session, Terry had developed a close relationship with Scott's brother, Ralph, who was serving his second term in the state senate. Terry had enthusiastically supported Ralph Scott's bill to create the North Carolina Milk Commission, a measure that drew criticism from the state's major newspapers for being monopolistic because it fixed milk prices at the producer level; supporters argued that it was necessary to ensure an adequate supply of North Carolina–produced milk. The two also shared an abiding interest in increased funding for public education. Ralph liked the young legislator from Fayetteville and talked to his brother about him.[39]

Ralph was Kerr's eyes and ears in Raleigh. On weekends, when he returned home from Raleigh, he would join his brother on Sunday mornings to walk the few miles from their farms to services at Hawfields Presbyterian Church. The two would talk politics to the very door of the church, enter for the service, and then pick up right where they left off for the return walk home. Sometimes, when Kerr couldn't wait to finish a sentence or when something occurred to him during the service, he would pass a note forward to his brother. In later years, Ralph joked that he learned all he knew about politics just walking to church.

When Ralph Scott learned that Terry was traveling to Greensboro one day in the spring of 1953 he suggested that he stop by the farm and talk to Kerr. After Terry finished his business and was headed back to Raleigh, he pulled off U.S. 70 and onto the road to Kerr's thirteen-hundred-acre farm that lay across the rolling hills near the Haw River. He found the former governor in work clothes and brogans and they sat at the kitchen table and talked.

Scott quietly pondered the suggestion from his brother and from his old friends Capus Waynick and Frank Graham that Sanford would make an excellent campaign manager. Terry was young, ambitious, and would give Scott needed exposure among the Jaycees as well as the university crowd and voters from the growing urban areas in the state, groups that did not know Scott well. Combined with Scott's own solid relationship with political leaders in the rural areas, this new coalition was neither east nor west, nor rural versus urban, but progressive, even liberal, and formidable if cultivated.

It was a delicate balance and a curious marriage of political newcomers settling in growing cities with the farmers and rural folk whose roots went deep in the soil. Economically, culturally, socially, Scott's Branch-head boys seemed to have little in common with the Jaycees and young professionals that Terry knew. Yet, they enjoyed a common bond, one that might prove strong enough to transcend differences. Neither crowd had enjoyed the comfort of being inside and in control of the state party organization that generally had resisted as too expensive the kind of progressive programs they believed necessary to move the state forward.

If Scott had his doubts about Sanford, Terry questioned whether he could work with Scott. It would be a challenge. Scott had never really had a campaign manager; he followed his own instincts and had run his own campaigns, saying what he wanted when he wanted. Terry was worried that Scott's impulsive behavior and occasional outbursts would only reinforce the impression that he was a bumbler and an embarrassment to the state, an image that Umstead's folks were sure to foster. Finally, the two reached an accommodation, with Scott agreeing to curb his tongue and at least speak from texts prepared by his campaign manager.

Terry's decision to throw in with Scott was not without risk. Some of his friends counseled him not to get involved. If Scott lost, they said, Terry's own political career would be damaged. And even if Scott won, there was no guarantee that his support would be transferable to another candidate; it had not worked with Olive. Then, Terry would be at odds with the dominant faction of the state's Democrats. He called on Frank Graham to talk about the offer. Certainly he should work for Scott, Graham told him, "he's one of us."

"I knew such a step was reckless," Sanford later wrote in a journal, "but sometimes it is good for the soul to be reckless, and I wanted to see Kerr Scott representing North Carolina in Washington."[40]

There were other considerations. At that time, political campaigns were low-budget affairs and there was seldom any money for the full-time help. Scott's effort was going to be no different, and Terry had a young family to support and a growing law practice that could easily wither and die if left untended.

That law practice was his bread and butter. Moreover, he had come to thoroughly enjoy the practice of law and was determined to achieve an A rating from Martindale-Hubbell, the national legal reference standard, by 1959, when he would have finished his tenth year of practice. Terry liked the competition and the verbal gymnastics of trial practice, where alertness and a nimble mind often determined the outcome of a case. The law practice also suited his personality. He liked flying solo, determining his own destiny through his creativity and the force of his enthusiasm, persuasion, and leadership. He was a loner, in a sense, but one who liked people. Yes, the practice of law suited him just fine.

Terry's association with Charles Rose Jr. had put him in a unique situation. He was, for all practical purposes, a single practitioner, but he enjoyed the benefits of association with an established law firm that brought him business and provided a measure of support. He juggled the demands of his practice with the requirements of the legislature by perfecting a process for closing real estate transactions quickly and efficiently. When he was absent from the office, the paperwork was prepared and made ready for his attention when he returned. This routine produced a steady income without the need to schedule court appearances.[41]

Scott's campaign would require a more extended absence, so in the spring of 1954, Terry asked Dickson Phillips to cover his cases and serve his clients while he was occupied in Raleigh. Phillips, who had entered law school literally overnight at Sanford's suggestion in 1945, had returned to Laurinburg upon graduation and was practicing with Donald McCoy, another boyhood chum of Terry's. During the busy months of the campaign Phillips shuttled the forty miles to and from Fayetteville and kept the lights on in the law office.

By early May 1954 the Scott-Lennon campaign was shaping up to be a classic political brawl. Some voters chose sides immediately when Scott declared his intentions. A friend of his once said, "Just as is the case with ripe olives and collards, people either like him or they thoroughly dislike him; there is no middle ground."[42] The months on the farm had served as a tonic for Scott's political spirit and the respite from active duty in the governor's office had taken nothing from his love for the rough-and-tumble of campaigning. Even before his formal announcement, he was making appearances at events like Benson's Mule Day, puffing on his familiar stogie or chewing a wad of Brown's Mule.

Scott's carefree nature belied the seriousness with which he and his followers approached the spring campaign. This fight was for more than a Senate seat. It was for revenge, particularly for the younger Democratic activists that Terry brought to the campaign. This was a chance to right the wrongs of 1950. For them, Lennon occupied Dr. Frank's seat, and they intended to reclaim it. They were working to win the "Third Primary." After Graham's defeat in 1950, Terry visited Graham and told him that his campaign was not over: "I told Frank Graham that he gave me and a great many others in our generation a real dedication to do something, to get even, to rectify that injustice. I felt all his boys had benefited, and had certainly been renewed in their desires to do good things by his defeat. His defeat spurred us on to somehow rectify the error of the people."[43]

Graham remained on the fringe of the Scott campaign from his base in New York, where he was working for the United Nations. From time to time, Terry received checks written by Graham to the campaign. He tore them up because he knew Graham's wife, Marian, probably didn't know about them, as her husband kept lousy records of his expenses. Graham also could not afford it. "He never had an extra penny and I thought he had given us enough," Terry later recalled.[44]

Scott made his headquarters at the Carolina Hotel, which had been his base in 1948. It was of a size and design comparable to the Sir Walter but a few blocks off the beaten path in downtown Raleigh and a bit down-at-the-heels. The *News & Observer* offices, where Jonathan Daniels, Scott's old friend and advisor, held sway, were a block away across a shaded square. The separation from the Sir Walter and the headquarters of the established Democratic organization symbolized his estrangement from the Old Guard running Lennon's campaign.

Throughout the spring Scott rambled across the state and enjoyed the satisfaction of immediate recognition. He campaigned vigorously in small towns and rural crossroads, climbing out of his car and sharing a cold drink with the men in bib overalls, passing the time on the front porch of a country store. He was a natural storyteller and found in his own experiences example after example of ways to reassure the farmers and working people who had helped him in the past. "You were in serious trouble when I visited here in the early Thirties," he told a crowd in Benson, a small town east of Raleigh. "I recall what happened and what we all came through. We found it didn't pay to plow little pigs under . . . [now] we see the cycle going all over again. They're plowing under little heifers in Texas." Tough times were ahead for farmers, he said, and they needed someone with his experience in Washington.[45]

Scott turned one rambling conversation into a headline-grabbing publicity stunt. Early in the campaign, he told a radio audience in Pink Hill, a town of about four hundred souls in eastern North Carolina, that when he was a young man he had turned down a taxi ride for the twenty-one miles to his destination because the driver was asking a fare of a dollar a mile. "Now," Scott said, "I have walked many a mile for nothing, and I saw a chance to make a dollar a mile that time." [46]

The story evoked such a response that Scott announced he would give a bull calf to anyone who finished a twenty-one mile walk in less than six hours, the time that it had taken him in 1919. In early May, a month before the election, he was back in Pink Hill to give away thirty-nine bull calves, including one to a mail carrier from Burlington who made the trek in four hours and eight minutes. Pink Hill hadn't had so much attention in years, and the mayor, Tom Davis, made the most of the occasion, organizing a parade that featured the band from B. F. Grady High School and an American Legion honor guard. Scott rode through town in a sulky pulled by two mules and received induction into the Athletic Order of the Survivors of the Great Bull Calf Walk. The calf walk story was revived in the novel, *Facing the Lions*, by *New York Times* columnist Tom Wicker, a native of Hamlet, North Carolina, who was working as a sports writer at the *Winston-Salem Journal* when Scott was campaigning for office.[47]

The campaign became a blend of old and new and included one extended television broadcast in which Scott stuck faithfully to a script written by his campaign manager. It closed with Scott sharing his World War I experiences with his son, who was headed to Army service in Japan. Young Bob wasn't due to report for duty until after the election, so a departure scene was staged at the Piedmont Airlines terminal in Greensboro.[48]

Scott's speeches were free of the bombast of earlier years. Instead, reporters fed on down-home homilies and rural chatter. Scott also talked about solving American farm problems by using food surpluses to feed the hungry abroad and as a way to stop the spread of communism. The theory that communist-inspired revolution thrived on the empty bellies of peasants in Third World nations was prominent in many circles. He preached conservation and the need to protect the water resources in the state.

Lennon, eager for attention, tried unsuccessfully to draw Scott into a fight but found himself on the defensive instead. For example, the Lennon campaign placed an ad in a veterans magazine to criticize Scott's limited exposure to military duty during World War I. Lennon then was forced to explain his own 2-A classification during World War II, when he escaped the draft. On the stump, and repeatedly in his ads, Lennon accused Scott of accepting honoraria for speeches while he was governor and abusing the power of his office to enrich himself. Lennon challenged Scott to release his tax returns and put his own on display. Scott ignored the slap, but one of the minor candidates in the field, Alvin Wingfield Jr., responded by saying Lennon couldn't have been much of a lawyer if he only had $6,000 in income, the amount Lennon reported on his tax forms.

Scott brushed Lennon aside, saying in a radio broadcast from Charlotte, "The issues at stake are too important for any of us to go off on a rabbit hunt at this stage of the national and international crisis and emergency. Let's keep our eyes on the target, and our finger on the triggers as we hunt bigger game than rabbits." Scott reminded his listeners that he would not be "diverted from the main issues. You, the people, who know me of old, know that I will not be diverted from the row I set out to plow. Call it stubbornness or determination. That is my way of getting things done."[49] The dodge worked and Scott's income tax returns remained private. Some years later, Sanford said he was worried that releasing Scott's tax returns could have been detrimental. The governor had paid virtually no taxes in recent years because of losses in the farming operation that allowed him to offset current income with the losses of previous years.[50]

The spring of 1954 brought a mixture of political currents, but the tide was decidedly to the right. Americans had been shaken by the discovery of Soviet espionage at home and the success of communist movements around the world. In early May, the French had been defeated at Dien Bien Phu in a corner of southeast Asia later called Vietnam. Americans may not have been able to pinpoint the places where communists enjoyed success, but virtually everyone knew the name of Joseph McCarthy, the junior senator from Wisconsin. The Scott-Lennon race was in the closing weeks when the Army-McCarthy hearings opened in Washington, beginning 187 hours of live coverage by ABC television. At their peak, the hearings were seen by more than twenty million Americans who tuned in to see McCarthy, then at the height of his four-year reign of Red-baiting.⁵¹

For the most part, McCarthy's ragings made no impact on North Carolina politics. Criticism of the Republican senator was vigorous, if not commonplace. At a spring gathering in Chapel Hill's Emerson Stadium, the governor's brother, John Umstead, accused McCarthy of deception while many national leaders were still uncertain about how to deal with the man. "Anyone who isn't honest with his god, his country or his fellow human beings, doesn't deserve to be called a public-spirited citizen," Umstead said.⁵²

All in all, for North Carolina at least, the issues that had kept McCarthy in the headlines had never played well in the state. Willis Smith had made little headway against Frank Graham in the first primary when he attempted to cast Graham as a socialist and soft on communism. Candidate Alvin Wingfield had kept up a drumbeat of opposition to the United Nations, but that world assembly was generally held in high regard in the state. During the 1953 General Assembly, a majority of the legislators had blunted an effort to rouse support against the United Nations and repeal resolutions passed by 1941 and 1949 legislatures. The 1941 bill called for a world federation of government and the 1949 endorsed a constitutional convention to make the changes necessary to achieve a world government. Sanford had joined others who not only supported the United Nations but argued for an organization with even stronger powers. The 1953 legislature withdrew the resolution calling for a constitutional convention, but support for the United Nations remained strong. Sanford wrote, "It is the belief of the General Assembly of North Carolina that efforts should be made to support the United Nations, so as to develop within it adequate powers to prevent aggression, to control the weapons of mass destruction, and to bring about law and order to the relationship among nations."⁵³

The campaign was not to escape events that were beyond the control of either side. The first occurred on May 12, after Senator Clyde Hoey returned to his Washington office following a committee meeting and settled into his chair for his customary afternoon nap. At 2:45 his assistant, Jack Spain, found him slumped over, dead from a stroke. Hoey was seventy-six and had become a near legendary figure with his claw-hammer coat, high collars, and "serene manners" reminiscent of an earlier era. He was the only man to have been a member of both chambers of the North Carolina legislature, a member of the U.S. Congress, and governor. He was the last reigning member of the old Shelby Dynasty, organized by his brother-in-law O. Max Gardner.

Scott was campaigning in Statesville when he learned of Hoey's death. He and his staff talked into the night about how to deal with this new advantage handed Umstead and the opposition. They were fully aware of the influence that the governor could bring to bear on politicians eager to win the appointment or have their favorite named to succeed Hoey. Indeed, Umstead now enjoyed a rare opportunity for a governor. Only the governor of Florida, in 1936, had before this time appointed two senators. In a close race, the added political leverage given Umstead could sway enough votes to provide Lennon with the last-minute boost he needed.

The Statesville strategy session was captured in photographs taken for a May 24 article in *Life* magazine that showed Scott and his friends huddled in a motel room. Terry was still enjoying the glow from such inexpensive and glamorous publicity when he got a telephone call from a friend in Washington. Prepare yourself, Terry was warned, the Court's decision in the *Brown v. Board of Education of Topeka* case, outlawing segregation in public schools, would be announced on Monday.

The Monday that Atlanta editor Ralph McGill had warned was coming finally arrived. The day that practically everyone had been expecting, some with fear and loathing, some with faith and hope, was here. "Those who took an active interest in the world around them knew that *Brown* was imminent," writer John Egerton wrote later. "They had seen it, or something like it, coming for a long time. It was like an earthquake or a hurricane: Your intelligence and your common sense told you it was bound to happen sooner or later, but it was still a profound shock when it finally hit."[54]

On Sunday, Terry did not join the crowd of eight thousand who turned out in Shelby for Hoey's funeral. Forty members of the Senate arrived aboard a special train that carried them to the small textile town in the foothills of the Blue Ridge, where they joined politicians from across the state for services. Instead, Terry was working on a statement for Scott to have ready on Monday, when reporters were expected to call for his reaction to the Court's decision. Neither he nor others at headquarters could forget that it was the Supreme Court's decision admitting black students to graduate schools, sent down as Willis Smith pondered whether to call for a second primary four years earlier, that had ignited the racial fires of Smith's campaign in 1950.

Scott was one of the few politicians in the state who had advance warning. Ed Rankin at the governor's office learned about *Brown* in late morning when a reporter called for a reaction from the governor. Immediately

Rankin got on the phone to the United Press office in Raleigh and began taking down the report, which was passed page-by-page to his boss. Umstead was "dumbfounded, really dumbfounded," recalled Rankin, and he told his aide to release only a brief statement saying he was "disappointed" and he would comment further after he had read the opinion.[55]

An eight-column headline, reserved only for declarations of war and other catastrophes, crowned the front page of Tuesday's News & Observer on May 18: "Segregation Is Declared Unconstitutional." In the accompanying stories the paper reprinted the entire opinion that Chief Justice Earl Warren had read from the bench. The paper also registered the outrage of public officials and others in North Carolina and throughout the South over the Court's unanimous decision. "There will never be mixed schools while I am governor," said Georgia's Herman Talmadge. "The United States Supreme Court by its decision today has reduced our constitution to a mere scrap of paper." South Carolina's governor, James F. Byrnes, a former member of the Court, said he believed the separate but equal provisions did not violate the constitution. "I am shocked to learn the Court has reversed itself." In Florida, Governor Charley Johns said he would call a special session of the state's legislature. North Carolina's speaker of the house, E. T. Bost of Concord, said similar measures might be necessary in North Carolina. The chief justice of North Carolina's supreme court, M. V. Barnhill, said the decision set race relations back fifty years. He claimed abolition of separate schools would produce serious handicaps for hundreds of black men and women who teach in the state's schools. Apparently it was inconceivable to the chief justice that whites would attend black schools or be taught by black teachers.

If there was a feeling of jubilation in the state's black community, it was not reflected in the daily news reports. Leading black educators such as Dr. Harold Trigg, the only black member of the state Board of Education, and Dr. F. D. Bluford, president of North Carolina A&T State College in Greensboro, declined to comment. Charlotte Hawkins Brown, president emeritus of Palmer Memorial Institute, said, "It's going to be a complex problem and will take some time to work out. Only time, patience and the spirit of Christ will work it out."[56] Dr. J. W. Seabrook, president of Fayetteville State Teachers College, suggested that open schools, with students free to choose where they would attend, were the most effective method of integration. He added that federal aid would be required to equalize school facilities. He also said gradual desegregation, beginning in the first grade, was another suitable option.[57]

The Raleigh newspaper carried Scott's extended remarks in full. He questioned the Court's decision, but his statement was free of the outright defiance heard from other quarters. "I feel certain that no candidate would favor the end of segregation, and I am sure they will join me in hope and prayer that we can avoid stirring up fear and bad feeling between races in North Carolina." Scott reminded voters that he had worked to improve black schools in the state and that he believed no one wanted the end to separate schools: "As a member of the United States Senate I would work in close cooperation with other like-minded senators to preserve our traditions. I urge that all fellow citizens, regardless of race, color or creed, remain calm and work together in an orderly fashion while machinery is being set up to avoid disruption of our pattern of school life. To this end, I shall fight."[58]

Lennon was caught as flat-footed as his sponsor, the governor. He registered shock and dismay and said he would say more at another time. Two days later he told a campaign rally that Scott "and certain of his top advisers and political associates have encouraged the abolition of segregation in our public schools for many years."[59] It was a clear reference to Scott's broad support from black voters and his allegiance to Frank Graham. The words drew a stiff rebuke from the state's leading newspapers, who accused Lennon of injecting race into the campaign, and Lennon never repeated the charge.

Umstead was torn by the decision. His initial reaction, one he expressed only privately, was not much different from that of other public figures quoted in the days following the Court's decision: he was mad. He believed the Court had usurped the powers of the states to spend their tax money the way they wanted. "He had the opinion of many thoughtful conservatives," Rankin recalled, "which is to say—to hell with it. Ignore them. Make them do something. We are going to do what we are going to do. This is our state, this is our tax money and these are our schools and they are not going to tell us how to do it."[60] At the same time, however, Umstead believed that a temper tantrum such as those on display by other public figures in the South was not only unproductive, it was undignified. He was as disturbed as they were about the Court's interference with the Southern way of life, but he respected the rule of law and would no more have dismissed the Court's order than his own mother's admonition to never touch a drink of liquor. He was also mindful of the cost in the upcoming election if he threw gasoline on the smoldering fire.

The Court's decision left many questions unanswered, and those in positions of public responsibility were unsure about what *Brown* meant. Segregation may be dead, but what was expected in the schools in the fall? What were school boards, teachers, students, and their parents supposed to do? How was the nation, the South in particular, supposed to respond? No one knew.

As subsequent events unfolded, it was as if nothing had changed but everything would be different. When President Eisenhower arrived in Charlotte the day following the Court's decision to attend a celebration of the 179th anniversary of the signing of the Mecklenburg (County) Declaration of Independence, he said nothing about the decision and was warmly greeted by Umstead and others from the West Point class of 1915 on hand to see him. On the following day, in Greensboro, the city's school board voted six to one in favor of a resolution to "let the community, the state, the south, and if necessary, the nation, know that we here propose to live under the rule of law" and directed school superintendent Ben E. Smith to "study ways and means for complying with the Court's decision." [61]

Meanwhile, on Wednesday, the state's Democrats began gathering in Raleigh for the party's annual convention. Lennon's campaign was installed in room 110 of the Sir Walter Hotel, just a few steps away from party headquarters. Scott campaigned throughout Wake County around Raleigh the day before the convention's opening gavel. Asked if he had any more bull calves to give away, Scott said, "All we are giving away now is blue-nosed mules," referring to his campaign slogan that he was "a blue-nosed, kicking-mule Democrat." [62] Riding with him through the countryside were his assistant county manager, Bruce M. Poole; his friend and aide from Rocky Mount, Ben Roney; and a volunteer from Clinton named Lauch Faircloth, who also had worked in Graham's campaign four years earlier.

Memorial Auditorium was crowded when the convention was called to order. Delegates and party faithful filled the folding chairs on the auditorium floor and seats in the balconies. The Brown decision had been a lively topic in the hotel lobby and hospitality rooms upstairs, where folks gathered for a soft drink or something stronger, but the published agenda was clear of the subject. The caucus in one congressional district had heard a resolution condemning the Court's order, but it had been defeated on a voice vote.

When Irving Carlyle, a distinguished lawyer from Winston-Salem, rose to deliver the convention's keynote address, he began with the kind of rousing party rhetoric reserved for such occasions. But Carlyle was no ordinary man. Some believed he was Umstead's choice to replace Hoey. The night before, he had written a one-paragraph addendum to his speech that brought a stillness to the hall after he had uttered the first few words: "I would like to say this: The Supreme Court has spoken. As good citizens we have no other course except to obey the law as laid down by the Court. To do otherwise would cost us our respect for law and order, and if we lost that in these critical times, we have lost that quality which is the source of our strength as a state and as a nation." [63]

The delegates had responded heartily to the early portion of Carlyle's speech, including a reference to the Army-McCarthy hearings, which he called a "disturbing and degrading spectacle." His delivery had been interrupted nearly two dozen times. When he concluded his remarks about the Court's decision, his audience erupted in applause. Some even rose to give him a standing ovation.

The dark skies that had brought a blustery late spring storm dumping up to six inches of rain on eastern North Carolina were beginning to clear as delegates filed out of the auditorium. There was another storm brewing, however, and it broke the following week, just four days before the election, in Carlyle's hometown, where readers of the *Winston-Salem Journal* found a curious advertisement on one of the paper's inside pages. At first glance, it appeared to be an ad placed by the Scott campaign. It bore the signature of J. H. R. Gleaves, the president of the city's Progressive Civic League, a black political organization, and praised Scott as a friend. A portion of the ad read: "[Kerr Scott] has demonstrated his interest in our race and has aided our case of non-segregation."

The ad was a surprise to Scott. Terry and others in the organization had never seen it, and the implications of such an endorsement in the highly charged political atmosphere were all too clear.

Terry had prepared for last-minute trouble. Based on the experience of the closing days of the 1950 and 1952 campaigns, he had alerted supporters at country stores and other likely gathering places to call the moment they saw anything amiss. While he was chasing down the source of the phony ad—which he learned had been prepared and paid for by Winston-Salem Mayor Marshall Kurfees, a Lennon supporter—he got a call from deep in eastern North Carolina. Charles Cohoon in Columbia telephoned that a bundle of leaflets featuring a reprint of the newspaper ad had been dropped off at his service station.[64] This late development could prove devastating, particularly in the wake of the emotional energy generated by the Court's decision. The Scott campaign had less than seventy-two hours before voters would begin marking ballots on Saturday. There were no opinion polls, just gut instinct, to suggest the impact of the racist twist injected by Lennon's supporters.

Terry was determined not to repeat the mistakes of the Graham campaign, which had failed to respond quickly and decisively to the racist leaflets and had allowed the opposition to gain the advantage. He had resolved after that experience that response should be swift and sufficiently strong to put the opposition on the defensive. What he needed now was solid evidence that Lennon's supporters were the source of the dirty tricks.

By the end of the day, Terry had a plan with enough cloak-and-dagger dimensions to satisfy his old boss, J. Edgar Hoover. He called Les Atkins, a Scott supporter in Durham, and asked him to have a member of the tobacco workers' union whom he could trust contact Lennon's publicity agent, C. A. Upchurch Jr., ask for some of the leaflets, and then bring them to the Scott headquarters. Atkins found his man, who not only received a bundle of leaflets from the Lennon campaign printer but received written instructions from Upchurch on how they should be left in rural mailboxes at night and on the front porches of houses in textile mill towns. Atkins's agent quoted Upchurch as saying, "They beat me with this [in the Graham campaign], and it ought to be good enough to try again." Terry took his man's statement, had it notarized, and salted him away for safekeeping in a Raleigh hotel room, where he was kept happy with steak and beer. He then carried everything to Jonathan Daniels at the *News & Observer*.

On Friday morning, twenty-four hours before the polls opened, a story about the leaflets filled the paper's front page. Daniels even held the presses for an hour to make sure every inch of the story made it into print. A two-line banner headline announced, "Alton Lennon Forces Flood State With 'Phony' Race Issue Leaflets." Underneath was a picture of a bundle of the leaflets and the card from Upchurch authorizing distribution. Terry was quoted as calling the scheme a "last-minute effort of desperate, panicky men who know their cause is lost. The Winston-Salem leaflet is a falsehood and the people who had it printed know it is a falsehood. It is dirty politics and the people who printed it know it is dirty politics." [65] Terry called for state and federal authorities to investigate the activities of Upchurch, as well as a top state official who had delivered the leaflets to Cohoon's service station and an attorney who Terry said was also involved.

Terry announced that he had sent telegrams to all of Lennon's county managers notifying them that distribution of the leaflets was illegal and that the Scott campaign would press for prosecution of anyone handing them out. He also announced a $100 reward for further information. The threat was basically empty, but it had a chilling effect and kept some of the leaflets out of circulation.

Saturday, election day, was warm and cloudy. The Scott campaign couldn't have asked for a better finish to a potentially disastrous episode that three days earlier had posed a serious threat. The *News & Observer*, along with other newspapers in the state, carried front-page stories on election day about a possible FBI investigation of the Lennon campaign. The reply from Lennon's camp—that they had reprinted the Winston-Salem newspaper just as a "talking point" for their supporters—was unrepentant. It sounded weak and suggested duplicity.

No one knew for sure whether the developments of the prior few days had moved voters one way or the other. Both sides professed confidence as voters streamed to the polls and cast ballots in record numbers.

Scott's election-night party got underway at the Carolina Hotel around eight, when a three-piece band began to play popular tunes. Supporters milled about the lobby and performed the election-night ritual of predicting the outcome of the election from meager early returns. Ten o'clock, eleven o'clock, and midnight passed without any definitive results. County returns showed that Scott was running well in eastern and rural areas of the state, except for the mountain counties to the west, which were reporting winning margins for Lennon. Lennon also was doing well in Mecklenburg County and Charlotte, the state's largest city, as well as Winston-Salem and Greensboro; he was losing Durham, and Wake County (Raleigh) was on its way to giving Scott a whopping margin of more than five thousand votes.

In the overall returns, Lennon trailed throughout the night, although he remained within striking distance. After midnight, however, the odds grew longer that he could overcome Scott's lead. Shortly before two o'clock, Lennon joined his campaign manager for a ride over to the Carolina Hotel to see his opponent. He hummed a tune as the car covered the six or so blocks to the hotel's front door. He walked into the lobby where he was greeted by Sanford. "Hi Al," Terry said warmly. "Hi Terry," Lennon answered.

"Sanford clasped his shoulder," the News & Observer's Jim Chaney reported. "They hurried, with Sanford as guide, to an elevator, for the short ride up to the Carolina's ballroom. Sanford broke a path through well-wishers and walked with Lennon to the front." Lennon wasn't there to formally concede, but he told Scott, "If the final returns show you are the nominee, I assure you of my support." Then he left.[66]

Scott stayed out of the public eye on Sunday. It wasn't proper to be politicking on the Sabbath, he said, and the campaign made no pronouncements. His staff stayed in close contact with their people and the Board of Elections as the remaining precincts finally delivered returns. At the end of the day, there were still two hundred precincts unaccounted for, but Scott's lead held at fifteen thousand votes.

Lennon's headquarters remained quiet as returns pushed the overall vote up and up. The record turnout and late precincts narrowed the margin. John Rodman, Lennon's campaign manager, ignored the News & Observer's editorial page, which declared Scott the winner and proclaimed the results "a rebuke to some politicians. It helped prove for elections to come that diminishing returns have set in for those who believe there is a personal profit in political well poisoning."[67]

Monday passed without a formal concession from Lennon. On Tuesday,

Terry called reporters to the Scott headquarters and claimed victory. He then promptly headed for a vacation at the beach. Rodman finally issued a brief statement two days later, after the Board of Elections formally declared Scott the winner with a majority of 8,374 votes.

The results were a comfort to Jonathan Daniels, who had retreated from the front lines of politics after becoming such a target in the 1950 campaign. Like so many others bitterly disappointed over Graham's defeat, he now felt vindicated. In his postelection editorial, he wrote, "North Carolina can feel cleared as a result of the election. Also, now it can get down to the difficult problem before us in race relations in North Carolina which requests the 'calm, careful and thoughtful study of us all.' " [68]

Indeed, a mood of optimism seemed to prevail. Ministerial associations around the state and regional religious assemblies adopted resolutions calling for implementation of the Court's decision. Raleigh's ministers adopted a resolution praising the Supreme Court's decision, saying that the Court had, "through the interpretation of the law, brought into clear focus the Christian principal of the equality of all men in the sight of God." [69] The annual gathering of the southern wing of the Presbyterian Church, meeting the same weekend as the North Carolina primary election, voted 236 to 169 to open all its institutions of higher education to all races, and to recommend the same action by the denomination's synods and presbyteries. It also issued a call to local churches to examine their own life and to practice no discrimination.

There was, of course, a more troublesome side clearly indicating that the debate of segregation in schools was not over. Two days before the election, Umstead released his considered response to the Court's decision. He had prepared a tightly woven argument, written in the style of a legal brief, that sounded more like a formal objection to the decision than a leader's message to his constituents. He had handwritten the statement, Rankin recalled, setting his thoughts down on a yellow legal pad in the quiet of his office. In clear, precise language, the governor said he believed that the Court's previous decisions upholding segregation had been correct. He called *Brown* "a clear and serious invasion of the rights of the sovereign states. Nevertheless, this is now the latest Supreme Court interpretation of the 14th amendment." [70]

Educators, parents, and others in the state who were looking for direction, or a hint of how North Carolina would face this sea change in life and culture, did not find it in Umstead's brief. Instead, they got a history lesson. He traced the issue of separate-but-equal back to the ratification of the Fourteenth Amendment in Reconstruction North Carolina. At that time, Governor William Holden had assured North Carolinians that adoption of the amendment would not affect segregated schools, Umstead said, suggesting that *Brown* was little more than yet another breach of faith by the hated Federals who had occupied the state following the Civil War.

In the days following the election, Umstead met with the Board of Education and made some modest adjustments to policy. Work was stopped on plans to distribute school building construction money based on racial formulas and the board would no longer indicate in its records whether a particular school was for white students or black students. On the bigger issue of moving ahead to integrate classes, the board decided to postpone any action until after a second round of hearings at the Supreme Court, scheduled for the following year.

Umstead refused to take questions from reporters about the matter, other than to say he would stay in contact with other Southern governors, who were scheduled to gather soon in Richmond at the request of Virginia Governor Thomas B. Stanley. He turned his attention to other matters, including selection of a replacement for Senator Hoey. The day after he met with the state Board of Education, June 4, Umstead telephoned Chief Justice Barnhill and asked him to call Justice Sam J. Ervin Jr. into his chambers so he could speak with him without alerting anyone else in the building. Barnhill summoned Ervin and handed him the phone. The governor told Ervin he wanted to talk with him but not in his office. Could the justice meet him at the mansion? A little after three in the afternoon, Ervin found the governor in the mansion parlor, where Umstead asked the judge if he would accept the Senate nomination were it to be offered. Ervin said he preferred his position on the court, but would accept.[71] The following Saturday afternoon at one o'clock, Umstead announced that Ervin, who was fifty-seven, would succeed Hoey.

Ervin's appointment was a surprise. The judge was known for precise and colorful legal opinions, sort of a mixture of Harvard Law School, from which he had graduated, and the Jack tales of the Blue Ridge Mountains, where he made his home in Morganton. In the news accounts of his appointment, he was labeled a moderate, not as conservative as Smith and not as liberal as Scott. When Terry heard the news he mused that if Umstead had known that Ervin's daughter had been a worker in Scott's campaign headquarters he might have chosen someone else.

Ervin was not a political unknown. Indeed, Umstead was sending to the Senate a man with established credentials as a former state legislator, superior court judge, and state supreme court justice. He had even spent a little time in Congress, serving the seven months remaining in his brother's term in the House after Joe Ervin's death in 1945. The experience left Ervin and his wife with a bad taste for Washington, but in 1954 they headed north on the train with optimism that this time things would be different.

With his appointment, Umstead was sending to the Senate the man who would capture the national spotlight as the leading legal theoretician for the white Southern partisans in their fight against civil rights.

CHAPTER EIGHT

A Dangerous Dream

✻

AS KERR SCOTT PREPARED for Washington, Terry Sanford was looking toward 1956, when he fully intended to have his own name on the
statewide ballot. Scott's successful campaign had forged a coalition of
the Branch-head boys and Terry's contemporaries that he believed had the
makings of a new political force in the state. If Terry had his way, he would
use it to produce another winning campaign in 1956, one that would put
him in the governor's office.

Scott's Senate office became one of Terry's main oars in the state's
political waters as he helped Scott gather his Washington staff. Among the
campaign insiders selected for positions were Ben Roney, a Rocky Mount
oil jobber who had been with Scott since the road bond campaign in 1949;
speechwriter Robert Redwine, who had handled odd jobs for Scott when
he was governor; press aide Bill Whitley, and two secretaries, Peggy Warren and Betty Carter. Terry also was trying to find a job on Capitol Hill for a
relative newcomer named Roy Wilder. Wilder was a journeyman newspaper
reporter and former war correspondent who claimed he had been the only
man on the Normandy beachhead in 1944 with both a bottle of bourbon
and a jar of chitlins in his satchel. During the campaign, Wilder had taken
over as press agent when Whitley was sidelined by illness.

This inner circle was a fiercely loyal and dedicated bunch, although a bit
rough around the edges. Roney and Wilder could turn the air blue with their
language and both liked their bourbon a bit too much. Roney often nursed
a drink well into the night, rousing Wilder at all hours with phone calls
when something came to mind. His habits were usually overlooked in favor
of his keen sense of the nuances of state politics and an unfailing memory of political transgressions and favors due.[1] Yet, despite their political
savvy, they were all as inexperienced as the senator in the inner workings
of Congress and unschooled on national issues. Terry had filled that gap

during the campaign with help from Bill Cochrane, who had returned to Albert Coates's Institute of Government after the war and a year at Yale Law School, where he had earned a master's degree. Cochrane developed position statements on key issues that helped offset Lennon's characterization of Scott as a hayseed who only knew how to build roads. At Terry's urging, Coates granted Cochrane a year's leave of absence to join Scott in Washington. He would never return to Chapel Hill, and in time became a Capitol Hill institution in his own right.

Scott took his oath of office on November 29, 1954, rather than in January, because he was filling the remaining few weeks of an unexpired term. It was a day of immense personal satisfaction for Scott and others who saw his victory over Lennon as sweet revenge for Frank Graham's defeat four years earlier. Sitting in the gallery that day, in a place of honor next to Scott's wife, Miss Mary, was their champion, Dr. Frank. When Senator Russell Long of Louisiana spied his former colleague seated among the visitors, he called him to the Senate floor, where Graham was greeted warmly by those he had gotten to know five years earlier.

Ten days before Scott joined the Senate, his colleague Sam Ervin Jr. had made his first important appearance on the floor with the presentation of a report of the committee considering sanctions against Senator Joe McCarthy. Ervin had arrived in Washington the previous summer having told friends back home that he didn't think old Joe was such a bad guy. Upon his departure, however, he had attended a Democratic Party rally in Asheville, where mountain Democrats, who had been fighting Republicans for generations, let him know they believed that McCarthy was the personification of evil.[2]

Ervin distinguished himself in delivering the committee's final report. His performance that day was the first of many demonstrations of his ability to tie a legal knot around an opponent as he convinced his colleagues, some of them still swaying with public sentiment for the Wisconsin senator, that it was really the Senate that was on trial. In December, Scott and Ervin joined sixty-five other senators who voted to censure McCarthy not only for mishandling of witnesses and contempt for the subcommittee investigating him, but for smearing the committee and the Senate itself.

The McCarthy era of witch hunts and Red-baiting was coming to a close. McCarthy never recovered from Ervin's recitation of his abuses of Senate privileges and the condemnation of his behavior by his colleagues. Yet, another issue had emerged that reached far deeper into the American psyche and threatened the accepted way of life, particularly in the South. The reaction to the U.S. Supreme Court's decision on school integration would separate the senior members of the Democratic Party such as Ervin from younger progressives such as Sanford. In time, the issue of civil rights would frame the public careers of both men. It also would upset Terry's own political timetable.

In the second week of April 1955, lawyers appearing in the second round of the Court's *Brown* decision arrived in Washington. Among those climbing the steps to the Court was I. Beverly Lake, an assistant attorney general from North Carolina who harbored angry contempt for the Court's interference in the Southern way of life. Lake was a Harvard-trained lawyer who had taught law at Wake Forest College and worked for a time in Washington before joining the staff of Attorney General Harry McMullan in 1950. He had studied utility law at Columbia University prior to the war and even published a book on the subject. In the attorney general's office, Lake earned a reputation as a consumer advocate with his handling of rate cases he argued on appeal from the state Utilities Commission, which tended to side with the power companies. Yet, it was race, not utility law, that would define his political reputation.

Lake was a reluctant participant in the hearings the Court had scheduled as part of its consideration of a date for implementation of the *Brown* decision. Lake and McMullan, plus every member of North Carolina's Supreme Court, had told Governor Umstead that the Court's invitation to North Carolina and other states to appear as amici curiae was a plot to draw these states directly into the cases consolidated for the *Brown* decision. Lake told the governor it was a "diabolical scheme" of entrapment. He argued that if North Carolina took any official notice of the proceedings, then the state would be directly subject to any orders the Court issued for the school systems in Virginia, South Carolina, and Kansas, which were parties in the *Brown* case.[3]

Soon after the May 17 decision, North Carolina leaders began desperately seeking a legally defensible policy that would stop or at least stall the integration of public schools. Despite the applause that had greeted Irving Carlyle's defense of the Court at the state Democratic convention, ready compliance was never considered a viable option. The governor and his advisors were no more willing to submit to *Brown* than they had been after the Court's 1950 decision ordering integration of graduate education in Oklahoma and Texas. North Carolina continued to block efforts by black students to enroll where they pleased until it was ordered by the courts. McMullan had never forgotten the stunning rebuke he had received in 1951 from the Fourth Circuit Court of Appeals when it rejected the state's arguments opposing the admission of African Americans to the law school at Chapel Hill.

In August 1954, a little more than sixty days after the *Brown* decision, Umstead appointed an eighteen-member biracial committee to study the school question and make recommendations on how the state should respond. Named to head the committee was Thomas J. Pearsall of Rocky Mount, a tall, silver-haired, eastern North Carolina plantation owner who was one of the dignified gentry of the region. He had been born to modest circumstances but had married the daughter of one of the largest landowners in Edgecombe and Nash counties. After practicing law for a brief period in the 1930s, he had assumed responsibility for his wife's family's vast expanse of farms, most of which were worked by tenants who had been on the land for generations. He had served as speaker of the house in 1947, and when he took the call from Umstead he was finishing work as a member of the state's new Milk Commission that Sanford had helped create in the 1953 legislature. He didn't want another unpaid state job, and he knew this assignment was perhaps the greatest challenge he would face in his lifetime.

Pearsall and his wife, Elizabeth, personified the way of life in rural Carolina. He now cared for farms where her grandfather, who had been called "Marse Mack," had once worked slaves. Overseers supervised the daily work of black tenant farmers, who with their families made up a community numbering more than a thousand. In addition to the farms, the family owned a peanut brokerage and a cotton brokerage, and Tom sat on the board at a local bank. The Pearsalls were as much a part of the community as the annual harvest rituals that typified eastern North Carolina farm life. Tom had served on the school board before going to the legislature, and Elizabeth was active in the Episcopal Church. They were Democrats, of course, and tended to side with the more moderate, even progressive side of the party. Their close friends included Kemp and Maude Battle, as determined a pair of defenders of the University of North Carolina and Frank Graham as there were in the state.[4]

Pearsall's agreeable nature had won him a reputation as an arbitrator, which was one of the reasons Umstead had chosen him for the Milk Commission job, where he had successfully negotiated a system of compensation between dairy farmers and bottlers. He also was known as an innovative farmer with a compassionate nature. The Pearsall farms were recognized as a model for the treatment of tenants. For example, newborns were cared for by a nurse paid by the farm; tenants also were encouraged to provide for themselves with a garden and cow and helped to produce food for their own table. Pearsall established a cannery for farm families, and each year at the farm barbecue at harvest time, prizes were awarded for samples of the best that families had set by for the winter.

Relations between whites and blacks had never been an issue in Pearsall's white world; segregation was just a fact of life. Yet the Pearsalls had exhibited a keener sense of the change that lay ahead long before many of their neighbors. In the middle of the Great Depression, Tom had introduced his wife to Charlotte Hawkins Brown, whose Palmer Institute in Sedalia, North Carolina, was one of the finest African American college preparatory schools in the country. A short time afterward, Elizabeth invited Mrs. Brown, the daughter of North Carolina slaves who had been educated at Wellesley College in Massachusetts, to speak on racial amity to a group of whites at her church in Rocky Mount. Several leading members of the parish issued bitter protests, but Mrs. Brown spoke nonetheless.[5]

Pearsall's Advisory Committee on Education effectively supplanted any action by the state's Board of Education chaired by Lieutenant Governor Luther Hodges, who was all but ignored by Umstead and virtually everyone else on Capitol Square. The committee represented a cross-section of prominent white North Carolina, and included three African Americans: Dr. F. D. Bluford, president of North Carolina A&T State College in Greensboro; Dr. J. W. Seabrook, president of Fayetteville Teachers College; and Hazel Parker, a home demonstration agent from Pearsall's own Edgecombe County.

The Pearsall committee was the only biracial group given such an assignment by a Southern governor. Virginia's Thomas Stanley had announced he would appoint African Americans to a similar panel for his state, but two months after the *Brown* decision, his initial call for moderation had hardened to an announced policy of obstruction. "I shall use every legal means at my command to continue segregated schools in Virginia," the governor declared on July 25. Stanley later appointed an all-white advisory committee and named as chairman state Senator Garland Gray, a prominent associate of Virginia's political boss, U.S. Senator Harry Byrd. Before the hot days of summer had set in, Gray announced his opposition to integrating schools.[6]

In comparison to the noisier segregationists in the Deep South, North Carolina's leaders appeared to be the model of moderation. Yet, behind the closed doors and out of earshot of reporters, about the only difference between Umstead and the others was their public image. Opposition to admitting black students to white schools was just as firmly held among state officials in Raleigh as it was in Montgomery or Jackson or Richmond. Umstead's old friends on the state's high court told him to do nothing; they recommended he ignore the Supreme Court's order and force the hand of the federal government, which, under President Eisenhower, appeared unlikely to put any muscle behind the *Brown* decision.[7]

The initial discussion by Umstead's advisors focused not on how to follow border states like Kentucky, Maryland, and Delaware into compliance, but on finer points of the legal issues, principally whether to acknowledge the Court's amici offer. Finally, Pearsall asked Albert Coates, whose staff at the Institute of Government had prepared an extensive study of the issue, to speak to Umstead about the necessity to be heard. Before the deadline in the fall, the governor ordered McMullan to notify the Supreme Court that North Carolina would participate.[8]

The burdens of office were taking their toll on Umstead in the fall of 1954. He had never fully recovered from his heart attack of the previous year and remained frail and sickly, his condition made worse by his conscientious attention to a heavy workload. On a Thursday afternoon in early November, the governor left his office and took to his bed at the mansion. His doctor was called and ordered Umstead taken to Watts Hospital in Durham for treatment. Umstead's office announced that a severe cold had sapped the governor's strength and aggravated his heart condition.

Despite his hospitalization, Umstead was determined to carry on with his responsibilities and packed important papers and documents he needed into a scuffed leather briefcase that went with him to Durham. He never got to them. Friday and Saturday passed with little improvement in his condition, and on Sunday, November 7, he died of congestive heart failure at 9:10 A.M. His wife and daughter were at his bedside; he was fifty-nine years old.

Umstead's private secretary, Ed Rankin, arrived at the hospital at ten and after calling the wire services to notify them of the governor's passing, he next rang Luther Hodges, who was at his home in Leaksville preparing to attend morning church services. Two days later, immediately after Umstead's funeral on the ninth, Hodges took the oath and became governor.

Hodges arrived in Raleigh a stranger both to the office and to many of the people who had run state government for years; he had not escaped the relative obscurity that accompanied the office of lieutenant governor. During his first legislative session, he had been required to vote only once, and that was to break a tie in favor of a bill to require drivers to relinquish their licenses when convicted of speeding more than seventy miles an hour. Now he found himself in the midst of preparations for a legislative session where an additional $52 million in revenue was needed to balance the state's accounts.

Pearsall was determined to see the result of his committee's work receive immediate attention. Shortly after the new governor was sworn in, he briefed Hodges and reviewed the details of a report due for the 1955 General Assembly set to convene in January. Included in Pearsall's package was a collection of bills to eliminate statutory references to segregated education and to give the authority to assign students to local school boards.

Accompanying the legislation was a strongly worded resolution declaring that immediate integration was not wise. The governor announced that the plan had the endorsement of all members of Pearsall's committee, including the commission's black members, who had voted with the white majority despite pressure by the NAACP to abstain from doing so.[9]

This initial round of legislation included a new pupil assignment plan that became law less than two weeks before Lake rose to address the Supreme Court on April 12. The changes were patterned on similar legislation adopted in Alabama, where parents who wished school assignments different from those the local board offered were required to go through a complicated process that could take as much as two years to complete, making a mockery of legal due process. The effect of placing control in the local school board was to remove the state as a potential target for court-ordered desegregation. Those who would use the courts to enforce the Brown decision in North Carolina would have to deal one-by-one with 175 individual school districts.

The resolution from the committee was enthusiastically adopted by the legislature. Declaring that "the mixing of the races in the public schools within the state cannot be accomplished and if attempted would alienate public support of the schools to such an extent that they could not be operated successfully," it was hailed as a victory for segregationists. The resolution was little more than bluster, but it was considered a triumph for those who felt a rebuke of the Court was good for the soul. The original language had included the modifier "immediate" before the phrase "mixing of the races," but Hodges feared losing control of the legislature to the growing sentiment for massive resistance and even stronger obstructionist legislation. He finally consented to the change to avoid any more provocative debate.[10]

The new legislation became Lake's legal armor, the justification for his argument that the Court had overstepped its bounds. Lake's lean figure and severe expression were matched by his stark prediction of dire consequences if the Court ordered immediate implementation of its 1954 decision: "We start with the frank recognition of the indisputable fact that in North Carolina—contrary to the condition in Kansas—there the overwhelming majority of people regard that decision as a serious blow which they did not expect in view of the circumstances under which their schools are being operated. And the suggestion in the opinion that at this term that decision might be implemented by a decree requiring that Negro children be admitted forthwith to the schools of their choice has hung like a veritable sword of Damocles over the public schools of our state."[11]

Lake had been called to present North Carolina's case during the afternoon session, and Chief Justice Earl Warren recessed proceedings before

Lake's time had expired. The next morning, Lake resumed, quoting from the report of Pearsall's committee, which concluded, "The mixing of the races forthwith in the public schools throughout the state cannot be accomplished and should not be attempted." By the time he finished, Lake, who answered questions from his former law professor, Justice Felix Frankfurter, had summed up the state's position. First, North Carolina challenged the authority of the Court to require changes in the operation of a state's public schools. Next came the threat: If the Court did require immediate implementation, then whites would withdraw their children in droves and the base of public support for schools would be destroyed. In his closing, Lake issued a sweeping judgment on the state of racial relations back home, one that he would repeat time and again over the coming years as he became the leader of the segregationist chorus that was gaining in voice. Lake said race relations in North Carolina should be used as an example for the free world, and anything to disturb them would bring

> bitterness and antipathies unparalleled in our state since those terrible days which called forth the original KKK.
>
> The people of North Carolina are convinced that a segregated school system is a just school system, and the only practical school system for their state. That is not an opinion which originated on some tobacco road. That is an opinion which is justified by a century of experience, which has demonstrated the wisdom of this agreement reached a hundred years ago by carpetbaggers, the scalawags, the Negroes, and the handful of Confederate veterans who comprised the legislature which adopted the Fourteenth Amendment in the name of North Carolina.
>
> The people of North Carolina want to go on educating those 288,000 Negro children and their children's children, as well as the white people of the state, and we respectfully ask this Court not to make it impossible for them to do so.[12]

On May 31, 1955, the Supreme Court ordered that segregated school systems should be dismantled with "all deliberate speed." The imprecise language was a relief to Hodges, even though states like North Carolina were put on notice that although the Court would allow time for change, there was no mistake that desegregation was the ultimate goal. Still, Hodges and his advisors looked for wiggle room. Some told the governor they believed the Court would eventually reverse itself in later opinions and permit segregated schools. Others clung to the notion that what the Court meant was that a state could not force students into a dual system, but *Brown* did not require a state, or local school boards, to pursue a policy of integration.

A few weeks after the second *Brown* decision, Hodges created a new advisory committee, this time composed solely of legislators, and he asked Pearsall to continue as its leader. African Americans were purposely excluded this time; the governor said later they could not be "objective."[13] After its first meeting, the committee recommended to the governor that local school boards be asked to study the situation in their local districts, but recommended that no integration take place in the 1955–1956 school year.

The strategy taking shape in Hodges's office was novel, if not realistic. The governor, Pearsall, and otherwise reasonable people of influence remained convinced that blacks were just as upset as whites at the prospect of changing generations of habit and losing their own schools. White school officials had made it clear that they had no plans to put white students under the care of black teachers; thus, the changes would clearly cost black principals and teachers their jobs, which were positions of considerable influence with steady income in the community. With this threat to their educational structure, Hodges and others believed that black leaders would agree to voluntary segregation.

In an effort to test the viability of voluntary segregation, the governor invited ten prominent black businessmen, ministers, school personnel, and others to meet with Pearsall and his committee shortly after the May 31 decision was announced. The meeting was a bootless exercise and only demonstrated the vast gap in understanding between the races in North Carolina. Those invited to the meeting told the governor and his white entourage they wanted nothing less than immediate compliance with the Court's decision and full integration of the public schools.[14]

Lake sat in on the meeting and was fuming when he talked next with Pearsall and told him he was afraid no one was going to stand up to the NAACP, whose Legal Defense Fund had destroyed with its lawsuits what Southern politicians had successfully maintained for generations.[15] For Lake, the NAACP was a subversive element as evil as the Communist Party and was bent on destruction of the Southern way of life. He believed the organization was inciting North Carolina's otherwise docile African American population for its own aggrandizement. To Lake, each NAACP-funded lawsuit was a direct assault on the tattered remnants of the unsurrendered Confederate battle flag that had been handed down to him by his grandfather.

Three weeks after the meeting, Lake opened a personal campaign against the NAACP that would only intensify with time. In a speech to the Asheboro Lions Club on July 12 he said that the Supreme Court had, in effect, put control of the state's public schools at the mercy of the NAACP. Lake argued that because whites would not tolerate blacks in their schools—and would desert the schools rather than submit to integration — public education was now in the hands of an enemy who could choose where and when to next force integration. Speaking to a luncheon audience in the small Piedmont textile town, Lake said,

> We shall fight the NAACP county by county, city by city and if need be school by school and classroom by classroom to preserve our public schools as long as possible, while organizing and establishing other methods of educating our children.
>
> It will be a bitter and costly fight. We can also make it a costly one for our enemies, both foreign and domestic. We shall not surrender. We call upon our Negro neighbors to assist us in this fight to preserve their schools as well as ours.

Lake proposed that local citizens establish nonprofit corporations that would be ready to assume the operation of public schools, which would surely close when school districts were ordered to integrate: "So long as public schools are operated, the corporation would merely stand by. As soon as public schools in the community are closed, the corporation would be ready to move." The corporation could run these quasi-private schools, hire the teachers, and admit students it desired. Students who could not afford tuition could receive "scholarships" from state money, much the same as returning veterans had been educated under the GI Bill.[16]

Such plans already were being drafted in neighboring Virginia, where parents in the Prince Edward County schools were awaiting a decision that, when issued a few days after Lake's speech, required school officials to prepare a desegregation plan for the 1956–1957 school year. In the meantime, officials were told not to bar any African Americans who applied for admission in the coming school year.

Hodges was not happy that Lake had chosen to open a personal and public campaign. The governor wanted time to develop a response to the Court's latest order and hoped to avoid arousing the voters. Parents and others already were in enough of a stir without Lake's interference. Hodges knew that until he had a plan he could put forward, something that school officials and his administration could embrace, the opportunity lay open for a firebrand to take up the banner for massive resistance and wrest control of the issue from his hands.[17] From Hodges's vantage point, Lake appeared to be a ready and able leader of such a movement. And it appeared to lead to a gubernatorial campaign in 1956, when Hodges himself would be eligible for election to his own term in office. Lake had already let it be known he was leaving the attorney general's office to enter private practice when he made his Asheboro speech, and he certainly felt no allegiance to

Hodges, who had passed him over as a replacement for Attorney General Harry McMullan, who had died in June.

The day after news reports of Lake's speech reached the governor, he issued a brief statement saying that Lake was speaking for himself, as a private citizen, and his proposal was not official policy. The same statement came from Lake's new boss, Attorney General William B. Rodman Jr., although he told reporters he had not asked Lake to refrain from future public appearances. The same day Hodges released his statement, a Federal Appeals Court panel ordered the Summerton, South Carolina, school district to proceed "with all deliberate speed" to operate on a racially non-segregated basis.

Kelly Alexander, a Charlotte undertaker who was state president of the NAACP, could not let Lake's speech go unanswered. He sent telegrams to Hodges and Rodman demanding that Lake be fired. Alexander said Lake had "uttered remarks capable of inflaming race hatred and possibly inciting violence." [18]

Alexander and the NAACP knew Lake well. He had argued the state's segregationist position in the defense of the lawsuit filed by the NAACP against the University of North Carolina after the school had denied admission to three applicants from Durham's Hillside High School. As it had four years earlier in the law school case, the state lost the case on appeal, and the three black undergraduates were preparing to enroll at Chapel Hill that fall.

Alexander's telegram arrived over the weekend while the governor was in the mountains of North Carolina knee-deep in a trout stream. Two of his staff members, Ed Rankin and Paul Johnston, met in the governor's office on a Sunday morning and drafted an answer that they cleared with Hodges by telephone.[19] It embraced Lake; the governor said he would do all in his power to keep him in public office. And it took the NAACP to task: "I am amazed that this private organization, whose policies are determined in its national office in New York, and are obviously designed to split North Carolina citizens into racial camps, and which I am convinced does not actually represent any substantial portion of our Negro citizens, should have the effrontery to make such a request."

Hodges continued to speak on the matter that following Monday, when he told the *Asheville Citizen* that he believed North Carolina would "seriously consider" abolishing public schools rather than face mass integration, but he said he did not believe mass integration would ever be put into effect in the state. He said the push for integration is being brought "by a bunch of misguided white people in New York" and was not the wish of parents locally.[20]

Lake soon was repeating his Asheboro speech at other appearances.

Clearly enjoying his position at the center of the storm and as spokesman for the state's segregationists, he told the *News & Observer* that he had first proposed his plan for private operation of public schools to the state of Georgia in 1950 and had been perfecting it ever since. He said it was a reasonable approach, one that would prove to be "lawful . . . practical . . . peaceful." If public schools were closed in North Carolina it would be the fault of those pushing for integration. He said the loss of public schools would be the "greatest tragedy our state has suffered since the Reconstruction era. I earnestly hope the NAACP will not force it upon us."[21]

By the end of the summer Lake had settled into his new law firm and became coy and guarded in his remarks about a campaign for governor. He told reporters that though some had suggested he run for governor, he had not made up his mind. If he did run for governor, he knew that he could not use Hodges as his doormat. The governor's spirited response to Alexander and his own attack on the NAACP had left Lake little room to maneuver.

In his response to Alexander, Hodges said he would soon announce a detailed plan for North Carolina. It was clear that the governor remained convinced that voluntary segregation was the answer. He found comfort in this idea from legal advice from all across the state, including an opinion by Judge John J. Parker of Monroe, who was the chief judge of the Fourth Circuit Court of Appeals.

Parker had said in the rehearing of the Summerton case that the *Brown* decision did not require integration, it merely forbade discrimination. If blacks and whites chose to remain in their own schools, Hodges reasoned, then the state could be in compliance with the Court's decision and nothing would have changed. The Parker Plan, as it became known, was great comfort to leaders like Hodges who resented the Court's interference and were looking for some otherwise legitimate stand to forestall integration.

As for Parker, he sent word to Hodges by way of Charlotte author Harry Golden that Hodges should offer some hope to those expecting change. He suggested that the governor at least acknowledge that integration would begin in "some places tomorrow, in others next month, in others next year, but we will make a start to do the best we can first thing in the morning." Hodges rejected the judge's advice, saying that public pressure was simply too great.[22]

In early August, as parents and schoolchildren were enjoying the last weeks of their summer vacation, Hodges announced that he would make a statewide radio address on school desegregation. Raleigh was hot, unseasonably so, and temperatures in the state government offices had climbed to 105 and 110 when, on August 4, the governor said that he had recorded the longest speech of his term — thirty-six minutes — and that it would be heard the following Monday evening, August 8. He emphasized to reporters at his weekly news conference that his talk would include a special message for African American citizens.

The day after Hodges's press conference, Roy Wilkins, executive secretary of the NAACP, was speaking at a Palmer Memorial Institute meeting of the Presbyterian men of the Synod of Catawba (Negro) and he took note of the recent flap over Lake's speech:

> He [Lake] is using his high office to tell white people how to deny black people their rights before the law. We dare the Lakes and the Hodgeses and the State Board of Education and the Negro stooges over the state to let the people decide their fate. The people are far ahead of the politicians on this matter and the children and young people are far ahead of even their elders.
>
> Personally, I have been disillusioned about this state. I had come to believe, as had most of the United States, that your declaration that you were the "most progressive Southern state in race relations" was true . . . your whole state was thought to be liberal on the race question, and far ahead of the rest of the south. Yet on this public school question, Texas and Oklahoma and Arkansas are far ahead of you.[23]

Hodges's speech did nothing to change Wilkins's opinion. North Carolinians heard their governor promote voluntary segregation as the only way to save the state's system of public schools: "Let us realize with full knowledge that if we are not able to succeed in a program of voluntary separate school attendance, the state within the next year or so will be face to face with deciding the issue of whether it shall have some form of integrated public schools or shall abandon its public schools." Sounding as combative as Lake, Hodges continued his war on the NAACP. African Americans should be proud of their culture, their heritage, and their public schools, the governor said. He argued that his quarrel was not with the state's black citizens, but with the NAACP, which

> has used every means at its command to convince you that you cannot develop your own culture within your own race and therefore that you must be ashamed of your color and your history by burying it in the development of the white race. In short, this organization would destroy your identity as a race.
>
> And so my earnest request of you Negro citizens of North Carolina is this: Do not allow any militant and selfish organization to stampede you into refusal to go along with this program.[24]

Near the conclusion of his address, Hodges announced a telephone number in Raleigh that parents and local school officials could call to request materials and technical support for developing a voluntarily segregated system. Hodges closed with a reminder that he stood as firmly as any Southern segregationist in the belief "that a system of separate schools for the races is in the best interest of us all and I pledge to you that I will exert every effort to maintain such a system."

Hodges's aide, Paul Johnston, reported the following day that public response was two to one in favor of the governor's plan. Even the *News & Observer* endorsed his program, calling it "Southern leadership at its best. It is a program which could be undertaken in full recognition of the dignity of both races. It is a proposal which involved no loud and impotent defiance of law. It is one which could assure the advance in education of both races and continue the good relations between both races in North Carolina." [25]

As expected, the loudest objections came from the NAACP's Alexander, who said that Hodges

> did not recognize any evidence of a plan or program acceptable to the freedom-loving Negroes of North Carolina to desegregate public schools.
>
> Our interpretation of the governor's address is an appeal to the Negroes of North Carolina to compromise on their fundamental constitutional rights; to forget they are citizens and their rights as citizens and appeal for them to delay in enforcing their constitutionally protected rights in the field of public education. For a high state official to encourage the continuation of public schools as they now exist on a segregated basis is not acting in good faith but contrary to the law of the land.[26]

The governor also drew criticism from a small but vocal liberal white element. Noted playwright Paul Green of Chapel Hill wrote Hodges that he was disappointed that his governor had joined the "old familiar message of a reactionary South. True, the job of carrying forward, however slowly, but still carrying forward, the challenging directive of the U.S. Supreme Court is a tough one. We all know that. But men grow great on tough jobs and so do states and nations." [27]

Hodges remained undeterred. He was so confident of the soundness of his plan, and its acceptance by African Americans, that he was shocked and deeply offended when a few weeks later the student body at Greensboro's A&T College interrupted his speech with a noticeable and deliberate shuffling of feet. The governor and most in public office discounted the expressions of the NAACP and the few leaders who were bold enough, or independent enough, to say what most African Americans believed: that it was past time for the state to honor the Supreme Court's 1954 decision.

Each time white leaders such as Hodges targeted the NAACP with their attacks, they demonstrated to African Americans just how far they were removed from blacks' world. North Carolina had one of the fastest-growing NAACP organizations in the nation. Alexander had been working since 1940 when he reorganized the dormant Charlotte chapter and subsequently became state president in 1948. Since 1950, he had been a member of the NAACP's national board. By 1955, he had organized eighty-three chapters and claimed more than ten thousand members. Alexander was the most admired among the state's black leaders, and school integration was the most important issue on the agenda of black citizens.[28]

Hodges and most white political leaders had little experience with the general black community's loyalty to the NAACP. The African Americans they called upon for advice knew better than to acknowledge sympathy for, much less membership in, the NAACP. Bluford, the conservative and autocratic president of A&T College in Greensboro, had survived in a "go-along-to-get-along" world and was not willing to risk his standing or funding for his school. Both he and Seabrook, who came from the same generation, tolerated little dissent in their faculties and membership in the NAACP was discouraged.[29]

Throughout the spring and summer of 1955, Terry Sanford had watched the unfolding of events as had every other parent whose children were caught in this upheaval in the Southern way of life. Terry believed he held a progressive, even liberal, attitude on race that was founded in both the compassion he had learned at home in Laurinburg and the quiet preachments of Frank Graham. There had been no epiphanic experience that reversed generations of prejudice; rather, his attitudes had been shaped by a series of small but meaningful incidents. He remembered the black man he had worked with at the grocery store in Laurinburg whose complaint about Jim Crow laws had stirred his conscience. He would never forget Frank Graham's inquiry about serving African Americans at table in Chapel Hill. He also could not forget an exchange in the summer of 1946 while he was preparing to take the state bar examination. He had encountered a black law student who accused him of slurring his pronunciation of "Negro," producing the disrespectful "nigra," which was little more than a Southern parlor version of "nigger." Terry confessed that he talked like a field hand and also mispronounced words like tomato and potato. But he was embarrassed, nonetheless, and improved his diction.

Terry lived as naturally in the "oddly intimate remoteness" of the races, as one writer called it, as any of his contemporaries.[30] He perhaps questioned the way things were, but at the same time he accepted them. The traditions and customs of the Old South were simply a part of everyday life in Fayetteville. Schools, churches, neighborhoods, bus seats, public facilities were all strictly segregated. Even the benches for waiting bus riders were set aside, white and colored, and doctors and dentists maintained separate patient waiting rooms. One of the leading department stores on Hay Street, which depended on black as well as white trade, maintained a bank of four water fountains; there were white and colored outlets for adults, and white and colored outlets for children. The array was such a strange sight to black soldiers serving their first stint in the South that they brought cameras into the store to snap pictures to send to disbelieving friends and relatives back home.[31]

In the summer of 1954, a few weeks after the *Brown* decision, Terry had made a gesture in behalf of advancing the Court's decision. He was attending the annual conference of North Carolina Methodists meeting in Fayetteville when he proposed a resolution to require that Duke University, nominally a Methodist institution, admit black students to its student body. Racial barriers were falling at state campuses, and the Presbyterians had opened their doors; Duke should do the same, he reasoned. The resolution failed, but passage would have not changed life on the campus. Terry learned just how little control the Methodist hierarchy actually had over the university that would later become a part of his life: even if the resolution had passed, it would have had no binding effect on Duke.

Fayetteville was different from most Southern towns in at least one important respect. Fort Bragg, just a dozen miles away, was an outpost of racial integration. Following President Truman's orders, the military had begun desegregating its units one by one. At Bragg, the post commander had dropped racial designations for housing and schools, and by 1951 children of servicemen in onpost schools were attending integrated classes. The Fort Bragg Officers Club was the only restaurant in the region where whites and blacks could be seated and served in the same room. Cumberland County civilians may have noticed that white and black MPs patrolled the soldier bars and hangouts in town, but, for the most part, affairs on this federal reserve were treated as if they were in another world.

Like other Fayetteville attorneys, Terry handled legal matters for clients on the post. That is where he met Harry Groves, then a second lieutenant in the Judge Advocate General Corps. Groves had been raised in Colorado, where he and his family were the only people of color in the entire town. He was a Phi Beta Kappa graduate of the University of Colorado and had earned his law degree at the University of Chicago before he was recalled to active duty during the Korean War and assigned to Fort Bragg in 1950. He was an artillery officer but requested a transfer to the JAG office. When he was released from active duty in 1951, he settled in Fayetteville and hung his shingle outside a small office over a small Greek restaurant on Gillespie

Street, a couple of blocks from the courthouse. He was the only black attorney in town, and he was successful from his first day, thanks in part to his Army contacts. In time, however, he even recruited a few white clients, which startled some in the Cumberland County courthouse.

Groves was impatient with the attitude of most African Americans he met in Fayetteville, but he realized that he was more aggressive than most, more impatient than most, and blessed with talents that allowed more freedom than most. He found some relief with a small group of other men of similar age, attitude, and situation. Included were better-educated, advantaged men such as an undertaker, a couple of doctors, a dentist, and a dean at Fayetteville Teachers State College who was a grandson of the nineteenth-century leader Frederick Douglass. They called themselves the Townsmen and together believed they could move African Americans to take greater control of their lives. The group met regularly over dinner to talk about issues important to their community. Sometimes Groves invited them to the Fort Bragg Officers Club for a rare experience of integrated dining; at other times, they would meet at a private home on the outskirts of town where a woman served sumptuous meals to small groups.

Groves liked Terry. Their paths had crossed once or twice on post and Groves had formed a good opinion of him; he believed him to be fair and decent and more liberal than most of the white lawyers he knew. When Terry was running for the state senate in 1952, Groves asked him to have dinner with the Townsmen to talk about political matters. Terry did not give Groves an answer immediately; later, Terry said he would like to meet the group, but he could not dine with them. Groves resented Terry's response. Yet, when he told the Townsmen their guest wouldn't be coming to dinner he learned his friends were not surprised. In fact, they thought Groves's offer was one that only a non-Southern black man would ever consider posing. "I understood it too," Groves said some years later, "because he had to win white votes and in that blacks could not have elected him. We could vote for him. We couldn't elect him. I guess he thought it would just cause him to lose the race."[32]

In the summer of 1955, as Terry considered his own future, he didn't have any answers to the issue of school desegregation, but he found the level of the rhetoric disturbing. Shortly after Hodges's exchange with Alexander, he stopped by the governor's office and asked Ed Rankin to pass word to Hodges that he should not join Lake in trench warfare against the NAACP.[33]

Hodges wasn't quite sure what to make of the young lawyer from Fayetteville. He was aware of Sanford's political ambitions and had heard the speculation that he might run for governor. "He thought I was a young upstart," Sanford later said. "I had never been one of his loyal supporters. In all fairness, I had never been. I sort of wanted to be. I think he saw me as a smart aleck." [34]

A few days before Lake's speech, Raleigh radio reporter Phil Ellis had broadcast a story saying that it appeared Terry was a candidate for governor. Ellis quoted Bruce Poole, comanager of the Wake County campaign for Kerr Scott, as saying "I haven't talked to him within the last few days but I am sure he will be a candidate, and I am just as sure that he will win." [35]

There was no question Terry was eager to run. He had begun early to cultivate news reporters around the state. While he was still a state senator, he had called Julian Scheer, who had recently moved from covering sports to writing a daily column for the *Charlotte News*, and asked if they could get together on his next trip to Charlotte. Scheer didn't know Sanford, had never even been to Raleigh, and was caught completely off guard. His usual range of columns included light pieces about folks in and around Charlotte and he was more accustomed to phone calls from irate coaches or sports publicity agents. Politicians did not call. He never forgot that Terry was among the first politicians to learn his telephone number.

A few days later, Sanford and Scheer were seated in a coffee shop across from the *News* building. Scheer liked what he saw and heard. Here was a young man—Terry was thirty-seven—but he talked with the maturity and deliberate and thoughtful measure of someone older. He didn't have pat answers and Scheer found soundness in Sanford's logic. Scheer also succumbed to Sanford's innate ability to draw a person, even someone he had just met, into his confidence. "I sensed I wanted to confide in him," Scheer recalled many years later, "but I didn't have anything to confide." [36]

Throughout the spring and summer of 1955, Terry had listened to encouragement from Ben Roney and Roy Wilder in Senator Scott's office. They were eager for him to run, and so was Scott. The senator had even given him his first campaign contribution, a crisp dollar bill. From time to time, Terry used the rail pass provided by one of his law firm's clients, the Atlantic Coast Line railroad, to board the northbound train at Fayetteville, pay an extra $12 for a Pullman berth, and arrive in Washington the next morning in time for breakfast with Scott or Roney. He would spend the day on Capitol Hill talking politics and meeting people. His first encounter with a tall Texan named Lyndon Johnson was late one afternoon when Scott took him by the Senate majority leader's office and introduced him. Johnson impressed him immediately. "You couldn't help but admire this big rough fellow who was getting things done," Sanford said some years later. "He was getting along with Ike and still maintaining the principles of the Democratic Party. He was not just submitting to Eisenhower." [37]

After a day in Washington, Terry usually took the southbound train home so he could arrive in Fayetteville the next morning, in time to meet his law partners at the office. On one trip in the summer of 1955, he spent the evening in a huddle with Roney and Wilder. The threesome found a corner in the bar at the National Press Club on 14th and F Streets, where they remained until closing time. To remain sociable while Roney and Wilder downed their usual quota, Terry sipped crème de menthe. He had never been much of a drinker, though he was beginning to acquire a taste for the occasional martini with a twist of lemon that Wilder introduced him to.

Terry was not committed to a campaign when he left Washington for home. Certainly, everything he had done so far was a prelude to a statewide campaign in 1956. Managing Scott's effort in 1954 had put him in touch with local politicians across the state. News reporters and editors now knew his name. He believed he could count on Scott's Branch-head boys, the Frank Graham crowd, his contacts in the Methodist Church, and his own following among young political leaders. The unknown was Hodges.

Umstead's death had thoroughly fouled Terry's plans, as well as others' in the state. North Carolina politics was a ladder-climbing event; virtually all the state's governors had started at the bottom rung and moved up from one office to the other. Whenever something unexpected happened, the system broke down. Now, neither Terry nor anyone, for that matter, seemed to know how to read Hodges, who had bypassed all the usual rungs and moved to the top. At times, Hodges could be terribly aloof and disdainful of the cozy familiarity of politics, yet he displayed the instincts of a pro. He listened to no one in particular, and the party faithful were scornful of his penchant for appointing Republicans to political jobs. Terry believed he knew how to run against the Old Guard, the conservatives whom Scott had beaten two times out of three, but Hodges? "I was very uneasy about his cleverness," Sanford recalled some years later, "and I knew that if I got beat, I would probably be through." [38]

The challenge of the state's direction in integration also loomed large. The next election could well turn on this one issue. If Hodges and Lake were in the race, the only place for another candidate was across the divide in favor of the Supreme Court's decision. It didn't take a genius to know that being on the "wrong" side of that issue would not play.

Finally, Terry decided that 1956 was not to be his year, and he sent Roney a message telling him of his decision. It was a sarcastic note: "Believe I will let Liverlips and Huckleberry Finn dance the interposition waltz while I wait at the Peace and Quiet Cafe." It was signed "Tare," which was what "Terry" sounded like after it was massaged by Roney's eastern North Carolina accent. [39]

Not long afterward, Terry heard from Scott, who asked to meet him in Haw River the following weekend. When Terry arrived at the farm he found Scott, B. Everett Jordan, and Jordan's brother, Dr. Henry Jordan, a dentist who had been one of the mainstays in Scott's administration in Raleigh. Terry was surprised to find the three together in light of Scott's tangle with Jordan three years earlier. He was even more surprised when the senator told him they were interested in running Henry for governor in 1956.

It wasn't that Terry questioned Henry Jordan's credentials as a candidate. He had chaired Scott's highway commission and had successfully campaigned across the state for Scott's $200 million road bond issue. But why does Henry want to run? he asked. The three convinced Terry that Henry Jordan's campaign was a way to head off Luther Hodges and prevent him from using another four years as governor as a launching pad for a contest with Scott in 1960. It was better to stop him now, they reasoned, rather than wait until he had been chief executive of the state after an unprecedented tenure.

What Terry found mystifying was Everett's enthusiasm for his brother's campaign. Everett Jordan had been one of those who had encouraged Hodges to run for lieutenant governor in 1952. The two were old friends, even business partners. Terry also had not forgotten the episode at the 1952 convention. "But you have never been for Governor Scott," Terry told Jordan. "I am now," Jordan replied.[40]

Terry told the group he didn't believe Hodges wanted to go to the Senate, and if that was the only reason for Henry to run then he thought he could settle the matter with a visit to the governor. A few days later, Terry and Bill Staton called on Hodges and asked him about his political plans. The governor heard them out and answered with a qualified no. He said he wouldn't rule out a race against Scott but he had no real desire to join the Senate. Henry wasn't satisfied with Hodges's answer and asked Terry to begin putting together a campaign.

If the Jordans were committed, Terry had no doubt the result could be formidable. North Carolina's one-party politics had always turned on alliances with local factions in the Democratic organization. A campaign could be won or lost by the width and breadth of commitments from party leaders of all stripes. The Jordans knew the men whose word and endorsement accounted for hundreds if not thousands of votes across the state. Throughout the fall, Sanford and Jordan rode across the state trying to turn these local wheelhorses into a column of strength.

Hodges was taking nothing for granted. He maintained a busy schedule during the latter part of 1955. On one trip through Fayetteville he called Sanford and asked him to meet for coffee at the Howard Johnson's restaurant on U.S. 301. When Terry arrived he found the governor settled into a corner booth. After he sat down, Hodges asked, "Why are you against me?"

"Now, governor," Terry began, "I am not against you. I am just for Henry Jordan. He is my friend and I am pledged to support him."

The two talked for a bit about the race, but settled nothing. Terry reminded Hodges of their earlier conversation and told him if there was something more to be said about 1960 then he could arrange for Jordan and Hodges to get together and talk. The two parted.[41]

Over the next few days, as Terry talked with Jordan, he sensed a growing vagueness about the financial support that he had been promised by his brother. Finally, over lunch one day shortly after the first of the year, Henry reported he was not going to be a candidate. He made a formal announcement on January 10 from his home at Cedar Falls.

Jordan's change of heart caught Terry totally unprepared. He had committed himself to Jordan's campaign, flatly taking himself out of the race in early January when reporters had asked about his own plans. Now he had no candidate, it was too late to reorganize for his own sake, and he was crossed up with a governor who faced no real opposition to four more years in office. Terry was upset with Jordan, who offered no explanation for his decision, and he was angry at himself for ignoring earlier signs that were perfectly obvious now. In December, when Terry had tried to hire Kays Gary, a popular columnist with the *Charlotte Observer*, as Jordan's press agent, Gary had considered it but declined, telling Terry he found Jordan too indefinite about his plans to throw over a prime writing job with one of the state's largest newspapers.

For the first time in his political career, Terry felt he had jumped from an airplane without a parachute. He was frustrated, angry, and hurt and began rethinking his earlier plans to run. He knew it was a long shot. North Carolina, with its one-term restriction on governors, had never seen a campaign against an incumbent.

The filing deadline for the spring primaries fell on a Friday, March 16. When it arrived, Sanford was still wrestling with his decision. That morning the air was cold and the skies threatening rain when he and Dickson Phillips left Fayetteville for a two-and-a-half-hour ride to Raleigh. He still might just file for governor; at any rate, he didn't want to be sitting in Fayetteville at 11 A.M. with no time to get to Raleigh if the spirit moved him. When the two arrived in Raleigh they stopped at the Carolina Hotel, where the manager knew Terry, and he cashed a check to cover the $150 filing fee.

Only a few minutes remained before the books closed at noon, yet Terry was no closer to a decision than when he left home. He suggested to Phillips that they walk around the block and if nothing happened to stop them, then he was ready to take his shot at a campaign for governor and gamble the political chips he had accumulated during the past eight years. They stepped off and turned the corner only to run into Stacy Weaver, a prominent Methodist layman, educator, and father of their law partner. "He talked and talked," Sanford later recalled, "and I looked at Dick Phillips and said, 'I think the Lord has intervened.'"

Sanford and Phillips forgot the Elections Board office and walked across Capitol Square to the governor's office. The two were sitting with Hodges, the cash for the filing fee neatly folded in Terry's pocket, when the governor's political advisor, Harold Makepeace, interrupted their visit to tell Hodges that he would face no substantial opposition in the spring primary. On his way back to Fayetteville, Terry recalled his lesson from the river. He had let the last good campsite pass, and there wasn't enough time to find another before dark.[42]

Some said a trio of hurricanes in the late summer and early fall of 1955 helped Hodges win the Democratic Party nomination for governor. As soon as the warning flags for Hurricanes Connie, Diane, and Iona were down and it was safe to travel, Hodges pulled on his rain gear and headed to the coast to survey the damage. Seldom had voters seen a governor in this venue, and Hodges's publicity man, Hugh Morton of Wilmington, made the most of it. An accomplished promoter and amateur photographer, Morton fed pictures of the governor at the disaster scene to the major daily newspapers, winning for himself a prize for one shot of reporter Julian Scher bent double and struggling to walk against a howling wind.

Hodges's success, of course, was due to more than that. During his first year in office he had been an enthusiastic chief executive who had turned in a solid performance, pushing forward all of the programs Umstead had prepared before his death. He had even been bold enough to ask for a modest tax on tobacco, but when revenue projections proved higher than expected he settled for increased taxes on beer and whiskey instead. He had suffered no serious missteps, and voters seemed to accept his years in business as a ready substitute for public service. He was the first corporate executive since the 1920s to hold the job that most often had been occupied by lawyers.

Hodges won good reports for his program, plus he looked the part of a chief executive. His energy and stature were certainly in distinct contrast to his sickly predecessor. Hodges stood a little better than average height, but his broad shoulders and sturdy build suggested someone much taller. He had an expressive face accented by a wide, deep smile, bushy eyebrows, and heavy jowls. His hair was gray and lay flat over his prominent forehead. He was perhaps the most urbane and sophisticated governor since O. Max Gardner, thanks to his years with one of the nation's largest retailers, which had shown much of the world to a lad born before the turn of the century in a ramshackle tenant house on a Virginia tobacco farm a few miles from the Carolina line. He also was one of the first to see the office as a step toward national office.

There was little doubt that Hodges would run for a full term; he announced his intentions on February 5, 1956, at a testimonial dinner in his honor in Leaksville, the textile town where he had begun his business career with Marshall Fields. Among the well-wishers who filled the hall was Henry Jordan. Kerr Scott did not attend, but he sent along a telegram of appreciation, as did other major party figures. Senator Sam Ervin Jr. gave an unqualified endorsement. A week later Hodges walked quietly into the state Board of Elections office and paid his filing fee. There were no reporters, no cameras, no fanfare. "It was just a case of a man parting with $150," one newspaper reported.[43]

Later, Hodges wrote that the only thing that gave him pause about running was a concern that an opponent would raise the race issue to a level of intensity that would be an embarrassment to the state. One minor candidate who filed for the office did claim he would challenge Hodges's record on integration, but little was heard from him after filing day. Hodges easily overwhelmed three opponents with 85 percent of the primary election vote and became the first sitting governor to be elected to the office in sixty years. His was such an effortless victory that when it was over he told his campaign manager to return the unused portion of his campaign fund, which amounted to about one-fourth of the $30,000 that had been raised on his behalf.[44]

Reflecting some years later on his impulse to run for governor in 1956, Sanford said he was glad he had pulled up short. He was not ready, not mature enough, he said, to take on both the challenge of unseating an incumbent and the dicey issue of school integration, which in the spring produced violent reaction across the South. In Alabama, a mob of students attacked Autherine Lucey as she attempted to enroll at the University of Alabama, and unknown assailants set off a bomb at the home of Dr. Martin Luther King Jr.[45]

The race issue simmered just below the surface in North Carolina. The spring primaries offered a demonstration of what could happen to officeholders who strayed too far from the prevailing point of view. Incumbent Congressmen Thurmond Chatham from the Fifth District and Charles B. Deane from the Eighth were defeated in their bids for renomination. Both had refused to sign the so-called Southern Manifesto that circulated among congressional delegations from eleven Southern states. The signers pledged resistance, by all legal means, to the Supreme Court's decision. One of Terry's friends in Winston-Salem wrote of Chatham's defeat, "Some folks thought he liked the Negro to [sic] much." [46] At the same time, however, Second District Representative Harold Cooley survived a challenge even though his name also was missing from the symbolic statement. Cooley retained his seat with a campaign of opposition to the Court's decision.

The massive resistance movement was taking hold in state capitols across the South. By the end of March 1956, at least forty-two pro-segregation measures had been recorded in Alabama, Georgia, Mississippi, South Carolina, and Virginia. White officeholders were using every device at hand to stall the NAACP's push for immediate integration. The organization was outlawed in Alabama, Louisiana, and Texas, and in Georgia investigators raided the chapter offices. The South Carolina legislature asked the U.S. Attorney General to put the group on the list of subversive organizations. In Virginia, the legislature passed seven laws designed to hamper the organization in raising money, arranging lawsuits, and engaging in "activities [that might] cause or tend to cause racial conflicts or violence." [47] One survey showed that at the first of the year there were at least 568 local pro-segregation organizations in the South, claiming a membership of two hundred thousand, nearly all of it in a few major organizations of which the White Citizens Councils were by far the largest. South Carolina claimed forty thousand members, Mississippi seventy-five thousand, Georgia sixty thousand, and Louisiana twenty thousand. A group called the Patriots of North Carolina was founded in May 1956 and included in its membership three former speakers of the state house, a university trustee, and other political figures of note. Their most often quoted public champion was former state senator Julian Allsbrook of Halifax County, who had been defeated in his bid for reelection by one of Sanford's friends, Lunsford Crew.

Harold Fleming, head of the Southern Regional Council in Atlanta, an organization dedicated to improving race relations and committed to desegregation, told writer John B. Martin the price was high for those who spoke out against prevailing segregationist attitudes: "You may lose your job or your chance for advancement. Your children may suffer—your neighbors won't let their kids play with yours. It may be rumored that you're a communist because you've been 'known to mix and mingle.' You develop a sense of alienation, which is the highest price of all—you feel alienated from the society in which you live. Very few people are so dedicated they are willing to pay this price. The opinion makers—businessmen, civic leaders, preachers, educators, politicians, newspaper editorial writers—all have forfeited leadership. Very few will say anything on this subject. They don't want to pay the price."[48]

North Carolinians of both races watched closely the unfolding events just across the state's borders, where two of the three cases decided in *Brown* had arisen. Now the governors of Virginia and South Carolina along with the chief executives of Georgia and Mississippi were embracing the nineteenth-century idea of interposition, which held that a state could nullify a Supreme Court decision. Serious arguments were being heard anew for this long-discredited doctrine that most considered settled by the outcome of the Civil War.

More alarming to parents and educators was reaction to the Court's orders directing implementation of *Brown* in the public schools of Prince Edward County, Virginia, a quiet farming region that was only a three-hour drive from Raleigh. In response to the Court's order to integrate, Virginia voters had approved by a two-to-one margin a constitutional amendment to permit payment of state funds as tuition for privately operated schools. At the same time, Prince Edward County parents were raising money locally to take over the public schools in a fashion quite similar to what I. Beverly Lake had proposed a year before. Public schools were about to disappear in Prince Edward County.[49]

Hodges avoided alliances with the governors and others preaching interposition and massive resistance, though he didn't condemn those who did. At his testimonial dinner, he told reporters he had often talked with Virginia's Governor Stanley, whose home was not far from his own homeplace just across the state line in Pittsylvania County. Hodges was searching for a plan that he could embrace and stay with. He had defended Lake when the NAACP complained, but few weeks later had said Lake's plan for tuition grants was only a "last-ditch effort." The man he named attorney general, William Rodman, had gone even further in dismissing Lake's idea of a system of public-private schools, telling a gathering of county officials in August 1955 that such a notion would never pass constitutional muster.[50] A study of the alternatives open to the state following *Brown*, put together by Albert Coates's staff at the Institute of Government, suggested the same thing, but the report was careful to draw no conclusions.[51]

At his announcement party in February, Hodges moved his position again, shifting himself closer to the hard-line segregationists. He said that if voluntary segregation didn't work, then it was time for "legislation which will provide tuition grants or transfers along the general lines of the Virginia plan."[52] By late spring he was preparing for a special session of the General Assembly in July, when legislators would consider a package of bills being put together by the second Pearsall committee to implement a strategy that in some ways was more extreme than that adopted in Virginia. Both plans provided tuition payments to parents who refused to send their children to integrated schools, but they diverged on the issue of local options. Pearsall's plan called for a constitutional change to allow local boards to close schools. The Virginia plan did not. One Virginia lawmaker told the *News & Observer* he believed a school-closing provision was not included because writers feared voter reaction: "The people would think we were out to destroy the public schools." Woodrow Price reported, "Apparently the Pearsall committee had no such qualms about North Carolina."[53]

Indeed, the cry "Save the schools" would soon become the slogan of proponents of the Pearsall Plan, replacing the earlier refrain "Preserve the schools." The two were close in meaning, but it was a time when people dwelled long on the meaning of even the simplest of words. Elizabeth Pearsall had lobbied her husband to discard "preserve" because she believed "save" lent greater urgency to the task at hand.[54]

Yet, for all the work and public bluster against *Brown*, those who crafted the plan acknowledged privately that the Pearsall Plan was little more than a device that would only postpone, not preclude, the integration of North Carolina's schools. Reviewing those days five years after the plan was proposed, Hodges's chief aide, Paul Johnston, said, "It was something to slow down the effect of the Supreme Court decision so that it didn't destroy our schools. That's really what it was. But so many of the legislators would take an attitude that this was purely for segregation purposes when they knew in their hearts, and they would say in private or they would illustrate one way or the other, that they knew very well that they were passing something to accommodate the decision."[55] In all truth, Hodges, Pearsall, and others in the inner circle doubted the school-closing provisions would ever be used. To gain the endorsement of one important educator, Dallas Herring of Rose Hill, Hodges had promised that he would do everything he could to prevent such a thing from happening.[56]

Pearsall and his committee carefully prepped legislators for the upcoming session, paying particular attention to incumbents in hopes of discouraging any firebrands from suggesting radical alternatives. The governor and Pearsall conducted these briefings in out-of-the-way locations that were guarded by state troopers who kept reporters at a distance. One by one, the leadership fell into step, including such hard-line segregationists as Senator John Kerr of Warrenton, a legislative veteran who later joked that when he gave his approval to the plan he became "Hodges' bell goat."[57]

The Pearsall Plan was ingenious in that it seemed to satisfy a majority of white North Carolinians. Segregationists endorsed it because it gave them something specific to show that they were prepared to keep black students out of white schools if lawsuits forced local boards to integrate. Moderates liked the plan because it left local school boards the option to integrate when they thought best. Of course, those who believed immediate integration was the answer took no comfort in it at all, but the scattering of whites who held to this view, along with the state's African Americans—who composed roughly one-fourth of the state's population—were basically discounted as out of touch with reality in the discussions held behind closed doors.

The state Democratic Party convention in late May demonstrated just how serious a grip the segregationists held on the state's political leaders. The platform committee was chaired by the Patriots' spokesman, Julian Allsbrook, who declared his support of a plank upholding segregation, saying the "fundamental issue is whether the Anglo-Saxon race is to become a mongrel race." Millard Barbee, a labor leader from Durham, warned that the party's continued appeal to segregationists would alienate African American voters who had embraced the party under Franklin Roosevelt. John Kerr roared back that the party had better think about working-class whites in the textile mills and on the farms.[58] The committee approved the strongly worded language condemning the Court and pledging resistance, but there were dissenting votes. One was cast by Barbee and another by Sam J. Ervin III, the senator's son.

Hodges steered clear of such internal debate and remained focused on the main event of the summer, the special session that was due to convene on July 23. The session opened with formalities on Monday at noon, and that night Hodges spoke to a joint session. It was only the fifth time in the state's modern history that legislators had met outside of their routine biennial schedule, and when Hodges stepped to the well in the house chamber, the hall was packed from the floor to the galleries, where temperatures were over ninety degrees. The governor laid out the details of the plan as its namesake paced back and forth behind the rostrum. From time to time, a baby wailed from the gallery audience. "We are not going to defy the Court," Hodges said, "but . . . we are going to use every legal means we can devise to insure that the effects of what we feel is an erroneous decision by the Supreme Court are not forced on our state in a fashion which would deprive us of one of our dearest possessions, namely our public schools."

Hodges's speech was well received. Legislators gave the governor a lengthy round of applause when he told them, "I do not agree with the Supreme Court decision. I do not favor integration. I believe the majority of white and Negro people of the state feel the same way. Anyone who says otherwise is twisting the truth."[59]

The session resumed with hearings the following morning and proved to be a model of decorum and public access. For the first time, the proceedings were broadcast live by University of North Carolina television cameras. Prior to the session, UNC President Bill Friday had convinced Lieutenant Governor Luther Barnhardt and House Speaker Larry Moore that the issue was too important to pass unrecorded. The two leaders had reluctantly agreed to allow cameras in the chambers only after they were given assurances that on a signal from Moore (a handkerchief dropped from his pocket) the broadcast would go off the air. Once the coverage began, Friday believed that would never happen. He was confident that neither politician wanted to be known as the one who blacked out television screens across the state at a crucial moment in history.[60]

The session had all the appearances of a lesson in the legislative process. On the first day, speakers of all opinions took the podium. Notable among the opponents was a Duke University Law School professor, Dr. Douglas B. Maggs, a specialist in constitutional law, who said the Pearsall Plan would never win the approval of the Supreme Court. Maggs said he endorsed a proposal by Irving Carlyle, who had urged North Carolina to begin integration at the lower grades. The Pearsall Plan was not a valid answer, said Maggs: "What the state has lacked is the leadership to persuade the people they must accept the inevitable."[61]

Speakers were given only twenty minutes each, but legislators kept Maggs at the microphone for more than an hour dealing with belittling questions, such as whether his residence in California twenty-seven years earlier had somehow clouded his legal judgment. Later, opponents challenged his credentials by suggesting he was associated with communists. Maggs was followed by others who also opposed the plan, including the president of the state Parent-Teacher Association Congress, Mrs. John Crawford of Raleigh. She argued that the provisions for tuition support to students who refused to go to integrated schools would drain needed money from public schools. State Senator Clarence Stone told a reporter the PTA "should stick to flower gardens and window shades."[62]

Testimony from black churchmen and community leaders was restrained and aimed more at the broader issues of segregation than at the specifics of the Pearsall Plan. John H. Wheeler, a Durham banker who spoke for a committee with representatives from all the state's counties, said, "We come today offering our counsel and pledging patience and understanding in any effort which is designed to place the operation of our public schools system in compliance with the requirement of the Supreme Court decision that we shall make a prompt and reasonable step toward full compliance." The Right Reverend Frank M. Reid of Kittrell argued that North Carolina should join the thirty-one states that have practiced "pure democracy" in their schools and urged a freedom-of-choice plan.[63] Members of the legislative committee sat through these presentations in silence and asked no questions.

Pearsall was pessimistic as the first round of hearings continued well into the night. He was not concerned about the shifting of votes; he and the governor believed they had more than they needed for passage. But he worried that statements from Maggs and others might leave some parents and local community leaders disturbed at the viability of the plan and encourage legislators to suggest alternatives.

Paul Johnston from Hodges's office moved into the Sir Walter Hotel for the duration of the session. When he arrived in the hotel lobby after the first day of hearings he found members furious over statements by Maggs and others. Some were talking of joining a rump group that had rallied around a bill prepared by I. Beverly Lake. Lake's bill had been introduced by Representative Byrd Satterfield of Roxboro in the house and in the senate by one of his former law students, Robert Morgan, who was a popular young politician from Harnett County. Senator Ralph Scott also was staked out in favor of Lake's proposal. Hodges worried that Scott's political organization could further unsettle matters out in the rural precincts.

Further confusing the issue was disagreement from within the Pearsall committee's own ranks. Pearsall had to furlough the committee's lawyer, a young attorney named Tom Ellis, after Ellis began to work against the Pearsall Plan in favor of more obstructionist measures such as those embodied in the Lake bill. At one point, Ellis and the committee's other staff lawyer, W. W. Taylor, produced a statement claiming that "the public schools of North Carolina had served their purposes, they were through and we had just as well start looking for another means of educating the children of North Carolina." [64]

The most significant difference between the Pearsall and Lake plans was that Lake's proposed amendment to the constitution would strip the requirement of a system of public schools in North Carolina; he would leave to the General Assembly the question of whether the state maintained any schools. Moving from spot to spot, Johnston didn't get to bed until just before dawn — "I never did so much talking in all my life," Johnston later recalled — as he fought to keep the members in line and focused on the Pearsall Plan.[65]

For those closest to the battle, it was not a fight over how to integrate schools, but rather which option would be most likely to discourage black students from attending white schools and to accommodate whites, who many believed would flee public schools for private. Lake's plan clearly would have more easily facilitated public financing of private schools, as the state would be relieved of a constitutional mandate to operate public schools.

Pearsall had hoped to offset the damage caused by Maggs by ending the first day with an appearance by Raleigh lawyer W. T. Joyner, the governor's legal wheelhorse, but as the session pushed into the evening, it was apparent that Joyner was just too tired to go on. The next morning he arrived fresh and at the top of his form. He was preceded to the podium by both a determined segregationist, the Reverend James Dees of Statesville, who cited biblical authority for separation of the races, and "an almost prayerful integrationist," as the *News & Observer* called Charlotte writer Harry Golden.[66]

Golden said the state had failed in establishing lines of communication and bringing leaders from the black community and parents of black students into the discussion: "This is where we have failed in our leadership, because we have not sat down with Negro leaders to hammer out a plan that would be somewhat in keeping with the traditions of the state."[67]

The erudite Joyner had a commanding presence—even Hodges honored Joyner's Army rank and called him Colonel—and he could easily quiet a distracted audience. He was the son of a former state superintendent of public instruction who had been close to the revered Governor Charles B. Aycock. His carriage and patrician accent, his demeanor and confident attitude set him apart from the run of politicians who frequented the warrens of state government. Standing before this emotional crowd, he spoke of the committee's thoroughness and serious approach to a most difficult problem, and he characterized the Pearsall Plan as one of moderation that offered a necessary outlet, or safety valve, for those parents so distraught by integration that they would withhold their children from public school. Joyner came closest of all the public speakers to the hope held by some that it was merely a device rather than a practical solution when he said, "We hope [it] will not be widely used."[68]

The Pearsall Plan did not go as far as some states, which passed nullification and interposition resolutions. But its complicated provisions produced the same effect as those that fostered outright defiance to the enforced change of generations of habit and custom. The legislation allowed cities and counties to delay the inevitable and gave moderates, who were anxious about the future, and segregationists, who vowed they would hold back the dawn, something to rally behind as the battles continued in earnest elsewhere.

The General Assembly approved the bills in short order, finishing work on Friday with the senate giving its consent without a dissenting vote. In the house, two members voted against the bills. One was Representative Dan Edwards of Durham, among whose constituents were some of the African Americans who had spoken against the measures; the other was a Wilkes County Republican. The house did turn back an interposition resolution, as did the senate, but not before Senator Kerr provoked a forty-five-minute debate with such a proposal. "I am irrevocably, unalterably, everlastingly opposed to integration in the public schools," Kerr roared. "We're not going to conduct a rebellion. We are not going to conduct a revolution. We are simply not going to integrate." He declared North Carolina should stand up and be counted along with her sister states of the old Confederacy.[69]

The Pearsall Plan was only as good as the portions that could win approval as amendments to the North Carolina Constitution. Hodges immediately mounted a campaign on its behalf in a referendum set for September 8. It was an aggressive effort that mobilized workers as much, if not more, than his own bid for the gubernatorial nomination a few months earlier.

A few days after the session concluded, the *Charlotte Observer* quoted Terry Sanford as saying he favored the Pearsall Plan.[70] This relieved some in the governor's office who weren't sure what Scott's supporters would do after the senator's brother had signed on with Lake. (He subsequently voted with Hodges.) Terry did more than offer an endorsement: he volunteered to speak on behalf of the plan throughout eastern North Carolina. Hodges dropped him a note of thanks, saying, "It would have been too bad to have had a factional split up on this important school matter."[71]

At one appearance in a rural precinct of Cumberland County, Terry arrived while an acquaintance from the American Legion had the floor. The man was a devoted segregationist and he was pledging his support to the Pearsall Plan. "Any red-blooded American with an ounce of white blood in his body ought to be for this," he said.[72] Years later, Terry chuckled at the mixed metaphor that his enthusiastic speaker had left dangling before his audience, who cheered wildly at his patriotic appeal.

In his own speeches, Terry argued that the plan simply offered a "safety valve" for local school boards if a community found itself in an "intolerable situation," a phrase that one supporting editorial defined as "forced mixing." A vote in favor of the amendments, supporting newspaper advertisements declared, "will guarantee that your child will not have to attend a mixed school and will provide a grant of state funds (local funds may be added) to educate your children in segregated schools."[73]

The legwork for the Pearsall Plan gave Terry an opportunity to expand the reach of public appearances. He went wherever he was asked, sometimes traveling with Lauch Faircloth, an ally from the Scott campaign who was busy starting his own business in nearby Clinton. In late August, Terry was in Ahoskie, deep in the northeastern part of the state, where he spoke to the Junior Women's Club. "The Supreme Court may be as wrong as Corrigan," Sanford said, "but our response must be calm, quiet and deliberate reason. You do not cure away the darkness of the night; you illuminate your way by holding up a light. The people of North Carolina have reasoned their way out of many difficult situations, and we will reason our way out of this one." [74]

Terry admired Pearsall and his finesse in handling a difficult issue. "I think Tom Pearsall did one of the most brilliant pieces of governance that I've ever seen, in the way he handled that," Sanford later recalled. "Tom understood the East and the black issue and the passion surrounding it. By the nature of it, he never was fully recognized for what I think was a tremendous service to this state because we didn't really do anything. But they gave everybody the impression that they were doing the best they could." [75]

Apparently lost amidst the emotional energy was the cost to individual families if a shift from public to private schools should occur. The *Charlotte Observer* sent a reporter out to Country Day School in Charlotte, one of only a dozen private schools in the state. At Country Day, tuition ranged from $485 a year for five-year-olds in preschool to $735 for ninth graders, a price that would consume roughly one-third of the average annual income of most white wage earners. The state's proposed grant of $135 could never make up that difference.

Golden proceeded to poke fun at the state's efforts to evade the Court with his own plan, which he called "vertical integration." He observed that whites and blacks were content to stand together in grocery lines and teller lines at the bank and wait side by side at drugstore counters; it was only when folks sat down that there was trouble. "Instead of all these complicated proposals," Golden wrote, "all the next session needs to do is pass one small amendment which would provide *only* desks in all the public schools of our state—*no seats.*" [76]

Proponents of the Pearsall Plan were not amused, and they hit back hard. In one advertisement they said that to oppose the amendments was to be with the "NAACP, headquarters New York City, Jonathan Daniels, Mark Ethridge, Jr." [77] (Ethridge was editor of the Raleigh *Times*, which opposed the plan, as did Daniels's *News & Observer.*) An editorial cartoon in the *News & Observer* that appeared the week before the referendum depicted a schoolhouse with a No Trespassing sign across the door. An accompanying editorial said, "Perhaps such a town (with no schools) is so fantastic as to be inconceivable. Even those who support the Pearsall Plan say that they hope no such community will ever be created under that plan. But the clear result of the Pearsall Plan would be to make such a community possible." [78]

Election day, September 8, featured typical late-summer weather, warm by midday and cool in the evening. In Raleigh, the sons and daughters of the state's wealthy and well-connected were preparing for a formal ball at which 172 young women would be introduced to society "in the setting of the Old South." Each debutante stepped through doors of "a Southern mansion" to be escorted across the floor of Memorial Auditorium. The vision of Southern belles in crinolined gowns competed with disturbing pictures published the preceding week from Sturgis, Kentucky, and Clinton, Tennessee, where National Guardsmen had been used to restore order. Violence had delayed the opening of school for a handful of black children who wished to join white classmates in the same room. In Clinton, the soldiers stood guard around the courthouse where a local judge had jailed rabble-rouser John Kasper, a segregationist who had defied orders to stay out of town.

Perhaps it was the fine weather. Perhaps it was front-page pictures of soldiers in gas masks, carrying M-1 rifles with fixed bayonets facing off against angry whites. Perhaps North Carolinians didn't need any stimulus to express the way they felt about school integration at this, their first opportunity since the 1954 decision. Whatever the reason, no election in memory had so united voters or their representatives. Hodges, Scott, Ervin, the state's entire political establishment spoke as one. Voters approved the amendments by a margin of four-to-one. In one county in eastern North Carolina, they passed twenty-seven-to-one. Two days after the election, Hodges said, "Against the background of the violence and turmoil in Tennessee and Kentucky, and some extreme legislative measures taken in other states, North Carolinians can take pride in this solid endorsement of a moderate approach to the explosive problems resulting from the decision of the U.S. Supreme Court." [79]

The state's approach had not been fully tested, however. No black students had appeared at white schools. Integration of schools in Gaston County in the Piedmont and McDowell County in the foothills of the mountains was still tied up in court. Three days after the referendum, however, twenty-two African Americans quietly and uneventfully enrolled as undergraduates at three state university campuses, including two women at Woman's College in Greensboro. During the summer, the city of High Point had opened a municipal golf course to play by all, but just fifteen miles away at a municipal course in Greensboro, black golfers had been arrested for trespassing when they arrived to play and refused to leave when ordered.

Perhaps nothing pleased Hodges more than the political drubbing he delivered to Jonathan Daniels, whose News & Observer had made his life uncomfortable the entire year. The landslide in favor of the amendments left

Daniels further distanced from the majority than he had ever been. "I guess I got worse beat on that than anything I ever undertook," Daniels said later. He still burned with resentment about a plan that most of his contemporaries praised as genius: "There isn't any question about that. But it was a devious device, and never once have they dared to use it. And to propose that it was just a plan to gain time is a lot of crap. It was exactly the plan that was proposed in Virginia. But instead of being undisguised massive resistance, it was sort of a halfway-disguised massive resistance."[80]

The objections raised by the *News & Observer* nettled Hodges, who believed the question was one not of race but of good order and reputation. He was determined not to be included with the other rebel-yell politicians who were held in such disdain by his old friends at the New York City Rotary Club, where he had once been president. That was bad for business. In this case, recruiting of new business and industry to the state was his measure of success for his administration, which counted every dollar spent on bricks and mortar at new plants and encouraged the increase in the state's industrial employment.

Hodges was his own man when he took the oath of governor for a historic second time in formal ceremonies in January 1957. In the previous thirteen-plus months he had been occupied with the unfinished business started by his predecessor, by his own election campaign, and by the demanding attention of school integration. Now he laid fair claim to the office with the most impressive electoral mandate since the legendary O. Max Gardner was unopposed for the Democratic nomination in 1928.

Hodges found a state in transition as he set his program in motion for the next four years. North Carolina remained heavily dependent on agriculture, and overall conditions for North Carolina farmers were improving. Nearly three out of four farm families now had automobiles, half had freezers, and a third had telephones. But mechanization and other factors were rearranging the landscape. Farm laborers, mostly African Americans, continued to leave the state for the promise of better jobs and better conditions overall in cities in the North.

At the same time, North Carolina's main industries, furniture and textiles, continued to enjoy prosperous years, a string of which had begun following the war. High Point was on its way to becoming the center of the nation's furniture industry. At the beginning of the decade, North Carolina textile plants produced 40 percent of all hosiery manufactured in the country, and the state led the South in production of woolens and worsteds. In 1953, Dupont had produced its first bale of Dacron at its huge new plant in Kinston; the local paper called it the beginning "of a new industrial era." Greensboro's Burlington Industries, built by J. Spencer Love, would soon become the world's largest textile operation. At its peak it would have 130 plants in sixteen states and seven foreign countries. The state's cities were growing in size, particularly Charlotte, which had surpassed Wilmington as the largest city just before the war; since 1940 it had grown by a third, increasing its population by about thirty-five thousand.

Hodges played to his strengths. He was a businessman with a wide range of connections in the international business community. He also knew the leaders of the state's largest businesses and industries and had earned their respect at their level prior to entering politics. The governor promoted tax concessions for business and rejuvenated the state's Department of Conservation and Development and, under the leadership of his old friend, William Saunders of Southern Pines, set it on a mission of identifying new corporate residents of the state and helping them locate their new plants and expanded operations in North Carolina.

This was an aggressive campaign reminiscent of Henry Grady's pumping of the New South at the turn of the century. Hodges organized traveling bands of North Carolina businessmen who called on prospects abroad. The state purchased special advertising sections in the *New York Times* in which Hodges announced that North Carolina workers were "ready, willing and able." Hodges promoted the clean, healthy environment of rural America, where employers could "draw upon a large and industrious labor supply." He also set about establishing industrial training centers to customize a workforce for a new industry. He insisted on hands-on training and prohibited these schools from maintaining libraries or taking on academic trappings of any sort, according to Dallas Herring, who was instrumental in opening the first such center in Burlington.[81]

The centerpiece of Hodges's program would in time become a new venture called the Research Triangle Park. Greensboro contractor Romeo Guest, Winston-Salem banker Robert Hanes, and others had been promoting the idea of combining tracts of land into a corporate research park at a location that provided easy access to the campuses of Duke University in Durham, the University of North Carolina at Chapel Hill, and North Carolina State College in Raleigh. Nine months after taking office, Hodges announced plans for the four-thousand-acre park situated in the middle of a triangle formed by Durham, Chapel Hill, and Raleigh. The vision of the park's promoters was confirmed when Chemstrand, a major supplier to the textile industry, announced in 1959 that it would become the first tenant.

The attractive features of the Park, plus North Carolina's "moderate" approach to school integration and apparent calm race relations, was alluring to any business seeking new locations in the South, according to George Simpson, who took a leave from the university at Chapel Hill to lay the organizational groundwork.[82] Chemstrand Corporation was looking for an alternative to its facility in Decatur, Alabama, when the state's name became synonymous with massive resistance to civil rights. A site in Princeton, New Jersey, had been recommended by its consulting engineers, but when they learned about the new development in North Carolina, the southern location moved to the top of the list.

For all of his finesse with businessmen, Hodges confounded the state's Democratic Party leaders. Some were still muttering about the accident of history that had placed him in office. On a more practical level, local county chairmen were not the least bit happy that Hodges often ignored the party channels and named whomever he wanted to state jobs. The governor said he just wanted the best man for the job, but that sounded like Republicanism to men who had delivered the party vote. When Republicans actually did receive plum assignments, these local chieftains were near revolt.

Chairing the party was John D. Larkins of Trenton, a lawyer who had been one of the faithful for more than twenty years. He had joined the insiders of the traditional party organization almost from the day he came to the legislature in 1937. In March 1957, on the day of the party's annual spring gathering, called Jefferson-Jackson Day, Larkins invited Hodges to meet with the county chairmen. Immediately, one man after the other roasted Hodges for not passing the names of potential appointees by them for approval before they were offered positions in his administration. Larkins, whose services Hodges had inherited from Umstead, acknowledged in response to a question from one of the chairmen that the governor had not consulted him either. The meeting closed with everyone unhappy and on edge. Relations between Larkins and the governor deteriorated further after an account of the meeting appeared in the *Winston-Salem Journal*. Hodges reportedly said he believed Larkins had betrayed him. The two men met to make amends, but Larkins later wrote, "I felt like he had called me a traitor in public, but he only apologized to me in private."[83]

There is perhaps no greater political reward that a governor can bestow than that of appointment to the U.S. Senate. Four of Hodges's immediate predecessors had filled vacancies created by the death of elected senators, a string of mortality seldom matched in the nation's history. The unenviable North Carolina record had prompted some who had been asked if they wanted an appointment to the Senate to respond that, no, they weren't ready to be carried home in a box. When Scott had arrived in Washington, he waited for an office to open for him rather than move into quarters last occupied by Hoey.

Such a record made all the more ominous the news on April 9, 1958, that Kerr Scott lay seriously ill in a hospital bed in Burlington, where he had been taken after suffering a heart attack while home on the Easter recess. Scott was sixty-one and, though he looked hale and hearty, a lifetime of barbecue, country cooking, and thick cigars had taken their toll. Miss Mary, his wife, and his son, Osborne, had delivered him to the hospital after she noticed that he was perspiring heavily and having trouble breathing as they returned home from Burlington, where he had gone to get his driver's license renewed. Miss Mary blamed herself for not keeping her husband on a restricted diet that doctors had earlier prescribed to help him lose weight. The night before the attack, she said she heard him rustling through the refrigerator preparing himself a midnight meal of leftover meatloaf.

The doctors' initial reports were serious, but after forty-eight hours their prognosis became more encouraging. Scott remained under an oxygen tent and reporters learned that he would be sent home soon for three months of absolute rest. "He's going to be a honey to keep in bed until he gets better," Miss Mary said. The senator was eager to get back to Washington to vote on the farm bill, which he feared was in trouble from the Republicans. She also said Kerr had begun to complain that he couldn't enjoy his customary cigar or a chew of Apple and Honey, one of his favorite brands.[84]

Miss Mary's comments helped to reassure those who had attended the series of funerals of the state's fallen representatives: Josiah Bailey in 1946, Mel Broughton in 1948, Willis Smith in 1953, and Clyde Hoey a year later. Four days after Scott entered the hospital, the chief of medicine at the National Heart Institute told reporters he didn't see why Scott couldn't campaign for reelection in 1960. After all, he said, President Eisenhower had recovered nicely from his heart problems to campaign in forty-eight states, not just one. News like this encouraged Scott, who enjoyed campaigning and seeing old friends at farm gatherings. When he spoke to one such group not long after he went to the Senate he said, "You know this convention has been a regular affair for Miss Mary and me. We look upon it as a real treat. As we Branch-head boys say, 'It's a trip to town.' "[85]

Six days after Scott was stricken his name slipped from the front pages of the state's newspapers. Then on the afternoon of April 16, just after four, while his wife was down the hall at the hospital visiting a sick grandchild, Scott suffered a coronary thrombosis and died. "There was no warning. No nothing," said one of his doctors, G. Walker Blair.[86] His death came on the eve of his sixty-second birthday. A nonfattening angel food cake with a decoration of sixty-two red roses had already been prepared.

The well-wishers, family friends, neighbors, and others who had drifted away after it appeared Scott was on the mend returned, and in swarms. Ralph Scott put in a call to Fayetteville and asked Terry to come to Haw River to give the family a hand with arrangements. He immediately headed

north, took a room in a Burlington hotel, and remained close by as preparations were made for a Friday afternoon funeral at Hawfields Presbyterian
Church.

Political funerals always draw large crowds. The small country church
where Scott had been an elder since 1933 was jammed, and thousands
milled around outside as services began. The number attending was larger
than the population of many North Carolina counties whose farm-to-
market roads Scott had paved. A delegation from the Senate arrived in
Greensboro and was driven to the simple brick church built in 1852. Among
the official honor guard were Olin Johnston of South Carolina, Herman
Talmadge of Georgia, and Milton Young of North Dakota. Senator John F.
Kennedy of Massachusetts also was listed as part of the delegation but
did not attend. Scott's old friend Frank Graham traveled alone to pay his
respects.

A convoy of thirty State Highway Patrol cars carried state leaders from
Raleigh to the funeral, where congregants sang Scott's favorite hymn,
"The Little Brown Church in the Wildwood." The gray-and-black patrol
cruisers crowded the road along with hundreds of other vehicles, from
long black sedans to battered pickup trucks. Some said they had not seen
such an outpouring of grief for a public man since Franklin Roosevelt's
train passed through the Carolinas on its way to Washington from Warm
Springs, Georgia.

Members of the Senate had grown as attached to Scott as his friends at
home. "Senator Scott was a great Southern liberal who recognized that the
purpose of our American system of self-government is to promote the welfare of the people," Senator Wayne Morse of Oregon said in a tribute. Some
recalled how Scott delighted in offering a chew to unsuspecting visitors to
the Capitol; others knew him from a Wednesday morning prayer breakfast
that he attended without fail. Senate Majority Leader Lyndon Johnson of
Texas recalled the red rose that Scott always had attached to his lapel. "Kerr
Scott loved people," Johnson said. "Kerr Scott's love was not an abstract,
academic love. He wanted to do things for them because he was of them."
The Republican leader, Everett Dirksen of Illinois, spoke of Scott's gentle-
ness and deep religious faith. Minnesota's Hubert Humphrey recalled that
Scott could never understand why the idea of a World Food Bank, which
would distribute food and fiber from this nation to those in need abroad,
had never been transformed into reality.[87]

Jonathan Daniels seemed to be in shock: "It seemed incredible that the
Squire of Haw River who stood so squarely on the North Carolina earth
could quickly fall. He was to the last the Branch-head Boy and he seemed
as eternal as the native spirit of North Carolina."[88]

One of the most poignant and accurate reflections on Scott's life was an editorial in the *Greensboro Daily News* written by William D. Snider, who had worked for a time as a publicist in Scott's highway department. Snider recounted Scott's legacy and said Scott

> saw his regime as an instrument of redressing the balance between lawyers and farmers—between moneyed interests and the boys at the head of the branch.
>
> Like Harry Truman's, his shadow grows larger every day. For Scott and Truman were alike; their hearts were in the right place, and they were sound on many large and memorable issues; they were sometimes wrong, and petty, on small ones.
>
> He was a bulldozer, not a diplomat, a doer, not a philosopher. He never plowed under false colors. If he is standing close to St. Peter this morning, we suspect he is advising to rip out all that gold facade and repave it with black Macadam.[89]

African Americans remembered Scott as much for what he had not done as what he had accomplished for them. Even as the pressure rose in the mounting debate over civil rights, Scott had avoided exploiting it. When the Senate was locked in a fight over Eisenhower's civil rights bills, a reporter had asked Scott if he would be the first from his region to publicly support the legislation. "You must remember that I'm a Southerner," he was quoted as saying, "and I'll always go along with the southern boys, but during this civil rights debate I'll have a word to say about the need for the preservation of our water resources." [90]

An African American newspaper in Durham, the *Carolina Times*, reflected the combination of sorrow and regret: "Even when he did just the opposite of what they [blacks] wanted him to do on issues involving their welfare, they took him to task with a kind of restraint that gave evidence of their abiding faith that beneath it all was a heart of pure gold and that when the chips were down they could depend on him to keep the covenant with his conscience rather than with some political clique." [91]

Governor Luther Hodges arrived in Haw River the day before the funeral to pay his respects to Miss Mary and the family. The governor's limousine (driven by Highway Patrolman Harold Minges, who had the same assignment when Scott was in office) stopped at the Scott farm, where Hodges learned the senator's widow was at the burial ground selecting a final resting place for her husband. Minges and Hodges met her there, and both expressed condolences. Hodges then drove on to nearby Saxapahaw, where Minges left Hodges for a private meeting with B. Everett Jordan.[92] Exactly twenty-four hours after Scott's funeral, on Saturday afternoon, Hodges announced that he was appointing Jordan to fill the balance of Scott's term.

The governor noted that Jordan and Scott were neighbors and even related by marriage (Miss Mary was Jordan's first cousin). It was an effort, though weak, to soften the blow to those in the Scott organization, who had lost not only their leader but their leader's hard-fought victory to the very faction they believed had opposed Scott throughout his entire career. Although Scott and Jordan had once been allies, with Jordan raising much of the money that helped Scott win in 1948, the two had drifted apart, and Jordan still smarted over Scott's passing over him for Frank Graham in 1950.

Many of those disappointed in Hodges's decision said Jordan was just a seat-warmer for the governor, who planned to run for the Senate himself in 1960. Jordan himself told his wife when they first talked about the appointment that he would be in Washington only two years. Southern Pines businessman Voit Gilmore, a Chapel Hill classmate of Terry Sanford, was one of those on the short list of possible replacements; he denied any suggestion of seat-warming had arisen when Hodges had talked with him about the job. Gilmore said Hodges disavowed any interest in going to the Senate.

The Scott loyalists were outraged and not silent in their anger. Scott aides Ben Roney and Roy Wilder quit on the spot. "He betrayed Kerr Scott and Kerr Scott considered him more concerned with special interests than with the good of the people," Roney said of Jordan.[93] They believed Hodges should have named Miss Mary as a stand-in replacement and let Scott's staff continue to run the office until the 1960 primaries and the election of a nominee. One man wrote to Hodges and attached a clipping that said Scott had once joked that three classes of people would attend his funeral: "those who were genuinely sorry, those who were curious and those who wanted to know if the SOB is dead."

"I attended Senator Scott's funeral," the letter writer said. "I was among thousands who were genuinely sorry—grieved beyond words. There were a few in the curious class. And alas! there was the governor of the great state of North Carolina 'politicking' in the church yard while his funeral was being held—Yep, Kerr Scott knew three classes would attend." [94]

It is doubtful that Hodges ever seriously considered naming Mary Scott to fill the remainder of her husband's term. Hodges told Gilmore that he had "some serious obligations out there" as he narrowed his list of potential nominees. Harold Makepeace, the governor's chief political advisor, thought attorney Ben Trotter, Hodges's hometown neighbor, close friend, and business advisor, would get the nod. Gilmore was on the list, of course, and then there was Jordan. The governor could not forget that Henry Jordan, Everett's brother, had forsaken his own ambition to be governor when he withdrew as a contender in 1956, leaving the field open for Hodges's spectacular victory.

Terry Sanford really didn't care who Hodges picked for the job, although his favorite was Gilmore. It bothered him greatly that Hodges presented Jordan, a staunch union-busting, conservative textile mill owner and founding member of the North Carolina Citizens Association, as a Kerr Scott kind of senator.[95]

Much more important to Terry than who was going to be sitting in the Senate four hundred miles away was how this change in the political landscape would affect his own plans to run for governor in two years. The immediate question was what would become of Scott's political organization. North Carolina politics was built on personal followings, and leaderless factions were soon picked clean of effective organizers by the competition unless one acted quickly. Ralph Scott was a likely successor. Ralph, however, was mindful of Kerr's commitment to Terry's plans to run for governor and readily deferred his claim to his brother's ambitious young protégé.

Terry had Ralph's support in his pocket as he prepared his response to Hodges's decision. If he expressed his indifference, news reporters would lump him with all the others saying the expected and run the story deep inside the paper. No, this was his opportunity to claim the leadership of the Scott organization that he believed was rightfully his. In his response he took aim at Hodges, not Jordan, and said the governor could name whomever he wanted but he was dead wrong in foisting off Jordan as a Scott man.

He succeeded. The morning after Scott's funeral, the *News & Observer*'s "Under the Dome" column, where the political gossip reported could make or break a candidate, noted that "the nucleus of [Scott's] organization is expected to gravitate to Terry Sanford, the young Fayetteville lawyer."[96]

CHAPTER NINE

Breaking in Line

❊

ON THE NIGHT OF JULY 23, 1957, school boards meeting simultaneously in Charlotte, Greensboro, and Winston-Salem adopted an integration policy approving the transfer of a total of twelve black children in the three cities to white public schools. The meetings were carefully orchestrated, as were the subsequent admissions, all of which took place on the same day in September. More than three years had passed since Greensboro's outspoken school superintendent Ben E. Smith had pushed for uncompromising acceptance of the *Brown* decision. Token integration was his reward.

Taunts and intimidation by whites and the threat of violence accompanied the black teenagers as they walked through crowds of jeering whites to start classes. The night before Yvonne Bailey was to begin her studies at Reynolds High School in Winston-Salem, someone painted "Nigger go home" in large letters on the driveway of her home. Whites threw eggs at Josephine Ophelia Boyd as she entered Greensboro's Grimsley High. Superintendent Smith received threats and a brick through a large plate-glass window at his home. Greensboro police officers were dispatched to stand guard.

It was a measure of the intensity of emotion that everyone—from the *New York Times* to Governor Luther Hodges—proclaimed the "integration" of North Carolina schools a success. Twelve black students, out of more than 275,000, had crossed the schoolhouse threshold with more than 650,000 whites. Indeed, schools in these three cities did open on schedule and remained open without interruption, unlike those in other southern communities of Little Rock, Arkansas, and Nashville, Tennessee, where an elementary school preparing to receive its first black student was bombed the day before classes were to begin. One subsequent North Carolina casualty was pretty Dorothy Counts, the teenage daughter of a theology professor in Charlotte, who withdrew after only two weeks from Charlotte's Harding High School where she had been repeatedly spat on and pelted with rocks.

If only by comparison, North Carolina was an island of reason in a sea of racial hatred. The state's reputation for moderation was enhanced by Hodges, who, as chairman of the Southern Governors' Conference, attempted to mediate a resolution to the violence that had closed Little Rock schools and eventually led to President Eisenhower's decision to send federal troops to Little Rock to restore order. A few weeks later, Hodges was interviewed on the United States Information Agency's Voice of America in a broadcast designed to counteract the growing reputation of America as a nation in racial crisis.[1] Hodges had stood his ground against white extremists who threatened to bring their campaigns to the state. In the fall, as schools were opening, he publicly warned John Kasper, who had led demonstrations by whites in Tennessee, to stay away. Later, in January 1958, he let it be known that he was pleased that a band of Lumbee Indians had routed a group of whites gathered for a cross-burning at a Ku Klux Klan rally in Robeson County.

Yet, Hodges continued to defend the Southern way of life and complain of federal interference. In a speech to his fellow governors meeting at Sea Island, Georgia, in 1957 he applauded Senators Richard Russell of Georgia and Sam Ervin Jr. of North Carolina for their opposition to civil rights legislation and for pointing out to the nation what could happen "if the Congress of the United States allowed casual emotion, half-baked information and partisan politics to dictate dangerous legislation." [2] He chastised Northern newspapers for singling out racial violence in the South while ignoring similar incidents in their own backyard. Hodges assured the governors that attitudes about race in the rest of the nation were not that different from those held by their own constituents.

Hodges wasn't the only Southern "moderate" who was receiving national attention. In Florida, Governor Leroy Collins had broken with the conservative crowd that controlled his state's legislature. At the Sea Island conference, he delivered a speech entitled "Can a Southerner Be Elected President?" Yes, Collins answered, but he warned that if "the South should wrap itself in a Confederate blanket and consume itself in racial furor, it would surely miss its greatest opportunity for channeling into a wonderful future the products of change now taking place. And we should face up to the further fact that it would also bury itself politically for decades to come." [3]

Collins was a Tallahassee lawyer in his mid-forties who had risen through the ranks of Florida politics and, like Hodges, been promoted by the death of the state's chief executive. In 1954 he had been elected to fill the remaining two years of Governor Dan McCarty's term after McCarty, a progressive in the mold of Georgia's Ellis Arnall, died the year following his inauguration in 1952. In 1956 Collins had gained notice outside the region when he won election to a full term by defeating outspoken segregationists, including former governor Fuller Warren, who called Collins the "curly-haired boy up in Tallahassee—the friend of the N-double-A-Cee-P."[4]

Collins captured nearly 52 percent of the vote in the first primary, and Atlanta editor Ralph McGill called it "a wholesome victory for all the South."[5] Some took Collins's success to mean that "racial moderates might be in the ascendancy." In his inaugural address in 1957, Collins spoke directly to the pressing issue of school integration, urging compliance: "In the first place, it will do no good whatever to defy the United States Supreme Court. Actually, this Court is an essential institution for the preservation of our form of government. It is little short of rebellion and anarchy to suggest that any state can isolate and quarantine itself against the effect of a decision of the United States Supreme Court."[6]

Like Hodges, Collins had begun traveling the nation urging businesses and industry to relocate to his state, and Florida was enjoying growth unseen since the boom times of the 1920s. At the same time, Collins was reminded shortly after taking office that state government remained in the control of rural legislators from northern Florida who were unmoved by the potential for industrial development in the metropolitan areas.

The first act of the 1957 Florida legislature was a resolution calling for interposition. Collins forwarded the resolution to Congress along with a personal message condemning it, after he publicly branded it a "hoax."[7] He did sign a subsequent anti-integration measure, one that would close any public school when federal troops were in the vicinity to enforce integration, saying, "It is almost ridiculous to assume that any sound education could be carried on under pressure of armed guards, and as a parent, I would rather have my children at home."[8] The legislators pressed him further, passing other bills similar to North Carolina's Pearsall Plan. Collins vetoed this package, calling it the "first resort of the agitator."[9]

The Pearsall Plan provided a measure of protection to white North Carolinians against the changes that had seemed so much a threat after the Supreme Court decision in 1954. It had worked so well that the issue all but dropped from public discussion after the 1956 referendum on the constitutional amendments enabling the plan. Even in private conservation, integration wasn't discussed on the patio by the barbecue grill as Terry Sanford and his friends gathered for weekend outings or later in the evening when the conversation turned to politics and Terry's plans to run for governor in 1960.

The Sanfords and their friends were part of a new, expanding, successful middle class that epitomized the years since the war. They were the children of the Depression, who had known war and hard times and now were determined to provide a better life for their families. After a decade of work, Terry and Margaret Rose were comfortable in their home in a quiet, shady neighborhood that was close enough to Fayetteville's upper-class precincts of Haymont to be well regarded. They were among good neighbors: the children's doctor lived next door; one of the town's leading bankers lived across the street. Betsee's school, Hillside Elementary, was at the end of the block, and Terry could walk to the office if he took a notion.

The Sanfords enjoyed a life with their friends that they had only dreamed of a decade before. Terry took special care with his weekend cookouts, where he experimented with his own creations, such as hamburgers he grilled with a slice of tomato in the middle. Popular evenings were twice-a-year dances at the country club. Terry had yet to perfect his moves on the dance floor, but Margaret Rose appreciated his efforts to at least try to remain current with the popular steps.

Terry preferred to spend his leisure time outdoors. The family had begun to follow a summertime routine of taking a cottage at the edge of Bogue Sound on Emerald Isle, a barrier island on the Atlantic Coast. Margaret Rose and the children stayed at the beach for most of the summer, and Terry came over on weekends. All the family enjoyed the coast—it had been a favorite of Terry's since childhood—and Terry taught the children to water ski behind a sixteen-foot motorboat he kept docked near the house. When the beach season ended, he towed the boat back to Fayetteville to be ready for outings on the Cape Fear River. Even short day cruises with a friend gave him a chance to relax with a cigar and a beer along a course that had changed little since he had set off as a teenager on his first river adventure.

The family took occasional summer vacation trips, including one to New York City, where Terry's fancy Chrysler conked out in the middle of the Holland Tunnel. The car's huge V-8 engine tended to overheat and when it happened again—this time in a funeral procession—Terry had the car towed to the dealership and turned it in for a Plymouth station wagon. So much for status.

The family's vacation travel was scheduled around Terry's obligations to the North Carolina National Guard. He had commanded the infantry company in Fayetteville until 1953, when he was appointed assistant G-2 and began reporting to the 30th Division headquarters in Raleigh. Promotions in rank came slowly, however, and when he learned he could make major by changing to the judge advocate general's staff he put in his application. His superiors liked him and his file bulged with glowing efficiency ratings that complimented his leadership abilities.

The law firm had moved into offices on the second floor of the new Grace Pittman Building on Hay Street. The building was owned by Dr. R. L. Pittman, a wealthy physician who had once operated a small hospital in an older rear portion of the property. The Sanford firm's offices were in a new addition fronting on Hay Street that had been built to accommodate Fayetteville's new J. C. Penney department store. From his window, Terry had a view of Hay Street and the Hotel Charles, another of Pittman's properties, where he regularly took lunch at the round table in the rear of the dining room with other lawyers and downtown businessmen. In the fall, when the World Series was on television, Pittman would invite Terry and others to watch the afternoon games and feast on thick steaks from the hotel kitchen.

The firm included Stacy Weaver Jr., who had first met Terry when he attended Boys' State; Dickson Phillips, who moved to town in 1957; and Donald McCoy, who was the last of the trio to leave Laurinburg for Fayetteville. Early in 1957 the firm received some public notice when a Cumberland County jury awarded their client damages of $120,000 in a personal injury case, the largest jury award in a civil suit in that part of the state. The firm represented the family of a man who had been killed when a bus hit his car, also seriously injuring his son. The bus company argued that their driver had swerved to avoid hitting another vehicle he thought was going to run through an intersection. The company turned down a settlement offer of $20,000 and the case headed to trial. While Phillips handled the legal research, Weaver found a witness whose testimony proved invaluable. Terry argued the case. Weaver would never forget his partner's ability to remain cool and unruffled in difficult situations, moving with the flow of testimony to work his own magic in the courtroom. The same agreeable qualities in his personality that served him well in politics encouraged jurors to like him, and to believe him.[10]

He brought more than charm to the courtroom, however. He had a keen legal mind, said Phillips, and could practice more law before ten in the morning than most lawyers could in a full day at the office. He earned his A rating in the Martindale-Hubbell directory honestly.

Terry's peripatetic nature and his engaging personality helped the firm land North Carolina Natural Gas Company as its biggest client and eastern North Carolina's latest new industry. Terry happened to be on an airplane that was forced to overfly Fayetteville because of bad weather and land in Jacksonville, Florida. During the trip, he struck up a conversation with another passenger headed to Jacksonville, who was in the process of creating the company out of smaller distributors, including Tidewater Gas Company, which Terry had represented before the state Utilities Commission. By the time Terry boarded his plane for Fayetteville the following day, he had convinced the man not only that the Sanford law firm should be appointed general counsel but that Fayetteville, not Raleigh, should be the company's home. The account would produce steady income for years.

The firm also handled many of the real estate closings for Fayetteville's newest subdivision, VanStory Hills, which was being developed by Paul Thompson and his partner, Thomas McLean. The new development was on a 250-acre tract just west of downtown that had been held in what most believed was an unbreakable trust agreement until Terry found a way to satisfy both the requirements of the trust and free the property for sale. Terry had first become interested in the VanStory land after he had arranged with Branch Banking & Trust Company to lease a small tract that had been isolated by the construction of Bragg Boulevard, a new thoroughfare linking Fayetteville with the military post. He and Thompson, who had become his closest friend since moving to Fayetteville, used part of the land to open the first automated car wash in Fayetteville. They leased the remainder to Durham businessman Frank Kenan, who was expanding his chain of Tops discount gasoline stations.

It was a busy time. Terry was building a law practice, dabbling in various entrepreneurial ventures, raising a family, and planning a political career. He juggled all these activities, sometimes blending one with the others, such as when he agreed to help Pittman raise money to bring a new liberal arts college to Fayetteville.

Officials at the North Carolina Synod, the governing body for the Presbyterian Church in the state, had called Pittman in 1955 and asked him to lead an effort to raise several million dollars to launch a new college that they said the Church planned to locate in Fayetteville. The Presbyterians wanted to consolidate three small colleges — Flora Macdonald in Red Springs, Peace in Raleigh, and Presbyterian Junior College in Maxton — and build a new one in a more urban location. They told Pittman they had chosen Fayetteville as the site because the school was to serve eastern North Carolina. They agreed to locate the new school there if the community would lend support. Pittman took on the campaign and enlisted help from Terry, who was just completing a term as the first president of Fayetteville's United Fund.

The Fayetteville committee succeeded beyond all expectations, collecting pledges of money as well as a sizable piece of land along the Cape Fear

River. To the dismay of Pittman and Sanford, however, the Presbyterians had begun entertaining invitations to locate their college in other communities as word of their plans spread. Sanford and Pittman protested, and the churchmen assured them that the interest in other communities was natural, but that the school would still go to Fayetteville. In the spring of 1956, however, the Synod announced that Laurinburg would be the home of the new school they planned to call St. Andrews College.

Terry was pleased for his hometown, and not surprised at the decision when he learned that the McNair family had made a sizable contribution to persuade church leaders to reconsider the offer to Fayetteville. At the same time, he and Pittman felt betrayed. But, rather than lose the momentum and community spirit that had been aroused, Terry approached officials in the North Carolina Conference of the Methodist Church with the idea of a new school.

The Methodist Church had been an important part of the Sanfords' life in Fayetteville. The family attended Hay Street Methodist, a sturdy redbrick church that was one of the most prominent in town. Terry had been a Sunday school teacher and chairman of the church's administrative board and had served as the district's lay leader. In 1955, he helped host the annual conference when it met at Hay Street. Terry knew Bishop Paul N. Garber and understood the complicated inner workings of the Methodist bureaucracy well enough to approach the conference with the idea of a new college. When the bishop heard his plan, he endorsed it without hesitation.

The proposal was taken to the Church's annual conference in the early summer of 1956. Though Terry had prepared carefully, Fayetteville's plan ran into trouble again. Once word spread that the Methodists also planned to build a college, local delegations began organizing their campaigns. The question finally settled on bids from two eastern North Carolina cities, Fayetteville and Rocky Mount. During the conference, the Fayetteville delegates huddled with the bishop and delegates from Rocky Mount. Ultimately, the conference endorsed the building of two schools, Methodist College in Fayetteville and North Carolina Wesleyan in Rocky Mount. Methodist College was chartered in the fall of 1956, and Terry was named chairman of the board of trustees. Less than two years later, he and four others, including Pittman, stood in a drizzling rain to pose for pictures at the formal groundbreaking ceremonies.

Terry was not keen on the idea of two campuses. He thought, in fact, that it was foolhardy and that the Church would be hard-pressed to support both campuses as it should. However, he agreed to the compromise because, he later acknowledged, he was mindful of his political career, and there was no need to alienate an entire community if he could avoid it.[11]

Terry's goal remained the governorship. His campaign had begun the moment he had walked out of Hodges's office in the spring of 1956. It now was a factor influencing every decision, occupying his time as never before. He looked for opportunities to travel around the state and readily accepted speaking engagements. In the spring of 1957 he sounded the first note in a theme song that would mark him as a candidate, as a governor, and as a public figure for years to come. The issue was education. It was not the narrow dimension of school integration—he earnestly hoped he could avoid a showdown on that—but rather the question of whether North Carolina was investing in its schools at a level sufficient to prepare students for competition in a world now frenetic over technology. By the end of the year, the space race would be engaged and Americans reminded of their second-place status by the incessant beeping of a radio transmitter on the Russians' Earth-circling orb, Sputnik.

In February 1957, when Governor Hodges outlined the details of his administration's programs for the coming four years, he unwittingly produced an opportunity for Terry to develop education as an issue. The governor was focused on the pursuit of industrial development. Included in his plan were tax reductions worth $8 million for corporations, development of vocational training, and a $100,000 twin-engine airplane to carry him and his scouts to industrial centers in the North and Midwest. His plan also included merit salary increases for state employees and teachers of about 10 percent, but that was about half of what leaders among the state's educators said was needed for teachers.

Hodges and his advisors had devised a "trickle-down" policy of economic improvement, one that would be revisited on the national level by Ronald Reagan nearly forty years later. If business and industry expanded, they reasoned, then the state's tax base would expand and there would be more money for schools and other state services. The program was supported by a package of changes in the tax structure that had been prepared by a study commission composed of leaders from the state's business establishment.

The governor's program seemed assured of passage, for Hodges controlled the legislature. The speaker of the house, the lieutenant governor, and all the important committee chairs were in his camp. But his allies undermined their own position when, on opening day, both houses quickly approved a pay raise of 20 percent for certain top state officials. Teachers, principals, and parent leaders of the PTA were outraged. They demanded to know how legislators could approve such a measure for high officials and ignore the 19 percent increase that had been requested for teachers and principals by the State Board of Education and the education establishment. *Greensboro Daily News* editorial cartoonist Hugh Haynie found a new favorite target. He poked at Hodges almost daily, depicting him as a white knight he called "Sir Luther," whose massive castle of industrial development rested on a rickety, patched framework that represented public education.

Less than two weeks after Hodges outlined his program, Sanford was on his way to Winston-Salem for a speaking engagement at a Young Democrats Club. In his pocket he had a prepared speech on constitutional revisions. The topic was dull, but this was a friendly crowd and he believed they would indulge him. On the way, however, he changed his mind and began outlining a different speech. Instead of delivering a history lesson, Terry turned his attention to Hodges, who, he said, had adopted an approach that was "dangerously wrong." The answer was not lower taxes to help one segment on the theory that benefits would trickle down to all others. What the state needed was a concerted effort to raise the standards of education. Then, new industry would be happy to settle in North Carolina without tax concessions.

Terry's delivery of the speech received only scant local coverage, but it drew statewide reaction after an editorial encouraging him appeared two days later in the *Winston-Salem Journal*. "We are testing everything we do in North Carolina by what it will do or fail to do for new industry. The school problem has been placed too far down the list when in reality, said Mr. Sanford, schools should have a higher place than the idea of decreasing taxes for industry."[12] The Greensboro newspaper followed soon with a front-page story noting Terry's criticism of Hodges's program and suggesting that a new leader was rising in the Democratic Party.

The statewide attention produced letters that stacked up beside the cigar humidor on the corner of Terry's desk in his Hay Street law office. He heard from parents, schoolteachers and principals, former legislators, political allies, and commentators of all stripes. "That was an excellent statement you made on the public schools," wrote Charlotte's Harry Golden, "and I am sure that the vast majority of the thinking people of North Carolina are with you on it."[13]

Terry stretched the truth when he said he wasn't making a political speech; he told reporters that he was just an interested parent. But, in fact, Bill Cochrane in Washington (who stayed on to work for Everett Jordan after Scott's death) was shipping him data on the problems of the state's educational system. "We'll be glad to supply enough ammunition for a whole series of safaris. You just keep shooting," Cochrane wrote in one letter accompanying a sheaf of papers. "Just make sure you see the flare before you jump. You've got one now, so don't faint heart."[14]

Not all were so certain the time was right. Ralph Scott warned Terry that his public exposure might be premature. "Your friends in the legislature are of the opinion your attack on the governor is a little early," Scott wrote him. "They are afraid it will wear out before '60 if you don't watch out." [15]

But Terry was convinced he had found an issue that, if developed properly, would be his for the campaign and beyond. Nothing consumed more of the state budget than public education. However, the question was not what percentage was being paid for education but how much was left undone. The National Education Association said the state needed nearly six thousand new classrooms to bring its schools up to the national average. In addition, many of the state's teachers were not properly trained: 90 percent of the state's twenty-one hundred part-time teachers had less than four years of education.

Parents and community groups wanted to know more, and Terry obliged. A few days after the Winston-Salem speech, he told a newspaper reporter that "the public school question is the most critical issue facing North Carolina today. We are not attracting new teachers. We could be damaging irreparably our schools for the next decade. What we do this year determines what kind of school leadership we have four and seven and ten years from now. . . . But we are not going to lift ourselves by our bootstraps if we wait for increased income from new business before we fulfill our responsibility to the public schools," he said. More funding for education and attracting first-class leadership, not expensive invitations to new industry, was the key to the future.[16]

The issue played as well in the rural areas as it did in the cities. Nearly 250 persons turned out for a Future Farmers of America meeting at Grantham School in rural Wayne County to hear Sanford in early 1958. "We would like to see us do for the public schools what Governor Scott did for the public roads," he said. "The rural school, which year after year sends forth graduates unable to compete with the graduates of larger, wealthier school systems in the state, needs to be lifted out of the mud. The schools which do not measure up because of inadequate state and local funds are blights on a state whose proud constitutional boast is 'a general and uniform system of public schools.' "[17]

Working well ahead of the typical campaign timetable, Sanford opened his first campaign office in Chapel Hill shortly after Kerr Scott's death. Scott's former aides, Ben Roney and Roy Wilder, plus two secretaries from the senator's office, Peggy Warren and Betty Carter, moved into a two-room office above a drugstore and started doing business as the Capital Typing Service. The women kept a bank of automatic typewriters churning out letters on Terry's behalf. Roney and Wilder roamed the countryside talking with members of Scott's political organization and feeding political rumor and fact back to Terry.[18] The first Christmas after Scott's death, Terry sent each of the county contacts a plastic-encased plug of the senator's favorite chewing tobacco. After the last box left Chapel Hill, Wilder wrote Terry: "The Capital Typing Service is again operating at near enough capacity, satisfactorily and, as always, unprofitably."[19]

The files at the Capital Typing Service contained the names of members of professional organizations and civic clubs as well as local political leaders. Some were old Scott allies who worked the precincts and country stores of rural North Carolina. They knew the patriarchs of local families in settlements off the main roads could produce twenty, fifty, or even a hundred votes with just a nod of consent. These folks were the bedrock of the Democratic Party, the so-called yellow-dog Democrats who claimed they would vote Democratic even if the party ran an old yellow dog. The files also included the names of many younger Democrats whom Terry had worked with in the state YDC, which claimed more than forty thousand dues-paying members.

Among Terry's allies within the YDC was Henry Hall Wilson Jr., whose term as YDC president coincided with the 1956 presidential campaign. During the months prior to the Democratic national convention in Chicago, Wilson had organized dinners and other events to feature the leading presidential contenders. Adlai Stevenson, New York Governor Averill Harriman, Senator John Sparkman of Alabama, Estes Kefauver, and even Kentucky Governor Happy Chandler visited the state. During Chandler's campaign stop he declared that he could beat Eisenhower because his service as commissioner of baseball would get him the male vote and he would count on the support of African Americans because Jackie Robinson had broken the color barrier and joined the Major Leagues during his term: "And I'm an extremely handsome fellow and that gets me all the female vote. So what else is there?"[20]

Harriman's visit was more problematic. Wilson discovered that the former New York governor was unwelcome in much of North Carolina after he endorsed school integration. Three towns withdrew an invitation to sponsor an event that featured him as the speaker. Finally, he arranged a rally in Asheboro, where folks seemed more concerned with less weighty matters. While the governor was standing with a small group of locals, one man asked Harriman how much he was worth. "Oh, about a hundred million, give or take ten," Wilson remembered Harriman's reply. "You know how real estate values fluctuate."[21]

Wilson and Sanford had worked for Kefauver in North Carolina but knew his cause was lost by the time of the convention. Most Southerners deserted him after he and the other senator from Tennessee, Albert Gore, refused to sign the Southern Manifesto. The Democrats finally chose Stevenson as their candidate with Kefauver as his running mate, which did not sit well with the North Carolina delegation. A majority of the state's votes went to Senator John F. Kennedy of Massachusetts, who had the support of Luther Hodges. Hodges wasn't smitten with this Yankee; rather, the Kennedy votes in the South were a snub to Kefauver.[22]

The maneuver caught the attention of writer Harry Golden, who observed in his newspaper, the Carolina Israelite, "We hate our own much more than we hate 'outsiders.' The Southern delegates, therefore, wanted Kennedy, a New England Roman Catholic, who writes articles in the Atlantic Monthly against the Southern textile industry. How do you like that for the renunciation of logic?"[23]

When the balloting began, Wilson was seated beside Senator Sam J. Ervin Jr., who had led the Southern delegates' fight against the party's civil rights plank. He later recalled that Ervin chose neither Kennedy nor Kefauver, but Gore. "This was a little curious," Wilson later wrote, "because Gore was more liberal than either Kennedy or Kefauver, as Ervin well knew, but Gore was Southern, and he wasn't Catholic, and he wasn't named Kefauver."[24]

The fall campaign season in 1956 was as tame as any North Carolina had seen in years. Hodges had token Republican opposition, and the other statewide contests were routine. One of the more rousing events occurred in Winston-Salem, where Kennedy spoke at the YDC's annual convention. Less than a month later, North Carolina Democrats carried the state for Stevenson, but with only a fifteen-thousand-vote margin.

Terry saw Kennedy again two years later, when Kennedy was invited to Charlotte to speak at a Chamber of Commerce dinner. The senator's intentions for a campaign in 1960 were clearly evident. After Kennedy accepted the invitation, he asked his hosts to invite delegates who had attended the 1956 convention and he sought out Sanford and Wilson — the only two who attended — to say hello and to introduce his wife, Jackie.

From time to time, Margaret Rose accompanied Terry to political events, but like Mrs. Kennedy, she would have preferred to be doing something else. She enjoyed music, had begun to paint watercolors, and had taken a new interest in gardening. As her husband prepared for a statewide campaign, she was involved with their new home, a large brick house set in a grove of trees just up the hill from a lake in a neighborhood of expensive homes. Moreover, she had to care for two young children as well as the family's two dogs, a dachshund named Coco and a white poodle named Nicky.

Nothing loomed as a greater threat to Margaret Rose's pleasant suburban routine than her husband's political plans. Yet, though it would mean change, she supported him fully. Terry was as sure of his plans now as he had been of anything in his life. The operations of his Chapel Hill office expanded as he enlisted additional help, including Thomas W. Lambeth, the son of a public school superintendent, who had remained on as director of the student union after graduating at Chapel Hill in 1957. Sanford met Lambeth when both served on a selection committee that recommended William Aycock as chancellor of the university. In 1958, Lambeth began making scouting trips on Terry's behalf to the state's counties, where he talked with political contacts and filed detailed reports on what he learned.

In the late spring of 1959 Terry was in Raleigh for the unveiling of Scott's official portrait. Artist Chandler Christy of New York painted the governor seated in a chair, cigar in hand, and gave him a stern expression that bothered Scott's son, Bob. He wrote Terry that he supposed the artist "painted what he saw—a mighty unhappy man. He had no way of knowing that Kerr's personality was anything but gloomy and that the expression was that of an active man forced to sit still for long hours." [25]

The house chambers were packed as legislators and others, including Terry, paid homage to the former governor. Standing in the rear of the hall that day was Hugh Cannon, a twenty-eight-year-old lawyer who was working his first session as a member of the Institute of Government staff. Cannon was seeking a gubernatorial candidate to support in 1960 and a friend had suggested he take a look at Sanford.[26]

Cannon was a native of Albemarle and had graduated from Davidson College before going on to Oxford University as a Rhodes scholar and earning a law degree from Harvard University. After law school, he had interviewed with firms in Charlotte, but nothing there seemed to satisfy his missionary zeal. He worked as a volunteer in an unsuccessful congressional campaign in 1958 before he accepted an offer from the Institute of Government, where he was assigned to track legislation in the senate during the 1959 session. It was a job that provided a perfect window on state politics and Cannon had developed a liking for Lieutenant Governor Luther Barnhardt, who was considered a likely contender for 1960, when he first heard of Terry Sanford.

Cannon had not been impressed with Terry's appearance at the portrait dedication, but J. Alex McMahon, a former Institute staffer and fellow Harvard Law graduate, urged him to take a second look. If he wanted to get a taste of politics, McMahon told Cannon, then he should talk to Sanford about a job in his campaign. Terry might not win the governorship, but if he lost, it would be with honor, Cannon later recalled McMahon saying. He asked McMahon to arrange an introduction.

The legislature was close to adjournment when Cannon showed up at

Terry's Fayetteville office for an interview. Terry assumed Cannon was look-ing for a job in the law firm, but Cannon explained that his ambition was more than that. He offered to write speeches, do research, fetch coffee, drive the car, anything. He confessed his political résumé was brief, but he passed along the names of those he had met in the congressional cam-paign. Terry made some calls and learned that though Cannon was short on experience, his coworkers had been impressed with his judgment. Three weeks after their first meeting, Terry asked Cannon when he could start. He was in Fayetteville within the week.

When Cannon arrived at the law firm, it was understood that his stay would be short-lived. Until the campaign began in earnest, he was assigned to work with McCoy and Phillips on the purchase of rights of way for the gas company's line connecting eastern North Carolina with the main feeder located farther west. Cannon had been there only a few weeks when Terry stopped by his office and dropped off some pieces he had written on education. It wasn't a speech exactly, more a collection of ideas, and he asked Cannon to shape it up.

Cannon approached this first project as if he were preparing a paper for a Davidson professor he hoped to impress. He found Terry's ideas not just good, but inspiring. Forty years later, Cannon still recalled his initial im-pression: Terry Sanford was not the average politician, hustling an angle on a popular issue, but "an absolutely brilliant man who could go with ideas and conceptualize at such a pace."[27] Cannon had been looking for a candidate who shared his desire to do something about the condition of the world (before the law, he had considered the ministry), and working through that first assignment he believed he had found him.

That summer, a year before the all-important spring party primary elec-tion, the *Associated Press* asked 140 news editors to pick the frontrunner among the possible candidates for governor in 1960. House Speaker Addi-son Hewlett of Wilmington, Attorney General Malcolm Seawell, Thomas J. Pearsall, State Treasurer Edwin Gill, and former party chairman John Lar-kins of Trenton all placed in the ranking. But 62 percent of those polled said Sanford was ahead of them all.

One name missing from the list was that of I. Beverly Lake, who con-tinued to be the leading spokesman for the segregationists. In a speech in Burlington that spring, he had accused Hodges of buckling under to the NAACP. The governor had been "blinded by the glitter of moderation," Lake told a civic club, while North Carolina had pursued a segregation-integration policy "of appeasement, of acquiescence in tyranny and judicial lawlessness of retreat, retreat, retreat." He accused Hodges of "fritter-ing away four, long priceless years" in the battle to maintain segregated schools. The speech was all but an accusation of political treason. The NAACP was "this invader," Lake said, and Hodges and his allies had done nothing to stop it.[28]

Terry was anxious about Lake, whose entry into the governor's race would surely bring the race issue to the fore. Lake's intentions were not clear, but late in the summer, Terry learned that Lake had visited Dr. Henry Jordan seeking his support. Jordan reportedly told him to raise a campaign fund and then they would talk.[29]

If Lake entered the race, Terry was sure that North Carolina would not escape the experience of segregationist campaigns that had become a staple of contemporary Southern politics. In Alabama, Attorney General John Patterson had become governor in 1958 largely on the basis of his legal fight to put the NAACP out of business. Dedicated segregationists, who vowed to fight to the end, also had won elections in Georgia and Virginia. Leroy Collins's popularity in Florida was fading. No one serious about any future in public life hinted of sympathy for integration, not in a time when even the so-called moderates such as Mississippi Governor J. P. Coleman were the targets of abuse. Coleman had taken a position quite similar to Umstead's in North Carolina, only to be forced to use a statewide radio and television broadcast to defend himself against criticism that he had been too soft on the integration question.[30]

The reputation for moderation that Hodges had cultivated for North Carolina remained intact. No federal troops had been necessary to integrate formerly all-white schools in Greensboro, Charlotte, Winston-Salem, and Durham. There had been no call for FBI agents to investigate lynchings, as was the case in Alabama. On more than one occasion, the governor and his attorney general had demonstrated no patience with the Ku Klux Klan's bluster in southeastern North Carolina.

In August 1959, Sanford celebrated his forty-second birthday. A decade earlier, he had been preparing to challenge the governor's handpicked candidate for the presidency of the YDC. At that time, he was a political unknown, just another young lawyer with ambition. Now he was the spokesman for a new political coalition that included Scott's Branch-head boys, associates from the National Guard, classmates from Chapel Hill, Methodist churchmen, Jaycees, lawyers, the American Legion, a few businessmen, and a host of contemporaries who saw in him a leader for their generation.

There was even money in the bank, some of it raised by Hargrove Bowles, a successful Greensboro businessman who had been collecting campaign contributions since late spring. Called Skipper since his days as the leader of a college dance band, Bowles was the brother of Terry's Swain Hall roommate, John, who now lived in Los Angeles, where he was head of the nationwide Rexall drugstore chain. Like his brother, Skipper had been successful in business and lived in a large, handsome home overlooking the well-tended fairways of Greensboro Country Club. When Terry and Paul Thompson arrived at Bowles's home to talk to him about raising a campaign war chest, they suspected that he might even be a Republican.

Terry's campaign infrastructure also was taking shape. Basically, it followed the familiar military chain of command, a pyramid structure like the one he had devised as a student at Chapel Hill. He was at the top, and immediately below were a select group of loyal and trusted friends called area keys. They, in turn, looked to their own county keys, who were the local campaign organizers with workers in the precincts.

On November 2, the area keys met for the first time at Greensboro's O. Henry Hotel, where Bowles had booked a meeting room. Present were Scott men Merrill Evans from the rural northeast, Jack Kirksey of Morganton, and Clint Newton of Shelby, who had helped in Terry's YDC campaign. Hector McGeachy of Fayetteville and Bill Staton from Sanford, who had run Frank Graham's campaign, were there. So was Jack Pool from Clinton, who had been student body president at Chapel Hill when Terry was a freshman, and Charlotte businessman Paul Younts, a retired general and one of Terry's allies from the American Legion. Others included Wadesboro lawyer H. Patrick Taylor Jr., the son of a former lieutenant governor; Kerr Scott's son, Bob; Raleigh lawyer Woodrow Teague; and Asheville lawyer Bruce Elmore. Over dinner, Terry talked about the upcoming campaign and outlined what lay ahead. Before these men left, they were assigned the counties they were expected to organize. That night, Terry left for a week on the road with Tom Lambeth at the wheel of a new car he had just purchased for his new job with the campaign.

The newcomer at that meeting was Bert Bennett, a tall, lean businessman from Winston-Salem who had just resigned as Forsyth County party chairman to sign on as Terry's campaign manager. Some of those present had known Bennett at Chapel Hill, where he had been student body president. Others knew him as a political leader closely aligned with the conservative business interests that dominated the party organization in Winston-Salem, home of Wachovia Bank & Trust Company and R. J. Reynolds Tobacco Company. Terry had chosen him for those reasons and others, and believed Bennett would add balance to the organization.

It was the beginning of a political alliance that would shape North Carolina politics for the next twenty years.

CHAPTER TEN

"Puddles of Poison"

FAYETTEVILLE ON FEBRUARY 4, 1960, was cold, windy, and far removed from that French hillside where Terry Sanford had sat in the grass warming himself in the spring sun fifteen years earlier. There in the backwash of war he had considered his future and the prospects of a life in politics. Now, on this day, proclaimed Terry Sanford Day in Fayetteville, he formally commenced a campaign for governor. He called it a New Day for North Carolina.

A crowd of five thousand filled the intersection and stopped traffic in front of the small stage built on the north side of the Old Market Building on Hay Street. Terry's family, his neighbors and friends, all were bundled against the brisk, chilly wind. Margaret Rose was beaming. Betsy Sanford wore a satisfied smile and held her chin high as she sat beside her husband, Cecil, who looked as steady and genial as ever. Mrs. W. Kerr Scott, the senator's widow, had even traveled down from Haw River with Kerr's brother, Ralph, to wish Terry well. There was no formal laying on of hands, but her very presence was an endorsement.

The ceremonies started at 12:30 in the afternoon and were replete with symbolism. Terry recalled the Scott tradition when he said it was time to quit "holding the line," a battle cry used by Scott against those in the legislature who thought his program extravagant. "I call on you to join with me to build a better North Carolina," Sanford declared. "The object is not to defend the goal but to score a touchdown. The touchdown for North Carolina is in expanding, growing, developing and building."

He spoke of improving schools and hiring more teachers, of catching the wave of industrial development rising in the South, of reforming the state's court system, of reordering agricultural marketing and building roads. North Carolina had yet to reach its full potential, he said, and "people are becoming more and more aware of our shortcomings and are determined that now is the time when something must be done. . . . This is a new day of opportunities. Let's make it a new day for achievement. We are ready to go."[1]

More than a decade of dreaming, planning, and plain hard work lay behind his words. The smoldering fire of political ambition had come to full flame. Everything—from the choice of Fayetteville as a place to live and raise a family to the countless nights on the road to attend some small gathering and deliver a fifteen-minute speech—had led to this day. No candidate in recent memory had ever brought such preparation to the starting line; Terry believed he would need it. Those who had all but anointed the governors of the past were just as determined as he was. This had the makings of a watershed year in North Carolina politics.

Terry's prepared statement was brief; it took but a tenth of the hour dedicated to the flag-waving, band-playing sendoff conducted beneath a huge banner carrying an outline of the state with the candidate's picture set in the center. Many in the crowd held homemade posters and signs. There were rousing marches played by the Fayetteville High School band, which also serenaded with the more gentle strains of "Carolina in the Morning." The entire affair was scripted to the last detail, including an endorsement from Mrs. E. R. McKeithan, president of the United Daughters of the Confederacy and a grand dame of keepers of the Lost Cause. She reminded all that Terry had helped save the Confederate Women's Home from closing when it needed money from the legislature.

The good feeling, enthusiasm, and uplifting spirit of announcement day climaxed a month of almost nonstop travel. In January, Terry had made appearances in all one hundred counties of the state. The itinerary had opened on the seventh in nearby Bladen County when a caravan of cars rolled into Elizabethtown for an 8 A.M. breakfast meeting and had concluded on the twenty-ninth, after a sweep through the far mountain counties on the Tennessee border that ended with a meeting in Charlotte. No candidate had ever tried such a tour, and campaign manager Bert Bennett would discourage anyone ever attempting it again.

It had been an exhausting exercise. Day after day, Terry and Bert, accompanied by one or more young aides, had been passed like Pony Express parcels from one auto convoy to another. The daily routine included meetings at eight and ten in the morning, then a luncheon, followed by afternoon sessions at three and five. At night, the candidate huddled with campaign contributors and local boosters who had accepted assignments to raise money on his behalf. Often, he made appearances in as many as five counties in one twenty-four-hour period. Instructions to local organizers had been precise: No meetings at the courthouse. That smacked of the old, not the new. Invitations were distributed generously, and in person. Terry wanted rally-size meetings but not so large that guests felt lost and out of touch.

The demanding schedule ground Bennett to a nub. Although he finally learned to catch naps in the front seat of the campaign car, as did his candidate, he didn't make every stop. The only person besides Terry to complete the entire trip was Wallace Hyde of mountainous Graham County, who had quit his job to work as a volunteer. Hyde almost missed claiming that honor when he lingered too long over a plate of country ham at his aunt's boardinghouse and the caravan left him behind. He caught up at the next stop.

Bennett marveled at Terry's stamina and his knack for working a crowd without missing a single hand, and seldom a name. The level of organization was equally impressive. Before each stop, Terry thumbed through a packet of "ICs," carefully notated index cards compiled by Peggy Warren, who had logged each letter written, every phone call made, virtually every personal contact Terry had made with hundreds of people across the state.

Bennett began to feel the life and vibrancy of the campaign when Terry spoke with folks he met at a breakfast meeting or around the drink box at country stores. This was the part of campaigning that Terry enjoyed the most. He genuinely liked people and they liked him, responding to the twinkle in his eye, his boyish grin and dimples, his firm handshake, and his good humor, a trait he inherited from his father. He demonstrated a rare ability to focus intently on each person as he moved from one friendly hand to the next. This close attention stirred something in people. His mother once told a friend that her son was simply "beguiling." [2]

For Sanford, the campaign was not a dash to the finish line, but a marathon whose every step moved him that much closer to his goal. Like an athlete encouraged by the last chip shot, bounce pass, or base hit, Terry drew on the nodding endorsements and firm commitments from those who extended their hands. He left each with a feeling that he had "won that one." This zest for the nitty-gritty of political life was as much a part of him as keen intellect and roaming mind. He was simply at home on the campaign trail.

At each of the January meetings before the formal announcement, Terry spoke of the days ahead and coyly introduced Bennett as the man who would be his campaign manager—if he decided to run, a phrase that always drew laughter. None mistook the visits for what they were, and Terry assured a crowd in Raleigh that this exercise was simply prelude to the main event. "We're not going to be sawing any limbs off behind our friends," he said, just in case some felt they were being led down a dead-end path, as he felt Dr. Henry Jordan had misled him four years earlier. [3]

Terry talked and he listened. When his Ford sedan, borrowed for the campaign, finally rolled into the driveway of his home on Sylvan Road after the last stop in Charlotte, he believed that two issues—education and roads—would make the difference in this campaign. Of the two, education was the most compelling, but it also presented the greatest challenge. Demands for more school buildings, higher teacher pay, and the necessities required to improve the state's education system would cost a lot of money. Luther Hodges had balked at the price tag and conservatives in the legislature, where the checks were written, would be hard to persuade. Yet Terry believed that parents of school-age children, as were he and Margaret Rose, would not stint when it came to providing for their children. They were willing to do what was necessary, he insisted, and to make his point he often joked about an incident during the campaign.

At one stop he had finished his usual speech about the needs of education in the state when a woman stood and asked bluntly where he expected to find the money to pay for all the things he promised. Terry wrote that he scouted the room for the presence of news reporters and seeing none, replied, "From taxes." The crowd applauded. Later, as he and Bennett headed out the door, he remarked that they had just witnessed something extraordinary: that crowd had enthusiastically endorsed taxes for schools.

Bennett, the realist, responded, "They thought you said Texas." [4]

Candidates had been promising better schools and more asphalt for years. There was nothing new here. At the core, roads and education were the staples of state governments across the land, and because there appeared to be more of the same ahead, at least at the end of January, news reporters were predicting another humdrum campaign.

The missing ingredient—the red meat of Southern politics that promised to bring news to a campaign—was the race issue. This issue worried Terry more than having enough money to pay campaign bills, more than building an organization, more than whether people would accept his vision for the state. He had seen what it had done to Frank Graham, and he had learned a thing or two about dirty tricks from Scott's campaign. Sanford had no patience for such demagoguery. Whatever happened, he told those closest to him, he would confront the race issue forthrightly, promptly, and he would not do or say anything that twenty years later would be an embarrassment. He felt he should be bold, but cautious. "I was well aware that it didn't have to bounce but a little bit off course to kill you," he later recalled. [5]

Since the *Brown* decision, the nation's attention on civil rights had been focused elsewhere, mostly in Arkansas and Tennessee and the Deep South states of Alabama, Mississippi, and Georgia. But just seventy-two hours before Terry Sanford Day in Fayetteville, four black college students in

Greensboro, North Carolina, took seats at a dime store lunch counter reserved for white customers, asked for service, and refused to leave when they were denied. The tactic had been tried three years earlier in Durham, but interest in that demonstration proved faint and failed to ignite any action. This time, however, things would be different.

Few blacks, and even fewer whites, fully understood the consequences of this simple act of protest. All were caught unawares, especially the daily newspapers in Greensboro. The first reporter to hear about the students was Jo Spivey, who worked for the afternoon *Greensboro Record*. Spivey's last edition was already on the front stoops of readers' homes when she arrived at the F. W. Woolworth store just before 5 P.M., as the store was closing and the students were leaving. When the young men returned the next day, she got the story for the early editions. Further accounts appeared the following day in the *Greensboro Daily News* and wire service accounts began to flow. Yet it was not until the third and even the fourth of February—the day of Sanford's announcement—that most newspaper editors gave the coverage more than cursory attention.

Before February, the race issue had not registered as a serious concern in a poll of North Carolina voters that Terry had commissioned Lou Harris to conduct, the first ever for a political candidate in the state. Harris was a Chapel Hill classmate who had learned polling techniques under Elmo Roper before setting up his own company, Lou Harris & Associates. He was now hip-deep in John Kennedy's bid for the Democratic presidential nomination and was on his way to interviewing more voters in one year than any pollster in history. When Harris contacted Terry late in 1959 about polling in North Carolina, he had found a willing client with a cautious campaign manager. Bennett finally agreed to this new campaign device but insisted that only he and the candidate see the results, and that may be "one too many," he noted in a memo.[6]

Bennett was not alone in his suspicion about political polling. The techniques of social scientists had improved significantly since the embarrassing gaffe of the early days, when the famous *Literary Digest* poll had predicted the defeat of Franklin Roosevelt in 1936. Problems were inherent in the science, however. One of the most important was the lapse of time between the interviews and the compilation and interpretation of the data. In later years, pollsters would begin analyzing polling data within hours after questions were asked. In 1960, the data might not be available for weeks, and much could happen in a campaign during that length of time.

Harris's interviewers began knocking on doors in North Carolina in January while Terry was on his hundred-county tour. What they found showed that the election was wide open. If it was any consolation, voters who didn't know Sanford—and eight out of ten did not—also drew a blank on the other likely candidates. Harris predicted a "nip-and-tuck race" with Sanford getting "not anywhere near the margin necessary to win without a runoff election."

Terry was particularly concerned about the poll's report of his apparent soft support among farmers and voters in the rural areas, where he had hoped his association with Kerr Scott would give him an edge. To Terry's satisfaction, Harris did report that the dominant issue on the minds of voters was education; ironically, however, voters did not identify education with Sanford but with John Larkins, who had announced his candidacy a few weeks earlier.

Terry had anticipated Larkins's candidacy. He was the kind of man North Carolina had been putting in the governor's office for generations. A politically active lawyer, former legislator, Raleigh insider, and eleven years Sanford's senior, Larkins had served as the state Democratic Party's national committeeman before Governor Umstead had named him state chairman. He had been the legislative liaison for Umstead and Hodges and for a time chaired the powerful state Advisory Budget Commission. He had been one of those who had stopped Kerr Scott in his tracks in 1951 and now pinned his own hopes of becoming governor on the help of the old party regulars, legislators and county sheriffs.

Before declaring himself, Larkins had carefully touched base with Hodges and with Senators Jordan and Ervin, advising each of his plans and describing himself as the conservative alternative to the "liberal" Terry Sanford. On January 19, in a statewide, thirty-minute television program broadcast right at the six o'clock dinner hour, he declared his candidacy.[7]

Larkins's real ambition was Washington, not Raleigh, and had been ever since Umstead passed him over and picked Alton Lennon as successor to Willis Smith in 1953. Before finally settling on a campaign for governor, he had considered a congressional race but decided not to challenge Third District incumbent Graham A. Barden. The incumbent rewarded him by announcing the day after Larkins declared for governor that he was retiring at the end of the term. When he heard the news, Larkins was shocked but stayed the course.

Barden's decision wasn't the first surprise to throw Larkins off step. On Christmas Eve, with his statewide broadcasts already under contract to television stations across the state, he took a call from his friend Woodrow Jones of Rutherfordton, who earlier had agreed to be his campaign manager. Jones told Larkins that the governor had prevailed on him to help put together a bid for the vice presidential nomination at the Democratic convention in July. Jones asked his friend to be relieved of duty, and Larkins agreed, reluctantly. It took him another six weeks to find a campaign manager.[8]

As the 1960 gubernatorial campaign began to take shape, Hodges became increasingly uncomfortable with the choices. The governor believed his administration had compiled an impressive record—moderation in race relations, industrial development, and clean government—and he was impatient with any who might put such a record to the test in a political campaign. Hodges believed that Larkins could not be counted on to defend him, and neither could Sanford. The governor and his chief political advisor, Harold Makepeace, were determined to have a candidate who would champion his administration.

Hodges's backstage maneuvering became decidedly public in mid-January, when he released a statement denying he had endorsed a candidate and adamantly declaring his neutrality. The governor might have given up his search for a candidate had it not been for I. Beverly Lake, who more than any political figure at the time was guaranteed to provoke him. For five years Lake had been Hodges's nemesis, especially on the race issue, and now he was being coy about his plans. He had told some of those encouraging him to run that he would consider it if they raised $50,000 to pay for his campaign.

The tide was building for segregationists in the South. Lake had to look no further than Virginia, where public schools in Prince Edward County had been closed and turned over to a nonprofit corporation, effectively eliminating public education for black children in the county along the lines of what he had suggested five years earlier.[9] South Carolina remained steadfast in its resistance to the Court, and in Florida, where Leroy Collins had created some excitement for liberals and moderates, conservative candidates appeared to be voter favorites.

In mid-January, Lake said he would announce a decision in thirty days at a YDC rally in the town of Sanford. Bill Staton, one of Lake's former students, encouraged Terry to be there too and to be prepared to say some nice things about Lake. Staton and others expected Lake to bow out of the race, just as he had four years earlier.

Terry arrived at the rally with campaign workers Hugh Cannon and Lauch Faircloth and found a crowd of six hundred filling the American Legion hall. The three men stood near the rear of the hall as Lake began his speech calling for tighter regulation of utilities and a more "businesslike administration" in Raleigh, a phrase calculated to unsettle Hodges, even if he said nothing more. He followed his familiar criticism of the Supreme Court's Brown decision and the Pearsall Plan with a firm declaration that if he were governor he would do something about civil rights demonstrations and not allow students attending state-supported colleges to march to and fro in front of a dime store entrance and block the way of paying customers.

Cannon couldn't help noticing that many in this crowd were not the kind of folks who made a habit of political meetings. The Lake people, as they came to be called, included good old boys off the farms and from rural communities who cheered lustily at Lake's statements of defiance to federal authority. There was no mistaking Lake's core following, and he demonstrated that he could rouse at least these angry whites whose daily newspapers carried one story after another of the growing sit-in movement. Yet, despite the obvious sympathy for his point of view and the enthusiastic response from this crowd, Lake announced that he would not be a candidate. He said he simply did not have the money to mount an effective campaign.

Relief showed on Terry's face as he joined Lake for a photograph with the rally organizers. Lake was grim and unsmiling as he stood in the center of the group; near the side, Terry wore a typical bemused expression. Terry picked his words carefully and told reporters that the decision by his "long-time friend has removed a heavy load from my mind. He would have been an able and formidable contender." [10]

The matter might have ended there except that Lake did not fully close the door. Before he left for his home in Wake Forest he said he would reconsider his decision if the money became available. Robert Morgan, the Lillington legislator who had sponsored Lake's countermeasures to the Pearsall Plan, told reporters that night that efforts were already underway to convince Lake he should enter the race. As Terry rode back to Raleigh with his friends, he did not believe that would happen.

Two days later, Terry opened his state campaign headquarters in three rooms on the fourth floor of the Carolina Hotel, Kerr Scott's old haunt, where he had been promised good rates by its owner, insurance executive Joseph Bryan of Greensboro. Peggy Warren closed the Capital Typing Service in Chapel Hill and relocated to Raleigh; so did Jeanne Nunalee, a secretary from the law firm in Fayetteville. Others taking up posts were Henry Hall Wilson Jr., Ben Roney, and Roy Wilder. Tom Lambeth and J. Phillips Carlton of Pinetops, a graduating senior from State College, reported to work as Sanford's drivers and traveling companions.

Later that morning, Terry walked from the hotel to the state Board of Elections office to pay his filing fee. Before he left his room, he slipped on his ring bearing a paratrooper's badge and pinned an old Frank Graham campaign button to the underside of the lapel of his suit coat. The mementos were a private reminder of the challenge that lay ahead. In his pocket was a check for $250 from O. Max Gardner Jr. of Shelby that he planned to use to pay his filing fee.

In a prepared statement, Sanford told reporters, "I am going to try to be as good a governor as Max Gardner, Sr. I am going to hope to be half as good a man as Max Gardner, Jr." [11] It could easily have been young Max filing for governor that day, had he not been stricken with multiple sclerosis. As Terry handed Gardner's check forward, he paid tribute to his friend, saying, "In health, he was a source of strength to his friends. In illness, he is a source of inspiration. His courage, his wonderful spirit, his determination and his happy outlook have lifted the lives of his friends." [12]

The Saturday newspapers that noted Sanford's official entry into the race also included Attorney General Malcolm Seawell's defense of the Hodges administration. Seawell, who was known for a quick temper and sharp tongue, expressed irritation at Sanford's coziness with Lake and told reporters that if no one else was going to speak up for the governor's record on integration then he would. He said Sanford's comments left the impression that "he was embracing the slap at the present administration. I don't say that he intended it that way. I just say that is the impression some got." [13]

Seawell's remarks surprised Terry, who had made a point of staying in touch with Seawell after he became attorney general. The two had talked often about their political ambitions, and Terry believed Seawell wanted a seat on the state's high court, where his father had once served; he planned to oblige him that honor if he became governor. At their last visit, which had been just a few days earlier, Seawell had said nothing about running for governor. [14]

There was no way that Terry could have anticipated events of the next few days, which would ultimately shape the outcome of the primary campaign. Hodges's determination to blunt Lake's attack on his administration would ultimately launch Seawell's candidacy for governor at the same time that the lunch-counter sit-ins would rouse angry whites to rally behind a candidate like Lake who would campaign for the separation of the races.

Within a week after the four scared young men had asked the waitress at Greensboro's Woolworth counter to serve them a cup of coffee, similar demonstrations were underway in other cities in North Carolina and the South. Word of their bold action spread quickly. On February 8, black college students in Winston-Salem and Durham took their places at lunch counters as the demonstrations expanded to Fayetteville, Charlotte, Raleigh, and High Point. The sit-ins were fully integrated now, with white students joining in to carry picket signs and endure the abuse heaped upon them from angry, taunting whites.

The situation was becoming volatile. A bomb threat emptied one store, and in Greensboro, whites ignited sheets of toilet paper and dropped them in the laps of students seated at the counter. In Raleigh, as a young black woman left Woolworth's, a heavyset, red-faced man raked the cigar in his hand across her sweater. "Did you burn it?" he asked sarcastically, unaware that a large portion of the fire had flicked into the crook of his folded right arm. A bystander finally warned him that the rising curl of smoke was from his own burning coat sleeve.[15]

Most encounters ended in stalemate. White store managers hunkered down and refused to extend service. The students sat quietly, expressionless and impassive, on the lunch counter stools while others marched outside with picket signs. There was some movement, however. In the little town of Ahoskie, deep in the heart of eastern North Carolina, Oscar Speed, manager of the Walter-Boone drugstore, said he did the right thing when he served a black couple who sat down in a back booth in his store.[16]

The governor and his attorney general stood back from the fray and left local officials and police to sort it out. At a news conference a few days after the demonstrations began, Seawell told reporters he knew of no law that prohibited mixed seating in restaurants, nor was there a statute that would require an owner to serve an unwanted customer. Both he and the governor said they didn't believe that the confrontations added anything to the future of race relations but simply made matters worse.

The demonstrations were beyond the understanding of North Carolina's politicians as well as of the newspaper editors struggling to cover the story unfolding before them. Nothing like this had ever happened. In the newsrooms, editors couldn't even reach a consensus on whether to describe the demonstrations as "sit-downs" or "sit-ins."[17] In the halls of power, police chiefs and mayors, even the governor, weren't quite sure how to deal with young people who seemed ready and willing to endure threats of jail and worse.

Gene Roberts of the *News & Observer* may have been the first reporter in the state to see that the spirit of the lunch-counter demonstrations wasn't limited to young people. The determination of the students had stiffened the resolve of young and old alike. On Tuesday night, two weeks after the demonstrations began in Greensboro, Roberts was at the White Rock Baptist Church in Durham to cover a community meeting where Reverend Martin Luther King Jr., the leader of the Southern Christian Leadership Conference, was scheduled to speak. More than twelve hundred people, including about fifty whites, jammed into the church. Earlier in the day King had met with about three hundred students from the larger black campuses in Virginia and the Carolinas who were meeting in Durham to discuss recent demonstrations. That night, at the church, Roberts heard

King say, "Let us not fear going to jail. We must show we are willing and prepared to fill up the jails of the South. Our ultimate aim is not to humiliate the white man but to win his understanding." [18]

King's words were a familiar refrain. But what followed this appeal impressed Roberts and convinced him that this time something was different. When King finished, the preacher at White Rock Baptist asked his flock to make their own sacrifice for the young people. Give up your Easter dress, don't buy that new spring outfit, he said, and Roberts heard the amens rise from every corner. The students were on the front lines, but Roberts saw that they would draw strength and support from their elders.

The spread of the demonstrations became the "liberals' horror," Roberts would say later.[19] Each news account of the lunch-counter demonstrations stirred the resentment of whites already angered by the threat to their segregated classrooms. Any hope by Sanford or Hodges that the state might skate clear of the race issue in 1960 died on the sidewalks where angry whites, some in Ku Klux Klan regalia, taunted and harassed students walking picket lines. A week after Sanford paid his filing fee, Seawell told reporters he would be a candidate for governor and declared himself the champion of the "splendid" record of Governor Hodges, including his handling of school integration.

Under other circumstances Seawell might have been Terry's candidate for governor. Tall, with a strong, chiseled look and the right amount of gray in his hair, Seawell was close enough in age for Terry to consider him a contemporary. They shared the Frank Graham tradition of Chapel Hill, and Seawell had preceded Terry as an associate at the Institute of Government. After the war, Seawell had compiled an impressive political record, beginning with his election as mayor of Lumberton. Later he had been elected district solicitor and prosecuted Klansmen when they tried to roust Lumbee Indians in Robeson County. His district included Fayetteville, and though Terry did not practice a lot of criminal law he had found himself across the table from the combative and intense prosecutor on more than one occasion. Seawell was a superior court judge when Hodges appointed him attorney general in 1958.

In his brief time in office, Seawell had proved to be an aggressive attorney general. He used his office to enforce fair trade laws on gasoline dealers and most recently had begun preparing legislation to regulate small loan companies. He also had vigorously pursued the conviction of labor leader Boyd Payton after Governor Hodges used National Guard troops on the streets of Henderson during a period of labor unrest in the spring of 1959. The latter episode, which concluded with a trial marked by dubious testimony against Payton, caused considerable concern among Seawell's friends who considered themselves moderates, even liberals. Most stuck with him, however, and applauded his credentials on race relations, particularly after he was presented a B'nai B'rith award for promoting interracial harmony. He was an outspoken defender of racial progress and enjoyed a strong following among black voters, particularly in Durham, the home of the state's oldest and most influential black political organization.

Lake answered Seawell ten days later when he announced that he would be a candidate. Standing with him at a Raleigh news conference was Morgan, who had forsaken his own campaign for reelection to the state senate to work for his old professor. Lake said he planned to talk about a range of issues: fiscal conservatism, regulation of utilities, overhaul of the state highway commission. After all that had come before, however, they were secondary to the issue that the Supreme Court's *Brown* decision had laid before him.

Despite what the state's attorney general might say, Lake said the Court's decision was not the last word, which was a curious interpretation for a serious student of the law. "I consider any condition and any policy of our government which causes the people . . . grave concern for their constitutional liberties, peace and good order of our state, and the future welfare of their children, a legitimate subject for public discussion in this campaign," Lake argued.[20]

His beliefs were not founded in hatred, he said, and he would not accept the support of "any person or organization whose program or statements are designed to create or increase tension and discord between white and Negro North Carolinians or to belittle the contribution of either to our state. The preservation of our social order, in which two great races live in peace as neighbors and friends, each proud of its own distinctive qualities and each regarding these as a trust to be preserved for future generations, is an entirely different matter. If I become governor, I shall use every power conferred upon me to continue that social order in North Carolina." Two years later, the newly elected governor of Alabama, George C. Wallace, would abbreviate Lake's lengthy declaration to two words: "Segregation forever."

Lake's decision to make segregation an issue in the campaign struck one state official as curious. "How in the hell can he do that," the *News & Observer* reported him saying, "in a state where I have personally never met an integrationist?"[21]

Lake made his announcement within hours of an appearance on NBC's *Today Show*, where he presented a segregationist's point of view in a panel discussion on the sit-in demonstrations. Appearing with him were Marion A. Wright of Linville Falls, North Carolina, who was vice president of the Southern Regional Council, a biracial group based in Atlanta; Mayor George B. Herndon of Fayetteville; and two black college students, Betty Johnson of Virginia Union and Lacey Streeter, a junior at North Carolina Central. Lake told the national television audience that if restaurants were integrated, "you would have chaos and confusion in eating establishments all over the Tar Heel state." [22]

Terry decided to let Lake and Seawell fight over segregation while he busied himself with other matters. Late in February he stood before a gathering of about two hundred women in Greensboro for a strategy session on his behalf. The woman who put the meeting together was the same Martha Clampett McKay who had pushed her way into the men-only world of campus politics twenty years earlier. After college, Martha Clampett had married Herbert McKay and settled down in Chapel Hill, where she had been a volunteer in local and congressional elections. She had no experience in statewide contests, but that didn't keep her from calling Terry in 1959 and volunteering to organize women in his campaign for governor. When the area keys met at Paul Thompson's cabin outside Fayetteville just before Terry began his hundred-county tour, McKay was once again the only woman present at a political strategy meeting.

Terry all but ignored his noontime hotel meal as he focused on what he planned to tell the women McKay had invited to Greensboro. This was more than an "eat-and-greet" function. He had plans for these women, who had arrived at midmorning for working sessions and who would remain until the afternoon to construct a clear strategy designed to engage women on his behalf. Sanford believed he could mobilize women to do more than lick envelopes and fetch coffee: he could give them an issue, a banner to carry, a mission. He gave them education.

"If you help elect me governor, and when our four years of service is done, I would want no higher tribute than for the citizens of North Carolina to say that I put education first," he said as he opened what was a brief but pivotal speech. He said he was not only their champion for better schools for their kids, but a champion for the beleaguered education professionals as well. He said he wanted higher teacher pay and would lead a revival of respect for the teaching profession. He spoke of the need for more teachers who were prepared to offer a wider range of courses and called for a long-range plan for education where progress would be monitored and adjustments made as conditions required. "There is one force in North Carolina which can overcome all of the forces of opposition. Women! Women determined to provide our children the finest in opportunities, women determined that our state will advance to its full potential." [23]

The Greensboro meeting was such a success that others were scheduled for Goldsboro and Charlotte. Working from an office in Chapel Hill that would eventually rival the activity of the headquarters at the Carolina Hotel, McKay produced position papers, organized letter-writing efforts, and designed brochures. Her volunteers dusted off Christmas card lists and mailed postcards produced by the campaign. It became, as McKay remembered years later, "a fight for education."

McKay equipped her army with brochures and materials highlighting the shortcomings and weaknesses in education, and each woman was given a hundred postcards that were to be returned with the name and address of each voter contacted. The crusaders reached thousands of new voters concerned about low teacher pay, crowded classes, courses of study that failed to meet the demands of a modern age, inadequate buildings, and an overall neglect of education that was sapping strength and attention from the state's teachers.

Almost simultaneously, the Sanford campaign launched a similar effort aimed at young voters. Led by Wilson Woodhouse, the group proved to be a remarkable launching pad for young politicians. Of the six members on Woodhouse's committee, Jimmy Hunt from Lucama, then a senior at State College in Raleigh, later would be elected to an unprecedented four terms as governor; Phil Carlton would serve on the state supreme court; and three of the other four would serve multiple terms in the state legislature. One of the three, Eddie Knox of Charlotte, would serve as the mayor of Charlotte and make an unsuccessful bid for governor.

After the Harris poll highlighted potential soft spots, Sanford moved to shore up support with North Carolina's farmers. He announced plans for developing food processing as well as food production in the state and called it the "second phase" of Kerr Scott's administration. He reminded farmers that Scott had promised to get them "out of the mud" with new roads; now it was time to "get the farmers out of the hole," and he enlisted Scott's son, Bob, to carry the story around the state. Terry also gained some attention in rural areas when he criticized Hodges's consolidation of the state highway commission districts. At one campaign stop, he told a crowd that a man couldn't get his road repaired unless he was a retired textile executive. He said the little man didn't stand a chance and promised to reorganize the highway commission once again. It was an old campaign song, but it never failed to draw a good response.

When Sanford declared that the state had a duty to pave every mile of school bus routes in the state, Hodges could contain himself no longer. That promise was outrageous, the governor said, and would cost $500 million and take twenty-five years to complete. Terry said, yes, it would take time, "but it will take forever at the present rate." [24]

In mid-April, Hodges all but endorsed Seawell, saying he was the candidate who "comes nearer to speaking out than any of the others. I like the way Seawell had the courage to speak out favorably on the things we are trying to do in North Carolina." [25] Sanford let the issue die. He had taken his shots at Hodges, in part to let any doubters know he wasn't Hodges's man, and to attract the attention of old Scott voters who were being lured away by Larkins and Lake. But Terry did not really want to fight with the governor or anyone else whose help he believed he would need later on. He was convinced that he would meet either Larkins or Lake in a second primary, and the difference between winning and losing could be determined by how quickly he could persuade Seawell's supporters that he was the best alternative.

Besides, it was fine for Terry that the former attorney general was taking most of the heat from Lake on the race issue. Harris's second wave of interviews, conducted after the sit-in demonstrations had come full flower, showed the race issue consuming far more of the political consciousness than a few weeks earlier. White North Carolinians did not like what they had been reading about in the newspapers, and Harris reported that attitudes on race were hardening. Whites favored segregation by a margin of two to one, with more than half those polled saying blacks had no right to be served where they were not wanted. [26]

Bert Bennett carefully tracked each step of the campaign from his posts at the Carolina Hotel and his office at Quality Oil Company in Winston-Salem. The campaign had proved to be a greater drain on his time than he had anticipated. After spending the entire month of January with Terry, he began dividing his time between business and politics. This was his first major campaign, but he was proving to be a master tactician and superb organizer.

In time, the candidate and the campaign manager would become legend, and the organization they were putting together would change state politics for the next generation. Yet, no two men could have been quite so different. The candidate had come from meager beginnings and worked his way through college; the manager graduated from prep school. The candidate enjoyed the law; the manager tried one semester of law school and headed home to learn the family oil business, where he was made a partner at the age of thirty-one. The candidate had poked and prodded the establishment; the manager had been embraced by the established party organization.

Bennett was a pragmatist, ever the businessman, studying the bottom line, looking for results. His language was marketing and his experience was in selling one of the most competitive American products, cheap gasoline. He was intrigued by Roney's old-boy network, but he wanted fresh insights. Early in the campaign, while all the candidates were hustling over the entire state, Bennett became intrigued with Hugh Cannon's analysis of voting results that showed that less than a third of the state's one hundred counties could deliver a winning margin. Bennett was so impressed that he posted a state map illustrating Cannon's research on the wall behind his desk as a daily reminder of where Sanford's "customers" were.

Bennett was more conservative in his politics than Terry, but he cared less about philosophy and more about ambition. He would later recall that at their first meeting, "The only thing I asked him was did he want it bad enough. The hell with what he brought with him. If he didn't want it bad enough, forget it." Terry had the fire all right, and more, Bennett learned: "He was a worker. You have got to work it. You can't oversleep or overdrink, or run around with women. You have to work it." [27]

Terry was what he called a natural. "Kennedy was a natural," he said. "They have got to love it. Damn, it is tiring, and [voters] don't give a damn when you come to a meeting at six in the morning and you haven't slept all night and the wife is giving you hell, the kids, this and that. They want you up. They don't give a damn if you've got a cold or sore throat. Get there and look fresh. They don't want your troubles." [28]

Bennett marveled at Terry's stamina and enthusiasm. He recalled one evening after Terry had received word from Margaret Rose, who was anxious about some situation at home. As he and Terry sat through yet another campaign dinner, Bennett slipped his friend a note that read "Terry, what makes you stay in this business?" Terry took the napkin and below Bennett's scribble wrote, "To keep the s.o.b.'s out." "And there is a lot of truth in that," Bennett recalled. "You really don't want that other crowd to have charge of it. I wouldn't want Lake to have control of it. Or Malcolm Seawell." [29]

Bennett worked tirelessly. He usually could be found at either the campaign office or back in Winston-Salem talking on the telephone to campaign keys who delivered daily, even hourly reports on the competition. He quickly processed what he heard and issued instructions in a flat, somewhat nasal monotone that could sound as cold as the numbers.

Bennett meshed well with most of those in the campaign inner circle. He enjoyed the confidence of Terry's law partners, Donald McCoy and Dickson Phillips; Bill White, a Fayetteville beer distributor who had signed on for the duration; Lambeth and Carlton, who dogged the candidate's every step; and Cannon. He especially liked the style and commitment of Paul Thompson, whose assignment was to raise the money to pay the bills.

Thompson had been a reluctant volunteer and joined the campaign only out of loyalty and friendship to Sanford, who considered him his closest friend. Thompson was quiet and thoughtful, laconic in nature and not easily excited by the ups and downs of politics. His favorite venue was business, with politics a distant avocation. With Thompson's relative detachment from politics, however, Terry knew that whatever advice Thompson offered was not colored by personal ambition or petty jealousy. Most important, he could be sure that after the election Thompson would not hand him a stack of due bills from contributors seeking a return on rash promises made in the heat of the campaign.

For the most part, the Sanford campaign ran more on energy and enthusiasm than hard cash. Cannon recalled that there was a constant struggle to keep the bills paid in the first primary. Sanford's recollection was different; money was not a concern, he said. No one will ever know for sure because the state's Corrupt Practices Act, a relic dating to 1931 that required reporting of contributions and expenses of political campaigns, was woefully outdated and barely covered the obvious.

The Sanford campaign's financial reports were as forthright, if not more so, than the competition's. Ten days before the May primary, when others submitted a handful of pages, the Sanford campaign turned in a hefty document more than two inches thick that included the names and addresses of hundreds of one-dollar contributors. The campaign reported more than $76,000 in contributions, with a like amount of expenses. The other three candidates, who had been working just as hard and spending like amounts, delivered reports accounting for one half to a third less than that.

In the face of a toothless law, the reports were never considered an accurate representation of the true cost of campaigns. For example, the law was unclear on whether contributions received before the year of the election were required to be reported. Sanford's first report included a $1.01 contribution from Kerr Scott that was received in 1958, but the same report omitted the names of some early contributors whose money was used to offset expenses of the Chapel Hill office. Some of this money was collected in 1959 by Bowles, who asked that the Sanford law firm send invoices to donors so they could report their contributions as legal expenses.[30]

Campaigns also were slack in accounting for in-kind contributions, even though the law specifically required reporting of any thing of value used on a candidate's behalf. Nothing appeared in Sanford's reports to account for the automatic typewriters, adding machines, and duplicating machines in the campaign headquarters that were on loan from Remington Rand in Charlotte. Henry Hall Wilson Jr. had simply put in a request for what he needed when he set up the Raleigh headquarters. "We do not need a Univac," Terry joked in a memo to Wilson giving the name of his contact at the company.[31] Later, Lou Harris returned a $6,000 check written for polling expenses and told Terry to use the money elsewhere. Another dodge that stretched the credibility of the reports was the practice of putting campaign employees on corporate payrolls; for example, during the campaign, Cannon was paid by a Pepsi-Cola distributor.[32]

For his part, Terry had attempted to change the way political campaigns had been financed. His strategy was founded in good politics as well as necessity. His list of wealthy donors was short, so Terry introduced a broad-based effort designed to enroll small donors who chipped in a dollar or two on his behalf. By announcement day in February, teams of volunteers in thirty-six counties were armed with palm-size coupon books and assigned to collect a dollar from ten people the first month, twenty people the second, and thirty people the third. Terry hoped to have enlisted as many as two thousand volunteers by election day. The plan produced much-needed cash and great public relations.

Terry made the most of a contribution from Charles A. Cannon, one of the South's best-known textile manufacturers, although the donation that he and Bert Bennett received from Cannon early in the campaign had been a disappointment. The two had flown to Kannapolis, the home of Cannon's vast holdings near Charlotte, for a private audience. Cannon seemed agreeable and impressed with Sanford's history with the State Highway Patrol, a subject of special interest to Cannon. As they were leaving, Cannon handed them an envelope that they tore open once they reached the privacy of their plane. Inside they found a rumpled dollar bill. It didn't pay any bills, but it did give Terry license to declare on announcement day that one of North Carolina's most influential businessmen was on his side.[33] The campaign later reported a $500 contribution from Cannon, but the early use of his name proved more valuable and helped ease the fears of businessmen anxious about the young Fayetteville lawyer with ties to Kerr Scott. R. S. Dickson wrote Skipper Bowles in mid-December 1959, "I just want to be sure that he does not reflect Scott's thinking and attitudes. If you will recall, when the labor union had taken over the Wake Forest cotton mill . . . when confronted by the owners for protection at Wake Forest by the National Guard, Mr. Scott replied to them that he did not recall anything they had done for him." [34]

Public disclosure of contributors cut both ways. In 1954, Terry worried about how to report $11,000 that Kerr Scott had received from international labor unions; it was reported, and six years later remained heavy baggage. Even before Terry formally announced, Larkins's supporters were circulating rumors that Terry had taken $100,000 from labor bosses. It was a preposterous claim, considering the feeble state of organized labor in North

Carolina, but it continued to dog Terry even after no less an antiunion textile man than Charles A. Cannon gave his endorsement.

Terry had some hope of reversing the usual flow of campaign money. In prior years, virtually all the campaign fund-raising was done by the state headquarters and money was then distributed to county chairs and area organizers to buy ads in local newspapers and hire campaign workers on election day. When they made their plans, Sanford and Bennett apportioned the cost of the campaign to the local chairmen, who were asked to send money to Raleigh as well as raise what they needed for their county efforts.

It is fair to say that Sanford hoped to enter office with as few obligations to contributors as possible. When he could, he avoided taking money directly. Once, when a contributor showed up at his house and gave him $300 in cash, he stuffed it in the sofa and didn't find it until months later. Terry usually tried to avoid uncomfortable situations; one arose when a supporter pressed several hundred dollars in his palm, at the same time telling him that he had his eye on a seat on an important regulatory commission. Terry made no promise and pocketed the cash. "I thought, by damn, now I have just committed the worst thing I could do," Sanford later recalled. "I have taken money on the one hand while I am told on the other hand that I want this. I said if I keep this money then I have got to appoint him. And if I keep this money this is kind of dishonest in my view of things. So I talked to Bert and we sent it back to him. Hurt [the man's] feelings." [35]

In 1960, the expense of television advertising was just beginning to raise the cost of running for office. More than a third of the Sanford campaign expenses were devoted to advertising, and a large part of that went to television, which previously had been used only sparingly by candidates in North Carolina political campaigns.

Ted Cramer, a High Point advertising man and former television station manager, produced Terry's ads after his agency took over the account midway through the spring. Working under a crushing deadline, Cramer and Cannon wrote new ad copy and the lyrics for a catchy jingle they sang over the telephone to a talent firm in New York that produced the soundtrack for the ads. At the same time, a camera crew filmed the candidate out among the people. The resulting thirty and sixty-second ads included Sanford talking with a farmer, his foot propped on the rear of a tractor while chickens clucked in the background; checking food prices with a housewife in a grocery store; standing before a huge map of the state talking about industrial progress; and talking with Jempsey Puckett, a former paratrooper who had jumped into France with him in the 517th. Each of the spots opened with the jingle and older footage shot on Sanford's announcement day that included, for some unexplained reason, a close-up of the sign with the word "governor" misspelled. For the time, the promotions were as good as any others on the air, with the candidate stiff as the studio props, eyes moving with the roll of the teleprompter.[36]

Then, as well as later in life, Terry's delivery of a prepared text was never very slick. His voice was flat, almost a monotone, and carried little excitement. Early in the campaign, Peggy Warren had passed along to him the comments of a friend in Chapel Hill who was a speech professional. After witnessing a Sanford appearance, she wrote, "There was no emotion, no soul, nothing except thoughts, cold and analytical. It is in you or so it seemed to me; but it was not in your speech." [37] Wilder arranged for him to receive some coaching in New York, and Cramer tried to help Terry in the use of effective pauses and voice inflection, but a lifetime of habit was hard to change.

In early May, with the election four weeks off, Bennett and Sanford received the results of a second poll from Harris. It confirmed what Bennett had been hearing from the area keys: Larkins, and maybe Seawell, were the candidates to beat. Larkins had the courthouse crowd, the county sheriffs, and the traditional party leaders on his side. Seawell, meanwhile, had Hodges's old organization shaking the bushes for him in the business community.

This poll showed that voters now knew Terry and for the most part liked what they saw. He had made education his trademark issue, and Harris advised him to keep "banging away at this same issue that so far has worked handsomely on his behalf." Sanford was only four points shy of winning in one primary among voters who had made up their mind. He had a two-to-one lead over Seawell and about the same distance lay between him and Larkins. The numbers showed Lake so far back in the pack that Harris wrote him off as a serious contender.[38]

Lake was a one-issue candidate, Harris wrote in his report, and "while most Southerners are still against integration, they do have some hesitation to place the matter in the hands of an extremist. As Beverly Lake becomes better known in North Carolina, it does not seem likely at this time that he will make any real inroads on the present situation of the other three candidates in the race for Governor."

The poll captured the single-minded nature of the Lake voter, nearly half of whom said they had no interest in any other candidate. But it failed to accurately measure the intensity and determination of the Lake support. Harris's interviewers didn't attend any of Lake's campaign rallies, which drew people from deep in the rural precincts of eastern North Carolina. Likewise, Harris had not felt the fever that would build in the crowd gathered on spring evenings for offerings of country music and barbecue before a warmup by John Burney, a husky bear of a lawyer from Wilmington, who would roar, "People ask what does the I stand for in Dr. Lake's name. I tell them I don't know, but it doesn't stand for integration."[39]

Reporters covering the race had begun to take notice of Lake's growing momentum, and by early May were reviewing earlier assumptions. Sanford had done far better than they expected and now, they wrote, appeared headed into the final four weeks with a substantial lead. But he was not far enough ahead to claim a majority in the first primary, so the question was which candidate would place second and force a runoff.

Four weeks out, the pace quickened. Larkins found himself about where he had been in January, holding on to old friends, but with little more. He continued to call Terry the handmaiden of organized labor and tried to cast doubt on Seawell's independence from Hodges, calling him the "crown prince." As for Lake, Larkins was mum. He and Lake had known each other since they were fraternity brothers at Wake Forest, when Lake was called "Ike." They were close enough friends that Larkins had even tried to get Lake to be his campaign manager when Lake was reconsidering his own candidacy. Now, Larkins clung to the hope that if he made it to a second primary he would inherit Lake's organization and consolidate conservative voters behind one candidate.

Seawell and Larkins both accused Sanford of promising more than he could deliver. Larkins tagged him "high-tax Terry" and said his own experience in government made him an expert on state spending. Seawell tried to saddle Sanford with an endorsement of a tobacco tax when Terry refused to rule it out completely as a source of revenue. Terry certainly wasn't advocating any new taxes, but he had made no promises to R. J. Reynolds Tobacco Company executives, who had invited him in for a meeting in the quiet of the executive level on the seventeenth floor of the company's Winston-Salem headquarters.

Terry seldom responded to the sniping. He called Larkins's efforts to link him to organized labor an "old-time smear campaign," and in an indirect challenge to Lake, he said those exploiting the issue of integration were spreading "a spirit of defeatism." For the most part, he followed a strategy of fighting fire with water, as he liked to say, responding in a way that would defuse an issue before it could spiral out of control. His quick wit and sense of humor were his best defense. When critics said his program—particularly his endorsement of a $100 million program from the United Forces for Education—was "pie in the sky," his Wake County supporters produced a huge apple pie and served it up under a banner that read, "If It's Pie in the Sky, Let's Start Cooking." A grinning Sanford, knife in hand, was photographed ready to slice and serve. Looking on was his frequent traveling companion, Lauch Faircloth, while a high school band played his peppy campaign song, "The Man on the Go—Terry Sanford" and everyone sipped Pepsis.

Terry answered those who said the UFE program was too expensive by saying that "children of the state cannot wait" for the trickle-down economics to produce the money needed. He was upbeat and optimistic, displaying the kind of confidence produced by ten years of preparation. His timing wasn't bad either. Shortly after he declared "Our tax structure will produce a substantial surplus, even this year. It could well be upwards of $50 million," Hodges announced the surplus would be $30 million. It was close enough that voters could glimpse a ring of truth in Sanford's predictions.

Yet, for all this byplay, Lake began to set the tone for the campaign as it reached its final weeks. He was unrelenting in his attacks on the Pearsall Plan, Hodges's handling of school integration, and particularly the NAACP. In early May, he called a press conference to announce that if he were elected he would "seek to create in North Carolina a clear, well-understood climate of public opinion against integration of schools."[40] Later, at a campaign stop in Durham, where the oldest and most effective black political organization often determined the winner in close contests, he declared that the NAACP was set on "an all-out attack to compel the complete intermingling of our two great races in all aspects of daily life."[41]

Lake blamed Hodges for making North Carolina the "softest spot in the South" for racial integrationists. He said if he were elected he would do whatever necessary to terminate integration, "whether by voluntary action of the school board or by compulsion beyond its capacity to resist."[42] At the time, with the school year drawing to a close, all of thirty-four black children were in formerly all-white schools.

Ten days before the election, at the state party convention, Hodges answered Lake. The governor picked his old ally from the Pearsall fight, W. T. Joyner of Raleigh, as the convention's keynote speaker. Joyner didn't mention any candidates by name, but he urged Democrats to "keep the school doors open to all North Carolina children. In these dangerous times, I come to call upon North Carolina Democrats as never before to keep your heads, keep your tempers, keep the state strongly Democratic and keep our schools open." He praised Hodges and the effectiveness of the Pearsall Plan. "The threat of a single order of statewide application has been met up to this time, because state officials have not attempted to interfere with local action. To this date, no court has issued any order taking charge of the admission of pupils to any schools, as unfortunately has occurred in other states."[43]

By election day, May 28, newspaper readers were ready for relief. If the election had not been lively enough, during the previous four weeks television's favorite couple, Luci and Desi Arnaz, had gotten a divorce, John Kennedy had won a surprise upset in the West Virginia primary pushing Hubert Humphrey out of the presidential race, President Eisenhower had owned up to sending a U.S. spy plane over Russia, and in California Caryl Chessman finally ran out of time and was executed in the gas chamber. All this passed as a blur for Terry, who on election day voted with Margaret Rose in Fayetteville and then headed to Raleigh. He was confident of victory.

Sanford took an early lead and held it throughout the night. The race was for second place, and the man pulling in behind Sanford was not Larkins, the only party pro, or Seawell, the voice of moderation on race, but Lake, who at midnight trailed Sanford by a little more than eighty-two thousand votes. When it was over, Lake had carried nearly two dozen counties, most of them in an arc across eastern North Carolina. He won 28 percent of the total vote to Sanford's 41 percent. Larkins and Seawell split the difference. The election had drawn more than 653,000 voters to the polls, the largest turnout in the state's history.

Hodges was shaken by the results, as were others who had discounted Lake as little more than a spoiler. Shortly after ten o'clock, when returns were far from complete but the trend was clear, Hodges appeared at the Sanford headquarters at the Carolina Hotel, pulled Bennett and others aside, and told them that he would do whatever was necessary to defeat Lake in a second primary.[44]

The thrill of victory was strong at Lake's headquarters. Nothing, except blind faith, would have allowed even the most devoted supporters—the true believers—to imagine that in ninety days Lake could overcome not one but two candidates and edge his way into a runoff. Even Morgan, his campaign manager, who had been drafted at the last minute, had given Lake little more than a slim chance. Lake had begun with no organization, no preparation, a modest bank account, and certainly no friends within the editorial offices of the state's major daily newspapers. The best to be expected might be a strong protest vote, little more than a tacking of Lake's segregationist manifesto to the state house door.

The campaign had tested Morgan's loyalty. He had as much reason as Bill Staton and others who came up in the YDC in the previous decade to be part of the Sanford campaign. Morgan and Sanford were friends and shared a common political heritage. Both had fathers who were devoted Roosevelt Democrats. Morgan was an admirer of Frank Graham, whom he had come to know during his months at Chapel Hill in the Navy's V-12 program; he had often joined the group at Graham's house on Sunday nights.

After the war, Morgan had planned to take a law degree from the university, but he couldn't find a place to live in Chapel Hill so he accepted an invitation to enter Wake Forest. There, he became a disciple of Professor Lake, who instilled in his students his own brand of populism that championed the little guy against the power companies, the banks, and large corporations.

Lake had been teacher, mentor, and friend to Morgan and a host of others who were jump-starting careers delayed by the war. He carried a special fondness for these men into his declining years, when he would reminisce about his class of 1950. Morgan had etched as clearly in his mind his final semester at law school, when he worked at the kitchen table in Lake's home to prepare an introduction for Frank Graham, who was due on campus the following day. Lake liked Graham and disliked his opponent, corporate lawyer Willis Smith, even more, and gave the kindly liberal from Chapel Hill his full blessing. That same spring, Lake encouraged Morgan to run for clerk of superior court back home in Harnett County. It was a long shot, the professor told him, and he probably wouldn't win, but if he lost, a lot of people would know there was a new young lawyer in town.

Morgan won that election and the one four years later when he ran for the state senate. He became active in the YDC, and Terry called on him in 1954 to help in the Scott campaign. Four years later, shortly after Scott's death, Sanford included Morgan in a meeting of Scott associates he wanted to work on his campaign for governor. As that session at Ralph Scott's farm ended, Morgan pulled Sanford aside and told him he could count on his support, unless Lake chose to run.[45] Terry said he understood, although he never imagined that Morgan would be the one to manage his opponent's campaign.

Morgan had run Lake's Raleigh office almost singlehandedly and without pay. The only other staff member in the campaign office was a paid secretary. It was not until the final weeks before the first primary that the campaign hired a press secretary. He was Alexander Hudgins, a Richmond, Virginia, press agent who had worked for that state's massive resistance movement. Charles Crone, from Lake's advertising agency, told reporters that Hudgins was the only experienced newsman he could find who would associate himself with Lake's campaign.

What Lake lacked in organization, money, and staff, he made up with what Bert Bennett called the "fire in the belly," although for Lake it burned not for the office but the South's second Lost Cause, segregation. Morgan complained that reporters weren't giving Lake a fair shake, focusing on his segregationist themes rather than what he had to say about fiscal conservatism and utility regulation. But it wasn't balancing the budget, keeping the power bills low, or overhauling the highway commission that gave Lake's campaign appearances their evangelistic flavor. Folks took to their feet and let loose their rebel yells when Lake talked about the threats of the NAACP and the Supreme Court to their segregated lives.

The old rules really didn't seem to apply. This was a crusade in the guise of a political campaign. Lake tapped into feelings with no other outlet. The Lake people weren't all just five dollars short of their Ku Klux Klan dues but included many respectable, church-going folks who believed that a way of life they had known, that their fathers and grandfathers had known, was being voided without so much as a by-your-leave. Their leader, their spokesman, was not some "gallus-snappin' redneck." He was Dr. Lake, a venerated college professor and former assistant attorney general who had stood at the well of the Supreme Court.

With Lake's surprising showing in the first primary, more people began to find their way to the Lake campaign headquarters on the tenth floor of a downtown Raleigh office building near the law offices that Lake kept with his partner, A. J. Fletcher. Lake had joined Fletcher in 1955 largely to handle the law practice while Fletcher pursued his varied business interests, which included Capitol Broadcasting Company, owner of WRAL radio and WRAL-TV, Raleigh's new television station that closed each day with a soulful version of "Dixie." Some of Lake's volunteers included those on the political fringe who would arrive unannounced at the Raleigh headquarters carrying copies of campaign advertisements with strong racist content that they had crafted on their own and paid to have published in a weekly newspaper around the state. On one occasion, Morgan asked a visitor where he had gotten the information he had used in one of these home-grown ads. "I got it the same place Terry Sanford gets his. I made it up," the man told him.[46] From time to time, when things seemed really haywire, the thought crossed Morgan's mind that within this ragtag collection were more than a few loose cannons or even a spy from the opposition.

In the first primary, Lake used television ads to bypass the newspaper reporters who he believed treated him shabbily by distorting his message and harping on his segregationist views at the expense of his other ideas. The result was an odd marriage. Stiff and formal, Lake was cold in the new electronic medium. His high forehead and balding pate shone in the bright lights and the production was ragged. But television connected the candidate directly to simmering segregationists who shared his opinions about the liberal press, the overreaching Supreme Court, the villainy of the NAACP, and, perhaps, even the extravagance of Luther Hodges.

It was no surprise, then, that on the Monday afternoon following Saturday's first primary, Lake ignored the traditional press conference and used television to talk to his people. In a twelve-minute political speech, carried live by WRAL television and radio and fed to a network of radio stations across the state, Lake announced that he was calling for a runoff and laid out the options for voters clean and neat: Vote for Beverly Lake and segregation will have a champion. Vote for Terry Sanford and the NAACP will be running North Carolina schools and classrooms filled with black children.

"This is not a personal fight," Lake said. "I have no quarrel with Mr. Sanford. He is personally attractive and I like him, but I am opposed to his economic policies and program and I am opposed to the mixing of white and Negro children in our public schools. . . . Mr. Sanford's supporters in the first primary have sought to mislead the people of North Carolina by saying that I will close your public schools if you elect me. That is a false statement. I could not if I wanted to and I do not want to." He offered up South Carolina, where no black child had crossed the threshold of a white school, as a state that had successfully resisted integration but had kept public schools operating: "There have been no closed schools, no invasion of federal troops, no violence and no integration in South Carolina, where the governor has developed a climate of public opinion against the NAACP."[47] He ignored the example of Prince Edward County, Virginia, where local officials had closed public schools rather than integrate.

Lake cast himself as the valiant underdog doing battle with labor leaders who were secretly backing his opponent, with the state's leading daily newspapers that carried their liberal bias to their news columns, with Hodges and his wealthy industrialists, and, most of all, with the NAACP. It was a preposterous coalition, but one against which he declared he would prevail. He noted the success of Farris Bryant, a segregationist who had just clobbered the moderate elements of Florida's Democratic Party to win the gubernatorial nomination the week before. And, before the day was over, he received a backhanded endorsement from South Carolina Governor Ernest F. "Fritz" Hollings, who, when asked about the contest in North Carolina, said he had heard Terry Sanford was a moderate, so "I necessarily stand for Dr. Lake who stands for segregation and our way of life."[48]

Whereas Lake avoided news reporters, Terry enjoyed the give-and-take with the press. He even fancied himself one of the boys, having briefly owned a struggling weekly newspaper in Fayetteville. Since the onset of the campaign, Terry had held two news conferences every week; one was scheduled for Monday mornings to give the advantage to the afternoon dailies, and the other for Friday afternoons, which provided fresh copy for the morning newspapers.

On the morning that Lake declared his intentions, Terry was ready for questions about the ordeal that lay ahead. The campaign's inner circle had already decided they would not make the same mistake made by Graham ten years earlier. Graham's first-primary lead had dissolved into defeat in a feverish, frantic four weeks largely because the genial Dr. Frank had waited until too late to deal with the wild charges and foul claims. Terry believed that the best strategy was an offense that would force Lake to respond to his agenda, thereby keeping the opposition off balance and, he hoped, slowing the momentum that had pushed Lake into second place.

When Terry arrived for his morning session with reporters, he felt a terrible burden. The election was now his to lose, not Lake's to win, and every word, every move counted as never before. He knew how to be tough and this was a morning for toughness. The newsmen did not find the candidate with his usual smile, twinkle in his eyes, or laughter in his voice when he declared that it was time to stop playing "race against race or group against group. Let's use our common sense and common decency. Let's use our brains instead of our mouths." A reporter noted a narrowing in his eyes and a deep v that formed in the middle of his brow, when he said, "I will not be abused. I'm going to run a positive campaign that I have been running." [49]

The warning shots across the bow were followed later in the day by a formal demand from the Sanford campaign that he be given equal time on the same radio and television hookup that WRAL had provided Lake. That night he prepared his own twelve-minute statement. For the first time in the campaign, he would have to deal directly with the race issue, and he wanted his statement to be something that he could live with after the election was long past. "We felt that at this important time in history," he said some years later, "the question should be put squarely. If we lost, at least it would be understood why we lost. . . . I had a fellow call me up about two o'clock in the morning saying, 'I got to worrying about you, Terry.' He said, 'There's a picture of you and the black American Legion leaders in Fayetteville. I want to get that picture and destroy it.' And I said, 'Don't you worry about that picture.' He said, 'And another thing, you can't shake hands with a black in public. You might have your picture taken.' I said, 'Well if I have my picture taken doing that I'll just have to have my picture taken, because I'm not about to take any such position as that.' That was the first time I explained to a fellow that you don't have to win when you run. You know that's not necessarily the most important thing." [50]

Terry picked his words for his statement carefully, well aware that the semantics of the race issue were inseparable from the social and moral questions involved. Three years earlier, Associate Justice William Brennan of the U.S. Supreme Court had struggled with a subtle but important change when writing the decision in the Little Rock case. Brennan finally took the suggestion of a friend, who advised that he substitute the word "desegregation" for "integration." Brennan later wrote, "I was taken with his suggestion that it made a difference to people in the South, and after all we were writing an opinion that we had hoped would find understanding and acceptance in the South as well as in the rest of the country."[51]

Terry knew that the I-word was the deadly third rail of Southern politics: a candidate was either for integration or against it. Lake had drawn the issue in clear black-and-white, literally and figuratively. Sanford was caught between saying what he believed to be the right course for the state and being the one setting that course for the next four years. "I was for the Supreme Court and for being fair to everybody. You could say those things and people understood what you were talking about. If you said, 'The only thing for us to do now is to move to integration,' you could have gone fishing and forgotten about it, because you were not going to get elected," Sanford recalled some years later. His final draft was crafted in such a way to give his old friends in the rural precincts something to hold on to for the rough ride ahead; at the same time, he renewed his own conviction that the rule of law was supreme.[52]

On Tuesday afternoon at four, Terry looked into WRAL's cameras and said he "was shocked to find that instead of running against me, whom he can't beat, Professor Lake tried to set up a straw man to run against. He is injecting a false issue on integration and it is false because I am, and he knows I am, opposed to integration. The difference is that I know how to handle it, and he doesn't. . . . Professor Lake yells about mixing of the races, about NAACP domination, and is appealing to blind prejudice for the pure and simple purpose of getting himself a few votes."

Sanford said Lake's "constant hammering on this appeal to blind prejudice has brought North Carolina to its most dangerous crossroads in this century. The people must stop before entering and must look for the signs before choosing the road to the future, because Professor Lake has put us in a perilous, dangerous position. His talk is not going to stop anything, but his reckless words could start something we can't stop. . . . Every time he opens his mouth he is building evidence which is going to be introduced in the Supreme Court to show bad faith on the part of North Carolina, in the event he is elected governor. And though we don't like it, the Supreme Court has the last word. He is inviting the Supreme Court to step into North Carolina."

Sanford embraced what he called "the North Carolina plan which has so well protected North Carolina, particularly eastern North Carolina. If [Lake] were elected governor, it would result in the Supreme Court throwing out the North Carolina plan as unconstitutional."[53]

By embracing the Pearsall Plan, Sanford actually appealed to the Lake supporters, in an ironic way. Although Hodges presented the Pearsall Plan as the model of moderation, the Harris polls showed that the most steadfast supporters of the Pearsall Plan were segregationists who believed it to be their defense against admitting black children to their schools. Whatever the nuances, Terry's allies had at least some defense and Roney could tell the older Scott crowd in eastern North Carolina with a wink and a nod, "You don't have to worry about old Terry on integration." In the coming weeks, such endorsements would prove the difference in holding Sanford's base of support in the east.

Terry's comfort level with his statement revolved around this curious interpretation of the word integration; thirty years later he said he could still defend his position: "I would suggest there is a difference between supporting integration and ending segregation. I never denied we were trying to end segregation. We did it without dishonoring ourselves. We never really denied where we stood on the schools and the court orders. You didn't want to make that the single issue. You wanted to keep that as far from the front burner as you could get it." [54]

If any were disturbed by Sanford's statement, they kept their objections to themselves. The question to be answered in the second primary, set for June 25, was whether North Carolina would fall in with the hard-line segregationist politics of Alabama and Mississippi or maintain its reputation for a slow, if not more civil, approach to dealing with the end of segregation. As Sanford put it, the question for voters was not whether white and black would sit together in a classroom, but whether there would be any public schools open under a Lake administration.

At his Monday news conference, Terry had boldly declared that he would again visit all one hundred counties; a few days later he withdrew this rash, impractical promise. His schedule was demanding and exhausting enough without stretching it for symbolic reasons, but he was determined to touch down in every section of the state before election day. Traveling by automobile, airplane, even helicopter, he appeared day and night, wherever he was needed. He departed at daybreak, needling and herding an assortment of companions into the waiting automobile. Stragglers were left stranded at the curb. David Cooper of the *News & Observer* complained in print that keeping pace with Sanford was like competing in the Indianapolis 500 on a bicycle.

Helicopters were Terry's personal favorite; they were a novelty and helped draw a crowd. When he had to, he would use a small plane, which created problems because some rural strips had limited lighting and access. The only time he said he feared for his safety was one night as the plane cruised over darkened fields of eastern North Carolina and his pilot started talking despondently about a love affair that had recently ended. "I thought, this son of a bitch is going to commit suicide with me in the plane," he later recalled.[55]

Wherever he went, Terry drew a comparison between what he called a reasonable, progressive program and Lake's one-note complaint about integration. He drew heavily upon a thick file of research of Lake's public and private careers that was essential to his strategy to bury Lake with his own words. Terry believed that though North Carolinians may not like integration, at least a majority were not willing to man Lake's barricades against the Supreme Court, the federal government, and the future.

The Lake dossier was compiled by Joel Fleishman, who had joined the campaign after his classes at Yale finished. Fleishman was exceedingly bright, a polished Anglophile who as an undergraduate at Chapel Hill smoked hollow-tipped Parliament cigarettes and read the *Manchester Guardian*. He had proved to be a masterful student politician while simultaneously earning degrees in law and drama before going on to graduate study in New Haven. Bennett assigned him to learn everything he could about Lake, and Fleishman soon produced files bulging with copies of Lake's speeches, newspaper clippings, legal opinions, and personal history, including detritus from Lake's Harvard days where, he discovered, Lake had been a classmate of accused Soviet spy Alger Hiss.

At one campaign stop, Terry quoted from a 1955 speech in which Lake told an audience in Gastonia, "We should be thinking about alternatives to the public schools." At another, he recalled Lake's notorious Asheboro speech that so inflamed Hodges and Pearsall. Hit. Hit. Hit. When Sanford and Lake met for a televised debate on June 13, Terry even suggested that Lake was a closet Republican and had taken a page from the GOP playbook with his "tax-and-spend" charges.

When Morgan charged that Sanford had won the so-called bloc vote, a convenient euphemism intended to tag Sanford as the favorite of black ward heelers, Sanford rebutted immediately. He didn't have unanimous support from black voters in the first primary, he told a rally crowd in eastern North Carolina. Malcolm Seawell had carried the black precincts in Durham, John Larkins was the favorite in Asheville, and, he claimed, Lake had won the predominantly black precincts in Iredell County. Some years later, Terry confessed that he really didn't know which of the candidates was preferred among black voters in Iredell County; all he knew was that Lake had carried the county and that a leading Lake supporter was known for his influence in black precincts. He also said he had urged his Durham supporters not to press for black support in the first primary so that he would have an answer to the bloc voting charge he anticipated coming in the second.[56]

At that same rally, after feeding barbecue to twelve hundred persons gathered at the local high school, Terry compared Lake to Senator Joseph McCarthy: "He has been talking about communists, and a left-wing press and dangerous enemies. The truth of the matter is that I am the only candidate who has been cleared by the FBI and I ought to know a left-winger when I see one." Then he returned to his steady theme: "Never before in this century have we had a man run for governor on the pure basis of racial hate. We do not need that kind of climate in North Carolina. We need a continuation of the sunny, bright climate to build for tomorrow."[57]

To underscore Sanford's claim that Lake's election would force the state into economic and social stagnation, the campaign sent a film crew to Little Rock, where interviews were collected from a leader in the Chamber of Commerce and a mother of schoolchildren, who testified on film that "the stakes in this emotional hate game are too high." The industrial developer warned that not a single new industry had approached the city since Governor Orville Faubus had allowed schools to close.[58] "We were trying to be defensive in a way that got the focus off whatever it was he said," Sanford recalled. "Generally, he would take our bait and start explaining himself."[59]

The Lake campaign seemed consumed by Sanford's aggressive strategy. Lake struggled to respond. Time and again, he insisted he had a program beyond fighting integration, and two days after he called for the runoff he gave a lengthy speech on fiscal responsibility to prove it. He denied he had said he would close public schools and challenged any to look at his public statements over the years. He used valuable time proclaiming his allegiance to the Democratic Party, denying he was a closet Republican. Two weeks before the voting, Lake was even forced to defend his record on segregation. Thomas Pearsall called a Raleigh news conference to challenge Lake's claim that he had written the 1955 Pupil Assignment Plan, the bit of legislative maneuvering that had been the state's first defense against a unified lawsuit that could have forced all the state's school districts to integrate. Pearsall said Lake's ownership of that bit of defiance was bogus and that the committee could not use what Lake had written for them. Lake fumed for days and pulled in his own witnesses to attest to his credentials.

Lake tried to establish his own drumbeat, claiming that Sanford's "tax and tax, spend and spend" approach would bankrupt the state. The state's current budget surplus was phony, he said, and the result of a windfall in income tax collections. Conservative business practices, he said, not extravagant promises were needed in difficult times. He called Sanford Santa Claus.

Sanford answered that North Carolina would never get ahead with such a defeatist attitude. He talked of building better schools that would lead to more opportunity. He was upbeat, optimistic, hopeful of a brighter tomorrow, with new ideas and energy to make things happen. With a cheering crowd before him one night in Hickory, he said, "If we can hitch up those reindeer and load up this bag with school opportunities, then I'm all for being called Santa Claus." [60]

Lake's lasting signature on the campaign was a series of evening rallies. Nothing before or since equaled this combination of camp meeting and political gathering, old-fashioned reunion and media event. Moms and dads, their kids holding balloons that read "For your children's sake, Vote for Lake," filled tobacco warehouses and other local venues for a night of free soft drinks and hard politics. Selected nights were recorded for paid television broadcasts, and Lake's arrival in a caravan was led by a siren-wailing police car and heralded by a lively rendition of "Dixie." Often, the warmup man was John Burney, whose booming voice equaled his considerable size. Burney coached the crowd like a sideman on a television talk show directing applause. "Now, when Dr. Lake comes down the aisle," he told a Durham crowd waiting for a television production to begin, "we are going to shake, rattle and roll." [61]

A week remained before election day. Lake's final eastern North Carolina rally was held in Lumberton with a crowd of over six hundred at the Robeson County courthouse. Burney advised the crowd, "You'll know when the television cameras come on because I'm going to ask, 'Are the people of North Carolina going to make Beverly Lake governor Saturday?' When I ask that question, you let me know. We want the people of North Carolina to know that we aren't sitting on our backsides and letting the newspaper roll over us." [62]

The News & Observer and the Charlotte Observer, the state's two largest daily newspapers, came in for special attention from Burney and Lake. That night in Lumberton, Lake restated his plans for "creating a climate of public opinion against integration," adding that "wittingly or unwittingly my opponent's program would permit the News & Observer, Charlotte Observer and their satellites and fellow-travelers to bring about a climate of integration." Gene Roberts, the News & Observer reporter assigned to Lake, was sitting at his usual spot at the side of the crowd. Before the rally concluded, a friend called him outside and warned him of trouble. They headed for the darkened offices of the Lumberton newspaper. A few minutes later, a group of toughs arrived looking for him. After they passed on, Roberts slipped out of town. A few years later, as a reporter for the *New York Times*, his paper often received the same abuse from George C. Wallace, who used the press as a punching bag. Yet Roberts said he never felt as threatened as he did that night in Lumberton.[63]

The Lake campaign tried its best to rattle Sanford, but their opportunities were few and their attempts awkward. Morgan accused Sanford of misrepresenting headlines in a newspaper, only to find that his staff had given him the wrong edition of the paper and his charge was baseless. About ten days from election day, Morgan raised the issue of union influence, citing the money given Scott in 1954. The Sanford campaign placed ads in weekly newspapers saying Terry Sanford would defend Scott's honor if no one else would. "He was doing some things that we had to react to," Sanford recalled some years later. "We couldn't get ourselves in a situation that Dr. Frank got himself into where he was on the receiving end and not doing anything about it. You had to figure out how not to ever let him get the initiative, how to keep the initiative at all times. That is one thing that I had concluded, that you couldn't let the initiative get away from you."[64]

There was no question that Sanford had an edge over Lake with reporters covering the campaign. While Lake retreated to his home in Wake Forest to write speeches, reporters often joined Sanford in his car, where they tapped out stories on portable typewriters cradled in their laps. They liked Sanford's phrasemaking, and he was quick to incorporate new material into his stock speeches. After he read that a Lake supporter had showed up one day to drive his candidate around in a Cadillac convertible, Sanford made reference to "foot-stomping, white-Cadillac-riding professors." He said, "North Carolina is not going to be fooled by fear even if it is dressed up by a combination of Bilbo and Daddy Grace." (Racist demagogue Theodore Bilbo was a senator from Mississippi; Daddy Grace was a flamboyant black evangelist and founder of the House of Prayer for All People.)[65]

What Terry feared most was some stupid mistake that would occur with too little time to correct it. It almost happened at a Raleigh news conference less than two weeks before election day, when a reporter tried to pin him with a question about Hodges's support. Terry said he had not seen Hodges since the onset of the second primary, which was true but only because he had talked to Hodges on Sunday just hours before Lake called for a runoff. Then the reporter followed with another question: Had he met with John Kennedy at a motel on the edge of Raleigh?

Running late and already miffed at the first question, Sanford answered, "No, I didn't see Jack Kennedy." He left immediately to catch a plane. As he rode for a campaign appearance, Terry was uncomfortable with the way he had left things in Raleigh. In truth, Sanford, Bennett, and Cannon had met with Lou Harris and Robert F. Kennedy, the candidate's brother, a few weeks prior to the first primary. The group took dinner in a Raleigh motel room mainly as a convenience to Kennedy, who was sick when he arrived. That evening, with Kennedy propped up in bed sipping soup, they talked, but Terry had made no commitment. It was clear to Terry that the reporter had simply confused the Kennedy brothers. As soon as he could find a telephone, he called Bennett in Raleigh and told him to put out a correction, but his campaign manager told him it was too late. "They've already charged that you saw him secretly and took $100,000," Bennett told him.

The Kennedy meeting was Terry's second lapse in an early resolve to remain out of the maneuvering for preconvention support by the presidential contenders. He had successfully stalled one Chapel Hill classmate who wanted a commitment for Missouri's Stuart Symington, an early candidate who was his personal favorite. As a favor to Robert Redwine, Kerr Scott's old speechwriter, he had met Redwine in the early spring. At that meeting, Redwine intimated that a few kind words from Terry on Lyndon Johnson's behalf—"Something you would say anyhow"—could produce a campaign contribution of five or six thousand dollars. Terry turned him down flat. He had finally accepted Harris's offer to meet with Kennedy after weeks of nagging and only after it looked as if John Kennedy might take the nomination.

In spite of his concern, the disclosure of the Kennedy meeting faded quickly, in part because Terry slipped word to a reporter that he also had met with contacts from the Johnson campaign, and Johnson was the favorite of most Southern politicians. After the Kennedy meeting was exposed, Terry sent word to the Johnson camp that he would sit down and talk. A few days later, Johnson's chief political aide, Bobby Baker, and Terry's old friend Bill Cochrane, who had stayed on in Washington to work for Everett Jordan, met him in Greensboro for an evening meeting.

By the final hours of the campaign, Lake was grim and drawn as he headed to his last rally in Rockingham, a county seat next to the South Carolina line, not far from Laurinburg. Pennants, balloons, and placards decorated the hall. Some in the crowd had driven three or four hours to be on hand. One man arrived with a red neon sign in the rear window of his car that read "Lake for Governor." Isaac London, editor of the pro-Lake Rockingham Post-Dispatch, billed the affair as "reminiscent of the white supremacy and Red Shirt campaigns of 1898 and 1900." Lake did not disappoint, promising to drive the "NAACP from North Carolina." Portions of the rally were broadcast on the eve of the election.

Terry also was physically spent, but confident. He believed Lake's high-water mark had been the day he had called for a runoff. At that time, some of North Carolina's businessmen were more concerned about the tax implications of Terry's education program than they were about the threat of a racist campaign. Even midway, the officers of one of the state's leading banks had carefully, quietly hedged their bets. Morgan said he got an unexpected $5,000 from a powerful eastern North Carolina banking family that he was told had sent a like amount to Sanford. With each day, however, Lake's support eroded while Sanford collected endorsements, including one, finally, from Malcolm Seawell, whose last-minute support came by way of a statement he had a friend read while Seawell went fishing. Among those who endorsed Lake were Mrs. William Umstead, the former governor's wife, and W. T. Joyner Jr., whose father, the colonel, endorsed Sanford.

Jonathan Daniels had his say the Sunday before election day on the front page of the *News & Observer* under the headline "For All Our Betsys." It was a poignant, focused reprise of Sanford's appeal for open schools that personified the issues in the future for the Sanford's own eleven-year-old daughter. The editorial was reprinted as an advertisement, coupled with a huge photograph of the candidate and his daughter.

Lake spent election eve in Charlotte in a last-minute television appeal that was carried by other stations across the state. He was still disputing Sanford's claims of black support in Iredell County and declaring his party loyalty. It was not a good night. Thunderstorms knocked out transmissions to stations in Durham and Greensboro and others received the signal with pictures but no sound.

Sanford's broadcast originated in Greensboro and went on the air at 8:30, two hours before Lake's. Appearing with him were Bennett, the incoming president of the state's education association, Winston-Salem lawyer Irving Carlyle, and the Reverend Charles L. Brown, a former paratrooper from the 517th who was now a Raleigh pastor. Sanford recalled the campaign, and told of walking across Raleigh's Capitol Square the Sunday before and seeing leaflets littering the ground that appealed to racial prejudices. He called them "puddles of poison."

"I am confident that the people of North Carolina are not willing to be led to destruction by a Pied Piper of prejudice," he said in his broadcast. "I am confident that the tons of leaflets prepared in desperation—distributed in dark of night oozing with hate and fear—will not fool people."[66]

The campaign was over. Twenty-four hours after Sanford began his election-eve broadcast, Lake was in his Wake County headquarters preparing to walk two blocks to the Carolina Hotel and acknowledge defeat. Early in the evening, the outcome was clear; Sanford led with fifty thousand votes. Even rural Harnett County, Morgan's home territory, didn't deliver much better than a 60-40 margin for Lake. When Lake told the three hundred or so persons jammed into the room that the campaign was over, they answered by singing "Dixie." They patted Lake on the back and offered encouragement before Burney declared, "This is the last of our camp meetings." But, he said, "we're going to continue to fight. We will never surrender the rights of the people to the NAACP and the AFL-CIO."[67]

A crowd followed Lake to the Carolina, where he forced his way through the jam-packed, hot, stuffy lobby to a waiting Terry Sanford, whose own face was wet with perspiration. Terry had been moving in and out of the big room during the evening, sometimes with Margaret Rose and the children in tow. Just before Lake arrived, Terry asked for courtesy: "I just want to say, let us act with the same kind of dignity when Dr. Lake comes in that has marked this campaign throughout."[68] All applauded.

When the two met, Lake wore a "pleasant expression, but did not smile broadly," a reporter observed. With him was Morgan, "who looked like he had been hit with a sash weight."[69] After paying their respects, the two left.

Sanford and Lake would never enjoy the genial relationship they had known before the primary. When Terry paid a courtesy call on Lake a few days later, Lake was angry and told him that he resented being likened to Bilbo and Daddy Grace and being called the Pied Piper of Prejudice. That was inexcusable, he said. Over the years their paths would cross. On one of the last occasions that the two spoke to one another, Lake told Sanford the South's defeat in the Civil War was the greatest tragedy ever to befall the region. He died believing as he had in 1960 that the Supreme Court was wrong. He said he held black friends in Wake Forest in higher regard than justices with whom he disagreed. He was not a racist, Lake told an interviewer in 1992. He believed in the pride of the races: "I'm delighted that I'm a white man, and I'm delighted that all of my descendants are white. I want that to be true. I think the white race is, in many respects, superior to the other races of the world in development. And we want to bring the other races up to our standard, rather than pull ours down to theirs."[70]

Terry's victory celebration continued well into the night, the crowd overflowing the hotel into Nash Square, a city park across the street. At one point, Terry joined them and was lifted over a hedge so he could wade into the crowd. At the election board offices, workers continued to tally the 638,000 votes that were cast. Finally, Terry retreated to a room in the hotel where he took a tall glass of ice water from Ben Roney and looked down at the jubilation below.

A block away at the offices of the *News & Observer*, editor Jonathan Daniels was finishing an editorial planned for the paper's front page that was inspired by the hopeful conclusion to a historic campaign. "Sanford is free," Daniels wrote. "He is bound only by his devotion to a great, better, richer North Carolina and one in which never again will any man dare put political hope in stirring bitterness and hate." [71]

CHAPTER ELEVEN

A New Day

ON JANUARY 5, 1961, as Terry Sanford took the oath as North Carolina's thirty-ninth popularly elected governor, the weight of the long campaign finally fell away and he felt a sense of excitement. His thoughts
turned to the future and the four years voters had given him to fulfill the
promise of the "New Day" that he had been talking about. He began his inaugural address with this familiar phrase, worn smooth after a year of use,
and was eager to get on with business.

He had struggled with the content and the length of his address, nip-
ping, tucking, measuring and weighing each word. He wanted to set goals
for an activist administration that would be driven by his belief that progressive public policy was more than mere abstraction. He came from the
tradition of Franklin D. Roosevelt and Kerr Scott, leaders for whom government was like a good neighbor offering a hand to the disadvantaged,
educating children, creating an environment for good jobs, and doing all
those things that made for strong families and communities. He hoped to
do no less.

He began his speech with a tribute to his predecessor, Charles Brantley Aycock, the state's icon of universal education, and then restated his
own commitment to better schools. "We must give our children the quality
of education which they need to keep up in this rapidly advancing, scientific, complex world," he said, his voice earnest and clear. "They must be
prepared to compete with the best in the nation and I dedicate my public
life to the proposition that education must be of a quality which is second
to none. A second-rate education can only mean a second-rate future for
North Carolina." [1]

Education would be the centerpiece of his administration, but he harbored an even broader vision. North Carolina had reached an important
point in its history. His ambition for the next four years was difficult to put

into words because it was as complex as the changing world around him and as simple as an echo from his childhood, when he learned to make each day amount to something, to make a difference in the world around him. "I wanted somehow to say North Carolina could achieve greatness," he later wrote. "I wanted people all over the country to respond with glowing reaction whenever the name of North Carolina was called. I wanted us to lead in everything worthwhile, to be the leader of the nation." [2]

Sanford believed it was time for North Carolina and the entire South to shake free from generations of suspicion and resentment that remained from that conflict of a century before. It was time for the South to gain full partnership with the rest of the nation. He was not speaking in hyperbole when he declared, "I want North Carolina to move into the mainstream of America and to strive to become the leading state of the nation. We can do it."

Sanford already had demonstrated his own willingness to break with tradition when six months earlier he had seconded the presidential nomination of a Massachusetts Catholic, Senator John F. Kennedy, rather than follow his elders in support of Texas Senator Lyndon B. Johnson. Now that Kennedy was headed to the White House, he had been given grudging credit for savvy politics, if not broader ambition. In the heat of the past summer, however, some of his best friends thought he had surely scuttled his chance to be governor, trading his victory over Lake for a footnote in national history.

Sanford had postponed declaring his presidential preference until he was sure of his own nomination. Then, before leaving Raleigh for a brief vacation with the family at a South Carolina beach house, he had retreated to a motel on the northern edge of the city to sort out arrangements for the transfer of the party leadership from Hodges to himself. His campaign manager, Bert Bennett, was installed as chairman, and Sanford prepared for the fall campaign against Robert Gavin, a political moderate and Sanford lawyer who was the Republican nominee. No Republican had ever collected much more than 45 percent of the vote for governor in North Carolina, so, barring anything extraordinary, Sanford would be governor-elect come November.

Hodges was preoccupied with his own ambition for the vice presidential nomination. His friends had produced a sixteen-page brochure, complete with a picture of the dilapidated log tenant house where the governor had been born, that would be delivered to every delegate at the national convention. The picture was an embarrassment to Mrs. Hodges, but the governor's team believed the "log cabin to White House" theme might make it around the track one more time.[3] On the Sunday following the primary election, when Hodges called to congratulate Sanford on his victory, he had asked him to lend support. Sanford said he would, but privately didn't give the governor half a chance.[4]

Sitting poolside at the motel after the primary, Sanford tallied the presidential options. Henry Hall Wilson Jr. was for Kennedy; so was Bennett, as were his law partners in Fayetteville. Ben Roney, the most experienced politician in the crowd, argued that he should back Johnson along with the rest of the North Carolina delegation. Certainly, the Texan was the safe choice, the accepted candidate, and even, Sanford believed, better prepared to be the leader of the free world. But he was tired of the old routine of Southern politicians backing a regional favorite to protect their reputations at home when they knew a Southerner would never lead the ticket. Roney wanted him to play it safe unless, he said, Sanford had some obligation to Kennedy that he didn't know about. Sanford told Roney he was obligated to Kennedy, and half suspected that Roney believed the rumors that he had taken money from the Kennedys to help pay for the recent campaign. That wasn't the case at all. Sanford believed he was obligated to a new kind of political thinking, not money, and rather than waste a vote on Johnson he believed he should support the candidate who was best able to defeat the Republican favorite, Vice President Richard Nixon.[5]

Kennedy was young, vigorous, and exciting and represented a new generation of political leadership, just as he did. Both men were sons of the twentieth century, veterans of combat, and eager to assume their roles in determining the country's destiny. Joining Kennedy now, Bennett told Sanford, would be something special, something different, something unexpected, plus it would give the state an uncommon entrée to the White House. "History knocks seldom," Bennett said, "and when it does, you'd better open up. And history is knocking in this opportunity."[6] Donald McCoy and Dickson Phillips agreed. But don't do anything foolish, McCoy had warned before he left the beach for the trip west to the national convention.

All hell broke loose when Sanford landed in Los Angeles and the Kennedy campaign trotted their Southern trophy out to meet the national press. Sanford not only endorsed Kennedy but succumbed to pleas from his brother, Robert, that he deliver a seconding speech as well. Hodges, Senator Sam Ervin Jr., and others were furious, scornful, and derisive. The imputed motives ranged from ego to payoff. Drew Pearson intimated in his syndicated newspaper column, which appeared nationwide the day of Kennedy's nomination, that Sanford's endorsement was in return for buckets of cash that the Kennedys had dumped into his gubernatorial campaign. Telegrams flooded Sanford's hotel suite and most were not friendly. His fellow delegates were angry to the point of embarrassing themselves. When Kennedy came to speak to the delegation, half of those in the room refused to extend the customary courtesy of standing as he departed. When the balloting began, Sanford delivered only six of the state's thirty-seven votes, and the twelve who cast their half votes for Kennedy came to be known as "the Dirty Dozen."

The trouble had just begun. When Sanford returned home he learned just how badly he had miscalculated the depth of prejudice in North Carolina, where only one in a hundred church members was a Catholic. Rum and Romanism, particularly Romanism, had moved North Carolina into the Republican column in 1928, when another Catholic, Al Smith, had lost the state to Republican Herbert Hoover. Some of Sanford's area keys telephoned to say that was going to happen again and destroy his candidacy with it.

Nothing disturbed Sanford more than reaction at his own church, Hay Street Methodist. When he learned that his pastor intended to preach an anti-Kennedy sermon, he sent word that if he was in the congregation he would walk out in protest. The pastor was even fretting over an invitation he had extended earlier to Sanford to deliver the Layman's Day address later in the fall. The candidate arranged to be unavailable.[7]

The innuendo of dishonesty and deceit in the Pearson column gnawed at him in the days following the convention. Sanford believed Pearson's source was Robert Redwine, the former Scott aide who had approached him during the campaign offering a contribution if he would endorse Johnson. When Sanford brushed him off, Redwine assumed that he had already taken money from the Kennedys.[8] Jonathan Daniels interceded and arranged for Sanford to visit Pearson, an opinionated traditionalist who harbored his own notions about Southerners. As the two sat down to talk in Pearson's Washington home, Pearson offered Sanford a drink, suggesting bourbon and water. Sanford, who never was much of a drinker, could have taken that as well as anything, but to abuse Pearson of at least one stereotype, Sanford said he would prefer a martini from the pitcher Mrs. Pearson was stirring for her husband. Pearson subsequently wrote a column apologizing for the suggestions of payoff, but it received limited circulation and the rumors would persist for years.

When the convention was over, the Sanfords rented a house in the North Carolina mountains on the Methodist assembly grounds at Lake Junaluska, where Terry hoped to relax and enjoy some time with his family before beginning the fall campaign. After Terry arrived, however, he found himself leaving the retreat for daily excursions into surrounding counties to douse fires ignited by the sparks of the convention.

The anti-Kennedy reaction only stiffened the resolve of Sanford and Bennett to mount a unified campaign for the fall, which would be the last in the century when the Democratic gubernatorial nominee stood shoulder-to-shoulder with the party's choice for president and presented a combined statewide campaign. They recruited Dr. Henry Jordan as the chair and borrowed $50,000 to meet the state's initial assessment due the national party, an ironic twist to the earlier rumors of cash from the Kennedys.

Among other things, the united effort sponsored repeated telecasts of Kennedy's Houston speech, in which he effectively buried the religious issue before a gathering of that city's ministerial association. The campaign also aired endorsements of the Democratic ticket from Ervin and Fourth District Representative Harold Cooley, who looked painfully stiff and anxious on film. These broadcasts and a vigorous campaign by Sanford helped offset negative advertising sponsored by the Republicans, who had organized groups of wealthy Democrats in Greensboro and Winston-Salem to endorse Nixon.

Sanford did salvage one important name for Kennedy. J. Spencer Love, the quirky chief executive of Burlington Industries, the largest textile firm in the state, declared himself for Kennedy. It was reported that after Love's announcement, the trash cans in the Burlington headquarters parking lot in Greensboro filled with Nixon bumper stickers hastily discarded by Love's subordinates.

Kennedy campaigned in the state in September, making stops at rallies in Greenville, Raleigh, and Greensboro, and was due to travel on to Asheville until bad weather set in. His back was giving him trouble and his voice was weak, but he drew enthusiastic crowds, particularly in Raleigh. A few days later, Nixon made a fateful appearance in Greensboro. While getting in an automobile, the vice president bumped his knee on the door; he ignored the injury and it became infected, knocking him out of the race for several days.

Throughout the fall, Sanford never failed to plug for the ticket. His endorsement of Kennedy became so familiar that some interpreted it as a message to voters that they should not vote for him if they couldn't vote for Kennedy. "I didn't say anything that dumb, but my campaign really was on that theme; that we're for Kennedy, that Kennedy's a great hope for the country," Sanford said some years later.[9] It was all a gamble, but Sanford believed that he could afford to share his comfortable two-to-one lead over his Republican opponent and keep the state Democratic.

When the polls closed November 8, Kennedy carried North Carolina by fifty-seven thousand votes; that was well below the margins of the good old days, but it was three times larger than Stevenson's showing against

Eisenhower in 1956. Sanford won with a margin of more than 120,000 votes, although he failed to gain majorities in cities like Greensboro and Winston-Salem, where Republican strength was beginning to build; he carried Charlotte, but just barely. Sanford's advantage over the Republican was in eastern North Carolina and in traditional party strongholds in small towns and rural areas of the state.

The Kennedy team was grateful. On inauguration day, Robert Kennedy and his wife, Ethel, joined the new governor and his family in the reviewing stand erected in front of the Montgomery Ward store on Fayetteville Street. It was a glorious day, sunny and bright, though cold. Because the ceremonies took place on a Thursday, state government employees were granted a three-hour holiday, and they joined a crowd that brought the city to a standstill.

The parade was the longest and biggest in recent memory. Air Force jets streaked across the sky and high school bands came from one end of the state to the other to participate. Ten thousand military troops—more than the population of most North Carolina towns—marched down Fayetteville Street accompanied by tanks, troop carriers, jeeps, and an Honest John rocket. When a unit of paratroopers from Fort Bragg reached the reviewing stand, Sanford rose, stood ramrod straight, and raised a salute. Earlier in the day, his wartime chaplain, the Reverend Charles Lynnwood Brown, who now had a Presbyterian pastorate in Raleigh, offered a prayer at the Memorial Auditorium ceremonies.

At midafternoon, Hodges and Sanford climbed in a cream-colored Lincoln Continental, one that had been specially built by Ford Motor Company for the presidential inauguration three weeks off, and rode to the governor's office, where Hodges delivered the state seal to Sanford's custody. The two motored on to the mansion, where Hodges's friends presented him with a new Ford Thunderbird that he drove to the house of a friend for an overnight visit.

Hodges was headed for Washington to become secretary of commerce. Some called the appointment "Sanford's revenge." The proud former governor knew he owed his place in the Kennedy cabinet to the very person whose gubernatorial ambitions he had attempted to scuttle and who had withstood his scorn in Los Angeles.[10] When Sanford met the president-elect in Georgetown about ten days after the election, he reminded Kennedy that amidst the heat and emotion of the convention in Los Angeles, he had told him, "If I ever recommend [Hodges] for anything in your administration, I hope you'll just kick me out of the office."[11] Now, with the election behind them, he was feeling more conciliatory and asked Kennedy for the appointment as a gesture of party unity and in recognition of

Hodges's work on Kennedy's behalf in the fall campaign, when he had led a businessman's committee for the Democratic ticket.

The Sanfords finished inauguration day exhausted but in good cheer at the head of a receiving line that did not end until after dark. The crowd emptied the mansion kitchen of food, and after the last guest departed, the family climbed the broad staircase to the living quarters on the second floor.

On Friday morning, a little before eight, Sanford walked into the governor's office and started earning his $25,000 a year. Bennett was only a few minutes behind. The office now reflected Sanford's personal touch. The portrait of Governor Aycock hung on the room's inside wall near a black-and-white, eight-by-ten photograph of Frank Porter Graham. A scowling Kerr Scott looked down from the wall across from the governor's desk, which sat in front of a huge fireplace with an ornate mantle and large mirror in a filigreed frame. On the outside wall was the portrait of Governor O. Max Gardner.

The twenty-four-by-twenty-two-foot governor's office has the charm of a small cave. The high, vaulted ceiling is held aloft by a thick granite pillar that stands in the middle of the room. Two large windows, set deep in the four-foot-thick granite walls, open to the west and the shaded lawn of Capitol Square. When Sanford arrived the windows were hung with heavy crimson draperies, the same color as the wall-to-wall carpet, and offered the sun only casual, indirect access. The new governor accepted the chunky, dark-stained period furniture as it was, adding only a small portable bar that he refitted for coffee service. The appointments suited him just fine.

In the governor's outer office, a larger space filling the building's southeast corner, Sanford installed four secretaries and Thomas W. Lambeth, who as administrative assistant was to be the office gatekeeper and scheduler. Tall and thin, Lambeth had a toothy grin and pleasant, youthful appearance. He was a true product of Chapel Hill, with courtly manners and a maturity beyond his twenty-five years. Few on the governor's staff held such a deep affection and abiding attachment to Sanford, which in Lambeth's case would continue throughout their years.

The other key staff member on hand was Hugh Cannon, whom Sanford already had designated as his legal counsel. Cannon actually had been on the state payroll since September, working as a liaison with Hodges, who had included Sanford in the budget-making process. Cannon's new office was right behind the governor's in an all-but-hidden chamber under the capitol's west portico.

The biggest change Sanford made to the governor's office was the creation of the office of press secretary. His predecessors Hodges and Umstead had handled inquiries from reporters through their private secretary, an official office they filled with former newsman Ed Rankin Jr. Sanford wanted a more active role with the media and appointed former newspaper reporter Graham Jones, his campaign press aide, as the state's first press secretary and announced a regular schedule for press conferences that he initially approached with uncommon vigor and enthusiasm.

Veterans in Raleigh were surprised to learn that Ben Roney was not at the governor's right hand. Roney remained part of the team, but he was installed as the secondary roads officer and given an office in the Highway Building across the street. It was an appropriate spot for a man for whom politics was a zero-sum game of political favors. Sanford had been warned that if an old party warhorse like Roney were put in the front office it would send the wrong message for someone talking about a New Day.[12] Roney was a good soldier and understood, but he never forgot the slight and swore it would never happen again. Eight years later, after he engineered the election of Kerr Scott's son, Robert, Roney staked out a desk not more than twenty steps from the governor's door.[13]

If there was ever an eager governor of North Carolina, it was Terry Sanford. None of his predecessors, save Gardner, had waited so long or followed so focused a path to the office. Sanford arrived fresh, invigorated, and challenged, not by the job but by its possibilities. He was comfortable with the power that came with public office and was committed to using it in creative ways to realize his vision for North Carolina. And he had a lifetime's accumulation of ideas. Some were products of the recent campaign and already had found their way onto his ever-present legal pad; others dated back to Laurinburg and Chapel Hill. When he moved into the governor's office he took with him a copy of *North Carolina, Economic and Social*, the book written by his old professor, Huntington Hobbs, who had proposed a progressive program for the state more than thirty years earlier. Hobbs's numbers may have changed, but Sanford knew North Carolina remained awkwardly poised between a rural economy and the new demands of an industrial, even space-age, America. North Carolina was blessed with a people strong in spirit and will, but many citizens remained ill-housed, ill-fed, ill-trained, and struggling to make it to the next day. Sanford believed there was much to be done. His administration later would be marked by themes — social programs, race relations, and the arts — but for the moment, two objectives were paramount: Increase the quantity and quality of jobs for North Carolina workers and give their children an education equal to the demands of a changing world and shifting economy. Sanford had begun to work on both fronts even before he took office.

He wanted to quickly put his personal stamp on the state's industrial development program and started with changes at the top. Shortly after the November election, Sanford had invited Hargrove "Skipper" Bowles on a hunting trip to Lake Mattamuskeet and chosen him as his shooting partner. Standing in a duck blind, cold and damp in the Carolina dawn, Bowles had accepted the governor-elect's offer to take the top job at the Department of Conservation and Development. Tall, handsome, wealthy, Bowles was a bubbling optimist whose secretaries typed in capital letters the slogan "WE ARE ON THE GO. LEAD — FOLLOW — OR STAND ASIDE" as a footnote to his correspondence. He was a super salesman with a keen business sense and extensive contacts among corporate executives through his membership on the board of First Union National Bank in Charlotte as well as a number of other companies. Two weeks after inauguration day, Sanford and Bowles were in an old Buick careening through Chicago behind a phalanx of motorcycle cops, their sirens screaming through thirty-two red lights and across a median, just so they could reach a meeting of national furniture executives, where the governor presented awards to North Carolina companies. Later trips were without the escorts that embarrassed the boy from Laurinburg, but he was determined to "out-Hodge Hodges," as one friend put it, and beat the enviable record of industrial development set by his predecessor.

Sanford had made his plans for education clear in late November, when he was the special guest at a Chapel Hill meeting and reaffirmed his support of the program put forward by the United Forces for Education, the coalition of statewide organizations such as the School Board Association, the Parent-Teacher Association, and the North Carolina Education Association. The UFE's request for an increase in school spending of $100 million was the amount needed to recover from years of barebones budgets. Most of the money would pay for a 22 percent pay raise for teachers; in addition, the program called for more than twenty-eight hundred new teachers to be hired in the next two years. Libraries and school supplies were to get a share of the money, and the program would provide clerical assistance for schools. Money also would go to staffing at the state Department of Education and in the new Industrial Education Centers that had been created in Hodges's administration.

The governor-elect's first major appointment was Dallas Herring, a quiet, serious businessman and Latin scholar from the tiny Duplin County town of Rose Hill, whom he named chairman of the State Board of Education. There was no single person more closely identified with the UFE's ambitious program, and the choice sent a welcome signal to the school lobby. Herring had supported Sanford's bid for office and was pleasantly surprised when on their first meeting after the primaries Sanford promised to help expand technical education beyond the high school by an amount greater than Herring had hoped possible.[14]

The particulars of the education program were not the issue; rather, Sanford's task was to determine how to pay for it. Hodges's budget assumed there would be a balance of about $30 million remaining at the end of the fiscal year, but Sanford would need an additional $70 million to pay for the full UFE program for two years. The governor was prepared to request higher taxes, despite the political consequences. Optimistic almost to the point of self-destruction, he seemed convinced people would understand. "If it takes more taxes to give our children this quality education," he said on inauguration day, "we must face that fact and provide the money. We must never lose sight of the fact that our children are our best investment. This is no age for the faint of heart."[15] As he spoke those words, he scanned the faces of the members of the legislature seated in the front rows for some indication of what to expect in the days ahead. He might as well have been reading tea leaves, but, he thought, they looked as receptive as any jury he had seen.

North Carolina's General Assembly was the most independent legislative body in the nation. When the state's first constitution was written in the wake of the American Revolution, the drafters were so wary of central authority that they denied the governor a veto, limited him to one term, and gave him precious little else. Over the years, the state's chief executives had learned how to influence legislation with their control of the budget and unfettered power of appointment. In his first year alone, Sanford would name nearly five hundred people to all manner of boards and commissions, to judgeships and to seats on regulatory boards that controlled everything from banking franchises to the price of milk and electricity.

Among those seeking the robes of a judge or the prestige and influence of a highway commissioner were the 170 members of the legislature, whose regular biennial sessions opened in early February and continued until June, when tobacco and other crops needed attention. The members were an everyday lot; among the 1961 class were one minister—Republican Representative Murray Coffey, who also claimed work as a stonemason— three physicians, two undertakers, two newspaper publishers, teachers, a barber, a beauty parlor operator, and one locomotive engineer. J. Henry Hill Jr., a Catawba County Democrat, ran a barbecue restaurant and newsstand. There were more lawyers and farmers than anything else. All were part-timers, amateurs in the technical sense, whose pay and expense accounts did not cover the cost of service. But they were experienced; well over half the members in both chambers had been there before and knew well the art of trade and negotiation.

For more than a hundred years, the state house and senate had been meeting in chambers on the second floor of the capitol, whose cornerstone was quarried on state land and laid in 1833. The 1961 session would be the last in the old building; construction was due to begin on a new legislative building of contemporary design a block away. The old chambers, their carpets worn thin, had heard the ring of secessionist oratory in 1860 and the impeachment trial of a Reconstruction-era governor. The members' desks were outfitted for inkwells and the sergeants-at-arms still polished brass spittoons, though they now were most often filled with the remains of cigars and cigarettes. The quarters were cramped and legislators often huddled on the second-floor balcony of the rotunda, where the Raleigh Junior League sold soft drinks and goat's milk. During the daily sessions, lobbyists leaned on the worn brass railing under the rotunda, cornering members and speaking in hushed voices.

The historic chambers preserved the legislature's nineteenth-century character and personality. Oratory remained a practiced art by some, especially members who had earned their reputation as country lawyers. Representative John Kerr had a booming voice and commanding presence and could draw attention by simply standing and asking for the floor. One of the more colorful speakers was Representative "Cousin" Wayland Spruill. Once, when he rose to complain that the speaker's quick gavel had denied him the floor, he said, "I don't care about speaking first. Even George Washington couldn't be first at everything. Old George was first in war, first in peace and first in the hearts of his countrymen. But, then he married a widow." [16]

When Sanford looked over the roll he found the names of many friends, including some who had carried the vote for him in important counties. Some had been around since before 1953, when he had served his one term in the senate. The 1960 elections also had produced a small contingent of Republicans who were led by a young Greensboro lawyer named William Osteen, but their numbers were modest and not a worry. In the house, where most of the Republicans held seats, the governor would have to depend on Speaker Joe Hunt, a testy conservative partisan with ambitions of his own, to keep them in their place and largely out of the way. In the senate, which was dominated by members from lightly populated rural counties, Sanford's principal ally was Lieutenant Governor Cloyd Philpott.

Sanford knew he was not a favorite of the old lions in the legislature, most of whom had probably favored another candidate for governor. A year earlier, Sanford had avoided the courthouse crowd, which was the base for legislators who depended on the favor of county sheriffs and local politicos to return to Raleigh session after session. Yet, when the new governor went looking for someone to shepherd his program through the 1961 session, he demonstrated his knack for finding the right person for the job, choosing as his legislative liaison former senator William Copeland of Murfreesboro, a village in the northeastern corner of the state. Sanford and Copeland had served together in 1953. In fact, he had been the very man who had so frustrated the freshman senator from Cumberland County when he wanted to debate Governor Umstead's budget bill. "I had made up my mind [in 1953] that if I got to be governor, I wanted that little bastard on my side," Sanford said years later.[17]

Copeland was cautious, conservative, and thorough, but he had a reputation as a steady team player. In the 1959 session, he had chaired the appropriations committee, skillfully defending Hodges's budget from attack and resisting efforts to increase school funding. He knew where the official and unofficial power resided in the General Assembly and knew how to count votes. His appointment sounded alarms among the school people, who had fought Copeland in the past, as well as Lieutenant Governor Philpott, but the governor assured all that Copeland would be loyal and effective.

If Copeland worried Philpott, Sanford was just as concerned about a key appointment by the lieutenant governor, who also had ignored tradition and chosen Thomas Jackson White, a newly elected senator, as the chair of the crucial finance committee. Though this was White's first term in the senate, he had served in the house, where he and Philpott had been seatmates. The two were almost polar opposites in their politics, but they respected one another and had grown close. White could still find the notches he carved in the desk to record the few times the two had been together on crucial votes.[18]

White was an experienced trial lawyer and a fierce competitor who disliked losing almost as much as he disliked news reporters, whom he once called the "worst freeloaders the Lord ever put on this earth."[19] He was conservative, independent, and arrogant and told the members of his committee that he knew they didn't like the gavel in his hand, but they'd have to work hard to beat him. He arrived at his desk at five in the morning and had done a day's work by the time his committee met at eight. Philpott reassured Sanford that White would give him no trouble when his tax bill came to a vote, and the governor took him at his word.

In the coming months, such alliances would prove essential, and none more so than Sanford's growing friendship with his lieutenant governor. Sanford and Philpott came from different worlds, but the two had grown close during the fall campaign. Philpott was a Lexington furniture manufacturer who was well respected in the state's business community. Before Philpott announced his own plans for public office, Sanford had considered him a possible manager for his campaign. He was a warm, friendly, unpretentious man who wore his thinning hair trimmed in a crew cut. He was eight years older than Sanford, but the two shared a common vision for the state. In his campaign, the lieutenant governor also had endorsed the UFE program and presented himself as a progressive alternative to two able primary opponents. In the fall, Sanford and Philpott had campaigned together; while traveling across the state with their wives the two couples had become close enough friends to laugh when the wives realized on inauguration day that they were wearing identical outfits. Margaret Rose said hers came from J. C. Penney; Frances Philpott said she shopped at Sears.

As her husband prepared for the start of the General Assembly, Margaret Rose was busy trying to establish a routine for her children, who had traded a comfortable suburban home for life in the governor's mansion, a drafty old barn of a house set on the edge of one of Raleigh's faded inner-city neighborhoods. Built at the turn of the century and set in the center of a square block of real estate shaded by huge oaks, the mansion was more a curiosity than a home, with its fancy scrollwork and doodads, assorted Victorian balconies and porches.

Behind this delightful façade was a building in much need of repair. The heating system was old, and in winter some corners of the house were cold and uncomfortable. There was no kitchen in the family quarters on the upper floors, although the Sanfords had use of a bomb shelter in the basement that was stocked with enough food and drink for them to survive for weeks. The main dining room could easily seat more than thirty guests, but an inventory of the china cabinet showed that dinner plates were worn, the colors faded, and the coffee cups did not match.[20]

Margaret Rose helped Betsee, Terry Jr., and two dogs find themselves in a new world. Both children felt awkward and out of place, particularly after the adventure of the first few days faded into a realization that their familiar home and friends were a hundred miles away. Terry was delighted to find a variety of color television sets to watch. Betsee was curious about the stories of ghosts said to haunt the place. Both were anxious about the future.

The Sanfords were the youngest first family the state had known since Aycock had the job sixty years earlier. None had ever faced a decision like the one that confronted Terry and Margaret Rose as they considered a new school for their children. They finally chose to enroll them at Murphy Elementary, an aging brick schoolhouse located two blocks north of the mansion. It was not the best school in the Raleigh system, nor the worst, but it was fair to say it was one of the schools that the new governor hoped to overhaul with his ambitious education program. The school was still adjusting to the admission of its first black student when Terry and Betsee walked in with their mother and Hugh Cannon after a Highway Patrol car let them off at the curb.

Margaret Rose had favored enrolling the children at Ravenscroft, a newly organized private school run by the Episcopal Church on Capitol Square, where they would get attention comparable to what they had received at the first-rate school they had left in Fayetteville. For Terry, there had never been any question that the children would attend a public school. Whatever their motives, placing the children in Ravenscroft would have been seen as running from an integrated school—and one that had only one black child among the sea of white faces. "Given everything that I believed in and was trying to do, it would have been disastrous if we put them in private school," Sanford said years later. If he and Margaret Rose had concerns about the quality of instruction at Murphy, "We just had to worry about that later on." [21]

The children had more personal concerns. Terry Jr. was glad that little Bill Campbell, a third-grader whose parents asked that he be assigned to Murphy, chose to break the color line. It helped deflect attention from him and his sister, both of whom were self-conscious and painfully aware of the stares that accompanied their first trip to the classroom.

Normally, Sanford would have accompanied his children on their first day at a new school. This year, he intentionally remained away, hoping to avoid media attention that would turn the routine into a public spectacle. That was folly. Reporters gathered for the arrival of the Sanford children, and in the following days the governor's office received news clippings of their reports from newspapers all over the world. The sensational slant on the coverage embarrassed Sanford. "I mean, gosh, 'Southern governor sends his children to integrated school,'" he recalled years later. "One poor little boy and we called it an integrated school." [22] (In 1993, Bill Campbell was elected mayor of Atlanta. His brother, Ralph, was elected state auditor in North Carolina in 1992.)

Sanford continued his morning exercise routine and often jogged by Murphy School on runs he took through the surrounding neighborhood. He usually rose before dawn, pulled on his sweatpants, and hoped the exercise would work off extra pounds that easily accumulated on his stocky frame. He enjoyed the fresh light of the new day and the solitude of the quiet streets in the early morning. It was a good time to think about the coming weeks and the coming legislative session, which, he wrote later, was "the most challenging, the most exciting, the most determinative, the most satisfying, the most pleasant, and the most dangerous task of a new governor." [23] The success of Sanford's administration would be determined within the first six months of his four years in office. If his years of preparation for the governorship were to mean anything, it was essential that he present a solid program and win its approval. There would be no second chance.

Sanford's first appearance before the legislature came February 9. The presentation of the annual budget message was a perfunctory affair, part of the opening ritual, in which the governor delivered a proposed budget for the next two years. For a new governor, it was more a program crafted by the previous administration than a plan for the future. But Sanford made some additions to the program, which became evident when he reached the portion of his speech dedicated to education. His pace quickened when he told the members jammed into the house chamber for the joint session that this budget did not do the job: "It can be argued that we can get along on this level of appropriations, and we can, but at this rate we will never achieve opportunities of education second to none. . . . I am sure, I am positive," Sanford declared, "that there is contained in this budget no implied admonition to 'hold the line' at the proposed figures. Rather, I am satisfied, I know that it was and is expected that this budget will serve as a 'line of departure' from which we will move to the objective of quality education to meet the demand of a rapidly advancing, changing, scientific, complex world." He said he would return in a month and have more to say on the subject.[24]

On inauguration day, Sanford had declared that education would be the "rock upon which I will build the house of my administration." As legislators visited him in the office, he believed that members generally favored his ambitious program. But he knew, and they knew, that they couldn't adopt his program unless an additional $70 million was found to pay for it. "There was an overwhelming determination to improve the schools even if we had to increase taxes," Sanford later wrote. "The test yet to come was what kind of tax would be acceptable. This was difficult. The opposition to any kind of tobacco tax was marked. Generally, there was a feeling that the easiest tax would be to increase the existing sales tax schedule to 3.5 or 4 percent. People talked about taxes on 'luxuries,' but they could never pin it down. One man's luxury, it seemed, was another man's necessity. Besides when you looked item by item you found these things simply would not produce appreciable revenue."[25]

The 3 percent sales tax had been enacted in 1933 to save the state from bankruptcy and keep schools operating in the face of financial crisis. At the outset, there were a few exemptions. For example, food was covered, but block ice, such as that used in home iceboxes, was untaxed, presumably for health reasons and the political risk of taxing water. Later, during World

War II, the legislature had begun granting exemptions so that by 1961 over fifty items, including food and medicine, were exempt from taxation.

Sanford hoped that North Carolina's existing taxes might generate the necessary money. The state, as well as much of the nation, was recovering from a stalled and stagnant economy in the 1950s. Yet, the closer he came to his date with the legislature, the more it was obvious that the state's economy was not growing fast enough to pay the bills and that new taxes on cigarettes, or soft drinks or liquor would not raise enough to get the job done.

He kept returning to the sales tax. Raising the total levy was the most palatable, although it would retain the confusing array of exemptions. Yet removing these exemptions, particularly those for food and medicine, was considered so dangerous politically that Jay Jenkins, the veteran Raleigh reporter for the *Charlotte Observer*, dismissed it completely as an option in a column he wrote before Sanford returned to the legislature. Sanford's closest friends reminded him of the risks. Paul Thompson and Donald McCoy made an urgent trip to Raleigh to convince him to look elsewhere. Copeland told him he was doubtful that legislators would ever adopt such a thing. Cannon and Lambeth were opposed for philosophical as well as political reasons. The only person with any sympathy was his new revenue commissioner, William Johnson; after only a few weeks in office, he had found the state laws designating taxable and nontaxable items to be a bewildering mess.

Sanford kept his own counsel. Whatever he chose was sure to be met with opposition and he didn't see any reason to give his enemies a head start by tipping his hand. The weekend before he was to make his special education address, he called Peggy Warren Satterfield, who had declined an offer to work in the governor's office in favor of marriage, and asked her to come to the mansion to type his speech. He also invited leaders of the school lobby, on whom he would depend for support, for a brief meeting on Sunday afternoon. Much to their surprise, they learned that Sanford meant what he had said in the campaign when he had endorsed the complete UFE program. "They were convinced I was going to cut it in half," Sanford later recalled. "But, I said absolutely not. We said this is what we are going to be for and this *is* what we are going to be for. They thought I was a politician and thought I was doing this talking and I was going to step back." [26]

On Monday, he was still tinkering with the speech when he slipped into the back of the governor's black Cadillac limousine and headed out of town with his revenue commissioner to deliver a Founder's Day speech at Johnson's alma mater, Campbell College in Buies Creek, a crossroads town in the rolling countryside of Harnett County. On the way, the two stopped to visit a school and talk with the students and their teachers. The details of his speech remained closely guarded until just a few hours before he stepped to the well of the house and began to outline his plans for what he preferred to call the school tax. His opponents called it the food tax, and later "Terry's Tax," and thus hung a label on him that would remain for his entire political career.

"I have explained to you my reasons for believing that the budget is inadequate to achieve the public education goals we must set for our state," Sanford told the legislators on March 6.

> I am sure that it is generally acknowledged that we have not done all we can do.
>
> I come to you now with the most difficult decision that I have had to make since assuming the office of governor, and, perhaps the most difficult of my term of office.
>
> I come to you now with the most difficult decision of your service in this session.[27]

He explained why he believed new taxes on tobacco, soft drinks, and liquor were unsuitable and then detailed his changes for the sales tax, acknowledging the regressive inequity of rich and poor paying at the same rate. Nonetheless, he said, "I predict [the poor] will be willing to do their share in order that we might have a strong tax structure which will support the schools which will give their children a better chance in life."

He asked that the exemptions be removed as of July 1 and that the proposition be submitted to a vote in the fall to determine whether it should be continued beyond an expiration date of July 1, 1963. He pledged to carry a campaign, a "crusade" he called it, to every county in the state to win public support for the tax if legislators would unite behind it:

> In this way the people will understand what we are doing, will participate in our decisions, and we in North Carolina will be ready to move.
>
> The hour is at hand when North Carolina can begin its bold march forward. We begin this march in these halls by reaching out and grasping the hands of our priceless possession, our children and our grandchildren.

Sanford's boldness caught most legislators completely by surprise. House Speaker Hunt told reporters he had expected the governor to offer a smorgasbord of suggestions, leaving it to the legislators to pick a few. He didn't know Sanford, who believed such a thing was nothing less than political cowardice for a chief executive. It was the governor's job to lead, he would explain later, and to duck the hard decision and leave the choice to the legislature would have been a dereliction of duty.

The public comments of legislators were cautious, reserved. Privately, however, the *Charlotte Observer*'s Jenkins said legislators thought Sanford "was simply off his rocker if he thought they would accept such a tax." [28]

The governor found little initial support from the editorial pages of the state's major daily newspapers. The usually friendly *Greensboro Daily News* questioned his choice and said that increasing the sales tax to 4 percent with the exemptions in place was a better way to go. The *Raleigh Times* called the food tax a "last-ditch resort." The conservative *Gastonia Gazette* said forget food, put the taxes on cigarettes and liquor. Editor Bill Moore of Sanford's hometown paper, the *Laurinburg Exchange*, was right when he observed that "Governor Sanford put his public career and himself on the spot."

Sanford presented his choice to the legislature in such a way that opponents shared the hot seat with him. Unless they wanted to be labeled as opposing education, "standing in the way of boys and girls," as Jenkins put it, legislators were forced to come up with alternatives, and they soon found that their options were no better than the governor's. At the same time, Sanford's package had a curious appeal to both liberals and conservatives. Those eager to get the state's education program moving were willing to swallow hard and accept the tax; conservatives, meanwhile, liked the fact that everyone would pay.

Nothing occupied more of Sanford's attention in the coming weeks than the education program, which was clearly the keystone of his administration. If he lost this battle, his promise of building a strong educational program would be voided. To build public support, he and Bennett mobilized campaign workers and allies in the education lobby to produce a series of "education rallies," including one where the governor's speech was carried over a statewide radio broadcast. The first took place in Smithfield two days after his legislative address, where hundreds of parents turned out to hear Sanford speak. The familiar environs of a political campaign suited the governor just fine. He was forceful, determined, and clearly fighting as hard for this program as he had for his own candidacy a year earlier.

North Carolina was at the bottom of the national educational heap, Sanford declared. Teacher pay was below average in 1950, and in the previous decade salaries had advanced less than in any other state in the nation. Forty states had lower teacher-pupil ratios, thirty-nine spent more on local schools. In North Carolina, an average of $240 a year went for each child enrolled; the national average was $369. The product of such neglect was devastating. The rate of illiteracy among Tar Heels rejected for the military was among the highest in the nation. Citizens in forty-six states finished more years of school than people in North Carolina. It was a simple equation: A good education was essential for survival. In North Carolina, ranked eighth in the nation in the number of children in school, the education system was struggling and losing ground:

> We have given proportionately less attention to the maintenance of schools than we have to the maintenance of wardrobes, our automobiles and our kitchen stoves.
>
> I hope that those who may be tempted to speak out against the food tax will suggest some painless way we can get the money. I hope they will explain why it is fair to tax the food which persons, including the poor, who must "eat out" pay on food at cafes and restaurants. As you know, we have been taxing that food since 1933.
>
> I hope also they will remember that if we tax bread we also will be taxing cake; if we tax fatback, we also will tax caviar; if we tax cornmeal, we also will tax filet mignon. No one is going to go hungry because of this tax.

Two days later, Representative Shelton Wicker from Sanford rose near the end of the day's legislative session and sent forward the governor's bill. "They said you should save the best for the last," he joked. Speaker Hunt, a reluctant supporter of the governor's program, responded dryly, "The last bill or the last of us?" [29]

Over the coming weeks, the governor transformed every speaking engagement, every public appearance, into a rally for education. Two weeks after he spoke to the legislature he was at the commemoration of the unfurling of the first flag of the old Confederacy in Louisburg where he compared the gallantry of North Carolinians in battle to the "fight for better education opportunity for our children and better opportunities for all people." Earlier in the day he had spoken of education excellence at the inauguration of Dr. Samuel Proctor as president of North Carolina A&T State College in Greensboro.

The crusade for education was unlike anything seen since the turn of the century and the days of Aycock. Sanford believed that aroused parents could add some backbone to legislators concerned about voting for higher taxes. At the same time, however, the governor knew that what he really needed was a working majority in the legislature. In the coming weeks, he would prove to be a masterful lobbyist and as persuasive as any man who held the office.

Sanford paid close attention to the members who daily filed past his office on their way to the chambers upstairs. When he needed to see a member, he posted Hugh Cannon at the door to shepherd him into the governor's office. One by one, the governor took the measure of his opposition. Most legislators told him simply, "I can't sell this back home. I can't come down here and vote a tax on food." After hearing that refrain over and over, Sanford recalled telling one man, a veteran from a district in the mountain foothills, " 'Well, Henry, look at it this way. That is not really important because you are expendable.' He laughed of course, and he voted with me and didn't get beat." [30]

The dining table at the mansion was seldom empty. Tuesday through Friday, when legislators were in town, Sanford made sure that platters of eggs, grits, sausage, ham, bacon, and biscuits were full and set for a crowd at breakfast. If the schedule permitted, a similar spread was ready for guests at midday. Once, after a luncheon, when Sanford learned one legislator was leaving on a long ride home, he packed his pockets with chicken and biscuits.

The lobbying was intense and involved every person within earshot of the governor's office. Staff members and department heads could expect calls at any time of the day and were often called at home in the evening to return for meetings at the mansion. The governor paid little attention to the clock. Cannon's wife, Jesse, finally complained that he was spending so much time at the mansion that the only difference between him and the round-the-clock security detail was that the state troopers wore uniforms.

Sanford followed the legislators to their haunts, particularly the lobby of the Sir Walter Hotel. In the evening hours, he moved among the members parked in the cushioned chairs and sofas puffing cigars and trading stories. Sanford chatted with those who needed special attention and then, on the ride back to the mansion, made notes on the lengthening list of favors suggested in the course of an evening's conversation. He once wrote that none of the trades were put as boldly as Alton Lennon's response to Kerr Scott; when the governor asked for his help, Lennon was said to have answered, "The question is, what's in it for Al Lennon?" [31]

Sanford was a practical, pragmatic negotiator who easily rationalized the concessions and favors he granted. As was his nature, he gave legislators the benefit of the doubt. "I did have people with road problems, parole problems, problems of admission to the schools for retarded, and jobs for constituents," he later wrote. "In all of these, with rare exception, they were not personally involved, but merely were reflecting pressure from their own constituents. I did what I could to help them. They are entitled to have influence in behalf of their constituents who elected them, and I held up their hands whenever I could." [32]

In mid-April, the education program made it past the first hurdle when it was approved by the appropriations committees. A few days before the vote, the governor's initiative won the endorsement of two important national figures, Admiral Hyman Rickover, the creator of America's nuclear navy, and Harvard University President Emeritus Dr. James Conant, both of whom had become leaders in a national education movement. Conant called Sanford's program "a landmark in public education." Rickover said, "I have been talking with your governor about his education program. He has more zeal for and dedication to education than any public official I have ever met."[33]

Even with such endorsements, the final committee vote did not come easily. Sanford was still talking with legislators just hours before the vote. Some members remained convinced that the education package was too extravagant and were persuaded by arguments of Senator Archie Davis, a respected top executive with Wachovia Bank in Winston-Salem, who carried a heavy briefcase stuffed with financial reports to show the state could not afford such an expense. Members argued that "you can't buy good teachers." The governor said they were missing the point.

When the bill was called for a voice vote, committee chairmen ruled in Sanford's favor. Opponents grumbled about heavy-handed tactics but did not insist on a roll call.

The appropriations vote was the first major test for Copeland and the governor's team of lobbyists that included Roney, Cannon, Bill White, who had left his business to head the state purchasing and contract office, and Bruce Poole of Raleigh, an old political warhorse and Kerr Scott ally. From time to time, Budget Director David Coltrane and Prison Director George Randall, two holdovers from the Hodges administration who got along well with legislators, were called in to help. At crucial committee meetings, Copeland's crew stood on the perimeter of the room, appearing to one who was there like "professional football scouts, looking for a hole in the line."[34]

Before the sales tax bill was called to a vote, Copeland urged Sanford to press forward with other parts of his program to demonstrate that he could get what he wanted from the legislators and to ensure that some additional appointments were in place. Accordingly, bills to reorganize and expand the Highway Commission and the Conservation and Development Board moved ahead and passed easily.

Despite this early success, Copeland's tally sheets showed that the margin of victory for the tax package would be slim when it was voted on in committee. Opposition had mounted from many quarters, including grocers and the food industry. The North Carolina Bakers Council weighed in against it; the council's lobbyist, William C. McIntyre, accused Sanford of taxing "innocent babies for milk they have to have." When Sanford learned McIntyre was a member of the state Milk Commission, he asked for his resignation.

At the same time, however, opposition outside of Raleigh had begun to soften. Newspapers that had been cool finally gave grudging support. By mid-May, the tax bill was due for an important vote when Sanford was out of town, courting industrial prospects in Ohio. He left the group of traveling businessmen and flew back to Raleigh after Philpott sent him a note reminding him that he shouldn't wander off again: "We might from time to time run into legislative or committee blocks which could be eliminated by your personal contact with one or several people."[35] The bill passed out of committee.

The battle was all but won, although last-minute skirmishes posed some threat. Sanford's allies had to turn back an effort to substitute the tobacco tax for the sales tax in the House Finance Committee, and some were anxious when the senate took up the measure. Just days before the vote, Cannon received a preliminary report showing that state tax collections were expected to be higher than predicted; he feared opponents could use this information to argue that new taxes were unnecessary and Sanford's initiative would collapse.[36] His concern was short-lived. The bill sailed through the senate by a vote of forty-two to eight; the margin in the house was eighty-five to thirty-one. Even those who didn't like it voted with the governor. Senator Jennings King, who had grown up with Sanford in Laurinburg, cast his vote with the majority but not before he declared the new taxes would lead to a "two-party system in North Carolina. The Democratic Party has been the party of the poor and oppressed. The food tax is a tax imposed by the comfortably well-to-do."[37] It became law on June 13.

Sanford's legislative victory surprised observers who had been watching the work of the General Assembly for years. Lynn Nisbet, a columnist whose work appeared in nearly all the afternoon daily newspapers in the state, called it the result of

> the most astute salesmanship campaign ever conducted by the chief executive of North Carolina.
>
> Governor Sanford has used to greater degree than his recent predecessors the art of moral suasion. He has "sold" legislators on the merits of his program. The majority of those who voted for his bills did not do so because of promises or threats, but because they had been convinced that it was the right thing to do.
>
> Men who swore early in the session they would stay here until Christmas before they'd vote for a sales tax on table foods were found in the front ranks of advocates three months later. Many of these men are not the kind who can be bought or threatened.[38]

Gene Roberts of the *News & Observer* wrote that legislators liked Sanford's genial nature and accessibility, which stood in contrast to Hodges, whom some found cold and aloof: " 'It goes without saying that the governor's down-to-earth politics has paid off,' one house member told a reporter last week. 'It's hard to vote against a man who has become your friend.' " [39]

That's not to say there wasn't plenty of horse-trading. Roberts reported that Sanford's lobbyists were sure to see "that legislators who 'vote right' are rewarded. Senator Luther Hamilton of Cartaret [County] had tried repeatedly—and without success—to have the legislature elect him to the consolidated University Board of Trustees. But when he rallied to the governor's program after opposing Sanford in last year's primaries, he found himself one of the leading vote-getters in the trustee selections." [40]

Before adjournment, some of the dissenters composed a ditty poking fun at the governor:

> Did he feed you tax expansion, when you ate up at the mansion?
> Did he put the food tax square upon your plate?
> If he fed you tax expansion, when he fed you at the mansion,
> Then we hope you choke on what you really ate.

And the refrain:

> If you acted very good and backed the tax on food,
> There'll be room for you, for sure, on C&D.[41]

Sanford praised the work of the General Assembly. And well he should have; it gave him virtually everything he asked for. In addition to the education program and taxes to pay for it, the legislators adopted new regulations on small loan companies, a deal brokered in Sanford's office when the session became deadlocked on the measure. The state minimum wage law was increased to seventy-five cents an hour, and welfare payments for the old, the disabled, and the hungry were boosted to help offset the cost of the new taxes the poor would pay for food and medicine. Sanford called the 1961 session a "legislature with a conscience," and in his speeches avoided mention of troublesome matters, such as the General Assembly's failure to reapportion the senate, defeat of an auto inspection law, and refusal to upgrade the state's antiquated court system.

Sanford and Philpott were in good spirits when they left Raleigh just days before the session adjourned and headed for the National Governors Conference, which was meeting in Hawaii. It was a welcome break from the demands of the previous months and Sanford made the most of it, waterskiing and enjoying what the island had to offer. He drew reporters' attention one night when he was refused entrance to Don the Beachcomber's, a popular tourist nightspot that required guests to wear regular shoes. Sanford's flip-flops didn't meet the dress code, but the matter was resolved when the governor promised not to dance. News accounts of the incident moved Eugene Price, editor of the Goldsboro *News Argus* to wire the governor of Hawaii, William F. Quinn, asking for some indulgence. "It being summertime, and all," Price wrote, "he probably didn't pack a pair of shoes. Brogans airmailed today. P.S. Don't worry about tar on heels. It won't come off." Quinn answered, telling Price not to worry. He had called for a special Terry Sanford Day "where nobody will wear shoes in memory of the valiant governor of North Carolina."[42]

Sanford arrived in Hawaii like a peddler with a trunkful of wares, touting North Carolina products and possibilities. One item that went on the plane with him was a straight-backed wooden porch rocker. He kept one in his office and had one shipped to President Kennedy, who said that it was the one chair that helped him withstand his constant back pain. Years later, the plain varnished model that sold for less than $30, cushions included, was auctioned as part of Jacqueline Kennedy Onassis' estate as the best-known piece of furniture from the Oval Office.

That summer there was a growing feeling in the governor's office that anything was possible, that any issue could be resolved. In late May, for example, the governor sent his young assistant, Tom Lambeth, to the mountain town of Mars Hill to help settle a dispute over the hiring of a school principal and end an eight-day boycott of classes by students. The governor freely weighed in to break the legislative deadlock over regulation of small loan companies. In midsummer, he wrote Agriculture Commissioner L. Y. Ballentine on behalf of migrant workers after state health inspectors reported a "wholesale disregard for minimum sanitary conditions" in nearly half of the camps visited.

The governor also enthusiastically joined in the efforts to save the decommissioned battleship *North Carolina*. Sanford endorsed a public campaign headed by Hugh Morton of Wilmington to raise $100,000, much of it in pennies collected by schoolchildren, to keep the battleship from the salvage yard. White House sympathy for the cause had helped save the ship, and on a visit to Washington in April, Morton, Sanford, and Skipper Bowles presented the president with a commission in the North Carolina Navy. When the ship arrived off the bar at the mouth of the Cape Fear River in late summer, it had been stripped of all essential military hardware, but its belly was full of diesel fuel, which was sold to aid the public subscription. Sanford climbed aboard a Coast Guard cutter, as eager as a kid with a new toy as he watched ocean tugs nudge the giant up the Cape Fear and into a permanent slip across from downtown Wilmington.

Every corner of state government got his attention. When the Institute of Government supplied him with a chart showing that more than 170 agencies and commissions reported to the governor, he said he would see that they did, regularly. Those in charge of major departments, and certain key state officials such as State Board of Education Chairman Dallas Herring, had standing weekly appointments. In his first summer in office, he also instructed every agency head to prepare a written report and oral presentation on where they wanted their departments to be in fifteen years.

Sanford was not satisfied with simply continuing the routine of state government. Early in the year, he began looking for someone to "pay attention to some of the things that we really ought to be thinking about." "What could we do that is different to make things better?" he asked his staff. He approached Dr. Hollis Edens, who had recently retired as president of Duke University, and asked him to become his assistant for special projects. "I said I want you to be in charge of things that are not in the regular run of the governor's office. We might want to touch some foundations for some money. We want to do some different things that ought to be done and I don't really know how to define any better than that right now."[43] Edens declined the offer, saying he needed time to rest.

Sanford's innovative spirit was infectious. "We would do anything, I mean we would try anything, anything that wasn't illegal," recalled Cannon. Sanford was "inspiring. He never talked about problems. He talked about what you should do and why you should do it. His favorite message to me was, 'Handle this.' He didn't tell me how, or when. He gave us a lot of leeway and told us to run. And we did."[44] There were limits, however. "Cannon was giving the university a little trouble one time," Sanford later recalled. "I said, 'Cannon, sit down here. I want to explain something to you. You don't turn down the University of North Carolina without my personal permission.' "[45]

Despite the youth and inexperience of his immediate staff, Sanford assigned broad authority and discretion to solve problems he dropped on their desks. Once, a woman arrived at Cannon's office with a note from Sanford that read, "Listen to this lady and see what you can do." She explained that she had a child who was both deaf and blind and she didn't know where to turn because the state's school for one disability would not admit the child because of the other. While the mother waited in his office, Cannon checked her story with department heads. When they arrived, he said, "I am going to go out for a few moments and one of you decide [who wants to take the child]. We could do things like that, and we did it. Everything was possible."[46] The freewheeling attitude that permeated the governor's office so disturbed the venerable state treasurer Edwin Gill that he arrived one day at Sanford's desk with a complaint, according to Hugh Cannon: "Mr. Gill said, 'The problem with your director of the budget is that he thinks everything is possible. That is not his function. His function is to restrain.' Terry said, 'Well, that is just a different way of looking at it.' "[47]

At midyear, new members began to take their places on state boards and commissions and in state departments. Sanford's appointees were a heterogeneous mix, reflecting the range of supporters who had been drawn to his campaign as well as personal considerations. His highway commission, the most politically sensitive group, included many of the area keys who had turned out the vote for him in 1960. Merrill Evans, from the state's northeastern corner, perhaps the state's most rural region, was appointed chairman, and campaign stalwarts such as Lauch Faircloth of Clinton, Clint Newton of Shelby, Clifton Benson of Raleigh, Jack Kirksey of Morganton, and James K. Glenn, who was Bert Bennett's business partner, took seats on the commission. Also included was a hometown member, Thomas McLean, the business partner of Sanford's best friend, Paul Thompson.

Conservative business interests who had gambled on his election were pleased with his new members for the state Banking and Utilities Commission. Major state banking interests such as Wachovia Bank & Trust Company and First Citizens Bank were represented. The only major change was his determination to give more jobs to women; Gladys Bullard of Raleigh became the first woman on the prestigious Board of Conservation and Development.

Everyone put in their requests, including Sanford's own father. Cecil Sanford wrote his son on behalf of John Lowry, a nominee for the board of trustees at Pembroke State College: "John is the man who came by when you and Cecil were gassed on the road below Maxton that night. He picked you up and brought you to see a doctor in Maxton and then on home that night, and would not take a cent for doing it." [48] Lowry didn't make it onto the Pembroke board, but in 1962 he was appointed chairman of the state Board of Water Well Contractor Examiners.

Roney stepped in to keep Dr. Lenox Baker chairman of the state Board of Health. Baker, a political conservative and accomplished orthopedist, had backed another candidate for governor and would normally have been replaced. Roney interceded on his behalf, telling Sanford about Baker's considerate treatment of his daughter. The governor passed over his own choice in favor of Roney's nominee.

No personnel decision more clearly demonstrated the new energy of the Sanford administration than the appointment of Hugh Cannon as director of the budget. He replaced David Coltrane, who had run the office since the days of William Umstead and who was the most respected senior member of the state government bureaucracy. Coltrane's assurances had helped calm nervous legislators in the recent session and his presence was a comfort to conservatives anxious about fears of runaway government spending. Cannon was half his age, with no experience, but Sanford wanted a budget officer who would expedite his program and not quibble over details.

For Cannon's replacement, he chose Joel Fleishman. As the governor's legal counsel, he would handle all manner of projects in the coming months, paying particular attention to civil rights and the arts, two issues that had yet to appear on anyone's agenda.

The pace at the governor's office slackened with the legislature gone from the building, but Sanford's schedule was seldom routine. Lambeth dutifully prepared a daily agenda that he constantly adjusted to accommodate last-minute guests whom Sanford treated like family. One day Lambeth told the governor about a man who day after day had showed up at his desk and asked to see the governor. Sanford told Lambeth to alert him if he called again. When he did, Sanford interrupted his day and invited the man into his office. He stayed a few minutes and then left. When he was gone Sanford told Lambeth of a similar visitor who had pestered Kerr Scott for attention. When Scott finally asked the man in, he walked to the door of the governor's office, looked inside, and then turned and left, saying, "Well, I just wanted to see you in the governor's office." Perhaps, Sanford told Lambeth, "that might be what folks want. They just want to see that I am here." [49]

On another occasion, a man showed up at the office with a newspaper reporter in tow. He was there, he told Lambeth, to be sworn in to a minor state commission. Lambeth checked and found that the post was to go to someone else. Rather than spoil the man's day, Sanford went ahead, signed the commission, and saved himself and his newest appointee from embarrassment in front of the home folks.

Sanford's office was open to anyone in state government. "All they had to do was walk in there and Tom would run them in," Sanford said later. "I think it just gets everybody involved. You learn something from everybody." A frequent visitor was Senator Ralph Scott, who usually sat in a rocking chair like the one Sanford had sent the president. "He would sit in that rocker and start complaining. I would say, 'Now, Ralph, I want you to come over here every morning at eight o'clock and get in that chair and stay there all day long so I can ask you about everything before I do it so I won't make any mistakes.' He said, 'Hell, no. I would rather complain.'" [50]

One day a woman arrived to tell the governor that the Lord had instructed her to travel to Raleigh and ask the governor to pave her road. She lived in the mountain foothills, where many roads had yet to see their first asphalt. Taken with the woman's sincerity, Sanford arranged for the road to be paved. Many years later, when he was in the U.S. Senate, questions arose about a road in the same vicinity that had opened valuable mountain property to a development owned by Republicans. Sanford inquired about it and was told by one of his old friends, "That's the road you and the Lord paved." [51]

Sanford's accessible style unsettled old-timers on the Council of State whose offices were in the capitol. State Treasurer Gill and Secretary of State Eure had been raised on tradition and decorum. Gill, who had been a fixture in Raleigh since Sanford was a youngster, seemed the one most disturbed by the changes. He had assumed an important advisory role with Hodges, who had come so unexpectedly to the job; when Gill presumed the same with Sanford, he was gently but firmly rebuffed. Some resentment began to build, Sanford said later, and Gill never forgave what he considered a humiliating slight by the boy who used to deliver his newspaper.

Eure had been in public office since the Depression. He was uncomfortable with the youthful exuberance of Sanford's staff, who on arrival had reduced the average age of capitol workers by at least a generation. Lambeth was only twenty-five, although a news release announcing his appointment fudged his birthdate to make him appear a year older. Cannon was twenty-nine. The eldest of the governor's immediate staff was press secretary Graham Jones at thirty-two. A headline writer at the *News & Observer* called them "Terry's Kindergarten," a phrase that stuck with Eure, who reminded Lambeth that he should refrain from addressing the governor by his first name.

Earlier in the year, State Auditor Henry Bridges had complained about the freewheeling travel budget of Skipper Bowles and his industry hunters at C&D. Such complaints were little more than a nuisance for a man who at first commuted to Raleigh in a chauffeur-driven Bentley before exchanging it for a more modest Chevrolet. Bridges finally lowered his voice after Sanford's friends in the legislature offered a bill to exempt C&D from Bridges's review.

In early July, Sanford announced an impressive agenda of eleven items that he planned to focus on in the coming months. He said he would continue his push for highway safety and build more secondary roads. State government could use some attention, and he said he planned to trim the excess and eliminate inefficiency. He planned to give more attention to water conservation and developing economic plans for all areas of the state, plans that would include provision for the corporate executives whom Bowles was showing around in the state's new twin-engine airplane. He also planned to get to the bottom of corruption in college athletics. The legislature had turned down a request for $50,000 to investigate point shaving in basketball games, but Sanford planned to push ahead, nonetheless.

Education remained the top priority. The governor's initiative on behalf of public schools had attracted national attention, and in his first summer in office he accepted invitations for appearances before education groups across the South. In mid-August he traveled to Nashville, Tennessee, to deliver the commencement address at George Peabody College for Teachers. Earlier, in July, he had spoken in Columbia, South Carolina, at a state education conference. His Columbia speech included a theme that would continue throughout his administration. When most other Southern politicians were clinging to the Stars and Bars of the Old Confederacy, Sanford found another use for the frequent references to the past. "The South is moving again into the mainstream of America," he told the South Carolina educators.

> The South is rising again! It is not rising again through secession from the union, nor through insurrection, nor through nullification. It is rising again through education, through industry, through commerce and through agriculture.
>
> The clarion call for better schools has replaced the rebel yell as the voice of the South, and it deserves the attention of a national audience which usually is only too willing to hear the opposite. Education across the nation is crying for direction and leadership. Well, let's lead.[52]

The Columbia speech was a call for unity of purpose and clarity of goals for a region that Sanford said should be bold and aggressive, not defensive or reactionary. Southern children could no longer afford to be shortchanged by provincialism in an age when they would have to compete in a national market. "The hour is at hand when South Carolina, North Carolina and all the South can rise again and march again. We will make this march not with bayonets but with textbooks. We will not be firing on Fort Sumter. We will be firing on the dungeons of ignorance."

Speaking at Peabody in August, he said,

> Our roadblock is the dead hand of the past which reaches out to hold us back. For many of us, our emotional commitments and our inherited value systems clash with our intellectual recognition of the need for change. We cannot make progress dreaming of magnolia trees.
>
> There is no way to live in the past. Marching boldly into the future is not an irreverent disregard of the deeds of our fathers; indeed, such boldness and determination are our inheritance and we honor the traditions of the South by moving into the mainstream of American leadership. If this becomes our theme, the first roadblock will disappear.[53]

Sanford's conviction that the South was ready to move from its past and drop generations of racial custom seemed farfetched in the summer of

1961. The nation had seen both blood and terror on the faces of Freedom Riders, a racially mixed group of courageous young people who had set out in early May on a bus journey to test the Jim Crow customs of interstate commerce. They passed through Virginia and North Carolina without serious incident before trouble met them at the bus station in Rock Hill, South Carolina. There, John Lewis, a disciple of Dr. Martin Luther King Jr., became the first casualty when he took a fist in the face after he refused to use the "colored" entrance to the bus station. Yet the Rock Hill fracas was nothing compared to what happened when the bus crossed the state line into Alabama. Outside of Anniston, while trying to outrun a caravan of angry whites, the driver was forced to pull his bus to a halt: the tires, leaking air from slashes at an earlier stop, went flat. He fled to the woods as the whites converged, smashed windows, and finally set the bus afire with the passengers trapped inside. Alabama state troopers, firing into the air, broke up the mob and drove several beaten and bloodied riders to the hospital.

Trouble continued in Birmingham, where white rioters even attacked John Seigenthaler, Attorney General Robert Kennedy's assistant, who originally had been sent south on something of a goodwill tour. Seigenthaler ran smack up against Governor John Patterson, who boasted that "there's nobody in the whole country that's got the spine to stand up to the goddamned niggers except me." [54] A few days later, while attempting to secure safe passage for a busload of Freedom Riders out of the city, Seigenthaler ended up in the hospital with others who were beaten while police remained a comfortable distance away.

Sanford despised grandstanding like Patterson's. In mid-June, when a secondgroup of Freedom Riders passed through the state, the riders walked past faded "white" and "colored" signs in the Raleigh bus station, which had been integrated. The day they arrived, Sanford was at his usual weekly press conference passing out samples of the year's peach crop to reporters, none of whom asked a single question about the integrated group of travelers who had lunched together two blocks away. A few weeks later, Sanford politely declined Mississippi Governor Ross Barnett's call to Southern governors to meet in Jackson for a strategy session to deal with the spread of demonstrations.

Before Sanford's first year in office came to a close, two events occurred that would shape the balance of his term. The first was the unexpected death in mid-August of Lieutenant Governor Philpott. The second was the defeat of a statewide bond issue that sent a chill through the governor's staff.

The Sanfords were in Manteo, attending a performance of *The Lost Colony*, Paul Green's outdoor drama about the first English settlers on the Outer

Banks, when they received word of Philpott's death. The lieutenant governor had been admitted to a Winston-Salem hospital two days earlier suffering from abdominal pains. Doctors diagnosed an aneurysm of the aorta and his condition became hopeless.

Funeral services were held two days later in Lexington, where Philpott had been mayor immediately following the war. Nearly twelve hundred people turned out for the funeral. Sanford said he would not forget Philpott's "warm, ready smile, the firm handshake, the sympathetic spark in his eye—all spoke a genuine interest that had an appeal. . . . No one could have asked for a dearer or better friend," the governor said, "and no one could have expected more conscientious and able service to the state to be served in so many ways." He recalled Philpott's support of the education program and said, "School children, and indeed all of North Carolina, will be the beneficiaries of his life's service for generations to come." [55]

Philpott's death was more than the loss of a good friend. Sanford had come to see him as a likely successor, who would continue initiatives begun in his own administration. Such talk had upset Sanford's critics, who already were complaining about the growing power of the Sanford political organization and Bert Bennett's smooth efficiency as state party chairman in clearing Sanford loyalists for state jobs and appointments. Indeed, Bennett had brought new discipline to the party organization, which had been allowed to atrophy under Hodges. After the election, Bennett continued to divide his time between Winston-Salem and Raleigh. He spent so much time in his car shuttling between the two cities that he had a Dictaphone machine mounted on the floorboard. An endless stream of brief, tersely worded memos flowed out to his contacts around the state, to the governor's office, and to Washington, where Henry Hall Wilson Jr. was a member of President Kennedy's staff.

Wilson worked under Lawrence O'Brien, the master strategist of Kennedy's campaign. The two had come to know each other in the fall, when Wilson had managed Kennedy's campaign in North Carolina. When O'Brien saw Wilson at the inauguration, he offered him a job as special assistant in the White House. Wilson's primary responsibility was to help move the new president's legislative package through Congress. He also became Sanford's principal contact in Washington for federal appointments and favors.

Bennett was on his way to achieving near perfection in the party discipline, from Washington to the county courthouse. His reach was considerable. At one point, he threw the support of his cadre of young college politicos behind the son of an ally who was running for student body president. On another, he asked Carl McCraw, the head of First Union National Bank, where he was a board member, to check on a teller he heard was telling customers about the virtues of an opposition candidate.[56] Bennett cleared virtually every appointment from the governor's office and most of those coming out of Washington.

Bennett had refined the nucleus of Sanford's winning organization. A coalition of forces had put Sanford in office, but under Bennett the old allegiances were erased to produce one network. Those who objected were frozen out. This rankled old Scott loyalists such as the senator's son, Bob, as well as former close associates such as Wilder and Roney, who felt they were never fully admitted to the Sanford inner circle once Bennett assumed command of the campaign.

Just two weeks before Philpott's death, reporters had pressed Sanford with questions about his political organization. Usually in good humor at press conferences, Sanford responded testily, with an impatience reserved for those who questioned his motives: "I am not interested in politics purely for the sake of politics. I am interested in a strong political organization because this is the way that good government is carried out. There isn't any other way. A good political organization gives stability to a party and thereby stability to government. My interest in politics is that it is an instrument of better government."[57] Sanford's answer was probably too high-minded for most to believe, or to understand. He later explained that what he meant by his response was that he never intended to become a "political boss" pulling strings for the sake of power, or even someone whose livelihood depended on a political job. Politics was merely a means to an end: he had wanted to be governor and he had to become a politician to get elected. Now, his political organization was available to others who might follow and he had hoped Philpott would be his successor. "There was not any question in my mind that we could start a team that would just be unequaled to anything we had ever seen," Sanford later recalled.[58]

The unexpected, and overwhelming, defeat of a $61 million state bond referendum in November also unsettled the new administration. The bonds were to pay for more classrooms and dormitories on state university campuses, new facilities at the state ports, juvenile training schools, prisons, and mental health hospitals. The bond package had not been part of Sanford's program, but he accepted responsibility for it nonetheless.

There had been no signs of serious trouble before the election. Most of the complaints about the sales tax had faded after the levy first showed up on grocery receipts, some of which accompanied letters to Sanford with the taxable amount circled in red. One group of Lake partisans organized a caravan and drove to Hillsville, Virginia, to do their grocery shopping. The town welcomed them with a banner across the main street. One car bore a sticker that read: "Tax and Spend: Don't Blame Me, I Voted for Dr. Lake."

In the days leading up to the November 7 referendum, there had been a scattering of leaflets that Sanford blamed on Republicans seeking to embarrass his administration. Yet, days before the vote, former Republican gubernatorial candidate Robert Gavin urged voters to approve the bonds.

Sanford made appearances at rallies organized by a citizens group supporting their passage. He told voters that though the bonds did not pay for one dollar of his education program, there must be buildings on college campuses if students were to succeed beyond high school. To Sanford, the bonds were part of a broader package. "Education is no TV dinner that you can open up and there it is," he said, "It is more like making biscuits from scratch. You have to put in the ingredients and do the stirring." [59] He urged supporters to vote and, at the last minute, mobilized some of his own campaign organization to boost the turnout.

Bennett and Sanford did not call on their people to rally voters as they had in the spring for the sales tax package, and the result was a searing embarrassment. More than 350,000 voters, one of the largest turnouts for a referendum in years, produced losing margins in ninety of the state's one hundred counties. A few days after the election, as he prepared for a press conference with his staff, there were exchanges of dark humor in the governor's office. The early reading was that voters' pent-up anger over the sales tax, complaints about the state's new airplane, even Sanford's own enthusiasm for new programs and innovations had overwhelmed reasonable arguments in favor of the much-needed improvements in state facilities. At the news conference, Sanford refused to be drawn into a lengthy post mortem. He said simply: "The people have spoken, and that's that."

The year that had begun with excitement and produced spectacular success was ending under a cloud. Some suggested that Sanford and his young staff had moved too far, too fast. "The governor and his administration had seemed to get out of touch with the grassroots," the editor of the *Greensboro Daily News*, Bill Snider, wrote in a Sunday column. "Highly organized and riding a wave of power, they had forgotten that the first rule of successful government requires some attention to the people's sentiments." Snider said Sanford may have redeemed himself in a thirty-minute televised broadcast in which he summarized his first year and put to rest any suggestion that the bond referendum would be placed on another ballot in the near future.[60]

Those expecting contrition from the governor were disappointed. As he would on numerous other occasions, he simply braved the cold wind of rejection and remained unrepentant, even determined to press forward against the odds. "All of us felt that it was a huge rebuke," recalled Cannon. "It was like a chill wind blowing. It was a huge emotional setback for all of us," said Cannon. Now Sanford said "Hell no. That's just a basic reaction to a lot of things." He said, "I'm not going to worry about it. We lost it and maybe if we'd known it was going to be like this we'd have done something different and maybe we wouldn't have. I'm just going to let that go and I'm not going to give it another thought." 61

Sanford refused to retreat on his decision to call for changes in the sales tax. When he delivered a summary of his first year, which was broadcast over a statewide radio network, he said,

> The General Assembly had the vision to vote for a program of school improvement for your children. The General Assembly had the courage to vote the taxes from the only adequate source. . . .
>
> Let me say this to the mothers of children. I share with you a desire to give your child the best opportunities in life. But we cannot improve our schools by just talking about it. You and I are doing something about it, and when we pay 15 cents on a $5.00 basket of groceries, you may do so with confidence that you are broadening the horizons for your child and all children.62

In the meantime, he asked people to consider the twenty-three thousand jobs created in his first year, the farm-to-market roads under construction, improvements in highway safety, increases in farm income, and a hundred other programs under the governor's office. Much had happened to move the state forward and more work was ahead:

> It so happened, that from the opinion I have of the urgent needs, I thought that the recent bond issues should be approved. I knew that failure of the bonds would mean your children and grandchildren, even if qualified, might be denied a college education. I knew failure meant your neighbor's crippled or deaf child might have no place to go for training. I keenly feel these needs, but even so, as I said the night of the election, it is not for me to quarrel with the decision of the majority of the voters.

His mood was serious, but not angry. The speech gave him the opportunity to answer many of the nagging questions from reporters and complaints from the opposition: Did he travel too much? Was his administration too political? Was he a spendthrift? Was he too young, too inexperienced for the job? Was he too liberal?

State government would live on what it had, Sanford said, and he would reshuffle priorities to meet the most urgent needs with the money at hand. Shortly after the first of the year, he announced that David Coltrane would lead an effort to find ways to trim savings from the state budget. Meanwhile, patients in mental hospitals and youngsters in need of help at training schools would be housed, but not treated. College students could take rooms in private homes instead of new dormitories. Privately, however, Sanford was reading results of a Lou Harris poll conducted after the bond referendum that showed his approval rating was in the tank: three out of five North Carolina voters were dissatisfied with his performance. In a curious turn, the popularity of John Kennedy, the man he had risked his own political standing for, was soaring. "His popularity now far exceeds the vote he received here a little over a year ago," Harris reported.[63]

Sanford called his troubles "a temporary setback." It wasn't his nature to complain and he was having far too much fun being governor to be worried about polls. He liked the perks, the attention, and the opportunities that came with the job. In the prior six months alone, he had spent time with the President of the United States, traveled to Hawaii, hobnobbed with movie stars in Hollywood, appeared on Jack Linkletter's popular television show, and led a trade delegation to Mexico. But, more important, he enjoyed the action and the options of a public office where he could take an idea to work with him in the morning and have something happen by noon. Terry Sanford was convinced he had the best job in the world, and with a four-year commission in hand, he was going to make the most of it.

Terry Sanford's father, Cecil Sanford.

Terry Sanford's mother, Betsy Martin Sanford.

Terry Sanford as an infant.

The Sanford family's home on Caledonia Road in 1995.

Young Terry with his sister, Betsy, who died of spinal meningitis when she was nine.

Terry Sanford as a teenager in Laurinburg.

The Laurinburg High School Class of 1934. Sanford is second from right in the back row.
Courtesy of North Carolina Division of Archives and History

UNC President Frank Porter Graham influenced an entire generation of students and opened the world to young men such as Terry Sanford. In this photograph, Graham is teaching a class in government at Boys' State, a program for high school students that Sanford managed for Albert Coates at the Institute of Government. Courtesy of Duke University Archives

While he was a college student, Sanford and a friend operated a boys' camp near Marion, North Carolina, until a flash flood spawned by a hurricane put them out of business. The two campers seated on the steps with Sanford are not identified.

Sanford was in law school when he was elected speaker of the student legislature at UNC. Other campus political leaders included (from left) Terrell Webster of Gastonia; W. J. Smith Jr. of Charlotte, who succeeded Sanford as speaker; Jick Garland of Gastonia; Sanford; Ferebee Taylor and Louis Harris. Later in life, Taylor was chancellor of the Chapel Hill campus, and Harris became one of the nation's best-known political pollsters. Courtesy of Duke University Archives

Sanford (seated third from left in front row) and his law school class at the University of North Carolina Law School before World War II. Courtesy of Duke University Archives

FBI Special Agent Terry Sanford (second from right in front row) with his training class in Washington, D.C., 21 March 1942. Courtesy of Duke University Archives

Terry and Margaret Rose Sanford in Laurinburg before the 517th Parachute Regimental Combat Team shipped out for Italy. Courtesy of Duke University Archives

Paratrooper Terry Sanford first saw combat against German forces in occupied Italy, where this picture was taken. A month later, in August 1944, the 517th Parachute Regimental Combat Team was part of Operation Dragoon in southern France, the largest night parachute drop of the war.

First Lieutenant Terry Sanford (left) and Daywell M. Anderson, a friend from Chapel Hill, standing in the doorway of a C-47 transport at an airbase in Italy in July 1944. Courtesy of the North Carolina Division of Archives and History

After Sanford finished law school, he returned to work with Albert Coates at the Institute of Government. Pictured with Sanford (far right) are (from left to right) Coates, North Carolina Governor Gregg Cherry, State Highway Patrol Commander H. J. "Doggie" Hatcher, and Patrol Captain David T. Lambert. Courtesy of Duke University Archives

Because of Sanford's service as a special agent of the FBI, Institute of Government Director Albert Coates (left) assigned him to assist law enforcement agencies in the state. In March 1947, Coates and Sanford presented FBI Director J. Edgar Hoover (center) with two guidebooks on traffic laws. Courtesy of Duke University Archives In September 1949, Sanford was elected president of the Young Democratic Clubs of North Carolina. The following year he sponsored statewide rallies that attracted national political figures, including Vice President Alben Barkley and Senator Estes Kefauver of Tennessee. Pictured with Sanford and Kefauver (second from right) are Basil Whitener of Gastonia (far left), who was later elected to the U.S. House of Representatives, and two other unidentified YDC members. Courtesy of Duke University Archives

Cover of brochure from Sanford's campaign for the North Carolina Senate in 1952.

TERRY SANFORD

FOR

STATE SENATE

Governor Kerr Scott (left) and his campaign manager, Terry
Sanford, during Scott's successful 1954 bid for the U.S. Senate.
Courtesy of North Carolina Division of Archives and History

Senator Kerr Scott at the Democratic National Convention in
Chicago in 1956. Courtesy of Hugh Morton

Sanford and Mrs. Kerr Scott at the dedication of her husband's
official state portrait.

The Sanfords at home on Sylvan Road in Fayetteville just before Terry began his campaign for governor in 1960. From left, Betsee, Margaret Rose, Terry Jr., and Terry. Courtesy of Duke University Archives

Sanford on the night of the second primary election in June 1960, after defeating I. Beverly Lake for the Democratic gubernatorial nomination. Courtesy of North Carolina Division of Archives and History

Terry Sanford delivered a seconding speech for presidential nominee John F. Kennedy at the Democratic National Convention in 1960. Courtesy of Hugh Morton

(Left to right) Sanford, North Carolina Governor Luther Hodges, and presidential candidate John F. Kennedy at the Democratic National Convention in 1960. Hodges and other leading state Democrats denounced Sanford for his endorsement of Kennedy. Courtesy of Hugh Morton

Sanford easily defeated Republican Robert Gavin and helped carry the state for presidential candidate John F. Kennedy. With Sanford are (left to right) campaign aide Roy Wilder, an unidentified office worker, and Graham Jones, Sanford's press aide. Courtesy of North Carolina Division of Archives and History

Governor-elect Terry Sanford met with President-elect John F. Kennedy on November 29, 1960, and urged Kennedy to choose North Carolina Governor Luther Hodges as his secretary of commerce. Sanford's campaign manager, Bert Bennett of Winston-Salem (center), attended the meeting at Kennedy's Georgetown residence. Courtesy of Duke University Archives

Sanford took his oath as governor on January 5, 1961. Courtesy of Duke University Archives

North Carolina Adjutant General Capus Waynick led the newly inaugurated governor and the official party from Raleigh's Memorial Auditorium to their cars before the start of the parade. Courtesy of Hugh Morton

Governor Terry Sanford with Lieutenant Governor Cloyd Philpott at the 1961 Azalea Festival in Wilmington. Philpott, Sanford's choice as successor, died unexpectedly a few months later. Courtesy of Hugh Morton

Sanford with (left to right) his sister, Mrs. Mary Glenn Rose of Telford, Pennsylvania, and his father and mother. Courtesy of North Carolina Division of Archives and History

Hargove Bowles of Greensboro (left) and Terry Sanford (right) with Paul Thompson (center) of Fayetteville. Bowles served four years in the Sanford administration as head of the Department of Conservation and Development; Thompson, who was Sanford's closest personal friend, was a member of the state Banking Commission. Courtesy of Duke University Archives

Governor Terry Sanford was determined to beat his predecessor's record on industrial development and led industry hunting missions around the globe. This group left Raleigh in February 1962 for Europe. The second man standing to Sanford's right is Charles B. Wade Jr. of R. J. Reynolds Tobacco Company, who was chair of the Duke University Board of Trustees that selected Sanford as president in 1969. Courtesy of North Carolina Division of Archives and History

Sanford borrowed a sailor's hat and slicker and boarded a Coast Guard cutter to watch the arrival of the battleship *North Carolina* off the bar at the mouth of the Cape Fear River. A Coast Guard officer mistook Sanford for one of his crew and ordered him below. Courtesy of Hugh Morton

Governor Terry Sanford built the reputation of his administration on advances in education. He promoted the cause with frequent visits to public schools around the state. Courtesy of Duke University Archives

At least a generation separated the governor and his young staff from most members of the North Carolina Council of State. From left, Labor Commissioner Frank Crane, Insurance Commissioner Edwin S. Lanier, Agriculture Commissioner Jim Graham, Superintendent of Public Schools Charles Carroll, Sanford, Treasurer Edwin Gill, Attorney General Wade Bruton, and State Auditor Henry Bridges. Missing from this photo is Secretary of State Thad Eure. Courtesy of Sanford family

Betsee and Terry Jr. in the governor's office with their father.

In the fall of 1962, as civil rights demonstrations were building to a peak, Terry Sanford announced the creation of the Good Neighbor Council, one of the early biracial groups in the South, and assigned it the task of removing racial barriers in the workplace. Seated to Sanford's right is David S. Coltrane, who led the council through its early years. Courtesy of North Carolina Division of Archives and History

On the evening of May 10, 1963, civil rights marchers in Raleigh crowded onto the lawn of the governor's mansion and refused to leave. Sanford left a white-tie fund-raising reception he was hosting for the North Carolina Symphony to speak to the crowd. At his right is State Highway Patrol Lieutenant Lloyd Burchette, who ignored Sanford's instruction to remain inside. Courtesy of Sanford family

Governor and Mrs. Terry Sanford in colonial costume at the Carolina Charter Tercentenary in Pinehurst, in April 1963. Courtesy of Sanford family

The 1963 General Assembly approved Governor Sanford's plan for the creation of the North Carolina School of the Arts. With Sanford are members of the school's first board of trustees along with Sanford aides Ben Roney (third from left), a wily politician who helped win legislative approval for the school; Hugh Cannon (on Roney's left), the governor's budget officer; and John Ehle (far right), who conceived of many innovative projects. Trustees in this photograph include Sanford, E. N. Richards, Roney, Cannon, Sam Ragan, Mrs. Everette Miller, Dr. Vittorio Giannini, Mrs. Paul L. Muilenberg, Dr. Benjamin Swain, Mrs. Wilbur Jolly, Dr. James Semans, R. Philip Hanes Jr., Mrs. James Boyd, Smith Bagley, and Ehle. Courtesy of North Carolina Division of Archives and History

Sanford enjoyed fishing, hunting, sailing, and cigars.

Franklin D. Roosevelt Jr. (seated second from right) was part of a presidential delegation that visited the state in 1964 to learn more about the North Carolina Fund. Pictured at the mansion are (seated from left) Sanford, H. L. Riddle Jr. of Morganton, Roosevelt, Budget Director Hugh Cannon; (standing from left) Tom I. Davis, and Graham Jones, Sanford's press secretary. Courtesy of North Carolina Division of Archives and History

President Lyndon B. Johnson with Governor Sanford during the president's visit to the home of a tenant farmer near Rocky Mount, North Carolina, in 1964. Seated beside Sanford is Johnson's daughter, Lynda Bird. Courtesy of Sanford family

In August 1964, Terry Sanford was host to the twentieth reunion of the 517th Parachute Regimental Combat Team. The occasion included an opportunity to jump from a Fort Bragg training tower, where Sanford showed his old form, keeping his eyes on the horizon. Courtesy of the North Carolina Division of Archives and History

Dr. Frank Porter Graham and one of his former students, Governor Terry Sanford. Courtesy of Sanford family

Dr. John R. Larkins (second from left) and Governor Terry Sanford with Jordan Kearney (left) and Thomas W. Young (right) of the *Norfolk Journal and Guide*, one of many African American newspapers that praised Sanford's 1963 statement on extending equal job opportunities to all North Carolina citizens. Courtesy of North Carolina Division of Archives and History

In 1964, Governor Sanford campaigned for the reelection of President Lyndon B. Johnson (above, with microphone to mouth), who appeared at a Raleigh rally that fall. Between the two is Sanford's successor, Dan K. Moore. This is one of the few pictures where Sanford is shown wearing glasses, which he kept stuffed in the breast pocket of his suit coat and resisted using in public. Courtesy of North Carolina Division of Archives and History

Mrs. Betsy Sanford and her son. The two corresponded regularly while he was governor. She offered encouragement in tough times and he told her about his travels and the people he met. Courtesy of North Carolina Division of Archives and History

In December 1964, Terry Sanford, his daughter Betsee (shown), the governor's legal counsel Joel Fleishman, and Hugh Morton visited Mrs. Jacqueline Kennedy in New York, where they presented the state's contribution to the John F. Kennedy Memorial Library. Hugh Morton photo courtesy of North Carolina Division of Archives and History

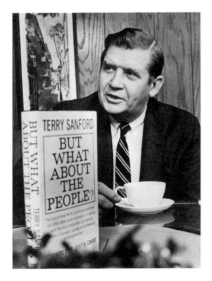

Sanford told the story of many of the accomplishments of his administration in a book he titled *But What About the People?* It was published in 1966. Courtesy of Duke University Archives

Sanford undertook a project in 1965 that led to the creation of the Education Commission of the States. A planning conference for the commission was held in Kansas City, Missouri, where former president Harry S. Truman welcomed Sanford and sixteen other governors and representatives from every state plus American Samoa, Puerto Rico, and the Virgin Islands. Standing at Truman's left is Governor and later U.S. Senator Mark Hatfield of Oregon. Courtesy of Duke University Archives

Governor Terry Sanford with Alabama Governor George Wallace and Massachusetts Governor Chub Peabody. Courtesy of North Carolina Division of Archives and History

Sanford was inaugurated president of Duke University on October 18, 1970, after having taken office on April 2 of that year. Taking part in the ceremony were University Marshal Dr. Jay Phillips (left) and Trustee Chairman Charles B. Wade Jr. AP Wirephoto courtesy of Duke University Archives

Amid antiwar demonstrations in the spring of 1970, Duke President Terry Sanford changed the way administration officials dealt with student demonstrations against the war in Vietnam. He remained accessible and spent time talking with them about their concerns. Courtesy of Sanford family

Charles B. Wade Jr. (right) and J. Alex McMahon (left) chaired the Duke Board of Trustees in successive terms throughout most of Terry Sanford's fifteen years as Duke president. Courtesy of Duke University Archives

The president's office was open to any visitors, particularly students, as long as Sanford was president. Courtesy of Duke University Archives

Sanford chose Law School Dean A. Kenneth Pye (left) as his chancellor and Dr. John O. Blackburn (center) as his provost when he took over the Duke presidency. Courtesy of Duke University Archives

It was Sanford's habit to rise early and exercise before beginning his day. At Duke, he would pull on a jump suit and leave the president's residence on Pinecrest Road for a run. Courtesy of Duke University Archives

As president of Duke, Sanford concentrated his energies on building the graduate schools. With him at the groundbreaking for the Fuqua School of Business were (left to right) Sanford, Atlanta businessman J. B. Fuqua, and Business School Dean Thomas Keller. Courtesy of Duke University Archives

One of Sanford's early speeches as Duke president was to the L. Q. C. Lamar Society, where he called for Southern states to join together in preparation for the future. With Sanford in Atlanta for that meeting were (left to right) Florida Governor Reuben Askew, Georgia Governor Jimmy Carter, and South Carolina Governor John West. Courtesy of Duke University Archives

In 1982, Duke University dedicated the Bryan Student Center, which Sanford called the school's "living room." Standing with Sanford at the dedication was Greensboro businessman Joseph Bryan. Courtesy of Duke University Archives

Margaret Rose Sanford carried a Duke pennant to the Great Wall during the Duke tour of the People's Republic of China in October 1975. Courtesy of Duke University Archives

As Duke President Sanford began his address on commencement day in 1979, he could not understand why his words were met with laughter until someone on the stage pointed out the banner that was being unceremoniously unfurled overhead. Courtesy of Duke University Archives

Dr. and Mrs. James H. Semans first met Sanford when he ran for governor. Sanford named him chair of the first board of trustees for the North Carolina School of the Arts. Mrs. Semans was a member of the search committee that nominated Sanford for the Duke presidency and later succeeded to the chair of the Duke Endowment. Courtesy of the Duke University Archives

Duke University President Terry Sanford and students in the fall of 1985. Courtesy of Duke University Archives

Addressing a press conference in Durham, Sanford announced in January 1976 that he was ending his campaign for the Democratic presidential nomination. Later that year, former Georgia governor Jimmy Carter fulfilled Sanford's ambition to become the first Southerner since Reconstruction to campaign for the Democratic nomination and be elected president. Courtesy of Duke University Archives

A Sanford supporter at the 1972 Democratic National Convention in Miami. Courtesy of Hugh Morton

Sanford (far right) joined the Democratic Party's 1972 presidential candidates after the nomination of Senator George McGovern of South Dakota (fourth from left) and running mate Senator Thomas Eagleton of Missouri (far left). Also at the podium were Senator Hubert Humphrey of Minnesota; Congresswoman Shirley Chisholm of New York; Senator Henry Jackson of Washington and Senator Edmund Muskie of Maine. Courtesy of Hugh Morton

Democratic presidential candidate Sanford arranged a meeting with Soviet Premier Alexis Kosygin during a trip to Moscow in 1975. Sanford was accompanied by Julian Scheer of Washington, who is seated beside Sanford. Courtesy of Duke University Archives

After Sanford left the Duke presidency, the school dedicated the Sanford Institute of Public Policy. Courtesy of Duke University

Sanford won the Democratic Party nomination to the United States Senate in 1986 and campaigned across the state, including this stop in western North Carolina at what he called his "Asheville Jubilee." With Sanford are basketball stars Tommy Amaker (left) and Tommy Burleson (right). Courtesy of Hugh Morton

U.S. Appeals Court Judge Dickson Phillips entered law school in 1945 at the urging of his friend Terry Sanford. On December 10, 1986, he administered the oath to North Carolina's new senator on the steps of the nation's Capitol. Courtesy of Hugh Morton

Senator Terry Sanford greeted Queen Elizabeth II at a reception in London. Courtesy of Sanford family

Sanford's Senate colleagues turned out in Raleigh on February 27, 1988, to help Sanford retire his campaign debt. Included in the lineup for the evening were (from left) Senator William Proxmire of Wisconsin, Senator George Mitchell from Maine, New York governor Mario Cuomo, Senator Ernest F. Hollings of South Carolina, Senator Daniel Inouye of Hawaii and Senator Dale Bumpers of Arkansas. Courtesy of Hugh Morton

Soviet Union President Mikhail Gorbachev with Senator Sanford at a function in
Washington, D.C. Courtesy of Sanford family

Senator Sanford and his Republican challenger Lauch Faircloth met for a debate
in September 1992 shortly before Sanford entered Duke Hospital for emergency
heart surgery. Courtesy of Hugh Morton

In 1994, University of North Carolina Television asked all the living governors to join in an evening of discussion. With Sanford are (from left) Republican Jim Martin, Democrat Jim Hunt, Republican Jim Holshouser, and Democrat Bob Scott.

Sanford aboard his sailboat, the *True Blue*. Courtesy of Sanford family

In 1988, the University of North Carolina presented Sanford with the University Award, its highest commendation, in recognition of Sanford's service to higher education. Courtesy of Hugh Morton

President Bill Clinton spoke at Chapel Hill October 13, 1993, as part of the bicentennial celebration of the University of North Carolina. Before his speech, he visited with (from left) retired UNC President William Friday, Sanford, and CBS journalist Charles Kuralt, a North Carolina native. Courtesy of Sanford family

After Sanford returned to Duke to teach, he met from time to time with historian John Hope Franklin, a professor emeritus at Duke who also was in retirement. One project they discussed was a national commission to deal with racial conflict in the nation. Franklin was later named to head such a commission by President Bill Clinton. Courtesy of Sanford family

Tom Lambeth (left) and Joel Fleishman (right), who worked with Sanford when he was governor, were among more than a hundred friends who turned out in honor of Sanford's eightieth birthday party at the Duke baseball field in September 1997. Courtesy of Hugh Morton

Sanford's last public appearance was in February 1998 at the governor's mansion for a fund-raising luncheon on behalf of the North Carolina Center for the Performing Arts. Sanford was joined by his law partner, former governor Jim Holshouser (left), and Governor Jim Hunt (right). Courtesy of Hugh Morton

Long-time friend and photographer Hugh Morton visited Terry Sanford with William Friday (right) on January 23, 1998, to look through a collection of photos Morton had taken of Sanford over a period of more than thirty years. Courtesy of Hugh Morton

Volunteers from the 82nd Airborne Division provided an honor guard for former paratrooper Sanford. His funeral was held April 22, 1998, at Duke Chapel. Photograph by Chris Hildreth and courtesy of Duke University

CHAPTER TWELVE

A Shore Still Dimly Seen

IN EARLY AUGUST 1961, Terry Sanford was in Los Angeles courting industrial prospects when he appeared on a radio talk show whose host opened the microphone to callers, some of whom were transplanted North Carolinians surprised to hear a familiar accent from home. As the evening passed, the topic inevitably turned to the race issue. One caller, a black woman, told Sanford, "I want to congratulate you for your stand on civil rights and integrating schools. Just keep up the good work. That makes our boys don't mind going over there and fighting side by side with our white brothers."[1]

Sanford politely accepted the caller's compliment, but he knew full well the difference between perception and reality. With modest exception, North Carolina had changed little since this woman had moved west. Only a handful of black children were preparing to enter white schools that fall and, except for a few lunch counters, most public accommodations were still for whites only. People of good will in Charlotte and Winston-Salem had formed biracial committees, but so far their efforts had produced little more than talk. Pickets continued their numbing passage in front of stores, restaurants, and movie theaters that refused to serve all customers. The demonstrations had become almost commonplace in the major cities.

Nearly ten years after the *Brown* decision, blacks in North Carolina remained frustrated by the promise that had not been fulfilled. No sooner had Sanford arrived home from Los Angeles than the United States Civil Rights Advisory Committee released a report on the state's pitiful progress in providing equal education. Among other things, the report said that of the 111 one-, two-, and three-teacher schools in the state, 79 had only non-white pupils. "There is a definite racial pattern in Negroes being assigned to these dinky schools," said Chairman McNeill Smith, a Greensboro lawyer and contemporary of Sanford's at Chapel Hill.[2]

Segregation remained the way of life in North Carolina and throughout the South. About the only change was a rising tension among whites whose fears rose from the new boldness within the black community, which heretofore had been held in check by custom, by tradition, and by law. Sanford was a product of this world. He had been raised in a small town where the divisions between races were clear and inviolate. He recalled that the white citizens of Laurinburg had treated their black neighbors in New Town with kindness and charity, but equality was never a consideration. It was just the way things were.

Yet the life ignored and unseen by most whites was one of opportunities and justice denied. As soon as young black children were old enough to consider a future, they boarded a train headed north, looking for a better life. They called it the "Chickenbone Special," a tribute to the fried chicken their mothers, aunts, or grandmothers prepared and packed in sack lunches for them as they left the South in search of jobs and opportunities in the North.

Blacks did not know if Terry Sanford would be any different from the average white officeholder. But he had honestly come by his reputation as the leading moderate—some even said liberal—governor in the South. After all, he had conducted the first successful one-on-one campaign against a segregationist and had demonstrated his own personal allegiance to integrated schools. All this was enhanced by his youthful appearance, easy manner, progressive outlook, and the distance that he was putting between himself and the racist politics making news elsewhere in the South.

Sanford had set the tone for his administration at his inauguration, when he asked North Carolinians to look to the future, not cling to the past. Near the close of his speech, he had declared, "We are not going to forget, as we move into the challenging years ahead, that no group of our citizens can be denied the right to participate in the opportunities of first-class citizenship."

Sanford had taken as much care with this simple statement as he had any of the words he spoke that day. He wanted people to know that his New Day for North Carolina was not only for education, but for human rights as well. Some, like Jonathan Daniels, had urged him to be even bolder, but Sanford believed a simple reaffirmation of the American creed served well enough. He was eager to plant the flag, as it were, but he was not prepared to sacrifice his administration for the sake of one issue.[3]

Sanford arrived in office with no agenda for civil rights and no plan for guiding North Carolina through what later would be called "the second American Revolution." All he had was a determination to do the "decent thing" within the limits of his authority. "I knew that when we reached the point where we could say that our policy was one of absolute fair treatment, that we would make those moves that proved that," Sanford later recalled.[4] In that sense, he was no different from any of the nation's other leaders. No one knew where the growing civil rights movement was taking America. Elected officials, from John Kennedy in the White House to beleaguered mayors in Southern cities, simply were reacting to demands from African Americans whose leaders had no common strategy, who disagreed among themselves, and who vied for public attention and support. While the older, established NAACP favored working within the system, James Farmer's CORE, the Congress of Racial Equality, pursued aggressive direct action such as the Freedom Rides. Dr. Martin Luther King Jr.'s Southern Christian Leadership Conference chose its battles carefully and struggled to remain viable from its base in Atlanta. Across the South, some older blacks remained uneasy with the students whose lunch-counter demonstrations and picket lines had inspired so many to civil disobedience.

Sanford's links to the black leadership in North Carolina were tenuous, some might even say nonexistent. Although race had been a pivotal factor in his election, it had been a contest among whites over white issues. There had been no blacks in his campaign organization, and contact with black voters was limited mostly to haulers hired on election day to take voters to the polls. His television ads depicted only white faces and voices, and Sanford had been warned to avoid situations where photographers could catch him shaking hands with a black person. After he became governor, the only blacks near at hand were the janitors at the capitol and the felons on the household staff at the mansion. The closest "advisor" who could offer a black point of view was Dr. John R. Larkins, a sociologist who was a consultant in the state education department. Yet Larkins himself worked in an office in segregated quarters blocks away from the whites in the Education Building on Capitol Square.

What would set Sanford apart from his predecessors and many of those occupying positions of responsibility elsewhere in the South was an understanding that equal rights was an issue whose time had come, and that it was his duty as governor to deal with it. "History had turned," he would say later. He was determined to try a new way. The young governor believed the way to meet the revolution was through communication and understanding rather than the obstructionist maneuvering and futile gestures of many Southern politicians.[5] These included North Carolina's senior senator, Sam Ervin Jr., whose mastery of the law and the Constitution helped segregationists drape their opposition in a cloak of legal respectability.

"I could have reacted to all of this by defensive measures," Sanford later wrote, "by adding to the insults, by giving them a wide berth and staying away from the strife by suggesting that these were only radicals, outside agitators (and some of them were), and making veiled suggestions that somehow the Communists were behind all of this mean business of stirring up our good Negro citizens. The emotional reaction to this kind of approach is tried and true."[6] Instead, he attempted to interpret the lofty precepts of justice and fair play and understand what a segregated life meant to a parent like himself, or children like his own Betsee and Terry. "Most of us have never experienced [discrimination] personally, so it requires sizable imagination to sense the feeling of oppression the American Negro feels," he wrote in an unpublished memoir.

> How can we understand the feeling of the Negro father who, on an automobile trip, never knew where he could buy a decent meal, or never was sure what service station would allow his little girl to use the rest room? How could we understand the feeling of a Negro mother who had to find words to explain to her little boy why he couldn't sit up front and watch the bus driver? How could we be expected to understand the feeling of futility of the Negro high school student who had observed the valedictorian of five years earlier now working on the city garbage truck? How could we understand that there would be resentment in the hearts of every Negro as he passed in front of public places where, even if he didn't have the remotest desire to enter, he couldn't, solely because of his color?[7]

Fortunately for Sanford, the movement spared North Carolina during his first months in office, when he had his hands full maneuvering his education package through the General Assembly. Demonstrations commemorating the first anniversary of the sit-ins were mounted in Greensboro but quickly fell into a routine. Most of the attention of the movement remained focused elsewhere, largely in the Deep South.

For a time, it seemed that the race issue had retreated from the public agenda in North Carolina. When the state's Baptists gathered for their annual meeting in 1961, they were more likely to be aroused over drinking and dancing on the church-supported campuses. Some quiet change took place as Duke University and Wake Forest University admitted their first African American graduate students and the Baptists desegregated undergraduate education at tiny Mars Hill College, where the first African American student was the granddaughter of a former slave who had once been held as security for a loan by the school.

Most whites were locked in position, awaiting the next demand. Even those sympathetic to the cause of civil rights proceeded with caution and discretion. When McNeill Smith of the Advisory Commission on Civil Rights hired a black secretary to work on commission matters, he bowed to pressure from the other women employed at his downtown Greensboro law firm who objected to the woman's using the same toilet. Rather than force the issue, he opened a separate office in another building.[8]

Sanford's initial steps were taken quietly, without fanfare and within the comfortable boundaries of old-style politics. In the summer of 1961, as he began extending rewards to political supporters by way of appointments, he added the names of prominent blacks to his list. By the end of the year, more than a dozen men of color were members of boards and commissions that had never had a black member before. With the appointments, Sanford hoped to demonstrate to the black leadership in the state that he was different from governors they had known before. He also hoped to open lines of communication to men like John Wheeler of Durham, who ran Mechanics and Farmers Bank and was one of the most influential leaders within Durham's considerable black community.

Midway through the summer of 1961, Sanford and Hargrove Bowles, his director of Conservation and Development, began talking about something far more significant than appointments. Despite Bowles's current wealth and servants, he had grown up poor and was a product of the Frank Graham school of social conscience at Chapel Hill. More recently, Bowles was upset by a "whites only" sign he had encountered at a diner outside of Greensboro where he and his black driver had stopped for coffee. "He would come in here furious about this fellow that had that sign up," Sanford later recalled.[9]

Tom Ellis, the new state parks superintendent, had been on the job only a few days when he received a summons from Bowles, whose department was responsible for the operation of the parks. Bowles asked Ellis to join him for a meeting with Sanford. Though Ellis had been with the department since before the war, he had never set foot in the governor's office, and when he arrived at the capitol he was anxious and full of questions. His anxiety turned to amazement as he listened to Sanford and Bowles talk about fully integrating all park facilities.

North Carolina's parks were not segregated by state law, but by custom and regulation. Black citizens could drive through Mount Mitchell State Park, for example, and hike the trail to the top, but park rangers would discourage them from using the picnic areas with whites. At the same time, Hammocks Beach State Park was considered to be a blacks-only beach park. Only a few years had passed since the state had purchased a high peak in Ashe County and changed the name as it appeared on U.S. Geologic Survey maps from Nigger Mountain to Mount Jefferson. The change was made not out of sensitivity but because some state officials feared whites would consider it a park for blacks and not use it.[10]

Ellis's first meeting at the governor's office was followed by another and another as Sanford and Bowles let him talk through the problems that he anticipated if blacks were allowed to use the whites-only overnight cabins, picnic areas, bath houses, restaurants, and the swimming pool at Morrow Mountain State Park. In addition to public reaction, Ellis was concerned about attitudes of members of his staff, some of whom he knew would resent the change. By the time the talking was done, however, Ellis said, "They had me thoroughly and totally convinced" it was the right thing to do.[11]

The three decided changes would be made and they would begin near the close of the 1961 summer season. They would begin with the integration of the swimming pool at Morrow Mountain, where blacks who had been turned away were threatening a lawsuit, and Ellis chose the last Sunday in August for the first day of integrated admissions.

He was on hand when the pool opened that Sunday. White and black swimmers entered the pool, and though both groups were uncomfortable and wary of the new arrangement, the day ended without incident. Ellis was surprised later that evening, when he got a call at home and heard Sanford say, "Tom, I hear you had a problem at Morrow Mountain and had to close the pool." Ellis explained that all swimmers were asked to leave the water when a thunderstorm threatened their safety, but after the clouds passed, most of the swimmers returned to the pool.[12]

In the spring of 1962, before the state parks opened for their periods of heavy usage, Bowles drafted a new state policy that he circulated to Sanford before passing it to Ellis for his department. "It is now the policy that no colored person shall be denied the use of any facility in any state park nor shall any employee by words or action make the impression that their use is not permitted," the statement said.[13]

The desegregation of the parks passed without incident or comment, which was remarkable for the time. America's reputation abroad was under attack after diplomats from African nations had been refused service at restaurants in the Greater Washington, D.C., area. Soviet propagandists were making the most of the nation's dual society, particularly on the African continent, where Russians were bidding for attention from emerging nations. Soviet Premier Nikita Khrushchev called for the removal of the United Nations Headquarters from New York City after a black diplomat was embarrassed there.

In September 1961, while Sanford and Bowles were negotiating the park desegregation, the governor dispatched Morganton lawyer H. L. "Chick" Riddle Jr. to a conference with the State Department's chief of protocol, Angier Biddle Duke, who met with representatives from thirty states (most Deep South states ignored the meeting) to discuss ways to ensure that traveling diplomats would be treated with dignity. President Kennedy was looking for something more than Virginia Governor Lindsay Almond's suggestion that foreigners wear identification so that they would receive "decent treatment."

Riddle was a man of wit and liberal orientation and one of the earliest Kennedy supporters in the state. The president had rewarded him for his help by naming him grand marshal of the inaugural parade, and the affable Southerner made the most of the connection. He frequently called at the White House and often charmed his way into Kennedy's office. Once, Riddle was seen late in the day with his feet propped on a desk enjoying a Cuban cigar with the nation's chief executive.[14]

Riddle's new assignment was a test of his cleverness. National restaurant and motel chains with establishments on the major highways in North Carolina refused service to black travelers no matter whether they were diplomats or ditch diggers. In North Carolina, foreign dignitaries had not even been welcome at the governor's mansion until the Sanfords moved in. In December 1959, Governor Luther Hodges had hosted a dinner for an African diplomat at the Morehead Planetarium in Chapel Hill rather than violate tradition. Riddle found Hodges's example useful, however. When a Liberian vice president was visiting Asheville, Riddle arranged for a private picnic at the Biltmore mansion rather than confront the problem of finding service at segregated restaurants in town. "This was done to prevent any possible incidents," Riddle wrote Sanford, "but was so successful that it was one of the highlights of the visit." [15]

With no coherent plan and public opinion clearly against change, Sanford found himself dealing with each situation as it arose. In the fall of 1961, for example, Jim Crow laws threatened cancellation of President Kennedy's visit to Chapel Hill, where he was to receive an honorary degree. Just a few days before the president's plane was to land in Raleigh, Sanford received a phone call from John Wheeler in Durham. Did he know, Wheeler asked the governor, that segregated rest rooms remained in the terminal building at the airport? Sanford assured Wheeler that Kennedy would never see the inside of the terminal, but he got the message. He turned the matter over to Hugh Cannon, who already had heard from John Seigenthaler in the Justice Department. While Wheeler was writing the governor, students from North Carolina College in Durham had wired the White House demanding that the president cancel his trip rather than use segregated facilities.

Seigenthaler told Cannon the trip would be cancelled unless he could be assured that the "white" and "colored" signs painted on the outer entrance to the rest rooms would be gone by the time Kennedy arrived. In something of a panic, Cannon telephoned the terminal management, which operated under an independent authority. Initially, he was told Kennedy could stay home if he didn't like Southern customs. State law required the signs, Cannon learned, although the authority no longer enforced use of the separate entrances to what was now a common toilet.[16] In fact, the question was largely moot; new regulations from the Interstate Commerce Commission prohibiting segregation in travel and terminals were due to go into effect within days.

Cannon quickly negotiated an arrangement that allowed the terminal management to save face and at the same time give him enough to inform Seigenthaler that the matter had been resolved. Rather than remove the signs, the terminal manager simply took out the doors. They were later reinstalled after some attempts to remove the racial designations, but a shadowy stain of "white" and "colored" remained faintly visible until they were replaced years later.

Although Sanford steered clear of public involvement in the confrontations that threatened the peace during his first year, he was drawn in on two occasions. The first incident occurred in mid-June and was over quickly. Trouble threatened the town of Trinity after a brawl erupted between whites and blacks that sent a white restaurant owner to the hospital. The night before the fight, a black youth had been attacked after he had appeared at the man's restaurant and asked for service. Sanford ordered a dozen State Highway Patrol cars into Trinity until order was restored and tempers cooled.

The situation in Monroe, a farming community east of Charlotte near the South Carolina border, was not so easily resolved. Throughout the summer, African Americans had persisted in their demands to use the city-owned swimming pool that was reserved for whites. Leading the demonstrations was Robert F. Williams, the president of Monroe's NAACP chapter, whose confrontational style was attracting national attention.

Williams called himself a revolutionary, and he shocked some and infuriated others after he raised a Cuban flag at his home. It remained there until a black paratrooper who was home on leave tore it down. Williams made no secret of his admiration of Cuba's new leader, the recently declared communist Fidel Castro. Williams's full beard, his dark blue beret, and the large pistol he wore strapped to his side completed a picture that was a nightmare to NAACP leaders already suffering under white suspicion that the civil rights movement was the work of communists. Williams vowed to meet "force with force" and had organized some of his neighbors into a paramilitary guard, complete with a charter from the National Rifle Association, where they bought ammunition at discount prices. The state NAACP stripped Williams of office, but members of the local chapter promptly reelected him president and his wife secretary.

Williams capitalized on a long-simmering dispute over the swimming pool. In 1957, blacks in Monroe had demanded admittance to the pool or, as an alternative, the construction of a separate facility of their own. Their protest evaporated following threats and intimidation by Ku Klux Klansmen, who rode armed through the streets. At the onset of the town's summer pool season in 1961, Williams rekindled the issue and led pickets at the pool after the city council refused again to admit African Americans, even on a limited basis two days a week.

Tensions increased after Williams claimed he was threatened and harassed by whites, and he appealed for help from a New York group called the Emergency Civil Liberty Committee, which sent a troop of young whites and blacks—called Freedom Riders by local authorities—to join the picket lines in Monroe. Williams demanded protection from the governor's office and also wired the U.S. attorney general claiming blacks could not expect justice in Union County. Kennedy's office pressed Sanford for details as pickets circled the courthouse with their signs.

Sanford received regular reports on all such disturbances directly from the State Highway Patrol, with whom he felt a close association dating to the Patrol School in Chapel Hill. Patrol Commander Colonel David T. Lambert had been one of his first instructors, as had other officers in Lambert's command. During the Freedom Rides, the patrol had reported regularly on the movement of the buses and kept an eye on suspected white troublemakers. On one occasion, a trooper found that a carload of so-called white hate riders, whom he had been following at a discrete distance, had stopped on a dead-end road near the state line. When they asked for directions, he sent them on into South Carolina.[17]

As the trouble in Monroe threatened to escalate, Sanford asked Dr. John Larkins to go to Monroe and file a report. Larkins met with his own contacts in Monroe and Charlotte, where leading blacks, including state NAACP leader Kelly Alexander, were as angry with Williams as anyone. They accused him of grandstanding and frustrating their own quieter efforts. Larkins also talked to Williams, whose guerrilla attitude and appearance was a shock to the prim and well-dressed academician. In his report, Larkins described Williams as "hoping to be attacked so that they could have a war and destroy the town."[18] Cannon, who had taken numerous phone calls from Williams, reported to Seigenthaler at one point, "I cannot help being pessimistic that sooner or later we will have serious trouble with Williams."[19]

Cannon didn't have to wait long. In late August, several demonstrators drawn to the protests by civil rights groups, including the Southern Christian Leadership Conference, were in the Union County Jail in Monroe. They were awaiting trial on charges filed after a middle-aged white couple returning home on a Sunday evening was snatched from their car, threatened with their lives, and then held in Williams's house. While they sat bound in a chair, they said Williams made a call to the sheriff's office to set up an exchange for the jailed protesters.

The couple was released unharmed within a few hours, but the abduction brought swift reaction from authorities, who issued arrest warrants for Williams and others on charges of kidnapping. A raid on Williams's home produced weapons and a box buried under a dog house that contained fifty-eight sticks of dynamite. Williams disappeared (he later showed up in Cuba and then China, where he remained for several years) and civil rights groups that had given Williams support were embarrassed. Eager to extricate their people as quickly as possible, they accepted suspended sentences and orders to obey the law. The town returned to segregated normalcy.

The troubles in Monroe gave Sanford his first opportunity to define the policy that would later mark his administration as different from others in the South. At a news conference he said, "I will say this about North Carolina, as a state, and its position. We have always attempted to be fair to everybody and to give everybody the degree of liberty guaranteed by the Constitution. The courts have been open to everybody, law protection to everybody. At the same time, we have followed another policy and I certainly intend to continue. We are not going to put up with violence in any form for any purpose. The sooner we make that clear to these people who come here from the outside as well as people who might already be here, I think the better it will be." [20]

He would modify his approach as the tensions in the state increased, but the statement put the civil rights leaders on notice as to what to expect in North Carolina. The governor would remain alert and ready to respond with police when needed, but he believed deeply in the constitutional rights provided citizens to redress grievances, including marching and picketing. To use law officers to break up legal demonstrations was simply wrong. The State Highway Patrol had not been sent into Trinity or Monroe to bust heads and pack protesters off to jail. Rather, the show of force was used only to protect demonstrators and innocent bystanders who might be injured in the sweep of events. "We were trying to take the attitude that it wasn't up to us to break up demonstrations," Sanford said years later. "But it was up to us to keep the order and let them demonstrate, which was constitutional. It was unthinkable to put them in jail for that." [21]

The governor's words of moderation gave blacks in North Carolina encouragement, but words alone would not suffice. Midway through his term, some of those whom Sanford had invited to the mansion for coffee or meals began to ask for more than Southern hospitality. They wanted action.

James Farmer and CORE set out to test the Sanford policy in the summer of 1962 with the continuation of the Freedom Ride campaign to open public accommodations. At the height of the summer travel season, Farmer announced that major motel and restaurant chains, such as Howard Johnson's and Holiday Inn, with facilities located along the routes from the northeast to Florida, would soon see pickets outside their doors if they refused service to African Americans. CORE's plans brought swift reaction from the Howard Johnson's chain, which negotiated a desegregation settlement for its Florida locations, and Farmer shifted his attention to North Carolina, where some local owners and managers had refused to budge.[22] CORE chose North Carolina because Farmer believed the state's reputation for moderation would produce a successful morale-building effort without risk to the lives and safety of demonstrators. On the other hand, Farmer later wrote, a North Carolina campaign would require a different approach from that used against segregationists elsewhere in the South whose violent reaction was guaranteed to provoke a national response.[23]

Ironically, the CORE campaign found its early success in a section of the state most notorious for its racist attitudes. The first Howard Johnson's locations that conceded to CORE demands were those along U.S. 301, which ran from the Virginia to the South Carolina state lines, right through the heart of eastern North Carolina. Three of these restaurants were owned by Tom Pearsall, the man credited with the school desegregation plan that had brought peace but little integration by 1961.

Sanford had talked often with Pearsall, consulting him first in May 1961, a few days before the first buses carrying the Freedom Riders entered the state. Pearsall counseled the governor to make a tough "law-and-order" statement and to be prepared to use the Highway Patrol to "meet mob violence." At the same time, however, he urged the governor to "approach the matter quietly, informally and without public notice. It is entirely possible," he wrote, "that we will have no incidents and we certainly should not stir up trouble and excite the public."[24]

Pearsall and his wife, Elizabeth, were wrestling with their own personal decisions. While attending a biracial meeting one night, Mrs. Pearsall was confronted by a black businessman who asked how she and her husband could defend whites-only seating at their restaurants. She told the man that she wanted to serve everyone, but that waitresses in the restaurants had told her they would quit because their husbands refused to allow them to wait on blacks. Shortly after this meeting, she later said, she was in one of the restaurants when a busload of soldiers en route to Fort Bragg stopped for a meal. The whites sat at tables inside while the blacks ate boxed meals outside. "The hostess is an older woman," she said. "She was trying privately to indoctrinate these waitresses and their husbands. But one of the waitresses was there where I was and I said, 'How did that make you feel? They're going off to risk their lives for us and yet they can't come in?' And this woman, the waitress, said, 'It makes me feel pretty bad.' "[25] The Pearsall's restaurants began serving all customers shortly afterward, joining one in Greensboro whose owner also changed his policy.

Other establishments in Durham, Raleigh, and Statesville remained steadfast in their refusal to break with tradition, and they became the target of demonstrations. In Raleigh, marchers were met with fire hoses. In Durham, after four persons were arrested and remained in jail rather than pay a $25 fine, a thousand marchers converged on the restaurant to protest. Statesville authorities produced the most embarrassing incident for Sanford; when Farmer and a group of six hundred marchers reached the county jail where protesters were held under arrest, they were met by a thick fog of insecticide laid down by police.

The demonstrations worried Sanford, who feared escalating countermeasures by local authorities, such as the use of the fogging machine in Statesville. He kept his distance, however, and relied on the Patrol reports that kept him posted on the mounting number of arrests. He also began reaching out to an increasing number of blacks, including Raleigh businessman John Winters, a newly elected member of the Raleigh City Council. A beefy man with a workman's build and bushy eyebrows that gave him a brooding appearance, Winters was called to Sanford's office by Hugh Cannon, who appeared at his real estate office one day and said the governor needed his help. Winters had never met the governor, though he had worked in his campaign and would never forget the night of the general election, when he and another black man had attended the Sanford victory party at the Sir Walter Hotel. No black person had ever been invited in to a white politician's celebration, and when Wheeler told his friends that Al Adams, Sanford's Wake County chairman, had insisted he come, they just stared in disbelief.[26]

Winters brought a perspective different from either the proper banker John Wheeler or the academic John Larkins. He had worked as a waiter at the Sir Walter, a porter at Raleigh's airport and train station, and driven a milk route for a Raleigh dairy before he started a home building business that was beginning to make him a wealthy man. Winters and Sanford were close in age and he easily spoke his mind as the pickets marched in the summer of 1962. One day as Cannon complained loudly about "outside agitators," Winters told him, "You don't understand. We're the outsiders. We've been outsiders and we're trying to get in." [27]

Another telling episode stuck in Winters's mind. He was in the governor's office when Sanford took a call from Robert Kennedy. The attorney general wanted Sanford to arrange hotel accommodations for a small group of African visitors headed to Raleigh. The governor said he would oblige and immediately put in a call to the manager of the Carolina Hotel, who booked the rooms. "When he finished," Winters recalled, "Hugh and I were standing there and I said, 'Governor, if you make arrangements for John Winters to go to that hotel and be accommodated like that then you wouldn't have to worry about these Africans.' " [28]

The CORE campaign had extended into the hot summer days of August before Sanford intervened directly. He believed the group's highway campaign would ultimately be successful because the national chains could not withstand the assault on their reputation for long. It was only a matter of time. Meanwhile, the risk of real trouble, violence and even bloodshed, loomed. He sent word to Farmer that he'd like him to come to the mansion to talk.

Farmer had been to the White House, including a private session with President Kennedy that he recalled as cold and insulting. But he had never been inside a governor's mansion nor had he met a Southern politician like Sanford, whom he described as "a fine and liberal gentleman, and highly competent." [29]

Accompanying Farmer at the meeting was Floyd McKissick, the Durham lawyer who had been the first black man admitted to the law school at Chapel Hill. McKissick's lawsuits had opened the university to black undergraduates and desegregated the Durham schools. He was an important figure in the Durham community, where he moved easily between CORE and the NAACP, merging the work of the two organizations. A year later, he would succeed Farmer as CORE's national chairman.

Sanford had asked for the meeting to take the measure of the man who seemed bent on disrupting life in his state. "The fact that he and I were never likely to agree on any approach is no argument for refusing to see him," he later wrote. "I told him I would not tell him to stop but that I thought he was doing more harm than good." [30] Sanford offered to negotiate a settlement if CORE would agree to a moratorium on demonstrations. Farmer and McKissick excused themselves from the mansion library to the hallway, where they talked briefly; when they returned they said they would halt demonstrations after one final large march that they would conduct with the proper permits in Durham. The march was concluded peacefully and featured a speech from Roy Wilkins, the NAACP's executive secretary, who had given his support to the CORE demonstrations over the objections of state NAACP leaders. A month later, however, after a group established by Sanford remained far from a resolution, the pickets returned in Statesville.

The race issue was a delicate balancing act. Although Sanford wished to move the issue forward, he remained obliged to a white constituency that he could not ignore. Early in 1962, he had taken up the cause of a contingent of white reservists from the state who had been assigned to a formerly all-black Army unit during the military buildup in reaction to the tension in Berlin. Sanford wrote his friends in the White House to see if the men could be reassigned. Presidential aide Larry O'Brien forwarded Sanford's letter to the Department of Defense, which responded that there was no valid military reason to make a change. "I am sorry that this matter cannot be handled to the entire liking of Governor Sanford," Air Force Brigadier General C. R. Roderick wrote O'Brien, "but I am quite sure that you will appreciate the many ramifications and the possible explosive situation if we go any further." [31] Sanford let the matter drop.

In the fall of 1962, the focus of the civil rights movement shifted to Mississippi, where James Meredith, a black veteran, was scheduled to enroll at the state university in Oxford. Governor Ross Barnett had vowed to resist integration and had delayed the opening of the fall term as he negotiated with the White House, which was intent on enforcing court orders admitting Meredith to the school. Barnett was still in Jackson as the other Southern governors gathered in Hollywood, Florida, for their annual meeting and President Kennedy ordered federal marshals and armed troops onto the University of Mississippi campus.

Sanford's reputation had preceded him to Florida. Only a few weeks earlier, *Look* magazine had featured him in a flattering article that said, in part, "Most politicians do what people supposedly want. North Carolina's 44-year-old governor often does the opposite." The story included a quote from Robert Kennedy, who said of Sanford, "He's going places." [32] The *Christian Science Monitor*, a national newspaper with a broad following, also had singled out Sanford, focusing on his education program and quoting from his Columbia, South Carolina, speech. In Florida, reporters were describing him as the leader of the "moderate forces" in the South. Sanford dodged the opportunity to lay claim to the title. He enjoyed media attention and saved enough news clippings during his term to fill ten large scrapbooks. But he was wary of reporters' attempts to pit him against Barnett and his Southern colleagues. By the time he left Florida, he had turned down three opportunities to appear on network television news programs.

He didn't shy from expressing his support for the president, who went on nationwide television to explain why he was ordering federal marshals onto the campus in Oxford. The morning after the broadcast, Sanford told a reporter, "I have never been prouder of our President." [33]

That opinion was not shared by other governors, at least not in print. Before the meeting concluded, the governors elected as their chairman Arkansas Governor Orval Faubus, who had been the first governor to defy court-ordered integration. During the four years he was part of the conference, Sanford would never be asked to join the inner circle, although he was twice elected chairman of the Southern Regional Education Board, a coordinating council dealing with higher education. "I knew the tunes," Sanford would joke later, "but that didn't mean I had to sing in the choir." [34]

Sanford's statement of support for Kennedy was not warmly received at home either. A political acquaintance in Monroe wrote, "It is much to my amazement how I could have supported you when you became governor of our state. Please stop running for higher office, maybe the Senate, and start being the governor." Another letter writer, the Democratic Party chairman in Montgomery County, wrote, "If we had more governors like Barnett and Faubus, we would win." [35] The Reverend James Dees of Statesville, leader of a small but noisy group of segregationists who called themselves North Carolina Defenders of States' Rights, sent Sanford a copy of a telegram he wired Barnett that read, "May God bless you in your stand for the basic principles of our republican form of government, for freedom and for your stand in defense of the American people against certain monsters in high places in these times of crisis." Dees demanded to know if Sanford was "using [the governor's] office to try to induce the owners of Howard Johnson's restaurants to submit to the integration demands of these CORE agitators, trespassers and disturbers of the peace?" When Sanford didn't respond immediately, Dees sent a second telegram. "You did not answer my question about your urging Howard Johnson to integrate." [36]

Dees got his answer. "I'm not using my office to do anything except to urge people to act as Jesus Christ taught us to act in dealing with one another," Sanford wrote the preacher.[37]

Sanford had entered office believing that persuasion, not force, and reliance on a basic sense of decency, not law, would lead to change. Like Frank Graham, he held a deep-seated faith in the basic goodness of people and often spoke of the progressive heritage of North Carolina. And like Graham, he was disappointed at the depth of feelings that he encountered. He would never forget that after the Campbell boy enrolled in the Murphy School, the PTA disbanded rather than hold a meeting that his parents might attend. It also stuck in his craw that state prison employees had suggested to Prison Director George Randall that a new black employee, a former professional football player named John Baker, shouldn't eat in the snack bar with whites. Randall dispensed with such foolishness by dining with Baker himself. (Baker was later elected sheriff of Wake County.)

After Sanford had appointed a black man to a state medical board, a Hickory physician wrote him objecting because the man would "have supervisory capacity over employees other than his own race. I do not believe that we in North Carolina have indicated that this is what we desire." The governor responded unapologetically to the doctor: "I cannot really believe it is necessary to defend the appointments of any fair-minded citizen of this state. It is inconceivable to me that many people would deny that representatives of more than a quarter of the citizens of this state should have a voice in the decisions of boards and commissions." [38]

Sanford found reactions to even his modest efforts disturbing as well as surprising. "It is hard for somebody who had lived here," Sanford recalled later, "to come to the realization that folks thought what they thought about the differences in the races." [39]

In the fall of 1962, with so many racial issues unresolved and positions hardening by the day, Sanford worried about the growing clouds of discontent. He believed something new was needed. He had talked with some community and business leaders who were willing to take some bold steps, but they were fearful of moving on their own. At the same time, Sanford believed that issuing sweeping orders from the governor's office would be counterproductive.

Ever since his early days in office Sanford had visited schools whenever he could and had set a goal of visiting classrooms in every county of the state by the time he left office. Teachers willingly turned their students over to him and Sanford enjoyed his time with young people. He often spoke of the virtue of working hard in school and the necessity for a good education. When he had the time — and he usually made the time — he would stop to chat with individual students about their hopes and dreams, bending close to give an eight-year-old his undivided attention. "I told the students across the state, white and Negro, that this is not the age for the common laborer; you must have a skill and you must work here and now to get it. Education is your future. That was my theme and it is eternally true." [40]

At the black schools he visited he was met by eager, excited young people, virtually none of whom had ever seen a governor in their community. He was not prepared for his own reaction, however. The night after he had been in one classroom he was so troubled by his conscience that he couldn't eat dinner. "Always," Sanford noted later,

I had the sickening feeling that every time I talked to them I was saying words that were a mockery, that I was talking about opportunities that I knew, and I feared they knew, didn't exist, no matter how hard they might work in school. All of my words had a shallow sound, at least to me.

I knew it could not come true for the Negro unless we could open up enough jobs so he could see success for himself. That kind of hope and expectation of success is another way of describing motivation. That is the kind of motivation which takes students to their books and classes."[41]

Sanford mentioned his concern to one of his staff members, novelist John Ehle, who would provide the inspiration for a variety of innovative projects. Untroubled by the complications of politics, Ehle responded with a blunt assessment that cut right to the heart of the issue. He told his boss that he could either change his speech or he could change the state. Sanford chose the latter and decided that jobs would be the fulcrum.

Equal employment had been on the agenda of the black leadership for months. Shortly after Sanford took office, John Wheeler had supplied him with a working list for his administration in a lengthy letter written on behalf of the Durham Committee on Negro Affairs. Wheeler presented an inventory of grievances, ranging from a statutory exclusion of blacks from membership in the National Guard to discriminatory hiring practices in state government that included classified advertisements stating racial preference.

In the fall of 1961, blacks had pressed their case with the governor after a series of stories in the *News & Observer* reported that fewer than a dozen black workers—out of seven thousand state employees in the buildings around Capitol Square—held jobs above the rank of janitor or messenger. After the news articles appeared, Sanford was visited by a delegation led by Kelly Alexander, who demanded changes in state employment. A month later, the governor came in for sharp criticism from Ralph Campbell, the president of the Raleigh NAACP chapter and the father of Betsee and Terry's classmate, in a speech to the association's annual meeting. "Several meetings have been held with Governor Sanford on equal job opportunities," he said. "The governor says he has to move slowly on this. Maybe he's moving too slowly. We're not asking them to give us anything. All we ask is to be hired on an equal basis."[42]

Almost a full year had passed since Campbell's criticism when, in October 1962, Sanford stepped out of his limousine into the evening air at Bracket's Cedar Park near Polkton, one of the rural precincts of Rutherford County west of Gastonia, where he was scheduled to speak to a group of Methodist lay leaders. "It is most appropriate," Sanford began, "that I announce some important plans at a meeting of church laymen because our most difficult problems of race differences must be worked out in the spirit of Christian fellowship." He then outlined a plan for a state-sponsored group to be called the North Carolina Good Neighbor Council, whose mission would be to open the way to better jobs for African Americans. The details would take some time to work out, he said, but "in these days in America, we need to show living proof that people of different backgrounds and races can work together. If we are true to our religious heritage in North Carolina and if we believe the lesson of the parable of the Good Samaritan, we should help those in need of help. It is as simple as that. But it is powerful in its capacity to achieve broader opportunities for everyone, the helped and the helpers alike." [43]

Biracial committees were not new. One of the earliest models from the post-*Brown* era was from Tampa attorney Cody Fowler, who chaired a commission appointed by Florida governor Leroy Collins to make recommendations on race relations. Sanford's minister in Fayetteville, Henry Ruark, had sent him a copy of the Fowler commission's report shortly after he took office. More recently, Sanford had seen similar models at work in Texas, where the state had created local groups to deal with discrimination aimed at traveling foreigners that had created such embarrassment for the United States in Latin America.

Sanford was testing the water with the Methodist laymen. He wasn't sure just how his own initiative would be received, but figured that no one could fault him for talking about human relations at a religious meeting. "But I knew that before I left office that I had to make a firmer determination of where we were headed," he later recalled. [44] The speech got surprisingly limited press coverage. The *News & Observer* used an Associated Press version of the story filed by the *Shelby Daily Star* but devoted more space to an article in which Sanford offered fatherly advice in the wake of a weekend of drunken partying that marred the annual state Debutante Ball. He suggested in a letter to the sponsors that in coming years the debutantes' escorts, most of them college men, be asked to take a pledge of sobriety for the weekend.

Sanford said nothing further about his proposed council in the ensuing weeks. When a reporter asked about his plans at a news conference in early November, he said he wasn't ready to announce anything.

The fall of 1962 was not the time for dramatic gestures, particularly on such a touchy subject as race. The state's Democrats were being hammered in the midterm elections by Republicans who had launched one of their most aggressive efforts in years. The party had mounted particularly strong campaigns against legislators who had helped Sanford move his tax bill through the 1961 General Assembly. Sanford campaigned for Democrats as if he were a candidate himself. While the Republicans talked about the food tax, Sanford developed a basic speech that he could deliver with uncommon conviction. David Cooper of the News & Observer reported that Sanford's "basic theme is this: North Carolina has enjoyed amazing progress under 60 years of Democratic administrations, and now stands at the forefront of the South ready to 'move into the forefront of the nation.' "[45]

In mid-October, Sanford joined Vice President Lyndon Johnson for a campaign tour through the lower Piedmont, where Congressman Charles Jonas, a Republican incumbent, had been forced into a pitched battle with incumbent Democrat A. Paul Kitchin as a result of the 1961 congressional redistricting. Sanford and Johnson also appeared on behalf of incumbent Democrat Hugh Alexander, who was facing a stiff challenge from an attractive young Republican named Jim Broyhill of Lenoir, who was the heir to the Broyhill furniture fortune.

In November, North Carolina Republicans enjoyed a victory such as they had not seen since 1928. Twenty-three Republicans were elected to the state house, more than doubling the number in the previous session. Broyhill edged out Alexander with just a little more than a thousand votes to spare and Jonas defeated Kitchin. In fact, Jonas had survived so many Democratic challengers since he had gone to Congress in 1953 that Republicans were touting him as the man who could capture the governor's office for them in 1964.

As was his habit, Sanford tried to put the best face he could on yet another difficult and embarrassing setback for himself and the Democrats. He claimed that only one legislator challenged directly on the sales tax issue was defeated, and that there were too many competing local interests to attribute all the success of the Republicans to discontent over the sales tax. But he failed to convince the Democratic slate in Guilford County that the tax issue didn't cost them votes. The party's entire legislative ticket was defeated, ending gubernatorial ambitions of former state House Speaker Joe Hunt Jr., who was running for the state senate. Hunt was bitter in the aftermath, and openly blamed Sanford for his loss. "It was a protest vote against his administration," Hunt declared.[46]

Sanford absorbed the criticism and tried to find some light in the Democratic gloom by pointing to the election of a Democrat in Mitchell County, a Republican stronghold in the mountains. He said a two-party system was healthy for the state and "part of the price for joining the mainstream of America." He also heard from Representative Jack Potts of Brevard, who turned around a sales tax campaign. "I told voters that I had never apologized for my vote," Potts wrote the governor, "since it was cast on the behalf of the school children of our state. It is my firm conviction that this ad turned enough voters to elect me." [47]

Whatever Sanford said, the returns had to be discouraging and highly visible confirmation of the low rating he had in the polls a year earlier. Yet he didn't complain publicly. In the face of difficulty, he remained confident that he would overcome the political drag that his initiatives had created for his administration. In a speech delivered in late November, he exhibited a renewed boldness, almost a defiance in the face of defeat, that had been missing since the glorious summer in 1961 before the unsettling months of racial unrest and growing discontent over "his" taxes. Sanford had risked considerable political capital for his education program. Now he was considering a move on civil rights that could prove just as costly.

When Sanford stood before the Commission on Secondary Schools of the Southern Association of Colleges and Schools meeting in Dallas, he was mindful of difficult days a century earlier, when the nation's chief executive, Abraham Lincoln, had wrestled with what was politic and what was right. The dual issues of race and education were now one, and promised to blend further in the coming months and years:

> We need our own and a new kind of Emancipation Proclamation, which will set us free to grow and build, set us free from the drag of poor people, poor schools, from hate and demagoguery. It has to be a bold dream for the future, realistic in terms of our country, and aware that the South is entering the mainstream of American life. This kind of proclamation can be written in one word, "Education."
>
> The South, and the rest of the nation for that matter, needs to take a long, hard look at itself to see where it stands now and to see where it hopes to stand twenty years from now. [48]

The speech was a prelude to what some would later consider one of Sanford's finest moments as governor. As he worked on ending the siege of street demonstrations and resolving the growing frustrations of both whites and blacks, he had been seeking a shore that remained dimly seen, in the words of the hero of his early years, Georgia's Ellis Arnall. His ideas had already found their way to his legal pad when he called Ehle to the governor's mansion. Ehle found the governor in the library, his favorite spot. A fire was crackling in the fireplace and Sanford handed Ehle a statement he had written in longhand on the yellow page.

"It was entitled 'Observations for a second century,' " Ehle recalled in his book, The Free Men, "and in it he discussed his views concerning racial intolerance. He said that this document was to be the topic of a breakfast meeting the next morning; we were to decide at breakfast whether the statement was a good one and if it ought to be released at all. I remember thinking that this would be the first time in history that a Southerner while governor of a state had taken a stand openly, avowedly, in favor of Negro rights."[49]

Terry Sanford was not going to rewrite his speech to North Carolina's schoolchildren.

CHAPTER THIRTEEN

But What About the People?

IN TERRY SANFORD'S OWN ACCOUNT of his four years as governor, a book he titled *But What About The People?*, he devoted fewer than two of the 165 pages to his January 1963 statement on racial equity that attracted international attention. This modest reference was not an attempt to minimize the importance of what he had to say as the South headed toward its most difficult, and dangerous, period of protests and demonstrations. Rather, it was a reflection of Sanford's conviction that no matter how large the issue loomed at the moment, racial discrimination was but one of the impediments to improving the quality of life in North Carolina.

The declaration he offered as he entered the second half of his term was a prelude to one of the most creative and productive episodes in state government. Under his leadership, North Carolina spawned an array of new programs in education, the arts, and improving the human condition. A 1990 Harvard University study would rank Sanford as one of the nation's ten best governors in the twentieth century. When Parris Glendening was elected governor of Maryland thirty years later, he opened his administration saying he planned to use Sanford as a model.[1]

Sanford had a way of confounding his critics, a game he seemed to enjoy. Those who believed that he would coast through his last two years in office, using the time to repair an image battered by voter discontent over the sales tax and bruised by the election returns in 1962, were disappointed. He had invested one-fourth of his life in reaching the governor's office, and he didn't plan to spend the remainder of his term as a caretaker.

Despite his problems, Sanford could think of no place he would rather be than in the governor's office, "where more good can be done than any other political office in the country," he told an interviewer in 1962. If the price for what he considered a successful term was political oblivion, then so be it, he said. "A governor is not worth his salt unless he is willing to go to the boneyard. If he is the kind of governor who is willing to face the problems, regardless of the consequences, then he will do his state some good."[2]

Sanford's third year in office was only a few days old when he set out to prove that was so, as he welcomed a select group of twenty-five men and women to one of his sumptuous working breakfasts. Country ham, biscuits, eggs, grits, honey, stewed apples, and trimmings filled the long table in the mansion dining room. Among those attending were his close aides and the people who made the wheels of his administration turn, as well as a handful of prominent black business and professional men from across the state. After the meal, Sanford read a statement on civil rights that he had been preparing for several weeks. When he finished reading the two hundred or so words, he asked for comment.

One of the first to speak was John Wheeler, the Durham banker on whom Sanford had come to call on for advice and counsel and who had never been shy about expressing his unhappiness with the governor's progress. When he spoke this morning, he told the governor his statement did not go far enough. What the state needed was a new Emancipation Proclamation, he said. State laws, not good words, were the weapons against discrimination.

Discussion quickly ensued and John Ehle later wrote, "I realized somewhere during it that John Wheeler, by attacking the statement for being too moderate, had got the group past the point of debating whether a statement ought to be released, and on to the question of whether the statement went far enough." And that, said Ehle, was probably what Sanford had in mind when he allowed Wheeler's reaction to dominate the discussion.[3]

Over the next few days, Sanford solicited reactions from others. Response was heavy, and generally favorable. Considering the wide range of Sanford's contacts, not all agreed. One associate was in the governor's office after receiving his copy. "The governor, smiling disarmingly, asked him if he had read the statement," Ehle wrote. " 'Yes,' the man said grumpily. He sat down and shook his head sadly. Then noticing that the governor was still smiling, he blurted out, 'My God, you're not going to release it, are you?' "[4]

He not only released it but chose the most public forum he could find. On the afternoon of January 18 in the ballroom of the Carolina Inn in Chapel Hill, he opened his remarks to two hundred reporters and editors gathered for the annual meeting of the North Carolina Press Association by saying, "I wanted to take this occasion, talking to people who have so much to do with the attitudes of the citizens of the state, to say something to you that I have long wanted to say, that I believe we must say and that I believe will mean much to the development of the life and character of our state." Then, he began.

The American Negro was freed from slavery one hundred years ago. In this century he has made much progress, educating his children, building churches, entering into the community and civic life of the nation.

After Sanford finished his opening sentence, a few became alert that the governor's speech was more than routine. As he recalled the moment in his book, *The Free Men*, Ehle "saw one of the deans of the university look up, startled; the Negro waiters stopped in place at the back of the room." [5] Sanford continued.

Now is the time in this hundredth year not merely to look back to freedom, but forward to the fulfillment of its meaning. Despite this great progress, the Negro's opportunity to obtain a good job has not been achieved in most places across the nation. Reluctance to accept the Negro in employment is the greatest single block to his continued progress and to the full use of the human potential of the nation and its states.

The time has come for American citizens to give up this reluctance, to quit unfair discrimination, and to give the Negro a full chance to earn a decent living for his family and to contribute to higher standards for himself and all men.

Slowly, the significance of the governor's words awoke even those who had slipped into a postluncheon stupor. Applause interrupted the governor, and he continued.

We cannot rely on law alone in this matter because much depends upon its administration and upon each individual's sense of fair play. North Carolina and its people have come to the point of recognizing the urgent need for opening new economic opportunities for Negro citizens. We also recognize that in doing so we shall be adding new economic growth for everybody.

We can do this. We should do this. We will do it because we are concerned with the problems and the welfare of our neighbors. We will do it because our economy cannot afford to have so many people fully and partially unproductive. We will do it because it is honest and fair for us to give all men and women their best chance in life. [6]

Finally, after two years, Sanford had defined the "decent thing." He then announced he was that day appointing twenty-four persons to the Good Neighbor Council he had proposed months earlier to work toward the elimination of discriminatory hiring practices. To show good faith on his part, he was asking the heads of all state agencies to immediately write nondiscrimination hiring policies for their departments.

"The talk lasted less than five minutes. The governor folded his papers and sat down," Ehle wrote. "There was a smattering of applause; then, as the editors began to respond to the importance of the occasion, they stood and gave the governor what can only be termed an ovation. They applauded what might prove to be one of the greatest political errors, yet one of the finest achievements, of Terry Sanford's life."[7]

In the aftermath, Sanford heard from all manner of people. Filmed news reports to the networks caught the attention of Attorney General Robert Kennedy, who called Sanford's office to say that when he heard someone with a Southern drawl talking about "good nay-bahs," he knew right away who was speaking.

The national press, particularly the African American press, was astonished, which was a comment on current feeling toward the South as well as on Sanford's remarks. He drew attention from *Jet* magazine, and the headline in the *Los Angeles Eagle* read "N.C. Governor (That's Right!) Urges Equality." An editorial in the *Los Angeles Times* said, "When Governor Sanford says in all honesty that he does not believe southerners are doing a good enough job in education, and in freeing themselves, 'from the bondage which has held them down,' it seems to me that his warning and his appeal applies to all of us. 'Hate and demagoguery' are not a special possession of the South. I am sure that the place to look first for reform is in the mirror."[8] A *Louisville Courier-Journal* editorial said, "North Carolina's Governor Terry Sanford has laid his political future on the line before by refusing to mouth accepted Southern dogma on segregation. But in his talk to the North Carolina Press Association, he hit directly at a by-product of segregation that is at once one of the South's most cherished institutions and greatest economic handicaps — cheap Negro labor."[9]

The governor received letters from North Carolina servicemen and their families posted overseas who told of the pride that swelled for their home state. America's reputation had been tarnished abroad by the growing conflict over human rights, they said. Sanford by word and deed had helped offset criticism they heard from people in the lands where they served.

At home, the *Greensboro Daily News* called his statement "a dollars-and-cents appeal, [which,] coupled with the prodding of Tarheelia's deeply ingrained fairness and honesty, augurs well for the program behind which the governor has thrown his leadership." Catholic Bishop Vincent S. Waters of Raleigh was pleased. "Congratulations. Spoken like a man, a governor and a Christian." Dr. Lewis Dowdy, acting president of A&T, wrote, "I could never explain to you what immeasurable motivation this statement has provided for our students." One of those seniors, Student Body President Ezell Blair Jr., who along with three others had launched the sit-ins three years earlier, also wrote to the governor: "You can count on our support concerning future endeavors of this nature to make our state a better place for its citizens to live, learn and lead. May God's blessing be upon you." [10]

Amid the hefty files of letters preserved in the state archives is a sheaf of papers mailed to the governor by Isaac A. Battle, the principal of the Amanda S. Cherry Elementary School in Harrellsville in Bertie County, a rural crossroads deep in the state's northeast corner. Battle had seen countless numbers of his students leave home on graduation day, boarding trains and buses to escape the dual diseases of grinding poverty and discrimination. Another generation of his students, perhaps one that could remain at home, had heard the governor's speech, and they wrote to tell him about new dreams. "I am glad to know that you feel that Negroes have as much right to vote, work, have nice jobs and speak in any other manner as well as whites," wrote Gene Earl Vinson in a clear but inexperienced hand. And young David Douglas wrote the governor, saying, "After we heard your speech we organized a better citizens club so we can qualify for any type of jobs." Jacqueline Harrell wrote, "To know that you are the only governor in the South to make such a speech to give the Negroes the opportunity as the whites is heart warming." [11]

But among the congratulatory letters and telegrams and positive news clippings there remained the angry voice of those resistant to the changes that threatened their traditional way of life. A few days after Sanford's speech, about four hundred persons attended a meeting of the North Carolina Defenders of States Rights in Caswell County, where black students had just begun attending school with whites. The public relations director of a Virginia group that sponsored private all-white schools offered advice on implementing the Pearsall Plan, and Bernard Dixon, a Caswell County farmer, denounced Sanford as a "carpetbagger." "He is against white people. It is reflected in his statements and the newspaper headlines he makes," Dixon said. "But Sanford is doing at least one good job and that is bootlicking the Kennedy brothers, and I use the word only because it is a polite term." [12] Before the meeting adjourned, the crowd endorsed a resolution dedicating their support to I. Beverly Lake should he run for governor in 1964.

By the end of the month, segregationists across the South were responding to a new voice of demagoguery. As Sanford sought consensus with words of hope and moderation, Alabama's Governor George Wallace delivered his declaration of "segregation forever" in an inaugural address that was as well received in many corners of North Carolina as it was in Alabama. The Caswell County crowd too had listened. "Brothers, [the U.S. Supreme Court] kicked the trap from under the gallows," Dixon declared. "Unless we take a firm stand and use the word 'never,' and that's what they're using in Alabama and Mississippi, we're not going to like this thing." [13]

Wallace's election quickened the pulse of Southern segregationists, whose leadership had been thinned by the election in 1962 of racial moderates in Georgia and South Carolina. From that point until the mid-1970s, when he closed his last presidential campaign, Wallace capitalized on the anxiety of angry whites in a movement that reshaped the politics of the region and ultimately the nation.

Sanford was not deaf to the rallying cry of states' rights that was raised in defense of the old ways and new politics. Of far graver concern, Sanford believed, was the failure of the states to meet the responsibilities to its citizens for decent schools, health care, prisons, good jobs, and paved roads. "If we will meet these responsibilities," he wrote at the time, "we will keep government closer to the people. Unless there is some reason for crossing state lines, dealing with broad economic measures that the states can not do alone, then the states can meet these problems." [14] This optimistic outlook came from the man considered to occupy the weakest governor's office in the land, at a time when many openly questioned the viability of or even the need for state governance at all. Sanford had no veto power to check the legislature, was limited to one term, and was already half through that. Yet, with his usual optimism, Sanford saw these limitations as the reason to move quickly and do everything he could before the last grain of sand ran out on his administration.

Sanford had finally found the person to put in charge of "good works," as he called it, in John Ehle, whom he would later credit with ensuring that innovation would be the trademark of his administration. Ehle, a quiet man of average build and height with sympathetic eyes and a creative mind, was an unlikely addition to any governor's staff. He was a writer, a novelist, and had only a passing interest in partisan politics. He had so little familiarity with Sanford that he misspelled the governor's name in a journal entry he made after their first meeting. Ehle's primary venue was the communications center at Chapel Hill, where he taught playwriting, produced award-winning radio dramas, and was preparing to write his fourth novel, one he would call *The Land Breakers*. In January 1962, he got a call from Joel Fleishman in the governor's office, who asked if he would meet Sanford one night at the mansion. Fleishman told Ehle that Sanford was intrigued by some ideas included in a newspaper article that Ehle had written entitled "What's the Matter with Chapel Hill?" It was a critical lament of the decline in the creative arts at the state's premier campus where, Ehle said, the university was permitting its cultural heritage to wither and die. Among the projects suggested in the article was a state film board that would produce feature-length motion pictures about subjects related to the state.

At their first meeting in the family quarters on the mansion's second floor, Ehle and Sanford covered a range of topics. Ehle liked the governor and was taken with his family. While they talked, Terry Jr. practiced rides down the banister of the mansion's grand staircase, an adventure Ehle considered dangerous given its very long sweep. Sanford touched on Ehle's idea for a state film board, but the two parted with nothing settled. Two weeks later, Ehle was invited back to the mansion for dinner.[15]

He found himself among a party of ten that after the meal adjourned to the library, where Sanford asked each person to suggest projects for the remainder of his term. This night Ehle felt he was of no help at all, and what he heard didn't appear to inspire the governor. One guest wanted the governor to spend his time promoting pig farming so North Carolina could unseat Denmark as the source of fine hams. Highway safety was a big item, but Ehle discounted what a governor could really do about that and actually held a higher opinion of the ham proposal. Sanford surprised Ehle when, as the evening drew to a close, the governor pulled him aside and asked that he come to work for him.

Ehle said he wasn't interested. He had heard some of the suggestions, and pigs and car wrecks weren't on his agenda. Moreover, he told Sanford he had accepted an advance from a publisher and arranged a leave from the university so he could move to New York and concentrate on his new book. Nonetheless, he was invited back for another dinner a few weeks later, when Sanford pressed him further. Ehle again declined, but this time he paid for his meal with a suggestion. He offered that the huge Biltmore mansion on the edge of Asheville, a mammoth survivor of the excess of the Gilded Age, would be the perfect location for a summer conference center for the arts. He also offered that the mansion and grounds would make a perfect location for a summer residence program for gifted junior and senior high students interested in the arts. The governor was so taken with the ideas that he asked Ehle to accompany him that weekend, when the two would put the idea to Biltmore's owner, George C. V. Cecil.[16]

The Biltmore plan died aborning. Cecil found more objections than Sanford had arguments. Along the way, however, Sanford convinced Ehle to rearrange his schedule and join his staff. "He said, 'Take the summer and write the book and come back in the fall.' He convinced me that there was a big opportunity and he was dead serious about the thing," Ehle later recalled.[17]

Before he left for the summer, Ehle prepared proposals for two projects.

One was the film board, which he modeled after the National Film Board of Canada, and a second was for a new kind of high school where competing disciplines such as science, the humanities, and the arts would cultivate talents often overlooked in a traditional setting. Ehle proposed to call it the Governor's School and suggested it be located at the Research Triangle.

Sanford dispatched both proposals to the Smith Richardson Foundation, where his old friend Capus Waynick held sway. The foundation headquarters was in New York, but the money flowed from the heirs to Vick Chemical fortune, whose most popular product, Vick's VapoRub, had been created around the turn of the century by a Greensboro pharmacist. At the time, the foundation devoted much of its resources to promoting grassroots programs on Americanism, but Waynick offered encouragement.

On July 31 Sanford announced a grant of $125,000 from the foundation to underwrite the film board, whose initial productions were to include some administration boilerplate, such as a promotional film for use in industrial recruitment and a feature on food processing. Ehle also salted the list with more poignant topics such as the plight of mountain folk that would illustrate a recently published Ford Foundation study that found poverty, ignorance, disease, and desperation throughout the mist-shrouded coves and hills. The Richardson Foundation was not interested in the Governor's School, which came as a disappointment to Sanford. Undeterred, he told Ehle to take the idea to the Carnegie Corporation in New York, where he met with Carnegie staff member Margaret Mahoney and unveiled his "hope-list" of programs.

The slower pace of a college campus had done little to condition Ehle for the urgency of Sanford's mission, something he would demonstrate time and again. Ehle's proposals had not even reached Carnegie when the governor announced the creation of a committee to study the prospects of a state music conservatory. The announcement came one day after Sanford paid a visit to a summer music camp at Brevard, where he had frolicked with students in a cold mountain stream and tried out a sousaphone. But he had not acted totally on impulse.[18] Brevard's Transylvania Music Camp had been created thirty years earlier by Dr. James Christian Pfohl to train young musicians. Sanford's visit was a day of appreciation for the governor, who a year earlier had arranged for Pfohl's summer symphony to play in the White House Rose Garden at a performance attended by President Kennedy. That night in Washington, at a dinner with the students, Sanford learned that if these talented young persons expected to pursue a career in music they would have to seek training elsewhere. There was no place in the South for them to go. The notion of a conservatory, a Juilliard for the South as it were, had been rolling about in his mind ever since.

On his return to North Carolina that fall, Ehle moved into the lieutenant governor's office, unused since Cloyd Philpott's death; these new quarters on the second floor of the capitol became an idea factory. He worked on the rim of the governor's official party, detached from the day-to-day distractions of petitioners and appointments. Initially, his pay came from a grant that Sanford arranged from the Mary Reynolds Babcock Foundation, so his salary wasn't even in the budget. He concentrated on proposals for the Governor's School and became Sanford's primary contact with the North Carolina Conservatory Committee, which was in place by the time he arrived back in Raleigh. At the same time, he helped the state's new film board take its first steps.

Ehle quickly caught on to Sanford's urgency. Some months later, after James Beveridge, a Canadian recruited as director of the film board, asked Ehle where he was supposed to get money to produce the first films, Ehle took him by the arm and, finding a crack in Sanford's schedule, slid in the back door of the governor's office to show him the kind of outfit he had signed on with. "Terry asked a couple of questions," Ehle recalled, "and said, 'I will have the money for you this afternoon.' He called the departments and said, 'We want to do a film on this and this and this.' He used their budgets. We had no money [for production]. We just had money for administrative purposes. Jim Beveridge was damn well impressed." [19]

Ehle continued to press for interviews at the nation's largest foundations. He had learned from Mahoney that Ford might be interested in programs regarding the arts, government, and education, and Carnegie might take on the Governor's School. Ehle lined up interviews at both foundations and Sanford flew in for a round of meetings all in one day.

The ambitious young Southern governor was regarded with some curiosity. He was the first governor to call on Carnegie, Ehle recalled, and "They didn't know what to do. They didn't know whether he was going to arrive with guards or if there would be an entourage of any sort or the protocol. Should they notify the police department or what?" Ehle assured them that nothing of the sort was necessary; Sanford traveled light, without a New York police escort. [20]

Sanford moved easily in the stiff and regimented atmosphere of the New York foundation world. He was as adept at charming foundation executives who jealously guarded their prerogatives as he was at convincing a rural legislator dangling his vote in trade for a few miles of asphalt. Almost instinctively he understood the desire of foundation executives to use their money creatively, and he was more than willing to find ways to satisfy them.

At Ford, Sanford's approach was totally disarming. In his initial meeting he told Ford President Henry Heald that he had not come to ask for money. Rather, he said, he was seeking ideas about what a Southern governor could do to improve conditions for people in his state. Most particularly, Sanford related his concern that even with the best educational system, many youngsters were doomed before they began. He related the stories of youngsters who were part of a generation lost to society because they were caught in a "cycle of poverty." [21]

"The disadvantages were varied and many," Sanford later wrote,

> but all of the disadvantages led to one common difficulty. These children came into a school system not organized to treat them. They came and found school a strange world they had never known. They had no idea of how in the world you might get something useful from a piece of paper with little marks on it. And they had no idea why you should want to get anything good from such a marked-up piece of paper.
>
> Later we were to find whole neighborhoods of children who had never even heard a nursery rhyme. They didn't know Cinderella and had never sung about the mulberry bush. They came to school without the advantage of knowing how to shape their names, without the advantage of being able to count even a few numbers. They came without knowing their ABCs, and as often as not, without knowing there were any ABCs.
>
> They might be Negro, white, or Indian, living on the farmland of the coastal plains, or the mountains or in the crowded housing areas of the Piedmont, the children of decent people, or irresponsible people, or criminal people. They were everywhere and anywhere. They were caught in a cycle of poverty, condemned to remain in poverty, and destined to raise their children in poverty.[22]

Ford had been experimenting with a new initiative called the "gray areas program." It had started in Oakland, California, with $1.6 million of Ford money; it was the foundation's first foray into direct action and was aimed at mobilizing residents of inner-city neighborhoods to deal with the compounding problems of urban decay. The nation's cities were losing the battle as the suburbs drained tax-paying citizens, leaving behind the poor and the unemployed, who lived in substandard housing, sent their children to inadequate schools, and suffered the worst of urban life. No one had a name for it yet, but the gray areas program was one of the first skirmishes in what later would be known as the War on Poverty.

Paul Ylvisaker, who created the gray areas program, was present for Sanford's first visit with Heald. He had already come to realize from the early work in Oakland that urban problems would be solved only with the involvement of state government. "The states had . . . the frozen potential,"

Ylvisaker said sometime later. "When Terry came along to the foundation one day, boy, what a breath of fresh air he was," Ylvisaker recalled. He was impressed with Sanford's approach, the breadth of his understanding of social ills, and his appreciation of the real and political difficulties in dealing with them. "I'll never forget when he came that first time. When Heald and I took him to the elevator, when he pushed the button and let them descend, Heald turned to me and said, 'Have you still got your wallet?' That was a time when we were really happy to be took, because here was a governor who had used up his equity in a one-term situation with the legislature who knew he couldn't get blacks into decision-making in a short run and here's where philanthropy really is of use." [23]

By the end of the year, the letters and foundation proposals that flowed from Ehle's typewriter had begun to produce results. In addition to the Governor's School and the film board, he had prepared requests for grants to pay for remedial programs for entering freshmen at black colleges as well as a special summer program for black youth. There was a proposal for a study of eastern North Carolina, where the average wage of a black worker in Greene County, the poorest in the state, was about $200 a year, just a little more than $4 a week. Likewise, Ehle was interested in creating an institute that would study the special social and economic problems of the North Carolina mountains, where poverty, disease, and unemployment were endemic. Ehle also was organizing a series of visits to North Carolina of some of the nation's leading thinkers, who would sit and talk with state leaders about the future. "We do not expect you to make a talk or to prepare a paper," Ehle wrote one invitee, "but we want your advice in as informal and natural a way as you care to present it." [24] During the coming year, six leaders in education and the arts, as well as dreamers such as Buckminster Fuller and scientists such as Dr. William O. Baker, the head of research at Bell Labs, came to call.

Before his session at the mansion, Dr. Edward Higbee, an expert in the relationship between technology and the environment, climbed in a state plane one night and flew with Hugh Cannon at a height sufficient to show how lights shining from North Carolina cities and towns below were evidence of a growing megalopolis. Later, at the mansion, he told a group of Sanford's invited guests that if the state did not act soon to preserve green space, then the strip from Raleigh to Charlotte would soon be paved over. By the end of his term, Sanford would create the Crescent 2000 Commission to prepare for orderly growth in the Piedmont.

In January, four days after Sanford announced the creation of the Good Neighbor Council, he also announced that a summer program for academically gifted and artistically talented high school students would commence in June with four hundred rising juniors and seniors from across the state.

The first session of the new Governor's School would meet for eight weeks on the Salem College campus in Winston-Salem, where local foundations and business leaders had raised half of the $450,000 needed to cover the first three years; the Carnegie Corporation had agreed to underwrite the other half.

Newspapers also carried accounts of a recently completed visit by a delegation from the Ford Foundation that had spent four days talking with educators, city and county leaders, newspaper editors, and state officials about urban and rural poverty, remedial education, health care needs, and local and state resources that could be marshaled to improve the quality of life in North Carolina. Included in the itinerary was a visit in the mountains, a layover at East Carolina Teachers College, and finally meetings in Raleigh and Chapel Hill. The visit concluded with a dinner at the mansion. Just before the group headed back to New York, Clarence Faust, a Ford vice president, assured the governor that Ford was eager to see a proposal for a major grant to North Carolina.

These early victories demonstrated a touch of genius in Sanford's approach to his "good works" agenda. By working outside the state budget he could bypass the General Assembly, where support for such notions, particularly in the arts, generally had not been well received. During the 1961 session, for example, a bill to create a state ballet company as a complement to the state-sponsored symphony had been hooted down. Moving unilaterally, Sanford could avoid embarrassing confrontations and, at the same time, save his political chips for those projects that might require legislative approval. Plus, he could move at his pace, not that of a legislative committee. His use of nonstate funds for what some would consider harebrained schemes and frills also helped offset Sanford's growing reputation as a spendthrift, due, at least in part, to his activist approach but largely the result of constant carping by Republicans and conservatives in his own party who harbored a different philosophy about government.

As the 1963 General Assembly gathered for the start of the session, Sanford's connections with the state's conservative members were tenuous. Many in the body considered him a liberal; more ascribed to State Treasurer Edwin Gill's understanding of government than Sanford's. Nonetheless, Sanford greeted the members with confidence and a level of comfort he had not known two years earlier, when his staff was new and unseasoned and when he was wrestling with the decision to ask for new taxes to pay for the education program. Now an expanding state economy was generating tax revenues sufficient to cover continuation of the education program begun in 1961 as well as pay for some of the new facilities whose construction had been delayed after voters had rejected the proposed bond issue in 1961.

Sanford's required address to the 1963 General Assembly covered fifty-four typed pages. He distributed copies in advance of his appearance on February 7, and Graham Jones, his press secretary, announced that the governor would not read every word. Instead, he said the governor planned to "just talk" about the progress of state government during the past two years.

Sanford droned on for nearly an hour. He offered an agenda that was ambitious but one designed to go down a little easier than what he had proposed two years earlier. Included were changes in utility regulation to provide for better consumer representation, a boost in the state minimum wage from seventy-five cents to a dollar an hour, minimum protection for migrant laborers, improvements in highway safety to remove drunk drivers and faulty vehicles from the road, and, what he would consider the keystone for the session, changes in the state's system of higher education, including the creation of a statewide community college system. He warned as he previewed his program,

> You will hear some whisperings abroad saying that we have done enough, have moved well and far and rapidly, and so it is time now to slow down, rest, and catch our breath.
>
> These whispers come from the fearful and those who have always opposed the accomplishments from which they now would rest. This cannot be and is not the spirit of North Carolina.
>
> Much remains to be done, to provide better educational opportunities for the competition our children will surely face, to encourage broader economic development so everybody will have a better chance to make a better living. Now is the time to move forward. Now is no time to loaf along.[25]

In the budget message he delivered two days later he softened up the opposition by proposing an increase in the personal income tax exemption from $300 to $500 as well as removal of the sales tax on over-the-counter medicines and newspapers sold by carrier boys. The governor hoped that this would forestall attempts by Republicans and sales tax opponents to repeal the changes adopted two years earlier.

Legislators were a bit glassy-eyed as they took in the start of the new session. Sanford's program was not that overwhelming, but none had ever seen anything to equal the new Legislative Building, finished just weeks before the opening day at a cost of $6.2 million. Designed by Edward Durell Stone, the building offered legislators a generous measure of space and comfort. For the first time, each member had his own office and telephone and committees had assigned meeting rooms. The design included plenty of polished brass, deep red carpets, marble, and columns, but the five high-peaked skylights and courtyards in each corner suggested a building for the performing arts rather than politics.

The building had been erected under the watchful eye of state Senator Thomas J. White of Kinston, whose command and defense of the legislative prerogatives were beyond question. The new building offered legislative comfort and public accommodations impossible in the cramped space of the old building, but gone was the coziness that had existed previously between legislators and the governor.

Perhaps the fascination with the new building and its amplified sound system and new furniture distracted the members, or maybe a world changing beyond belief upset the pace of the session. Whatever the reason, the record of the 1963 General Assembly was mixed for the state. At the end, Sanford would defend legislators against criticism of lackluster performance, only to see members in the final hours produce the most troublesome bit of legislative chicanery in modern time.

On the plus side, members followed Sanford's lead and endorsed a continuation of his education program and approved another $51 million for teacher pay raises, reduction of class size, and more clerical help and teaching materials. The changes adopted for post–high school education would become a model for other states. A new plan for a system of community colleges was approved as part of a bold plan that was more than simple expansion of the industrial training centers begun by Luther Hodges. The new institutions would provide junior college classes for commuter students not yet able to attend a four-year institution as well as job training for those seeking a new skill or career. All classes would be open to any student, regardless of previous education record, and promised to expand post–high school education to virtually every corner of the state.

Sanford came to the legislature dedicated to making the community college system the cornerstone of his education program. His goal was to have a school within commuting distance of every North Carolinian, and at a cost that working people could afford. In endorsing the plan in a speech the previous November at Methodist College in Fayetteville, Sanford said, "If you [students] have the will and the skill you can go to college. We must make it our policy to provide the classrooms, to establish the loan funds, to employ the college teachers, and to have the teaching facilities and everything needed to match the ambitions of our youth." [26]

The college-level courses and additions of libraries were too much for some, including Hodges, who favored hands-on training over books and social studies. When he first proposed the technical institutes, Hodges had prohibited training institutions from opening libraries. One weekend, the former governor paid a special visit to a new campus with State Education

Board Chairman Dallas Herring, who explained that the demands of the modern job world required students to be able to read and understand history as well as a training manual.[27] In later years, Sanford would count the creation of the community college systems, shepherded into being by Herring, as one of the outstanding accomplishments of his term.

The community colleges were only part of a legislative package prepared by the so-called Carlyle Commission that had been created to end political logrolling begun in the 1961 General Assembly, when political power threatened to undermine the governance of the state's system of higher education. Sanford named the study commission, which was headed by Irving Carlyle of Winston-Salem, after a visit from Herring and University of North Carolina President William Friday, who laid out the need for better planning for postsecondary education. Also included in the commission's report were recommendations on expansion of the university system that would lead ultimately to new campuses at Wilmington, Asheville, and Charlotte. Sanford initially endorsed the commission's recommendations on changes for the state's colleges and universities, but after he learned that a legislative fight over this part of the study might jeopardize his plans for the community colleges, he withdrew his endorsement.[28] The issue would remain unsettled for another eight years until the sixteen-campus university system was established under Governor Robert Scott.

Against considerable odds, Sanford also succeeded in winning approval for the North Carolina School of the Arts after opponents had all but killed the enabling legislation in committee. The governor's study group, the Conservatory Committee formed the year before, had carefully prepared the way. Its meetings throughout the state had involved leading arts supporters in the major cities, as well as some key legislators. Ehle had even prepared a book on the proposed school that Sanford had arranged to be printed at Central Prison. The sentiment for the arts school was not unanimous, of course, and even some in the state's arts community objected to the notion of creating a separate institution. Some even formed a curious alliance with legislators who considered the school a waste of money and just plain silly. Supporters of the music program at Woman's College (later the University of North Carolina at Greensboro) mobilized coeds who arrived en masse to argue that money for arts education should go to established music programs on their campus and not to a new school. Opponents derided the measure as the "toe-dance bill"; one member rose to oppose it saying, "Do you think I could go back home and tell my people that I voted to spend $325,000 of their tax money so some guy in a bikini can get on the stage and do a toe dance?"[29]

Sanford appealed to state pride and the excitement of innovation. State

Senator John Kerr of Warrenton endorsed the school in a ringing speech in which he said, "The beauty and glory of ancient Greece have not faded one iota. Why should we not take the leadership in this? Let's build something for the future." [30] Endorsements like this and a number of political favors saved the bill.

Essential to passage was the work of plainspoken Ben Roney, who rescued the measure from a committee where it was considered all but dead. The governor's secondary-roads man negotiated with reluctant legislators who reportedly were promised miles of new asphalt for their support. When the school later honored those who had midwifed it into existence, "Maestro" Roney, as he became known, was credited with "paving" the way. Roney later said that the governor called him in to help near the end of the session because he was the only one who had anything to trade.[31]

Sanford also succeeded in passing the first significant highway safety bills in a decade. Legislators approved the use of chemical tests on suspected drunk drivers and requirements that seat belts be installed in all automobiles; however, Sanford did not get an automobile safety inspection bill he had sought.

Not all his victories showed wide margins of support, but that did not bother the governor. He worked majorities where he could and believed that all he needed was the one vote that gave him more than half. He later explained, "I've always been a 51 percent man, and thought that if we could move as far as we could and still carry 51 percent, then that was the responsibility of leadership." [32]

The legislature was winding down in mid-June when Sanford used an appearance at the annual meeting of the state's broadcasters to review the session. He defended the General Assembly's record even though he had been handed losses along with some surprising victories. Instead of a dollar-an-hour minimum wage, the General Assembly approved an increase to eighty-five cents. The senate had refused to agree on reapportionment of its districts. And he didn't get all he had asked for in utility regulation. Yet, the governor said, "the members of the 1963 General Assembly cannot honestly be criticized for 'doing little.' . . . This General Assembly truly has compiled a record that is fiscally sound and forward bound." [33]

Less than a week later, however, Sanford would be hard-pressed to deliver such praise after the passage of the so-called Speaker Ban Bill, legislation that Sanford said later he would have vetoed "in a second" if he had had that power. The law, which banned communists from speaking on state-supported campuses, passed both the house and the senate in a matter of hours. Both Sanford and UNC President Friday were caught totally off guard. Their allies scrambled to recover, but efforts to recall the bill were unsuccessful. North Carolina higher education would be hamstrung for years by this limitation on an essential element of academic freedom, free speech.

The Speaker Ban Bill was passed in a fit of pique as the answer of many legislators to week after week of civil rights marches and demonstrations that had disrupted life in North Carolina's major cities. A week before the bill passed, the house had approved other punitive legislation raising the penalties for conviction of trespass and contempt of court. Before the vote, Rowan County Representative George Uzzell simply told his fellow members that they knew what the bill was for; it was approved with no debate. One day later, the house narrowly defeated two states' rights bills calling for amendments to the federal Constitution, but passed and sent to the senate a resolution calling for the creation of a court higher than the U.S. Supreme Court. Sanford's old legislative roommate, Representative Ike O'Hanlon of Fayetteville, said the measure would "be taken certainly as a protest vote about what is going on throughout our beloved North Carolina." [34]

Though legislators never publicly criticized the governor for his initiatives on civil rights, Sanford's own reading of the General Assembly showed his sentiments were not shared by the membership. Many members hailed from small towns and villages where suspicion of the motives of the civil rights movement led some to believe that communists and other subversives must have a hand in it. In these communities, segregation remained an established way of life, no matter what the high court and federal judges might say or do.

In February, at budget hearings for his institution held just two days after Sanford's Press Association speech, A&T's Dowdy had taken the brunt of the legislative anger over demonstrations in Greensboro. Senator John Kerr publicly upbraided Dowdy. "Didn't students from your college take part in the sit-in strikes in Greensboro trying to do away with segregation?" he demanded angrily.

"Yes," Dowdy replied.

"And you come down here begging the white folks to give more money to your school. . . . some of us are getting tired of it," said Kerr.

Dowdy's pride in his school, his students, and his race ran deep. But the browbeating from Kerr was unnerving and he answered diplomatically, even apologetically: "We know that young people in our city, our state, and all over the world, are seeking for improved behavior patterns. This does not mean that we at A&T are not putting forth every effort to bring about improved behavior patterns on the part of our students." [35]

Kerr's opinion was shared by many in the body, including Clarence

Stone, the chamber's presiding officer in the absence of a lieutenant governor, even though Stone liked the young governor. Prior to the opening of the session, he had been the Sanfords' guest for Christmas dinner at the mansion and had repaid his friend with a quick gavel that moved Sanford's program through with dispatch. But Stone cherished the memory of the Old South. When he traveled with Sanford to a reenactment of the battle at Gettysburg he excused himself from the official party, found the monument to a Union general who had raided his hometown, and relieved himself on the cold stone in broad daylight.[36] As one who harbored such deep resentment, it was not surprising that he had little patience with marching students intent on changing his world. When a bill for state-paid grants of $50 for North Carolina residents attending private colleges in the state reached the floor for debate, Stone argued that if the bill were approved, "You'll be giving those marchers fifty dollars to march." [37]

Regardless of the sentiment in the legislature, Sanford pushed forward. He arranged for introduction of two bills that repealed the last of the state's Jim Crow laws. One removed racial restrictions on membership in the National Guard, and the other repealed a state requirement for separate toilets for the races. Both passed with little comment. He also announced he was assigning Dr. James T. Taylor, the only black state official with statewide responsibilities in the Employment Security Commission, to devote full time to opening job opportunities in state government to African Americans.

In speeches and public appearances, the governor continued to encourage goodwill and cooperation if whites and blacks were to live together. "We must move forward as one people, or we will not move forward at all," the governor told a campus gathering at A&T in April where he was honored as Citizen of the Year by Omega Psi Phi fraternity. A week earlier in Little Rock, Arkansas, he had said, "We will begin to realize our great potential when, and only when, we give equal employment opportunities to Negroes." [38] In February he had spoken on Brotherhood Sunday at White Rock Baptist Church in Durham from the same pulpit Dr. Martin Luther King Jr. had used two years earlier.

As demonstrations in the state's major cities grew larger and more intense, however, Sanford was learning that Wheeler had been right. Those leading the marches in the streets of Greensboro, Durham, Raleigh, and Charlotte were no longer content with speeches and sympathetic counsel: they wanted action from the governor, and they wanted it now. It was not long before Sanford found himself wedged between two angry, competing forces, one in the Legislative Building and the other in the streets.

In Greensboro, demonstrations that had begun in the winter and carried into spring were growing steadily in size and frequency under the direction of Jesse Jackson, a popular A&T football player and rising student leader. By April, in Charlotte, the NAACP was pressing its campaign and threatened to picket an international trade fair where visitors would see not only the state's best products but its worst prejudice. That same month, Chapel Hill also became an NAACP target; about forty pickets paraded outside the ceremonies dedicating the new $2 million School of Public Health to protest segregated wards at the university's medical center. One of the honored guests that day was Frank Porter Graham.

Momentum also was building in Raleigh, where the focus of the demonstrations was the intersection of Fayetteville and Davie Streets. On the southwest corner sat the Sir Walter Hotel, the Raleigh home of legislators, some state officials, and lobbyists who watched the nightly marches from under the Sir Walter marquee. Directly across Davie was the S&W Cafeteria, where legislators enjoyed home-style cooking at prices that fit their expense allowance. Both establishments offered service to whites only.

Frank O. Sherrill's S&W Cafeteria was the largest eating establishment downtown, and as such set the pace for restaurants along Fayetteville Street. His other locations in Greensboro and Charlotte also had become the focus of demonstrations after the initial success at dime store lunch counters. Pressure was building as demonstrators in Greensboro moved beyond picketing and finally were arrested when they entered, took seats at dining tables, and refused to leave. In late April, the same tactics were adopted in Raleigh, where eleven demonstrators were arrested.

It was no surprise, then, that a week after the arrests in Raleigh the S&W manager refused to serve thirty-five-year-old Angie Brooks, who after being turned away at the Sir Walter Coffee Shop—whose manager first asked if she had come to apply for a job—crossed Davie Street with three college students and North Carolina State College professor Allard Lowenstein and challenged S&W's service as well. Brooks was from Liberia, where she had been an acting president of her country before joining the Liberian delegation to the United Nations. She had been educated at Shaw University and had spoken there the day before after attending a colloquium on developing nations on the state campus.

Students at Shaw had been part of the civil rights movement since before Sanford had been elected governor. In February 1960, it was the birthplace of the Student Nonviolent Coordinating Committee, which now provided many of the foot soldiers and leadership for street marches across the South. Its location on the southern edge of Raleigh's downtown business district, along with a close relationship with nearby St. Augustine's College, guaranteed a good turnout when pickets or marchers were needed on Fayetteville Street. That these students were now supported by white college professors on the state payroll was all the more exasperating for many legislators, who now had the civil rights movement brought literally to their front door.

The legislature was heading into its final weeks as the civil rights movement in the South experienced its most stunning scenes and shocking tragedies. The Children's Crusade in Birmingham, Alabama, began the first week in May, and the world watched as authorities used police dogs and fire hoses to turn back children marching peacefully for civil rights. Later in the month, Alabama's George Wallace would make his defiant trademark appearance in the doorway at the University of Alabama. A few weeks later, civil rights leader Medgar Evers would be dead from a sniper's bullet in Mississippi. More than fourteen thousand demonstrators were to be hauled off to jail across the South in 1963 and many in that number would be counted in North Carolina cities. By mid-May the jails in Raleigh and Greensboro were packed full of demonstrators, most of them college-age people who had adopted the SNCC tactic of filling the jails to strain the system until the barriers fell on the outside.

The marchers filed into the jails despite intolerable conditions. In Raleigh, a cell designed for six women held thirty-one. When the county jail was full in Greensboro, demonstrators were hauled off to the county farm, housed temporarily in the National Guard armory and finally a county facility that had once been a hospital for treatment of polio victims.

The sacrifice by the students was not lost on Sanford. On May 10, as his friend John Winters helped coax students from the jail in Raleigh after a city court judge pleaded with them to return to their campus without condition, the governor was at Pembroke State College for the school's Diamond Jubilee. Speaking to an audience that included mostly Lumbee Indians who had suffered discrimination as oppressive as that visited on blacks, he said,

> I don't know and I don't suppose anybody really knows, the full answer to the tension of Negro youths who feel, apparently with justification, that they are left out of the full advantages of American citizenship.
>
> While I don't know the answer I believe I know the reason — communication. That means people must talk about their complaints, difficulties and hopes with people against whom they complain. This means goodwill. It means maturity. It means you become civilized in the deepest meaning of the word.[39]

By the time Sanford returned from Pembroke that day, the demonstrators were leaving the Wake County Jail. As they walked free, they were met by hundreds of supporters who formed a line of march that proceeded up Fayetteville Street, around the capitol, on to the Legislative Building, and back to Shaw. Later in the evening, the marchers headed out again. This time, when the group reached the vicinity of the capitol someone said, "Let's go to the governor's mansion." [40]

It took only minutes to arrive at the mansion, which was ablaze with light. They had chosen as their evening for protest the governor's annual fund-raising ball for the North Carolina Symphony. Inside, the Sanfords and hundreds of guests in formal wear had just returned from a cocktail party at the Sir Walter (no alcohol was served at mansion affairs) and the crowd was waiting for the evening's honored guest, Eleanor Steber of the Metropolitan Opera, to descend the grand staircase. Marchers filled the broad lawn, crushing in on the azalea bushes beneath the porch on the mansion's south side, where some stood sullen and glaring while others sang freedom songs and gospel tunes.

After about twenty minutes, Sanford decided to speak to the crowd. Before he stepped out the side door onto the porch, the symphony's director, Dr. Benjamin Swalin, begged the governor to send him as a replacement, Sanford recalled: "He said, 'Let me go out there. I know how to deal with them. I've played in a great many Negro schools.' I said, 'You stay in here. I'm walking out there as a single human being and I am going to talk to them.'" [41]

The governor told Trooper Lloyd Burchett to remain inside, but the patrolman stayed on his heels, stiff and watchful in his starched gray uniform. The Sanford children, Terry and Betsee, who had been aroused by all the commotion below, were perched on a second-floor balcony. Betsee would never forget the scene, nor a corresponding incident months later when protesters with a different message left a burning cross not far from where the singing crowd now stood below. [42]

Sanford emerged from the mansion to a crowd of more than seven hundred. The mood was tense. Those in the front ranks already had refused to speak with Tom Lambeth, who had stepped out to meet the marchers shortly after they arrived. Lambeth, whose sympathies clearly lay with the marchers, was stunned by their reaction. "They stared at me. It was heated," he recalled. [43]

Sanford had no problem with the demonstration, but he was miffed that what had begun as a pleasant evening to boost the arts had been interrupted. He stood on the porch looking at the crowd that tossed epithets his way and did not say a word until someone yelled, "Let our great governor speak." He expected no trouble, but when he heard that call, he was reassured that he had no cause for alarm. At the same time, he remained alert. "I'll be glad to talk to you about any of your problems, any of your grievances, any of your hopes. This is not the time, or the place. . . . You are not bothering me at all. You can stay here another hour or so, if you like. I've enjoyed the singing."

From the crowd, someone shouted, "We are not here to entertain you, governor."

"You are not here at my request either, friend," Sanford shot back. "If you want to talk to me at any time about your plans and your problems, let my office know. You have not come to me with any requests."

One of the demonstrators yelled that the governor "should have known our troubles."

"I'm not a dictator, son. You're in a democracy," Sanford replied.[44]

Sanford's appearance ended the demonstration. The marchers remained a bit longer and then headed back to the Shaw campus. Winters walked along with the young people and found himself wrestling with his own conscience. He was eager to seize this moment in history and do what was right, but he also was cautious and mindful of political reality. "There were some that really wanted more from Sanford, who felt that as governor, he was supposed to issue an Emancipation Proclamation, or whatever was necessary to address the issue," he later recalled. "But there were some of us cooler heads that knew [that] the governor's authority and that of the General Assembly was one that had to be balanced."[45]

The constant pressure of the demonstrations was beginning to have the desired effect. In the week after the march to the mansion, the Raleigh Merchants Association adopted a resolution urging the city council to adopt antidiscrimination ordinances. Sanford worked with Winters and Raleigh's Mayor William G. Enloe, who was an executive for a theater chain, to meet in Washington at the Justice Department, where Robert Kennedy had called in the head of the company whose movie houses in North Carolina and other states barred black customers. Winters sat outside Kennedy's office with Enloe as the attorney general argued for change. Then, he said, "we all met and they agreed on a plan for desegregating the theaters of North Carolina, starting with Greensboro, and I think Winston-Salem was next, Charlotte, Durham and Raleigh. . . . I remember Bill Enloe said to me, 'John, why didn't you put Raleigh first?' I said, 'Because Raleigh was the least volatile. Thanks to you and other council members, here we had a better climate. We really need to do it in Greensboro where we had a hot bed.' "[46]

Greensboro's jails and temporary holding facilities were strained after eleven consecutive nights of marches and more than twelve hundred arrests. Similar conditions existed in Durham, where one night four thousand marchers conducted a mass meeting outside the Howard Johnson's restaurant, the object of demonstrations nearly a year earlier.

On two occasions, Sanford alerted the National Guard to readiness in Greensboro, but no soldiers ever appeared on any North Carolina streets during his term. Instead, the governor stayed in constant contact with local authorities and augmented their beleaguered forces with more than fifty units from the Highway Patrol. The governor hoped that by keeping his distance, working in the background, he could avoid complaints of "outsiders" telling local officials what to do.

He continued to apply pressure where he could. After restaurant owners in Charlotte said they wouldn't budge until s&w took the first step, Sanford flew to see Frank Sherrill at his mountain home near Flat Rock and urged him to open the doors of his cafeterias to all. Sanford had known Sherrill through his church work and considered him a decent and honorable man. He also found him to be like many who ran downtown businesses who were fearful that a life's work would disappear if they broke with Southern custom and permitted whites and blacks to sit side by side. No one wanted to be first. Sanford left empty-handed that day. Sherrill held out for several weeks more before finally agreeing to a timetable that ultimately opened his restaurants.[47]

City officials made some headway in Raleigh, and in Durham newly elected mayor R. Wensell Grabarek negotiated a truce, but Greensboro remained difficult. In an effort to relieve the tension building in the city, Sanford arranged with authorities to release students without bond and sent Dowdy to get them back to campus. Dowdy was troubled by the governor's instructions and struggled to find an alternative, but finally conceded to the orders from his boss. When a number of students still refused to leave, they were carried out of their cells.

Students resented Sanford's intrusion. So did Bennett College president Dr. Willa Player, who later told historian William Chafe, "I was not going to let a private school be dictated by the governor." She urged her students to remain in jail rather than, as she saw it, turn her campus into a prison.[48]

Dowdy had issued orders that students continuing to participate in demonstrations jeopardized their standing at the university, but it was an empty threat. Clearly, Dowdy knew he could not expel his entire student body and the governor knew "they couldn't kill a spirit unwilling to be killed."[49]

Later, Sanford said: "I was trying to say [to the college presidents], 'Don't worry about it. You support your students and you won't get crossed up with me.' I said, 'I know that when they get back on campus they might go out again, but you just do the best you can because you've got to represent the students and I'm not asking you to do anything you don't want to do.' "[50]

CORE's James Farmer was totally unprepared for Sanford's orders. "It was the first and only jail lock-out in the movement," he wrote in his autobiography *Lay Bare the Heart*, "following what I believe to have been the largest jail-in for civil rights activity in this country." [51]

By the last week in May an uneasy truce prevailed in Greensboro, Durham, and Raleigh when an extended CBS news report compared demonstrations in North Carolina to the often violent confrontations on the streets in Alabama. Reporter Nelson Benton quoted black leaders who hoped "they [could] force North Carolina leaders, proud of their pretensions, to live up to their promises." The NAACP's Roy Wilkins voiced some hope for Durham, where he was impressed that Grabarek had appeared at one mass meeting and listened to what blacks had to say. "That kind of man has to be honest," he said. But Farmer said demonstrations would not end in Greensboro until it was an "open city." [52]

Some took hope when the desegregation plan for the theaters was announced, the result of the negotiated settlement at Attorney General Kennedy's office. If those gains had been won, perhaps others were just ahead, and demonstrations resumed.

Patience was wilting in the June heat in Greensboro, where both sides were nearly exhausted. Police were edgy, pushed to the limit; march leaders were beginning to worry about outbursts from new participants who had not been trained in nonviolence. On the night of June 5, Jesse Jackson led yet another mass demonstration into the city's main intersection, where he vowed to return in twenty-four hours to "take over the city of Greensboro." Forty miles away, in Lexington, North Carolina, a white man was killed when shots were fired as a crowd of whites gathered to retaliate against a black neighborhood where residents had organized demonstrations and marches. In Raleigh, marchers returned to the Sir Walter Hotel, where they settled into the lobby with suitcases for a "check-in" sit-in.

For Sanford, the resumption of demonstrations came at a most difficult time. The legislative committees were taking action almost daily on his program at the same time he was reading reports from the Highway Patrol that carried little good news from the streets. Sanford showed little of the strain when he did see reporters, and they got little from him on the racial situation.

On May 21, as students were being carried out of the Greensboro jails, he told the media simply, "We are watching this and keeping in touch. We don't intend to let it get out of hand if we can help it. The answer to these problems is good sense and I think we have an abundance of good sense in North Carolina." When reporters pressed him further, he said, "Do you have any questions about the wheat referendum?" referring to a pending congressional matter. "I think it ought to be passed." [53]

Legislators were asking the governor, "Why do they turn on you—as much as you have done for them?" Others found outlets for their anger. The university's public television budget was eliminated after members discovered one of the regular marchers was associated with UNC-TV. The money was later reinstated after Senator White called committee members together and told them to use their influence to see that the university got its money.

Senator Ralph Scott, whose credentials were solid in the conservative ranks, ran interference for Sanford when and where he could. At one point, he told some colleagues who were deeply suspicious of the governor's handling of the situation that they shouldn't worry about old Terry, he knew what he was doing. Scott convinced some that Sanford was using his old friend Allard Lowenstein, the State College professor who had been on the streets with Ambassador Brooks, as a mole within the movement.[54]

Sanford remained particularly close to developments in Greensboro, where Mayor David Schenck finally issued a statement on June 7 putting the weight of the city behind desegregation of businesses. Sanford saw that the White House was aware of Schenk's decision to open his city; the president praised Schenck at a news conference with the nation's mayors who were meeting in Honolulu. By the middle of June the crisis had passed in Greensboro and Charlotte as theater managers began making arrangements for the seating of their first black customers.

On June 18, Jackson and two others from A&T sat down for a meal at the S&W Cafeteria in Greensboro. That same day, Sanford appeared in a special broadcast from the UNC television studios that set in motion a series of events that he hoped would reduce the growing tension in the streets where, he feared, demonstrations and counterdemonstrations led by Ku Klux Klansmen and their sympathizers could lead to serious injury. In the brief statement, Sanford called for an end to street demonstrations that he said had reached the point of diminishing return for those seeking change. He announced that he was inviting protest leaders to a meeting in Raleigh "to place before the public in an orderly manner their hopes and aspirations, with the hope that this will promote better understanding which will enable citizens to resolve the differences which have arisen." The demonstrations were counterproductive, he said, adding, "Anyone who hasn't received this message doesn't understand human nature."[55]

The next morning, he served breakfast to a small group of black leaders, most of whom regarded him with more sympathy than did the impatient young people. Yet Sanford aide Hugh Cannon wasn't sure that Sanford's call for an end to demonstrations, the only thing that had won significant gains, had not alienated even these men. Cannon recalled his relief when he heard one man tell the governor not to worry about those who might consider his statement to be a retreat. "We remember back in the Civil War," the man said, "Stonewall Jackson was the most beloved man of the Confederacy but he made a horrible mistake one time. He got too far in front of his men and they shot him. I understand you can't get too far out in front of your people in North Carolina. You will get shot." [56] Later that day, President John Kennedy sent to Congress the most comprehensive Civil Rights Bill ever prepared.

Sanford's appeal for a halt to demonstrations brought the first full night's sleep some local police officers had known in weeks. The state NAACP called a moratorium on marches. In Raleigh, police officers were taken off alert, and two days later, the Associated Press reported that during the previous week several restaurants in Asheville had admitted blacks for the first time. Nearly one-fourth of the more than 460 restaurants in Charlotte were desegregated, and in Fayetteville, spokesmen for downtown variety stores and department stores had announced they would hire employees on a nondiscriminatory basis.

The governor's office coordinated the meeting with Floyd McKissick of Durham and chose as the site the old house chamber, where Reconstruction-era Republicans had controlled the state when the last black members had served there. It must have appeared to Secretary of State Thad Eure that a similar revolution—this one inspired by communists—might well be underway. As Sanford prepared for his meeting from his office on the south end of the first floor of the capitol, Eure, from his quarters in the opposite corner, was preparing to take the starch out of those on the state's campuses who were lending support to the civil rights movement. Three days after Sanford's televised statement, Eure contacted his counterpart in Ohio and asked for a copy of a proposed new Ohio law banning communists from state campuses; he and others had heard about it in a WRAL-TV commentary broadcast by Jesse Helms, who had joined the station in 1960 to run the station's news operation and present daily commentaries of a decidedly conservative point of view.[57] Some might even credit Helms with providing the spark that ignited the Speaker Ban fire. His praise of the Ohio legislators was only the latest in a round of editorials that, from his debut in November 1960, had raised the specter of communist influence on college campuses. He frequently characterized college students as naïve and gullible, calling them innocent victims of college administrators who put forth a bogus argument that communism deserved full debate. "Educational institutions are serving no good purpose in permitting Communists to propagandize students," he opined that April. "To contend otherwise is the same as saying the colleges and universities would be justified in offering instruction in safe-cracking or pornography or murder." [58]

On Tuesday, June 25, many of those who had been part of the street demonstrations across the state filled the old house chambers and waited for Sanford. The large contingent from Durham included McKissick's daughter, who had spent time in jail; Jackson and others came from Greensboro. NAACP President Kelly Alexander and Dr. Reginald Hawkins, who had led marches in Charlotte, were on hand. So was Golden Frinks, the leader of Dr. King's SCLC chapter in eastern North Carolina. NAACP officials from outside the state attended. Altogether about 150 packed into the hall.

It was clear the meeting would include no cheering section for the governor. The day before, McKissick had offered to Sanford, and the legislators meeting a block away, a preview of what to expect when he released a list of grievances and demands. The carefully prepared memorandum asked for nothing less than state action to remove segregation from every aspect of life. It called for legislation where necessary and immediate response from state and local officials, boards, and agencies to create a truly open society, from public accommodations to political affairs and education.

The crowd in the house chamber was tense when Sanford arrived. Walking with him to the front was Capus Waynick. The script worked out with McKissick called for the governor to make a statement and then depart. Sanford believed it was time for venting, but he had no intention of letting the office of governor be submitted to verbal abuse.[59] Waynick would hear everyone out, along with David Coltrane, who was representing the Good Neighbor Council, and make his report.

Described as a "salty, crusty trouble-shooter," Waynick was the perfect surrogate. A retired general by virtue of his service as state adjutant general under Luther Hodges, Waynick had been in similarly difficult situations during a lifetime in newspapers, international diplomacy, and politics. In the 1930s he had helped defuse tense situations in High Point when labor unrest threatened the peace. Later, he was the Truman administration's man in Nicaragua and Colombia and ran Truman's Point Four Program in Latin America. He was in retirement at his home in High Point, having only recently left the Richardson Foundation, when he got a call from Sanford, who asked him to help guide his administration through the current storm.

"You are here this morning at our invitation to indeed find a better way to express your hopes, desires and aspirations," Sanford began his remarks to the group.

> You must find a way that not only expresses the depth and breadth of your dissatisfaction, but which also encourages people to assist in opening up jobs and other opportunities.
>
> The demonstrations have shown just how unhappy and discontented you are, how anxious you are to remove, and remove right now,

the indignities and injustices which have been visited upon your parents and their parents.

The demonstrations had produced results, Sanford said, but they had reached "the point of diminishing returns in the latter days, destroying good will, creating resentment, losing friends and not influencing people."

Returning to a theme voiced two years earlier in his speech to educators in South Carolina, Sanford said,

> Your enemy and mine is a system bequeathed to us by a cotton economy, kindled by stubbornness, intolerance, hotheadedness, north and south, exploding into war and leaving to our generations the ashes of vengeance, retribution, and poverty.
>
> The way to fight this common enemy is education, up and down the line and across the board.

The governor argued that negotiation, not marching, would lead to progress.

> That is why you are here. The story this morning is not the story of mass demonstrations. The real story is not beclouded by the story of possible violence, of the force, the danger, with failure to establish clearer understanding.
>
> The story this morning is the reasonable story of what you think and what you believe. I think that is important.

Before he left, he said that if this forum worked, then other meetings would follow with mayors and local officials. "Now is the time for men and women of good faith to put North Carolina above the distressing clamor of racial conflict," he said.[60]

At Sanford's departure the group stood and offered courteous, perfunctory applause. Judging from the response, it seemed doubtful he had convinced any that demonstrations had not brought change and that more demonstrations would not bring more change. Blacks had been listening to promises of tomorrow for too many years, and Sanford's speech was "brainwashing," said John Brooks, a national NAACP official. What North Carolina needed, he said, was for all to "go home and plan bigger and better demonstrations." A traveling corps of "NAACP commandos" was promised for small towns across eastern North Carolina.[61]

McKissick told the group, "We fear the governor misunderstands the situation. It is utterly necessary that the people see the point of the demonstrations, not just the governor. And every indication is that the majority of the white people in North Carolina have not begun to grasp the point of the demonstrations." He recited instances of duplicity and humiliation: a Methodist Church conference had endorsed a resolution calling on businesses to accept black customers, but the same conference had refused to admit black Methodist churches to membership; civic clubs spoke of goodwill but refused to admit black members, and little further action had followed in the cities since demonstrations were halted. "The governor has emphatically stated that 'law and order' must be maintained in the state," McKissick continued.

> We are in favor of the maintenance of law and order. There are two concepts of law and order today. The first concept is that concept of law and order which requires Negro citizens to accept segregation which whites and Negro citizens alike, know to be morally and legally wrong as well as degrading to Negroes. We do not accept this concept but we are in favor of "law and order" in truth and in fact. Is it "law and order" when a law grants certain privileges to white citizens and denies these same privileges to Negroes because of their color? This concept of law and order we reject.
>
> The second concept of law is simply—where all citizens are accorded the same privileges and rights—the concept that law is color blind.[62]

Waynick absorbed it all. More than a generation separated him from McKissick and even Sanford, but he was enough of a populist, enough of a Kerr Scott–Harry Truman Democrat, to know that what the crowd before him was asking for was right and that its feelings were justified. Some years later he told an interviewer "that if I'd been a Negro, I'd have been causing trouble a long time before they were." At the time of the Supreme Court's *Brown* decision he had "recognized the beginning of the new day and that the quicker we conformed to reasonable acceptance of changing circumstances and philosophy, the better it would be for everybody concerned." Like Sanford, and Frank Graham, who was Waynick's classmate at Chapel Hill, Waynick believed that the road to change would be successful only if attitudes, as well as laws, changed.[63]

After the meeting, Waynick traded words with McKissick's daughter, who challenged him to join her for lunch at the Sir Walter Hotel. He declined because, he said, he had plans to meet the head of the state restaurant association. But he told the young woman, "I'm afraid they'd do me like I heard happened to a man at another place under similar circumstances when the management said, 'Why, we'll have to feed this Negro, but you white so-and-so get the hell out of here.' "[64]

By the time the meeting concluded, Sanford already was on his way to a routine appearance out of town. He felt confident that Waynick would represent him well and believed his choice was rather clever, that the group would be impressed with his military title and take him seriously.

While the governor was away that afternoon, the General Assembly passed the Speaker Ban Bill. Over the next twenty-four hours, Sanford and Friday considered their options for reversing the precipitate action of the legislature. A recall vote was attempted the next day, just prior to adjournment in the senate, but fell short of the votes needed. Some UNC loyalists later faulted Sanford for not throwing his full support behind the recall effort. But, according to Sanford's own head count and a reading from his friends on the floor, the members were in no mood for arm twisting: "To get in there and say vote against it now would have made them look foolish back home. This wasn't a reasonable thing to do politically. But we gave it serious thought." [65]

The governor was as eager for the session to end as the legislators were to leave. He was only days away from announcing perhaps the most ambitious project of his administration: a multimillion dollar program to attack the causes of poverty. The continued turmoil in the streets presented no fit climate for the introduction of a program that would require a united effort of blacks and whites. A week later, Waynick, Sanford, and Coltrane followed up the Raleigh meeting with the second step to finding an alternative to street demonstrations.

Within days of the capitol meeting, the governor's office issued more than 350 invitations to city officials to meet July 5 in Greensboro. Despite the conflicts created by a holiday weekend, more than two hundred mayors, city council members, and city managers responded to Sanford's call and were on hand at the Woman's College campus. They were eager to find help, and Sanford offered them a new Mayors Coordinating Committee, whose first members were Charlotte's Stan Brookshire, Schenck from Greensboro, Grabarek from Durham, as well as High Point Mayor Floyd Mehan and Mayor M. C. Benton from Winston-Salem. All had won their share of battle ribbons in previous months.

The governor urged local leaders to be fair and not to "suppress the full expression of all aspirations." He said he would be firm: "So long as I am governor, the state is not going to take its cue from the fear of masses or mobs. The state of North Carolina is not going to be frightened into any position on any subject, and certainly the governor of North Carolina is not going to respond to pressure of any group, or any situation. On the one side, we will keep the peace and dignity by whatever steps are necessary, or on the other side, we will insure that all be accorded the full rights and advantages of first class citizenship. I do not intend to dance to the tune of the extremists on either side of any question." [66]

Operating on the belief that elected officials had asked for the job and were aware of the burdens they assumed by taking office, Sanford encouraged the mayors and council members to become leaders in resolving issues in their own towns and cities. "I simply call on you to deal with the situation, to work at it, to display wisdom and courage, to understand that every child of God on earth desires a chance in life and human dignity along with it."

He concluded, sat down, and braced for reaction. "I fully expected some would rise to say, 'Why don't you stop them, why do you let them get away with this?' I knew there was no answer to this except that it couldn't be stopped, that this was the sweep of history that was going to roll on, and events have borne out this judgment," he wrote a year later in an unpublished account of his administration.[67]

To his surprise, Sanford found almost unanimous support for his approach. The city officials were eager for guidance. None had ever experienced anything like this before, which gave some impetus for a guidebook that the coordinating committee prepared and distributed a few weeks later. Most of those who spoke were encouraging, their responses thoughtful. "I have no fear of our Negro population," the former mayor of a small Piedmont town said, "but you do have to prepare a majority of our people to accept the colored people. If we don't, the integrating motels, hotels and restaurants will be strictly for the birds."[68]

Just prior to meeting with city officials, Sanford attended the first meeting of the Good Neighbor Council. Its mission, he said, was to open job opportunities, not through force but persuasion and by appealing to the conscience of the state's employers. "There will not be any discrimination in state jobs," he said. "Such discrimination is both unconstitutional and undemocratic. Negroes are invited to apply, just as all other citizens, to Walter Fuller, State Personnel Officer, and their applications will be judged on merit and ability."[69]

The Council's mission eventually blurred when Coltrane had to replace Waynick, who was sidelined with a heart attack, no doubt encouraged by the late hours, long rides, and pressure of constant negotiations in towns across the state. Coltrane performed masterfully and traded on his years in state government that had earned him a reputation as a solid, conservative public man who could be trusted. Some old Scott hands had never forgiven Coltrane for his slight of Scott a decade before, but Sanford's talent for finding the right person for the right job prevailed over such objections. Coltrane brought maturity, patience, and familiarity with North Carolina to a job totally unsuited for any of the younger men of Sanford's inner circle. "He was more austere, he was more reserved," recalled David Gergen, who later became an advisor to both Presidents Ronald Reagan and Bill Clinton. Gergen spent many hours with Coltrane as a summer intern. He was Coltrane's driver and traveling companion, and saw him as few others did. "He was so obviously committed to it, and he didn't try to ram things down anybody's throat. He stated clearly that this was in your interest and this is what we want to do, can't you get your community together? . . . He didn't mind casting any arguments in terms of their self-interest," Gergen recalled. He said Coltrane would tell local white leaders, "You don't want violence here. You don't want the national press here. We are all better off if we don't do these things." [70] Sanford later told Coltrane he had performed some of his most valuable service to the state in his leadership of the Good Neighbor Council. He stayed on the job until his death in 1968.

It would be years before the last sign-carrying line of pickets disappeared from the streets of North Carolina cities. The summer summit did not stop demonstrations, and the continuing racial tension never fully cleared from Sanford's agenda. Yet the meetings in Raleigh and Greensboro and constant attention from Coltrane produced the desired effect. The state had seen the last of mass demonstrations for a while.

Across the nation that summer, blacks were preparing for a mass march on Washington that was scheduled for late August. In advance of the march, one Southern politician after another appeared on Capitol Hill before a Senate panel conducting hearings on the administration's Civil Rights Bill. The measure included provisions for public accommodations, greater powers for the Justice Department to initiate school desegregation suits, provisions for the withholding of federal funds for programs and activities where discrimination occurred, and new programs to ensure fair employment. It was the most comprehensive civil rights measure ever put forward, and Kennedy worried that continued demonstrations such as the March on Washington would complicate his efforts to win passage of even a portion of the proposed legislation. Three days before Sanford's meeting with demonstration leaders in Raleigh, the president held a similar session at the White House, where he asked civil rights leaders to cancel the march. CORE's Farmer told him that was not possible. "We understand your political problem in getting the legislation through, and we want to help in that as best we can," Farmer said. "But the civil rights forces have their problems too. We would be in a difficult if not untenable position if we called the street demonstrations off and then were defeated in the legislative battle." [71]

Two Senate committees had commenced hearings. In the Judiciary Committee, chaired by Mississippi's James O. Eastland, North Carolina's Sam Ervin Jr. spun mountain stories and parried points of constitutional law with witnesses, including the attorney general. No one expected anything to come from Judiciary, which had traditionally bottled up similar legislation. Supporters held out more hope for the Commerce Committee and favorable treatment from its chairman, Warren Magnuson of Washington. Among Magnuson's committee members, however, was South Carolina's Strom Thurmond, who in late July invited I. Beverly Lake to testify. "We wanted to have someone from North Carolina," a Thurmond aide told reporters, "and we thought he'd be a good man. He's spoken out pretty strongly on this subject."[72]

The fire of segregation burned as brightly as ever for Lake. A few weeks before Thurmond invited him to Washington, a reporter visiting Lake in his Raleigh law office noted a plaque framed and hanging on the wall that read "The principles for which we stand are eternal—I. Beverly Lake." In the course of the interview, which touched on his continuing interest in a reprise of a campaign for governor, he proposed a new program of technical education: "We ought to have three regional junior colleges—one such college for Negro boys in eastern North Carolina, one for white boys in the Piedmont and another in the west."[73]

Lake followed George Wallace and Ross Barnett to the witness table in the hearing room. They claimed the current unrest was the work of communists and criticized the administration for not attacking the subversives who were undermining their way of life. Lake told the committee that if the public accommodations bill passed, white people would not stand for it: "They will resort to their constitutional right to keep and bear arms and, when tempers flare, those arms will be used." Taking a page from his 1960 speeches, he said the bill "would fan racial differences to the white heat of hatred and would change the image of the federal government from that of a beloved and respected protector of justice and liberty into that of a feared and despised police-state monster."[74]

Sanford considered an invitation to appear before the committee and devoted some time to preparing a statement. In it, he echoed Frank Graham's response to the Truman report on civil rights more than a decade earlier. More laws were not the answer, he wrote. The answer lay in the hearts of men. But he finally decided against going to Washington. He believed his appearance would have been a vain gesture that would have accomplished little and only stirred the dust at a time when he needed to see clearly what lay ahead. "Politically, I could not have testified for the public accommodations," he said later. "I just couldn't have unless we wanted to destroy our effectiveness."[75] Besides, neither side would find satisfaction in his words. His friends, or at least those who believed the bill was necessary to break the barriers of segregation, would have been disappointed when he could not deliver forthright support. Yet his remarks were certainly no comfort to segregationists either.

He stuffed the draft of his statement in his files, which was unfortunate. His voice could have added to better understanding. The themes he chose and the words he used clearly expressed his concern for the real issues and a hope for the future. They would have added some light to the heat coming from the witness table. "Must we take each painful step by difficult demonstrations," he wrote,

> followed by agonizing debate over federal legislation, for each bit of human progress achieved?
>
> How do you open up job opportunities for Negroes?
>
> How do you see that they get a fair chance at promotions once they get jobs?
>
> How can you inspire ambition in a young person who knows that the school leads nowhere, that he couldn't go anywhere without schooling?
>
> How can you do away with bitterness, and distrust, and opposition, and foot-dragging, and hatred?
>
> By legislation? I don't know. It hasn't seemed to work.

Yet he held to the need for change. "Freedom is involved, surely," he wrote.

> To walk by public places daily where you may not enter is debilitating to the spirit—even if you do not have the remotest interest in going in. To travel without knowing when or where your children might have a meal or use a bathroom is far more than just inconvenient. It challenges the very faith of mankind.
>
> Freedom is involved also in the rights of the owners of property and businesses. I'm not speaking of property rights but of something deeper—the freedom to improve, to correct error, to do right.

He remained optimistic and hopeful, as Graham had been before him.

> I insist that man is good, is moral, has a conscience that seeks the right. I insist that man does not have to be made good by the force of federal courts. Indeed, man is good, and if timidity and a desire for surface conformity cause him to transgress for a time, his innate sense of fair play will ultimately triumph. Leadership, clarity of purpose, understanding of the full weight of the burdens of integration, injustice, and inequities will cause our people to seek to do the things that are right.
>
> I say, don't defeat it and don't pass it. Rather, re-word it to state that free access to public policies is the American policy, stated by the Congress of the United States, supported by the President of the United States, promoted by Senators, Congressmen, the President, state legislatures, governors.[76]

More than 250,000 persons arrived in Washington on August 28 and jammed the Mall. The crowd spilled out from the Lincoln Memorial, surrounded the reflecting pool, and continued on beyond the Washington Monument. Nothing like it had been seen before and King's "I Have a Dream" speech eclipsed virtually everything said that day. To Sanford's surprise, he received a mention from Roy Wilkins, executive secretary of the NAACP, who began his speech by noting, "We come to petition our lawmakers to be as brave as our sit-ins and marchers, to be as daring as James Meredith, as unafraid as the nine children of Little Rock, as forthright as the governor of North Carolina, and as dedicated as the Archbishop of Saint Louis." Sanford was overwhelmed by Wilkins's unexpected reference and privately considered it a very personal reward for his efforts to bring North Carolina along a difficult road.[77]

As the draft of his congressional testimony indicated, Sanford was thinking beyond the immediate issues of whether a man could buy a hot dog at a restaurant in North Carolina. Rather, his concern was with entire families, white and black, whose poverty left them beyond the pale of opportunity. Throughout the spring, Ehle and others in state government, including George Esser from the Institute of Government in Chapel Hill, refined Sanford's ideas into specific grant requests designed to mount a comprehensive statewide attack on the causes of poverty. The total of the foundation requests came to $7 million. Sanford planned to match that with smaller amounts of state money and support from North Carolina foundations to create the North Carolina Fund, the first statewide program of its kind.

Ford had never approved such a project for a state, or for so large an amount. The ambitions of the Fund were such that Ford President Henry Heald broke with his own routine and traveled south to talk in person with those involved. He paid a call on John Wheeler in Durham, which in itself was a historic gesture. "[It was] the first time anybody from the Foundation's top echelon had gone to a black man," recalled Paul Ylvisaker. As far as Ford was concerned, Wheeler's participation and approval was crucial. From the beginning, the foundation insisted on supporting the rights of black North Carolinians and looked to Wheeler for approval of the governor's plans. A nod from Wheeler could have scuttled the entire program.[78]

Heald also met with Charles Babcock, who exerted considerable influence on the foundations supported by the Reynolds tobacco fortune. Babcock had married R. J. Reynolds's daughter, Mary, and the two lived at Reynolda, the family estate outside Winston-Salem. Babcock was a private man, an avid reader and amateur botanist who held a deep interest in his adopted hometown. He worked quietly to reshape the city and was instrumental in the relocation of Wake Forest University there in the 1950s.

"Charlie and Heald met in the rotunda of the state capitol like two Indian chiefs," Ylvisaker recalled. "They walked in from separate sides, they can't have said more than about two paragraphs of words, but they communicated at a very gutsy level in which Heald, in effect, said, 'Look, old man of the establishment down here, you know what position I'm in. Is this good?' And Charlie Babcock said, 'Look, old man of the Northern establishment, I wouldn't be in it unless I'd thought this thing through damn carefully. It's a risk we're going to have to take and I'll ante up the money.' " [79]

Ehle recalled the meeting with less dramatic overtones. He said Heald was mostly concerned with whether Sanford planned to use the Fund for political purposes. Babcock assured him he did not.

The Fund was perhaps the most audacious program of Sanford's administration. It was creative, even revolutionary, and produced self-sustaining programs that remained a generation later. It also was not without risk. At the height of Sanford's promotion of his state as a home for new industry and business, where the trademark was "Variety Vacationland," the governor put a spotlight on the darker side of North Carolina, where poverty, ignorance, and desperation were common. At a time when citizen action was in its infancy, the Fund bypassed local officials and promoted community-based citizen groups that challenged the status quo and empowered poor people in a way they had never known before. Ylvisaker called it "one of the best projects we ever came out with because it grew with the times."

In his book, But What About the People?, Sanford traced the genesis of the Fund to a visit to a poor mountain school he had made with Ehle. There they saw a blond-haired little girl named Melissa, whose teacher said she just didn't "fit in." The governor asked Ehle to quietly learn more about Melissa. He returned with a profile that Sanford had known since childhood. Melissa was a child of poverty and for her, Sanford realized, "improvement of schools wasn't enough. Not nearly enough. If school was to have any meaning for them, these children first had to be put in a position to understand why learning was important, to comprehend what school was all about. That was the only way they could break out of the cycle of poverty in which they were trapped." Sanford came to realize that while trying to better educate children, he had "stumbled into the whole confusing pattern of poverty in America." [80] Billy Barnes later wrote of Sanford's discovery that "these children have so many distractions—hunger, sickness, crowded living and poor studying conditions—coming between them and their lessons that they can't take advantage of what the school has to offer." [81]

Perhaps more than his education program, more than doing the "decent thing" on civil rights, he now had found something that represented the essence of a governor seeking to use resources at his command to improve the lot of his constituents. "It was difficult to say where the idea came from," Sanford said later. "It is just one of the things that had plagued me all my life. When I got [to be governor], I began to say what can we do about it."[82]

Sanford announced the creation of the Fund on July 18. Signing the organization's charter with him were Babcock, Wheeler, and C. A. McKnight, editor of the *Charlotte Observer*. Twelve others, representing a broad cross-section of community leaders, educators, and members of Sanford's administration, made up the board of directors. The incorporators cosigned a note at Wachovia Bank to pay the electric bill for the first thirty days, but lenders knew a check for $2 million from the Ford Foundation was on the way. Before the Fund closed its doors on schedule a little more than six years later, the Ford Foundation and the Mary Reynolds Babcock and Z. Smith Reynolds Foundations would have invested nearly $10 million in Fund programs.

The early agenda touched every corner of the state. "Twenty or more rural and urban communities will be selected for special help by the organization," Sanford said in announcing the Fund. "These communities will develop their own comprehensive programs for making improvements, using schools, welfare, public health and other agencies." Another early initiative would be a statewide effort to improve academic performance of children in the first three grades at more than a hundred schools and a new method of introducing vocational education in high schools.[83]

If Oakland was a skirmish in the nation's War on Poverty, then the North Carolina Fund was its initial battle. The first shot was fired in a Southern state with pockets of high unemployment and where basic needs such as decent housing, a balanced diet, and adequate health care continued well after Franklin Roosevelt's initial assault on the plight of the rural South thirty years earlier. Just how large a foe existed in city slums and rural communities was never clear. One Ford study said half of the state lived below the national poverty line; a later study found more than a third of all North Carolina families had annual incomes of less than $3,000 and one in ten had incomes of less than $1,000. Whatever the numbers, Sanford knew poverty sapped the strength of his state and wasted the investment in education, which was the first step to a decent life:

> Some of this poverty is self-imposed and some of it is undeserved. All of it withers the spirit of children who neither imposed it, nor deserve it.

These are the children of poverty who tomorrow will become the parents of poverty.

We hope to break this cycle of poverty. That is what the North Carolina Fund is all about.[84]

The North Carolina Fund became the responsibility of George Esser, who left the Institute of Government to direct the program. Esser had been raised in western Virginia, where his father was a supervisor at a coal mine. He was the product of the Virginia Military Institute and one of Albert Coates's recruits from Harvard Law. When Esser arrived at the Institute in 1948, Sanford had recently left to open his law practice in Fayetteville.

At the Institute, Esser had focused on urban issues, developing short courses for mayors and city managers. He was already familiar with the Ford Foundation's gray areas program, and when he learned that a group from Ford was due to visit the state in January 1963, he prepared a memo on the new Ford ideas. "I helped them focus on this by describing what was being done in Oakland," he later recalled. "I tried to help them realize that you cannot deal with the physical problems of the city unless you deal with the problems of the people in the city."[85] One study of the Fund described Esser as a man of "humane instincts."[86] He was that, plus he had an appreciation of the challenges of such an ambitious undertaking, not the least of which was Ford's activist approach to integration. Yet he was still surprised when Ehle told him the governor hoped he would take the job as director. He had never managed anything more complicated than a church committee.

The initial programs were to operate on two levels, but both were essentially educational. Sanford later wrote, "We wanted to say to the community leaders, let's see if we can show how education, combined with welfare, health, employment, and other public and private services, can be used to stop wasting lives and burdening American society with a handicap it need not carry."[87]

The Comprehensive School Improvement Program was aimed at improving teaching methods in the first three grades plus preschool. Local school superintendents shaped programs to fit their schools and then submitted proposals to the state Department of Education, which managed $4 million in grant money. Out of this came demonstrations of team-teaching, the influence on reduced class size, ungraded classes, and the benefits of teachers' aides. The impressive evidence of benefits of preschool training on the learning curve of children led to the creation of HeadStart, one of the most successful of Lyndon Johnson's Great Society programs.

Little else in the Fund's existence sparked more change, or more local self-examination, than Fund-supported community action programs, which were the second major component. Communities across the state were invited to submit proposals to attack the causes of poverty in their own backyard; by the deadline in early 1964, fifty proposals covering sixty-six of the state's one hundred counties had been submitted. The ideas were as varied as the perceived need: day care for working mothers, job training for the under- and unemployed, health care and birth control, kindergarten instruction, summer camps and day camps with an educational tilt, neighborhood centers for school readiness, health maintenance, job opportunities, and tutoring utilizing student volunteers. Throughout the spring, Fund board members visited each of the communities and then awarded grants to eleven programs. "For the first time in many instances," Sanford wrote, "the hazy, dimly seen figures who move about the shanties in a dreary pantomime suddenly were brought into clear focus as human beings whose mode of life made an ironic mockery of the Chamber of Commerce sign at the city limits: 'A Good Place to Live and Work.'"[88]

The Fund also supported the North Carolina Volunteers program, which recruited young people to work in the summer of 1964 at subsistence wages in community action programs and other local agencies. This was a forerunner to VISTA (Volunteers in Service to America), another of the programs begun by Johnson's Great Society initiative.[89]

But the Fund was more than money and programs. It introduced into local communities concepts that challenged the status quo. Local organizations were required to involve blacks and whites in their leadership. The integrated Fund staff, young and active, was the first of its kind. "It was the first thing in the state of North Carolina that had an integrated staff," Nathan Garrett, a Durham accountant and Fund staff member later recalled. And local organizations were required to bring the poor into the decision making. Billy Barnes, who chronicled the Fund's work as its public relations manager, said, "We wanted to create an atmosphere in which, for the first time, low-income people of both colors were asked, 'What do you think about this?' It was helping people get food stamps and shots for their babies. But more so, it was teaching people who need a fish to fish. It was where low-income and particularly black people started to grab a piece of the action in our state."[90]

The creation of the Fund invigorated Sanford, who told people well before his term was nearing its end that four years just wasn't enough time to get everything done. Like a mechanic who has just learned the use of all his tools, he was eager to deal with as many of the state's problems as he could. "My timetable for everything is Let's get on with it right now," he once said at a news conference.[91]

He found private money to establish the North Carolina Traffic Safety Council and set up a commission to develop new concepts in traffic law enforcement. In the fall of 1963, he established the Commission on the Status of Women, one of the first of its kind in the nation, and named Dr. Anne Scott, a faculty member in the history department at Duke University, as its chair. He asked the commission to study a wide range of women's issues, including discrimination in jobs and pay, and report back to him by the end of the following year. Throughout his administration, he had had Martha McKay looking for women to be nominees to state boards and commissions. "Hell, the women elected him," Martha McKay recalled some years later. "I don't think there is much question that women made a major difference to his campaign." After the election, McKay remained involved. "I looked at every appointment and every committee to see if it had the right women, and enough women, and all that. I asked him for a council for women and he said, 'Yes, go ahead.' " [92]

Even before the commission was established, Sanford had shaken the state's judicial establishment when he elevated Superior Court Judge Susie Sharp to the State Supreme Court. The governor later recalled that when he informed retiring Chief Justice Wallace Winborne of his plans, the severe and proper justice drew upon all his dignity and objected, saying, "But governor, this is a man's court." [93]

The state prison system had not seen such attention from a governor in years. Sanford worked closely with Prison Director George Randall, a former textile executive who had taken the job in the closing days of Luther Hodges's administration. Sanford revived the state's probation services, which he believed were underutilized by judges. In late 1962, he fired the probation director and used emergency funds to hire ten new probation officers. When the 1963 General Assembly came to town, he added another fifty positions. Sanford backed Randall's use of work release, an idea imported from Wisconsin, and added an emphasis on job training and education. At a ceremony at a women's prison marking the first class of graduates to earn their high school equivalency exams, Margaret Rose Sanford delivered the commencement address. By Sanford's final year in office, the state's prison population was declining while the state's general population was growing.

People outside of the state were beginning to take notice that something was happening in the South besides civil rights demonstrations. In the summer of 1963, the NBC *Today Show* broadcast a feature on the Governor's School, a racially integrated, eight-week program for four hundred students with extraordinary talents in the arts and sciences. Barbara Walters, the show's cohost, opened her interview with Sanford by calling him the "education-minded governor." (Two years earlier, the governor had declined to appear on the program after producers said the only thing they were interested in talking about was race relations.)[94]

To Sanford, it seemed that anything was possible with enough time. Then, in late November 1963, the world changed for Sanford and the nation with the assassination of President John Kennedy.

The governor was lunching in Winston-Salem with Bert Bennett, James Gray, publisher of the Winston-Salem newspapers, the *Winston-Salem Journal*'s editor Wallace Carroll, and James "Scotty" Reston, a columnist for the *New York Times*, when a runner from the *Journal* newsroom alerted them that Kennedy had been shot. Reston departed immediately for Washington. Sanford headed back to Raleigh with his Highway Patrol driver Lloyd Burchett at the wheel. He instructed Burchett to avoid any delays at cities along the way and rode silently, absorbed with his thoughts. He learned from the Patrol dispatcher before he arrived at the mansion that the president was dead.

For all of Sanford's public presence, his friendly, disarming nature, he always kept part of himself completely private. His personal reaction to Kennedy's death joined other life-shaping experiences in that place. He never wrote about the feelings of loss that enveloped him on November 22, and in later years he would turn the talk away from his feelings when the subject arose. He would say only that Kennedy's death changed the direction of the world and that from that point on the country lost its sense of purpose and would be long in finding it again.

The official statement from his office on the Friday of Kennedy's death was brief, only ten words; it said simply that the tragedy was "overwhelming." A longer statement, issued the following day, revealed more of what he felt had been taken from him and the American people:

> With passionate concern for all people, often harassed from both sides and from behind, President Kennedy set his strength determinedly for human understanding and world peace, remaining resolute in his faith, undaunted and unafraid.
>
> The valiant soldier of freedom is dead.
>
> All mankind is less.[95]

Six months later Sanford was due to deliver a speech at a memorial tribute in Chapel Hill, but, he said, "I couldn't write a speech. I kept sitting there trying to write a speech and I just couldn't write it."[96] Instead, he crafted a column of verse that included the following:

> The memory of John F. Kennedy
> will be housed in the minds and hearts

of every nation
as long as man is free
as long as men hope to be free.⁹⁷

As soon as arrangements could be made, the Sanfords left Raleigh for Washington to attend the president's funeral. Before the services began, Sanford walked to the White House from his hotel and worked his way through the crowd gathered on the sidewalk across from 1600 Pennsylvania Avenue. When he attempted to cross the street, a policeman pushed him back and refused to let him pass, despite his credentials. Sanford finally talked the officer into taking him by the arm, as if under arrest, and leading him across to the other side. At the White House, Sanford spoke briefly with Robert Kennedy and then left.

Sanford had always felt as if he had a hand on that torch that had been passed to his generation. Kennedy's administration, like his own in North Carolina, marked the beginning of a new era for the nation. Three months before the assassination, on August 10, Robert Kennedy wrote Sanford to commend him on his management of difficult times. "You have shown leadership in this effort," the attorney general wrote, "which could well be followed by many chief executives in the north as well as in your part of the nation." Penned at the bottom was a postscript: "I hope I am not causing too much trouble for you down there. Just deny you ever met me. That is the only advice I can think to give you. Bob." "I haven't denied you yet," Sanford responded in a note.⁹⁸

There were reports in later years that Kennedy planned to dump Lyndon Johnson in favor of another vice presidential nominee in 1964. Mrs. Evelyn Lincoln, Kennedy's secretary, wrote that Sanford was the substitute. Sanford discounted the reference and said that if such a thing had been suggested to him he would have rejected it. To Sanford, replacing one Southerner for another would have made no political sense and only created more problems for a Kennedy reelection campaign, which already was in trouble in the South.⁹⁹

Despite his entrée to the White House, Sanford saw Kennedy infrequently, working most of his requests through Henry Hall Wilson Jr. The governor passed up invitations to state dinners at the White House, if only to show his critics that he was no Kennedy groupie. At one point, Margaret Rose asked why others from North Carolina were dining with the president while they stayed at home. Terry told her that there would be plenty of time for that during Kennedy's second term.

For the most part, Sanford's requests amounted to relatively minor business such as citizen concerns over a Navy bombing range on the Carolina coast and the preservation of the battleship *North Carolina*. During Kennedy's visit to the state in 1961, Sanford also passed along a request from the Special Forces troops at Fort Bragg that they be allowed to wear their green berets as part of their official uniform. As a chief executive himself, Sanford was mindful of how petitioners drained time and attention, and he was reluctant to intrude on a president burdened with the threat of nuclear war and constitutional challenges at home. He asked for so little in the first two years prior to the 1962 elections that Bennett told the governor that the party's fortune, and Sanford's own reputation, would be improved if Sanford could land some bit of pork from the White House. "These little jobs here and there are fine," Bennett wrote, "but there is nothing like that big thing coming to North Carolina." [100] Sanford was working on placement of a major federal health research facility in North Carolina when Kennedy was killed.

Sanford had looked forward to a second term for Kennedy, but knew his reelection would not be easy. The president's popularity had plummeted in the South with the introduction of the Civil Rights Bill. The legislation had angered many of those who had tolerated his enforcement of court orders desegregating the universities in Mississippi and Alabama, but who fiercely objected to federal laws that they believed intruded on the rights of private businesses. Traveling across eastern North Carolina in July 1963, the News & Observer's Roy Parker Jr. visited counties where feelings ran strong. "I'm so mad, I don't want to talk about it," he quoted a young woman he found at the Goldsboro gas company. "It's the Negro thing." [101]

The Civil Rights Bill accelerated the growing discontent of white voters with the Democratic Party. David M. Britt of Fairmont, a former legislator and later a federal judge, wrote Bennett in January 1963, "The main trouble is that we have alienated a large conservative element in our state that have heretofore been loyal to our party on the state and local levels." Britt described himself as a "non-skid" Democrat but warned that whereas "there are thousands like me who are sticking, it is obvious that thousands are leaving us and in my opinion our state leaders in 1963 must strain every nerve to determine the trouble and to attract these people back into the fold." [102]

Bennett was concerned about the angry mood of voters. Writing Raleigh lawyer William Joslin in the fall of 1963, he cast the upcoming campaigns in stark terms: "As you well know, this is basically a race with the John Birchers, the Whiteners and Lennons [conservative members of the state's congressional delegation], against the so-called Bennett-Sanford way of doing business in North Carolina." [103]

But the "Bennett-Sanford way of doing business" was not sitting particularly well either. In midsummer the governor was embarrassed by a letter from one of his appointees to David Reid, the president of the state Young Democrats Club. After Reid moved a YDC meeting from the Sir Walter to the Carolina Hotel, which permitted an integrated meeting, Utilities Commissioner Sam Worthington wrote Reid: "My compliments to you and your nigger constituents. I hope the NAACP and CORE send a raft of them and you get a complete belly full of niggers until they actually spew out of your ears." Sanford cut off a reporter in midsentence when he asked about the affair, saying he was sure Worthington didn't expect such language to appear in public print.[104]

It was assumed by virtually everyone, including Sanford, that Bennett would be the gubernatorial candidate in 1964. Certainly the governor was interested in continuing the momentum of his administration, and after Philpott's death in 1961, Bennett appeared to be the man to do it.[105] Bennett, however, was having second thoughts, and while playing golf with Sanford over the July 4th weekend, he told the governor he was not going to run. Years later, Bennett said he did not have the deep desire required for a successful campaign. Others said Bennett did not want to be on the losing end of a contest with Republican Charles Jonas, the congressman from Lincolnton who had defeated five Democratic challengers. Polling data indicated a strong Republican effort led by Jonas might produce the first GOP governor of the twentieth century.[106]

Bennett's decision came as a surprise to J. Phillips Carlton, whom Bennett had already engaged to direct his campaign. For the past three years, Carlton had attended law school at Chapel Hill while working in the governor's office, where he managed gubernatorial appointments as well as other assignments for Bennett. By the summer of 1963 Carlton had his law degree and was preparing for the campaign when Bennett called him to his Winston-Salem office and told him he was not running. Before they parted, Bennett asked Carlton to stop by Greensboro on his way home and meet U.S. District Judge L. Richardson Preyer of Greensboro, and "do for him what I was planning on doing for Bert." [107]

Preyer had an impressive résumé: grandson of Vick Chemical Company founder Lunsford Richardson, Princeton graduate, distinguished Navy war record, and Harvard Law School. He had practiced law in Greensboro before moving to the state superior court bench. In 1960, he had considered running for attorney general and had thought about a campaign for governor in 1964 until President Kennedy appointed him to the bench.

Preyer had emerged as an attractive and likely candidate after Bennett and Sanford met with Luther Hodges in Washington and Hodges told the two Preyer was someone he could support. "I thought that was a ten-strike," Sanford said later. "You know Hodges and I were not the most intimate of friends [and] this is Hodges's candidate and we can support him. That is a big asset because this more conservative element would tend to look to Hodges and not to me." [108]

A news report in late August of Bennett's decision not to run forced Sanford and Bennett to move quickly. They organized a meeting on September 8 with about fifty veterans of the 1960 campaign who gathered at a Holiday Inn in Greensboro. Shortly after the meeting began, Preyer's name was brought up and one of the group was dispatched to ask the judge to join them. Some took his quick appearance at the door to be manipulation; others later said the meeting had been arranged for Preyer to meet many of those who would handle his campaign across the state. Whatever the underlying purpose of the meeting, which would be an issue months later, Preyer was already prepared to run and announced the following day that he would resign his judgeship and become a candidate.

The entire affair was too closely stage-managed for some. Old-time Scott loyalists felt left out of the decision making and were openly skeptical of the voter appeal of a candidate who was the epitome of wealth and refinement. They couldn't picture a man with degrees from Princeton and Harvard sitting around the country store, pulling on a soft drink and talking about the crops. At one point in the meeting, Lauch Faircloth tapped Bob Scott on the shoulder and whispered, "I haven't heard him say damn yet." [109] Many of Kerr Scott's supporters already believed they were being edged out of the Sanford organization and later floated a trial balloon promoting Bob Scott as a candidate.

There was even deeper concern about the Sanford political apparatus from party conservatives; they feared that if given another four years in office, it would dominate the state for many years to come. One of this group was former superior court judge Dan K. Moore from the town of Canton in the western mountains. Moore had left the bench to become legal counsel for Champion Paper Company and he was eager to run. At age fifty-seven, he believed he didn't have time to wait. When he determined in mid-August that another conservative favorite, I. Beverly Lake, also planned to run, he made his move. A week before Bennett's meeting in Greensboro, Moore phoned the *Asheville Citizen* and announced his candidacy. A few days later he was endorsed by Dr. Henry Jordan; support followed from Senator Sam Ervin Jr. Just after Thanksgiving, on November 30, Lake made his expected announcement and the 1964 field was complete.[110]

From the outset, Lake and Moore tried to make Sanford the central issue of the campaign. Both accused him of trying to pick his successor and campaigned against the "Sanford-Bennett political machine." Sanford attempted to slough off the attacks and said a political machine was just something you called the opponent's organization. If the candidates would just leave him alone, he said in January, he could do his job. He then recited a list of eighty projects on his agenda.

The real wild card in the campaign was once again the race issue. Public attention was focused on Washington, where the Civil Rights Bill would soon carry the full support of President Johnson, who stunned many in the South with his vigorous endorsement of the bill and the entire movement. In North Carolina, the bill would become a political litmus test for candidates in much the same way the Supreme Court's Brown decision had been used four years earlier. Moore and Lake both condemned it. Lake vowed he would not enforce any law he believed unconstitutional. Moore called the bill a "constitutional mockery." Preyer hedged, saying he objected to provisions of the bill, but it should be obeyed as the law of the land if passed. Sanford's chief concern was that a renewal of civil rights demonstrations during the heat of the spring primary campaign would work to Preyer's detriment. Throughout the fall of 1963, Sanford continued to focus the attention of troubleshooters like Coltrane on potential hot spots around the state while he concentrated on meetings with black leaders.

In mid-September, Sanford called a private meeting at the mansion of prominent black leaders from around the state. Included in the group were those who had organized many of the demonstrations. Sanford told them he believed there must be a better way than mass demonstrations and he won some support. Sanford's legal counsel, Joel Fleishman, wrote a friend after the session: "It is an interesting thing to note that the Negro leaders present, in fact, agreed with the governor. They have set about trying to work out additional means of focusing attention on their grievances, and I am hopeful that we might come up with something." [111] Some of those who attended also publicly discouraged a march on the state capitol planned for early October by Golden Frinks, an organizer in eastern North Carolina for Dr. King's Southern Christian Leadership Conference.[112]

The campus at A&T in Greensboro finally was relatively quiet. Before classes resumed in the fall of 1963, Mayor Schenck had pleaded with Sanford to meet with college administrators to pressure them to keep students on campus and off the streets. Sanford urged the mayor to talk to Waynick, thus dodging personal involvement. In a confidential note to Waynick, he said he had no intention of pressuring college presidents: "You should stress the point that they cannot substitute force of this kind in place of creative leadership in solving the problems. If would simply be a matter of deferring what is obviously going to come in Greensboro, and soon." [113]

Indeed, the governor had found an ally in Jesse Jackson, who had returned that fall as president of the student body. Jackson was a natural leader who carried his college honors with no lack of humility. When A&T President Samuel Proctor resumed his duties that fall after a leave of absence with President Kennedy's new Peace Corps, one of the first persons at his office door was Jackson. Proctor's secretary had scheduled Jackson for an appointment later in the week, after Proctor had first talked with his deans, but Jackson broke in line. "Jesse was standing outside my door at 7:30 in the morning," Proctor recalled, "He said, 'As one president to another, I thought you and I ought to talk.' I had not thought of him as being the president of anything. He thought of himself as president equal with me in running the school. That was Jesse." [114]

Proctor shared none of Dowdy's misgivings about Sanford's intervention the previous spring. He liked the governor and the two talked often, speaking candidly about any situation on campus. "We 'the people' trusted. That meant that when he decided to do things for us it had almost absolute approval because people trusted him so. I don't know why, but he was never looked at as one of the rank-and-file politicians. He was always looked at as someone who came at it from another point of departure. Politics was politics generally, but now and then somebody emerges who looks like he is above the pack. Terry Sanford looked that way." [115]

Jesse Jackson came to enjoy his new entrée at the governor's office, where he had been hired to coordinate the production of a series of films on civil rights, one of the ideas broached by Sanford at the meeting in September as an alternative to street demonstrations. In late October, Jackson asked Sanford to issue an invitation to a mansion luncheon for three to four students from each of the black campuses in the state. "I would like to talk with you before the luncheon, so that we may synchronize our thoughts and efforts," Jackson wrote the governor. "I prefer just students—no civil rights officials, college presidents or anybody. I have four students from here." [116]

Altogether four films were produced and gave voice to the frustrations of the young black people who made up the crowds that had marched in Greensboro, Charlotte, Durham, Raleigh, and other cities. In one, titled *Good-bye to Carolina*, a senior in engineering at A&T explained that a lack of jobs in North Carolina meant 90 percent of his class would seek employment outside the state after graduation. "I would much rather stay in the state and work. But things being what they are, it is impossible," said another. Another film, produced under the title *We're Not Alone*, included observations from a Panamanian student studying at Bennett College who talked about discrimination exported by whites abroad: "Americans try to make you feel that you are so much inferior."

The black students expressed themselves in a way that many whites probably had never heard. Their stories broke through the stereotypes and simple language of picket signs and the carefully framed demurrals that their elders who worked as maids and mechanics reserved for conversations with white employers. "Ever since I have been a small child," one young woman said, "my parents taught me to stand up for what I believe in. Demonstrations for me are a last resort. I feel that by moving to the streets Negroes are trying to awaken the consciousness of white America to the injustices of so many years." Many had been not only on the streets, but in jail. "In all of that noise and all that filth, I felt I had found sanctuary . . . and for the first time I think I believed in God."

"There is a tendency of many in the older generation to advocate a go-slow policy, but they are now being run over by the militancy of the Negro student movement," said James Ferguson, president of the student body at North Carolina Central. "This freedom must come and it must come now." [117]

Sanford also gave Jackson a taste of Democratic Party politics. New YDC chapters on black campuses had come out of the summer summit in the house chamber and Jackson was proving to be an astute strategist and effective political organizer. "In my own subtle manner," he informed the governor in the fall, "I have generated the desire for a voter-registration project here. (In so doing, some of the Demonstration Extremists have been absorbed.) If we handle ourselves properly, we can swing a helluva lot of votes out of this county for Preyer, also." [118]

In late January 1964, Jackson joined the state YDC delegation in Las Vegas for the national convention, where Al House, a thirty-two-year-old lawyer from Roanoke Rapids, North Carolina, was making a bid for the national presidency. The arrival of North Carolina's integrated delegation attracted attention, particularly from House's opponent, who was from Massachusetts, which sent an all-white delegation. Jackson found the convention a welcome new sea in which to swim. He would disappear within the crowd, where he met Willie Brown, a Californian who would later be mayor of San Francisco, and Harold Washington, later mayor of Chicago.[119] He spoke well of his governor, telling a reporter, "He became governor at a very difficult time, a time when the state was moving out of an old political era into a new one. It has taken courage." [120] Many years later, in a speech to a gathering of young black leaders, Jackson would credit Sanford with giving him a rare political opportunity at an early age.

The civil rights demonstrations resumed in 1964 in the most unlikely of spots, Chapel Hill, where more integration had taken place than in any other city in the state. Only a handful of the more than two hundred businesses in Chapel Hill still refused to serve blacks. Black students attended all public schools, and the school board had had a black member since 1953. In late January, James Farmer, flanked by CORE's new national director, Floyd McKissick, threatened massive demonstrations unless Chapel Hill became an "open city" by February 1.

Sanford answered Farmer's challenge immediately, issuing a stern rebuke—stronger than even his troubleshooter Capus Waynick could endorse—and said neither the town nor the state would be threatened. He promised full support for town officials and set up another showdown with CORE.[121] "I felt that I had been pushed around long enough," Sanford later recalled. "When Farmer and McKissick promised to shut down the government, I reminded them that they didn't have the power and I wasn't going to let them do it. I talked very tough to them and I should have talked tough to them."[122]

All the Democratic gubernatorial candidates supported Sanford's tough stand, but the exchange offered Lake an opportunity to get in a lick at his old competitor. Sanford's statement was "three years too late," Lake told reporters; he said if he were governor he would fire any faculty member, university employee, or student who took part in a demonstration, a threat he would repeat throughout the campaign.

There was no mistaking the tension building in the state. Ku Klux Klan membership was growing rapidly; burning crosses on courthouse lawns and at rallies in towns across the state were seen with greater frequency than ever before. As this kind of activity increased, Sanford asked Hugh Cannon to get what information he could on the Klan from the FBI. When the agency reported back with little useful information, the governor used an undercover agent from the state Department of Motor Vehicles to infiltrate the Klan. "Within a week he was in eastern North Carolina," Cannon recalled. "He had a pickup truck with Mississippi tags on it, had a Mississippi driver's license and said he was in the cattle business." The agent eventually gained the confidence of Klan leaders, whom he allowed to win some of his state expense money in late-night poker games. He eventually became so involved that he was elected an officer in a local Klavern. "He wrote up a report after about two or three months of all they planned to do and we got it typed up and sent it to [the U.S. Justice Department]," Cannon said. "About two months later, the FBI announced that North Carolina was one of the biggest Klan memberships in the nation."[123]

Sanford's aides also were briefed regularly on the work of a second informer, who was recruited by the American Defamation League of B'nai B'rith and who reached the upper tier of the Klan organization run by Grand Dragon Robert Jones of Granite Quarry.[124]

The thirty-eight-year-old Jones was a salesman who discovered he could make more money running the Klan than he could selling lightning rods. He was a flamboyant speaker who traveled the state in a Cadillac with a pistol in the front seat and the trunk full of overpriced robes, pamphlets, and Klan paraphernalia. Beginning in early April, he began a series of weekly rallies that always ended with a fiery cross. As the primary election neared, he pledged to burn crosses in fifty of the state's one hundred counties as a demonstration of Klan strength.

Bennett remained fully confident of victory and believed the campaign would be a repeat of 1960, with Preyer leading in the first primary and then defeating Lake in a runoff. A few weeks before the election, however, Preyer's pollster, Joseph Napolitan, showed Bennett numbers that put Moore, not Lake, in second place. Bennett didn't believe him and sent Napolitan back to check his numbers. He returned with the same standings. "It surprised the hell out of me," Bennett later recalled. "We had a conduit to the Lake group. We sent word that "We hear you are in third place, we'll help you. Leave the word 'help' open." We got word back that 'You are going to need the help. I am in first place.' That was the word we got back." [125]

Most knew where Sanford stood, though he never declared himself publicly and refused to respond to most of the attacks from Moore and Lake. Questions about the campaign were off limits at his news conferences, which provoked the *Charlotte Observer*'s Jay Jenkins to complain that "to make these topics taboo you revert to innocuous inquiries which could just as well be handled in sign language." [126]

Remaining out of the fight ran against all Sanford's instincts and those of his wife, who urged him to do as had the governor of her home state of Kentucky and vigorously defend his administration and publicly support his choice of successor. He did what he could behind the scenes but feared public involvement would only raise the visibility of the kingmaker claims. In later years, Sanford said he regretted he didn't do more.

As election day approached, Sanford did urge Hodges to declare himself for Preyer when he saw Hodges in Reidsville shortly before the election: "I said if you will come out for him, we don't need but a few thousand votes. [Preyer] wasn't going to win in the first primary, but it would have shifted the one-two from Preyer and Moore to Preyer and Lake." [127] Hodges made no pronouncements, and Sanford called it a "real betrayal" by the man who had been instrumental in Preyer's candidacy in the first place.

On election night, when it was clear that Moore, not Lake, would face Preyer in a second primary, Bennett knew it was over. "You could almost just fold the tent," Bennett said. Yet the Preyer campaign went through the motions to enlist Lake's support, although all realized it would strain the credibility of both men if the most conservative candidate endorsed the most liberal. A few days later, Carlton and Nat Townsend, a Raleigh lawyer who was Preyer's official campaign chairman, paid a call on Lake to see what he would require for an endorsement. After the meeting, they found Sanford and Bennett standing in the trooper's station on the first floor of the mansion and made their report. Lake wanted one-third of all appointments and a guarantee that if Preyer were elected he would not appoint either Sanford or Bennett to the U.S. Senate if a vacancy arose. Both men immediately agreed to Lake's stipulation about the Senate, but word was sent to Lake that his price was too high.[128]

As expected, Lake endorsed Moore in a political swan song that compiled all the sins of his opposition for more than a decade. Lake said he had his concerns about Moore's connections to big business, but Preyer's affiliations with liberals was a greater sin. Judge Preyer was a nice man, Lake said. He was earnest and honest, but he was the representative of liberals, communists, civil rights demonstrators, the NAACP, and the "noisy clique of professional liberals at Chapel Hill who are a red and festering sore upon the body of the great university." [129]

The close of Preyer's campaign came on a Friday evening at a television studio in Charlotte with the broadcast of endorsements of his candidacy from Tom Pearsall, L. P. McLendon of Greensboro, and Sanford, who readily agreed to publicly declare himself when Preyer asked for his help. "I knew I wasn't going to change anything," Sanford later recalled, "but I figured that, by God, if everybody else went down with the ship then I would be on it. I made a damn good speech, I might say." [130]

Tom Lambeth remembered it as one of his best. The night before his appearance the governor asked for suggestions from his staff. He called Ehle to join him at the mansion to craft a speech. "We're trying to fill an inside straight," he told Ehle. The novelist pitched in that evening, as did others, but Sanford ended up writing most of his speech in the limousine on the way to Charlotte, pecking it out on a typewriter balanced on the jump seat.

Sanford gave a robust defense of his administration, acknowledging that not everyone had agreed with his way of doing things. But why, he asked, would the state's next governor want to dismantle the Good Neighbor Council or educational programs like the Learning Institute of North Carolina? He reached into his childhood, recalling the relay races with other boys at Roper's Farm when each was expected to do his best:

> I am pleading that we let the great race for progress in North Carolina be run by the candidate who wants to run—not walk—and is willing to run hard, who wants to win for North Carolina.

You alone make the decision—you choose the runner. I have one vote and I'm not telling you how to vote. But I'm saying, please put the man in who is willing to run the race all of the way.[131]

On election day, Terry and Margaret Rose voted and the family headed to the mountains for a few days of rest. Along the way, Terry told the family Preyer would lose, and that was the last said about the campaign.[132]

In addition to his disappointment over Hodges, Sanford felt a deep sense of betrayal by civil rights leaders who had persisted in demonstrations in Chapel Hill. The marches, sit-ins, and protests were a reminder for a majority of voters who had long lost patience with the movement. Had they not taken their challenge to Chapel Hill, Sanford believed the race issue might not have been as significant a factor in the primaries: "Basically they were good crusaders, and what they basically wanted to achieve was proper, [but] to come here in the middle of a hot campaign, where the old racist, Dr. Lake, was running again and to deliberately plan to have a confrontation couldn't help but elect Lake, or certainly defeat the more enlightened candidate."[133]

The vote for Moore was overwhelming, and Lake called the outcome a repudiation of Sanford's administration, but Sanford refused to be drawn into a public fight. "You know I refrained from entering any kind of debate with Mr. Lake for a long time and I think I can restrain one more day," he told reporters. The governor said he was more inclined to accept the winner's analysis that people were voting for Dan Moore, not against Terry Sanford.[134] But that was simply slicing the same cake another way. Moore had made Sanford and his administration an issue in the campaign, and much of what Sanford had begun was in jeopardy. Ahead lay four years of conservative government. Moore's judicial temperament and passive style suited his coterie of conservative supporters just fine.

In the six months that remained in his term, Sanford began looking for ways to secure his programs that might be vulnerable to a new administration. Before he left office, he asked the governor-elect's wife, Jeannelle, to join the board of trustees of the North Carolina School of the Arts. She accepted and formed a fast friendship with Mary and James Semans of Durham, the school's most steadfast benefactors and supporters. The school survived its formative years and grew in strength during the next four years. A summer internship program in the governor's office that immersed college students in state government was shifted to the Institute of Government in Chapel Hill. The North Carolina Fund added Ed Rankin, who was destined to be the governor-elect's chief aide, to its board of directors and at least provided a linkage of understanding. The Fund programs that Moore had found so objectionable in the campaign were paid for by private money and beyond his reach. In fact, the antipoverty efforts expanded during the next four years as North Carolina and other states took advantage of a flow of federal money pouring out of Lyndon Johnson's Great Society programs.

Yet there were casualties. Sanford's efforts at reforms in corrections later were cut short when Moore replaced Prison Director George Randall with his own appointee, who was a man with a decidedly different attitude. Randall's progressive programs of rehabilitation, education, and counseling were curtailed and allowed to wither. Within a year, the state had its first major prison riot. The Film Board was not refunded, although it was picked up by the North Carolina Fund and continued for a brief time.

Moore retained the Good Neighbor Council and left Coltrane in charge, but it was renamed the North Carolina Human Relations Commission and tucked into the folds of state government. Efforts to boost employment of blacks were curtailed, and Sarah Herbin, who had led recruitment of black candidates for state jobs, returned to her home in Greensboro. However, the governor's emphasis on hiring had had its desired effect. Eight months before he left office, the state's largest textile mill had hired more African American workers than in the previous ten years combined, retail stores were adding clerks, and in state government "Negroes have been employed in the following non-traditional areas: draftsmen, park rangers, counselors, factory inspectors, tax auditors, parole and probation officers, dental technicians, prison guards, accounting clerks, duplicating machine operators and maintenance mechanics." And there were 255 black students on traditionally all-white campuses.[135]

Few governors leave office as popular figures, but Sanford was probably less popular than most. He had asked for higher taxes, introduced more new programs than people could count, and pulled North Carolina along the road to racial integration faster than many whites had wanted to go. In August 1964, the charred remnants of a crude burned cross were found on the mansion lawn. But as the administration was drawing to a close, Bowles gave a spirited defense when he spoke to a Goldsboro civic club in November. "I know full well that a sizable percentage of you men in this room don't care for Terrible Terry," he told the Goldsboro crowd.

> You've made up your minds that he is a sorry governor and you don't want me or anybody else to confuse you with the facts. I only ask that you give me the courtesy of your attention. Try to listen without punching holes in what I'm saying as I go along.
>
> This, gentlemen, is a lesson in history—hot off the stove—for

you've watched history in the making these last few years, these fast, furious, fruitful years of the Sanford administration.

First of all, he promised so much that it would take all of my allotted time to go over the list. He was full of ideas. Second, he not only delivered all that he promised but he gave us many bonuses. He told me a few months ago that he would have promised more than just his thirty-two-point program, but he just didn't realize that so much needed to be done and could be done in this office of governor.

Bowles tallied the score: improvements in education unequaled since Charles Aycock's term a half-century earlier; more roads built and paved than by Kerr Scott; more new jobs created and industry expanded than by Luther Hodges. And he applauded Sanford's reasoned approach to civil rights. "It truly has been a new day in the old North State," he declared.[136]

Bowles had come in with Sanford and stayed to the end as a loyal ally. In early December he presided at a tribute to Sanford that drew a crowd of six thousand to the State Fair Grounds in Raleigh, where Bowles presented a mock check made out to "Ole Terry" for $25,000 signed by "Skipper and a gang of friends." (Sanford sent the real one to Methodist College to become part of a scholarship fund.)

Most in the Sanford family were ready as the date approached for the return to their Sylvan Drive home in Fayetteville, eager to settle into a normal home life. "I like politics," Margaret Rose told a reporter, "and I think I'll always be interested in it. Sometimes, I'd like for Terry to go back home and make some money. We'll just barely break even in these four years. You can't make anything at this job."[137]

As for the governor, Sanford joked that he felt like the beauty queen who was having so much fun she was reluctant to give up the crown. He spent five days on the Yale University campus in November as a Chubb Fellow talking with students about his administration and a life in public service. He told them, "Public service enables you to accomplish things that all your life you wanted to do, but never could." As he finished one of his end-of-term newspaper interviews, he told a reporter, "I'd do it again, yes sir. And I may."[138]

At the time, *Time* magazine called him "one of the most memorable instances of progressive southern leadership in recent history."[139] Yet, there also was a gnawing in his gut that he had so much more to do. The schedule in the closing months was as busy as when he first took office. He urged the Research Triangle Institute to begin work on developing low-cost housing and he organized the Crescent 2000 Commission to study the future of the state's rapidly growing Piedmont. He traveled to Washington to sit for his official portrait and went on to New York with daughter Betsee to call on Jacqueline Kennedy, where he, Hugh Morton, and Joel Fleishman presented the state's contribution for the construction of the Kennedy Library. "Remember 1960?" Mrs. Kennedy asked the governor. "Wasn't it a wonderful year?" Before they left, she borrowed Morton's camera to snap a picture of her visitors from the South.[140]

In early December Sanford commuted the active prison terms imposed on a dozen of those convicted as a result of protests in Chapel Hill in a long, publicized trial before an uncompromising judge. *Chapel Hill Weekly* editor Jim Shumaker wrote that the commutations "might come back to haunt Terry Sanford, since there doesn't seem to be an outside chance that he is taking the veil for good. Although aware that this might cost him later on, he did what was right, and even for an honest and courageous man that is not always an easy thing to do." [141] He also signed a pardon for Boyd Payton, the labor organizer whose sentence he had commuted three years earlier.

Finally, almost as he was reaching for the door, he announced that the federal government was locating a $25 million environmental research facility at the Research Triangle Park. The political pork that Bennett had asked for two years earlier had arrived after years of cajoling and maneuvering, first with Kennedy and later with Johnson. North Carolina succeeded in winning the site despite heavy lobbying from a half-dozen other states.

There was other unfinished business. Sanford was disappointed that hiring of black employees in state government had not moved at a faster pace, and he regretted not earlier turning his attention to changes in the state's prisons. "One of the most elusive efforts, one that will continue to taunt my imagination was our effort to reform the prison system," he later wrote.[142] Sanford was most concerned for the average inmate and the "hopelessness, the inadequacies of penal reclamation and rehabilitation." He remained personally ambivalent toward the death penalty and did not stop the execution of Theodore Boykin, a thirty-one-year-old black man convicted of rape and murder, who died in the state's gas chamber on October 27, 1961. Boykin's execution passed with little public notice and no thorough review by the governor. Even his lawyer wrote Sanford to say that justice was served.[143] Two years later, however, as the state prepared for two more executions, Sanford commuted two death sentences, including one involving the death of a policeman in Charlotte, after a judge familiar with the case wrote him expressing doubts that justice had been served. The letter troubled Sanford, who thoroughly investigated the case before issuing a commutation. Boykin was the last prisoner executed in North Carolina until 1984, after the death penalty was restored following a 1972 U.S. Supreme Court decision that ruled prior procedures were unconstitutional.

Just prior to January 4, 1965, Sanford went to the studios of WTVD-TV in Durham and taped his last report to the people. In the studio with him was a group of students from his daughter's high school in Raleigh. For thirty minutes he talked to them about his administration in a relaxed, conversational style, roaming from topic to topic, more like a teacher or friend than a governor. It was an engaging performance that was a blend of FDR's fireside chats, Sunday nights with Frank Graham, his mother's classroom, and supper table conversations with his father. He was earnest, understanding to the point of simplicity, and talked of the importance of creating new jobs, improving education, building roads, changing the way the criminals are housed and the mentally ill are treated, and planning for the future.

> In North Carolina, we believe we can lead in the advancement of civilization, and as I've said before, I hope we can become the most civilized community in all the world.
>
> We're going to do it by concerning ourselves with people, working with people and providing for them a better opportunity in life. And I believe if we put our trust in people, and if our weapon against poverty and bigotry is education, we can conquer all the battles and make North Carolina a leader of all the rest of the nation.
>
> You can be a part of that leadership. That's what this administration has been about.[144]

During his term, Sanford did the things most modern governors were expected to do. He built roads, boosted education, and recruited new industry that created jobs. Measures of his administration were the miles of asphalt, the additional dollars in a teacher's paycheck, and the number of new factories and businesses. There had been no scandals, although there were the usual complaints of cronyism in highway construction. He had cleaned up a few messy situations during his term, and had insisted on a full investigation of a college basketball point-shaving scandal. Despite its early anxiety, the state's conservative business establishment had received treatment as good as if not better than what it had enjoyed under Luther Hodges. Sanford had not disturbed the cozy relationship among bankers, power companies, and others dependent on state regulation for their growing profits.

At the same time, life was changing in North Carolina and elsewhere in the South. Sanford sounded proud of his role in effecting that change in an article he wrote for *Look* magazine that he titled "The Case for the New South." In it Sanford argued that the stereotypes of the South no longer applied. Leaders like himself who had been born in the twentieth century "have resolved to improve the South's economy by improving all of its parts, and to bring about the orderly acceptance of the Negro into the Southern community, guaranteeing him every right and privilege granted under the law." Prejudice would fall under the weight of economic progress, he said.[145]

Outside of North Carolina, Sanford's administration would be remembered for its moderate, even liberal approach to civil rights. *Look* reported that during his term Sanford had "supported the Negro first for equality more vigorously than any public official in Southern history." [146] He would see his four years as much more than that.

Sanford's real legacy was his energizing spirit and innovative programs and initiatives in education, the arts, job training, and community building. For four years, the state had been a laboratory for ideas and a demonstration of what could result with a creative chief executive who enjoyed using the power of the governor's office to make things happen.

CHAPTER FOURTEEN

New Horizons

MOST OF THE FORMER GOVERNORS of North Carolina had left office late in life. If they had further ambitions, they were usually political. Clyde Hoey, J. M. Broughton, Kerr Scott, and Luther Hodges had all ended up in Washington. Terry Sanford had no such plans. He was forty-seven years old when he opened a new law practice and the family returned home to Sylvan Road in Fayetteville. They had teenagers in tow, and Margaret Rose was hoping that life among familiar faces and places would bring some semblance of normalcy.

Mansion life had presented the children with experiences available to a limited few. When the daughter of the President of the United States visited North Carolina with her father, Betsee set a prim and proper pose for cameramen when she greeted Lynda Bird Johnson. Terry Jr. got his picture in the paper receiving an autographed baseball from New York Yankee Roger Maris, a meeting that almost didn't take place because the boy was miffed that Maris, not his hero Mickey Mantle, had broken the home run record of Yankee slugger Babe Ruth.

Margaret Rose had tried to maintain a sense of balance during the family's stay in Raleigh. She and Terry had talked to the children about not taking advantage of a staff of household servants and others who responded to their whims and wishes. Yet, one evening, only minutes after a fatherly chat, Terry heard his son call from the top of the grand staircase, "Hey, somebody get me a Sun Spot." Such convenience was just too tempting, young Terry later recalled.

Margaret Rose hoped her son would acquire a taste for music, so she bought him a guitar. She paid for lessons, but soon found that he was learning blues licks from a prison department trusty, one of the mansion staff who lived in the mansion basement. One of the other trusties with a couple of seasons in semipro baseball in his past gave him tips, and another taught him how to throw a punch after Terry arrived home a bit bruised from a schoolyard scuffle. He wasn't going to be picking up an education like that on Sylvan Road.

Sanford was virtually starting over. To avoid conflicts of interest when he became governor, he had severed connections with his law firm in Fayetteville and resigned from the board of directors of an insurance company he had represented. He had remained as chairman of the Methodist College board, but he figured no one could find fault with that. A few months before the end of his term, Sanford agreed to form a new firm in Raleigh with his budget director Hugh Cannon and John Hunter III, one of Cannon's classmates from Davidson College, along with Charlie Rose III, the son of his first Fayetteville partner. Sanford planned to commute from his home in Fayetteville.

The partners arranged for space in a new high-rise office building under construction on Fayetteville Street in Raleigh that housed the offices of Branch Banking & Trust Company. When the building was not ready in January, the four took rooms at the Carolina Hotel, dodging about town to meet clients at their offices. Eventually, Sanford's corner office on an upper floor of the BB&T building gave him a clear view up Fayetteville street to the state capitol. He covered one wall with a map of the world.

The law firm provided a supporting platform for Sanford's wide-ranging interests, and he was a productive member, not just a name on the door. When the firm opened its doors, he had retainers from Southern Railway and Coronet Films, a division of Esquire magazine that produced educational materials for classroom teachers. Others seeking an entrée to state government followed. Some were disappointed. Although the firm took clients whose business required appearances before state regulatory agencies, where his successor Dan K. Moore would be naming members, Sanford prohibited legislative lobbying to avoid the appearance of trading on past political favors.[1]

Sanford did not plan to spend all his time unraveling the problems of his legal clients, however. Before he left office, he had talked to Paul Ylvisaker of the Ford Foundation about undertaking a study of the American states. In April 1965, the Ford and Carnegie Foundations announced that Sanford would lead the $280,000 project from a base at Duke University.

The American states study was tailor-made for Sanford. Scholars had begun to seriously question the viability of state governments and whether they could survive in the modern age when the nation's problems spanned political boundaries. If anyone could find some hope for state government, it might be Sanford, whose administration was regarded as one of the most creative in the country. Joining him for the work were Eli Evans, a Yale law graduate from Durham who had worked in Richardson Preyer's campaign; political scientist Thad Beyle, who had worked in the governor's office as a faculty fellow; and writer David Ethridge, a Chapel Hill graduate who had been editor of the *Daily Tar Heel*.

Much of that first year was devoted to implementation of an idea with broader implications. Before Sanford left office, he had received a copy of James B. Conant's book, *My Several Lives*, from John Gardner, the president of the Carnegie Corporation. The book was the concluding work in a series of studies of American education in which the former president of Harvard proposed the creation of a nationwide educational policy to be developed cooperatively by twelve or fifteen of the larger states. This interstate compact would examine issues in education and suggest roles for the states and the federal government.

Conant admired Sanford's education initiatives as governor and was delighted when he agreed to undertake the creation of what later came to be known as the Education Commission of the States. Conant readily accepted one major modification at Sanford's suggestion: Instead of commission members receiving their appointments from legislatures, Sanford argued that governors were better suited to initiate new programs. He also proposed that all the states, not just a few, be included. By the middle of 1965, Sanford had gathered enough evidence of the need for such a compact, and he had produced an outline of the project that he took to the National Governors' Conference sessions in Minneapolis.

In his autobiography, Conant wrote: "Governor Sanford had envisioned a body in which governors, state legislators and educators from all the states would come together to share their knowledge and discuss plans for the future.... I began to realize what a master workman had taken over the task of creating a new educational agency. The combination of Sanford's boldness, ingenuity and charm carried all before him."[2]

That September, Sanford presided over a planning conference for the commission that he scheduled for Kansas City, Missouri. The location was convenient to travelers coming from east and west, and Sanford offered the lure of an opportunity for the governors to meet former president Harry Truman, who lived in nearby Independence. A year later, the commission opened a headquarters in Denver, with Wendell H. Pierce as executive director. Thirty years later the commission was still thriving and honored Sanford at its James Bryant Conant Symposium.

Sanford also was finishing work on a book about his governorship. He titled it *But What About the People?* and it was published in 1966, with Conant writing the preface. Sanford took the title from a line in a Carl Sandburg poem, "The People Yes." A year later he published a second book, *Storm*

Over the States, which was the product of the American states study. Sanford had surprised his assistants by crafting the books with more detail than they had expected. "He sketched out what he thought the chapter should be like. He had thought a lot about these questions and in a way we were being peppered with memos and ideas all the time," Evans recalled later. "This was not our book, it was his book."[3]

In the summer of 1967, the Sanfords headed to Europe. Sanford had been asked to participate in a month-long seminar on American education at the Salzburg Institute of American Studies, where students from around the continent gathered at Schloss Leopoldskron, a palatial estate where much of the popular movie *Sound of Music* had been filmed. In late summer, the family packed for the trip and left a month early to allow for personal travel before Sanford was due in Salzburg.

They sailed on the SS *France* to England and then traveled on to France, where Sanford rented a car and drove the family east into Belgium and the village of Joigny, where he was billeted in the months after the Battle of the Bulge. The town had changed little in the twenty-two years since the war's end, and Sanford took his family to the courtyard where the 517th's colors had been lowered on the day he and the other survivors of the brutal winter campaign shipped out for the States. He drove to a large military cemetery to visit the grave of a cousin who had been killed just two or three days after entering combat. It was a moving experience and one that left him with questions. "I noted with some perplexity that the keeper of the grounds, the person with whom we talked and who gave us directions, was a native German," Sanford later wrote. "I never hated the German people, even when I was engaged in he middle of combat. Still, there was a symbolism here which I could not then define, and one that has puzzled me since. Here . . . was a German tending the graves for the United States government of our comrades who had been slain by his countrymen. It was not that I resented it. I knew he was too young even to have been involved."[4]

The trip was a refreshing break for the family. Never far from Sanford's mind, however, was the question of his own future. The law firm was successful, and he had enjoyed the travel and work on the Carnegie and Ford projects that had introduced him to a wide range of leaders in public offices around the country. But he was ready for a new challenge.

A return engagement as governor was always possible, but never clearly defined. No North Carolina governor had ever returned to office, which made the notion all the more enticing to Sanford, who believed he had left unfinished business behind. For the present, he believed the state was standing still, if not moving backward. He never spoke unkind words about his successor, but he was disappointed in Moore's administration.[5]

The differences in politics and style between Moore and Sanford were striking. Moore approached the office as a judge, ruling on proposals that crossed his desk, unlike Sanford, who daily looked for new approaches to old problems. Sanford embraced the ambitions of the national Democratic Party; Moore kept his distance. At the 1964 Democratic National Convention in Atlantic City, a whooping, orchestrated anointing of incumbent President Lyndon Johnson, Moore had denied the party's civil rights platform plank and refused to withdraw his appointment of an ally who had signed a petition in support of George Wallace's short-lived campaign for the presidency. In the fall, Moore had avoided close association with the Johnson-Humphrey campaign while Sanford campaigned heartily for the president at home and in other states and rode every mile of a cross-state whistle-stop tour with Mrs. Johnson. Moore's wife, Jeanelle, came along for the train ride, but her husband only reluctantly joined in a campaign that produced the last great Democratic landslide election of the century.

Sanford's administration had been clean and productive, but Moore acted as if his predecessor had spoiled the nest. He had little interest in Sanford's programs and initiatives. With the party's conservatives re-installed in state government, Treasurer Edwin Gill renewed his entrée to the governor's office. Even ambitious improvements in the community college system were sidelined as too extravagant. Early in Moore's term, Dallas Herring had appealed to Gill for help in restoring some of the cuts, only to learn that Gill himself had written the reductions in state spending into Moore's budget address. And, at his first opportunity, Moore had appointed Beverly Lake to the state supreme court, filling part of the bargain made after the first primary. Lake supporters also took important jobs in the administration.

The 1968 political season was approaching as Sanford returned from Europe. As much as he might want to make an unprecedented run for a second term, Sanford deferred to the ambitions of Bob Scott, who had been elected lieutenant governor in 1964 and was preparing a campaign for governor. The only other office that held any interest was the U.S. Senate seat currently occupied by Sam Ervin Jr., who had never faced a serious challenge. Sanford considered him beatable.

Relations between Sanford and Ervin had not improved with time; the two remained at opposite poles. Sanford considered Ervin to be a "constitutional racist"[6] who had used his influence in the Senate to impede the progress of civil rights. Sanford's defection to Kennedy in 1960 remained a source of irritation for Ervin. "To this day [he] has never gotten over it," Sanford recalled in a 1971 interview, "and he keeps telling people that I'm a liar because when I told him that we ought to have a dozen people for Kennedy, that I didn't tell him that I might be one of them. And from that day to this he has been very vicious in his comments about me, but I don't care."[7]

Ervin, and to some extent Jordan as well, had never done any favors for Sanford in Washington. In August 1964, after Preyer's defeat in the Democratic primary, Ervin was asked by a Johnson aide to comment on a Sanford appointment to the president's antipoverty program. "I would say politically he is somewhat poverty-stricken," the senator said. The aide further reported to Johnson that "Senator Jordan, without a second's hesitation, replied: 'I don't think much of him,' and asked that he not be quoted."[8] Two years later, White House aide Marvin Watson reported to the president that Ervin might approve of a Sanford appointment to a State Department post: "He said he thought that would be fine and he would be good for it. Senator Ervin said it would get Sanford out of the State and get him far away. Senator Ervin said Governor Sanford had been saying he may run against him and he thought it would be good if he could get an appointment out of the country."[9]

Sanford's interest in a Senate campaign seemed to rise more from his boredom on the sidelines of public life rather than any ambitions to become a senator. He had never been as interested in joining the Senate as he had in being governor and had said so on numerous occasions. He was convinced that the office of chief executive was far superior to being one of a group. As governor, he could control his own destiny; the Senate's clubby nature discouraged individual initiative. A governor could get something done; a senator could work for years and effect little change. A governor could speak for his state; a senator shared his voice with others. A governor was close to the people he served; a senator was stuck in Washington most of the year.

Despite any misgivings he might have about the Senate, Sanford told a Greensboro television station in November 1967, "I would very much like to run for the United States Senate." At the time, he had already begun mapping out plans to open campaign offices in Raleigh, Asheville, Charlotte, Greenville, and Kinston and was looking for a hundred people to put up $1,000 each to finance the initial expenses. He also was reading the results of a recent survey of North Carolina voter attitudes. Voters tended to like Sanford, the poll showed. He was seen as a sincere man of conviction, a friendly young man, who as governor had produced a good record for education and highways. Even the negatives on the "food tax" appeared to have faded. Two out of three said he had done a good job as governor, just the reverse of the numbers after his first year in office.

Yet a campaign against Ervin would not be easy. Fewer voters could position Ervin on the political spectrum than they could Sanford, but those who knew the senator put him right where North Carolina voters thought their elected representatives ought to be. "Today," the poll report said, "Ervin is only 2 points more conservative and Sanford is 22 points more liberal than these voters think of themselves." If Sanford ran, the pollsters advised, he would have to use words in his speeches and campaign literature like "thoughtful," "down-to-earth," "level-headed," "mainstream," "responsible," and "moderate." "In a very real sense, Mr. Sanford must play a game of semantics."

The race issue was a factor. After a summer of televised reports of urban riots—Detroit had exploded in flames and mayhem—half of those interviewed *volunteered* concern over race. Overall, segregationist sentiment outweighed pro–civil rights declarations by three to one. "The entire matter of race for Mr. Sanford is rife with danger," the pollster reported. If he ran, he was advised to take an early position for "peace in our cities" and urge the use of National Guard troops and police to use force at the first sign of civil disorder: "We counsel the governor to talk to this point even when there are sizable numbers of Negroes in the audience." [10]

It was a troubling report. North Carolina voters were angry about the war in Vietnam, and angry about what they saw happening in the streets; it was clear that if Sanford were to position himself as an alternative to Ervin he would have to repudiate his own record. He had refused to use displays of force by armed troops five years earlier—how could he advocate it now? Voters were also looking for someone to take on Lyndon Johnson, whose ratings in North Carolina were pitifully low.

Despite these negatives, plus an early reading that Ervin held a three-to-one lead, Sanford continued with his plans. In early January his campaign office sent letters to two hundred thousand Democrats in selected precincts across the state. The message over Sanford's printed signature was brief, just six paragraphs long; the language reflected some of the readings from the poll. "I want to go to the Senate," Sanford wrote, "because the national government is too big, tries to do too many things, and is gradually overwhelming state and local governments. We do not need more government; we need less government to get more done. Endless talk will not bring more decisions back home. This can be done with a positive champion of the states in Congress." [11]

Some wrote back with words of encouragement. "How lucky this state is to have someone with your record ready to furnish an alternative to stone-age Sam," one friend in Durham wrote. A young woman who had been fourteen when she first campaigned for him in 1960 and now was studying political science in college volunteered to work in his campaign. A friend in Weaverville wrote: "Be assured that I will support you 100% in any political endeavor you attempt, even the presidency." And there was contempt. "If you feel you must run against someone, run against Jordan," one man responded. "The ham and egg, two-bit, yes man, rubber stamp 'Great Society' politician is a dime a dozen in Washington and if you were elected you would be no novelty. Why don't you try to get a job somewhere and get off the taxpayers' payroll?" A Statesville businessman responded, "At the present time, I think the senator we have in Washington who has done the most good to protect our constitution and prevent the spread of big government is Senator Sam J. Ervin, and I certainly intend to support him for reelection." Even some Sanford might otherwise count on for support begged off if he were to oppose Ervin.[12]

The initial campaign letter was followed by another round of polling in the area where the letters had been targeted. The results showed that the media attention and the interest generated by the first mailing had improved Sanford's chances. The pollsters told him he was gaining on Ervin: "Ervin would be a formidable opponent, of course, but not invulnerable. Even more encouraging, Governor Sanford has the momentum, having come from behind to achieve a standoff."[13] At the same time, Sanford's reading of the numbers left him worried about the effect of such a campaign on the state party and his own relations with Ervin's son and daughter, who were good friends.

Sanford believed he could defeat Ervin, but the campaign would be divisive, even destructive to the entire Democratic ticket, including Bob Scott. The race issue, which Sanford had held in check in 1960, would be far more difficult to finesse this time. Sanford was clearly identified by the majority of those surveyed as being on the "wrong" side of an issue that had catapulted George Wallace into national prominence as the most viable third party candidate for president since Theodore Roosevelt ran on the Bull Moose ticket in 1912. In late January, Sanford sent word to Ervin that he would not run and then made a formal announcement withdrawing as a candidate.

There was a smell of trouble in the air in 1968, particularly for the Democrats. Two years earlier, Republicans had scored surprising gains around the country, most especially in the South. Claude Kirk had been elected governor in Florida, and Jim Gardner of Rocky Mount had defeated the aging Harold Cooley in North Carolina's Fourth Congressional District. In Georgia, Barry Goldwater had helped elect the first Republican congressman since the Civil War, and Howard "Bo" Callaway almost snatched the governorship in 1966 until a Democrat-controlled legislature decided his close race in favor of Atlanta restaurant owner Lester Maddox. Maddox had made a name for himself in defying desegregation and passing out trademark pick handles to chase away those who attempted to integrate his business. Richard Nixon was fashioning a Southern strategy designed to appease South Carolina's Strom Thurmond, the GOP's most prominent defector, who had become the bell cow for other conservatives in the South.

The national press was also beginning to take seriously the "Dump Johnson" movement led by Allard Lowenstein, whose army of students was working the precincts of snowy New Hampshire and turning what appeared to be an unlikely effort for Minnesota Senator Eugene McCarthy into reality. On March 12, McCarthy nearly upset Johnson in the first primary of the season. His "children's crusade" had done the impossible. With the energy and enthusiasm that can only come from young novices who didn't know better, they had given their laconic, poetry-quoting candidate surprising legitimacy.

Popular commentary held that McCarthy's vote was a victory for the peace movement. Yet, a later study of polling results showed the New Hampshire voters supported McCarthy out of the same kind of frustration that was being registered in states like North Carolina. Americans were fed up with the war in Vietnam, not as doves, but as hawks who believed American soldiers were pawns in a deadly political game. Never before had Americans engaged in a struggle like the one in Southeast Asia, and the experience was tearing the nation apart. If McCarthy had been campaigning in North Carolina rather than New Hampshire, he might have succeeded there as well. Sanford's polls showed that 80 percent of North Carolina voters disapproved of Johnson's handling of the war.

No one was more surprised than Sanford when Johnson announced on March 31 that he would not seek reelection. Sanford had just left a meeting at the White House where he had agreed to be the president's campaign manager when Johnson announced his decision. Just two weeks earlier, Johnson had called Sanford urging him to take on the campaign. That call was itself something of a turnabout for the president, who in 1960, after Sanford's declaration for Kennedy, had told his aides not to ever mention Sanford's name in his presence.[14]

Sanford genuinely liked Johnson, the last of the New Deal champions, and had been impressed with him ever since Kerr Scott had introduced him to the big, tall Texan. Sanford's defection from the Southern ranks in 1960 had stalled their friendship, but Johnson later called on Sanford for help with his War on Poverty and other Great Society programs. In May 1964, the president and a swarming entourage had descended on the faded home of a tenant farmer near Rocky Mount in eastern North Carolina to dramatize the plight of Americans in need. (Sanford was convinced that Johnson had selected the site of the visit thinking he was headed to the hills of the

Blue Ridge Mountains and that no one on his staff was bold enough to tell the president he was going in the wrong direction.)

The North Carolina Fund had provided an early demonstration of what could be done with the nation's poor and disadvantaged and proved a useful testing ground for a national effort that Johnson was eager to get underway. Early on, however, Sanford had become disillusioned with the work of the Office of Economic Opportunity. He had never believed that poverty could be eliminated and reminded federal bureaucrats, whose own salaries inflated the cost of the programs, that this was not a "war on poverty," but a war on the "causes of poverty." No one in Washington seemed to appreciate the difference.

Johnson was struggling with his own future when he called Sanford in mid-March and asked him to come to the White House and talk about managing his campaign. Sanford was sure the suggestion came from Lawrence O'Brien, one of the few from the Kennedy years who had stayed on with Johnson after 1965. In the intervening years, Sanford had remained in touch with O'Brien and with Henry Hall Wilson Jr., one of the more experienced Washington hands on O'Brien's staff. Finally, Sanford agreed to come to the White House for a campaign strategy session on the afternoon of Sunday, March 31.

Taking on Johnson's campaign was sure to cut deeply into Sanford's personal life and pull him away from the law firm where he finally was producing a comfortable living for his family. Yet, if he was to ever seriously consider a presidential campaign, being on the inside of this one would be good experience, just as helping Scott in 1954 had proved valuable. He prepared to devote most of his time to 1968 and asked Hugh Cannon to join him for the meeting in Washington.

The day before he was due in Washington, Sanford and Terry Jr. were scuba diving in the Florida Keys. This was an important trip for Sanford, who was concerned about his son. Young Terry had run into his own problems since returning to Fayetteville and was having trouble in school. His father felt partly to blame; he suspected that his son's teachers were being soft on him because he was the son of "their" governor. Sanford finally suggested to the principal at Terry's school that his son was a good candidate for admission to the Advancement School. Created in the closing months of Sanford's administration, the Advancement School was located in Winston-Salem and was designed for eighth graders with recognized potential but poor classroom performance. In a short time, it was able to demonstrate that education, properly administered, could rescue youngsters before they slid further behind their classmates and ultimately dropped out of school. Young Terry would become an example of the school's success.

From the Keys, father and son flew to Washington, where Terry Jr. was put on a plane home to Fayetteville. At the airport, Sanford met Cannon and a driver from the White House. Sanford was relaxed and even playful, completely nonplussed by the task ahead of him. As the two walked through the terminal building, they passed a ringing pay phone and Sanford stopped to answer it. Recalled Cannon: "I said, 'We're going to the White House to see the President of the United States. Why are you answering that phone?' He said, 'Well, somebody's calling.' "[15]

Waiting for them at the White House were O'Brien, presidential aide Marvin Watson, and others, including one Texan who had been working as an interim chairman for the campaign. On the way in from the airport, Sanford read the advance text of a speech Johnson planned to deliver that evening and he was pleased that the president planned to announce his decision to halt the bombing of North Vietnam. Although Sanford had taken no public position on the war, he had first declared his concern three years earlier when he told students at Harvard that he believed continued involvement in Vietnam was a tragic mistake. "I thought it was not a justifiable war. I couldn't see any good coming out of that. We were beating up on those little so-called communists who weren't any threat to us," Sanford said some years later. "I must say I would have been even more violently opposed to it had I realized how many people it would suck into it. It just thought it was wrong and that we were just throwing our weight around."[16]

Sanford had written Johnson several times urging him to bring the war to an end. He also had told Johnson when he called to ask him to manage the campaign, "I can't be your campaign manager if you don't stop the bombing and start getting to the peace table and bring this war to an end. Why the hell should I or anybody else be your manager because you are going to get beat if you don't do it. That's why I was pleased on that Sunday because he was saying we are going to stop the bombing as the first step in negotiations."[17] Sanford believed the decision could ultimately salvage a president who had performed splendidly for education, civil rights, and, for all its faults, the poverty program.

The meeting at the White House lasted several hours. Late in the afternoon, Watson was called out to speak with the president, who was in the family quarters upstairs with weekend guests. He returned and then left again. Later, as the meeting broke, Watson pulled Sanford aside and asked where he would be at eight o'clock, the hour when the president was to begin his speech. "I can be anywhere you want me to be," Sanford answered. But, he said, he planned to return home, collect some things, and while there alert Governor Moore, Lieutenant Governor Scott, and other party figures that he was going to be signing on with the Johnson campaign. It was better to cover his bases early, rather than have leading Democrats at home react to calls from news reporters. "That's all right," Watson told him. "But call me as soon as you get there because I think the President's changing his mind about how he wants to do this." Watson's caution caught him by surprise. "That son-of-a-bitch in the Texas crowd wants to continue being the manager," Sanford thought. But he covered his initial reaction and replied blandly, "That suits me just fine." That Johnson would announce he would not seek reelection never crossed his mind.[18]

Sanford was on the flight home when Johnson reached the part of his speech — which had not been distributed beforehand — where he declared he could only do his duty if he concentrated fully on the job at hand, undisturbed by a political campaign. After Sanford's plane landed, he put in a call to Watson before beginning the ten-minute drive to his house. Watson's secretary was excited when she answered and told him her boss was with the president, but that he wanted to talk. "You just can't believe the reaction to the speech," she said. Sanford, puzzled at the comment, ignored his curiosity and left word for Watson to call him at home.

Still unaware of the full content of Johnson's speech, Sanford drove home through the darkness totally disconnected from the swirl of political events. His excited family was waiting at the door as he pulled into the driveway.

"Well, what do you think of that?" asked Margaret Rose.

Thinking she meant Johnson's call for the bombing halt, Sanford said, "I thought it was good."

"Did you know he was going to say that?"

"I read the speech," he answered, a bit pleased with himself.

The conversation was still on two tracks as Margaret Rose began reciting the names on phone messages that had accumulated in the wake of the speech. Sanford still wasn't clear what had happened when the phone rang again. It was Manly Eubanks, who had worked for a time in the governor's office.

"Did you know that was going to happen?" Eubanks blurted out.

"Manly, I just got in from the plane. What the hell happened?" Sanford said. He finally learned he was out of a job.[19]

Among those trying to reach Sanford Sunday night was Robert Kennedy, who had infuriated party liberals by entering the race after McCarthy's surprising showing in New Hampshire. Now Kennedy's prospects were improved considerably. It was Monday before Sanford could reach Kennedy, who asked him to join his campaign. Sanford liked Kennedy and had probably spent more time with him than with his brother, but he begged off a commitment.

McCarthy might have called too had he not thought he had already been turned down by Sanford. In December, while Sanford was still considering his own race for the Senate, Paul Ylvisaker at the Ford Foundation told Sanford that McCarthy might ask him to manage his campaign. Sanford agreed to talk to McCarthy but offered no encouragement. Some months later, Sanford saw Ylvisaker and told him McCarthy had never called. Ylvisaker said McCarthy told him he had called, but " 'got such a cold reception you turned him off.' And, I said, 'I never gave anyone a cold reception, certainly not Gene McCarthy.' " Sanford said Ylvisaker later discovered that McCarthy had mistakenly called Carl Sanders, the former governor of Georgia.[20]

Sanford never learned why Johnson had gone through the motions of bringing him to the White House to talk about a campaign that apparently was not to be. According to Johnson's own report of those days, recorded in his memoir, *The Vantage Point*, the president had made up his mind against running well before the March 31 meeting.

Through the remaining spring primaries, Sanford remained loyal to the party's leading contender for the nomination, Vice President Hubert Humphrey, whom he believed was best prepared to be president. Sanford traveled regularly on Humphrey's behalf and visited delegations in Georgia, Illinois, Oklahoma, and California. He kept an office at the Humphrey headquarters in Washington until it was overrun by summer interns, a measure of disregard that nettled him. By the time of the Democratic Party convention in Chicago, it was clear that Humphrey would be the nominee.

Sanford arrived in Chicago with Margaret Rose and Betsee, who was a sophomore at East Carolina University, amid talk that he should be Humphrey's running mate. The *New York Times*'s Tom Wicker had written that Humphrey would need either Sanford or Georgia's Carl Sanders or Oklahoma Senator Fred Harris if he expected to carry the South.[21] Earlier, Senator Everett Jordan had talked to Humphrey on Sanford's behalf and a budding campaign began to take shape. Cannon and Eubanks established a Sanford headquarters in a suite of rooms at the Blackstone Hotel. Most of the Sanford foot soldiers and some of the old allies were on hand: Eli Evans from the American states study, late from a stint as a White House speechwriter, had come in from New York; Joel Fleishman, who had returned to Yale after leaving the governor's office, joined in to help, as did Bill Cochrane from Jordan's office.

The city was in turmoil. For weeks, Chicago authorities, under the control of Mayor Richard Daley, had been bracing for the convention as thousands of antiwar demonstrators filled Grant Park on the edge of Lake Michigan. In the early part of the week, delegates walked through the park mixing with the young people, stepping over sleeping bags, ogling the conglomeration of hippies, yippies, folk singers, and odd-lot activists drawn to what looked like the nation's largest counterculture party. Betsee sought out a young man she knew who was in one of the National Guard units that had been drafted for crowd control. Though she was dressed more modestly than those in tie-dyed shirts and floppy sandals, Betsee carried the same antiwar commitment as those she had seen pushed behind the police barricades. Coming of age in Fayetteville, an Army town, she had had many friends, including a former boyfriend, shipped out for Vietnam. Some of them had not come back. At East Carolina, she had helped organize an antiwar group even though she found herself in a distinct minority on the conservative Greenville campus.

On Wednesday night of convention week, Betsee and Penny Teague, a friend from Raleigh, were standing on Michigan Avenue near the corner at their hotel when police covered a crowd of demonstrators with tear gas and then began swinging batons indiscriminately. The sight horrified the two, who feared they would be caught up in the thousands of young people fleeing police. They struggled to reach the safety of their hotel where, fortunately, someone recognized them as guests and unlocked the doors to give them refuge. Across the way, the Hilton had become a triage ward; wounded young people sat there amidst broken glass and the detritus of the melee.

When the Sanfords and other delegates staying at the Blackstone returned by bus from the convention hall, nothing appeared amiss. Police had cleared the streets and even washed away blood spilled in the fight. They found Betsee in her room. "I was just hysterical," Betsee recalled, "trying to tell my parents that this really did go on, and they said it couldn't have, it couldn't have, and, of course, it did." [22] The shock of that night would remain etched in memory for Betsee as it would for many who came to measure the summer of 1968 by the vivid images of police brutality broadcast internationally by the networks.

Humphrey secured the nomination, but the Democratic Party was in shambles. It was out of money, torn bitterly from within, and the nominee was carrying the political weight of an administration held in contempt by activists on the left and on the right. In the South, Republicans were picking up new registrations in the suburbs of such cities as Atlanta, Charlotte, and Charleston while George Wallace was threatening the party's traditional base among farmers and blue-collar workers.

The convention left Sanford both tired and disappointed. It bothered him that Johnson had been so roundly ignored in Chicago, like some crazy relative everyone was afraid to talk about in polite society. Sanford knew

Johnson was unpopular, but he was the president and due respect. He was so put out that party leaders had virtually ignored Johnson throughout the convention that he intentionally included praise for him in his seconding speech for Humphrey, a chore that he had reluctantly agreed to when the vice president called. "I was pissed off at the whole crowd," he later recalled.[23]

On the night of Humphrey's acceptance speech, Sanford remained in his hotel and watched the convention on television. Before the night was over he called Johnson at his Texas ranch and wished him a happy birthday. An appreciative Johnson was in a chatty mood. He told Sanford he wanted him to be his secretary of agriculture for the remainder of the term. "It won't hurt you," the president said. Sanford said he would pass.[24]

The convention had proven one thing to Sanford. He believed that he could do as good a job at running the party, and the nation, as any other candidate who had been considered. Perhaps, he thought, he should have handled the vice presidential bid a bit differently. Sanford had wanted the nomination enough to encourage efforts on his behalf, but he had refused to go to Humphrey and ask for the job. Instead, he sat in his hotel room on Tuesday night like the teenager waiting to be asked to the prom. There was hope in his heart, but he knew when Humphrey called on Wednesday morning to ask him to deliver a seconding speech that the vice president had picked someone else. He later learned that Humphrey retreated to the safety and familiarity of the Senate club in selecting Edmund Muskie, the quiet, steady senator from Maine, a good Roman Catholic. Sanford believed that Muskie brought nothing to the ticket to hold the disaffected Southern Democrats from moving in droves to support Nixon and Wallace.

On the flight home from Chicago, Sanford left his seat and sought out Sam Poole, a Southern Pines lawyer whom he had seen when he and Margaret Rose came aboard. Poole was a former state YDC president and had been working for much of the year organizing young voters for the Humphrey campaign. He had grown up with politics a frequent topic around the family peach orchard in the North Carolina Sandhills. His father had been one of Kerr Scott's early supporters, and Poole remembered the day the governor's limousine rolled up in the yard while he was out raking leaves and Scott stepped out and asked to see his father, Hawley. The elder Poole later joined forces with Sanford, who introduced Poole and his peaches to the capitol press corps that day in 1961 when the Freedom Riders visited Raleigh.

Sam Poole had not met Sanford before he arrived in Chicago, but he called on him for help in pleading his case to Chicago authorities to open Soldiers Field to the demonstrators and release some of the pressure of the crowd building at Grant Park. Mayor Daley had refused and responded instead with force. As he headed back home, Poole was exhausted and disgusted. He told Sanford he was through with the campaign and was going back to his law practice and his family in Southern Pines.

A few days later, Sanford was in bed nursing an attack of viral pneumonia when he got a call from Humphrey. The vice president opened the conversation by saying that Everett Jordan had talked to him about choosing Sanford and he had told him, "I'm very fond of Terry, and Margaret Rose, too," Sanford recalled. "And I said, 'Hubert, don't give me that bull.' I said, 'I didn't ask you.'" Then Humphrey got to the purpose of his call: "You've got to come up here and take charge of this campaign." Sanford protested, but agreed to meet him in Washington to talk.[25]

After the meeting, Sanford enlisted Cannon and Bert Bennett to help and he put in a call to Poole. "We're going back to Washington," Sanford told Poole.

"I'm not," Poole answered.

Sanford pressed further. "How about if I go back and take over the campaign?" He explained that Humphrey had called and asked him to chair the Citizens for Humphrey-Muskie Committee, the nuts-and-bolts portion of the campaign organization. "I said you have to have two or three things," Poole recalled. "One of them is control of purse strings, another is complete autonomy to bring your people in and so forth."

"If I get all that, will you go back?" Sanford asked. Poole said he would.[26]

Sanford arrived in Washington right after Labor Day. At the time, Humphrey was twenty points down in the polls and out of money. He had only the semblance of a field organization, no clear strategy, and his campaign headquarters was vacant space in an unfinished floor of a Connecticut Avenue office building.

The eight weeks remaining until election day became a scramble of days. The first problem was money, and Sanford helped Humphrey raise an initial $5 million needed just to get the offices open and television time booked. Until the cash arrived, Sanford's staff lived on credit cards, hoping for reimbursement at the campaign's end. At one point, Cannon was in Los Angeles and called Bennett to tell him that though he had a credit card to pay for a rental car, he did not have enough money in his pocket to park it. Bennett wired him $200.[27]

For Bennett, it was 1960 all over again. Instead of organizing a hundred counties, he was organizing fifty states. In some states, he was starting virtually from scratch. Poole drew young voters back to the Humphrey campaign with the help of some of those who had been in Grant Park in Chicago. He also worked his contacts with Young Democrats, some of whom he had known since 1963 when he was a member of the state's delegation to Las Vegas.

The Humphrey campaign finally began to gain momentum about three weeks prior to the election, after Humphrey broke with the Johnson administration over the conduct of the war. The vice president's speech in Salt Lake City was one that Sanford had advised him to deliver when he had visited Humphrey's home in Minnesota early in the campaign. He had urged Humphrey to resign from office and establish his independence in a dramatic fashion. Sanford said Humphrey waited too long to break with Johnson because he enjoyed the trappings of office too much, and because he did not want to upset Johnson. "He's so nice that he's almost yellow-bellied," Sanford recalled. "He was just scared to offend Johnson. I think he felt so grateful to Johnson that he didn't want to do anything to embarrass him. That was his nature. He just really was such a good, extraordinarily nice person that he never could come to hard decisions." [28]

After the Salt Lake City speech, money began rolling into the campaign and crowds were larger at Humphrey's appearances across the country. As he headed into the final week, he was gaining in the polls; Sanford later believed the Democrats would have defeated Nixon if given more time.

Nixon's victory signaled the end of the solid Democratic South. He carried North Carolina and would have swept Republican Congressman Jim Gardner into the governor's office had Gardner not alienated the traditional Republican base with an outrageous flirtation with the Wallace vote. Instead, Bob Scott was elected governor.

Nixon's election did not settle the national debate over the war. The turbulence continued into 1969, particularly on the college campuses, where antiwar demonstrations were creating problems for college administrators and state officials. In February, Governor Scott directly intervened and sent state troopers onto the Chapel Hill campus to secure a dining hall that had been occupied by demonstrators. Two months later he ordered armed troops to clear the campus of North Carolina A&T State University in Greensboro after demonstrations broke into violence. Scott Hall, a dormitory named for his father, would bear the pockmarks of .50-caliber slugs for years to come.

The student unrest had even spread to Duke University. Known for its civility and Southern hospitality, Duke had remained relatively quiet through the election year. On the night after Martin Luther King Jr.'s death in April, more than fifteen hundred students had conducted an around-the-clock silent vigil on the main quad. It lasted four days as students drew attention to demands for minority rights and higher wages for the black employees on the university payroll who cleaned rooms and served meals.

Duke trustees had little patience for such insolence, and although President Douglas Knight was sympathetic, he was prepared to be tough. Later that year, after officials closed San Francisco State because of student protests, he was asked what he would do if students tried such a thing on his campus. Knight told the student newspaper, the Chronicle: "It would be a great error. . . . It had damn better not be [done]." [29]

Student discontent carried over into the new year. On February 12, after students at the University of Chicago took over the school's administration building, about sixty black students thrust Duke into the national spotlight when they did the same at the registrar's offices on the first floor of the Allen Administration Building. They declared the building to be the Malcolm X School of Liberation and issued a list of thirteen demands, including establishment of a black studies curriculum, a black student union, and elimination of the SAT as a requirement for black student admissions.

Knight, who was attending a fund-raising breakfast in New York City at the time, reacted quickly. He chartered a plane and within hours was back on campus. He knew the patience of his board for such trouble had worn thin and those who resented the admission of black students in the first place would be loud in "self-congratulation and hot for the severest punishment" of the rebellious blacks.[30] Knight sent a message to the students that he would begin negotiations only after they left the Allen Building. The students refused. Meanwhile, pressure continued to build. Alumni, parents, outsiders, and board members called. Some offered advice and others issued orders for Knight to squelch the rebellion as soon as possible, using whatever means necessary. Even more disturbing, Knight later recounted, were reports of locals armed with shotguns circling the campus in their pickup trucks waiting for night to fall. Feeling an urgency to resolve the situation before dark, when he feared serious violence would erupt, Knight set up a command post in the alumni building on the edge of the West Campus and called Governor Scott, who agreed to send the Highway Patrol onto the campus. He then made one last call to the students occupying the Allen Building. They again refused to budge, and around six that evening, police rushed the building, only to find it empty.

All the commotion had attracted a boisterous crowd of twenty-five hundred students, most of whom had poured out of nearby dormitories. Believing they were in danger of being attacked, the riot-equipped police fired tear gas canisters into the crowd. Within thirty minutes, the demonstration was over and no one was seriously hurt. The crowd had been dispersed, but not without inflicting grievous wounds on Duke's reputation.

The following Sunday Knight spoke over Durham's WDBS radio to give a progress report on the "misunderstandings" between his administration and the black students. He was unrepentant for the actions of recent days. "I put the freedom of the university above force used by the black students," Knight told reporters.

The stress and strain of the episode weighed heavily on Knight, who started carrying a pistol in the pocket of his dressing gown when he made his 1 A.M. tour around campus with a guard. "My mother remarked later that when she saw the first news story describing me as 'Yankee-born and Yale-educated,' she braced for trouble. As I tell this difficult part of the story, I must say that I tried even then—and much more now—to understand the depth of the anger. It was everything that had happened since 1954, all concentrated in one episode. Inevitably, I was seen as the man who had somehow mysteriously caused it to happen. At the very best I had lost control of the situation; at the worst I was at the heart of the problem." [31]

Knight believed he had saved the university from even deeper trouble. He feared violent attacks, particularly from the ninety black students enrolled at Duke. But he knew that his days at Duke were numbered, judging from the reactions of various members of the board of trustees. When board chair Charles Wade convened a special meeting for March 27, Knight decided he would opt for the honorable way out. He resigned effective June 30, because "to fight a motion of dismissal would simply add further confusion to the university and our private lives." Two months later he told an Atlanta news media gathering, "I have been severely criticized for being too lenient, but I was the only university president within 600 miles who called in the police." [32]

The board named a three-man committee composed of Chancellor Barnes Woodhall, Provost Marcus Hobbs, and Charles Huestis, the school's chief financial officer, to run the university while it looked for a new president. They soon became known as "the Troika," and prepared to keep things on track for an unknown period of time.

At first, the search for a new president centered on the conventional candidates, such as young leaders in higher education as well as candidates from the Duke faculty. Then Duke board member Mrs. Earl Brian offered an idea: Why not Terry Sanford? She had known Sanford for years and served with him on the original board of trustees of Methodist College in Fayetteville. Brian, the wife of a Raleigh physician, had been impressed with Sanford's leadership style as chairman for the young school and believed he had a level-headed approach to solving problems and building the institution.

Brian found other Sanford supporters on the Duke board. Among them were Mary D. B. T. Semans, a granddaughter of Benjamin Duke, brother of the school's principal benefactor, James B. Duke; Nancy Hanks of the

Rockefeller Brothers Fund in New York City; and Wade, a top executive at R. J. Reynolds Tobacco Company in Winston-Salem. Wade had been named chairman in December 1968, succeeding Wright Tisdale of Detroit, who had held the position for five years.

Semans was enthusiastic. She had met Sanford in 1960 when he was campaigning for governor and was impressed with his honest answers to her questions. Later, as governor, he had drawn her and her husband, Dr. James Semans, who was a member of the Duke Medical School faculty, into public service when he picked Dr. Semans as the first chair of the board of the North Carolina School of the Arts. Together, the couple had successfully lobbied Governor Dan Moore and countless others to secure funding for the school in its formative years, when its future was tenuous. Later, she would say Sanford had changed their lives by involving them in the school and extending their circle of friends into politics and the arts.[33]

Another Sanford booster was J. Alex McMahon, who, as president of the Duke Alumni Association, was automatically a member of the search committee. McMahon was president of North Carolina Blue Cross and Blue Shield in Chapel Hill. A 1942 Duke graduate who had received his law degree at Harvard, McMahon had succeeded Sanford as a staff member at the Institute of Government in Chapel Hill and had closely watched Sanford's administration as governor when he left the Institute to become the legal counsel and lobbyist for the North Carolina Association of County Commissioners.

The board cleared an early impediment to Sanford's nomination by changing a requirement that the president hold an earned doctorate degree, a stipulation adopted to satisfy faculty members at the time of Knight's selection. It was changed to include the equivalent of a broad university academic background and earned doctorate, and Sanford soon emerged as one of the top three candidates of the three hundred names considered.

Before anyone at Duke made official contact, Sanford had heard that the search committee might be interested in him. He had discounted the rumor, although he mused that the Duke presidency would be an interesting challenge in difficult times. It was the kind of job he'd like to have, but it was unlikely that he, a University of North Carolina graduate, would be chosen. All the same, he thought, if it were offered, he'd probably take it.

During his lifetime, Sanford had imagined himself in a number of careers: an Arctic explorer, a Boy Scout executive, a lawyer, a doctor, a writer, a businessman, a governor, and even President of the United States. In the four years since he had left the governor's office, he had fulfilled some of those ambitions, but public service remained an unsatisfied desire. Stirring within him was an ambition to mount a campaign for the presidency. But unlike in the years prior to his election as governor, he was not as clearly focused on how he might accomplish such an improbable, if fascinating, ambition.

In the summer of 1969 Sanford was preparing to settle into a routine that he hoped would allow him more time at a vacation home that he and Margaret Rose had bought at Hound Ears, a golf and ski resort near Boone. The development was one of the early ventures of Grover and Harry Robbins, two brothers who had turned an old railroad line into a theme park called Tweetsie Railroad at Blowing Rock. The Robbins brothers had done well and, with help from Sanford's law firm, were expanding to develop Beech Mountain, a ski resort at much higher elevation where their principal attraction was to be a re-creation of the Land of Oz. At one point, the Robbinses even sent their public relations man, former *Charlotte Observer* columnist Kays Gary, to Hollywood to buy the red slippers worn by Judy Garland in the classic movie.

While Sanford occupied himself with the law firm, he fielded several other opportunities, including some that would have considerably fattened his bank account. He had become a member of the board of directors of Esquire Incorporated, which owned Coronet Films, one of his early clients, and at one point seriously considered joining in a venture to buy the company. He pulled out and said later that at the time he thought, "Why do I want to turn my attention to grubbing in a business now at this late date?" [34]

He also had talked with William Benton, the chairman of the board of Encyclopedia Britannica and an influential figure in national Democratic Party politics, who early in 1969 offered Sanford the presidency of the company. The salary was well into six figures, and he told Sanford he could probably parlay the job into a cabinet position with some future Democratic administration. The offer was inviting, Sanford wrote Benton, but he said he had not "given up the thought of running for governor or the United States Senate, or maybe something else" and would not want to forsake his North Carolina base for Chicago, where the company had its headquarters. [35]

When the Ford Foundation was looking for a replacement for Henry Heald, Sanford's name appeared on the list of candidates. He was invited to New York for conversations about the job, but when he let it be known that he probably was not through with politics, he was dropped from consideration. He also turned down an offer to run the Chicago Board of Trade, the nation's primary commodities market, where such things as pork bellies, wheat, and corn futures were traded. That job also would have required relocation to Chicago, and he passed the opportunity on to Henry Hall Wilson Jr., who easily swung into the position after leaving the White House in 1968.

It was not that Sanford disliked business. He had dabbled in entrepreneurial ventures ever since he was a young lawyer in Fayetteville, first buying a car wash and later owning a local weekly newspaper. He still held a controlling interest in an insurance agency and in 1969 had begun talking about a barbecue restaurant franchise operation with actor Andy Griffith of Mount Airy, who had turned Mayberry into North Carolina's best-known fictional town. But nothing Sanford had done or seen dissuaded him from seriously considering a campaign for the nation's highest office, probably in 1976 after Nixon had served two terms. Managing Humphrey's campaign "gave me the idea that I could do a whole lot better than they were doing," he later recalled, "and why didn't I aspire to move on to the national level? I suppose when Bert and I went up there we at least had a kind of lurking feeling that we ought to explore this area. But I wasn't so set on it that I was deliberately maneuvering myself in position." [36]

By the fall of 1969, he had fashioned a rough campaign plan that he presented to a small group of friends who joined him at Hound Ears one weekend in October. Included were Cannon, Eubanks, Evans, Poole, and Spencer Oliver. Oliver was a former national YDC president who had worked in the Humphrey campaign and had stayed on in Washington on the staff of the Democratic National Committee. Late in the afternoon, after finishing a round of golf, the group was gathered in a sauna when Sanford announced that he planned to take the Duke job if it were offered, and run for president in 1976.

"I will never forget this," recalled Poole. "He looked at us and we were all sitting there with no clothes on, towels wrapped around us, and [Eli Evans] said facetiously, 'I'd like for the record to reflect that the temperature was 155 degrees, in October, when you said that.' That was the beginning. It wasn't the beginning in his mind. He had thought about this." [37]

Not all were in agreement. Cannon warned that the Duke job could embroil Sanford in internal affairs at Duke and compromise any chance he had to build a national constituency. Sanford explained later, "I thought that I'd take that chance. Being president of Duke would be a life-time achievement in itself. I thought I would be there about four years. I saw it not as a negative but as a positive. I was thinking, 'When you leave Duke, you will have been president of a great university.'" [38]

Sanford's undeniable political ambition troubled members of the Duke board. While the selection process progressed, Board Chairman Wade asked James V. Johnson of Charlotte, a soft drink distributor who had run

Bob Scott's campaign for governor and stayed as state party chairman, to call Sanford and ask about his political plans. Sanford later recounted his conversation with Johnson in a diary: "I told Jimmy, who is an old friend of mine, that I would say definitely that I would not run for Senate or governor again. I did not qualify it: I simply intended to read myself out of ever occupying those two offices. Since I had been prominently discussed as a possible candidate for vice president along with Hubert Humphrey, Jimmy mentioned, not as a principal point of the discussion, that it might be that I would seek national office. I told him that I would not rule out this possibility, and that he should pass the message on with both of those aspects to Mr. Wade." [39]

In committee discussions, McMahon argued that Sanford was the perfect choice because, not in spite of, his political experience. "It was a recognizably political job," McMahon recalled. "Balancing constituencies and being a good listener were the things that were very attractive about Terry. The question of what Sanford might do in the future was irrelevant. . . . 'He's the right guy for the job now,'" he told committee members. "'For heaven's sake, let's not go into speculation about what he is going to do in the future. He seems to be amenable, so if he gives us a few years we need some stability around this place.'" [40]

In late October, the first official contact with Sanford by the search committee came when its chairman, Dr. John McKinney, the dean of the graduate school of arts and sciences, called Sanford at his law office and asked for an appointment. Sanford obliged and a few days later the two talked at length about the possibilities. Sanford allowed that he was interested but qualified his response, telling McKinney that he had turned down other offers and he might do the same with Duke. He did want to pursue the matter, however, and a week later McKinney invited Sanford to a dinner meeting with the committee at the "old president's home" at Duke. McKinney asked if he needed directions and Sanford said that he knew where it was.

Sanford was running late as he left his Raleigh office for Durham. On the way, he realized that he had left the list of the committee members behind. He pulled up at what he thought was the official residence of the Duke president just off the campus circle and was surprised to find the building empty. The campus was nearly deserted as Sanford, now late for his meeting, poked about trying to find help. He ended up at the Duke Medical Center, where he found a telephone and called McKinney's residence. It took some convincing to pry the meeting location out of McKinney's daughter, who had been instructed not to reveal where her father was that night. Sanford finally convinced her that he was the reason for the meeting and she directed him to the president's residence, located off campus in a wooded neighborhood. The house that Sanford thought was the president's home had been turned into alumni headquarters and a new one had been built during Knight's administration.

Sanford was an hour late. "In any event," he later noted in his diary, "the cocktail party was still in swing and I managed to have one and to have a delightful dinner sitting with Semans and McKinney. After dinner we sat around several hours talking, with me answering questions and the committee members asking questions. I had decided that I should not be too eager, in fact was not too eager. I answered everything exactly as I saw it, and figured I had best not accommodate any expressions to anything that I might judge to be the thinking of any particular committee member. I thought it all came off very pleasantly." [41] Indeed, Sanford had impressed the search committee with his appreciation of the board's ambition to build a national reputation for Duke, something they asked Knight to start, as well as resolve the current unrest and turmoil on campus.

Semans reported to Cannon, who was handling legal affairs for one of her family's foundations, that the meeting had gone well. "He never de-emphasized the fact that we needed to be a national university and he never detracted from that approach," she later recalled. "But he also said we had to do a lot of work at home. I thought he would bring Duke back into focus as the kind of place Mr. Duke would have wanted. It had drifted away from the South but also from North Carolina, and I knew he wanted to do something about that." [42]

The search committee had two other finalists besides Sanford, but on November 21, the Duke student newspaper reported that Sanford had the "inside track." In fact, Sanford had already begun talking with Wade about what he would expect should he take the job. The two arranged a meeting at a motel near Greensboro, where they thought they could meet without drawing attention, at which Sanford explained his professional obligations, including additional responsibilities with the Robbinses' business interests.

Sanford was surprised to learn that the president's annual salary was $60,000. He thought that was a rather large sum and asked if some of it could be deferred, since he had no other source of retirement income. He also told Wade he would want a term appointment. Wade objected, but Sanford explained that he did not look forward to spending the rest of his life doing one thing; also, he believed it might suit faculty members better if they knew he was to be in charge for a set period of time.

Wade released Sanford from absolute secrecy so that he would be free to seek advice from others. One of the first he called was Fleishman, then part of President Kingman Brewster's staff at Yale. Fleishman urged Sanford to take the job. So did Eli Evans, who prepped Sanford with some background on the Duke Endowment and offered some questions for him to put to the search committee.

Bert Bennett was another matter. Over breakfast one morning, the two talked about the future of the so-called "Sanford wing" of the state Democratic Party. Bennett was eager to keep it a functioning, viable organization. With its leader cloistered at Duke, Bennett saw it withering away and urged his old friend to remain free to run for statewide office in 1972. Sanford told Bennett that he himself should run in 1972, perhaps for governor or for Everett Jordan's Senate seat. Jordan already had indicated he would retire at the end of his term if Sanford would agree to run. Bennett dismissed the idea.

Sanford had brought his family into the discussion early. Margaret Rose was skeptical that the Duke board would choose a Carolina graduate as the school's president, but she told her husband to take the job if it were offered. Betsee believed her father's plan was super. After Thanksgiving, as Terry Jr. rode with his father back to Asheville, where he was attending Christ School, he told his father he should take the job at Duke. "You've already proved you can be a great governor," he said.[43]

The week prior to the board's meeting on the weekend of December 13, Sanford was in the Virgin Islands with Grover Robbins. He told Wade that he would not be returning to North Carolina until late Friday, the twelfth, and gave him the phone number at his home at Hound Ears where he would be on Saturday when the board voted on the search committee's recommendation. Before he left on the trip, he prepared two letters. One of them was brief and thanked the committee for its consideration but asked that his name be withdrawn. In the second, he said he would welcome the opportunity, but with some conditions: he wanted assurance of less involvement of the Duke Endowment in the affairs of the university, among other things. He asked Margaret Rose which one to mail. She chose the long one.

Before leaving on his trip, Sanford arranged for a phone call on Friday night from Cannon, who anticipated hearing from Semans after the search committee made its decision earlier that day. The committee was pledged to secrecy, however, and she never called. Late that evening, when Cannon called to tell Sanford he had no news, Sanford assumed that the conditions he had laid down had eliminated him from consideration. So be it, he thought.

Yet, the next morning he waited for more news and listened for the phone to ring. He was unaware that Semans had called Cannon that morning, anxiously trying to locate him. It was nearly noon when the phone finally rang at Sanford's house. It was Wade, who said, "Mr. President?" when Sanford answered the phone. "Oh, my," Sanford replied.

Wade said the board had chosen him and wanted to announce his appointment the following day at a press conference in Durham. Sanford accepted, assuring Wade that he was eager to get started and looking forward to the job.

Just before receiving Wade's call, Sanford had started a fire in the fireplace, and had thrown some packing material from a new mirror onto the flames of the kindling. Just as the phone rang, Sanford realized something was wrong as the room began to fill with smoke. "Hold it a minute," Sanford told Wade. "The house is on fire." [44]

He hung up and grabbed a fire extinguisher to stop flames that now had escaped the fireplace and set fire to a plaque over the mantle. After he grabbed some tongs and dragged the burning logs onto the lawn, averting a disaster, he discovered he must have knocked the damper shut when he put one of the packing boxes on the fire. When he finally had things under control, he called Wade and they finished their conversation, completing details for a formal announcement the next day.

Sanford immediately tried to reach Margaret Rose in Fayetteville to tell her he had accepted the office, but it was late in the day before they talked. She already had heard the news and was not thrilled. She told him she had encouraged his interest but had never really believed he would be Duke's choice. "I felt [her reaction] was partially a put on," Sanford later noted in a journal, "although I was certain that anybody would look on this new responsibility with considerable dismay, especially since everything was going fairly easy for us for the first time in our lives." [45]

Sanford arrived home very late, having stopped in Taylorsville to make a speech that had been on his calendar for some time. The next morning, he asked his wife, "Did you ever think when you came to Chapel Hill twenty-five years ago as a coed from Hopkinsville, Kentucky, that you would wake up in bed with the president of Duke University?" [46]

At the Sunday press conference back in Durham Sanford received a hearty welcome from board members, faculty, staff, and a few students. He was calm and poised, as usual, and said he wanted to work with the students on their agenda. However, he said, "if trouble comes, I assure you I'll not panic and we will handle it." Someone asked what he would say to faculty members who questioned his lack of a doctorate degree. "I won't hold it against them because they don't have a law degree," Sanford responded with his sly smile. Margaret Rose was with her husband. She had come around, at least publicly, and displayed none of the hesitancy she had expressed privately. Asked whom she would root for in future athletic contests between UNC and Duke, she replied quickly and forcefully, if tongue-in-cheek, "I hate Chapel Hill." [47]

Public reaction was positive. Even the *Chronicle*, whose editors had been nothing but an irritant to Knight and most of Duke's board members, welcomed Sanford in an editorial that quoted Knight describing him as a man of nerve and principle. Asked if he had any advice for his successor, Knight replied to the Chronicle, "De illigitimies non carborundum," which translates to "Don't let the bastards grind you down." Over the following weeks, Sanford received hundreds of letters, including one from an old political foe, who wrote, "You are amazing; in one single act you have pleased both your friends and your enemies."[48] A few days after the press conference, Sanford performed his first official duty as Duke president when he signed Christmas checks sent each year to retired Methodist ministers, a duty given to Duke presidents under a provision in James B. Duke's will.

CHAPTER FIFTEEN

A Tar Heel Blue Devil

THE WEST CAMPUS of Duke University is a symphony of Gothic slate-roofed buildings of gray-blue Cambrian volcanic rock that was quarried in nearby Hillsborough. Gargoyle downspouts and decorative sculptures of human and animal forms carved in the archways stare down on the green lawns shaded by huge oaks. The campus has that classic, ivy-covered-halls look, with arched passageways and leaded windows under spindled gables. All this and the interiors of polished dark wood suggest tradition far older than reality. Construction on the West Campus began less than fifty years before Terry Sanford arrived in 1970 when a small Methodist school called Trinity College was renamed Duke University.

From the windows in the president's office on the second floor of Allen Building, Sanford could see the eight-foot bronze statue of James Buchanan Duke atop a twenty-five-ton Cape Anne granite pedestal in front of the campus's majestic chapel in the main quadrangle. Strategically situated, the administration building put Sanford, the school's sixth president, only steps away from important student gatherings that usually took place in front of the chapel. He would have it no other way.

Sanford reported for work on April 2, 1970, purposely avoiding taking office on April Fool's Day. He was inheriting a host of problems, including an unsettled mood over the war in Vietnam among students and faculty, tensions over black studies, a threat of labor unions from hourly employees, and even allegations that Duke had become a slumlord by accepting a gift of substandard housing. He also was greeted with the university's first budget deficit, fading and discouraged support from alumni, and a federal lawsuit charging Duke with underpaying nonacademic employees, most of whom were the black workers who served the meals, cleaned the rooms, and groomed the handsome campus for students from well-to-do families. Sanford felt confident that he could handle all the items on the agenda in the five or so years he planned to be at Duke, not as some interim caretaker, but as a leader who could continue the mission begun under his predecessor, Douglas Knight, to make Duke a great national, even international, university.

If there was any regret, it was that his father, as steady a churchman as John Wesley ever imagined, was not there to see him assume responsibility for the campus he had proudly showed his son years before, when an education at Duke was well beyond the family's financial reach. Cecil Sanford had died in 1966, just prior to his eightieth birthday, due to surgical complications after he suffered a fall. Terry missed his quiet humor and steady hand. "The breaks were frequently against him and his luck was always bad. But he always kept his dignity, and his sense of humor and his happy, if sometimes resigned, outlook on life," Sanford would later write of his father.[1] Meanwhile, his mother took pride in this new challenge in education that had been handed her son. She was doing well at home in Laurinburg, where neighbors marveled at her stamina and steady service.

Sanford had his assignment from the board: Restore stability to the Duke campus and rebuild student and faculty confidence in the administration, repair the deteriorating relations with alumni, and return the school to its North Carolina heritage, with a continuing ambition to raise Duke up as an institution whose name would appear on anyone's top-ten list of great universities. It was a tall order and just how Sanford would accomplish his mission was not at all clear. Not long after his arrival he interviewed Bill Green, who was being recruited for the university's public affairs job. Green asked, "What are you doing here?" Without hesitation, the new president replied, "I'm going to identify creativity and leadership and bring it here and make it better."

"How are you going to do that?" Green asked.

"I don't know," Sanford said bluntly.[2]

Sanford approached his new responsibilities at Duke with the same high ambition that he had carried into the governor's office. This time, however, he had the benefit of experience working with an institution as awkward as state government and talented people upon whom he could draw for execution of the ideas that poured from his office. It wasn't too far a stretch to say that Duke's board of trustees could be no more difficult to deal with than a legislature or that the students and faculty were nothing more than separate constituencies with their sometimes overlapping and conflicting agendas. "I was here to be president of the university," Sanford said later. "I wasn't here to fix anything, but I thought I could elevate Duke to national and international status and that was always it from the very beginning. . . . They asked me to come in here at a time of turmoil," he said. "Several people said, 'Well, he'll come in here as a great fund-raiser.' I said, 'I'm not coming as a fund-raiser. I'm coming as president of the university and as the president of the faculty. That's my position.' So occasionally when somebody wanted to categorize me and say, 'Well, he's not really a Ph.D., he's here for this,' I slapped that down right then and there. I said, 'I'm president of the university from start to finish.'"[3]

The job could not have come at a more propitious time in Sanford's own long-range plan. He was well aware that this new challenge offered him a unique opportunity to personally join the national debate on issues that occupied the nation. This forum in higher education could supply possibilities for him to talk about the war in Vietnam, race, jobs, and other topics on the agenda of those in politics, the arts, and the media. Although it was not his reason for taking the Duke presidency, Sanford knew that if he performed well in this assignment, there would be no reason why he couldn't become the nation's new president in six years.

On the morning of April 2, Sanford's alarm roused him at five thirty and he struggled out of bed. A reception the night before for former governor Luther Hodges and his new bride had kept him and Margaret Rose out late. He exercised for a half hour, dressed, and drove to the campus to begin his first day. When he arrived outside of Allen Building just before seven, the sky was gray, it was raining and looked like the start of a miserable day. Bob Felman, the outgoing student body president who had been on the search committee, and Allen Albright, a Duke law student and former Morehead Scholar at Chapel Hill, met him when he arrived. They were joined by Hutch Traver, a junior from Durham who was slated to become Felman's successor in office. Traver's long hair, mustache, and patched jeans reflected his politics; he had been elected after leading a protest the year before against CIA recruitment on campus. Together Sanford and the young men walked across the quadrangle to the dining hall to join a group of students that Felman had invited to breakfast with the new president.

For the previous four months, Sanford had immersed himself in the mechanics of the job. During that time, he had picked Duke Law School Dean Kenneth Pye as his chancellor, a job Sanford envisioned as his chief of staff, and chosen a provost, Dr. John Blackburn, from the economics department. He had met several times with the board's executive committee and even made some calls on Duke's behalf to foundations in New York. Meanwhile, he pored over hefty briefing books that the interim management "troika" had produced to bring him up to speed. Among other things, Sanford had discovered that the Duke budget was in the red, a condition that no one had mentioned to him in the fall. As he walked the fifty yards across the quad to breakfast with his hosts, he put the mechanics aside and just hoped that at least a few of the students had answered Felman's invitation rather than rolling over and sleeping in on a cold, wet morning.

The turnout was impressive; waiting for Sanford were about 150 young people. He filled his tray in the food line and sat down to eat before moving around the hall to shake hands and speak to individual students during the next hour and a half. He had never left a political gathering without speaking to all he could, and this appearance bore a striking resemblance. He expected the cynics to call his outing a stunt, but for Sanford it was as meaningful a reminder of what he was doing there as the photograph of Frank Porter Graham that he had mounted on his office wall. Later in the morning, he paid a courtesy visit to the Durham City Council and pledged support for civic endeavors, then attended a chamber of commerce reception. The next morning the newspapers had pegged the story on Sanford leaning close to young people with their long hair and bell-bottoms. He had accomplished what he had hoped for on his first day. "I am sure it made the point that I wanted to make," he noted a few days later in a journal he started with his new job, "that the university starts with students and that is the purpose of it, and that I wanted to keep in touch with them."[4]

Courting students was not what some had counseled. He had been advised to first win the support of the faculty. As was often the case, Sanford took a contrary approach to the conventional wisdom, drawing on the experience of Yale's Kingman Brewster, who had won high marks for his handling of disruptions on the New Haven campus. "I said, I have a different approach: Get in solid with the students and the faculty will petition to let them in too," Sanford noted later that day in his journal. "Presidents have to be the representatives and have to have common purpose with the students. That is why the institution is here."

As for the students, they weren't sure what to make of the new president. Some dismissed him as a hack Southern politician just a few notches to the left of George Wallace. His nonacademic background, plus his Southern roots, automatically made him suspect among Duke's large contingent of students from the Northeast, who distanced themselves from their Southern peers,[5] whom they called "grits" regardless of whether they shared radical politics and wore the same hippie uniform of shaggy hair and fatigues.

"You were a grit and a grit produced offspring, which were called 'gritters,'" recalled Tom Drew, who was a sophomore from Anderson, South Carolina, when Sanford arrived. "Gritters were the little children that you saw going through the chapel and the dining hall and the library on tours and would look at you like you were real strange because you had long hair and a beard and a tie-dyed shirt."[6]

Sanford also arrived burdened with the suspicions that attended anyone connected with university administration. "The university seemed to mirror the nation," recalled Tom Campbell, who was a *Duke Chronicle* editor when Sanford arrived. "[It was] bent on ignoring urgent questions of race, war, and peace. The only way to effect change seemed to be through raised voices and confrontation."[7] Students had no reason to think Sanford would approach them any differently than had his predecessor. Campbell was among many who were surprised at the changes Sanford would bring to the campus, starting within his first few days on the job.

The changes started in Sanford's office, where his ready accessibility to visitors, especially students, shocked his secretary, Mrs. Christine Mimms, a proper and experienced gatekeeper who had served five of his predecessors with devotion. Sanford had been in office only a few days when he heard Mrs. Mimms tell a student that he couldn't see the president without an appointment. The new president stopped what he was doing and called for Mrs. Mimms to usher a surprised undergraduate into his office. He was no less approachable as he rambled around campus looking into its nooks and crannies.

Mrs. Mimms soon was busy extending invitations to all manner of folks. Campbell later recalled his meeting: "Terry came around his desk, warmly shook my hand and sat in a chair facing mine. He got me a Coke. We made small talk in the time-honored Southern style of easing into the business at hand. He asked my opinions on issues facing the campus and the country, listening closely to my answers. When we agreed he usually mentioned a plan that he had in mind for action, for change. Where our opinions differed he would talk some in that amazingly non-confrontational manner that he had—not opposing your position exactly, but just 'exploring' things from a somewhat different point of view."[8]

At a meeting with students a few weeks after taking office Sanford suggested with a tone of uncommon confidence in the young people that they set about raising $1 million as a challenge to the university to build a student union. He had been surprised to find that there was no common meeting place for students other than the chapel steps, and he asked one of his assistants, Vic Bubas, who had been a highly successful Duke basketball coach, to resurrect a study that had been prepared earlier for such a building.

Certainly no one in the top levels of the Duke administration had ever provided a more receptive ear to student concerns about public issues. Sanford had been in office a week when Traver led a delegation of students to ask if Sanford would help bring *New York Times* columnist Tom Wicker, an outspoken critic of the war, to the Duke campus. Sanford had anticipated that students would press him early to declare himself on the war, and he was ready. "I already knew how I felt about the war," Sanford wrote in his journal, "namely that it ought to be stopped, and I already knew that I would support the students. I knew also that if I hesitated and studied it, and told them to let me talk to some people and to come back, that I would have lost whatever advantage I otherwise would have gained. And so, without any hesitation, I said, 'Why, certainly I would be delighted to, and we can have it at the President's Home.'"

Sanford's immediate and positive response startled Traver and the others. They had anticipated equivocation and delay while Sanford checked with the deans and others in the administration. Instead, they found him steadfast in his declaration even after the *Daily Tar Heel* inaccurately lumped Sanford together with the radical antiwar activist Rennie Davis as the co-sponsor of an upcoming "antiwar festival" in Chapel Hill. Against advice from some who said he should protest, Sanford let the story stand without objection. A few days later he was quoted in the *Chronicle* saying, "Personally I feel the time has come to bring the war to an end. I'm certainly in favor of students expressing their position on the war. I'm glad this is happening."

The Wicker visit could not be arranged, but Sanford recruited a substitute speaker in Vermont Governor Phil Hoff, another critic of the war, and hosted a reception for him at the Alumni House where he passed along a $1,000 contribution to organizers. The money was from North Carolina native and successful Texas oilman Walter Davis, whom Sanford had seen the night before and who offered financial support to the students.[9] The event occurred with little objection, although Sanford did receive a note from the Duke chaplain, who complained about a "cocktail party" on school property. Sanford responded by explaining that the cocktails amounted to fruit punch.

Sanford believed he could do more. In the middle of April, he wrote in his journal, "What I would like to do now is find a new approach, a new device, for using this office and this forum to present the cause for getting out of Vietnam. I realize this cannot be my main business at Duke, but I believe it can be a useful part over the next year." A few weeks later, as the growing unrest over the war erupted into deadly violence, he was handed an occasion that erased any doubts of those who suspected him and his motives.

In early May, news that President Nixon had secretly ordered the bombing of Viet Cong positions in Cambodia produced a new round of campus demonstrations. Nothing shocked the nation more than what happened on a working-class campus in northern Ohio. On Monday, May 4, at Kent State University, National Guardsmen opened fire on a crowd of a thousand students, killing four and wounding six others. Student reaction on campuses across the land, including Duke, was swift. Campus leaders called for a May 6 boycott of all classes and a vigil and a fast in front of the chapel. Sanford told the *Chronicle* he had no objections to the boycott, but he had no intention of suspending classes.

Sanford remained alert. He was determined to maintain peace on the campus and continue all university operations. He was bothered that Traver, at a meeting on the eve of the demonstrations, had decided to take a more militant stance in favor of a strike, not a boycott. At the same time, Sanford believed in the students' right to speak their minds in the same way he had supported black citizens of North Carolina a decade before.

Sanford believed the best strategy was to put himself in the middle of the action, to be seen as available to any and all who wanted his attention. One hard-core group of students seemed determined to close the university and had taken issue with Sanford's support of plans for an ROTC ceremony scheduled for the same day as the demonstrations. The campus was swirling with talk, and on the eve of the demonstration Sanford wasn't sure what would happen next.

On the morning of May 6, Sanford met for breakfast with a group of students that included Bill Garrison, a law student and son of one of his steadfast political supporters from the North Carolina mountains. Since the reception for Hoff a few weeks earlier, Sanford had been talking to Garrison and leaders of the moratorium about alternatives to mass protests. He had gently suggested that the men trim their long hair, find more presentable clothes, and carry their protest to the greater Durham community to collect signatures on petitions that he would see were forwarded to Washington. Over breakfast, Sanford heard about the plans of some students to distribute leaflets supporting nonviolent demonstrations, and he took this as a good, even hopeful, sign that the protests would not lead to serious trouble.

By mid-morning on the next day, May 7, more than a thousand students had gathered in front of the chapel where the assistant chaplain, Elmer Hall, had arranged to toll the bell in memory of the students killed at Kent State. The sound of the bell quickly drew a crowd of students that turned its attention to Traver, who was using a bullhorn to try to move the crowd to action. Traver had just declared that the students should "take over the Allen Building" when he was surprised to see Sanford standing in the crowd gathered around him. Traver asked Sanford if he wished to speak and the president stepped forward, stealing the moment when he told the crowd that if they were going to take over the administration building they should "take me with you. I've been trying to occupy it for a month and have not been able to stay there very much." His humor broke the tension and then, in a serious, steady cadence he explained his position on the war and urged the students to think in terms of influencing national opinion, not just the powers that be on the Duke campus.

The demonstration broke up but students continued to mill about. Sanford remained visible, as did others from the administration whom he had deputized. The day before he had ordered all those reporting to him to remain visible, with no two standing together.[10] He had shut down his predecessor's so-called war room in the university's development office, where administration officials had huddled during previous troubles. All had been ordered to remain on the move, watching and reporting regularly to his office.

Sanford was determined to maintain control of the campus without becoming heavy-handed. When one of his vice presidents urged him to call Governor Bob Scott and ask for help from the Highway Patrol, Sanford heard him out before dismissing the suggestion; likewise, he had no intention of calling for reinforcements from Durham police. As if to demonstrate his own confidence in the course he had set, Sanford headed downtown at noon to meet a speaking engagement at the Lions Club. He delivered a prepared speech about Duke's relationship with the community and told the men he was pleased the campus was calm. "Of course," he later noted, "I had my fingers crossed and was tapping on the wood of the podium."

Events escalated that afternoon when a crowd of several hundred students filled the traffic circle just inside the main entrance to the West Campus. Several buses and a television news van were trapped. The group sent a delegation to Sanford demanding that university employees be sent home, which Sanford considered a ruse by protest leaders who wanted to claim they had closed the school. Sanford told the students he had no plans to close anything and he headed for the circle.

When he reached the traffic circle, he found a crowd of students sitting on the grass and in the roadway. The mood was no less tense than that of eight years earlier when hundreds of civil rights demonstrators had filled the lawn of the governor's mansion. But these young people were considerably more belligerent as they interrupted him with catcalls and obscenities after he was invited to speak his piece. He tried to diffuse the tension with humor, as he had the morning before, saying, "Just because I wear shoes and a tie doesn't automatically entitle me to your disrespect. It's just a bad habit that I picked up and can't break."

Students continued to interrupt him as he talked and, finally, when he had had enough of the epithets, he feigned anger, put down the bullhorn, and turned to leave. As he stepped away, he heard some in the crowd urge those causing the disruptions to be quiet and to let him speak. He stayed.

"Don't fight your university," he told the students. "Let us all fight Washington together." He announced that he had sent a telegram to President Nixon registering his opposition to the war and that the telegram carried the endorsement of the chancellor and forty-two other faculty members. The telegram said, in part, "We implore you to consider the incalculable dangers of an unprecedented alienation of America's youth and to take immediate action to demonstrate unequivocally your determination to end our military presence in Vietnam." [11]

Sanford told the crowd that he planned to speak at five that afternoon at Page Auditorium, where together they could make plans to organize their efforts into something more meaningful than blocking a few cars and buses. He rejected all demands that the campus be closed and declared it would remain open as long as one student wanted to go to class.

The auditorium was an appropriate enough venue. It was named, in part, for Walter Hines Page, an irreverent writer and publisher who had given his professors at old Trinity hell, writing as he departed the campus after just a short stay that the faculty looked like they "ought to be worming tobacco." By the time Sanford arrived, the fifteen hundred seats in the hall were filled and he walked to the microphone without introduction.

He commended the students for their orderly protest and expressed his opposition to the war as well as regret and sorrow over the students who had been killed and injured at Kent State. Students applauded when he declared that he would not bring police on campus "under any circumstances I could imagine." He startled some when he announced that he had asked the undergraduate faculty council to consider a pass-fail alternative that would allow students time off to work against the war beyond the campus. And he urged students to move out into the neighborhoods of Durham and talk to people about their feelings about the war, offering to help in organizing a citywide canvass. Sanford also announced that he was appointing a committee to influence the nation's foreign policy through student activity. He said that Chancellor Pye and five student leaders, including Felman, would be in six different places to meet with students to hear their ideas about what should be done. The tactic was designed to clear the hall and to give the students something concrete to do rather than to continue to stew among themselves.

As Sanford left the stage, a student rushed to the microphone to exhort the students to stay to plan a "real demonstration." Sanford picked up a chair, returned to the stage, and sat close to the speaker. Apparently, this action cooled any thoughts of such action and the crowd began to depart.

By the time he finished, Sanford believed he had successfully redirected most of the protesting students into the discussion groups where they could vent the emotion and energy that had been building throughout the day. About two hundred headed back to the circle and then marched through the quadrangle chanting, "We're on strike. Close it down."

Sanford headed home to a dinner party with Margaret Rose that had been planned by Durham businessman Frank Kenan and his wife, Betty. Just as the meal was about to be served, the telephone rang and Sanford was called back to campus, where a crowd had gathered outside the library while others had moved into the Allen Building. Some had entered the library and set off fire alarms, temporarily causing confusion and provoking students who had stayed clear of the turmoil to concentrate on their studies.

At the suggestion of Duke Chaplain Howard Wilkinson, Sanford asked the crowd to move into the chapel, where he spent the next several hours answering questions and talking with the students. This time he made it clear that he believed in vigorous dissent, but would brook no trouble. "I'm going to be a strong president, not high-handed, arbitrary or dictatorial, but I'm going to have to be the final referee between all points of view," he said. "I'm not afraid of you. I welcome your thoughts. I don't have any personal position to enhance. I did not come here to have any part in the downfall of Duke University, and I don't intend to let the university be torn apart." [12]

One of those in the crowd that night was Steve Schewel, who would later be elected student body president. Later, he wrote:

> He stands before us illuminated by the chapel lanterns and listens. Hospital workers talk about their working conditions and wages. Students and faculty talk about the war we hate. Sanford's attention is intense. He drinks it in, soothes, calms, never says "no," promises future action on all our causes.
>
> He holds us, comfortable, in his palm, but as he leaves one student raises a bullhorn and challenges him with angry words to act, to act now. There are shouts, all eyes on Sanford in the midst of the crowd. The image that burns: His eyes flash, his chin lifts, his jaw sets, he is still, and there suddenly descends the kind of remarkable, deep quiet that can inhabit Duke Chapel.
>
> He is in full command. The crowd once more is his. He calms us again, and he is gone. [13]

Before he left the chapel, Sanford agreed to a meeting the next morning to discuss student demands. Their list was extensive, as if the students had been waiting a long time for the right moment for someone to listen. Their agenda ran the gamut from issues Sanford could do nothing about, such as ending American involvement in Indochina, to issues over which he had some control, such as ending the military presence on campus and the "repression" of all workers, especially blacks and women, and endorsement of a union vote by nonacademic employees at Duke Hospital.

The union issue was one that had been smoldering since the so-called Silent Vigil of April 1968, begun in response to the murder of Dr. Martin Luther King Jr. The day after King's death, five hundred students had marched to President Knight's official residence to deliver a demand that he immediately double the salaries of Duke's black employees. Half the group ended up crowding inside the large, rambling home, where they remained for more than a day. The demonstration then continued on the main quadrangle, where the numbers swelled to more than fifteen hundred participants. After four days, the vigil ended with some concessions to raises for employees, but no answer on the union question.

The chapel meeting was an instance of the student protests that were gathering momentum across the country. At Chapel Hill, more than five thousand students had turned out for a rally where student body president Tommy Bello called for a strike of indefinite duration. In a front-page editorial, the *Chronicle* urged Duke students to "strike in an effort to peacefully shut down the University." In fact, the editorial urged students at all universities and colleges to strike until Nixon stopped American involvement in Southeast Asia.[14] Some campuses did close. In California, Governor Ronald Reagan shut the entire university and college system for a week. Pennsylvania closed its eighteen campuses. At Notre Dame, administrators followed a tactic similar to Sanford's and excused students from classes one afternoon to enable student-faculty discussions on the war. At Oberlin College in Ohio, students began organizing a march on Washington, D.C., for the coming weekend.

Through it all, Duke remained open. Students began a citywide canvass, knocking on doors and telling surprised residents why they were against the war. There were some problems, and Sanford took angry calls from some who students had visited, telling him, "I don't want those dirty, long-haired hippies coming to my home."[15] A few weeks later, a student delegation arrived in Washington where they met with Senator B. Everett Jordan, himself a Duke trustee, who pledged his support to end the war. They even got themselves photographed with the aging Jordan, a man of no liberal bent, raising the peace sign.

As calm began to return to the campus, Sanford reflected on the events that had been thrust upon him in his first weeks on the job. "All in all," he wrote in his journal, "I consider that I am extremely lucky to have come through this first test on fairly good terms, and I think with a fairly good degree of acceptance. It probably will be very good for me in the long run to have had this kind of confrontation now."

From the outset, Sanford had been bombarded by advice and suggestions on how to do his job. Some senior faculty had argued that he should
clear the campus, using force if necessary. Concerned parents and anxious
trustees had offered similar get-tough suggestions. He photocopied a few
of the letters from these hard-liners and mailed them to trustees to help
them "understand some of the burdens of putting up with this kind of
advice." By and large, the board members were impressed with Sanford's
cool handling of the demonstrations.

The entire episode enhanced Sanford's stature and would become part
of the legend of his administration, but he still faced other urgent issues,
some of them nettlesome matters that unsettled certain board members
who wanted tougher measures from their president. The board had extended unanimous support in his election as president, yet there were
trustees who remained skeptical about his motives for taking the job. Sanford also knew that certain members of the executive committee were accustomed to micromanaging the school. At one meeting, the group spent
two hours debating whether the school owned a two-acre plot and consumed enormous time naming buildings and reviewing details of budgets.
He became determined to direct their attention to a broader vision and to
end this intrusion in administrative matters after his first meeting, where
he had witnessed trustees treating university staff members with discour-
tesy to the point of rudeness.[16]

At an early meeting of the board's executive committee, Sanford was
pressed with a demand by some members to do something about the
Chronicle, which had published a series of articles about substandard housing that once had been the mill village of Erwin Cotton Mills. The articles
had embarrassed the university and Burlington Industries, which had made
the gift to the university, since the old houses now were in serious disrepair.

Sanford subscribed to the James B. Conant philosophy of student journalism, that campus newspapers should "be as free as the wind and never
read by adults."[17] He had no intention of putting the Chronicle out of business, but at the same time, he was bothered by some of the things he had
seen in the paper. The articles about the mill village contained inaccura-
cies, but he was disturbed more by the editors' casual use of obscenity in
print. With Chairman Wade's help, he steered the angry trustees onto other
matters while he nudged the editors toward a more acceptable standard
in their editing, eventually gaining adoption of a code of ethics and a vul-
garity clause for the paper. "If the editor will stand responsible for this,"
Sanford noted in his journal, "I will let him off from everything else."

Overall, Sanford believed he could work well with the board. He had
known the chairman since 1959, when Wade was the only top R. J. Reynolds

executive who had supported his campaign for governor. Sanford had rewarded him with appointment to the prestigious Board of Conservation and Development, and over the years the two had become friends. Because Wade lived in Winston-Salem, and not in Detroit as had his predecessor, he was close at hand when Sanford needed counsel and advice.

The board included other old friends such as J. Alex McMahon and Mary Semans, who was a devoted supporter. She had high hopes for Sanford; walking with him across the campus one evening she told him that her ambition for his administration was to reconnect Duke with its heritage and base in the Carolinas, where the Dukes had made their money. She told him that while she loved the school she could not abide its estrangement from the state: "It simply is snobbish. It's not acceptable and it has not opened up its doors to the state and the people around it who are just terribly important."[18]

An important concern for the board was Duke's sagging financial condition. Most particularly, annual giving from alumni was not growing fast enough to offset rising costs, and for the first time since it opened under its name in 1924, Duke was running a deficit of more than $1 million. Although the Medical Center was paying its own way, much of the rest of the school was in the red. Sanford had only begun to get a grasp on the extent of the problem when his chief financial officer, Charles Huestis, and others on his administrative team informed him that the athletic budget alone was three-quarters of a million in the hole for the coming year.

The declining financial condition was complicating more than the bottom line. Sanford learned that the interim management team had postponed an overhaul of the school's dormitory visitation policy, which students had turned into coed housing, growing in popularity on a number of campuses. The administrators feared tougher restrictions would cause students to pull out of the dorms in favor of apartments off campus, thus costing the school rental revenue. The permissive policy insulted Sanford's sense of decency. Regardless of the potential for lost revenue, he pressed ahead with new rules to prohibit cohabitation. Rising one morning at three, he wrote the outline of new regulations that prohibited overnight visits and added visitation limits to the annual rental contracts.

Sanford wasn't going to wait for miracles, or for the Duke Endowment to bail out the school. "At the first trustees meeting they said, 'This is the first time Duke has ever had a deficit; how are we going to conceal it?' I said, 'Conceal it? We're going to announce it, say we're going to do something about it, say we haven't had enough alumni support, that the alumni figured Mr. Duke financed this place and that's all we needed. We're going to start a new campaign.' I just took that and turned it into a positive."[19]

When he learned that the athletic program was in trouble, he assigned the school's popular baseball coach and later athletic director, Tom Butters, to spend the summer raising money, something that had never been done. When professors complained that their office windows were dirty, Sanford jokingly told them they could pick up cleaning supplies from the maintenance department. And when Huestis suggested replacing the carpet in front of the president's desk that was worn through to the floor, Sanford told him to hold off. "I don't want you touching this rug," he said. "You don't know it but that rug is worth several million dollars if you leave it just the way it is." [20]

The school needed new levels of giving from alumni and from foundations if it was going to achieve the goals that Sanford and others had in mind. In his initial meeting with Frank Ashmore, Duke's development officer, Sanford told him he should clear away any assignments that didn't deal with fund-raising and concentrate on his main job. He then informed Ashmore that he wanted his term as president to be known as the high mark in improving the school's endowment. In a short time, a goals committee was established and came up with a wish list that was trimmed to $100 million. After Sanford looked it over, he doubled it.[21] "They said, 'We've never raised $100 million,' and I said, 'We're not going to raise $200 million either.'" But, Sanford believed, the school would never have reached the lower level if it had been allowed to stand. "We finally raised around $160 million or so and I called victory."

Raising money was nothing new to Sanford. He had never felt uncomfortable asking those who had resources to part with them for his causes. As he made the introductory rounds upon taking office, he included visits to the major foundations, where he was well received and given some assurances of support. Three weeks after he took office, he even brought home a pledge for $750,000 from the William R. Kenan Jr., Charitable Trust to endow a full professorship, money that he later thanked Bill Friday at Chapel Hill for helping Duke to get.

The situation was serious but not overwhelming, Sanford allowed. In an interview with the Chronicle, he said, "I do not think this university is in as tight a pinch as most private universities in this part of the country and in this state in particular. But we are in a fairly tight situation." [22]

Sanford believed salvation lay in the potential of Duke's alumni base, much of it in North Carolina. When he visited alumni clubs in the Carolinas he made sure he traveled with a student from that city or from the state in an effort to remind the locals of Duke's North Carolina roots. He focused on a group of fifty prospects who had the means to ease the strain of Duke's financial burden. He would later joke that Duke's problem was a product of simple math: the school had simply not been around long enough to have an alumnus die of old age.

Duke University inaugurated Terry Sanford as president on October 17, 1970. It was a beautiful fall day as visitors filled the seats in the white wooden folding chairs on the chapel quadrangle about two hours before the ceremony was to begin at three-thirty. Among the guests were Sanford's mother, actor Andy Griffith, Washington Redskins football coach George Allen, and two of Sanford's mentors, Frank Porter Graham and Charlie Rose Jr., his former law partner from Fayetteville. Invitations were accepted by enough presidents and chancellors of other institutions for their names to fill more than four pages of the official program.

As he stood at the podium to receive his oath, a breeze shifted his blond hair about his forehead. Around his neck he wore for the first time in ceremonial use a heavy sterling silver chain holding a gilt medallion. Sanford crafted his speech about a theme he called "Toward a Re-personalized Society." It was a message of hope and a promise of an uplifting mission for a university seeking to move into the mainstream, just as he had hoped his state could do a decade earlier.

"Duke University can lead, therefore Duke University must lead," he began. "We can afford to wait no longer for constructive leadership from our federal government," he said. "For the sake of America, we must move democracy within this university community and among its members, as far as we can consistent with the viability of the university."

He could have been describing his own ambition when he told the audience, "In a time when the problems of our nation are so complex and difficult, we cannot be content with graduating people who will just fit into what is going on, and who will survive within the system in their own private worlds." Rather, Duke must develop in students the brain, the heart, and the courage to lead the kind of life that makes a difference in this world. Such a graduate would seek workable solutions and find workable ideas to improve the quality of life, he said. "It will be the creative leader's ability to influence, his will to initiate, his determination to seek the right, and his moral concern for all people, that will help to give constructive shape to our society's future. . . . I want to see for Duke University a spirit that makes a Duke graduate a Renaissance Man with a purpose," he said. He closed with a demanding quote from Walter Hines Page, who Sanford said had written a friend at Duke many years before: "Let's keep sounding the note of leadership, and the next generation will *hear* it, and take it up, and *do* it, praise God!"[23]

Alumni who returned to Duke for the inauguration couldn't help but sense a new spirit on the campus, as well as some changes. Students had moved to the forefront with Sanford's administration, and the new president closed his first year urging the board of trustees to admit its first student representatives. Sanford recruited juniors and seniors to work in his office, often handing them research assignments for information that might as easily end up in a speech as in a new policy for the university. He also had begun a series of social sessions, "Tea with Terry," as they came to be known, where all the entering freshmen were invited in small groups to meet at the house for several hours of conversation. It was heady stuff for young people for whom adults seemed not only remote but irrelevant. He assigned his student assistants to greet important visitors at the airport and drive them to the campus. No matter seemed too important or of too much consequence to involve students. Sanford shifted responsibility easily to those who seemed to camp at his office. "The more authority I gave the students, the more responsibility they came forward with," he said some years later.[24]

Even his critics on campus were stymied by his disarming style. "The radical students on campus believe it's impossible to outfox him," a *New York Times* article said. "He's just plain smarter than the radicals are," the paper quoted Mark Pinsky, a Duke graduate and writer for a local underground newspaper. "He's co-opted the hell out of them. And when he deals he doesn't just promise—he delivers." [25]

An example was Sanford's handling of student demands that they be allowed into trustee meetings, an issue that had been raised before Sanford's arrival on campus. At one of Sanford's early meetings with the board, students entered the room with the trustees and then refused to leave when the meeting was called to order. "Sanford walked over to us and we told him why we had remained," recalled Clay Steinman. "Come on into my office," Sanford told them. "Let's talk this thing over."

"We did. He asked us to let him see what he could do. He left and came back with an offer: [a *Chronicle* editor] could stay and cover the meeting, except for personnel matters. A committee would consider an open-meeting policy. We agreed. Subsequently, the board did open its meetings, and after a similar incident the following year, the board opened its committee meetings as well." [26]

Duke's heritage became a subject of considerable interest for the new president, particularly after he discovered in his talks with students that they had little understanding of the university's history. Sanford had always enjoyed history and he told Margaret Rose he might begin teaching a course linking Duke's heritage with contemporary events. At the same time, his speeches began to include frequent references to his predecessors. He never organized a formal classroom session on Duke history, as he had hoped, but he did create the Duke University Archives and oversaw the selection of Dr. William King as the school's first archivist.

In the fall of 1970, Sanford followed through with his promise to allow students time off to work in congressional campaigns. It was a numbing political year, with Americans in retreat from the turmoil of the spring. Turnout in the midterm elections was low. Across the South, however, there was a new stirring of spirit among the Democrats, now rebounding from the raids by both Republicans and George Wallace. Voters chose a new crop of governors whose election revived the turn-of-the-century talk of a "New South." Dale Bumpers won in Arkansas, Reuben Askew was elected in Florida, John West in South Carolina, and in Georgia voters chose as their governor a peanut farmer from Plains named Jimmy Carter. Sanford had watched the Georgia returns closely after Carter defeated a bid for a second term by his old friend Carl Sanders. That had been a bruising affair, with Carter cozying up to white racists and accusing Sanders of pandering to "special interests," meaning black voters.[27] Sanford was not pleased with the result—and never forgot that Carter used the race issue to defeat his friend—despite the bold and progressive statements on race that Carter made in his inaugural speech.

The election of this new crop of Southern governors provoked renewed interest in the region, which was becoming increasingly popular for new industry. Corporate relocations from old industrial bases in Ohio and Pennsylvania were beginning to change the population mix in such cities as Charlotte, Raleigh, Greenville, and Atlanta.

Sanford's earlier vision of a day when the South would shed the scales of the past and move beyond the scars of Reconstruction appeared closer than ever before. Sitting in his office one weekend, with the pounding bass from a rock music concert in the football stadium clearly audible through his closed windows, he sketched out his thoughts for the future as he prepared the keynote address he was to deliver before a new organization called the L. Q. C. Lamar Society.[28] The society was the creation of interested academics, journalists, and political leaders from the South who had adopted the name of a former senator and Supreme Court justice from Mississippi who spoke out for national reconciliation after the Civil War.

"The question is, what can the southern states do about their own future to avoid 'northern mistakes in a southern setting?' " Sanford said in a May 1971 speech he delivered in Atlanta to an audience that included the four new governors, Senator Edmund Muskie of Maine, and Mayor Moon Landrieu of New Orleans. "The South's time has come," he said, "after a century of being the whipping boy and the backward child. The time has come, finally come. The South can lead the nation, must lead the nation—and all the better, because the nation has never been in greater need of leadership." [29]

Sanford suggested that the southern states, led by the new crop of progressive governors, should agree to work together to solve regional problems. Over the coming months, he used the resources of Duke, the Society, and others to create the Southern Growth Policies Board, whose mission was to study and recommend solutions to common regional interests such as transportation, tax structure, population groups, and industrial locations. An interstate compact by the southern states "could be our instrument for showing the way in preserving and developing cities as cultural centers, and in the maintenance and improvement of schools," he suggested in an interview with the New York Times.[30]

In keeping with his ambition for the university to prepare students for the world, including the world of public service, Sanford succeeded in bringing Joel Fleishman to Duke in 1971 to develop the Institute of Policy Studies and Public Affairs. After leaving the governor's office, Fleishman had returned to Yale, where he proposed a curriculum that would combine a variety of disciplines—economics, political science, history—into a unified course of study at the undergraduate level, with students taking on a policy problem and seeking solutions. Sanford liked the idea of "inoculating" young people with a dose of public interest and responsibility: "Sure, we wanted a graduate program and we wanted to train professionals, but my own experience had been that just training professionals at the graduate level missed the point of creativity, missed the people who were going to be officeholders, people who were going to be influential in state and local governments without being an administrator." [31]

Though reluctant to leave his beloved New Haven, Fleishman came to Duke and opened the new institute in January 1972; he was producing graduates before the curriculum he had recommended at Yale enrolled its first class.

The Duke presidency proved to be all that Sanford had hoped it would be. And his performance on the job was attracting attention. Look magazine published a profile on him, and Time mentioned him favorably. He even found a place on the editorial pages of the New York Times with a piece entitled "A Memo to Mr. Agnew." In it Sanford scolded Vice President Spiro Agnew for his attacks on student protesters. "The deep troubles of our society do not begin on college campuses, are not bred there, and are not centered there," Sanford wrote. "Instead, our possibilities for resolving these troubles find their greatest hope on our college campuses." [32]

A New York Times article, published just before Sanford's inauguration, observed:

In an age of campus unrest, the closest some politicians allow themselves to get to a university today is a National Guard command post. But in two weeks Duke University, with pomp and ceremony, will officially install a politician as its sixth president.

Some people on campus think that the political skills the 53-year-old Mr. Sanford learned in the state house in Raleigh are peculiarly adapted to tricky problems of higher education. Moreover, Mr. Sanford's success at Duke over the next two years could enhance his standing as a choice of the Democratic Party for vice president in 1972. The prospect already has widespread currency because of Mr. Sanford's ability, as a progressive Southerner, to fit well with almost any Democrat now contemplated as a candidate for the presidency. Indeed, there are those who believe Mr. Sanford could become the Democratic answer to Vice President Agnew and his repeated sallies against much of the academic community.

Sanford told the *Times* reporter that when he took the job at Duke he had ruled out any statewide political office through 1972, but had not made the same promise about national office. "I won't campaign for it, but I've never made a Sherman-like statement that I wouldn't accept it."[33]

Since his arrival at Duke, Sanford had devoted all his time to the university, setting his political interests aside. "Of course, old friends would call and I would give them encouragement," he said. "I had to avoid getting in there. We had too many Duke people on both sides. If I had come over here as a political figure, pretty soon they would have found a reason to get rid of me. . . . I figured that if I set myself a goal of five or six years I could get out of it decently, but I could see a longer range thing here. I could see that there was so much to be done here, so much to work with and so much to build on. I thought that [a limited term at Duke] was kind of a safeguard. They were firing presidents [of universities] right and left. If I was going to leave, I wanted to say I'm leaving on schedule."[34]

One who remained in regular contact was Bert Bennett. Just a few days before Sanford began his work at Duke, Bennett arranged a reunion of the old crowd from 1960 to coincide with an annual Democratic Party gathering in Raleigh. About forty of the county chairmen and area keys from that campaign showed up for a private breakfast with Sanford, and later that day a thousand friends turned out for a reception. The party happened to coincide with a solar eclipse, and Sanford observed that he was not leaving politics for good; he promised to return like the sun.

In the plan that Sanford had unveiled that fall in 1969 at Hound Ears, the last date on his chart was 1976. He fully expected Nixon to complete two full terms in office, and though he had briefly explored the possibility of running in 1972, he had put such thoughts aside by the time a group of students approached him in January asking permission to mount a petition campaign to put his name on the ballot. Sanford was pleased, yet at the same time he found himself in a difficult position. "I did not stop them," he later wrote, "primarily because, I suppose, I thought this was a pretty good exercise in democracy, and I knew anyhow that the Duke trustees would not go along with it, and nevertheless we would have seen a position made that these students are not satisfied with the Democratic field."[35]

The early groundwork for the petition drive was the work of Bill Garrison, the son of a school superintendent in western North Carolina and one of Sanford's supporters in his gubernatorial campaign. During his senior year at Duke, young Garrison had worked for Sanford in the president's office before heading to law school in Chapel Hill. Garrison had proved helpful in staying in touch with students during the tumultuous early days in May 1970 and he remained a regular visitor to Sanford's office. Working with Garrison on the petition drive was William Blue, a former president of UNC student government.

As the 1972 presidential primary season approached, Sanford had no plans to be publicly involved, although he had entertained some calls from those who believed the Democratic field was weak and that he had a chance. Sanford encouraged Hubert Humphrey to again seek the nomination because he was not impressed with Senator Edmund Muskie, who was gaining endorsement from party regulars. He feared that the party was headed down a disastrous path with the liberals forming behind Senator George McGovern. McGovern and party liberals had used a commission created following the disastrous Chicago convention to produce new delegate selection rules that diluted the power of the power brokers and party regulars who had controlled conventions in the past. A by-product of the changes was new delegate selection procedures that tended to favor issue-oriented candidates such as McGovern. It also was clear that George Wallace would once again be a factor.

Sanford's exit was to be provided by the Duke trustees, whom he believed would never approve of his entering a political contest. Thus, he reasoned, when the board turned him down, the petition campaign would quickly end. A week before a scheduled board meeting in January he sent each trustee a note explaining that he had not planted the speculation about his candidacy in the press. "When we meet here next week, I will tell you all about it," he wrote.[36]

Sanford also called McMahon, who had succeeded Wade as chairman of the board, and alerted him as soon as talk of the draft movement became public. McMahon was surprised but did not discourage him. As he began fielding phone calls from board members prior to the meeting, McMahon defended the notion, even against those who complained that Sanford was doing just what they had suspected, using Duke as a political stepping stone. He told board members they were "dead wrong. Even after a few years, if he leaves us, he has made the place better already." Besides, he argued, "who will be hurt? The flak is going to come from people who are opposed to him no matter what he does. Besides, what are you going to do about it, ask him to resign? It doesn't make sense to do that." Others were supportive, McMahon said, and recalled that it had not hurt Princeton University to have Woodrow Wilson in the White House.[37]

On the day of the board meeting, Sanford walked into his office and was handed an envelope by Mrs. Mimms, who told him it was from Thomas Perkins, whom Sanford knew to be a staunch Republican and a close friend of Richard Nixon. As the head of the Duke Endowment, Perkins carried considerable sway within the board of trustees. "I opened it up as if it might blow up," he later recalled. "Dear Terry," Perkins's note began. "I understand that the students have petitioned you to run for President. I understand that the filing fee is a thousand dollars. I enclose my personal check."[38]

At the meeting, Sanford was about to outline to the board how the draft movement had developed and then excuse himself while the trustees discussed the matter. Before he could begin, Washington lawyer Charles Rhyne, another Nixon Republican, told him he didn't need to leave and proceeded to deliver a statement that "could have passed for a nominating speech."[39] Judge Braxton Craven followed in the same spirit as Sanford sat stunned. He had never taken a poll, but he believed most of the board were probably Republicans, and conservative Republicans at that. He knew that if he had had to count on them to be elected governor, he would still be practicing law in Fayetteville. To his profound surprise, he found he had the board's approval to run.

The board's decision was not that clear-cut, recalled McMahon. And he didn't give Sanford much chance of winning anyhow. "So, what the hell. Let him run and have his fun, because a political animal is a political animal, meaning, you can't stop those people from being politicians, and he certainly was."[40]

Even after the board decision cleared the way for his candidacy, Sanford postponed an announcement. There was much to consider. He also knew the odds on his winning the nomination were long and that he would be entering the presidential contest woefully late. Outside of enthusiasm, he had little else to work with. He had no organization and no money and he faced an uphill battle to win credibility in his home state. He couldn't even count on support from his own governor. Bob Scott already had declared himself for Muskie and was not happy when he learned of Sanford's candidacy. "It irritated me that Sanford would do that," Scott later recalled. "He had a huge ego. He didn't figure he had to consult with too many people to ask their opinion. I felt like I had gotten out there on a limb—by his being here in the state—and got that thing sawed off behind me." [41]

Some of his closest friends tried to talk him out of entering the race and asked Tom Lambeth to argue their case with Sanford. "I was the one who was supposed to convince him not to run for president," Lambeth recalled. "I got up there and he told me a story about lying on a hill during the war and looking at a church, and then there was something about going to somebody's funeral. All I know is that I left there wondering, who are these fools telling him not to run? What am I doing here? I would rather be one of the ones remembered as one of those who agreed with him." [42]

Bert Bennett told him a presidential campaign "doesn't ring a bell with me" and turned his attention to building the political career of a young Wilson lawyer named Jim Hunt, whom he had first met in the 1960 campaign when Hunt was a senior at State College. Bennett's decision to take on Hunt's campaign for lieutenant governor, which was considered a second-tier campaign by many old-timers, began a political association that culminated with Hunt's unprecedented four terms as governor.

Sanford was not deaf to his friends. "I think it is true that they didn't think it was a serious campaign," Sanford said years later. "You could interpret that as 'Who is this jerk think he is running?' or you could have interpreted it in a kinder way, that I prefer to do, that the climate was not right. We probably could have changed the climate. But it was a question again, if they were skeptical, so was I." [43]

Before he announced any decision, he and Margaret Rose flew to Florida in late February where he had arranged a meeting with Muskie, who was struggling to revive his candidacy in the Florida primary. Sanford asked Muskie to release Scott from his commitment, but Muskie refused and discounted Sanford's reading that he, Muskie, would lose the North Carolina primary. Muskie did agree to talk to Scott, and he and Sanford parted on good terms.

The campaign could have ended there. He suggested to Margaret Rose that they remain in Florida for another day or two, relax a little in the sun, and then return to Durham where he would figure out a way to handle the student petitioners. Then facetiously he told his wife, "If the Lord wants me to save these people, I've got to see a burning bush."

The next evening, as he watched the television news in their hotel room, he was startled by a report from New Hampshire where Muskie had staged an appearance outside the offices of the *Manchester Union Leader* to protest disparaging articles that had been published about his wife. Muskie was so upset that he was moved to tears as he defended his wife's honor. "As it came on color television," Sanford later recalled, "when he began to cry, the color did something that his face, already reddened, exploded into a flash of red. And I said, 'There's the burning bush.' " [44]

Actually, Muskie's campaign was already in trouble before the Manchester episode. He had done poorly in New Hampshire and like the rest of the Democrats trailed far behind George Wallace, who swept the Florida primary with 42 percent of the vote, carrying every county in the state. Within a few weeks, he was drawing oversized crowds in Wisconsin, and his rousing rhetoric against busing, federal judges, and "pointy-headed pseudo-intellectuals who can't park their bicycles straight" touched raw nerves in voters who seemed fed up with candidates toeing the traditional political line.

If there was anything that moved Sanford to make the leap in 1972, it was probably his desire to challenge Wallace and show the nation that all Southern politicians were not demagogues. Defeating Wallace, particularly in his own region, was the kind of challenge that appealed to his competitive spirit and supreme self-confidence. If he could beat Wallace and at the same time extend his reach into other parts of the country, then it was possible for him to arrive at the Democratic National Convention in Miami not only as a compromise candidate, but as something of a giant killer.

Wallace represented the worst of Southern politics, Sanford thought. Sanford believed he understood the racist attitudes of men of another generation, such as Mississippi's Ross Barnett, who truly believed segregation was the proper order of things. Wallace was different. Sanford believed the Alabama governor was an opportunist who used this volatile, dangerous, and divisive issue to win votes. It was a most cynical approach and it deeply offended Sanford, who considered politics to be a force for good, not a lever to increase personal power and glory. "I always thought George was just a pure hypocrite, unlike Ross Barnett, who felt that God had intended things as they were. George started out as kind of an enlightened integrationist and then made his famous speech that he would never be 'out-segged again.' I think George saw it as just a great game, just another issue to be played, and he played it the way it was an advantage to play it," Sanford said later. [45]

Three days before he announced his candidacy on March 8, Sanford attended a conference on Southern politics at Loyola University in New Orleans, where he said that Wallace was not representative of the South.

"We have the kind of new politics that has broken the old cycle of fear and hate," he said.[46]

At a press conference the following day, Sanford said, "There comes a time in a man's life, despite the odds, when he is compelled to do what he thinks should be done, be it personal, public or political. That time has come for me." He defended his decision to remain at Duke while campaigning for office, saying, "Duke University and what we are trying to accomplish at Duke are too important for me to neglect in any degree, but holding that position or any other position neither disqualifies me nor relieves me from the duties of citizenship."[47] He said he would campaign on weekends, on his own time, and concentrate his efforts in North Carolina. He hoped to go to the Democratic convention in July in Miami with about a hundred delegates. That was far less than he needed for the nomination, but he knew it was too late in the political season to claim anything more.

Some initial reaction was positive, but the *News & Observer* discounted his campaign. Even an editorial in the *Chronicle* questioned whether, although his candidacy would increase the possibility of greater recognition for Duke and of financial contributions, it was wise for Sanford to spend so much time away from campus on nonuniversity business: "If it turns out that Sanford can effectively handle a campaign and his presidential duties at Duke, then we will consider the question of endorsement. But for right now, we just want to see what this campaign is going to do for Duke."[48]

The *New York Times* commented a few days later, "Mr. Sanford was an excellent Governor of North Carolina and is now widely esteemed as a university president. In another year and under different circumstances, it is even conceivable to think of him as a possible president of the United States. Certainly, he was high on Hubert Humphrey's list of Vice-Presidential possibilities in 1968 when the decision went instead to Senator Edmund S. Muskie. But in this year's heavily overcrowded field of Presidential contenders, Mr. Sanford's belated candidacy only further divides the already fragmented liberal center of the Democratic party."[49]

There remained a glimmer of hope, however. Well-known political pollster Joe Napolitan, who had done work for Sanford in the past, outlined the chances in a long memo he circulated around the country: "I think that for the first time since 1952, the convention will go more than one ballot, and if it goes more than three I think there will be an opportunity for a compromise candidate." Sanford could be that candidate, he argued. "I don't know anyone in politics who doesn't like Terry Sanford or respect his intelligence and ability. He isn't well known to the people, but if he should get the nomination, we can take care of that easily enough. He is a new face on the national scene and that's certainly an advantage."[50]

When filing closed for the North Carolina primary, Sanford found himself in a field that included Muskie, Senator Henry Jackson, a conservative from Washington state, and Shirley Chisholm, a black congresswoman from New York. McGovern and Humphrey stayed out.

The *News & Observer* called the race the "Dixie Classic," but it was a one-sided fight. Wallace had vowed to shake up the Democratic Party "to its eye teeth,"[51] and paid little attention to Sanford, dismissing him as a "high-type" individual, an expression he could deliver with a slight sneer and considerable disrespect. At one point, he told a reporter for *Newsweek* that Sanford was dull and uninteresting. "Have you ever heard him make a speech?" Wallace was quoted as saying of Sanford. "He'll bore your ass off." (Sanford responded, "I remember the time he heard me speak. Sure he was bored, because I was talking sense.")[52]

Wallace's 1972 campaign appeared to be going every bit as strong as his bid in 1968, when he had won the electoral votes of five states. "Send them a message," he said as he preached against busing for school integration and talked about what he would do if any antiwar protesters lay down in front of his car. He capitalized on a growing alienation of white voters from a government that they believed had grown too large and too generous with welfare at their expense. People liked what they heard.

In the weeks prior to the North Carolina primary, Wallace was also campaigning in Wisconsin and Indiana, two states where he got a strong popular vote but not a proportionate delegate count. Wallace made several campaign stops in North Carolina, moving from appearances in small towns such as Statesville to rallies in Asheville, Winston-Salem, and Greensboro. Traveling with him was his second wife, Cornelia, who would huddle in the corner of the cabin of his private jet wrapped in a white fur coat while her husband chatted easily with a traveling reporter. As his plane made the short hop from Statesville to Asheville he reminisced about a time in his youth when he worked his way across the state selling Bibles door to door. His rallies produced large and enthusiastic crowds.[53]

Sanford struggled for attention in the midst of it all. Most North Carolina voters seemed more interested in the other races on the ticket. Republicans and Democrats had full slates of candidates for governor and the U.S. Senate. At campaign stops, he talked about ending tax loopholes for the wealthy, putting price controls on all foods, a 25 percent increase in Social Security payments, equal rights for women, and establishment of national health insurance. He also advocated decentralization of power to the states, a theme he had developed in his book, *Storm Over the States*. As for Wallace, Sanford told voters the Alabama governor had "stood in the school-house door, [while] I was opening the doors to education to everyone."[54]

In an appearance before a group of business leaders in Birmingham, Alabama, deep in the heart of Wallace territory, Sanford spoke to the voter discontent that had swept Wallace into the mainstream, but he offered a response quite different from Wallace's. "[People] are fed up with a purposeless circular war that has gone on. They are fed up by an economy that got overheated by war and which is now out of control. Housewives are alarmed by day to day realities of inflation." Beneath the surface of this national mood, Sanford said, the specific grievances of Americans add up to one passionately felt conviction: "that government is not working."

Speaking to a nonpartisan crowd, Sanford did not refer directly to Wallace's campaign against the federal government, but he spoke to the same concern in more measured words:

> We must find a way to make our government work. We must find a way to involve more people in the decisions that affect their lives.
>
> We can revitalize government in America. The South does not exhibit a negative spirit. The answer to all problems . . . is not to scream at the problem but to be sane and reasonable and calm and determined to find intelligent solutions. If we do not like Washington and centralized super planning—and I for one have been leaning against it for twenty years—then we have to have local planning. In the South we still have an opportunity if we look to the future . . . to avoid most of the mistakes that have been made by northern cities.[55]

Sanford received a temporary boost in mid-March when his name was placed on the ballot for the May 4 presidential primary in Tennessee. (It was later withdrawn, however, by the Tennessee secretary of state on the basis that his candidacy was not widely enough known.) His campaign would rise or fall in North Carolina, however, where he recruited Clint Newton, the textile company executive from Shelby who had helped him in his bid for the YDC presidency in 1949, to coordinate the work of the young people led by Blue and Garrison. Newton moved to Durham and devoted full time to the campaign. On March 17 Sanford opened a headquarters in Durham and named as comanagers Lee Wing of Durham, a former member of the state Democratic executive committee, and C. Woodrow Teague, a Raleigh lawyer who had worked on his campaign for governor. Teague's appointment proved a severe disappointment for Bert Bennett, who had counted on Teague to help him elect Jim Hunt lieutenant governor. Sanford's raid into the ranks of the old organization widened a growing gap between Sanford and Bennett, whose political interests were on separate tracks.

At the same time, a national campaign organization was coming together under John Hoving, a veteran Washington insider whose career had begun with Estes Kefauver and who had come to know Sanford in the

Humphrey campaign, and Julian Scheer, the former *Charlotte News* reporter who had his own public relations business in Washington after many successful years in charge of public affairs at NASA. Scheer drew on others in Washington, such as Duke graduate and Washington lawyer Anthony Harrington; Gael Sullivan and Michael Murray, experienced lobbyists from Capitol Hill; and Spencer Oliver, who was on the Democratic National Committee staff as coordinator of the state party chairmen.

In early April, Jeffrey Kurzweil, the student member of the Duke board of trustees, was appointed Sanford's campaign manager for the June 6 New Jersey primary; Robert Morgan, Beverly Lake's campaign manager in 1960 who was now North Carolina attorney general, volunteered to go to New Jersey to pay Sanford's filing fee.

All the flurry of activity seemed bootless in the face of the momentum gathering behind the candidacies of McGovern, Wallace, and Humphrey. McGovern moved ahead in the delegate count after the Wisconsin primary. Sanford was encouraged as a few moderate and conservative Democrats shuffled about looking for an alternative to McGovern. On April 5, Senate Majority Leader Mike Mansfield predicted that a new face like Sanford or Florida Governor Reuben Askew might wind up with the Democratic nomination. Sanford's own campaign surged with new life as he picked up a $300,000 loan from Mrs. Frank Forsyth, the daughter of Z. Smith Reynolds of the Reynolds tobacco fortune in Winston-Salem, who had worked with Sanford on the North Carolina Fund.

Returning from one campaign trip in the West, Sanford stopped at the LBJ Ranch in Texas. The former president met him at the ranch's air strip in his famous white Lincoln convertible and played the warm and gracious host. Sanford said he seemed eager for visitors. On another visit, Johnson gave Sanford a copy of his recently published memoir, *The Vantage Point*, with a $500 campaign contribution tucked inside. The man who once had directed the nation now had other, less weighty matters on his mind. "He got in and drove on up by the barn," Sanford recalled. "There is a great big fellow with overalls on, old time gallus overalls. He is standing there, chewing tobacco, and Johnson stopped and the man says, 'Why I had the cultivator out there and it broke, and I was trying to plant some peas. Now, I don't know whether to plant the peas or fix the cultivator.' There was Lyndon Johnson making those kind of decisions." [56]

Sanford took heart in some polling data gathered just before Muskie withdrew from the race that showed Wallace with 33 percent of the North Carolina vote compared to his share of 28 percent. Sanford believed that if he could pick up Muskie's 14 percent he could push ahead of Wallace. [57]

The same poll showed Chisholm with less than 10 percent of the vote, but as primary day neared, Sanford was worried about her appeal to black voters. Sanford knew he would need black voters to defeat Wallace, and as unlikely as Chisholm's nomination appeared, her candidacy stirred strong response among blacks who had never before had a chance to vote for a black presidential candidate on a major party ballot. It was impossible for a white candidate, even one as sympathetic to civil rights as Sanford was, to overcome that relationship.

On election eve, Sanford sponsored a television appearance relayed across the state and took phone calls from voters. Produced in an era before such productions were finely tuned with staged questions and responses, the show had a roughness and spontaneity that was fast disappearing from politics. The candidate responded directly to callers, whose questions reflected the issues of the campaign rather than a producer's script. He talked about welfare costs, the rising cost of medical care and a college education, busing, the lifetime tenure of Supreme Court justices, the war in Vietnam. And there was the inevitable question about the "food tax." Sanford fielded each with calm, deliberate, and uncharacteristically brief answers, expanding a little longer on the tax question. But it was the first question he took that created his biggest headache in the campaign and frustrated him until the day the polls opened. Was he a serious candidate, or posturing to become a vice presidential nominee, a student from Elon College asked. "I certainly wouldn't be sitting here if I were not a serious candidate," Sanford answered. "I'd rather be president of Duke University than vice president and furthermore I'd rather be unemployed than be in the cabinet." [58]

Wallace easily outdistanced Sanford at the polls and captured more than 40 percent of the vote. The final count gave Sanford 304,000 votes to Wallace's 408,000. Chisholm got 61,000. It was a thorough drubbing. Sanford carried only four of thirty counties in which he had won a majority in 1960. Wallace's margin had increased over the vote he received in the state in the 1968 general election, from just less than a third to more than half of all votes cast. Even if Sanford had received all of Chisholm's vote, he would have carried only a few more counties in the Piedmont.

Sanford had suffered defeat at the polls before, but none of them—Graham's loss in 1950, the bond referendum in 1961, and Preyer's defeat in 1964—cut as deeply as this. On election night, his daughter Betsee stood at the rear of the headquarters as the results came in, tears streaming down her face, asking a friend how North Carolina could desert her father at such a time. [59]

"He can give you his own impression," Sam Poole later said, "but my impression was that the people of North Carolina were rejecting something that he had spent all of his political capital developing and that Wallace came in and turned the whole thing around. There were a lot more things involved in it than that, but that was really a very low point in his life." [60]

Virtually everything Sanford had been able to count on in past campaigns had failed him. Old loyalties had been complicated by his late entry and changes in political fortune. Scott had discounted his campaign. And Sanford would never forget the man who financed Chisholm's campaign was John Wheeler, the Durham banker whom he had arranged to be seated in 1964 as the state's first black delegate to a Democratic national convention. "That's a terrible irony," Sanford would later say. "She came out attacking me, and not Wallace." [61] Sanford gained the endorsements of some black leaders, such as Kelly Alexander, the head of the state NAACP, but Reginald Hawkins of Charlotte, who had run for governor in the Democratic primary in 1968, argued that winning delegates for Chisholm was more important than repudiating George Wallace.

"Nobody thought Wallace was going to be president," Sanford reasoned some years later, "but a whole lot of people thought Wallace had a message that ought to be delivered. And I didn't have a message. I would be the person who didn't have a chance, a person who was on an ego trip, a person who was 'What in the world is he doing in the campaign?' " [62]

The campaign thoroughly strained Sanford's relations with many old friends, including Hargrove Bowles, who won the Democratic primary for governor in May after a bruising contest with Lieutenant Governor H. Patrick Taylor Jr. Both men had been part of Sanford's campaign in 1960 and both had visited Sanford in search of endorsements. Although Sanford felt particularly close to Bowles, who had served his administration for four years, he did not endorse either man. [63]

For others, such as Bennett, the 1972 campaign was a turning point, when the man who had brought him into statewide politics went one direction and he went another. From 1972 on, Sanford's supporting cast began to shift from those friends with purely state interests, such as Bennett, to Duke associates such as Bill Green and Sam Poole, who had become his chief political aide.

Despite the outcome of the North Carolina primary—almost in spite of the outcome—Sanford was not ready to quit. He had said he would not continue if he failed to carry his home state, but after the primary he announced he would take his campaign on to Miami and praised his band of student volunteers. He claimed that he had "won" because he had talked about real issues: "We have said what ought to be said to America." Against considerable odds, he claimed he had done well in the short campaign, tripling support in just six weeks. "My concern for the future of our country has not diminished," he said. "In fact, the last few weeks have convinced me more than ever that the nation is in deeper crisis than many of us in public life have acknowledged—a crisis of trust and despondency, over a war that we have prolonged and mismanaged, over an economy reeling with uncertainty, and a government structure demanding sweeping reforms to respond to the problems of the average man."[64] To continue meant working only a few weeks more, Sanford said, and it would make life more exciting, particularly for the young people who were being given uncommon responsibility.

"We've got nothing to lose," Sanford campaign worker Julian Scheer told the *Winston-Salem Journal* in July as the convention opened in Miami. "We didn't come down here trying to be a front-runner, and we're not trying to make any deals. We got started because a bunch of these kids wanted a chance to work within the system and because we had some things to say. When anybody asks me why we are staying in, I just say, 'Why not?'"[65]

Tom Drew was one of those in the "kiddie corps," as Clint Newton called the student volunteers. "I graduated on May 9 and on the Monday after graduation they gave me a travel advance and sent me and my brand new graduation present, an automobile, to Florida to work the entire Florida delegation," Drew said. "I'm going to talk to Wallace delegates and black delegates about being Terry Sanford delegates. I talked to 85 percent of the Florida delegation and I probably generated more first ballot votes for Terry Sanford than anybody." When he was through there, Drew went on to Sanford's Washington headquarters, where he worked delegates from other states, including South Carolina, where he met a young Bill Clinton, who was an organizer for McGovern. Drew later joined two busloads of students, with the formidable Mrs. Mimms as den mother, and headed off for Miami. "We didn't have a care in the world, and we were still hoping for a deadlocked convention," Drew said.[66]

The final weeks before the convention in Miami were without any real hope of success. "We were getting great coverage in the press," recalled Scheer. "We were getting a fair amount of delegates. Everything was happening except the sort of spark that would make him the nominee. The philosophy was that if Humphrey didn't do it, the convention would have to turn to somebody else and standing there in the wings with a respectable number of delegates, with no blemishes, with a great record, was Terry Sanford."[67]

For the most part, Sanford spent convention week renewing contacts and enjoying the excitement of his volunteers, who otherwise may never have seen the inside of a national political convention. Some later counted Sanford's minicampaign as their start in politics. Bob Weiss, a Duke student who later went on to mount a successful campaign for Congress in West Virginia, worked in the Sanford boiler room where delegates were tallied. Wyche Fowler, later a senator from Georgia, was a student at Davidson College when he signed on with Sanford.

Two days before the nominating speeches, the all but lifeless body of the campaign quickened with one last surge of hope when Sanford was told that Humphrey was pulling out of the race and throwing his support behind Sanford. "We had a modest celebration that night," Scheer recalled. "We knew the long shot of politics, but we had a chance and our dream could become reality in just a few hours." [68] When Humphrey made his announcement, however, he released his delegates without directions. "Our campaign was over," Scheer said.

Sanford refused to end it there, and Hodding Carter III, a newspaper editor from Mississippi whose father had won a Pulitzer prize for his courageous editorials on race relations, delivered the nominating speech. Chapel Hill Mayor Howard Lee, the first black man to hold that office, and Virginia Attorney General Andrew Miller gave seconding speeches to delegates who paid little attention and were eager to get to the voting.

Sanford received 128 votes on the first ballot, which may have been a source of pride to his "campers" but meant little as far as the nomination was concerned. McGovern had captured the nomination with room to spare. Senator Henry Jackson was his closest contender with 534 delegates. Sanford's final count dropped to just under 70 votes, behind Wallace and Chisholm, and he was lumped in the "others" category by most writers.

After Miami, Sanford returned to the quiet of Durham and to Margaret Rose, who had been impatient with the campaign from the outset and its disruption of home life for six months. She never knew who she would find sleeping in the large, rambling president's home that became a virtual dormitory for young campaign workers. She had asked her husband time and again why he was running. Finally, he asked her, "What were you doing in the spring of 1972? She said, 'I don't know; what do you mean?' And I said, 'Well, whatever it was, you'll never forget the spring of 1972.' " [69]

If he took any comfort in the exercise, and that was his habit, Sanford believed he had cut a new path for Southern Democrats. "I proved my premise," he later told a reporter, "which is that the Civil War is now over. Before now, the South could never have had a president." His sentiment was shared by others. Robert Sherrill, writing in the Saturday Review prior to the convention, had said, "The South, which always used to settle for the vice presidential sop, seems to be brewing a new revolt." [70]

The 1972 general election produced a landslide victory for Richard Nixon, who won every state except Massachusetts. In North Carolina, Republicans broke the back of the Democratic Party by carrying eastern North Carolina and electing the first Republican governor since Reconstruction and the first popularly elected U.S. senator. That new senator was Jesse Helms, the editorial voice of Raleigh's WRAL-TV, who had been Sanford's nemesis when he was governor. Elected governor by a slim margin was Jim Holshouser, whose victory over Bowles came as a complete surprise to the state and to the candidate. The top-ranked Democratic officeholder in the state was Hunt, Bennett's candidate for lieutenant governor. The Republican revolution in the South had finally claimed North Carolina.

The Nixon victory left the Democrats fractured and angry. In January 1973, the party moderates and conservatives wrested the party leadership away from Jean Westwood of Utah, who had been a prime mover in the McGovern campaign, and installed as a new chair Robert Strauss, a Texas lawyer and wily party insider and fund-raiser. One of the last things Westwood did before leaving office was appoint Sanford to chair the Democratic Charter Commission. The creation of the commission had been ordained at the national convention where, almost unnoticed, a midterm convention also had been ordered. The commission's assignment was to prepare the party's first charter and attempt to repair some of the damage done by the delegate selection rules that had tipped the balance in favor of issue-oriented campaigns like McGovern's.

In the spring of 1973, Sanford began to assemble a staff for the Charter Commission and chose Clint Newton as director. He shuttled back and forth between the commission's headquarters in Washington and an office in Durham, rented rooms over Ken's Quickie Mart at 2526 Erwin Road. The 164-member commission scheduled its first meeting for April in Washington and kicked off an extensive slate of public conferences in May in Des Moines. Sanford originally had planned to hold conferences in each of the states but soon had to scale back due to time constraints. As many conferences as possible were scheduled for weekends to encourage participation from party members and to reduce the number of days Sanford would be absent from his duties at Duke.

The political advantages of the assignment were not lost on Sanford, who knew the commission work would give him a chance to travel the country, meet party leaders at all levels, and enjoy some attention from the national media. As he put the commission staff together, the group included experienced strategists from the McGovern campaign as well as his own close aides such as Sam Poole and Spencer Oliver, formerly with the Democratic National Committee staff, both of whom had attended the Hound Ears weekend back in 1969. For some of the Sanford partisans on the commission staff, the mission was clear. "For the next four years Terry

Sanford would be able to go around and meet all the key leaders of the Democratic Party and lay an incredible groundwork, grassroots network for a possible run for the presidency in 1976," said Tom Drew, who worked out of the Durham office. Sanford saw it differently, but did not deny the potential. "I wouldn't let them call it the Sanford Commission, which indicates I wasn't trying to use it," he said. "But I saw it as an opportunity to meet a lot of new people. That's about as far as it went. It wasn't a hidden agenda that, 'Now, oooh, I can get into the race.'"[71]

Most of the commission's early work in the spring and summer of 1973 was overshadowed by events in Washington, where another North Carolinian, Senator Sam J. Ervin Jr., was leading the Senate Judiciary Committee through an investigation of presidential misconduct. It was the beginning of the end for the presidency of Richard Nixon as an inquiry into a bungled burglary of the Democratic National Committee's headquarters at the Watergate complex in Washington escalated into a crisis of unimagined proportions.

A month before Nixon resigned in disgrace in August 1974, the work of the Charter Commission was largely completed. Sanford told a National Press Club luncheon in July that the party's new charter would abolish quotas for women, minorities, and other groups, end winner-take-all primaries, and provide for national goals. If adopted, the charter could help bind the party following its battles of 1972.

Sanford received high marks for his performance, but the process had not been without its divisive moments, among them tangling with Party Chairman Strauss. Sanford had known Strauss since before World War II, when both men were FBI agents in Ohio. The association did little for either man, and a generation later Strauss was more inclined to listen to another ambitious Southerner, Georgia Governor Jimmy Carter, whom he had chosen to head the Democratic Campaign Committee to help Democrats get elected in 1974.

With his toothy grin and inaugural declaration on civil rights, Carter had emerged as the symbol of the New South governors. He had dipped his toe into national politics at the Miami convention, where his aides had suggested to McGovern that he would be a perfect running mate. McGovern spurned the offer, but Carter and his friends went home convinced that he could do as good a job as any of the candidates he had seen.[72]

Carter also had convinced Strauss to add Hamilton Jordan to the national party staff in Washington, where Jordan was in a prime position to further Carter's interest and keep an eye on the competition. That included Sanford. Six months into the commission's work, Jordan sent a memo to Strauss in which he argued that Sanford had clearly sided with the party's dissidents and not with Strauss and "elected leaders" and that the commission's work was damaging the party. He said, "Sanford and his staff need to be slowed down and hopefully stopped," although he warned that a public confrontation should be avoided. Rather, he suggested, Strauss should leak to political columnists that the Charter Commission work was undermining his own efforts to rebuild the party.[73]

Sanford survived the political infighting and reached a peace with Carter when he postponed the midterm convention until after the fall 1974 elections. In December, the commission presented its final product with a proposed charter titled "We Reform That We May Preserve" to more than two thousand delegates meeting in Kansas City. By most accounts, Sanford was lauded for his skillful and egalitarian handling of the assignment, helping avert a last-minute walkout by black delegates. "As always in times of trouble," Sanford told the delegates, "Americans are turning once again to the Democratic Party for hope, for concern, for solutions. We cannot, we dare not, we will not fail them."[74] The convention proved to be an experiment that was never repeated.

Carter's campaign for the presidency was underway by the time of the gathering in Kansas City. He joined other early contenders such as Senators Henry Jackson and Lloyd Bentsen and all but ignored the convention agenda, instead working the state delegations in preparation for the 1976 presidential nomination. Like Sanford in 1972, Carter was met with the same doubting questions from reporters who were skeptical about the prospects of a one-term Southern governor.

Sanford had organized a Citizens Committee in 1974 and recruited as chairman former West Virginia governor Hulett C. Smith, but he waited for the close of the Kansas City convention to begin active campaigning. One of the early events in the spring of 1975 was a campaign fund-raiser in New York City that featured as a special guest former vice president Hubert Humphrey. On June 1, 1975, Sanford officially declared his candidacy at a press conference at the National Press Club Building in Washington and announced that his national campaign director would be Jean Westwood. He would begin campaigning full time in January, when he planned to take a six-month leave of absence from his duties at Duke. "I promise a bold campaign and a bold administration," he declared, "determined to put into practice the radical promise of the American Revolution, determined to talk sense and issues, openly and candidly, pledged to make the government join the people, to put people first in all our affairs and aspirations."[75]

Sanford even made an effort to shore up his shortcomings in foreign affairs, and he began making plans for a trip to Russia. Prior to his departure, Sanford and Julian Scheer visited the Russian embassy to talk with Ambassador Anatoly Dobrynin about the details of the trip. As they talked, it became apparent to Sanford that the officials he would be meeting with in Moscow were little more than minor functionaries, not the Kremlin leaders he needed to see to add substance to his political credentials. After Dobrynin finished, Scheer remembered, Sanford leaned close to Dobrynin and said in carefully measured tones, "I know you have to weigh my chances of being the next President of the United States when you advise Moscow on how to receive me." Then Sanford paused, leaned forward until he was just inches from the ambassador, and said, "But you must remember when you pose that question that he might just be." Then Sanford got up and left.

Scheer said Sanford took a leisurely stroll getting back to the campaign headquarters and when they arrived, a secretary came running down the hall. "Governor," she said excitedly, "Ambassador Dobrynin is on the telephone."

Scheer said Sanford told him to pick up another phone and listen in.

"Governor Sanford," Dobrynin began, "while we were enjoying ourselves so much and chatting, I failed to check the cables on my desk. There was one that said Premier Alexis Kosygin will see you Thursday in the Kremlin."

"I hung up and gave Terry a how-come-you-knew look," Scheer said.

"Diplomacy," Sanford answered.[76]

By the time he entered, the field was full. U.S. Senators Henry Jackson of Washington, Fred Harris of Oklahoma, and Lloyd Bentsen of Texas were in the race; so was Congressman Morris Udall of Arizona. And there were now two other Southerners, Carter and Wallace. Though confined to a wheelchair since an attempted assassination in 1972, Wallace and his team were putting together their best-financed and -organized effort ever.[77] "Too many people have been cozying up to him," Sanford told a reporter at his news conference. "Some people are afraid if they say something bad about him they'll upset him. I'm the nearest thing to him. I came up at the same time in similar climate, region and crucial times and it is my responsibility because of that to challenge him."[78]

Sanford said he planned to enter twenty primaries and hold "citizen assemblies" around the country where voters could discuss issues. The first was the following day in South Carolina where he told party leaders Charles "Pug" Ravenel and Lieutenant Governor Brantley Harvey and others that one of his main themes would be proposals to cut the federal budget. "He [President Gerald Ford] doesn't understand the economy and he continues to mess it up," Sanford was quoted in the *Charlotte Observer*.[79]

His request for a leave from his duties at Duke marked the end of five and a half years there. He had said that he intended to spend no more than six years at the school and he believed he had accomplished what he had originally set out to do.[80]

Since his arrival at Duke in April 1970, Sanford had mounted successful fund-raising campaigns and presided over the opening of a new telephone communications building, an eye center, an aquatic center, new campus apartments, nursing school additions, a new music building, and a new marine laboratory. Additionally, the board of trustees had added student membership at his request, the budget was into the black, and he had exposed the student body to dozens of prestigious speakers and lecturers from all walks of professional life by encouraging greater exchange with the day-to-day world.

There was a new vibrancy on the campus as Sanford began showing Duke University to the world. He engaged in what some considered shameless self-promotion, up to and including the production of a sixteen-page advertising supplement in the *New York Times*. Bill Green put the supplement together using faculty members and experiences from the Duke campus as a forum on the future of higher education. "There really was a sense that Terry was intent on leading Duke to new heights," Joel Fleishman would later say. "Terry had a vision for Duke that was larger than the existing vision, and he was willing to get behind good ideas. And that is in fact what happened."[81]

The labor troubles on campus had been resolved. A contest between rival unions had extended the issue for months after his arrival, but workers finally decided to accept representation by AFSCME on January 27, 1972, by a vote of 491 to 100. Seven months later, the union and the university signed a three-year contract with wage increases of up to 3.5 percent per year.

"At the end of five years I had done about what most people perceived I had come here to do," Sanford said. The sabbatical would give him a chance to try to fulfill his presidential aspirations. If at the end of those six months his chances didn't look good, then, in typical Sanford fashion, he would decide what else he might do. "I had pledged to come back and then if the trustees wanted me to and if I wanted to, I would continue for a few more years," he said.[82]

Through the summer and into the fall, Sanford squeezed in whatever campaign appearances he could fit into his schedule at Duke. He started in New England, where he began putting together organizations in New Hampshire, scene of the first state presidential primary, and Massachusetts. He made trips into the Northwest, and in Iowa developed a following among educators. In his remarks before a group in Houston he harkened

to the old Democratic Party and the alliances that had proven successful in the past. Democrats must be "bold, decisive, and inspirational," he
said; the nation needs "the spirit of John Kennedy, the vision and faith of
Franklin Roosevelt and the honesty of Harry Truman." [83]

Sanford's prospects looked as promising as other candidates' but he still
had to convince doubters who questioned the viability of a campaign that
had sputtered and failed four years earlier. He was more prepared and determined than before, but voters at home still were not ready to take him
seriously.[84] Elsewhere in the country, his themes never seemed to strike a
responsive chord. Jules Witcover later wrote, "His invocations of his record
on civil rights fifteen years earlier, with pointed references to the New Frontier, only reinforced the impression that he was a politician of the past." [85]

Even before the campaign began, another experienced Washington observer, William Greider, told Bill Green to advise Sanford to forget the
language of traditional politics. "Don't even be tempted to slip into customary politicking. It's lethal," Greider suggested. Sanford "is going to
have to be straight-forward. He cannot allow himself to use some of the
rhetoric he has been using and is accustomed to using. Tell him to talk not
like a politician but like a university president." [86]

In fact, Sanford had not found one compelling campaign theme. Rather,
he was still piecing together an agenda in the months leading up to his
formal announcement. He touched on issues such as controlling hand-
guns, campaign finance reform, aid to disadvantaged schools to relieve
the need for busing, tougher environmental laws, deregulation of the railroads, a national land use policy, and tax laws that gave the working person
the same breaks as the wealthy.

That fall, Sanford's Duke calendar remained full. In addition to the
usual events of a new academic year, he was preoccupied with a major
fund-raising campaign, the largest to date in Duke history. When he could,
though, he booked trips out of the state to weekend political meetings and
took advantage of other breaks in the university schedule.

Immediately after the Christmas holidays he headed north again. He had
been campaigning in neighborhoods for about a week when, in Marblehead, Massachusetts, he complained of chest pains and was admitted to
nearby Salem Hospital. His press secretary, David Ethridge, explained to
reporters, "Well, he's been on the go lately. I guess one meal a day and
twenty-five cups of coffee was just too much for him." [87] Stuck in a hospital bed, hundreds of miles from home, Sanford was deeply troubled by
this unexpected development. He had always been in good physical condition and had come to know the familiar rhythm of his feet on the running
machine he used when weather kept him from his morning jog outdoors.

Before this setback, he believed he was in excellent health and had no complaints of physical ailments.

What he discovered at Marblehead was that in his rush to get his campaign started, he had taken the bitterly cold weather for granted and ignored sound advice. Most of the time, he had worn only a suit, deciding against a heavy overcoat because it would have been cumbersome. "It had never occurred to me to look out for my comfort," he said later. "It was freezing cold, well below zero." As he moved from the cold of the outdoors to the warmth of houses, he began to feel a sharp pain from the middle of his chest and into his right arm almost to the point of numbness. At first, he shook it off, but at one stop, after the pain became severe, he asked if a doctor was in the crowd. When a guest answered his call, he hoped it would be a cardiologist, but learned the man was a dentist. He pushed on to other stops until the pain was too intense for him to continue. He feared the worst and expected to collapse. "Finally I said to myself, 'Well, you old fool, you will die up here of a heart attack to the great embarrassment of your medical center.'"[88]

Doctors in Salem determined that he had not had a heart attack, but they discovered a heart murmur that probably had been exacerbated by the repeated and extreme shifts in temperature. Texas oil man Walter Davis arranged for his blue-and-white Lear jet to stop at Duke, where it picked up cardiologist Robert Whalen before flying on to New England to collect Sanford on January 14 and return him to Durham. Back home, Sanford told reporters that he was "absolutely" still in the race. He said he planned to remain at Duke Medical Center for a few days of rest before returning to the campaign trail.

The statement did not betray questions that Sanford had begun to ask about the price of political ambition. At the hospital, lying flat on his back with the threat of serious health problems looming, he realized that he was causing strain on his family and putting his own future in jeopardy. In addition to everything else, Sanford was just about broke; he told one friend he owned only two suits. He also realized just how much the six-month delay in entering the race had cost him. Opponents such as Carter were far better organized and financed. And, for the first time, he considered the possibility that he might not be physically active until he was at least ninety-five years old.

"It scared him to death," said Sam Poole, who was out with student volunteers preparing for the New Hampshire primary when he got word Sanford was in the hospital. "He was jeopardizing his family in his quest for the presidency and it overcame him."[89]

Two weeks after returning to Durham, on January 25, Sanford withdrew from the race. "The ordeal of running a political campaign from a non-political position is tougher than I anticipated," he read from a prepared statement while Westwood and two other key supporters, Vermont Governor Philip Hoff and West Virginia Governor Hulett Smith, looked on. "I conclude that I cannot put together a winning campaign. I am not going to put my friends through the ordeal of a needless venture. I have no alibis and no complaints. I made my honest effort, and now I am content to close the book." [90]

On January 27, Eric Severied took note of Sanford's departure from the race in his commentary on the CBS *Evening News*. "The first dropout from the Democratic presidential race is Mr. Terry Sanford who may well possess higher qualifications of experience, wisdom and character than any of the others running. Something is wrong." [91] Six months later, Jimmy Carter won the Democratic nomination for president. His campaign got a significant early boost with a strong showing in the Iowa caucuses and a plurality in the New Hampshire primary. He carried the Florida and Illinois primaries, forcing Wallace to second place in each contest. By the time of the North Carolina primary in May, Wallace was all but through. Carter effectively co-opted Wallace's antigovernment themes as he and other candidates ran as outsiders of the Washington establishment and thus untainted by Watergate. Indeed, Sanford had been right; a Southerner could run and win the presidency.

CHAPTER SIXTEEN

"Outrageous Ambitions"

❀

THE OPENING OF DUKE UNIVERSITY'S 1981 fall term was still several weeks off when Terry Sanford called on former president Richard Nixon in his New York City office. As Sanford remembered it, the former president at first thought he was seeking a contribution to his alma mater (Duke Law '37) and tried to turn the conversation to the school's miserable gridiron record, offering to talk George Allen into forsaking his job as head coach at the Washington Redskins to rebuild the Duke football squad.

No, Sanford told him, he wasn't after money, or a football coach. He was interested in where the former president planned to archive the official papers of an administration that Sanford believed would intrigue scholars, writers, and students of history and public policy for generations to come. To Sanford's mind, for Duke to become the center of such study and research would be yet another step toward national and international recognition as an institution of outstanding quality and scholarship. This particular quest, however, would turn out to be the most controversial episode of all Sanford's years at Duke.

After shelving his ambitions for the presidency in the winter of 1976, Sanford had returned to his duties at Duke with his vigor, energy, and creativity. The five or six years that he had committed at the outset to the university had come to an end, but since arriving in 1970 he found that he thoroughly enjoyed what he was doing. There was no other place that offered such stimulating challenges in such a creative environment. He willingly extended his original timetable. "I was far fascinated with running Duke," Sanford later recalled.

> I was in love with Duke. I thought it would be great to be the first Southern president but not all that damned great. I really didn't push and concentrate on it and when the situation in Massachusetts gave me an opportunity to step aside I didn't do that with any regret.

I had accomplished more than I thought I was going to, but I saw how much more I could accomplish here. I could see how this would be a worthy ambition in anybody's life if they didn't do anything else. I was really dedicated to Duke and that's probably why I was reluctant to leave in the fall.[1]

He had entertained other options, though only briefly. In the summer of 1977, President Jimmy Carter asked him to become ambassador to France.[2] The job had little appeal for Sanford—first of all, he didn't speak French—so he waited a decent overnight interval before calling Secretary of State Cyrus Vance to tell him to find another candidate. He did use what influence he had to encourage Carter to choose Duke professor and Women's College Dean Juanita Kreps as his secretary of commerce. Sanford had recruited Kreps to become a vice president at Duke in May 1973.

Certainly, Duke's board of trustees were happy enough for him to remain. The prestige of the school was growing, the balance sheet was stronger than ever, and the school was alive with new and expanding programs. In addition, Sanford had successfully drawn the Durham community closer to the university; the city was transforming itself from a cigarette manufacturing town to the City of Medicine, largely because of the expanding medical complex of Duke Hospital and Medical School.

Sanford had a smooth working relationship with board chairman J. Alex McMahon, who had taken office in May 1971. While Sanford concentrated his energy on the main campus, the law school, and graduate programs, McMahon, who was president of the American Hospital Association, worked closely with Dr. William Anylan, who ran the huge Duke medical complex. McMahon recalled, "[Sanford] said, 'Alexander, you go up and keep an eye on the Medical Center. You and Anylan let us know if there is anything we need to do.' Terry didn't want to mess with the Medical Center. He didn't understand it, and didn't want to learn it."[3]

He was attuned to all phases of Duke life, but concentrated on fundraising, speechmaking, athletics, and relations with the trustees and left much of the rest of the administrative responsibilities to his chancellor and to administrators. Keith Brodie, who succeeded A. Kenneth Pye in the job when Pye was chosen as president of Southern Methodist University, later wrote that he handled the "mysteries of administering the arts and sciences and the law, divinity, engineering, forestry and business schools" under Sanford's watchful eye. "Essentially, I served as his alter ego, coordinating and integrating administrative and auxiliary services and collaborating with the provost in shaping and supporting the academic mission of the university."[4]

McMahon played to Sanford's strength: "He's got vision. He's got implementation capacity. I used to say the great thing about Terry Sanford is he just loves to talk to rich people and we need rich people to become interested."[5]

When Sanford began raising money for Duke, one of the first to receive a call was Joseph M. Bryan of Greensboro, easily one of the wealthiest men in North Carolina. Sanford had known Bryan since the 1950s, when Bryan had been one of the few businessmen in the state to support Scott. Later, gubernatorial candidate Sanford had rented rooms in one of Bryan's properties, the Carolina Hotel in Raleigh, and one of Sanford's closest friends, Lauch Faircloth, had later married Bryan's daughter, Nancy, whom he met when she was working as a volunteer in the Preyer campaign.

As Sanford told the story, Bryan asked him how much money he wanted. "All you've got," Sanford replied.

Duke did not get it all, but did receive $3 million of the $16.5 million needed to build the school's first student union, a project that Sanford found had real appeal to Bryan, who had rejected others. Bryan later wrote another check for $10 million for a cancer research facility at the Medical Center.

When Sanford learned that as a young man Atlanta industrialist J. B. Fuqua had borrowed books by mail from the Duke University library to study banking and finance, Fuqua became someone to see. Sanford had met Fuqua when he was governor and the two had remained in touch over the years through Democratic Party politics. After Sanford went to Duke, Fuqua invited him to join the board of Fuqua Industries, and in 1973 Fuqua became a member of the Duke board.

During one of Fuqua's trips to the campus, Sanford told him that if he would pledge $10 million toward establishing a graduate school of business, Duke would match it with $20 million more and the new school would bear Fuqua's name. Sanford told Fuqua that such a gift "would enable us to get the immediate attention of virtually every corporation and business leader in the country." When Fuqua left that day, the only thing Sanford had for his efforts were insistent refusals. But, before Fuqua's private jet reached its destination, he called to tell Sanford to sign him up for the pledge. "He used the argument that to have a complete university you had to have a school of business, and that's the one thing they didn't have," Fuqua recalled. "Duke University is one of the great universities and I think I have made some contribution to its greatness by the philanthropic investments I have made in it."[6] The university broke ground on the new business school in February 1981 on Science Drive near the Law School. Fuqua later gave Duke $20 million more for various projects because of

Sanford's influence. "He was a very persuasive person and yet a very sincere person," Fuqua recalled. "He was a person of tremendous vision. He had visions for the university and I think he contributed more to it than anybody else ever did."

Sanford moved easily in the world of corporate politics and successfully recruited other successful business leaders, including David Thomas of Wendy's restaurants, who contributed $4 million for the David Thomas Center, a residential hall and eating facility at the Business School. Dillard and Nello Teer of Raleigh helped build the Engineering School, and Asheboro textile man David Stedman was a major contributor to the Medical Center. ITT Corporation gave $1 million to the Business School and another million for an endowed professorship at the Institute of Public Policy, later renamed the Sanford Institute.

When Sanford came to Duke he had resigned from the board of directors of Integon Corporation, a Winston-Salem–based insurance company, and other boards, just as he had when he became governor to avoid conflicts of interests. Later, as opportunities arose, he rejoined corporate boards because he believed board membership was an asset for a university president, particularly one from a private institution that relied heavily on outside support. The relationships served him and Duke well; none offered more varied experience than his fifteen years on the board of ITT.

Sanford first came to the attention of the ITT leadership when he was chairing a company-sponsored student exchange program for students from the United States and sixty other countries where the company did business. In 1973, Sanford received a letter from a member containing allegations that the company was involved in the overthrow of Chile's socialist president Salvador Allende. The letter writer, another college president, urged Sanford to follow his example and resign.

Sanford declined, responding that there was no evidence ITT had done anything illegal, and he remained as chair of the committee. He sent copies of his correspondence to ITT Chairman Harold Geneen, who liked Sanford's feisty defense and offered him a seat on the board. "I thought it would be very interesting," Sanford later recalled, "and it paid a few thousand dollars in honorarium, which a struggling college president could use." [7]

Sanford's involvement with ITT became an issue on campus in 1977. In November, a campus group called the Radical Academic Union demanded that Sanford resign from the ITT board because of alleged illegalities by the corporation in South Africa and lingering questions about its role in the coup in Chile. Again, Sanford stood by the company and subsequently was named to a committee of board members to investigate whether a stockholders' suit should be brought against the company. He and the other committee members carried out an extensive investigation that determined that ITT was not guilty of any irregularities in Chile, Algeria, or Spain. Sanford wrote a report that totally exonerated the company. He subsequently emerged as an influential member of the board, a position he held for ten years, long enough to qualify for a handsome pension.

Sanford was as interested in increasing the stature of the Duke faculty as he was in raising new buildings. "We recruited at least forty major faculty positions of people like James David Barber [political science]," Sanford said, "but I could go right on down through anthropology and chemistry and foreign affairs."[8] Perhaps the best-known faculty addition was John Hope Franklin, a distinguished black historian who joined the Duke faculty in 1982 with a James B. Duke professorship, Duke's highest faculty post. Another coup was Phillip Griffiths, who gave up an endowed chair at Harvard to become James B. Duke Professor of Mathematics and Duke's provost in 1984.

Sanford never took a direct hand in faculty appointments, reviewing résumés as some presidents did. Rather, he encouraged department heads to seek the best and to diversify the Duke academic family. He ordered search committees to hold appointments open for at least thirty days to ensure that all candidates, particularly minority candidates, were considered. Bringing minorities onto the faculty proved as difficult as recruiting black students. In 1981, ten years after Sanford arrived, only 10 of the more than 540 faculty members were African Americans, and the school had fewer than a hundred black students in the entering freshman class.

Yet, Duke continued to improve its ranking in published lists of popular and influential campuses. By the early 1980s, the New York Times called Duke one of the nation's "hot colleges." It was competing with the nation's best schools—Harvard, Princeton, Yale, and Stanford—for its freshman class. It also was becoming the campus of choice for emerging faculty.[9]

Sanford's own involvement in national higher educational organizations increased as he served as the president of the Association of American Universities and as the first chairman of the National Association of Independent Colleges and Universities.

The Fuqua School of Business joined other Duke fund-raising trophies, such as a Flentrop organ at Duke Chapel, new buildings and treatment centers at the Medical Center, marine research vessels, and innovative programs. "[Sanford] opened up Duke to the outside world," recalled Joel Fleishman, whose public policy institute was a source of campus pride. "He brought the world of affairs and the world of practice onto the campus across the board. The consequences of that were that all of a sudden people began to know about Duke, because you can't have many people from the outside world coming to the campus and seeing what it is like and meeting faculty members and meeting students without carrying the word back out there." [10]

Nothing extended Duke's name around the country more than an innovative program begun in 1977 by Bill Green, the school's director of public affairs. Green invited working journalists to the campus to spend a month away from daily demands to pursue a course of intense study on anything in the school's academic catalogue. During their stay, they could talk with any professor, monitor any course, or just roam about the place. The program began with writers and editors from the *Washington Post* but was expanded to other news organizations. When the writers returned to their jobs, those they had met on campus became sources in their news stories, and Duke's name began appearing in print all across the country.

Despite his continued success, Sanford knew he occasionally needed some unfettered time to think, to recharge his mental batteries, and he embarked on a one-year leave of absence in July 1979. He planned to spend his time raising money and working on one or two books that he had started. He left his responsibilities in the charge of Chancellor Kenneth Pye, the former dean of the Law School. During the year, Terry and Margaret Rose traveled to Japan, Europe, Saudi Arabia, China, and Great Britain. He rafted down the Green River in Utah and spent more than a week in Colorado on an Outward Bound wilderness experience with a group of business leaders. He also took an extended trip to China as part of a group sponsored by the American Council of Young Political Leaders.

One of the fruits of his sabbatical was *A Danger of Democracy*, a book in which Sanford described the flaws in the presidential nominating process. He urged radical reform in the way Americans choose their presidential candidates for the general election and recommended that all present methods of selecting delegates to the Democratic and Republican national conventions be changed. Instead, voters would elect delegates from small districts who would be empowered to represent them in choosing the candidates at a wide-open convention. In addition, Sanford urged states to abandon binding presidential primaries. The primaries could remain to showcase the candidates, but delegates should be free to vote the wishes of their districts. Such a system of "thinking delegates" would prevent the primary contests, which are most beneficial to issue-oriented candidates, from overwhelming candidates who rise through the traditional political process.

"The danger of democracy is that we will use its name in vain," Sanford wrote, "and in its name so unstructure our political institutions that nothing can be decided, or decided wisely. There is considerable evidence that we have come close to doing just that to our political parties."[11]

Presidents were too important to be chosen by a popularity contest such as the primary system, which highlighted mistakes instead of focusing attention on reasoned and informed choices, Sanford wrote. "We do not expect to decide a national energy policy by referendum, voting on eight or ten proposals put forward by eight or ten groups. That issue is too complex even for 535 members of Congress. . . . Yet we expect to pick our president, a far more complex determination and infinitely more important than even an energy policy, by participatory disorder that knows no equal in American society."[12]

Sanford used his study as the platform for a national project to study ways to reform and improve the presidential nominating process. In January 1981, he announced the creation of the Duke Forum, a panel of prominent Democrats and Republicans who would preside over discussions among five thousand political leaders from across the country to consider suggested changes to the presidential nominating process. Sanford served as chairman and named Joel Fleishman as director and James David Barber as moderator. Among the panel members who participated were Vernon Jordan, executive director of the National Urban League; Robert Strauss, former chairman of the Democratic National Committee; and Elizabeth Hanford Dole, a cabinet officer under President Ronald Reagan.

In late July 1981, the summer doldrums had settled on the Duke campus. Many faculty members were either gone or planning trips in early August before classes resumed late in that month. On July 28, Sanford paid his call on Richard Nixon in his office at the Federal Plaza in New York City. As Sanford approached the meeting, he believed that within the school's grasp was an opportunity to become the center of a study of the American presidency that would attract worldwide attention. Sanford believed scholars would come seeking the details and nuances of a failed presidency while others would focus on Nixon's remarkable achievements in foreign affairs, including his opening of relations with China.

As the two talked, it was clear that Nixon was interested, but he told Sanford he didn't know where things stood on establishment of an official library and suggested that Sanford talk with his lawyer. A few days later, Sanford talked with the former president's lawyer, who said Nixon was ready to move ahead. Nixon's representatives told Sanford that Duke had better act quickly or the library would go to the University of Southern California, where plans had been underway to announce placement of the library there.

Sanford checked with McMahon and found him as enthusiastic as he was. "Terry called me and said, 'What would you think about having a Nixon library at Duke?'" McMahon recalled. "I said, 'I think it would be a great idea." My heavens, this is a university. He is one of the most significant political individuals of our time, [with] a significant presidency that ended up discredited, but my heavens, think of all the things to learn. I said absolutely, we take any store of scholarly materials."[13]

In a confidential letter dated August 8, Sanford told the executive committee of the trustees about his talk with Nixon and described the proposed library as a repository of "all of his papers and tapes [as representative, senator, vice president, and president], and memorabilia, similar to the LBJ Library at Austin and the Truman Library at Independence." Duke would provide the land, Sanford said, but the library would be administered by the National Archive Research Service and the General Services Administration.

"President Nixon is ready to announce that Duke has offered a site and that he has gratefully accepted," Sanford wrote. "Probably he, Mrs. Nixon, and children would come to Duke for the announcement, but likely we will instead have a press conference in New York. They want to make the announcement on August 19. These are the most significant presidential papers, from an academic and research point of view. I think we should go through with this arrangement, and I consider the Nixon decision to be a real coup for Duke."[14]

As he wrote that memo, Sanford believed he may finally have achieved his long-standing ambition to reconnect Duke with one of its best-known graduates. One of the first letters Sanford had written when he became president had been to Nixon, whom he asked to consider accepting an honorary degree. It would be good for Duke, Sanford had reasoned, plus it would remove a stain he believed sullied the school's reputation. In 1954, when Nixon was vice president, he had been due to deliver the commencement address but canceled after faculty members angrily objected to granting him an honorary degree at the same time. Shortly after writing the president in 1970, Sanford was in Washington to attend a conference of university presidents, where he saw a Nixon aide who told him the president had received his letter. He said Nixon had pulled it from a huge pile of correspondence and put it with others that he planned to answer himself.

Nixon still held warm feelings toward his alma mater, Sanford learned. He had graduated third in his class of twenty-six, had been president of the student bar association and an editor of the law review. He played softball for the law school team and attended nearly every dance. He wrote in his memoirs that he lived in a rooming house off campus where he paid rent of five dollars a month and sometimes Milky Way candy bars were his main daily meal. As a scholarship student, he took a job in the dean's office that paid thirty-five cents an hour. "As I look back," Nixon later said, "I am amazed that we lived so long and so contentedly in such primitive conditions, but at the time it seemed exciting and adventurous."[15]

However, Sanford was told that Nixon had no intention of risking embarrassment again and routinely refused such requests, although in this case Sanford hoped the president would change his mind. In the diary he was keeping at that time, Sanford wrote, "I felt that Nixon had been done an injustice by Duke in publicly turning him down for an honorary degree. It's one thing to decide not to give somebody an honorary degree, but to have it highly publicized is inexcusable."[16]

Sanford continued to court Nixon with invitations to visit his old law school. In January 1972, he offered the campus as the site for a national address on the United States' new relationship with China following Nixon's historic visit there. Nixon replied by letter that he thought it was a good idea but that his schedule made it impossible. A year later, in March 1973, Sanford wrote to the president's friend and fellow Duke law alumnus Charles Rhyne of Washington, "I would like for you to go to see President Nixon, if you think well of this, to talk with him about the possibility of locating the library at Duke University. There are many things to be said for having this library on this side of the country, and many things to be said in favor of having it at his law school alma mater. We are in a position to provide the setting, the property on the edge of Duke Forest, and certainly the library and academic backup."[17] Rhyne, a North Carolina native and former president of the American Bar Association, was eager to cooperate.

At the same time, Sanford wrote Nixon. "I hope you will consider Duke University as the location for the Richard M. Nixon Presidential Library," he said. "Duke will provide necessary land for the Nixon Library in a satisfactory location on campus, perhaps in the wooded area adjacent to the Law School. . . . I hope that this request communicates our pride in your relationship to Duke University, and the honor that your Presidential Library would bestow upon us. I feel also that there are compelling considerations for placing your Library at Duke, and I would be most grateful for the opportunity to visit with you to discuss this."[18]

Nixon aide David N. Parker responded for the president. He wrote Sanford to say that "demands on the President's official time do not allow him to be personally involved in the many decisions regarding the proposed library and its eventual location." Parker suggested Sanford talk with Leonard Firestone, the president of the Richard Nixon Foundation.[19] In fact, Nixon would never return to the subject, as the Watergate scandal consumed the White House; it would ultimately bring down his presidency, and Sanford's offer with it.

In the summer of 1981 Sanford was speaking with a visitor to the Duke campus who had been a member of the Nixon administration when he learned that Nixon had asked for advice on what to do with his papers. That was all Sanford needed to renew his campaign. He knew it was a bold step, and one that was sure to bring objections. After Nixon's resignation, his portrait had been removed from the law school and still remained in storage in the art museum vault. But Sanford prided himself on his ability to build consensus and confidently wrote the trustees:

> The faculty reaction will be mixed, but I expect Dean Crauford Good-win will overcome much of the negative attitudes. ("We are glorifying Nixon, Duke's reputation will be sullied," etc.)
>
> Obviously time is of the essence. They had expected to announce on August 19 that the library would be placed at the University of Southern California. They reversed this decision after my conference with President Nixon on July 28.[20]

(Sanford would say later that it was apparent Nixon's lawyer had overstated the case, leading him to make the situation appear more urgent than it really was.)

In an effort to bring the faculty into the process, Sanford called Dr. Richard L. Watson, acting chairman of the history department and a former head of the Academic Council, on the same day that he dispatched his confidential memorandum to the trustees. Watson had been a member of the Duke faculty in 1954, when he joined the campaign to deny Nixon the honorary degree. Now, on learning from Sanford that one of the nation's most dishonored political figures might have his library at his university, Watson was more than alarmed.

Among Watson's concerns, and an issue that eventually became the focus of the entire debate, was whether the library would be a center of scholarship as Sanford described it or a museum paid for by Nixon's friends and dedicated to his glorification. Watson later wrote Sanford, "As historians we would welcome the acquisition of collections of papers by Perkins Library whether they be those of poor or rich, of famous or infamous, of Woodrow Wilson or Richard Nixon, of Adolf Hitler or Winston Churchill, but we would draw the line at having a building named for some of these persons on this campus."[21]

Sanford recalled Watson's telling him that "as a historian I suppose I should be for this but I can't stand that son-of-a-bitch." The reaction surprised Sanford. "He was saying, 'My professional standards are in conflict with my personal emotions,'" Sanford recalled. "He said that as a historian, 'I suppose I should be for it.' It turned out that he wasn't for it so the personal emotions overrode the professional judgment."[22]

On the following Tuesday, Sanford received a letter from Watson and his successor as department chair, Dr. Anne F. Scott. Both expressed their reservations and said they did not believe the library would be useful for academic research because most controversial papers would be excluded. Also weighing in against the idea was Barber, who had built a national reputation with his study of presidential character. Sanford agreed to postpone action until the Academic Council could meet.

By mid-August, the debate had broken free of the confines of confidential memos and meetings on the Duke campus. Reports of the negotiations with Nixon appeared in the Durham and Raleigh newspapers and reached WTVD-TV, a primary broadcast news outlet in the area. On August 16, a story also appeared in the *New York Times*. Sanford responded two days later with a letter to sixty-five thousand Duke alumni in which he outlined the bare bones of the proposal. Enclosed with his letter was a copy of a letter to him from English professor Dr. Edwin H. Cady that reflected Sanford's own idea that the university should look to the future and not respond to present-day feelings about Nixon. "What's mistaken, as I see it, about wishing to spurn a documentary treasure of inestimable value is that the opposers operate in too narrow a time frame," Cady wrote. "They are far too now-minded. A great university lives in a time frame wholly other from the brief spans of the people who build at it through centuries as others erect cathedrals. If we get the Nixon Papers, he and we will be matters of history very shortly. The documents will be there for history, for our successors, very likely for centuries. To professors who do not grasp what access to a great documentary center means to a university, I am afraid it is not possible to explain."[23]

Sanford found some support off campus in editorials from the *Charlotte Observer* and the *Washington Post*. "President Sanford has acted in the national interest by offering the integrity of Duke as trustee for the Nixon files, and the university's reputation can only be strengthened in the public mind should his negotiations succeed," the *Washington Post* said in a September 6 editorial.

But Sanford had misjudged the depth and breadth of feeling within the faculty. While returning students seemed mildly interested in the issue, it quickly embroiled the faculty in bitter debate. Some of them issued angry demands for Sanford's resignation and made unwarranted charges that he was promoting the library as a means of favoring his own business interests.

Much of the opposition sprang from the history department, which Sanford found both surprising and disappointing. Feelings about Nixon ran deep elsewhere within the faculty, but Sanford would never forget one historian who told him, "Well, I'll be damned if I want to go to those scholarly meetings around the country and have people making fun of me for being at Nixon's university. I didn't want to put up with the gaff." [24] Opponents accused Sanford of trying to slip the issue past the faculty by pushing it in August, when the campus was virtually empty. They also questioned the propriety of mass circulation of the Cady letter. And the actual value of the papers became an issue. Existing restrictions on use of the Nixon archive had prevented any independent analysis of what such a collection would actually contain when or if it arrived at Duke.

News reporters flocked to the campus for an open meeting of the Academic Council, where any faculty member was allowed time to speak. Opponents outnumbered supporters six to one during the two-and-a-half-hour session attended by more than four hundred faculty members. A position paper prepared by Barber and published in the Chronicle summarized the arguments against the project. He argued that the Nixon correspondence, tapes, and other material probably would be relatively meaningless to scholars doing research on the former president because most important papers would be retained elsewhere. He touched on the belief of many that the Nixon library probably would follow the fate of other presidential museums, which had become "showplaces where modern audiovisual technology exhibits a president in his most favorable light, with film and tape and photomontage. No genuine objectivity is allowed to intrude upon the atmosphere of enthusiastic boosterism." In addition, Barber claimed, it was unlikely that Nixon and his family and friends would ever allow educational programs emphasizing his misdeeds in office. "We have a profound responsibility to our students," Barber wrote, "not to mislead them, not to sponsor or endorse or condone the falsification of history, but to insist on teaching the truth. That is a struggle professors have been waging for centuries, staving off those who would exploit us for their own purposes." [25]

On the day following the meeting, the Academic Council met again. This time, Sanford made his pitch for proceeding with negotiations, but after three hours of talk that included humor mixed with rebukes, the Council voted thirty-five to thirty-four in favor of a resolution calling on the board of trustees not to proceed with negotiations. Sanford could have turned the vote in his favor, but neither he nor others on his staff with ex-officio privileges voted. The focus now shifted to McMahon and a meeting of the executive committee of the board of trustees, which was scheduled for the next day.

McMahon told the board members, "This is the most controversial if not the most important decision that the executive committee and the board have been called on to make." Before voting, the members heard from faculty representatives that included Anne Scott, history department chair. She told the trustees that in accepting the library, Duke "would be inextricably involved with rehabilitating the career of Nixon . . . and the name of the University would suffer," according to the *Chronicle* report of the meeting. Another faculty member, English professor Carl Anderson, said, "I warn you not to discount the anger as a temporary thing. It is deep and it will not die." [26]

The executive committee voted nine to two to proceed with negotiations but with "severe restrictions" on the museum aspect of the library. Final approval would be contingent on the archival and scholarly aspects of the facility. The two opposing continuing negotiations were Isobel Lewis of Lexington, North Carolina, and John A. Forlines, a banker from Granite Falls, North Carolina. Forlines, a 1939 graduate, said, "I felt it would be best to go back to Nixon and say thank you, but no thank you. It's clear to me that the friends of Nixon are not going to donate $25 million to $30 million and not want to honor the man." [27] McMahon was mindful of the intensity of the campus debate, and the anger of opponents that had begun to focus on Sanford. Faculty members also were upset with McMahon's reminder to the executive committee of the closeness of the vote at the Academic Council. He told Sanford to let him carry the battle forward after the board approved continued negotiations. "I told him that we can always get a new board chairman, but I don't want to go through the process of getting a new president, so you stay quiet and let me do this," McMahon later said.[28]

Some opponents grew serious about Sanford's removal. James B. Duke Professor of Physiology Charles Tanford circulated a letter on department letterhead to the trustees that blistered Sanford for his performance and accused him of overplaying his hand as president. He urged the trustees to either abandon the library or request Sanford's resignation. "Mr. Sanford has been arrogant, devious and divisive. The rift between him and the faculty (ordained, as I have said above, by his own misconception of his role) is irreparable." [29] Attached to a copy of the letter in Sanford's files was a handwritten memo from his old friend Lauch Faircloth: "Terry, I would fire this son-of-a-bitch if it was the last thing I did. Lauch."

Sanford was not without his defenders among the faculty. Professor and novelist Reynolds Price told one national magazine that he favored having the papers at Duke: " 'If you tore down every building in Europe that bears the name of a morally reprehensible person, it would be a bare scene.'

Moreover, he notes, 'Nixon was one of ours. There's a certain amount of owning up involved.' "[30] Seventy-four faculty members, including Price, Fleishman, and Goodwin, released a statement of support for the library to counter the widespread impression of overwhelming faculty opposition.

"It was, for me, a rare experience," recalled Bill Green, who chronicled the affair in Duke publications. "Everyone was voting, taking sides, on the basis of principle. No funny business, no intrigue. Principle." He would never forget Sam Cook, the first black faculty member at Duke, pounding the table at a board of trustees meeting and comparing the Nixon library to the F BI headquarters in Washington. "When I walk in front of that J. Edgar Hoover Building in Washington, I want her to tremble, because she will recognize how bad it can be," Green quoted Cook. "I made the decision with Terry's approval that everything would be public. When we published the alumni magazine, we put the case that Larry Goodman on the history faculty violently opposed it. We put that right in that book. There was no attempt by Terry to muffle anybody or to keep even university publications from giving full ventilation to that argument, which gives you a flavor of the kind of public affairs instincts he has."[31]

After the decision by the trustee executive committee, Sanford assumed more of a moderating role in the issue. He subsequently agreed to continue negotiations and made an unscheduled appearance before a meeting of the Academic Council. "I don't intend to let one incident destroy the steady forward progress. It is apparent that faculty members, with considerable justification, feel they have been left out of a major decision," he told the council. He said he regretted sending the Cady letter, and offered to delay the negotiations until the faculty could put together its own agenda of conditions under which they would accept the library. He assured the council that no final action would be taken without faculty consultation, a stipulation included in the council's earlier resolution.[32]

It was at about this time that Sanford thought he had an answer that might satisfy those resisting the archives because of the museum dimension and, at the same time, bring the Nixon papers to the state. Rather than put the library on Duke property, he suggested it be located within the Research Triangle Park, a proposition that seemed to sit well with Chancellor John Caldwell of North Carolina State University, William Friday, head of the UNC system, and William Bennett, director of the National Humanities Center. Another person excited about the idea was Archie Davis, a highly respected retired banker and leader in the development of RTP. "We must look fifty years ahead," Friday told the group, according to notes that Sanford scribbled after the session concluded. Davis was so enthusiastic that he picked a site and even walked the property on foot to get a better feel for the lay of the land.[33]

Sanford talked with Nixon early the next morning and learned he was pleased with the multicampus sponsorship. "My brother received a degree from State College," he told Sanford, and he commented on the quality of the journalism school at Chapel Hill. He questioned some of the restrictions that the Duke trustees had offered before they would approve the deal, but Sanford said they would have to stay in place. Finally, he said okay, but, he added, to be sure that the announcement "does not look like the crazies ran us off." Nixon asked whether the restrictions were necessary. "Most of them," Sanford responded.[34]

Before the proposed news releases could even finish circulation for approval, the plan died. A few days after the initial meeting, Friday called to say that faculty members on the Chapel Hill and NC State campuses were just as aroused as their counterparts at Duke. That opposition combined with other complications killed the idea.

The turmoil subsided as negotiations with the Nixon representatives poked along. For Sanford, it had been a discouraging exercise and one that he found to be a profound embarrassment for Duke and himself. "A president of a great university is entitled to expect better," he wrote in a draft of a letter to the faculty that he never mailed, "and is entitled to a procedure and conduct that prevents this kind of assault because he dared raise an issue for debate." [35]

In his September 1981 report to the trustees, Sanford wrote, "I do not accept the proposition that lasting bitterness will follow a final university decision. That would not be characteristic of an academic community. For those who have been worried by the debate and controversy surrounding the placement of the Nixon archives here, I must say that I consider the exercise a healthy one for our students. Making public decisions is not easy, and students must learn to examine facts, verify facts, assemble facts, and measure facts against goals and objectives that they must also have formulated and defined." [36]

In October, the Academic Council voted unanimously to reject consideration of a Nixon museum and recommended limiting the library to fifty-five thousand square feet instead of the proposed building three times that size. It amounted to a compromise on the faculty's part, but Nixon and his supporters didn't see it that way. "The well had been poisoned," Sanford said later, "and Mr. Nixon then became the reluctant one." [37]

As a result of the library debate, the Academic Council changed its structure to eliminate voting rights for the president and others in the administration. Subsequent council chairs believed the episode increased the stature of the faculty in the governance of the university. Some of the faculty concerns proved accurate. Nixon's presidential library was later opened in Yorba Linda, California, where it became a monument to the man. In addition, legal action over public access to his papers would keep many of the files closed for years.

Two years later, the experience lingered in Sanford's mind as he drafted a speech on academic freedom on the occasion of the eightieth anniversary of the Bassett Affair, in which the Duke board of trustees withstood public clamor for the dismissal of a professor who had favorably compared turn-of-the-century black educator Dr. Booker T. Washington with Robert E. Lee. Sanford called his speech "On Doing the Right Thing" and reminded the Duke faculty that issues of academic freedom aren't so clear in modern society. Academic freedom is impinged by racial discrimination and more subtle forms of pressure from peers who might not be accepting of new lines of study or research or from those afraid to speak their minds to achieve acceptance. "I was going to reassure you that you could be critical of the president, but I don't know why I should assure you of that," he said. "The eightieth anniversary of such a notable event as the Bassett Episode is a good time to remind ourselves of the intellectual honesty upon which Duke University was founded, and I can put it in even simpler language by reading against what Chairman Southgate said: 'These men have got up here and talked and talked and talked about the expedient thing to do. I'm not looking for the expedient thing to do. I am looking for the right thing to do.' That's a pretty good test any time we make a decision." [38]

Sanford had planned to retire in 1982, when he reached the age of sixty-five. But as the date approached, he began to have second thoughts and found the trustees willing to let him remain. The debate over the Nixon library was rising to its highest crescendo in September 1981, when trustees announced that Sanford had agreed to extend his tenure for an additional three years. In a rather unusual move coupled with the extension and that appeared to be an unstated vote of confidence, they asked Sanford to hire a replacement for Kenneth Pye, who had left the post of chancellor, with the knowledge that that person was a likely choice as his successor.

Sanford was happy to stay on. He had unfinished business that included a major fund-raising campaign for the arts and sciences, faculty enrichment, and further development of the Business School. Plus, he said some time later, "I wanted the Nixon thing to cool off, but I wouldn't have stayed just for that. We just needed to round out some of those things. At the same time, I was well aware of the fact that there comes a time when a man ought to step out of this kind of job." [39]

By 1983, Sanford's efforts at building Duke into national prominence were clearly evident. In ten years, the number of applications had increased from 7,100 for nearly 1,200 spots in the freshman class to more than 10,000 applications for just over 1,400 places in 1983. And applications were increasing at 10 percent per year. It was regarded as one of the top six institutions in the country.

Sanford's warm, receptive relationship with students had become a trademark of his administration. Since his arrival on campus, students had been in and out of the president's office. He used some as researchers and aides, but he also drew them into policy discussions, where their judgment was given as much consideration as any administrator's or educator's. He challenged each freshman class to devote time and energy to improving the university, a charge that he took seriously. He asked the class of 1982 to prepare the school's first honor code and "to raise the banner for integrity. Your institution, Duke, is not only willing to accept your word, it maintains that personal honor, truthfulness, individual integrity, concern for others, intellectual honesty and decency are some of the traits of character that must be part of your education." [40] He had never forgotten the impression that a commitment to Chapel Hill's honor code had made on a freshman from Laurinburg more than fifty years before.

Nothing reinforced the president's connection with the student body more than events in early 1984 after Duke students embarrassed him at a Duke-Maryland basketball game, where they shouted obscenities and threw women's panties at a Maryland player who had been accused of a sex crime. A few days later, every Duke student received a letter from Sanford he titled "An Avuncular Letter."

Addressed "To My Duke Students," the letter encouraged student enthusiasm, but gently chided them by saying they had stepped over the line and traded their enthusiasm for cheapness. "Resorting to the use of obscenities in cheers and chants at ball games indicates a lack of vocabulary, a lack of cleverness, a lack of ideas, a lack of class, and a lack of respect for other people," Sanford wrote. "We are, I am sorry to report, gaining an unequaled reputation as a student body that doesn't have a touch of class." He urged the students to police themselves. "This request is in keeping with my commitment to self-government for students. It should not be up to me to enforce proper behavior that signifies the intelligence of Duke students. You should do it. Reprove those who make us all look bad. Shape up your own language. I hate for us to have the reputation of being stupid." [41] He signed the letter, "Uncle Terry," a nickname that stuck and found its way onto the cover of a football program that fall. At the next game in Cameron Indoor Stadium, students responded by chanting "We beg to differ" at the referees when they disagreed with a call.

Sanford made his last presidential address to the faculty on October 25, 1984. He gave a glowing pep talk about the history and integrity of Duke University that, like his earlier address, had some haunting refrains from the debate over the library. "Any view of a university's future should be a long, hundred-year view. That does not mean we need to wait one hundred years to perceive results, but it does mean that what is done today will still have an effect on this University a hundred years from now." Sanford encouraged them to hold to what he called "outrageous ambitions" that could not be reached easily. "The ultimate measure of a great university is the quality of its supply to the ranks of university scholars and teachers, that endless intellectual column which marches into the future to mark and transform society," he said. "That is our ultimate mission, not only to seek truth, but to enlarge and perpetuate the search for truth. If all of that is seen as outrageously ambitious for Duke University, then let it be, but nevertheless let us set it as our goal." Urging faculty members to continue their quest for excellence, Sanford concluded: "Finally, the stamp of Duke University and its continuing goal ought to be the unrelenting search for excellence in all of its endeavors. Duke aspires to leave its students with an abiding concern for justice, with a resolve for compassion and concern for others, with minds unfettered by racial and other prejudices, with a dedication to service to society, with an intellectual sharpness, and with an ability to think straight now and throughout life. All of these goals are worthy of outrageous ambitions. Thank you, and even eight months prematurely, thank you for making my time at Duke the best years of my life." [42]

On December 7, 1984, Keith Brodie, his chancellor and former chair of the psychiatry department, was chosen to succeed him as president.

More than a thousand friends and supporters turned out on May 3, 1985, to honor Terry and Margaret Rose at a retirement party at Cameron Indoor Stadium. Three gifts totaling $2.5 million to establish the Terry Sanford Endowment for Public Affairs were announced as the first toward a $10 million goal. "It has been the greatest pleasure of my life to see Duke grow in service to humanity and to see what it can be yet," Sanford said. "I believe Duke is poised for a new kind of greatness in its service to humanity." [43] On July 4, the Sanfords marked their last day at Duke along with their forty-third wedding anniversary.

During his tenure, Sanford had been responsible for forty new buildings costing more than $190 million. Of the new structures, twenty-three were in the Medical Center, with the most significant being Duke Hospital North, completed in 1981 at a cost of about $95 million.

The Chronicle gave Sanford credit for being a strong advocate for the university. "Raising money has always been one of Sanford's strong points," the newspaper said in its special edition on the Sanford years, noting his success in two fund-raising campaigns of more than $235 million and then $200 million.[44] Duke's alumni giving had risen to nearly $6 million per year, compared with $750,000 in 1970, and the endowment had more than doubled to $200 million from $80 million. In addition, the Institute of Policy Sciences and Public Affairs had developed into a major national program. He had recruited the American Dance Festival to Duke each summer and established the Institute of the Arts, which sponsored visits by distinguished artists, and the Duke in New York Arts Program. He had expanded the university's international studies program to 460 students studying in twenty-seven countries. In the city, he had led the Durham Progress group, an effort to revitalize downtown Durham that helped the city become an All-American City.

Sanford had signed his name to 37,813 degrees. He had accumulated nineteen honorary degrees of his own and was a member of twelve boards of trustees and twelve boards of visitors at other colleges and universities. "Spectacular is the best word that comes to mind," said McMahon as he summed up Sanford's years for the Duke alumni magazine. "He never sought out or never said, 'This is my doing.' He never had to. There were other people who would say that for him."[45]

John Brademus, the president of New York University, said, "Few American leaders have so perceptively appreciated the close interconnection between, on the one hand, economic development, social justice, and educational opportunity and, on the other, electoral politics. As president of Duke University, he employed his extraordinary experience, his wit and charm and considerable political talents in the service of one of the nation's leading centers of learning."

Accolades poured in. "The historians of higher education will doubtlessly credit you, as they should, with a strengthened program of arts and sciences, the new Institute of Policy Sciences and Public Affairs, the school of business," wrote U.S. Secretary of Transportation Elizabeth Hanford Dole, a Duke graduate. "They will write that it was during Terry Sanford's presidency that Duke became a truly national university."

"Certain historians believe that in a time of crisis a leader appears," wrote trustee Isobel Craven Lewis Drill, who had opposed Sanford on the Nixon library and also chastised him for lighting the Duke Christmas tree in the midst of the nation's energy crisis. "You were the leader Duke needed during perilous days of student unrest and academic uncertainty. My strongest recollection of you is your courageous action in restoring our university to its intended purposes."

"You have shown us that Duke can be itself—that it does not have to emulate the pattern of other institutions," wrote Mary and Jim Semans. "Duke University under your leadership has become a family again."

"It is a source of great pride to me that you stayed sixteen years at Duke instead of the five or six that you promised," wrote Charles Wade Jr., "and it is with even greater pride that I view your accomplishments. You took the presidency at the most perilous time in the history of Duke. The serenity of Duke is frequently shattered by an intellectual turmoil born of freedom and social consciousness. That is as it has been and always shall be, but it should never be as you found it—threatening its existence with violence and destruction. You set these forces to rest more satisfactorily than was done in any major worthwhile university in America."

"Terry Sanford had been an aggressive public figure whose political skills served Duke well, bringing the institution into the national limelight and building the strong alumni network this relatively young university needed for financial stability," Brodie later wrote.[46]

None of the tributes was more telling or personal than that delivered by Thomas W. Lambeth, the executive director of the Z. Smith Reynolds Foundation, whose association with Sanford spanned nearly thirty years. "Terry Sanford gave us our sense of our own greatness," Lambeth said, turning serious after reciting humorous anecdotes of his friend's remarkable career.

> What he led us to believe about him is not really so important. What is important is what he helped us to believe about ourselves.
>
> Terry Sanford paid to us as citizens the ultimate tribute: He asked us for our best. In North Carolina in the second half of this century there has grown a tradition that says that we can set our goals by how audacious we are in our dreaming and by how strong we are in our doing and that excellence is the aim of all our endeavors.
>
> That tradition has a name. The name is Sanford.[47]

Without the pressing responsibilities of the president's office, Sanford enjoyed a new freedom, considered his options, and indulged his hobbies: reading, sailing, gardening, and a little golf. In the spring of 1985 he began turning the soil in garden plots for onions, carrots, and radishes beside the home that he and Margaret Rose recently built south of Duke's West Campus on a heavily wooded, eight-acre lot. When they moved into the house in 1983, it was a welcome change from the university's official residence, where they had never felt comfortable. With four levels, eight bedrooms, and seventeen telephones, the president's home was built more for accommodating out-of-town visitors than for use as a private residence. The Sanfords' new home, which they designed themselves and which was built by a construction company run by their son, was comfortably arranged on one level with yards of glass that opened rooms to the surrounding woods. With a broad cedar-shake roof and wood siding, the house blended easily into the sloping hillside.

Retired at last, Sanford dug into his considerable library. Reading had always been a passion. When he was governor he enlarged the collection of the mansion library. By the time he left office, the shelves contained more than three hundred titles, many of them by writers from North Carolina and the South. His favorites were biography and history, and as he settled into retirement he reread *War and Peace* and finished William Manchester's biography of Winston Churchill.

His professional haven was again his law firm in Raleigh; he had not drawn any compensation from the firm, but he had maintained an interest throughout his time at Duke and his name stayed on the door. From time to time, he recommended Duke Law graduates to the firm's managing partners. One of the early hires was a young black man named Dan Blue, who later was elected speaker of the North Carolina House of Representatives.

Sanford also turned his attention to various business interests, including plans announced in 1984 to develop a community called Treyburn in northern Durham County. The $2 billion project called for four thousand homes as well as apartments, golf courses, shopping areas, hotels, parks, and medical facilities. Sanford's partners were his son, Durham businessman Clay Hamner, former Duke trustee Thomas Keesee, and Frank Kenan. The group, which incorporated as Durham Research Properties Inc., bought three northern Durham County farms, Stagville, Fairntosh, and Snow Hill, for more than $12 million and combined them to form the boundaries of the new development. They chose the architectural firm of Edward Stone, Jr. and Associates to design it. "Our assumption for [Stone] is to build a model for the whole country for years to come in terms of style, environment and community workability," Sanford said.[48] The development would become one of the showcase projects in the area.

Some duties remained at Duke, where he continued to help with fundraising. He also had his corporate board memberships at Fuqua Industries, ITT Corporation, Golden Corral, a restaurant chain run by an old college friend, and he was a member of the board at Howard University in Washington and the National Humanities Center in Durham. "You know I didn't just want to retire to the rocking chair," Sanford told the *Chronicle*.[49]

Regardless of whatever else arrived on his agenda, he never strayed far from politics. In January 1985, he sought the national chairmanship of the Democratic Party but the job went to Paul Kirk, a former aide to Senator Edward Kennedy. Sanford insisted at the time that he wasn't too disappointed. "I only wanted to be chairman long enough to reform it," he said.[50]

Sanford had maintained close ties with state Democrats. He was never more than a phone call away from Jim Hunt, who, after his term as lieutenant governor, had been elected governor and then had been the first to take advantage of a constitutional amendment and succeed himself in office. Despite Hunt's success, the Democratic Party had steadily lost the dominant position that Sanford had enjoyed in the early 1960s. In 1978, Jesse Helms won reelection and in 1980, Republican John East captured the state's second Senate seat with the help of Helms's National Congressional Club, a well-financed and closely managed political arm dedicated to electing conservative Republicans. The party's decline continued in 1984, when Hunt lost in a bitter challenge to Helms, and Republican James Martin was elected governor.

As Sanford prepared for his departure from Duke in the summer of 1985, the ranking Democrat in the state was Lieutenant Governor Robert Jordan. When a reporter asked Sanford if his plans included another political campaign, he replied that he had not ruled out entering the race for U.S. Senate in 1986, but made no commitments: "I've said all along that it hasn't been one of my ambitions to have 'U.S. Senator' written on my tombstone. On the other hand, because right now I think the national policies are being reshaped and priorities reordered, it's a good time to participate. And there are a lot of ways I can participate in the ongoing task of government without running for office."[51]

Indeed, the Senate had never held any real attraction for Sanford. He had flirted with a campaign in 1968, but when Senator B. Everett Jordan had offered to retire in his favor in 1972, Sanford found he was involved elsewhere. The Senate was no more appealing in 1985 than it had been before, but Sanford maintained an intensely personal determination to do what he could to revive the Democratic Party, as if to let it down now in its time of need would be a desertion in the face of the enemy. In addition, he was eager to face down the Congressional Club, which had made a reputation for producing hard-hitting campaigns. "Part of my motivation was to demonstrate that we could campaign against that kind of vicious campaign," he told a reporter.[52]

At first he tried to nudge as many people as he could into the race. One was Raleigh lawyer Wade Smith, the state party chair, who declined his entreaties to run. Another was William Friday, who had recently retired as president of the state's university system. Sanford believed Friday would be a strong candidate with good name recognition, a spotless record as the leader of the university for thirty years, and a host of friends and countless supporters. "I thought it would be an ideal cap to his career and also would give him that political experience that I felt was always a part of his makeup," Sanford said later.[53] When Sanford saw Friday at Brodie's inauguration, he invited him back to his campus office and the two talked about a campaign. Friday told Sanford that he was afraid his candidacy would draw negative attention to the University of North Carolina system. "The university didn't need that," he told his biographer, William Link. He agreed to consider it, but gave Sanford little hope.[54]

Time was running out to mount a strong campaign, and Sanford's list of viable candidates was getting shorter. Another logical Democratic contender was Hunt, but on September 12, the former governor took himself out of the race. The following day, Sanford announced he would run, not to put himself in the race, he would say later, as much as to discourage minor candidates and hold a spot for someone else.[55]

The initial reaction to his announcement was not encouraging. "It has been 25 years since voters elected him to office," the *Charlotte Observer* said in a news story on September 14. "The last time his name appeared on the N.C. ballot, in the 1972 Democratic presidential primary, Alabama Gov. George Wallace routed him, 50 percent–37 percent." The story described him as a "drawling grandfather" and questioned his ability to attract young voters. One of the state's Democratic congressmen, Representative Bill Hefner from Concord, told the *Observer*, "I think Terry's been out of the arena too long." One unnamed Democratic official was quoted as saying, "Nobody says it out loud, but everybody says it in private: He's outdated." Even his old friend Bert Bennett offered little encouragement. "I just didn't get the reception out there for Terry," he said.[56]

Sanford's name joined those of former national Young Democrats Bill Belk of Charlotte and Marvin Blount of Greenville as the only announced candidates. The complexion of the race changed almost within hours of Sanford's announcement, when on September 17 Senator East said that he was too ill with a hyperthyroid condition to seek reelection. That would appear to have strengthened Sanford's chances, but on September 24 Sanford reversed field. "I am not going to run for the U.S. Senate, although I find the prospect very appealing," he said in a statement issued from his Duke University office. "I have received tremendous support throughout the state and believe that I would be of useful service to people as a senator. But I believe I also can accomplish more worthwhile things without being a senator. In the final weighing, I do not want to exclude from my life those many projects and ideas that I have put aside during the many years in which I have been busy."[57] Friends said he had bowed to the wishes of the party under Jordan's leadership in favor of Friday's candidacy.

The situation remained in flux. A month later, another potential candidate dropped by the wayside. He was Lauch Faircloth, whom Sanford had supported financially and otherwise in 1984 when he had run unsuccessfully for the Democratic nomination for governor. "I intend to stay here and work within our state for progress in jobs, education and human services rather than traveling to the distant shores of the Potomac," Faircloth told reporters. "Frankly, I enjoy being around the people in North Carolina and living here and don't want to give those things up."[58] Friday also announced he would not run, and a day later Seventh District Representative Charles Rose told reporters he believed he could accomplish more as a result of his experience in the House and would seek an eighth two-year term.

In November, Sanford headed off on a sailing trip in the Virgin Islands aboard a forty-four-foot sloop he owned with Sam Poole. Sanford had taken up sailing during his years at Duke and became convinced he could make some money by owning a boat and leasing it to a sailing school. The business was a bust, but he thoroughly enjoyed adventures on The Blue Devil. With him on this trip were Poole, Paul Vick from his Duke staff, and Heman Clark, a long-time friend and law partner. Cruising from island to island they fished and enjoyed themselves and talked politics.

Sanford and Vick had become as close as brothers. Vick was director of Duke University's alumni affairs and had helped Sanford turn his personal financial situation around. By managing his investments, Vick had taken Sanford from virtual bankruptcy in the wake of his abortive presidential bid in 1976 to a net worth of more than $1 million. Poole, meanwhile, remained his closest political assistant. At the same time, he developed a successful law firm in Southern Pines and would later serve as chair of the board of governors of the state university system.

The trip ended with Sanford's political future unresolved. It was clear that if a strong candidate did not emerge, then the party risked losing the Senate seat for another six years. The possibilities nagged at Sanford. A political poll that he and Faircloth had commissioned jointly showed that his prospects were stronger than early newspaper commentators had suggested. Faircloth's were less so.

Democrats would need a strong candidate to recapture the seat. The Republican most likely to succeed East was U.S. Representative Jim Broyhill of Lenoir. First elected to Congress when Sanford was governor, Broyhill represented the more moderate and traditional Republicans in the state. Over the years he had successfully defended his seat in spite of repeated redistricting designed to help Democratic challengers.

In early December, word reached Sanford that Faircloth was reconsidering his position after being promised support from Tom Ellis, leader of the National Congressional Club. Ellis reportedly had discounted the club's chances in defeating Broyhill in a primary and planned to extend the club's influence into the Democratic Party by backing Faircloth and then beating Broyhill in the fall.[59]

Sanford remained eager to prove there was still life in the state's most senior Democrat, despite what had been said about him. He liked challenges and this was a whopper. Moreover, he was bored with business and wanted to get back to public service. Adding up all the factors, he decided that he could and should run.

On Christmas Eve, Sanford appeared at the door at Poole's home in Southern Pines. "Let's run," Sanford said.

"What about Lauch?" Poole asked.

"I'm on my way to see him," Sanford said.[60]

Two weeks later, Sanford and Faircloth were still talking and met for a final time at the Crabtree Marriott Hotel in Raleigh, where a meeting of the Democratic Party's state executive committee was underway. Sanford's friends say that the conversation was inconclusive and left each man thinking he had talked the other out of running. Sanford said he told Faircloth he was going to run, and Faircloth reportedly told friends he understood Sanford to say he would not run and planned to support Faircloth's campaign.

The following day, Sanford issued a press release saying he was back in the race. Faircloth learned of his decision when a reporter asked for a response. The "misunderstanding" effectively shut Faircloth out of the campaign and it embarrassed and angered him when he was told that Sanford had boasted to friends that he could easily beat him.[61] Faircloth hid his anger and disappointment, but a fifty-year friendship was in the trash. The two would not speak again until a few weeks before Sanford's death.

Sanford announced his candidacy: "I have been considering this decision in great depth became so many people who care about North Carolina have asked me to reconsider. I want to campaign for what I think is the soul of America. This nation grew great because we cared about people who needed our help. This nation became strong because we invested in education and personal opportunity. This nation led in productivity because we supported basic research. This nation became the world's leader because we stood for human dignity, freedom and individual rights everywhere. All of that, it seems to me, is in jeopardy."[62]

About 150 students surrounded Sanford at his announcement. Many of them had been recruited by J. B. Pritzker, the scion of a wealthy Chicago family who had enrolled at Duke the previous year. His first year in school had been a bit ragged, but with some attention from Sanford he had finally earned his degree and was grateful for the guidance he had received. He signed on as a full-time, unpaid volunteer. "One of the things we needed to show was that Terry Sanford was still appealing to young people," Pritzker recalled.[63] Although his studies suffered that spring, Pritzker learned how to run a political campaign as he put together a Students for Sanford organization. Before the year was over, he was organizing rallies and setting up Sanford's campaign appearances. He had learned from a professional, his mentor Jerry Bruno, the legendary advance man from John Kennedy's presidential campaign, who had retired to Chapel Hill and volunteered to help Sanford.

For a rich kid from Chicago who had grown up in California, North Carolina politics was like nothing Pritzker had ever seen. Often, those he was told to contact to prepare for a campaign event were men well beyond their political prime who were rallying for their man yet once again. They were old soldiers from the campaigns of the fifties and sixties who cautiously eyed younger workers, particularly someone like Pritzker, who was of Russian-Jewish background. He was not deterred. In rural precincts, when he was met with a you're-not-from-around-here look, he just introduced himself as "J. B. from Durham."

Wide-eyed and open to anything, Pritzker and other youthful workers logged long hours on the road, marveling at Sanford whose energy outlasted their own. Late at night, after a day of shaking hands, speeches, and travel from town to town, Sanford would invite his young aides in for a chat, drawing from them their reactions to the day's events and ideas about issues as he sipped a Scotch. "He treated us like adults," Pritzker recalled some years later, "and gave us adult jobs to do and relied on us like we were adults. I am not sure that even I, now that I am thinking about running for Congress, would treat a twenty-one-year-old as an adult and rely on his opinion about something." Pritzker got a glimpse of politics as it had been before television began to change the process. Sanford could still create excitement in the crowds that came to high school gyms and other venues for the free hot dogs, barbecue, and lemonade. "I was young and I had not known him during the gubernatorial campaign, but you could tell there were people there who saw him as John F. Kennedy. This was their touchstone to everything good about America. He dealt with that so well. He was just a decent guy."[64]

By the 1980s, the movements and words of most political candidates were carefully managed by media advisors and analysts. Not so with Sanford. As he had in 1960, he ran his own campaign and decided on a strategy that would promote his record as governor and president of Duke. His speeches and television ads were to remain positive from beginning to end.

The overarching goal was to produce a clear victory in the primary to demonstrate that Democrats were united behind him for the general election.

It was a formidable challenge. By the time Sanford entered the race, the field was confused with the activities of lesser-known candidates, including former state insurance commissioner John Ingram, a perennial candidate, Charlotte business executive Bill Belk, Mecklenburg County Commissioner T. L. "Fountain" Odom, and Ted Kinney, a Fayetteville real estate agent who had been encouraged to run by black political groups in the state.

Sanford quickly emerged as the front-runner, and when the votes were counted on the night of the primary, May 6, he had captured nearly 60 percent. Ingram was a distant second place at only 19 percent. It was a resounding victory.

The Republicans chose Broyhill, who defeated David Funderburk, a conservative Campbell College professor who had the nominal backing of Helms's Congressional Club. With Broyhill's more than a quarter century of participation in state Republican Party affairs, his nomination was really never in doubt. He drew on the support of old-line party workers who lived mainly in the Piedmont and mountains of the state. They did not respond to Funderburk's attack ads that challenged Broyhill's loyalty to the conservative cause, citing his votes on abortion and the national holiday for Dr. Martin Luther King Jr.

Sanford was ecstatic with his victory. "This is the beginning of a campaign to put a different voice in Washington," he told supporters at a victory party in Raleigh. "I intend to shape an agenda that will serve America with wishes and hopes and determination. . . . I intend to take to Washington a North Carolina voice, expressing North Carolina values."[65]

The matchup of Sanford and Broyhill offered some promise of a civil discourse on issues, said the *Charlotte Observer:* "Mr. Sanford represents the best of the moderate, progressive tradition North Carolina's Democrats have built over the past 30 years. Based on the records and personalities of the two candidates, a Broyhill-Sanford contest might be a relatively low-key affair. But it is likely to be a contest based on real issues and real records, not rigid ideology and distortions. And it should be one from which both candidates and the state can emerge with pride and honor intact, whatever the outcome. That would be a refreshing change."[66]

The complexion of the campaign changed on June 29, however, when Senator East was found dead at his home, the apparent victim of suicide by asphyxiation. On July 3, Governor Jim Martin appointed Broyhill to fill the unexpired portion of East's term. Broyhill resigned from his House seat and moved into East's office on the seventh floor of the Hart Senate Office

Building. The appointment gave him new status as an incumbent, which Republicans hoped would give him an advantage at the polls. Privately, Sanford worried that the appointment added credibility.

As the campaign headed into the final eight weeks, Broyhill's advertising took on a tone reminiscent of the attack ads that had been used against him in the spring. He called Sanford "a Teddy Kennedy liberal . . . supported by left-wing activists and special interest groups." His campaign constantly reminded voters that as governor Sanford had asked the legislature to extend the state sales tax to cover food. During the televised debate with Sanford, Broyhill said, "I just question, as I did twenty-four years ago, why we had to select the cruelest tax of all, the tax on basic necessity of life." [67]

Negative campaigning was becoming more and more a feature of the state's biennial political landscape, and Sanford advisors argued in an October memorandum to the candidate that he should become more aggressive. "We find ourselves with a 3 point lead that was once 17 points," the memorandum said. "And we know that the 'food tax' and 'national Democrat' arguments hurt us." [68] Sanford reviewed a round of ads designed to respond to the Broyhill attack, but discarded those with negative overtones. He argued that he was "not going to fight fire with fire." Nor was he going to ignore the barrage, as Democrats had done before, "thinking that it was virtually harmless, that nobody would pay attention to such ridiculous charges." Instead, Sanford continued his strategy of turning potential negative positions to his favor. For example, Broyhill's "food tax" ad featured a woman complaining about the tax; Sanford began laughing about "the 'whiny old woman,'" he later said. "Everywhere I would go I would sort of mimic her. I would say, 'Well, I'll tell you a whole lot of people can forgive me, including that 600,000 going to the technical schools across this state.' I made a damned good speech out of it." [69]

He organized a helicopter tour of the state's community colleges, which he said were the beneficiaries of the tax that also paid for more teachers, libraries, and expanded educational opportunities for youngsters. The tax cost the average family just eighteen dollars a year, Sanford argued, making it "the best buy that North Carolina has ever gotten."

When Broyhill suggested that Sanford might be soft on defense spending, a hot-button issue in the years of President Reagan's military buildup, Sanford pulled on an old leather bomber jacket, slipped his paratrooper ring on his finger, and let voters know about his record as a World War II paratrooper. In a short time, the Sanford campaign insignia became a miniature gold pin of a man dangling from a parachute.

The helicopter tour and the bomber jacket seemed to shave years off his age. Though Broyhill was fifty-nine, ten years younger than Sanford, one of Broyhill's friends said Sanford "looked damn good. . . . We took an image drubbing."[70]

By election day, the race was considered too close to call. Shortly after the polls closed, Sanford was sitting with some of his young workers watching television when the television networks predicted a victory for Broyhill. Sanford arched his eyebrows, but said nothing.[71] A short time later, the networks revised the projection after it was discovered that the early returns used in their analysis were those cast for the unexpired portion of East's term, not for the full six-year term. Sanford finally pushed ahead in both and won with a margin of about sixty thousand voters, or nearly 52 percent to 48 percent.

"I was lucky to win," Sanford told reporters at a press conference at his Raleigh headquarters, noting that Broyhill had raised nearly $5 million to his $3 million. And much of that came from Sanford's own pocket. He mortgaged his share of the Durham development for $970,000 to pay for the campaign. But it was worth it. "It finally put to rest the sales tax issue because that is the first thing they brought up against me," he said later.[72]

"They figured Terry Sanford had lost his wallop," the Durham Herald crowed. "They were wrong. Incredibly wrong. Mr. Sanford completed a political comeback Tuesday night unparalleled in North Carolina." The Charlotte Observer's Jack Claiborne editorialized, "The Sanford victory should call attention to what is an under-appreciated fact of N.C. politics. It is that, regardless of party registration numbers, the state's political allegiances are now so evenly divided between Democrats and Republicans that a slight shift in loyalties can alter an outcome. Jesse Helms won by a thin margin in 1984, and Terry Sanford won by a thin margin in 1986."[73]

Sanford's pollster, Harrison Hickman, said, "There are about 15 percent of the people in North Carolina who are truly ticket splitters. They make up their mind on the basis of this year's election and this year's factors. Where Sanford really won it was among independents." One key factor was Sanford's capturing of at least 95 percent of the black vote, his consultant for minority affairs, Ken Spaulding of Durham, told the media.[74]

Broyhill also was handicapped by a low turnout of Republicans. "A lot of people just stayed home," Senator Jesse Helms told the Charlotte Observer.[75] In 1984, when Helms was on the ticket with presidential candidate Ronald Reagan, 68 percent of the state's registered voters had gone to the polls; in 1986, only 51 percent voted.

A month after the election, Sanford had his Washington staff organized and was preparing to be sworn in to serve the remaining weeks of East's term. With more than twelve hundred persons scheduled to attend the ceremony on December 10, Sanford moved the occasion to the steps of the capitol. His old friend and law partner, Dickson Phillips, whom President Jimmy Carter had named to a seat on the U.S. Court of Appeals in 1978, administered the oath of office under as sunny a sky as North Carolina Democrats had seen in many years.

CHAPTER SEVENTEEN

Never Look Back

SHORTLY AFTER NOON ON January 6, 1987, Jesse Helms escorted Terry Sanford to the front of the Senate Chamber and presented him to take his oath for a six-year term. This biennial ceremony was a routine episode in the ongoing life of the Senate, but it represented much more for North Carolina. Of all the public men who had emerged since the end of World War II, no two better personified the competing forces that had shaped North Carolina politics than Sanford and Helms.

Helms had led the defection of Democrats after the party of Roosevelt and Wilson became the party of John F. Kennedy and Lyndon B. Johnson and carried the imprimatur of the Great Society and civil rights. Johnson had been correct when he said upon signing the Civil Rights Bill of 1964 that it was the beginning of the end for the Democratic Party in the South. The irony was not lost on Sanford that the Republicans had won succeeding victories across the South with the race issue, not unlike the Democrats, who had used it to rid North Carolina of Republicans in 1900.

Since Helms's election in 1972, the state had known its first Republican governors and elected a second archconservative Republican, John East, to the Senate. Helms himself looked unbeatable after winning reelection in 1978 and defeating former governor James B. Hunt, a Sanfordesque Democrat, in 1984 when he sought a third term. When he welcomed Sanford to the Senate he was easily the nation's best-known, and certainly its most outspoken, right-winger. He voted and talked as if he were on a mission from God to save the nation and personally restore decency, morality, and honesty.

Almost from the start of their public lives, Helms and Sanford had been on opposite sides in North Carolina politics. In 1950, Helms was the news director of spunky WRAL radio, a low-power Raleigh station, when he rallied conservative Democrats with eleventh-hour broadcasts to persuade

Willis Smith to continue his campaign to unseat Frank Porter Graham. Ten years later, the fire and passion of I. Beverly Lake's campaign still burned as Helms went on the air as the editorial voice of WRAL-TV, a relatively new station owned by lawyer-businessman A. J. Fletcher, who had been Lake's law partner for five years. A staunch conservative, Fletcher promoted his station as the "Voice of Free Enterprise" and was set on establishing WRAL-TV as an alternative to the more liberal opinions of the *News & Observer*.[1]

The first of Helms's nightly editorials was broadcast just weeks before Sanford took his oath of office as governor. During the ensuing eleven years he warned that liberals of Sanford's ilk were only socialists in disguise, that communists were infecting the minds of young people on college campuses and outside racial agitators were the cause of discontent among Southern blacks. The stridency and temper of Helms's broadcasts, which often carried over into the station's news coverage, rose to such a pitch during Sanford's term that some of the governor's friends complained to the Federal Communications Commission. Relicensing of the station was stalled but eventually approved after WRAL agreed to air opposing points of view.

In 1972, Lake was part of a delegation that persuaded Fletcher to release Helms from his contract so he could campaign for the Republican nomination for the Senate.[2] A few months later, Helms won his first statewide election on the same primary day that North Carolina Democrats humiliated Sanford in his first presidential bid and voted overwhelmingly for George Wallace. That fall Helms's statewide vote total in the general election was second only to Richard Nixon's as Republicans broke the Democrats' hold on conservative voters in North Carolina.

Subsequent Republican victories confirmed Sanford's oft-quoted explanation that only a few percentage points distinguished the politics of North Carolina from that found in the other states in the Old Confederacy. By the time Sanford reached the Senate, the balance clearly had tipped in favor of Republicans, and Helms's personal political organization, the National Congressional Club, had emerged as not only the most powerful independent political force in the state but influential in the conservative movement across the land.

For his part, Sanford believed that the campaigns of 1984—when the Democrats not only lost to Helms but forfeited the governorship as well—had been a wasted opportunity. From his corner on the Duke campus, he had counseled Hunt to avoid joining Helms in mudslinging (Hunt's rebuttal ads characterized Helms as being responsible for the deaths of women and children in Latin American dictatorships), but Sanford eventually was frozen out of the strategy sessions, or "expelled," as he later put it. "I kept saying, 'You can't be negative,' and they more or less forgot to tell me when the meeting was. I think they thought I was a bother."[3] J. Phillips Carlton took many of the calls from Sanford; recalling them later, he said, "He may have been right. He didn't like the television ads, the hard-hitting stuff. He would call me. He would call Hunt [and say] this is not the North Carolina way. People in the state will understand if you talk to them—lay out your business."[4]

The thought of challenging Helms himself had quickened Sanford's political pulse. But it was Hunt's turn to run and a campaign would produce a ragged end to his career at Duke. "That would have been rank disloyalty for me to have run," Sanford later recalled. "It was his time, and he would have been successful then had he not made all those errors."[5] Instead, Sanford found himself defending the Democratic Party in 1986 in a contest with Jim Broyhill, a leader of the state's Republican moderates, thus forever leaving open the question of whether the positive, upbeat style of campaigning that he had preached to Hunt could have succeeded against Helms, who had refined the art of negative campaigning.

Sanford was keenly aware of this history as he approached his Senate service. He knew some believed his mission for the next six years was to be an antidote to Helms. There was no question their votes would likely cancel each other out, as there was little on which they would agree, but he had no intention of reducing six years of work to such a state.

Certainly Helms's position and seniority would have to be reckoned with. Helms was a master at using the Senate rules and parliamentary behavior to get his way, or to get in the way of someone else. He had not been in the Senate long before his obstructionist behavior on legislation and appointments had earned him the nickname "Senator No." Reflecting later on their time opposite one another, Sanford said of Helms, "I was determined that I was not going to get in a knock-down, drag-out that I couldn't win. He could obviously stop anything that I wanted to start, and he did several times, but generally I beat him on policy issues because I had a margin of two on the Democratic side."[6]

Sanford knew that he and Helms were certain to clash, but he intended to be cordial and to work with Helms when the needs of the state required a united front. "I made it my business and he made it his business for us to stay civil and not get caught," Sanford said later. He wasn't going to pick a fight on his first day, and late on the afternoon before the swearing-in he called Helms and asked if he would introduce him to the Senate. Certainly, Helms quickly replied, adding that he would have been offended if he had not been asked.[7]

Sanford may have been a newcomer to the Senate, but he was no stranger to many in Washington. On Capitol Hill, Republicans John Chaffee of Rhode Island and Mark Hatfield of Oregon and Democrat Ernest "Fritz" Hollings of South Carolina had served as governors during his own term. He had worked with leading Democrats on the party's Charter Commission and in national campaigns dating from 1960. Familiar veterans as diverse as Lloyd Bentsen of Texas and Edward Kennedy of Massachusetts gave him welcome. New York Senator Patrick Moynihan was an associate from the 1960s, when both had been involved in a nationwide project called Urban America. Wyche Fowler, the newly elected senator from Georgia, had worked in his 1972 presidential campaign when Fowler had been a student at Davidson College. His Duke connections included Congressman Bob Wise from West Virginia, a Duke graduate who also had his first taste of politics with Sanford, and a host of Washington insiders, many of whom had college-age children return home singing the praises of "Uncle Terry."

He also knew members of President Reagan's cabinet. Secretary of Education William Bennett had begun his climb to political prominence after Sanford and University of North Carolina President William Friday had helped elevate him a few years earlier to the directorship of the National Humanities Center, based in the Research Triangle. Secretary of Transportation Elizabeth Dole, the wife of the Senate Minority Leader Robert Dole, was a North Carolina native and a Duke trustee, who told people that Sanford was her political mentor. At a White House dinner for new members held shortly after he arrived, Sanford even renewed an acquaintance with the president's daughter, Maureen, who had attended one of his fund-raisers in the 1976 presidential campaign and had made a modest contribution. Countless Duke acquaintances turned up in the most unlikely places, including one recent graduate who introduced himself as he drove Sanford's limousine to a swank Washington dinner.

The Duke connections played well with the Washington press corps. Many journalists at the *Washington Post* and the *New York Times*, plus the networks and news magazines, had taken advantage of the month-long sabbaticals offered on the Duke campus. Some had returned to Durham on occasion for one of Sanford's "Varmint Suppers," a banquet of wild critters that offered roasted 'coon and possum, smoked catfish, venison marinated in moonshine, squirrel stew, fried rabbit, and mud turtle soup. According to Sanford, most of the fare was "cooked on instinct."[8]

Yet, for all the familiar faces, the Senate was a new and different environment where for the first time in more than thirty years he was not in charge, a fact that he was reminded of daily in the early weeks as he waited for his betters to assign him a permanent office. Sanford faced a blur of activity with committee meetings and countless invitations to evening events that tended to blur one day into the next. When he saw the signal for his first roll call on the floor, he dropped what he was doing and rushed to the chamber, only to find it virtually empty. He decided right then that in the Senate, being on time was being early. "All this running around, of course, causes me to reflect on the usefulness of what I am doing," Sanford noted in a journal he had started keeping to record his life in Washington. "I suppose that it is worth it if I can get focused on a few things where I might be able to make a difference. The problem has been that the pace is so terrific that even if something worthwhile is being accomplished, a great deal of unnecessary dashing about is a price that has to be paid, I suppose. . . . But it is not the purpose of this log to make that point very often, except to remind myself in future years when I might possibly be reading this, to remember that we always moved on a hectic schedule to maintain a snail's pace. We get so little done for all of the energy we expend."

A most visible and embarrassing stumble in the first few weeks quickly reminded Sanford of his vulnerability. Though he rationalized his reversal of a vote for an important highway bill as a simple misunderstanding, he appeared as one who was out of his league and totally befuddled by Senate procedures.

The highway appropriations bill was up for an immediate vote when Sanford arrived in January. He didn't like it because of the way the federal government redistributed the federal gasoline taxes—North Carolina as well as other states received only 20 percent of what they collected at the pump and sent to Washington—and he told the Democratic leadership that he intended to vote against the bill as a demonstration of his concern, but only if there were sufficient votes to ensure passage. Majority Leader Robert Byrd told him the Democrats had a comfortable margin and accepted Sanford's offer. The bill passed with his dissent by a vote of seventy-nine to seventeen. In late March, however, it was headed back to the floor with a Reagan veto attached.

Prior to the Senate vote to override Reagan's veto, Sanford had talked with North Carolina Governor Jim Martin and Transportation Secretary James Harrington and told them that he planned to continue his protest and support Reagan's veto. Splendid idea, the governor said, we're with you. Sanford noted in his journal that Harrington told him that if the Reagan veto held there was enough cash in the bank to cover immediate needs and road construction would not suffer. Sanford also checked with Democrats back home, where he got mixed messages. Some expressed concern that he would damage his position with the Democratic leadership; others were adamant that he follow the party line and oppose the president. At the same time, Sanford was mindful that if he voted with the majority, Republicans would accuse the Democrats of effectively cutting the state out of $150 million in federal highway money by continuing the inequitable distribution.

Sanford was resolved to stand by his protest and on the evening of April 2, when the voting began, he was at the rear of the Senate Chamber with a small group of senior Democrats, including the majority leader. As the roll was called, it became apparent that the outcome would be much closer than Democratic Whip Alan Cranston of California had anticipated. Earlier in the day, Cranston had told Sanford he could continue his opposition to the bill and vote with the president, for the Democrats held a comfortable margin. That obviously was not the case when Sanford's name was called. The clerk was waiting for his response when Byrd told him to vote "present" and slip out of the chamber. Sanford did what he was told, but when he reached the Cloak Room, he was reminded by senators standing there that a present vote was not allowed under Senate rules. He would have to declare himself. He returned to the chamber where he voted "no," which gave Reagan the margin he needed. Before the vote was recorded, Byrd switched his vote in a parliamentary maneuver that allowed Democrats to rally overnight in time for reconsideration the next day.

Sanford left the chamber for a late dinner with his staff, most of whom thought he was wrong to uphold the veto. The resolve of Democrats back home was fading as well, as organized labor nudged party leaders to bring Sanford back in line.[9] After finishing his meal, he returned to the floor, where he told the Democratic leadership he would switch his vote to override when the bill was called the following day, effectively registering yes, no, and present votes all on the same bill.[10]

"There's no question that was inexperience," Sanford said later, recalling the episode. One of his staff members, Jennifer Hillman, later blamed Sanford's difficulties on a sloppy vote count and an inexperienced staff. Had Sanford known just how thin the Democratic margin really was—intelligence that a good aide would have provided early—he could have avoided being caught in such a difficult position. Further complicating the matter was the confusion introduced by Byrd. "There's no question that Byrd misled me," Sanford said.[11]

"I certainly had never intended to kill the bill," Sanford later wrote in his journal. "I had thought that my vote would send a message of protest about the way North Carolina had been treated for the past thirty years in the highway funds, and to emphasize the fact that I was totally dissatisfied with the report of a few days earlier that North Carolina was on the very bottom of the list of all states in funds received from the federal government."

None of this was clear to those who watched Sanford's rotation of voting choices; he simply looked like a freshman who couldn't make up his mind. "The *Washington Post* the next morning had anything but a nice story," Sanford's journal entry said, "that I had voted twice, first 'present' and then 'no,' and then had announced that I would vote to override when the bill was reconsidered. They played it in its worst possible light. Nevertheless, I had done my duty."

Back home, Martin capitalized on Sanford's discomfort. "He told me that he would continue to vote [to sustain the veto] until I told him to vote otherwise," the governor told reporters on the capitol steps in Raleigh. "I can assure you that I have not told him, or anybody, to vote for that bill." And the state's Republican leadership began to make hay out of Sanford's switch, calling him "Turnaround Terry" in the media. The *Durham Herald* even took him to task, calling his performance "the Sanford flip-flop." "He is not known for being wishy-washy. But even Mr. Sanford's best explanations have not offset the widespread perception that he simply caved in to political pressure," the *Herald* said. The *Charlotte Observer*'s political cartoonist, Doug Marlette, drew Sanford and Helms seated at separate desks with name plates that read "Senator No" and "Senator Whatever." [12]

Although the episode was a most unflattering introduction to Washington, Sanford brushed it aside and rationalized the damage. "It all blew over," he wrote, but he never entirely shook it. A reference to the affair always seemed to make it into reporters' accounts of his first term. But Sanford had never been one to dwell on the unpleasant. If anything, the mishap simply stiffened his resolve to make the most of the six years that lay ahead, beginning with the item at the top of his agenda, a creative initiative that he hoped could bring stability to Central America.

The continuing war in Nicaragua, where a leftist movement had ousted the corrupt Somosa dictatorship eight years earlier, had spilled over into neighboring nations and now the entire region was in turmoil. The Reagan administration's response to Nicaragua's new Sandinista regime was to supply military equipment and other support to the right-wing rebels, known as the Contras, who were using neighboring countries as safe havens from which to launch their attacks. The war had left thousands dead. Entire villages had vanished as a result of the fighting.

Washington seemed intent on a military solution. A year before, as the 1986 political season was getting underway, the Reagan administration had announced that the United States would seek $100 million in support for the Contras even as a delegation of eight Latin American foreign ministers was preparing for a visit to Washington to ask the president to put its weight behind a Central American peace effort.

As Sanford campaigned for the Democratic nomination, he was determined not to be caught in the crossfire on this issue, which had crippled Hunt, whose opposition to the Reagan strategy had left him vulnerable to the charge that he was sympathetic to the leftists supporting the Sandinistas. "I was absolutely determined that I wasn't going to be caught being wishy-washy on the Contra war," Sanford later recalled. "I said that I didn't agree with the president's decision on the Contras, but I was not going to Washington to try to pull the rug out from under him. Instead, I was going up there [to] suggest a different approach that will mean much to the United States and much to Latin America and much to Central America. That rang pretty well on the campaign trail." [13]

The turmoil in Central America touched few North Carolinians directly. Opponents to the Reagan administration's hard-line response mounted protests on college campuses and the Contra issue figured in the political rhetoric when conservatives used the threat of communists in the Western Hemisphere as a rallying cry for voters. But other issues ranked well above foreign affairs, which had never aroused much reaction in North Carolina elections. Reporters covering Sanford's campaign did not press him for specifics on his plans for the region, and that was just as well. He didn't have any. The Marshall Plan model sounded good, but he really didn't have an idea how that would work. [14] By the time he arrived in Washington, however, he believed that he could find a solution. It was a bold, even audacious, ambition for a freshman senator who didn't even have permanent office space, but Sanford was eager to push ahead as soon as possible. He planned to make the most of his opportunity, and within hours of taking his oath for a full term, he met with his staff to talk about Central America.

The Marshall Plan, named for World War II General George Marshall, remained the best model. Forty years earlier, when Europe lay devastated after the war, the United States had pledged assistance to help the nations rebuild under plans they themselves designed. "Marshall had said to Europe, 'You come up with a plan and we'll help you,'" Sanford later recalled. "Well, I didn't think they could quite come up with a plan in the way Europe was able to, but that began my thinking of what to do." Sanford believed the same could work in Central America, but this time there must be some sponsor other than the United States, whose credibility in the region was low, particularly in light of revelations late in 1986 that the Reagan administration had secretly sold arms to Iran as part of illegal military assistance to the Nicaraguan Contras. [15]

From his seat on the Senate Foreign Relations Committee, Sanford was well placed to hear the latest from the region as Reagan administration officials trooped to Capitol Hill to lobby for a Contra aid bill that was due for a vote. Sanford poked and prodded witnesses where he could, seeking information on what those familiar with the region believed would happen when the fighting stopped. After one hearing, where he sensed a veteran state department official had more to say than what the White House would allow, he invited him to his office for a more frank exchange and learned that Oscar Arias, the president of Costa Rica, was working toward a meeting of the presidents of the other Central American democracies. Sanford also learned about an upcoming meeting of ministers from European nations that did business in Central America. The issues were complicated, but there appeared to be an opportunity to work with these nations and others whose concern went beyond the shooting war.

In late February, Sanford made his first trip to Central America, traveling with Senator Christopher Dodd of Connecticut, another Democrat with a deep interest in the region. Sanford took with him his senior assistant, Bill Green, who had left his job at Duke to follow him to Washington. Green was older by a generation than others on Sanford's staff and tested by his years handling many touchy issues at Duke. Hillman, who had known Green from her own days at Duke, described him as "the resident best friend" among the decidedly youthful staff, meaning that Green was someone closer to his own generation with whom Sanford could relax and talk without restraint. Green was to be his lead staffer for Central America.

The trip coincided with the meeting called by Arias of the leaders of the other Central American democracies—Honduras, Guatemala, El Salvador—that felt threatened by the shooting war underway on the borders of Nicaragua. Sanford was in the audience when Arias and the other presidents signed an agreement to meet later in the year and begin talks they hoped would lead to peace and security in the region. Though Sanford was traveling with no official status or portfolio, he called on Arias and outlined his ideas for a multinational group that would work with the democratic governments, as well as the Marxists—if indeed they were Marxists—to rebuild the region once peace was restored. Arias immediately warmed to the senator's idea. Three days later, the leader of the Sandinista government, President Daniel Ortega, agreed to meet with the Arias group when it convened in the summer.

Shortly after his return, Sanford took the Senate floor for his first speech of any consequence. His subject was a resolution commending Arias and encouraging American support for the Costa Rican peace initiative. It was the first positive piece of legislation on the region to be considered in years and Sanford carried with him the endorsement of thirty members. The resolution praised Arias and the summer meeting in Esquipulas, Guatemala. It passed by a vote of ninety-seven to one; even Helms, one of the staunchest supporters of Contra aid, voted for it. Prior to the vote, Sanford assured him that the resolution carried no implications for approval of the peace plan nor was it designed as a short circuit to Contra military aid.

The resolution was the first step to the creation of the "mini-Marshall" plan, as he began calling it in conversations with other members. With the leaders moving toward peace on their own accord, Sanford felt the time was right for an effort to provide help in rebuilding their countries. It would need to begin soon and would require a new sensitivity to the politics of a region suspicious of North American motives and impatient with repeated slights that made for difficult relations. Only months before, when former secretary of state Henry Kissinger released a report on development in the Caribbean basin, he failed to have Spanish translations available. After learning of this misstep, Sanford vowed that his report would be prepared in Spanish with English translations.

In late June, less than six months after he arrived in Washington, Sanford announced the creation of a multinational commission that would prepare a plan for rebuilding the economies of the Central American nations in hopes of returning social and political stability to the region. The study would be coordinated through Duke University's Center for International Development Research and include representatives from the Central American countries as its senior members.

Sanford's organization of the commission demonstrated a keen sense of the possible and a genius for avoiding the typical Washington pitfalls, where good ideas often died aborning. Rather than fight a legislative maze to gain funding for the commission, he appealed to private foundations for help. It was an end run around potential opponents on Capitol Hill and reminiscent of a similar strategy twenty years earlier when he raised foundation money to launch the North Carolina Fund and a host of other projects rather than seek an appropriation from the state legislature. First on board with planning money were the Carnegie Corporation, with which he had a long association, and the Z. Smith Reynolds Foundation of Winston-Salem, now run by his former gubernatorial aide Tom Lambeth. Reynolds later had to withdraw because of its restrictions to grants within the state of North Carolina, but it was replaced by the Mary Reynolds Babcock Foundation of Winston-Salem. Additional start-up money came from the ARCA Foundation of Washington. Later, the commission drew on support from the Ford and MacArthur Foundations, which sent grants to Duke University, where William Ascher, codirector of Duke's Center for International Development Research, had been chosen as the lead staff person.

By the time of the commission's first meeting in December, Sanford had recruited forty-seven members, twenty of them from Central America, from twenty nations. Many were nongovernmental people recommended by universities and embassies. Business leaders, labor organizers, and social scientists came from Spain, Germany, Switzerland, the United States, Japan, Canada, Mexico, and a number of nations in South and Central America. Sweden's senior diplomat joined college presidents, scholars, and economists. Socialists sat down with capitalists. Sanford particularly liked having aboard former undersecretary of state Lawrence Eagleberger, whom he had come to know through his work on the board of ITT. Officially called the International Commission for Central American Recovery and Development, it was also known as the Sanford Commission, although he was not a member.

The composition was typical of Sanford's approach to problems, recalled Green. "What does he do?" Green said. "He reaches out for people who can implement the idea. He does that over and over again. Here it is a little larger scale with five countries participating and eventually Sweden, France, Japan, Canada, Mexico, Venezuela, and others." [16]

Named as cochairs were Dr. Sonia Picado, a former dean of the law school in Costa Rica who was the executive director of the Inter-American Institute of Human Rights, and Arthur Levitt Jr., chairman and chief executive of the American Stock Exchange. Picado would later serve in Washington on her embassy's staff in preparation for a political career of her own. Sanford was impressed with her energy, intelligence, and command of respect in a region that had been slow to accept women in professional or leadership roles. Recalling her first meeting some time later, Picado said she was taken with Sanford's cordial and warm attitude and his capacity to visualize the future for a region that most people seemed to take for granted. "I was surprised by his knowledge of Central America," she said. "It was extremely encouraging that he would know so much of Central America. He was convinced that the commission could bring peace." [17]

Levitt and Sanford had met in 1972 when Levitt's father was a Democratic candidate for mayor of New York and Sanford was running for president. "My first impression of him was that he was a distinguished, soft-spoken patrician, a real gentleman," Levitt recalled. "He had a wonderful sense of humor and eyes that laughed." About ten years later, Sanford's classmate Paul Colton was on the board of the American Stock Exchange when Levitt was hired as chairman and Sanford himself became a member of the board. [18]

In 1980, during Sanford's sabbatical at Duke, the two spent several days together in the wilderness of western Colorado on an Outward Bound trip. "Terry went down the Rogue River with me," Levitt recalled later. "They had what they called 'A Leap for Life' off a forty-two-foot cliff into the

Rogue River. Terry told nobody that he had a bad back and jumped anyway, cracking a vertebra. Rather than be carried out of there like most people would have done, he completed the trip flat on his back on a board down the Rogue River."

When Sanford asked him to cochair the commission, Levitt readily agreed. Although he had never been active in foreign affairs, he saw the assignment as an opportunity to be involved in something that had a chance to make a real contribution toward peace in Central America. "The Sanford Commission was kind of a crazy idea," Levitt said. "Whoever heard of a United States senator coming up with his own commission, not just another photo op?"

Sanford made several trips to the region, including one with a group of Senate observers of the Arias peace process. His visits criss-crossed boundaries and political alliances. On one trip he boarded an aging Huey helicopter for a ride in the jungle for a meeting with Contra leader Colonel Enrique Bermudez. "When I saw his miserable little army in there I took new courage that they weren't going to amount to too much." [19]

As Sanford rode about the countries, the damage of years of war affected him as much as the destructive influences of poverty and ignorance that he had found in mountain hollows and the back reaches of the state when he was governor. "You could see poverty all around," Sanford wrote about a visit to Nicaragua in November 1987. "It is touching to see little children, some of them dirty and unattended, and such scenes as a pregnant wife hanging on to her husband at a bus stop, he being subject to call up by the Sandinista army or kidnapped by the Contras to serve. It is all such a pathetic poverty-ridden sight that it's too bad that we have been adding to the misery by promoting, if not insisting upon, war. I am sure others would take issue with that evaluation, but in the final analysis this has never presented any danger to us, no matter what kind of government they had." [20]

In December, the commission members gathered for their first meeting in San Jose, Costa Rica, where they were welcomed by Sanford and Arias, who had since been named to receive the Nobel peace prize for his work in moving the peace process forward. In the weeks leading up to the session, Sanford practiced his language skills, fully intending to deliver his remarks in Spanish. Just as he was about to speak, Ascher urged him to stick to English, which he did. Sanford was amused when Ascher then promptly delivered his own speech in Spanish.

"The commission comes to the table as an independent body, owing allegiance only to human aspiration," Sanford told the group. "And it has great resources including the lessons of the past. Among those lessons is that mutual respect among nations is essential. Equally compelling is the lesson that strength doesn't create a nation's freedom. Freedom creates a nation's strength." [21]

It was an exciting time. Picado announced, "The meeting will bring together for the first time an array of experts from three continents. And for the first time in history, Central Americans will be full partners in planning the growth of our region." [22]

Sanford returned from the meeting optimistic about the future of the commission. He and Margaret Rose prepared for the Christmas holiday that they planned to spend with his mother, who no doubt was pleased with her son's efforts to fashion a forum for antagonists to meet and work out their differences. She would have expected nothing less.

Betsy Sanford was in her one hundredth year and remained a marvel to her neighbors in Laurinburg, some of whom had talked to her son about their concern over her continuing to drive a car. She did not get behind the wheel quite as often as before, but she maintained a busy schedule, including visits to the "old folks" in nursing homes and participation in the Methodist Church, where two Sunday school classes were named in her honor. Her own vigor and stamina were an inspiration to her son, who often countered any disparaging remarks about his age by referring to his mother's long life. On Christmas night, Betsy Sanford went to bed and died in her sleep. She was buried next to her husband and young daughter in a small family plot in Laurinburg.

The commission broke into study groups following the Costa Rican meeting before the full body gathered for two combined sessions, the first in Stockholm and the second in Washington. Within a year, it was ready with a report. In February 1989, Sanford returned to Guatemala as the commission gathered for a final round of sessions and personally delivered copies of the report to the Central American presidents. Sanford was absolutely buoyant with anticipation. "What impressed me was the energy and enthusiasm of the gathering group, which was such that you could feel it," he noted in his journal. "This project, so far anyhow, has been a tremendous success. It is their product. Reading the report, the emphasis is on what they can do. True, they need help. That is spelled out. But this is not an extension of our AID programs, and this is not just another aid to Central America or Latin America program designed by the United States. You could feel the difference."

The commission's recommendations covered a wide range of proposals, from more financial aid from the international community to renewed regional cooperation among the five Central American governments. Immediate action was needed in seven principal areas: food security, health and nutrition, basic education, safe drinking water and sanitation, temporary housing, infrastructure, and fundamental rights. "For the next five years Central America will need $2 billion per year of financial aid—up from current aid levels of $1.5 billion per year," the commission concluded.[23]

The report was endorsed by the presidents of all five nations, and some of the background studies generated for the commission contributed to the formulation of the Central American presidents' Joint Economic Plan of Action for Central America, which was signed at another presidential summit meeting in Antigua, Guatemala, in June 1990. It also was endorsed by the governments of Germany, Spain, and Sweden.[24]

Shortly after the delivery of the report, Ferrel Guillory, a News & Observer columnist who had traveled with Sanford to Central America, wrote that the commission illustrated Sanford's skill in conducting public policy. Whereas Helms threatened further military aid if Nicaragua's Ortega failed to uphold his promise of free elections, Guillory noted, Sanford brought people together to plan for the future. "Without engaging Mr. Helms directly in debate," Guillory wrote, "Mr. Sanford has challenged the essence of his approach to Central America over this decade."[25]

"I consider it the most significant thing I did in Washington," Sanford said some time later. He believed that the commission's work played a significant role in stopping the war in Nicaragua and pointing the way to economic recovery. "We certainly unified worldwide support for what was going on down there," Sanford said. "Given what you can normally do in a Senate seat, I thought it was a pretty good accomplishment."[26]

According to Picado, "The process of the commission itself was a victory. It was the first time the FMLN [Farabundo Marti National Liberation Front] and the Sandinistas met and talked. Everybody was suspicious of each other. It was very difficult for Central Americans to work together. The Sanford Commission created a space for dialogue in Central America that is still alive. . . . You have no idea how much respect and love I have for [Sanford]. I cannot think of anybody who worked as hard for Central America," Picado said. "I was impressed by his modesty. He said he didn't want it to be [his] personal project. He always wanted Central Americans to be on an equal basis and he did not want to impose the commission on the Central American people."[27]

"In some ways," Levitt later recalled, "it set the stage for the Central American peace. It gave it a basis for a peace that is continuing in terms of economic development and set the stage for relations between various countries on a continuing basis."[28]

Sanford's work brought plaudits from Arias and other leaders, including Ortega, who had not received a State Department visitor for three years until one arrived with Sanford when he delivered his report. As Sanford was leaving that meeting, he was called back by one of Ortega's ministers, who asked him to wait momentarily because his president had a present for him. A few moments later he returned with a painting of a young, sad-eyed Nicaraguan girl seated on a hillside by a flowering tree. The colors were rich and deep and set the scene against a background of furrowed hills and rising mountains. It was titled "Remembering in Silence" and Sanford had seen it hanging on the wall in Ortega's office. Written on the back in Ortega's hand was the message "To Terry Sanford, with the affection of the people from Nicaragua and the recognition for your involvement in bringing peace to our country, a sister nation."

Some of his fellow senators took notice of the commission's work. Kansas Republican Bob Dole wrote Sanford, "You have helped produce an impressive piece of work which should be of great value as we pursue the important issues of development in Central America." "You are to be commended for not only your efforts in bringing the International Commission into operation," Massachusetts Senator John Kerry wrote, "but also your persistent efforts to ensure that the recommendations of the Commission are incorporated into legislation. I agree that it is vitally important for our government to ensure that recovery and development in Central America will be high on our agenda, particularly in the face of developments in other areas of the world that could diminish the level of much-needed resources for this important region." [29]

"I didn't do it as a senator as much as I was a senator and I could do it," Sanford later recalled. Although he was forced to work at a slower pace than as a university president, or as a governor, he was pleased with the result while mindful of his mother's admonition to make something of each day. "That's the motivation, that you're doing something that makes a difference in people's lives. You've got to have a reason." [30]

Later in his term, Sanford attempted to gain a modest appropriation to continue work of the commission and follow through on recommendations made in the report. It was largely a bootless exercise that underscored the problems Sanford would have faced had he adopted a conventional approach at the outset. It took three years for Sanford's bill to reach the Senate floor for debate. In committee and on the floor, Sanford fended off efforts by Helms, who wished to turn the legislation into a statement by the United States that the Central American nations adopt more free enterprise initiatives. That was just the kind of attitude that Sanford hoped to change. "It was a bunch of right-wing blunder that would attempt to direct what the Central American countries could do, quite contrary to the philosophy of self-help and self-direction embodied in my bill." [31]

In September 1990, Sanford noted in his journal:

I got a note from Jesse [Helms] saying that he would support the bill with the addition of his enclosed amendment, which set out a lot of things that were totally inappropriate, and saying that while he noted that I had said that we should not be trying to tell these people precisely how to run their countries, that we certainly should tell them if we were going to spend taxpayers' money to help them.

Since he has never voted for any kind of foreign assistance, I don't believe we would get his vote if we took his amendment, and in any event, this is not an AID bill and not an authorization bill. I will gently tell him that by letter, and then proceed and see if he has the bad judgment to hold the bill up. I assume that our bill has virtually unanimous support. It certainly is a pain for me and everybody else to have to put up with Jesse Helms.

Sanford's bill finally won approval on September 30, 1991, when the Senate voted an appropriation of $500,000 to create the Central American Development Coordinating Commission—but the money never materialized.[32]

The Central American project provided Sanford with some relief from the glacial pace and irritating turf wars of Capitol Hill. The Senate had proven to be everything he had heard about and seen, only worse. He was usually in the office by eight to begin a daily schedule that included committee meetings, visits with delegations from back home, and action on the Senate floor. "There are constant telephone calls, individual staff conferences, dashing back and forth to the floor to vote, committee or caucus meetings, people stopping by, so that it all amounts up to a mad fourteen-hour-day rush generally speaking," he noted in his journal, "and even then it is difficult to keep up with personal mail that I have to see, and the larger amount of personal mail that I have to sign."

Most nights he arrived home late, but he continued to rise early and often took long walks from his apartment about a block from the Capitol around the neighborhood and beyond. As the city was waking, he found it a relatively quiet time when he could reflect on ideas and also see a different side of Washington. One morning he came upon a group of young people outside the Hart Office Building, where they had spent the night as "space savers" for lobbyists eager to secure one of the reserved seats at a hearing. The scene reminded him of Duke students who camped out overnight in lines for tickets to basketball games.

He did like the odd lot of people attracted to seats of power. One of those he remembered in his journal was Joseph Vincent MacHugh, whose passing he recorded. "He was 91 years old. He was an old man, trim, alert, with gray hair, who stood almost every day on the Capitol side of the subways, greeting senators by name and passing out some little tract that he had written. The first inclination would be to consider him some kind of nut, but he wasn't at all intrusive or aggressive. He didn't move out of position more than a step or two, and certainly was not an offensive buttonholer. I doubt that many people took him seriously, but they took his paper courteously and no doubt sometimes read them. Actually what he was writing was very good.

"What he didn't understand," Sanford noted, "was that we are probably not educable."

The Sanfords' social schedule was always overbooked. His membership on the Foreign Relations Committee brought invitations to many embassy receptions. These events, coupled with others sponsored by special interest groups and Democratic Party functions, left little time during the week for retreat from a busy schedule. The only time he could count on being away from the press of business was the four-and-a-half-hour ride from Washington to Durham. Usually a staff member drove while Sanford caught up on paperwork and correspondence, prepared speeches, or sorted through details of legislation. Sometimes he just talked with his aide or slept.

Most weekends were spent at home. On the rare occasion when he did not have some political event or occasion at Duke, he would putter about and tend to a small garden in the driveway loop at the front door, or work on a book about aging that he later titled *Outlive Your Enemies, Grow Old Gracefully*. Sanford enjoyed writing and the use of language. He had a knack for remembering details and incorporated personal recollections and anecdotes into his work to help readers understand his point of view. In addition to the aging book, he also was gathering material on a book about the education programs fostered by Lyndon B. Johnson, a work he planned to title, *The Lasting Lyndon*.[33]

The time he reserved for his journal was often his only time for reflection on current events, his own performance, or the worth of the entire exercise. By the time he finished his six-year term, he had filled nine three-inch ring binders with typed pages of single-spaced transcript. He noted his aggravation with the creaky legislative process, the deference to seniority over good sense, rules that defied understanding, and turf battles among committee chairs that led to shallow treatment of serious ideas. He also was discouraged at what he believed was a loss of the Senate's ability to compromise, something he had witnessed during his visits to Kerr Scott's Senate office in the days of Lyndon Johnson and Everett Dirksen. "I had been up there with Kerr Scott and had met Dirksen and Johnson and they had mutual respect for one another," he later recalled. "They were up there doing a job and they had their viewpoints to address, but they could get together and work out those viewpoints. They weren't doing it now. They didn't really care." [34]

The deep divisions between Republicans and Democrats was most evident in his first year as President Reagan pressed for Senate confirmation of Robert Bork to the U.S. Supreme Court. The nomination was voted out of committee but Democrats objected to Bork's hard-line conservative philosophy and had not forgotten his role as Richard Nixon's solicitor general, when he was suddenly elevated by the resignation of Attorney General Elliott Richardson and the firing of Special Prosecutor Archibald Cox during the height of the Watergate investigation. Conservative Republicans were bent on forcing the issue as pointedly as possible and characterized the opposition as a lynch mob. When Reagan mounted a televised appeal for Bork, Sanford's Democratic colleagues chose him to deliver the party's response.

In his televised speech, he said Bork was unqualified because the hearings proved that he wasn't a legal scholar and had misinterpreted the meaning of the Constitution. "My problem with Judge Bork is that he does not stick to his views. Over and over I get the impression that he follows his narrow interpretation only when it leads to the result he wishes it to lead to. That is not consistent scholarship." [35]

The nomination failed, with the Republicans mustering only forty-two votes in Bork's favor. Sanford was satisfied that another ten or fifteen Republicans would have voted against the nomination except that they didn't want to alienate the Reagan White House. "I voted against Bork," Sanford noted in his journal, "because I thought that he had supplied us with ample evidence over a long period of time that he had very strong, hard positions on every conceivable issue, and that if he had a chance to rule on anything pertaining to one of his preconceived opinions, he would decide the case and then work the argument to justify it."

Since coming to the Senate, Sanford had shouldered his share of the duty of presiding over it, an assignment that rotated through the Democratic majority. Sanford remembered that when Harry Truman was in the Senate, he would write letters to his wife while he was in the chair, but televised proceedings had changed that. Majority Leader Robert Byrd admonished presiding officers to remain alert and not bring work to the desk.

To occupy his time during the Bork debate, which featured heated partisan exchanges, Sanford took the measure of his Senate colleagues, particularly Republicans. Among the more obstinate members, he noted, were Gordon Humphrey from New Hampshire, a reactionary even more zealous than Helms. During the debate over the Bork nomination, Humphrey had attached his name to a campaign mounted by the National Conservative Political Action Committee that used computer-generated telephone calls to contact voters in states whose senators opposed the nomination. The nation's court system was in jeopardy, callers were told, and they should both contact their senator and send the committee money. Sanford returned one weekend with a handful of affidavits from those who had been called, and along with other Democrats challenged Humphrey's tactics on the Senate floor as an example of the politicization of the nomination process.

Ranked just behind Humphrey was Dan Quayle from Indiana, whom Sanford considered a dilettante and as "obnoxious" as Humphrey, "only louder." Next was Steve Symms of Idaho, with whom Sanford had traveled to Central America. He described Symms as a "likable John Bircher" who seemed only interested in the military operations in Central America, not the broader, long-range issue. At one point on the trip, Symms passed up a chance to meet with Costa Rican President Oscar Arias at his home in order to stay at the hotel and watch a football game.

Sanford likened his North Carolina colleague, Jesse Helms, to "the lad with his finger in the dike, keeping true democracy from totally overwhelming America. I think his service in the Senate has been largely of zero value to North Carolina. . . . He has a negative attitude about everything, and it is very difficult to find anything up here that he has done that has any lasting value," he wrote. "I would be expected to make that kind of judgment about him. He has done a good job of convincing people that he is just a good 'ole boy, a good 'ole conservative, just trying to keep those liberals from despoiling the political landscape."

Southern cordiality masked the relations between the contrasting voices of North Carolina. Helms and Sanford appeared together at functions and even posed for photographs on the Capitol steps with visitors from the state. On at least one occasion, Sanford helped Helms release a judicial appointment that was held up in the Judiciary Committee where Democrats and Republicans, irritated with Helms's politics, had refused to bring the nomination to a vote. Helms's colleagues had scores to settle, Sanford observed, and they weren't above settling them. Sanford responded to a request from Joe Bryan of Greensboro who asked him to see what he could do for Carlton Tilley, whom Helms had nominated to a district court judgeship. Tilley was eventually confirmed.

One of their most visible confrontations occurred in connection with their joint service on the Foreign Relations Committee. Late in 1988, Helms was forcing a point on behalf of Marine Lieutenant Colonel Oliver North as the committee considered enforcement of a subpoena for documents in

North's possession. Helms was asked if he had read some documents prepared in behalf of enforcement. When he said he had not, he challenged members to a show of hands on whether they had read the opinions. A few members raised their hands; Sanford did not and drew a glare from Helms. "I've read it, but I just don't raise my hand," Sanford said aloud, drawing laughter at Helms's expense.[36] Helms left angry, after snorting that Sanford was too old to raise his hand. "Later that day," Sanford noted in his journal, "he made some rather outrageous statements to the newspapers that I was lying, that I was dumber than he thought, and he certainly violated the normal rules of courtesy observed by senators."

Helms later called Sanford from the Senate floor to make peace. In the course of their half-hour conversation, he apologized for his outburst and extended his hand. Sanford described the meeting in his journal: "He said he wanted to be my friend, that we ought to work together on North Carolina matters, and would I shake. I shook. I am skeptical enough to know that he is not going to be an ally. It may be that he wants to get me off his back, and it may be that he genuinely wants to work in a more harmonious situation. I am sure he has not been accustomed to having people take shots at him in the Senate, and that may be a reason. It may be a more generous instinct. In any event, I think that was a thirty minutes well spent."

In his journal, Sanford referred to Ronald Reagan as "the master of deceit" after hearing his State of the Union address in 1988. "He went through his old litany of prayer in the schools, abortion, the line item veto and the constitutional amendment requiring a balanced budget. I suspect that this has been in every one of his speeches. Not only is it deceitful, it is certainly playing the right wing in a shameful manner. I don't doubt that the President believes all of this trash, but I think he is realistic enough to know that it's not something he's going to champion too strongly. He has given them this line right along, but he has never done anything about trying to get the legislation passed, and that is a redeeming feature at least."

He did not discount the impact of Reagan's appeal. "Yellow-dog Democrat that she is, Margaret Rose thought it was a splendid delivery," Sanford noted in his journal. "Nevertheless, sitting there watching him, knowing the facts behind his glib statements, had to be depressing."

The unrestrained spending of the Reagan years had been terribly damaging to the nation, and Sanford once facetiously told a group that the Republic had not suffered such an assault since the British burned the White House in 1812.[37] During Reagan's two terms, the nation's debt spiraled to record heights, despite ineffective stop-gap measures adopted by the Congress, which seemed as unconcerned as the president about the deficit. Sanford was bothered most by the administration's use of a surplus in Social Security collections to offset the rising cost of government.

The administration's maneuvering to deal with the deficit had troubled Sanford from his early days in the Senate, when he had an opportunity in committee hearings to question budget officials from the White House. Near the end of the second year of his term, Sanford began putting together the details of what he would come to call his "Honest Budget Bill." He attempted to put in one bill a requirement for a balanced budget, a proposal to reduce the national debt with new taxes if necessary, and a separation of Social Security and other trust funds and more investment flexibility of trust funds. Sanford reasoned that this money could be put in state and municipal bonds, where it would earn interest and support public works and education at the same time. Sanford's budget plan attracted attention. "Sanford has done his homework," wrote *Washington Post* columnist David Broder. "He understands that the annual autumn ritual in which the President and Congress congratulate each other for 'reaching the target' set by the 1985 Gramm-Rudman-Hollings deficit-reduction law is a charade." [38]

As the 1988 presidential elections approached, Sanford harbored some hope that Democrats might recover after eight years of Ronald Reagan. For all its shortcomings, the Senate gave Sanford an opportunity to participate in the preprimary maneuvering, which had never been a possibility in Durham. It was a side of Washington life that he seemed to thoroughly enjoy even though his first opportunity in the fall of 1987 was not entirely satisfactory.

Sanford had hoped Arkansas Senator Dale Bumpers would get in the race. One day, as Sanford was headed to a committee meeting, he was pulled aside by Bill Clinton, the young governor of Arkansas, who Sanford knew was interested in the nomination. "I went straight to the point to forestall my consideration of that," Sanford noted in his journal. "He seemed pleased enough. I said we simply have to go outside of the Democrats who have filed so far and find someone who can come in and who can serve. I said that if for any reason Bumpers backed down, we would have to go find someone else. I suspect that he thinks that he is the someone else, but time will give us a chance to take care of that."

Bumpers's campaign never materialized, and late in the year Sanford tried to convince New York Governor Mario Cuomo to run. Sanford liked Cuomo's politics, which harkened back to the New Deal roots of the Democratic Party. As governor he had demonstrated a concern for the welfare of people and he seemed to have a vision for moving the country forward. Sanford called it "the kind of vision that would return the Democratic Party to its traditional role," meaning a more moderate, centrist approach that would appeal to Southerners grown cautious about the shift of the party to the left. In December, Sanford and Sam Poole flew to New York City in hopes of getting Cuomo to change his mind, but the governor told them he had meant what he said when he took himself out of the race earlier in the year.

Finally, Sanford found a safe haven with his endorsement of Senator Al Gore Jr. of Tennessee. Gore was young, untested, and stiff in front of a crowd, and Sanford was bothered that Gore made too much of his Vietnam service; veterans would resent that, he noted to himself. But Gore showed some promise, was smart, and came from a political culture that provided some comfort for Sanford. Before announcing his support for Gore in January 1988, Sanford put in a call to Jesse Jackson, whose own ambitions for the presidency were causing concern within the ranks of the regulars in the Democratic Party.

Jackson had far outstripped his own youthful boasting twenty-five years earlier, when he had walked into the governor's office for a meeting with some of Sanford's aides, took a seat in the governor's chair, and declared, "One day, I am going to sit in this chair." [39] As the 1988 presidential primaries approached, Jackson was the best-known black candidate in the nation. Sanford had followed Jackson's rise with a combination of pride and bemusement over Jackson's knack for the dramatic and grand gesture. On occasion, when Jackson had seen Sanford, he had greeted him by dropping to one knee and kissing Sanford's hand, a gesture that Jackson employed with others as well. When Sanford reached Jackson by phone to tell him he was supporting Gore, Jackson "pretended to be disappointed," Sanford noted in his journal. "I pointed out to him, [when] he suggested I had some obligation to him, that he had campaigned against me in North Carolina for Ted Kinney in the primary. It would have made no sense for me to have supported Jackson, who obviously has no chance of winning the nomination."

There was more to it than whether Jackson could win or lose. Sanford clearly saw Jackson as a charismatic leader and a brilliantly skillful speaker, but he didn't like the politics that Jackson was preaching. After one meeting with Jackson, Sanford wrote in his journal, "If he were a white Baptist preacher instead of a black Baptist preacher, and even if he were more eloquent than he actually is as a black, he would not have had any showing at all. He has run a purely racist campaign. It is the kind of thing that we have condemned for years. It is exactly the same thing that George Wallace did, urging people to vote for him for the reason that he was black. Obviously he made an appeal to white voters, and very badly wanted white voters, but the vast number of the seven million people he is talking about voted for him, quite properly, quite understandably, but nevertheless quite truly because he was black. He seemed to be insisting that he had a right to the vice presidency, if he wanted it."

In fact, Sanford found little to be hopeful about in 1988. Gore's campaign ended early, and Sanford finally joined other Senate Democrats with an endorsement of Massachusetts Governor Michael Dukakis, who had done well in the spring primaries. The Dukakis managers expressed little interest in Democrats from Southern states such as North Carolina, and Sanford found them slow to return phone calls as the fall campaign got underway. Sanford was fed up by the time he joined other Southern congressmen for a meeting with Dukakis aides in October, where he told them theirs was the worst-managed campaign he had ever seen. "I'd have to say that they received this without profanity," he wrote in his journal,

> but I am sure that nothing will be done about it. Here we have an example of a self-satisfied crowd, now admittedly worried and harassed, but a group that admits no error, and has no doubts.
>
> It's . . . one of the worst mistakes that campaigners can make—they win a primary and then think that they know everything, and that they have everything under control, and that people who were not for them in the primary are just trying to get on board somehow for their advantage. I have seen many races lost because of this smug and possessive attitude. They in all likelihood are going to lose the election, and I don't know what can be done about it.

Back home, North Carolina Democrats also were in trouble. Sanford campaigned as he always had in the past, but this time he had little heart for the fight. He surprised even himself with his resignation to defeat. "If we win, great," he wrote. "If we don't win I can exist and get along, and probably do just as well."

That November, Governor Jim Martin won a second term and Jim Gardner, who had first run for statewide office twenty years earlier, became the first Republican elected lieutenant governor. George Bush carried North Carolina along with thirty-nine other states. The Democratic Party in North Carolina had never been in such a sorry state.

The election outcome capped two years that had been the most numbing Sanford had ever known. As 1988 came to an end, facing the prospect of another four years of Republicans in the White House, he wrote in his journal, "I have had some misgivings of whether or not anything worthwhile can be accomplished. We have a tremendous plan for Central America. The chances for getting it adopted are not at all certain. We have a great idea for how to put the president in a position to handle the massive and rapidly growing debt, or to put him on the spot for failure to do so, but I doubt very seriously that it will get anywhere because almost everyone in the Senate has an agenda, and it is very difficult to get their attention to something else." Yet he tried to remain hopeful. He had never quit a job in his life and he had been raised to find solutions, not wallow in defeat. "I am in the Senate, and I cannot leave now, so I will make the most of it, and by the time the gavel sounds again I am sure that I will be enjoying it very much."

CHAPTER EIGHTEEN

A North Carolina Regular

❀

IN ITS DAY, THE OLD BURKE COUNTY courthouse in the middle of Morganton's tree-shaded square was the political and judicial center of this peaceful county in the foothills of the Blue Ridge Mountains. North Carolina's legendary "country lawyer," Sam Ervin Jr., practiced law there, as did his father before him. Countless political candidates climbed the distinctive curving steps to the balcony to deliver speeches to crowds gathered on the lawn below. One of them was president-to-be Ronald Reagan, who came through Morganton in 1976 on his way to the Republican National Convention. In the spring of 1989, Terry Sanford stepped into the old courtroom to a warm reception from friends and allies of more than a generation of political contests.

This visit closed an invigorating day that had begun with a trip to the campus of the local community college and continued at a senior citizens center. From there he went to an elementary school where the first-graders were practicing their Spanish, and after lunch he stopped at two textile mills before heading to the old courthouse. There, Sanford enjoyed a reunion with old friends such as Sam J. Ervin III, the son of the senator whose seat he now held, and steadfast supporters such as Jack Kirksey, who had been politicking with him since his bid for the YDC presidency nearly forty years before.

By the time Sanford reached Morganton, he had been on the road for three days and the trip was proving to be a needed tonic. "I was finding that I was enjoying this more than anything I have done in a long time," he later noted in his journal. "I think my natural habitat is the campaign trail. My spirits rise, I don't get tired, and I find it to be tremendous fun, even, I might say, exhilarating."

Sanford was recovering from a disheartening start to the year. He had wished President George Bush well when he saw him presiding over the Senate for the last time as vice president, but he had found nothing inspiring in the new president's inaugural address. Jim Martin's second inaugural in Raleigh had been just as tedious and the ceremony inappropriately partisan, he thought. When the gunners from the National Guard fired the nineteen-gun salute, he was reminded of his own inauguration when, on hearing the cannons' report, one wag said, "They missed him." This snatch of humor did little to offset his impatience with the ceremonies and Republican folderol that increased as he and Margaret Rose sat in an open car parked at a standstill in the middle of the street for forty-five minutes waiting for a place at the end of the parade. Finally, he and two of his successor governors, Democrat Bob Scott and Republican Jim Holshouser, had their drivers pull their cars out of the line and turn back to the parking garage, where they left for home.[1]

The 1988 elections had left the Democratic Party a tumbled mess. As the state's top-ranked elected Democrat, Sanford had a hand in the selection of a new chairman. He was Raleigh lawyer Lawrence Davis, a lobbyist associated with the state's business interests, and his election upset the party's liberals and African Americans, who complained loudly about being ignored and taken for granted. Sanford left the meetings with a sense of foreboding about the future, noting privately the unspeakable: If the Democrats continued their course away from mainstream America, he might have to distance himself from it four years hence.[2]

Ever optimistic, he was sure it would not come to that. Even when the Democrats had drifted far to the left with McGovern in 1972, he had campaigned for the nominee. Such loyalty had confirmed the claims of his opponents that he was a liberal, as dangerous a label in contemporary Southern politics as "integrationist" had been twenty years before. In an effort to duck the "L word," he began describing himself as a "North Carolina regular" and suffered like his one-time hero, Georgia Governor Ellis Arnall, who took to calling himself "a Democrat, with a little d; though that, too, is inexact and cumbersome."[3]

No matter what label he put on himself, thirty years in public life had created an indelible impression among voters. During one of his trips into the eastern part of the state after the visit to Morganton, he was asked by a businessman he had known for years why he always voted with Senator Ted Kennedy, whom Jesse Helms had used as his favorite campaign punching bag. "Who told you that?" Sanford asked.

"My friends," the man responded.

"They're all Republicans," Sanford answered. A few months later, Sanford might have had the conversation in mind as he maneuvered to a seat away from Kennedy when members of Congress gathered to hear President Bush deliver his State of the Union address. Just when Sanford thought he had a safe spot, Kennedy took the chair right behind him.

Of greatest concern was the certain election of Washington insider Ron Brown as national party chairman. Brown had the backing of liberals such as Kennedy and the endorsement of organized labor, as well as overwhelming support among black activists. He was a polished, well-connected lawyer who in the summer of 1988 had worked the national convention for Jesse Jackson. Since the election he had continued to ally himself with Jackson, who appeared set on running again in 1992. There seemed little Sanford could do to stop the Brown election, which was certain to cause more trouble for Democrats in the South.

Prior to the meeting of the Democratic National Committee in January, Sanford had approached Kennedy in the Senate Cloak Room, where he argued that Brown was the wrong man for the job, if for no other reason than that he was too closely identified with an active candidate. The party needed an unaffiliated voice as chair, Sanford argued. Moreover, Brown seemed unconcerned about changes in the party that Sanford believed were necessary to move it toward the center before it lost all touch with its traditional working-class base, particularly in the South.

What bothered Sanford most was that with Brown as chairman, it would appear the party had been delivered over to Jesse Jackson. "I think that his election will be a tremendous body blow, if not a death blow, in North Carolina," he wrote in his journal. "Our problem has been that we have had great difficulty in getting back to the middle, to the moderate voter, the voter who thinks, perhaps with the residual prejudice that he was raised with, that the Democratic Party has become the party of the blacks, no longer concerned with equal rights for white males."

The entire affair proved awkward for Sanford, who worried that Kennedy might believe his opposition was founded in Brown's race, not his politics. But his credentials on race were solid, and Kennedy knew when they talked that Sanford had shouldered more than his share of the burden in the sixties and defended his brother's actions in Alabama and Mississippi. This also wasn't just a Southern phobia, Sanford argued, for if voters came to associate the party with Jackson and black issues, then all Democrats would be in trouble. He noted in his journal: "It is obvious that the Democratic Party is suffering tremendously because it is perceived by far too many people as being the black man's party, with the Democrats perceived as giving in to the blacks on every demand or petition. While this is not so, it is very difficult to overcome that image. It is also true that the blacks, or so it seems to me, are far more interested in having some participation and part, and taking over to the extent that they can, than they are in having a winning candidacy."

This was not the first time Sanford had been troubled by the changes that had crippled the Democratic Party in the South. During the 1988 primary season, he became visibly angry at a party meeting in Durham, where African Americans controlled the local organization. Sanford was asked why he had participated in a movement to stop Jackson in the presidential primary. He had done no such thing, Sanford replied, and furthermore he owed Jackson and the Durham black political committee nothing, particularly after they had recruited a candidate to run against him in 1986. As Sanford was on his way out, a preacher stopped him to say he was wrong to show such emotion. "I looked at him and said, 'Well, then I hope that you will pray for my forgiveness.' "

Later in the year, Sanford ran into similar complaints—"vanities of reverse racism," he called them—at a Charlotte gathering where a speaker demanded to know why North Carolina Democrats had not gerrymandered a congressional district where a black candidate could be assured of winning. Writing in his journal later, he said he was bothered by "their feeling that the Democratic Party would not be successful at all if it were not for them. The truth of the matter, historically, is that the Democratic Party took on the burden of bringing the blacks into American society, and paid dearly for this effort. Were it not for this, there would be no such thing as a Reagan Democrat, or certainly not very many of them. It is a sad commentary, but the lingering race prejudice does, indeed, drive a great many white people away from the Democratic Party."

As the 101st Congress prepared for business, Sanford focused his thoughts on the remaining four years in his term. He decided that he would continue to work on his economic plans for Central America, and his budget bill was a top priority. But he also believed the nation needed a new science policy, and there were unmet concerns in rural life, particularly housing for people who lived beyond the boundaries of urban areas. As the new members of the Bush cabinet made their rounds of introductions on Capitol Hill, Sanford lobbied for his pet projects and slipped material about the Central America development project into a packet he prepared for incoming secretary of state James Baker. He held out some hope that the Republicans might exchange their policy of a military solution for something more positive and forward-thinking.

Sanford was impressed with Baker but was furious over the president's nomination of John Tower as secretary of defense. After reading the confidential FBI reports on Tower, Sanford was convinced the man was unfit for office not only because of a record of drunkenness and womanizing, but because of Tower's role in the arms-for-hostages deal with Iran and the so-called October surprise. Suspicions remained that the Reagan campaign had negotiated with the Iranians not to release hostages held in the U.S. embassy in Tehran until after the November elections, when incumbent president Jimmy Carter was defeated. Tower had found Bush innocent of any wrongdoing, but Sanford concluded from the FBI reports that his work was little more than a whitewash. "I came away from reading that in a furious attitude," Sanford wrote in his journal. "The very idea of that kind of sabotage, that kind of double dealing, that kind of dishonest assumption of fair and impartial judge, convinced me that under no circumstances could I vote for John Tower."

After six months in office, the Bush administration was proving no more satisfying than what he had seen under Reagan. Bush was trivializing government, Sanford believed, by expending his energies on issues of immediate emotional and political gain that carried no long-lasting value for the country. The president's insistence on removing the capital gains tax had "wrecked the budget process," Sanford noted, and his continued saber-rattling over Central America helped postpone any real progress for rehabilitating the broken economies and societies in that region. Particularly troublesome for Sanford was Bush's proposal for a constitutional amendment to protect the American flag.

In midsummer, the Supreme Court had thrown out the conviction of a Texas man who had burned an American flag in a political demonstration outside the Republican National Convention in 1984. Sanford had no patience with flag burners, but he found the president's reaction more alarming. He believed the constitutional amendment that the Republicans hastily drafted to protect the flag was a far greater threat to the Bill of Rights and the American tradition of political dissent than any individual's abuse of a banner, no matter how hallowed. The president's response was base political cynicism, Sanford believed. Bush "was following a demagogic, vote-getting, low-principled course," he wrote. "First of all, he knows that the protection of the minorities is unpopular and that gains politically come from waving the flag, and oppressing the minorities. He knows very well that in the United States, the majority does not rule. The majority governs, but it does not rule. That was the point of the Bill of Rights. We protect the minorities. The President's repair to the Iwo Jima monument for his press conference, about the amendment, was thoroughly obscene."

Although the president acknowledged that the flag-burning amendment might be ruled unconstitutional later by the Supreme Court, he denied that he was using the issue as a political gesture. "It isn't wrapping myself in the flag," he said. "It is that the flag is unique and, in my view, should be protected by this change."[4]

For Sanford, the issue laid bare the frailties of current politics. He found normally principled members suddenly shaken by visions of the thirty-second television spots that opponents in the next election were sure to use against them if they voted against the amendment. There was another way, Sanford argued. The Democrats should turn the issue around and explain to the people that the president "was getting ready to violate and desecrate the Bill of Rights, which the flag stands for." His colleagues were not convinced. South Carolina's Fritz Hollings "said I didn't know what I was talking about, that we would all get defeated if we didn't vote for the Constitutional amendment." [5]

Public sentiment for the amendment was building as Sanford made plans in July to attend a reunion of the 517th Regimental Combat Team. When some members of his young staff questioned whether he really cared about spending a weekend with these comrades, most of whom couldn't vote in North Carolina, he told them, "I walked with all of these people, risked dying alongside all of them, and in spite of the fact that scattering kept us from maintaining close friendships, I felt close to all of them." [6] The reunion was just the venue for Sanford to test his flag amendment counteroffensive. As the talk around the bar shifted from war stories to contemporary issues, he heard the kind of patriotic response he expected from combat veterans. When he suggested that patriotism threatened to overshadow weightier issues, such as protection of liberties guaranteed in the Bill of Rights, he drew nods of agreement. Sanford returned to Washington convinced he was on the right track.

Sanford launched his own personal campaign for the Bill of Rights and for weeks carried printed copies of the document with him wherever he went, handing them out to whomever he saw. As he traveled about the state, he was surprised to find so few people with an understanding of the true meaning of the first ten amendments to the Constitution. At the same time, he remained troubled by the reluctance among his Senate colleagues to oppose a bill they believed was wrong. "It is a fact of Washington that when the issue presents a choice between [principle] and the next election, the next election prevails," he observed in his journal.

> That should not be surprising. Survival is about the strongest urge of the living being. It is the force of that instinct for survival that accounts for evolution, for the very presence of human beings. Even so, it is disconcerting to see senators figuratively testing the winds with a wet finger in the air as they go down to the well to vote.
>
> The skillful wind-tester will assess the risk of voting on what he considers high principle, and determine whether it is a risk he is willing to take. If he concludes the risk is too great, high principle has to lose.
>
> I have always thought that you ought to stick with high principle

but that one in public life was entitled to make some concession in order to stay in public life. There might very well, indeed, have been some high principles that should not be abandoned even if one is to lose the next election. Some of the questions that came up during the period of integration would fall in that category. On the other hand, I have said that if one is to commit political suicide, one is entitled to pick the instrument of death.

Sanford had his say on the flag amendment on October 17, two days before the vote. Speaking from notes instead of the usual prepared text he preferred on special occasions, he thought the speech was one of the best he made during his term. The issue was not desecration of the flag, he said, but desecration of the Bill of Rights, and he recalled the conversations with his buddies from the 517th to make the point.

> I said to each one in turn, but what about the Bill of Rights? I thought we were over there fighting to protect the Bill of Rights. I thought we were fighting the concept of Hitler that did not put up with any kind of protest, and that did not observe any kind of civil rights. Almost to the person, they agreed, "Well, I hadn't thought about that."

Americans had a right to protest against government, he said, although some people wouldn't like it.

> Protest is often offensive to those who have to endure the protestations. I know, as the former president of Duke University, I did not like to see people protesting against the university and the Vietnam War. But I knew very well that anybody in the academic world who did not understand that students had every right to stand up and condemn the governmental action, to stand up and condemn the administration of the university, simply did not understand the fundamentals of freedom in America.

Political grandstanding would help solve nothing, Sanford continued.

> To protect the flag against desecration, we do not need to tinker with the Bill of Rights. It is the document of fundamental freedoms for this country and for people everywhere all through the world that care about and seek freedom.
>
> This is the great message to the world. This is the great message of freedom that a strong democracy, a government of the people can stand—indeed, I would say, can invite—protest. When we come to the point at which we cannot absorb protest, we will no longer be a great freedom-loving nation.
>
> We know very well that our flag will fly higher and brighter all the

time, if we protect the freedoms for which it stands. Nobody can truly destroy that freedom by burning a flag. But if we begin to whittle away at those freedoms, we will soon see that the flag does not go up in flames but people who have been watching all over the world will see the brightness of those colors fade as they lose faith and confidence in our kind of government.[7]

When Sanford finished, Missouri Republican John Danforth, one of the cosigners of the bill, took the floor. He had made a mistake, Danforth said, and had rushed to judgment on the bill: "I will not vote for this constitutional amendment. I will vote against it."[8] Danforth's reversal caught Sanford by surprise, as did the vote two days later of archconservative Gordon Humphrey, who joined the opposition. In fact, backers could muster only fifty-one votes in favor of the amendment, fifteen short of the necessary two-thirds majority.

As the clerk called the roll, Sanford watched his fellow Southerners line up without him once again in the traditional conservative coalition of Southern Democrats and Republicans. During his two years in the Senate, Sanford had voted with this bloc less than one-fourth of the time. In 1988, the American Civil Liberties Union and the Americans for Democratic Action scored Sanford at 76 and 85, respectively, while the American Conservative Union, which gave Helms a score of 100, rated Sanford at 8.[9] Some months later, after Margaret Rose chided him as "dishonest" for voting against a Senate pay raise although he believed it was indeed needed, he told her "that was probably right and that kind of thinking had given me the reputation of the most liberal record of any southern Democrat and that I was just as glad to miss the bullet this time."[10]

Sanford counted his opposition to the flag amendment as one of his more satisfying moments in the Senate. It was a flickering candle of hope amid distressing times that by late winter left him "fed up with the whole process." Congress and the president—he laid most of the blame on Bush—continued to do nothing about the mounting national debt. In the Senate, he grumbled that members were more interested in personal credit than in accomplishment.

His frustration at the pace and quality of work in the Senate was compounded by personal problems. He discovered he needed a hernia operation at about the same time that Margaret Rose was hospitalized with an attack of phlebitis. Then, as he headed home for the Thanksgiving recess, he discovered that his accountant of thirty years "was about to break me financially." Stocks had been sold with no reserves for taxes and his tax returns had not been filed on a timely basis, costing him $11,000 more than anticipated. He had to take out a bank note to cover the shortfall, with no real idea of how he would repay it. "From a personal point of view, the Senate seat had been a considerable financial loss," he noted in his journal. "I had given up income that will amount to one and a half million dollars and already has cost me close to a half million."

Sanford had never accumulated much wealth, although he had attained a certain level of comfort by the time he left Duke. Then, he had used much of his savings for his Senate campaign and had little left in the bank after three years in Washington. He was even turning down appeals from friends and organizations that he had supported without question in the past. Before he learned the bad news at Thanksgiving, he had written a friend who was soliciting a donation for Outward Bound that "I simply do not have the money. I have taken a tremendous diminution of income in order to serve here. I had to totally separate myself from the law practice, and had to quit all boards and get out of all businesses that I was in, under the very proper rules of Senate ethics. I am actually digging into savings in order to keep up two homes, do the traveling that I must do, some of which is reimbursed, but none is reimbursed for Mrs. Sanford." [11]

Some of his savings had been used to recover from another disappointment brought on by a long-time friend and associate. Early in 1988, Sanford found himself explaining how a building that he owned with Paul Vick, his administrative assistant, had ended up being sold to new owners and then leased back for space for one of his Senate offices. One of his other offices in the state was in a building owned by his son. The entire affair was checked by the Senate Ethics Committee and though Vick and Sanford were cleared of any wrongdoing, the incident remained an embarrassment and smacked of double dealing. Sanford reimbursed the government for the cost of the offices from his own pocket and paid the resulting lawyers' fees that had accumulated during an Ethics Committee investigation provoked by newspaper accounts of the deal.

In February 1990, Sanford was in eastern North Carolina holding hearings on an issue close to coastal fishermen when he decided to remain on for a few days at his condominium near Morehead City. He relaxed and walked on the beach and reflected on his situation. For the first time in his life, he seemed to have no real objectives and examined serious doubts about his use of the time that remained in his life. "It may be that I am coming to the end of the road, and don't want to think of being in my last job," he wrote in his journal. The prospect of reelection weighed heavily. "I have to start running for re-election now. That can't be put off, and I can't avoid saying that I am running. The last possible chance that I could decide not to run would be shortly after the 1990 elections."

Republicans had begun touting Jim Martin as their candidate for the Senate, and the possibility of a contest with the popular governor stirred Sanford's competitive spirit. "He is the thrust of the new Republicanism in North Carolina," he noted in his journal. "If he were to run, and I were to beat him, we would have put to rest that particular Republican surge, which I think would be a great benefit for the state of North Carolina. For that reason, I would welcome an opportunity to run against Martin. If I lost, then I would have lost, but I look forward to the opportunity to take him on." Sanford also was put out with Martin, whose wife, Dottie, had produced a book on first ladies of the state and failed to include a picture of Margaret Rose; his own photo was none too flattering. (Near the end of his term, Martin would forsake politics altogether and retire to Charlotte.)

At the same time, however, the vision of retirement lingered and he daydreamed about writing, fishing, or helping his daughter, Betsee, in her business of selling home-grown North Carolina products. "It is useful to know that I have a great many projects after I leave the Senate, and that perhaps will help me to put in better perspective my efforts while I am in the Senate." Among the possibilities was the creation of a Carolinas law firm with former South Carolina governor Robert McNair. The two had been talking about it for several months.

He considered his own record in Washington, which was uneven at best. Certainly it was clear that four years in the Senate paled beside four years in the governor's office. "Its usefulness, its contribution to the nation and the state . . . was marginal," he wrote in his journal. He was still put out about an episode the previous month that had set him to wondering whether anyone really cared. On January 29, he held the first of a series of monthly press conferences in the state in an effort to reconnect with home. It had been well attended by reporters, but the next morning's *News & Observer* did not carry a single word. He was disappointed and sent a note to publisher Frank Daniels Jr. saying he had hoped for at least "a note in the 'Personals' that 'former Raleigh lawyer returns to town.'"

"This episode brought all my private deliberations about future Senate service into sharp focus: I don't need to run for re-election. I do not need to continue this tremendous personal sacrifice. The truth is that this job is not very important comparatively." He could do more at home in a community activity, he registered in his journal, without the pressure and "without the tremendous amount of running around the squirrel cage just to get a few nuts cracked. . . . In any event, I have done my duty. At best I have 20–25 years left, if I am lucky enough to avoid accident or disease. I have so much I wanted to do. Do I want to waste my life as Helms has? Do I want to stay on the treadmill that Lloyd Bentsen has trod with such pride? The time of decision has arrived. I do not have to run for re-election. That is a powerful decision for me. I am not quite ready to decide not to run, but I am nine-tenths there."

One friend who saw him at that time was convinced he was completely there. Before returning to Washington, Sanford stopped in Chapel Hill to speak at a function at the UNC Law School. State Supreme Court Justice Willis Whichard of Durham, who had managed his 1976 presidential campaign in North Carolina, was seated beside him at dinner when he innocently asked how things were in Washington. Sanford unloaded his complaints. It's no sure thing he would run again, Sanford told Whichard, who went home that night believing the party would have to find another candidate in 1992.[12]

For the moment, the only change of routine that accompanied Sanford's tentative decision was a reduction in fund-raising activities. He had retired most of the $1 million debt from his 1986 campaign, with half of that coming in during the spring of 1988 when seven of his Senate colleagues appeared in Raleigh at an event on his behalf. But his fund-raiser, Paula Levine of New York, already had begun scheduling the events necessary to raise the average $12,000 per week that Public Citizen, a Ralph Nader-founded advocacy group, said was necessary for a member to prepare for the next election.

Campaign fund-raising was an onerous task that no one enjoyed, least of all Sanford, who, though never bashful to ask for money for Duke and uncounted causes, remained reluctant to do repeated, hard solicitation on his own behalf. He complained in his journal, "I find it almost intolerable. I don't mind asking people for money, but I don't like to hound people all the time. I don't like a staff person constantly reminding me that we need to get a contribution from this person or that person. I have absolutely resisted any temptation to take any position with the thought that I might get a contribution."

He had hobbled his own postelection fund-raising by joining about twenty-five other senators who declined honoraria. A member could pick up thousands of dollars simply by delivering a speech or making an appearance at a corporate luncheon or breakfast meeting. Sanford joked that these payments were extravagant enough to make a Wall Street lawyer blush.[13] At the same time, he knew some of his colleagues depended on this money to make ends meet. One freely admitted to him that speaking and appearance fees had paid for his son's college education.

Sanford was not above taking money from political action committees, and while a member of the Senate Banking Committee he had used contributions from the banking industry to help retire his campaign debt. At the same time, he let it be known shortly after arriving in Washington that he did not accept quid pro quo contributions from individual companies. He had been in office only a few weeks when word spread that he had kicked a lobbyist out of his office. Indeed, Sanford had complained to the man's superiors after he arrived at Sanford's office and loudly threatened to cancel a fund-raising event planned on Sanford's behalf because Sanford had not voted to suit his clients.

He created a fine line of difference, he admitted, but one that he tried to maintain despite the brutish nature of the entire business. "I have to be very careful to keep fund-raising separate from Senate business," he wrote in his journal. "It is a difficult balancing act. I certainly do not intend to let any contribution interfere with any vote or any action I take, on the other hand, we have to go forward with fundraising to reduce the campaign debt. It is a bad system, but it has to be done, and it means that I am going to do all that I can to change the system of exorbitant campaign costs."

Sanford personally liked many of the lobbyists, or "Washington representatives," as he called them. Some, like John Hoving, he had known for years. Others he got to know better over breakfasts that he cooked and served in his apartment. Because he was an early riser, he decided to show off his skill in the kitchen for guests who were served fried apples, sausage and bacon, cheese grits soufflé, and a specialty of eggs, creamed cheese, and chives that he called Eggs Eli. Sanford's ground rules for the breakfasts precluded lobbyists from talking shop, although they were free to ask questions on any other subject.

The breakfast meetings became a novelty on Capitol Hill: "Senators don't cook for lobbyists," Paula Levine said. She was no better prepared. When she arrived for the first meeting she found Sanford in the kitchen busy with preparations. After she admitted she had no cooking skills, Sanford asked her to make coffee, but she failed even at that; she loaded the coffee maker incorrectly and brewed coffee was flowing off the counter onto the floor when the first guests rang the doorbell. While Sanford cleaned up the mess and hid her mistake, she answered the door. Later events went more smoothly and, in time, she began receiving calls from lobbyists asking when they might be added to the guest list.[14]

Levine was a stylish New Yorker who favored striking fashion and flair. Sanford nicknamed her the "New York Flash" after she appeared in his office one day wearing spats. The two met while working on the Democratic Senate Campaign Committee after Sanford volunteered to help in the 1990 senatorial races. After the election, Sanford encouraged her to set up her own fund-raising business and offered to be her first client. She was utterly charmed by this Southerner who impressed her with his grace and hospitality, thoughtfulness, honesty and loyalty, quick wit and good humor. She never failed to get a thank-you note after an event and had never seen a politician stop to speak to everyone, including the kitchen staff who prepared the fund-raising dinner. She later said she discovered that "if you were a friend, you were a friend for life." She was working on Sanford's behalf when she contacted the head of a large New York advertising agency she knew to be an active and generous contributor to Republican candidates. She was surprised when this Duke graduate told her he would be "honored to help Terry Sanford" and turned the event into a Duke alumni reunion.[15]

Sanford remained quiet about his own plans as North Carolina Democrats focused more on the political future of Jesse Helms, who was facing reelection to a fourth term, than they were on him. Sanford talked to a number of people about running, including former governor Jim Hunt and William Friday, whom he invited to his home one Sunday afternoon in the fall of 1989 for a long talk. Sanford believed Friday could beat Helms, but if he were to run he would have to forsake his comfortable and well-paying assignment as head of the William R. Kenan, Jr., Fund, where he had gone upon his retirement from president of the university system. Friday declined to enter the race, as did Hunt.

The race for the nomination became a contest between Mike Easley, a district attorney from the southeastern corner of the state, and Harvey Gantt, a Charlotte architect and the first African American elected mayor of that city. Gantt had approached Sanford early in his campaign, but Sanford did not take sides. Privately, he remained closer to Easley than to Gantt, who won the nomination in one of the most civil, issue-oriented primaries the state had seen in years. Immediately upon his defeat in a runoff election, Easley endorsed Gantt without reservation.

With the nomination, the Senate contest in North Carolina took on historic dimensions as Gantt, who had been the first black student at Clemson University in 1963, prepared to challenge Helms. When Gantt came to Washington in the summer of 1990, Sanford was encouraged by the support he found among the Democratic members of the state's delegation. At the same time, he was worried that the Gantt campaign suffered from what he called the "Dukakis Syndrome" and would fail if Gantt was unable to unite the party for the hard work of the fall.

A month before the fall campaign was due to begin in earnest, partisan politics fell to the back pages of the newspapers when on August 2 Iraqi forces invaded Kuwait, a rich oil-producing neighbor on the edge of the Persian Gulf. Iraqi troops looted Kuwait and threatened further trouble in the region against American allies such as Saudi Arabia and Israel. In response, President Bush initiated a military buildup in the region. At the request of the United States and other nations, the United Nations Security Council approved sanctions against Iraq that would remain until its leader, Saddam Hussein, ordered a retreat and Kuwait was returned to the control of its ruling family.

The specter of war grew with each passing day as Sanford listened to witness after witness called before the Senate Foreign Relations Committee to report on developments in the Middle East. The growing fever for military action bothered him, as it would have his old mentor, Frank Porter Graham, whose later years were spent as an emissary of the United Nations to trouble spots around the world. Sanford began to openly question the buildup and saber-rattling by the United States, and speaking from the Senate floor in mid-September, he said, "There is no reason for us to get involved in a shooting, killing war to take Kuwait. We can deny Saddam Hussein the fruits of his aggression simply by an embargo that prohibits him from selling any oil from Iraq or Kuwait." [16]

At a joint session in September called to hear President Bush speak on the growing tension in the Middle East, Sanford was not encouraged by the aggressive course set by the administration. "I got the feeling from looking at the four, bull-headed, four-star people sitting directly in front of me, and listening to the Republican side of the house responding to whatever it was he said, that there were quite a few people who would storm in right now with our young troops in an effort to 'take Saddam Hussein,'" he noted in his journal. "The great danger is that the President will get bad advice, some incident will occur and we will be committed before we know it."

Sanford's reluctance to join the growing patriotic parade for a military response was not popular and caused problems from the outset. After his remarks on the floor in September, he made an appearance in Jacksonville, North Carolina, which was home to many of the Marines stationed at nearby Camp Lejeune. His local campaign manager told him that his caution was being interpreted as a lack of faith in the military. "In truth," he noted in his journal, "I am simply trying to keep [American troops] from being sent unnecessarily into a needless war."

He urged more pressure from the United Nations to require Saddam to not only withdraw, but to destroy weapons of mass destruction. "It seems to me that we are going to be left holding the bag on a snark hunt if we simply say that he must unconditionally withdraw," Sanford noted for himself. A few weeks later, when Secretary of State James Baker and Secretary of Defense James Cheney appeared before the Foreign Relations Committee, Sanford bristled at the administration's apparent determination to move with or without congressional approval. "I think these people are headed in their own direction, not caring what Congress thinks, and determined to do whatever they want to do. I am afraid they are going to take the country to a real disaster." [17]

Sanford observed that many of those who spoke the loudest in favor of combat had seen none of it. He was one of only five members of the Senate who had combat experience, and he was reassured in his position after the most decorated member, Senator Robert Kerrey of Nebraska, who had been awarded the Congressional Medal of Honor for action in Vietnam, also publicly questioned the call for military action. Bush continued to send more troops into the Persian Gulf region until the number reached more than four hundred thousand, with a quarter of the total coming from North Carolina bases.

The continuing trouble in the Middle East kept Helms tied closely to Washington. He was late in starting his campaign while Gantt had been busy since early September. Liberals rallied to Gantt's cause, as did the arts community, which was still sputtering over Helms's ridicule of some avant garde productions as obscene and sacrilegious. Money poured into the state on Gantt's behalf. In October, polls showed the two candidates in a virtual dead heat.

Two weeks before the election, however, Helms's campaign began to air a television commercial that showed the hands of a white man slowly crumpling a job rejection letter. "You needed that job," an announcer said in a voice-over. "And you were the best qualified. But they had to give it to a minority because of a racial quota. Is that really fair? Gantt supports Ted Kennedy's racial quota law that makes the color of your skin more important than your qualifications." It was a devastating ad, and for Sanford reminiscent of the leaflets on the stoops of mill houses from forty years before. In this one simple commercial, the Helms campaign had neatly stitched together a message that touched all the hot buttons of Southern politics and raised the specter that Sanford had warned Kennedy about a year before.

The ads brought a stumbling response from Gantt's campaign. Sanford urged Gantt's managers to counter immediately with a voice-over ad of their own stating that Helms's description of the Kennedy bill was a distortion, "designed to be false and prejudicial. And then I wanted to quote Mr. Welch when he asked Joe McCarthy, 'Have you no decency left, sir?' " [18] His advice went unheeded. Gantt never recovered and the ad was cited as a major contributor to Helms's victory.

While Sanford was home in the days following the election, he asked Duke law professor Walter Dellinger, a specialist on the Constitution who later would serve as Acting Solicitor General under President Bill Clinton, to prepare a brief on the president's war powers. Specifically, Sanford wanted to know if sending troops to war without congressional consent was an impeachable offense. Dellinger outlined his argument that indeed it was, a conclusion he reported was shared by William Van Alstyne of the Duke Law School.

The United Nations had set January 15, 1991, as the deadline for withdrawal of Iraqi troops from Kuwait. On January 4, Sanford announced that he planned to introduce a resolution asserting that the president was bound by the Constitution to obtain a declaration of war from Congress before launching military action. A news service reported that Sanford's voice trembled with emotion as he said, "A great many people in the Senate have forgotten about war, but I can think right now of mothers who lost sons in World War II who literally never smiled again." [19] A few days later he repeated his position on the NBC *Today* show, where Kerrey and Republican Warren Rudman, who had served in Korea, also were interviewed.

Sanford shelved his own resolution, but on the evening of January 11 he rose in the Senate to speak in favor of a similar measure that had been introduced by Senator Sam Nunn of Georgia, the chairman of the Armed Services Committee. Sanford was composed and steady as he outlined his position. He was opposed to a shooting war and this was one

> that certainly does not need to be fought—the most unnecessary war in the history of this nation and a war that could have disastrous effects.
>
> Mr. President, it has always been easier to settle an argument with a gun, and it is much more difficult to settle one by other means. People throughout the world have been struggling all of this century and longer to find a way to resolve national differences without war. We finally have an opportunity today to make real and important progress toward a better way of resolving conflicts and at the same time get the job done in Iraq and get it done right.

Sanford argued for continued sanctions as a way of solving the impasse and said that going to war instead would suggest a lack of real courage.

> Mr. President, risking lives in a war is not to be taken lightly. Almost one-quarter of the troops deployed in the Middle East right now have come from places in my home state of North Carolina. I know many of their families, and I know their living conditions, and I know their communities. I know these fighting men that have gone out from those bases to the Middle East are to be commended. They are to be respected. They are to be honored. They have moved into their positions and carried out their duties with the utmost in professionalism.

They would, if summoned, serve this nation with outstanding competence and valor. However, I do not believe, as I see them and their wives and their children and their parents, I should vote to risk their lives until we have let the economic squeeze of the embargo run its course, because I believe it will work.[20]

On the following day, the Senate defeated the Nunn resolution and voted fifty-two to forty-seven to give the president power to send American troops into battle against Iraq. For Sanford, "This may very well be the worst day in the recent history of the United States of America. We will see, and we can hope and pray that it will not turn out as bad as it could turn out."[21] A day later, Sanford reflected on the swirl of events. "This is the end of a week that is historic. We gave the President authority to go to war, and I am convinced that for years historians and other observers will talk about what a stupid move this was. I am convinced that the President has already made up his mind to use this authority." When Bush launched an intensive air attack against Iraq on January 16, Sanford was in his car headed for Durham. He learned by phone from his office that members were being advised to remain close, and he had his driver turn around and head back to the Capitol.

Once military action commenced in the Middle East, Sanford voted for a resolution supporting the troops, but his outspoken position against military action had already made him vulnerable back home. A Mason-Dixon Opinion Research statewide poll taken in early February showed that 65 percent of the voters disagreed with the position he had taken on the war. Sanford said he was not worried that his stand might hurt his reelection chances. "I certainly didn't do it for political gain," he told the *Charlotte Observer*. "You have got a sacred obligation in public office to do what you think is best, not to read the polls and do what the polls say to do. . . . Sure, there are going to be people who say, 'He didn't support the President.' Well, I didn't support the President because I thought the President was wrong. And I would have been wrong if I hadn't voted for what I thought was right." For the record, he was confident, even cocky. "Right now, they don't have anybody," he said of the Republican opposition. "There's nobody on the scene that would be a formidable candidate. I'm not saying I can't be beat. I'm saying they don't have a candidate at the moment."[22]

Privately, Sanford had made up his mind to retire from the Senate on the weekend after the first bombs fell on Baghdad. The ruminations about his future and distress over wasted effort in Washington that had been a constant companion for a year were now ended. On Tuesday, January 22, he told Levine and Poole that his decision to retire was firm, and they talked about proper timing of an announcement. A few weeks later, Bill Green received a draft of a statement that began, "I have decided to step out of public office while I am still young enough to do a great many things I have wanted to do. I was drawn back into public office because I believed that for the good of the state of North Carolina the Democratic Party should be resuscitated. That has been accomplished." Sanford said he planned to practice law, work on corporate and charitable boards, and give attention to education. "I will read more, write more, spend more time with my family, and, as is said, take more time to smell the magnolias. To paraphrase Robert Frost, I have fields to plow, streams to wade, hills to climb, and years to go. You can't do much of that kind of thing in Washington." [23]

Another life, another career lay just ahead, he thought. "I can do a lot of things over the next twenty-five years if I live," Sanford wrote in his journal, "and the odds are in my favor, but if I am going to pick up this fourth or fifth career I would be better off starting at age 75 rather than 81, which age I would be at the end of an additional term."

While the nation poised for military ground action in the Middle East, Sanford asked Levine, Poole, and Green to keep his decision in strict confidence. "I cannot announce it right now, with all of the interest in the war, giving the appearance that I am running out on something, or quitting because my position on our conduct of the war is contrary to what was finally adopted, so I will wait and watch for a few weeks to see how things do develop." At the same time, he told Poole, he was under "under no compulsion to re-examine this position." [24]

Three weeks later, Sanford learned that Lauch Faircloth had switched his party registration and planned to seek the Republican Senate nomination to run against him in 1992. In April, Helms's National Congressional Club endorsed Faircloth's campaign and the *Charlotte Observer* reported that Club Chairman Tom Ellis, who was also cochair of Faircloth's campaign, planned to make Sanford's war vote the issue. Ellis wrote supporters in a fund-raising letter, "Lauch Faircloth supported President Bush's decisive action to defeat Saddam Hussein—while Terry Sanford opposed the President." He also included a news item about the National Taxpayers Union's ranking of Sanford as one of the Senate's big spenders. The fact that Faircloth had been a Republican for only a few weeks should help, not hurt in a race against Sanford, Ellis told supporters, because his reputation as a conservative Democrat would attract that type of voter to the GOP column in November 1992. [25]

"There is no vendetta against Sanford," Faircloth told reporters. "Terry Sanford is a gentleman. I can say that as well as anyone, having known him for 40 years." [26] Privately, Faircloth was smarting from what he considered rough treatment in 1986, when reports reached him that Sanford and one of his political assistants had mocked his chances in a statewide contest.

"There were two things that triggered him to run against Terry," recalled former governor Bob Scott, who had known both men. "[Harrison] Hickman wrote Faircloth off. Terry said something to the effect that if Lauch wants to see how bad he can get beat, he can take me on. That really set Lauch off. It was clear from what Lauch [told me] that the statements of those two people made him think, 'Then by God, I will show them.'" [27]

Faircloth's decision shocked Sanford. He knew his old friend's politics were far more conservative than his own, and he had heard rumors that Ellis had been courting Faircloth. All the same, the two were products of a generation where loyalty was valued above all else. Even when it had been clear that Faircloth's prospects at winning the Democratic gubernatorial nomination in 1984 were slim, Sanford had helped raise thousands of dollars to buy additional television time for him. As Faircloth began making plans to run against him, some of those loans remained unpaid.[28]

Sanford kept his own plans, and his thoughts about Faircloth, to himself when he scheduled a trip into the state in late March. Reporters trailed along as voter reaction to Sanford became an early litmus test on the war issue. Sanford was not the only member of the state's legislative delegation to vote against the Republican war resolution, but he had been the most visible, and even the *Washington Post* sent a reporter along. Reviews were mixed. In Asheville, a self-described peace activist praised his vote and more than a third of the 350 people at a forum on his behalf stood and applauded. Later in the day, a Westinghouse plant supervisor was quoted as saying, "I would not vote for him because he didn't support the president." [29]

The White House had taken notice of his position. Sanford was invited to a reception there for the Duke University basketball team after it won the NCAA men's championship, but as the president made his way along the front row where Terry and Margaret Rose were seated, he reached over Sanford, stepping on his toes in the process, to shake hands with a former Republican congressman seated behind him. The president then passed on without saying a word. Bush's social secretary also left the Sanfords off the guest list for a state dinner honoring Nicaragua's new president, Violeta Chamorro.

On March 8, as state officials gathered to welcome a contingent of nine hundred soldiers returning from the Gulf area, Republicans took notice that Sanford did not have a speaking part in the ceremonies. In fact, Sanford had been asked to speak at the ceremonies at Pope Air Force Base, but he had declined the offer. He had stood in ranks himself after arriving home from combat and sympathized with the soldiers' anxiety as politicians' speeches separated them from their waiting families. Indeed, Governor Martin overstayed at the microphone and his speech was interrupted by calls of "Let them go, let them go" from the wives, children, and sweethearts eager to wrap their soldiers in hugs and kisses.[30]

Sanford appeared with Martin at a parade in Raleigh in June to welcome home the troops, but dreaded every minute of it, he wrote in his journal, because "it is obvious to me that this was nothing but a Republican rally, an orchestrated effort from the President on down to exploit the military forces who did indeed perform extremely well in the Middle East." He noted that he had "a rising suspicion that the President welcomed, perhaps slightly prompted, the conditions permitting him to go to war. . . . There are 250 mothers in this country whose lives are forever blighted because of President Bush's unnecessary action, and certainly I can hardly see how a great moral nation can joyously claim that it 'feels good' to use the President's term, once again confident that America can lick the [world]. Well, that is nonsense. I felt that way a year ago, two years ago, and three years ago. Of course, we can do about anything we want to militarily, now that Russia has stepped aside."

While the war appeared to be over in the Middle East, the Kuwaiti government gave Helms $100,000 to help recreate a model of his Senate office at Wingate College, but left Sanford's office to deal with some of the unpleasant consequences of the war. Before the outbreak of hostilities, some Kuwaiti residents had fled the country for safety in the United States. After Iraqi troops were sent running back across the border, Kuwait's rulers allowed only Kuwaiti nationals to return. Refugees who couldn't prove Kuwaiti citizenship were refused entry, although many had left homes, businesses, and possessions. More than four hundred persons were stranded and virtually homeless in Raleigh and other American cities as a result of "freedom flights" from Kuwait. The disregard for their welfare by the Kuwaiti government only confirmed Sanford's private feelings that the ruling family was arrogant and racist. He noted privately, "It makes me even happier that I did not vote to help restore them to the throne."

As chairman of the Near Eastern and South Asian Affairs Subcommittee of the Senate Foreign Relations Committee, Sanford convened hearings in August 1991 on the plight of the refugees. At the time, he said the State Department, the Immigration and Naturalization Service, and the Kuwaiti government were guilty of "a serious dereliction of responsibility and duty" toward the evacuees.[31] As the United States sorted out the cases individually, Alice Glover in Sanford's office arranged for temporary housing for fifty families at the Raleigh-Durham Airport. "These people have been neglected by the Kuwaiti government, by the U.S. State Department, and more or less jerked around by the U.S. Immigration Service," Sanford noted in his journal.

Sanford was disgusted with his nation's performance in the Middle East. By using force, the United States had abrogated its role as the leader in the so-called New World Order proclaimed after the fall of the Soviet Union. The war also failed to meet any reasonable objectives. "I do not think that we really accomplished anything except to put the Emir back on the throne," he said some years later. "If I had my way, I would have turned the country back over to the people."[32]

Sanford maintained his silence about his own future throughout the spring and into the summer. As late as July, he still planned on ending his Washington career when he informed his news secretary, Ken Friedlein, on a ride back to Washington that he planned to retire.

Congress went into recess in early August and Sanford took advantage of the break to spend some time at his home at Hound Ears and at the coast. He always found these trips home refreshing for body and spirit. The sight of the sun setting behind Grandfather Mountain or rising from the Atlantic reconnected him with home. He enjoyed seeing old friends, walking on the beach, reading, and writing. He finally was making some progress on his book on aging and he found a relaxation he had not enjoyed for months. As was his habit, however, he could not escape politics.

Bush's postwar jump in popularity was giving all challengers second thoughts. The military victory seemed to have assured the president of re-election. Sanford had never discounted the ambition of Arkansas Governor Bill Clinton. The two had met again in April 1989, when Clinton was on hand for the inauguration of Arkansas transplant Lloyd "Vic" Hackley as the new president of Fayetteville State University. At home with old friends on the Fayetteville campus, Sanford told people that Clinton had designs on the Democratic nomination, but Clinton did not figure prominently in Sanford's discussions about a challenger for Bush.

Sanford's candidate was Senator Jay Rockefeller from West Virginia. Earlier in the year, he told Rockefeller that he probably would not be running for reelection and thus would have time to spend on a presidential campaign. When Rockefeller came to North Carolina in the spring as the featured speaker at the North Carolina Democrats' Jefferson-Jackson Day dinner, Sanford ushered him about and made sure he met local party people who could be helpful to him. In August, while Sanford was at Hound Ears, Rockefeller called to say he definitely was not going to run. A few weeks later, while on a sailing trip with Poole and Harrison Hickman, Sanford raised the possibility of his running again for president. "I could tell that there wasn't any wild enthusiasm for it and I didn't have that kind of enthusiasm myself," Sanford noted in his journal.

While he was in the mountains, he took some time to try out a new fly rod in a trout stream along the Blue Ridge Parkway. As he fished, he thought about the attractive alternatives to life after the Senate. He had continued to talk with McNair about their two-state law firm; it was clear that with the prominence of the two named partners, they could expect to do well. He also had talked with Duke President Keith Brodie, who urged him to consider returning to Duke as president emeritus.

Yet despite the attractiveness of opening yet another new chapter, Sanford could not bring himself to declare an end to his political life. It seemed that the longer he stayed away from the daily demands of Washington and the more time he spent talking with people in the state, the more his spirits were revived. Things might be different on his return. Just before the recess, he had been given chairmanship of the Ethics Committee, which added some stature and meaning after five years of steady service.

But the committee was also a trouble spot. Sanford had referred to his membership as his "favorite incarceration." The committee's work consumed countless hours, and once again he seemed "paired" with Helms, who was one of the Republican members along with Senators Trent Lott and Warren Rudman. The investigation into the so-called Keating Five had dragged on for nearly two years in the wake of the massive savings and loan association failures in the eighties. Democratic Senator Alan Cranston of California and four other senators were accused of attempting to interfere with federal regulators on behalf of Charles Keating, a California savings and loan executive, at the same time that they had received more than $1 million in campaign contributions from Keating and his associates. Keating's Lincoln Savings had been seized by regulators in 1988, and its failure cost taxpayers an estimated $2.3 billion when the government bailed out depositors. Keating was tried and convicted in federal and state courts. He served four years of a twelve-year state sentence for fraud before his conviction was overturned; in 1998, a new trial was ordered on the federal charges.

At the height of the Gulf War, on February 27, the committee announced reprimands against Democratic Senators Dennis DeConcini of Arizona, Donald Reigle of Michigan, and John Glenn of Ohio and Republican John McCain of Arizona for their roles in the case. Several groups, including the citizens' lobby Common Cause, criticized the committee's decision as "a cop-out and a damning indictment of the committee" and "a triumph for the [Senate] club." Sanford fired off a letter to the group angrily denying the allegations and telling them, "I am ashamed of you" for taking what he considered a cheap shot. He believed that the four had done nothing more than others in the Senate and were being made scapegoats.[33]

"I have lost more sleep over the Ethics Committee hearings than I have any other subject in my entire lifetime," he wrote in his journal in February. "I have worried about it. I have felt that we were doing a great injustice to drag these senators out in public, suggesting that they had done something terrible when in fact they gave constituent services, in a regular manner, called it off as soon as it became apparent that intervention wasn't appropriate, all in all had no more than two meetings with regulators, and made a few phone calls about related matters, but not to carry out Keating's wishes about the examination. There is nothing that they have done that shouldn't be done."

Sanford believed the five were being held to a phony standard and were the scapegoats for any number of transgressions that occurred routinely in Washington. He was satisfied that Cranston was doing nothing more harmful to the integrity of the Senate than any member "sitting at a table at the Monocle [a favorite Capitol Hill watering hole] and talking with bankers about their problems and taking away an [honorarium] of a thousand dollars or more." [34] And that behavior was not only accepted but protected from criticism by Senate rules.

As he prepared for his chairmanship, the committee had yet to reach a consensus on the case against Cranston, who had been given a serious reprimand for his part. Sanford was resisting Helms's efforts to take the matter to the full Senate, and a *Congressional Quarterly* article questioned whether Sanford could be tough enough for the Ethics Committee assignment. Noted were Sanford's votes against removal of two federal judges whose cases appeared conclusive. Sanford said he objected to investigative tactics of the Justice Department. As for Cranston, the article quoted Tom Lambeth, who said Sanford "does not want to be responsible for people losing their jobs." He said he had urged his old friend to be tougher. "I think he felt sorry for Cranston," the publication quoted Lambeth.[35]

Lambeth spoke from experience. His old friend had always been a soft touch, although he might talk tough. When he was governor, his budget director, Hugh Cannon, finally took on the job of booting those with unsatisfactory records after he learned after one episode that Sanford could not resist appeals from appointees or employees who should be on their way out to be given just one more chance. The same was true in the Senate.

In late August, Helms prematurely released the committee's confidential report recommending Senate censure of Cranston. The leak left the committee members looking as if they were engaged in a cover-up. Sanford found Helms's performance on the committee to be vindictive and improper, and agreed with Cranston's attorney that Helms should have recused himself from the hearings because of his feelings toward Cranston.

(Cranston helped Gantt raise campaign funds in 1990.) Other Democrats on the committee were bothered that Helms took such a hard line against Cranston while at the same time taking money from the Kuwaiti government and corporate sponsors for his museum at Wingate College.

August also brought another measure of dissatisfaction with his Senate duties. Sanford had begun to set in motion an investigation of the "October Surprise" by his Foreign Relations Subcommittee. A few months later, however, his resolution to launch an investigation failed to win approval when it reached the floor of the Senate.

Just before Labor Day, Sanford headed back to Washington after a month in the mountains and at the coast. On his way, he stopped in Durham to have breakfast with a group of women he called "Terry's Angels." They had helped with the details of his 1986 campaign and they wanted to talk about the upcoming race. Rather than tell them about his doubts, he sat down and began sketching an outline for a campaign that would begin in December with a series of community meetings across the state.

Then, three days after his meeting with his Angels, Sanford tossed his misgivings aside. "I awoke at 3:30 having concluded in mind exactly where I would put all the pieces in my decision of to run or not to run," he wrote in his journal. "I decided I had to run. I could find no decent way to be a lame duck. I shouted 'hurrah' and went back to sleep."

This time he didn't wait for second thoughts. By the end of the day, he had phoned Paula Levine and put her back on the payroll. He called Robert Squire, the campaign consultant who had created his 1986 television ads, and Sam Poole and told them he was going to run. By the end of the day, he gleefully told a reporter with the *News & Observer* that he was in the race. "I had set the course. Here it is announced to newspapers," he later noted in his journal. There was no turning back.

In truth, Sanford probably could not have reached any other decision, despite all his misgivings. Once he postponed an announcement in the spring, he had put the party in a difficult spot to recruit a replacement. He knew just how difficult because he had been scouting for replacements and come up empty. Congressmen I. T. Valentine of the Second District and Charles Rose III of the Seventh had both told him they would not run. Poole had not been receptive and Hunt had said no. Thus, by waiting, Sanford had let the decision be made for him, and he succumbed to the pitch that was irresistible. "I think we prevailed on him that it was his duty to the state," Poole said. "We talked about the fact that the easiest way to hold that seat was for him to run." [36]

His own pride, and supreme self-confidence, would never let him admit he could be beat, least of all by Faircloth and the Republicans. And there was more. "I had a certain amount of vanity that I thought I was the Democratic Party," Sanford said later. "I'd been there longer than anybody else. I was on the scene. And you know the attractiveness of the chase. I like candidating. It's a lot of fun getting out and seeing people and making sure you stress that point in the right way." Setting aside politics, and this time it would be for good, had just too great a cost. "All of my life I have been sort of motivated, sometimes not enough, by my mother's general philosophy [that] you ought to do things that make a difference. You ought not to just be here. And so as it turned out I could have gotten into various other things, but I got into the political campaigning and political activity and I liked it. There's not any question that you can make a quicker difference there than almost anywhere else." [37]

At the same time, he comforted himself with private thoughts of the possibility of relinquishing at least a portion of his term, particularly if a Democrat were elected governor in 1992. "My own financial problems and my desire to get out of here and my opportunity to go to Duke under very favorable circumstances would fit in very nicely because once reelected, and especially if we got Jim Hunt reelected, I would have that option. I can not at the moment say I will take that option but I will certainly have an option to step aside if I decide that is in my best interest and can be done in a graceful and proper manner," Sanford said in notes for his journal.

Sanford never entertained the thought that he might lose reelection, regardless of the complaints he had heard from voters upset with his voting record. He was confident that once he had a chance to talk to voters about the positions he had taken in the Senate they would understand why he did what he did on the war, the flag amendment, and anything else others believed would cause him trouble. He was entirely comfortable with positions that could cause him trouble politically, including his latest decision to oppose the Supreme Court nomination of Clarence Thomas, whose nomination by Bush appeared aimed at gaining support of African Americans eager to have a man of color replace retired Justice Thurgood Marshall.

When Thomas's name was first announced, Sanford had consigned himself to accepting him, even though he did not believe he was the best man for the job. No less a figure within the black leadership than Washington insider Vernon Jordan told him that if Thomas was rejected, black leaders feared that Bush would simply send another nominee who might be even worse. Jordan told him that Bush counted on support from Southern Democrats whose constituencies include large numbers of black voters. Sanford asked for a private meeting with Thomas and the two talked in Sanford's Senate office.

I told him in diplomatic and polite words that I thought he had not supported the advancement of blacks as well as he might have. But I understood that in order to get where he was he had to appease the Reagan types who brought him to this point of prominence. I pointed out gently that catering to those attitudes and those people now was coming to an end, that on the Supreme Court he would be totally free, that he did not have to account to Reagan or Bush or anybody else, except history.

He had no choice except to be polite, since I have the vote. I did have the feeling that he understands the need to continue the fight for civil rights. I pointed out to him that I had done far more for civil rights than he had so far. He had the final word, final position and he could do a great deal to improve attitudes in America.

He gave one example—when I said blacks suffered from discrimination—of the difficulty he had in getting a cab even though he is a member of United States Court of Appeals. He said recently he was in Georgetown and finally asked a [white] friend to hail a cab for him and when he did one cut through three lanes of traffic to get over there in a hurry.

We agreed that a great many people had hailed cabs for him through various stages in his life. Now he was free to do whatever he wanted to do. I just do not know what it is that he always wanted to do. We will see. I do not believe that enough opposition will be generated to defeat him.[38]

After hearings started on the nomination in September, Sanford began to have doubts, particularly when Senator Howell Heflin, a former state supreme court justice from Alabama, announced he would not support him. Sanford was also listening to African Americans whom he respected. Among them was Dr. John Hope Franklin, the prominent historian he had brought to the Duke faculty, who urged him not to support the nomination. He also took a call from Cathy Thompson, the daughter of his old friend Paul Thompson, who confirmed the credibility of Anita Hill, whose charges of sexual misconduct by Thomas transformed the hearings into the liveliest show in Washington. Thompson, a lawyer in Charlotte, told Sanford that Hill had been a classmate at Yale and was totally reliable. When the Thomas nomination reached the floor, Sanford voted no.

Sanford launched his reelection campaign in Laurinburg on December 2, a month after a physical examination that produced nothing of consequence. After the initial flurry of activity, he turned back to Washington. There would be no primary opposition to worry about.

The endorsement of Helms's political apparatus, the National Congressional Club, gave Faircloth an edge in the Republican primary. In addition to support from Club organizer Tom Ellis, who had been with Helms since the beginning, Faircloth won the endorsement of Charlotte lawyer Bob Bradshaw, a Republican aligned with Governor Jim Martin.

Faircloth was clearly the better known of the other leading Republicans, Charlotte Mayor Sue Myrick and former congressman Gene Johnston. There was no corner of North Carolina that Faircloth had not visited during a career that had begun as a driver for Kerr Scott, who later helped Faircloth cut short his draft obligation with a hardship discharge so he could return home and tend to his many business interests, most of them related to construction and farming. Even before Sanford's 1960 gubernatorial campaign began in earnest, Faircloth joined his friend on the road, often as his driver. Sanford once recalled that the two ended up sleeping in the same bed when overnight accommodations ran short one night on the road. "As I recall, he didn't snore," Sanford told reporters. Faircloth missed much of the campaign in 1960, however, after he was injured when a horse threw him. Sanford rewarded Faircloth for his help in 1961 when he named him to the state highway commission. In a subsequent *News & Observer* profile of Sanford's youngest highway commissioner—Faircloth was then only thirty-four—the governor remarked that Faircloth was one of the few men in the state he knew who wore Brooks Brothers suits and chewed tobacco.[39] In 1964, Faircloth supported Richardson Preyer, but he was more at home with the Scott side of the "Sanford wing" of the party and in 1968 helped Kerr's son, Bob, in his bid for governor. Scott named Faircloth chairman of his highway commission.

With the organizational power of the Congressional Club behind him, Faircloth depended so heavily on television ads in the primary campaign that his opponents called him the "stealth candidate" because he made so few public appearances compared to the opposition. Nonetheless, he won the nomination with 48 percent of the vote. Myrick was closest at 30 percent; Johnston gathered only 17 percent.

"The battle with Sanford will not be a grudge battle," the sixty-four-year-old Faircloth said on the night of the primary victory. "The battle with Sanford will be two clear ideological differences; he is a liberal spender, I am a conservative non spender." From Washington, Sanford, who had no primary election opposition, said, "I like Lauch personally, but it certainly will not keep me from insisting that he talk about real issues. There's nothing personal, no animosity from my end."[40]

While Faircloth was involved in his primary, Sanford's springtime political activity related mainly to raising money. His office began preparing a record of his term, and the report fairly well matched Sanford's own early assessment. He had proposed many things, but few had been adopted.

Some of his ideas about budget reform had been incorporated into other bills and he amended a national housing measure to offer more opportunities for prospective homeowners in rural areas. But legislative records rarely include home runs. The summary noted that Sanford had "laid an important foundation for the future."[41]

An attempt to win tribal recognition for the Lumbee Indians in North Carolina ended in February 1992, when Helms called on Republican support to effectively kill the measure. Ironically, the vote fell two short of what Sanford needed and came on a day when Democrats Bob Kerrey and Bill Bradley were out of town campaigning for president.

Before Sanford could begin his campaign in earnest he was sidelined with health problems. In midsummer, he began running a low-grade fever and experiencing flulike symptoms, and when both persisted he entered Duke Medical Center. On June 25, his doctor announced that he was being treated for an infection of the aortic valve of the left heart ventricle and that surgery may be required to correct it. Sanford downplayed the need for an operation and declared himself in good health by announcing that he had accepted invitations from seven groups seeking to sponsor debates between him and Faircloth. Nonetheless, he underwent two weeks of intravenous treatment in the hospital before he was released on the condition he continue self-administered treatments at home. In late July he returned to his Senate duties and declared himself recovered. "That's totally behind us," he told the Associated Press. "I'm raring to go."

As in previous campaigns, Sanford was the captain of his campaign team and made decisions that most modern-day candidates left to managers, staffers, or paid consultants. He drafted the outlines for ads, including a documentary that he scripted down to suggestions for photography and music. He wrote his speeches and planned to turn his campaign into a "crusade for children," as he called it, reminiscent of his crusade for education in 1960.[42] Once again, he committed himself to a hundred-county campaign. Early reports put him well ahead of Faircloth and polls showed he was the voters' choice against all comers, with a lead of more than 50 percent.

"Visiting four or five counties a day," a reporter noted in mid-August, "he is practicing retail politics in a world increasingly dominated by the wholesale politics of television. For the most part, his stops are in small towns, such as King and Yadkinville, that are removed from the state's major media markets."[43]

Faircloth cast Sanford as the liberal wanting bigger government and higher taxes. Sanford characterized Faircloth as the hard-line conservative critic of big government seeking drastic cuts in the role of government.

Based on the rhetoric alone, it was the classic contest between a New Deal Democrat who was optimistic and dedicated to using government for the common good and a nineties Republican whose evil empire was Washington and those within it. Faircloth was not nearly as articulate as Helms, but his message was the same. Faircloth also accused Sanford of succumbing to special interests, particularly the financial institutions whose political action committees had helped Sanford retire his campaign debt from 1986. Sanford had received $75,000 from various political action committees in 1991, but his receipts were equal to those of Helms. (Six years later, Faircloth would be forced to defend his own record of contributions from political action committees, one that prompted *Forbes* magazine to feature him in an article about "senators for sale.")[44]

Sanford and Faircloth met in a televised debate in September. Sanford showed experience and looked alert, strong, and vigorous, with a command of the facts. Faircloth stumbled on specifics, including details necessary to support the charges he had leveled in his campaign ads. When Faircloth began his litany of accusations that Sanford was a spendthrift, Sanford responded cleanly and coolly with the outline of his bill requiring a balanced budget and curbs on spending. Sanford's performance gave his supporters such confidence that some relaxed their efforts on his behalf and contributions actually fell off.

In late September, Sanford discovered that his health problems were not behind him. In fact, they had really just begun. On October 8 his office announced that he would undergo an operation to replace the infected heart valve. Sanford's response was stoic. "There are rare times in one's life when decisions must be made when it is just not convenient to make them," Sanford said at a Durham news conference shortly before entering Duke Medical Center. He said he would be back campaigning before the November 3 election.[45]

No one said publicly that his situation was critical. In private, doctors told him "this was a death-threatening thing and you can't wait."[46] Any who knew him, however, were aware that nothing short of life-saving surgery could keep him from campaigning. A medical team at Duke had discovered that the antibiotic treatments he had continued to administer to himself after leaving the hospital in summer had not controlled the infection, which had grown worse directly beneath the heart, where it had been hidden from view. The prescribed procedure was replacement with a valve taken from a pig's heart, which prompted some of Sanford's friends to joke in black humor that they hoped the replacement part would not come from a pig from one of Faircloth's farms. Physicians gave Sanford an excellent prognosis for recovery after four to six weeks.

Faircloth expressed his concern for Sanford in a statement and subsequent television ads, but the promotional condolences only highlighted the questions he had raised about Sanford's health and age since the medical problems of the summer. Faircloth's use of the issue angered Sanford's friends, but even Sanford's hometown newspaper suggested that perhaps the job was too much for him, and the Durham Herald-Sun reported that the surgery "could raise doubts about his ability to serve a full six-year term in the Senate."[47]

Sanford's weakened condition encouraged rumors that had circulated a year before that he was running for reelection only as a placeholder for another Democrat. Republican Sue Myrick had predicted in September 1991 that if Sanford won he would give up the seat if a Democratic governor was also elected. In eastern North Carolina, Republicans said his replacement would be Harvey Gantt.

Sanford was leading in various voter polls when he entered the hospital, although not by the comfortable margin that he had enjoyed earlier in the year. As he lay immobilized in recovery from debilitating surgery, he knew that he was losing ground with each passing day. As soon as he was able, he met with Poole and others to talk about ways they could recover from the setback. Lying in his hospital bed, he asked about using outtakes from the televised debate, where he had done so well, and discovered to his chagrin that a campaign aide had agreed in negotiations with the Faircloth campaign that neither side would use taped segments from the debate in subsequent television ads. That was a deal, he said later, he never would have cut. But it was done and he would honor it.[48]

Two weeks after the surgery, Sanford walked out of the hospital, pronouncing himself in good health. It was a heroic effort that was taken against the orders of his doctors, who said when he entered the hospital that they did not expect him to return to the campaign. He looked pale and wan; his cheeks were hollow and he had lost so much weight his clothing hung loosely on his once stocky frame. He immediately taped new television commercials and the change in his appearance was striking.

Sanford discovered that his hands-on approach to campaigning now was his greatest liability. With the decision maker laid up in a hospital, the campaign had drifted and "just sort of went on hold," Democrat Mike Easley, who was running for attorney general, told the Charlotte Observer.[49] Sanford knew he had blundered badly in not withdrawing when the first signs of medical problems arose in the summer, when the party would have had a better chance of finding a replacement. Now it was too late for regrets.[50]

Friends from Washington came to help. Senators Rockefeller, Kerrey, Nunn, and Bradley made appearances on his behalf. In Greensboro in late October, Sanford and Bradley toured a community college together, where Sanford brushed off questions about his surgery, calling it "this little operation." That same day, however, he had to cancel an appearance so a nurse could change his dressings and check the needles that remained in his chest to allow for drainage of fluids produced by the surgery.[51]

In the final days, Sanford's campaign took on a character and tone of desperation. Though he had avoided personal attacks on opponents in the past, he questioned Faircloth's early discharge from military service when Faircloth challenged his vote on the Gulf War. And he found himself in a losing exchange with Faircloth over requiring welfare recipients to work. It was a difficult time, and Sanford knew he had lost the momentum and was campaigning on his opponent's agenda, not his own. He had little choice, however. Asked why he waited until six days before the election to personally answer Faircloth's attacks, Sanford told a reporter, "I intended to do this a month ago, but I had a slight interruption."[52]

Faircloth had successfully planted doubt in voters' minds that Sanford was capable of serving out a full term, plus he had reshaped the Sanford image as that of a Washington insider, which was perhaps the most bitter irony of all. Sanford had never become a member of the Senate's "club"; in fact, one of his lasting achievements during his six years in Washington, his initiative on behalf of Central America, had come about because he had gone around the Washington bureaucracy.

As Sanford watched the returns from his home in Durham on election night, November 3, it became apparent early in the evening that he would lose decisively. About an hour before the eleven o'clock newscasts, he got in a car with Poole, Bill Green, and his son and the four rode to the North Raleigh Hilton, where campaign workers and friends had gathered. He was facing a loss of a hundred thousand votes, about the same margin that had separated him from Wallace in 1972. He was weak, and in pain. Just the day before, as he walked into a park in Durham, he had grabbed a companion's arm to keep from collapsing. "My stitches have popped," he said, "and I am bleeding. I will try to keep from passing out."[53]

He entered the hotel through a back entrance so that he would not have to make his way through the crowd. As soon as he entered the room, however, women greeted him with hugs of sympathy, unaware that each embrace pressed hard on IV needles and sent stabs of pain through his chest. He finally made it to the stage and began what Green remembered was one of his shortest but most heroic speeches.

In the face of his own defeat by a hundred thousand votes, Sanford declared victory as Democrats put Bill Clinton in the White House and returned Jim Hunt for his third term as governor. "If you think I'm going to bring any gloom to this meeting, you don't know me. This is a great night for the Democratic Party. We have the nation on the right track again. We have the state on the right track." [54]

Driving home to Durham with his son at the wheel, Sanford turned to Terry and said, "You know, this is going to sound kind of funny, but the craziest weight in the world has been lifted off of me." [55]

The Eternal Boy Scout

TERRY SANFORD'S BODY WAS LAID to rest in the crypt at Duke Chapel on April 22, 1998, following an "old-fashioned Methodist funeral." As the capacity crowd began to make its way out of the cavernous sanctuary, one old friend rose from his seat and said, "He might not have been elected president of the United States, but he got buried like one."[1]

The cancer that had been diagnosed four months earlier and that ended Sanford's life had been totally unexpected. He had been careful about his health and believed without question that he would live to be a hundred, just like his mother. He had been saying it for so long that those who knew him believed it too. Even as the news of his death finally settled on his friends, it was hard to believe that he would be gone. Sanford had figured prominently in the public life of North Carolina for so long that many had come to take him for granted. He had been there before, and he would be there again, it seemed.

He approached his death with the same stubbornness that he had always exhibited when handed a setback. He had too many things yet to do and wasn't ready to quit. Somehow he would overcome his illness.

The years since his release from the Senate had played out much as he had hoped. Within thirty days of the election, Duke University announced that President Emeritus Terry Sanford would teach in the Sanford Institute for Public Policy. In the semesters that followed, his course, Creativity in State Government, was filled whenever it was available. His office on the second level of the Institute became a way station for juniors and seniors who, after spending a term with Sanford, looked at the world of government from a different perspective. "People appreciate his personality, his candor and the fact that he's been there," said William Ascher, who was then director of the Institute. "He has anecdotes that can illustrate any point we scholars might want to make. He conveys not only the normative side of things, but also practical experience. He can put all the flesh on the bone." [2]

At the same time as his appointment, he was awarded Duke's University Medal for Distinguished Meritorious Service. The parchment read in part: "A visionary who balanced the budget; an innovator who cherished history and tradition; a cosmopolitan ambassador who revitalized our North Carolina roots even as he enticed the world to our doorstep; he led Duke University into a new era of growth and achievement. Today we look upon the lasting imprint of his courageous leadership and acknowledge that Duke is a different place because of the imagination, the breadth, the wit and the genius of Terry Sanford." Numerous other awards and honors for his contributions to the arts, education, and public service followed in succeeding years.

To his students, Sanford was something of a curiosity. In a time when conservatives were chopping away at government and politicians were held in low esteem, Sanford remained an unreconstructed New Deal Democrat who believed to his core that government could be a force for good and that public service was an honorable career. A few in Washington finally came to understand what he had been talking about when he wrote *Storm Over the States*. At the height of the congressional debate over state management of welfare and Medicaid a year after he left the Senate, *Washington Post* columnist Edwin Yoder suggested that reformers take a look at Sanford's book and his advice that "federal-state relations need not be adversarial and might be cooperative . . . [like] a marble cake, not a layer cake." [3]

He organized a new law firm early in 1993 with former South Carolina governor Robert McNair. The McNair-Sanford firm grew with offices from Charleston to Washington, D.C., but the marriage did not last. Sanford eventually withdrew, opening his own firm in Raleigh and later expanding it to include former governor James Holshouser. A bemused smile would spread across his face when anyone suggested treason for taking such a high-profile Republican as his named partner.

Writing remained a favored avocation. While he was in the Senate he had begun two books. One, *The Lasting Lyndon*, was to be a tribute to Lyndon Johnson's contribution to education. That manuscript was left unfinished; Sanford did not progress much beyond recollections of his own early association with the president. In *Outlive Your Enemies: Grow Old Gracefully*, he delivered a thorough and readable narrative on aging and health as told through the conversations of six elderly men who met at a corner diner each morning for breakfast. Sanford illustrated his story, which featured characters modeled on his own buddies, with his favorite anecdotes, such as the lesson learned about camping along the Cape Fear. "Odd how a little thing like that can be a big lesson in life," his character Will Mack tells his friends.

> I don't worry about what I might have done. It is behind me like that campsite. Go on to the next, and when they are all behind us, they are gone forever.
>   The river flows on, and we can't turn back upstream. Our life runs on. It is where we are that we can handle, not where we might have been." [4]

Later, when the friends had finished their self-taught symposium on health, another character in the book, Henry, tells his buddies what Sanford took as his own prescription for good living:

> "Keep involved. Care about others. Use your brain. Stay active. What I've gotten out of all this is that it can be exciting to fight old age. It is as exciting a challenge as we have ever had in our lives."
>   "Sure is," another answered, "to beat the odds. That is what we have been trying to do in everything since the first grade. Beat the odds." [5]

He finished six chapters of a novel he had been working on for a couple of years. From time to time Sanford would slip away from the Institute to a hideaway on the West Campus. It was a small, narrow office with good windows and a heavy wooden door that muffled most of the chatter of students passing below on their way to the student union, the school's "living room," as Sanford called it. Here in this retreat he escaped the stream of visitors and worked with fewer interruptions. As he finished pages he wrote in longhand, he passed them on to his long-time assistant Marsha Vick for transcription.

John Ruemmler, a novelist in Charlottesville, Virginia, helped Sanford shape Outlive Your Enemies and was continuing to advise on the novel. The two met through the Writer's Digest School, where Sanford had applied for a mentor. When Ruemmler was asked if he would take the assignment, he said, "You mean the senator?" [6] To the clerk at the Digest offices in Cincinnati, Sanford's application had looked like any other from an aspiring novelist. Ruemmler was impressed with Sanford's work and called him an excellent writer with a storyteller's eye for detail. The novel, which he planned to title Top of the World, was Sanford's assessment of what he considered the three main issues of the twentieth century: racial and gender discrimination, decent jobs, and education. He was telling the story through the lives of a newspaper man and his family.

All the while Sanford continued his fascination with business and new enterprises. He created one company to import reproductions by Russian artists of works by the European masters. He dabbled with an idea to sell books over the Internet well before Amazon.com entered the market. He continued to work with his daughter, Betsee, whose company, Carolina In The Morning, produced homegrown food items for sale in specialty shops and gourmet stores, and with his son, Terry, on a major real estate development north of Durham. Perhaps his grandest venture was a study of a new canal for Central America to replace the aging cross-isthmus facility in Panama. He had become fascinated with the idea while working on his economic plan for the region, and after leaving office he continued to meet with engineers investigating a revival of the original route across Nicaragua.

Young politicians aspiring to public office, some of whom he called "my boys," made their way to his door. He always offered encouragement and help where he could. One of them, a Raleigh lawyer named John Edwards, told Sanford he planned to run against Faircloth in 1998. Seven months after Sanford's death, Edwards defeated Faircloth as Democrats also regained control of the North Carolina General Assembly and fared far better than predicted in congressional elections.

President Bill Clinton remained in touch and sent Sanford a personal note on his first day in office. Later, on the fiftieth anniversary of the Allied invasion of Europe, the president invited Terry and Margaret Rose to the White House for a gathering of distinguished leaders and scholars who were all veterans of World War II and included him in a delegation that attended ceremonies in Europe.

One intermittent luncheon companion was retired historian and Duke professor emeritus John Hope Franklin. The two talked of many subjects and issues, but particularly about the nation's continuing struggle over the issue of race. In the summer of 1996, Sanford wrote Franklin that a recent series of church burnings in the South created "a tangible presence" of "stubborn, lingering racism in America." It was time, Sanford said, to convene a planning session for a commission that would begin a national discussion of the issue.[7] Their conversations eventually led Sanford to write Clinton's chief of staff, Erskine Bowles, who was the son of his old ally Hargrove Bowles, to urge the president to devote the energy of his second term to improving race relations. When the president created his Advisory Committee on Race in 1997, he picked Franklin to chair the panel.

Of all Sanford's activities, Duke remained foremost in his life. In addition to teaching, he took any assignment from his successors in the president's office, from settling disputes to raising money.

He seemed indefatigable. Once he had fully recovered from his heart surgery (he returned to the hospital for treatment immediately after the election), he followed a regime of exercise and sound diet and appeared to enjoy good health. His vices were few. He had never been much of a drinker, although he enjoyed an occasional martini or a glass of wine in the evening. He smoked an occasional cigar, but never cigarettes. In 1964, when the first Surgeon General's report on smoking and health was released, Sanford had defended the tobacco industry and lit up a cigarette as a public demonstration of support. An aide watched anxiously as Sanford fumbled with the match and said, "Damn, he doesn't even know how to hold it." [8]

In spite of all his confidence that he would live to be one hundred, Sanford was curiously anxious about a public celebration of his turning eighty, the age at which both his brother and father had died. When friends pressed him for approval of the occasion, he conceded to a midday gathering of barbecue and country music that turned out to be part reunion, part political rally, and not quite a birthday party. On a bright, sunny Saturday in mid-September 1997, as a cooling breeze blew across the green grass of the Duke baseball field, Terry and Margaret Rose stood in the shadow of the stadium and visited with a crowd of a hundred or so persons who had been a part of their lives in Fayetteville, Raleigh, Durham, and Washington. Former Senate office aides such as Jennifer Hillman, a Duke graduate and Washington lawyer, mingled with old-timers who had elected Sanford president of the YDC.

Less than three months later, in early December, Sanford was scheduled to be in New York for a special Christmas party but begged off at the last minute because of a low-grade fever that had nagged him for several days. The symptoms were similar to those that had preceded discovery of his heart infection in the summer of 1992, and he entered Duke Medical Center so doctors could investigate. After two days of tests, he returned home, relieved at news that his heart was fine, and he awaited his doctors' report. A week later he learned the cause of his trouble was cancer that had been found in his esophagus and liver. There was no explanation. It was just as he had written in Outlive Your Enemies, when Joe tells the others, "Bad luck plays a big part, I'd say. Cancer just happens. You can't get vaccinated."

Sanford was told he could expect to live another six months, and he responded with characteristic optimism. He told his doctors that he was in the best medical facility in the world and that they had just begun to work, so he expected an improvement in their prognosis. He entered the hospital on December 28 for the first round of treatments; when he returned home a few days later he had lost weight and looked tired, but he was upbeat and optimistic. "They said it was inoperable, but they didn't say it was incurable," he told a reporter. [9]

Just weeks before his diagnosis, Sanford had embarked on his latest grand venture, a campaign to raise $100 million to build a state performing arts center in the vicinity of the Research Triangle Park. In February, he made his last public appearance on behalf of the center at a fund-raising reception at the governor's mansion. He told visitors that such a goal was the kind of thing that could get him going.

The center was at the top of a list of items in a memo he wrote that he titled "When I Get Well." The schedule he outlined for himself included finishing his novel, shedding some business ventures that were losing money, teaching, and launching an ambitious new project he called Poverty USA. This was to be a national effort similar to the North Carolina Fund that would combine public and private resources in ten states to demonstrate what the states and local communities could do with volunteers and foundation support to deal with the causes of poverty.[10]

Although he steadily grew weaker, he remained alert and as active as his strength would allow. One after another, reporters from newspapers and television stations across the state came to the house for interviews. Friends from around the country made their way to Durham. A delegation from Terry Sanford High School in Fayetteville sent him a framed varsity letter and poster-size get well cards. He denied no one his time and sorted through his affairs with patience, dignity, and defiance. Death had been a companion through eighty days of combat, he told a reporter. "I can face it one more time without any problem."[11]

Sanford died at 11:30 A.M. on April 18 at his home. With him were Margaret Rose, his wife of fifty-five years, and his son, Terry, and daughter, Betsee.

Before his death, Sanford had told Thomas Langford, the former dean of the Duke Divinity School, that he wanted an "old-fashioned Methodist funeral." He got his wish, or at least as much of it as possible in a cathedral as grand as Duke Chapel. Langford programmed two old hymns, "Nearer, My God, to Thee" and a Sanford favorite, "In the Garden." The 82nd Airborne volunteered to provide military honors, and soldiers in crisp beribboned uniforms, shiny black jump boots, and crimson berets carried Sanford's casket to the front of the chapel and stood watch until services began on April 22.

The chapel filled early on the day of the service. All manner of people came to pay their respects. Seated at the front was an array of public figures that included four former governors, seventeen senators, a hundred members of the North Carolina General Assembly, the White House chief of staff, and the North Carolina council of state. On the end of one row was presidential friend and advisor Vernon Jordan, while at the other end was

Senator Jesse Helms, recently recovered from surgery and gripping a cane. Senator Lauch Faircloth, with whom Sanford had visited before his death, sat near the front, just behind the pallbearers. The fifty-one rows of pews were filled with friends, acquaintances, and those who had never met him but who felt they should come just the same.

Many had their private stories. Oscar Dantzler, the chapel housekeeper, told a reporter that he had been fishing at a pond at Treyburn when Sanford happened by and sat down to talk. It was the first of several visits. "You learn from Senator Sanford," Dantzler told a reporter. "The little man is just as important as the big man. Power don't mean nothing unless you can associate with all types of people." [12]

As is customary at funerals in Methodist churches, friends offer recollections of the deceased. They talk of good times and fond memories. They talk of deeds done. There are stories, laughter, and tears. If that is what Sanford had in mind with his instructions to Langford, whose eulogy recalled Sanford's love for the Methodist Church and his wife, Margaret Rose, then he would have been satisfied with remembrances that covered the full range of his remarkable life.

Governor James B. Hunt asked the crowd to "imagine what North Carolina would be like if we had not had Terry Sanford striving for us all these many years." Former speaker of the North Carolina house Dan Blue recalled the fatherly advice he received when he joined the Sanford law firm as one of the first African American lawyers hired by a mainstream firm in the state. "Let me say," Blue concluded, " 'Dear Lord, open your gate wide for Terry Sanford. He opened gates for me. Dear Lord, open wide for Terry Sanford, he opened gates for all of us here on earth.' " [13]

Mary Semans, the chair of the Duke Endowment, spoke as a friend and workmate at Duke and in countless community projects in Durham. "A man from Durham County called me and asked, 'Do you think we could come to Terry Sanford's services? He was my friend.' I'm sure he's here today because all of us know that we are all his friends. That man knew that all of Terry's friends were real, they were forever and they were sincere."

Joel Fleishman called Sanford "a great-spirited, great-souled man, a man of passion, a man with a conscience that had real bite, a man of loyalty. But most of all, Terry Sanford was a creative genius, but a thoroughly practical one who transformed everything he touched into something finer, better, worthier and more useful to the world. If I had to call him by a single phrase, it would be the 'great transformer.' " Duke President Nannerl Keohane said he was a "leader-hero," someone on whom she had come to depend for wise counsel and advice.

But it was Dickson Phillips who had known Sanford the longest, and perhaps the best. The two had shared their youth together in Laurinburg and later life experiences in the paratroopers and as law partners.

> And looking back, it all seems very simple to me: why he was what he was, and did what he did, and persevered to the end. He took an oath when he was 12 years old and kept it. It started out, "On my honor, I will do my best to do my duty to God and my country," and included such things as "help other people at all times." He believed it: he was the eternal Boy Scout. It is just that simple.
>
> He kept the oath about as well as it can be kept by one in the heavy engagements of an active uncloistered life. The simple compass at the core held him true on course to the end. That is why in the words he liked to quote about his great personal and political friend, Kerr Scott, "He plowed to the end of the row. His furrow was deep."

Phillips finished his prepared remarks and paused at the podium before returning to his seat. Then the tall distinguished judge, who had spoken in such soft tones of reverence and love, looked at the row of paratroopers seated on a front pew, raised his fist in a high salute to the casket and said, "Airborne, all the way."

As the service concluded, a bugler from the 82nd Airborne played taps while his comrades slowly folded the American flag that draped Sanford's casket. The division's deputy commander, Major General Thomas H. Needham, presented the flag to Margaret Rose before his soldiers carried her husband's casket to the crypt below.

Notes

1 Double Moons over Laurinburg

1 Bill Sharpe, *A New Geography of North Carolina* (Raleigh, NC: Sharpe Publishing, 1965), 4:2069.
2 Josephus Daniels, *Editor in Politics* (Chapel Hill: University of North Carolina Press, 1941), 290, 294.
3 Betsy Sanford, interview with Terry Sanford, 16 March 1981, Laurinburg, North Carolina.
4 Mary Glenn Rose and Helen Wilhelm, interview with authors, 25 June 1995.
5 Terry Sanford, interview with authors, 17 March 1995.
6 Ibid.

2 Runnin' on Rims

1 Reginald McCoy, interview with authors, 14 July 1996.
2 Terry Sanford, unpublished manuscript, Terry Sanford Papers, Duke University Archives.
3 Terry Sanford, interview with authors, 17 March 1995.
4 John L. Bell Jr., *Hard Times: Beginnings of the Great Depression in North Carolina, 1929–1933* (Raleigh: North Carolina Department of Cultural Resources, Division of Archives and History, 1982), 15.
5 John L. McNair, interview with authors, 18 June 1995.
6 Terry Sanford, unpublished manuscript, Terry Sanford Papers, Duke University Archives.
7 Scrapbook, Terry Sanford Papers, Southern Historical Collection, University of North Carolina, Chapel Hill.
8 Sanford, unpublished manuscript.
9 "Governor Speaks at Rotary Meet," *News & Observer*, 15 May 1934.
10 "Armed Strikers Object of Shots," *News & Observer*, 2 June 1934.
11 Reginald F. McCoy, interview with authors, 17 March 1995.
12 John Henry Moore, interview with authors, 18 December 1995.

3 The "Promised Land"

1 James Vickers, Thomas Scism, and Dixon Qualls, *Chapel Hill: An Illustrated History* (Chapel Hill, NC: Barclay Publishers, 1985), 131.
2 "Graham Explains Aids for New Men," *The Daily Tar Heel*, 26 September 1935.

3   William D. Snider, *Light on the Hill: A History of the University of North Carolina at Chapel Hill* (Chapel Hill: University of North Carolina Press, 1992), 209.

4   Jonathan Daniels, *Tar Heels: A Portrait of North Carolina* (New York: Dodd, Mead, 1947), 267.

5   Fred Hobson, ed., *South-Watching: Selected Essays by Gerald W. Johnson* (Chapel Hill: University of North Carolina Press, 1983), 185.

6   Ibid., 188.

7   Terry Sanford, interview with authors, 14 January 1993.

8   "Freshmen Take Pledge of Honor," *The Daily Tar Heel*, 4 February 1936.

9   Sanford interview.

10   Terry Sanford, interview with Brent Glass, 20 August 1976, Southern Oral History Program, Southern Historical Collection, University of North Carolina, Chapel Hill.

11   Alexander Heard, interview with John Egerton, 17 July 1991, Southern Historical Collection, University of North Carolina, Chapel Hill.

12   Sanford interview, 14 January 1993.

13   Dickson Phillips, interview with authors, 25 April, 1996.

14   Terry Sanford, interview with authors, 13 December 1995.

15   Sid Moody and High Mulligan, "Class of '38," *News & Observer*, 2 June 1963.

16   Sanford interview, 13 December 1995.

17   Ibid.

18   Terry Sanford, unpublished manuscript, Terry Sanford Papers, Duke University Archives.

19   William McCachren, interview with authors, 11 April 1995.

20   Sanford, unpublished manuscript.

21   Sanford interview, 13 December 1995.

22   Ibid.

23   Anthony J. Badger, *North Carolina and the New Deal* (Raleigh: North Carolina Department of Cultural Resources, 1981), 76.

24   Jim McAden, "Roosevelt Defends Policy of Liberalism," *The Daily Tar Heel*, 6 December 1939.

25   Badger, *North Carolina*, 67.

26   Ibid., 26.

27   Sanford interview, 13 December 1995.

28   Ibid.

4   Albert's Boys

1   Albert Coates, *What the University of North Carolina Meant to Me* (Richmond, VA: William Byrd Press, 1969), 67.

2   Albert Coates to Betsy Sanford, 12 November 1970, Terry Sanford Papers, Duke University Archives.

3   Terry Sanford, interview with authors, 20 December 1995.

4   William McWhorter Cochrane, interview with authors, 17 May 1995.

5   Martha Clampitt McKay, interview with authors, 9 March 1996.

6   "Legislature Approves Student Fees Amendment," *The Daily Tar Heel*, 18 April 1941.

7   Cochrane interview.

8   Terry Sanford to Mr. and Mrs. Cecil Sanford, March 1941, Terry Sanford Papers, Duke University Archives.

9   Ibid.

10   Ernie Frankel, "Pacifist Ericson Changes in Favor of All-Out Aid," *The Daily Tar Heel*, 24 September 1941.

11   Anthony J. Badger, *North Carolina and the New Deal* (Raleigh: North Carolina Department of Cultural Resources, 1981), 83.

12 Sanford interview.

13 William McCachren, interview with authors, 11 April 1995.

14 Sanford to Mr. and Mrs. Cecil Sanford.

15 Margaret Rose Sanford, interview with authors, 7 September 1995.

16 Ibid.

17 Coates to Betsy Sanford.

18 "Graham States University's War Policy," *The Daily Tar Heel*, 9 December 1941.

19 Sanford interview.

20 "U.S. Trains More Parachute Troops," *Life*, 12 May 1941, 111.

21 Sanford interview.

22 Terry Sanford, unpublished manuscript, Terry Sanford Papers, Duke University Archives.

5 The Battling Buzzards

1 Clark L. Archer, *Paratroopers' Odyssey: A History of the 517th Parachute Combat Team* (Hudson, FL: 517th Parachute Combat Team Association, 1985), 6.

2 "U.S. Trains More Parachute Troops," *Life*, 12 May 1941, 111.

3 Don Wharton, "Jumping Through Georgia," *Readers Digest*, November 1941, 81.

4 Terry Sanford to Mr. and Mrs. Cecil Sanford, 29 December 1943, Terry Sanford Papers, Duke University Archives.

5 Richard R. Clarke, "Paratrooper Writes Home," *American Magazine*, May 1943, 10.

6 Archer, *Paratroopers' Odyssey*, 21.

7 Terry Sanford to Mr. and Mrs. Cecil Sanford, 9 July 1944, Terry Sanford Papers, Duke University Archives.

8 Ibid.

9 Terry Sanford to Mr. and Mrs. Cecil Sanford, 17 July 1944, Terry Sanford Papers, Duke University Archives.

10 Terry Sanford to Mr. and Mrs. Cecil Sanford, 3 August 1944, Terry Sanford Papers, Duke University Archives.

11 "A Paratroopers Load," *New York Times*, 5 June 1994.

12 Terry Sanford, interview with authors, 14 January 1993.

13 Terry Sanford to Mr. and Mrs. Cecil Sanford, September 1944, Terry Sanford Papers, Duke University Archives.

14 Ibid.

15 Archer, *Paratroopers' Odyssey*, 54.

16 Margaret Rose Sanford to Mr. and Mrs. Cecil Sanford, 31 August 1944, Terry Sanford Papers, Duke University Archives.

17 Terry Sanford to Mr. and Mrs. Cecil Sanford, 3 September 1944, Terry Sanford Papers, Duke University Archives.

18 Sanford was proud to be called Terry and was amused when a person who did not know him well introduced him at public functions as James Terry Sanford.

19 Terry Sanford to Mr. and Mrs. Cecil Sanford, 13 December 1944, Terry Sanford Papers, Duke University Archives.

20 Ibid.

21 Ibid.

22 Terry Sanford to Mr. and Mrs. Cecil Sanford, 5 October 1944, Terry Sanford Papers, Duke University Archives.

23 Terry Sanford to Mr. and Mrs. Cecil Sanford, 3 October 1944, Terry Sanford Papers, Duke University Archives.

24 Unit Records, 517th Regimental Combat Team, U.S. Military Records, National Archives, Washington, DC.

25 Ibid.

26 Stephen E. Ambrose, *Citizen Soldier* (New York: Simon & Schuster, 1997), 351–52.

27 Terry Sanford to Mr. and Mrs. Cecil Sanford, 28 December 1944 and 29 December 1944, Terry Sanford Papers, Duke University Archives.

28 Efficiency Report, United States Army, 1 July 1945, U.S. Military Records, Terry Sanford Papers, Duke University Archives.

29 Terry Sanford, unpublished manuscript, Terry Sanford Papers, Duke University Archives.

30 Ibid.

6   The Third Primary

1 Terry Sanford, interview with authors, 20 December 1995.

2 "Campus Returns to Normalcy," *The Tar Heel*, 8 September 1945.

3 John Egerton, *Speak Now Against the Day: The Generation Before the Civil Rights Movement in the South* (New York: Knopf, 1994), 211.

4 Frank Porter Graham, interview with Charles Jones, Anne Queen, and Stuart Willis, 9 June 1972, Southern Oral History Program, Southern Historical Collection, University of North Carolina, Chapel Hill.

5 Douglass Hunt, letter, *The Tar Heel*, 8 December 1945.

6 Rudolph Pate, "Student Assembly Adopts Motion to Invite Negroes," *News & Observer*, 2 December 1945.

7 Ibid.

8 Frank Porter Graham, letter, *The Tar Heel*, 11 December 1945.

9 Ibid.

10 Quoted in Egerton, *Speak Now*, 456.

11 Sanford interview.

12 Quoted in William D. Snider, *Light on the Hill* (Chapel Hill: University of North Carolina Press, 1992), 233.

13 Frank Porter Graham, interview with Hank Patterson, James Wallace, and Joel Fleishman, 10 June 1962, Southern Oral History Program, Southern Historical Collection, University of North Carolina, Chapel Hill.

14 Egerton, *Speak Now*, 476.

15 Quoted in Nadine Cohodas, *Strom Thurmond and the Politics of Southern Change* (New York: Simon & Schuster, 1993), 177.

16 Quoted in Stephen Lesher, *George Wallace: American Populist* (Reading, MA: Addison-Wesley, 1994), 81.

17 *Remarks Presented in Eulogy of William Kerr Scott, Late a Senator from North Carolina* (Washington, DC: Government Printing Office, 1958).

18 Quoted in ibid.

19 David Leroy Corbitt, ed., *Addresses and Papers of Governor Kerr Scott* (Raleigh: North Carolina Department of Archives and History, 1953), ix.

20 Capus Waynick, interview with Bill Finger, 4 February 1974, Southern Oral History Program, Southern Historical Collection, University of North Carolina, Chapel Hill.

21 Ibid.

22 Scrapbook, Terry Sanford Papers, Southern Historical Collection, University of North Carolina, Chapel Hill.

23 Ibid.

24 Jonathan Daniels, interview with Daniel Singal, 22 March 1972, Southern Oral History Program, Southern Historical Collection, University of North Carolina, Chapel Hill.

25 Quoted in Julian M. Pleasants and Augustus M. Burns III, *Frank Porter Graham and the 1950 Senate Race in North Carolina* (Chapel Hill: University of North Carolina Press, 1990), 15.

26 News clippings, Terry Sanford Papers, Southern Historical Collection, University of North Carolina, Chapel Hill.

27 Quoted in Pleasants and Burns, *Frank Porter Graham*, 54.
28 Clint Newton, interview with authors, 12 July 1995.
29 Terry Sanford, interview with authors, 27 January 1993.
30 Scrapbook, Sanford Papers.
31 William Staton, interview with authors, 24 April 1995.
32 Sanford interview, 27 January 1993.
33 Staton interview.
34 Sanford interview, 27 January 1993.
35 Pleasants and Burns, *Frank Porter Graham*, 217.
36 Scrapbook, Sanford Papers.
37 Pleasants and Burns, *Frank Porter Graham*, 198.
38 Terry Sanford, interview with authors, 12 December 1995.

7   The Branch-Head Boys

1   Julian M. Pleasants and Augustus M. Burns III, *Frank Porter Graham and the 1950 Senate Race in North Carolina* (Chapel Hill: University of North Carolina Press, 1990), 248.
2   Ibid., 249.
3   Terry Sanford, interview with authors, 27 January 1993.
4   Quoted in Pleasants and Burns, *Frank Porter Graham*, 249.
5   David Leroy Corbitt, ed., *Addresses and Papers of Governor Kerr Scott* (Raleigh: Council of State 1953), 127.
6   Ibid., 306.
7   Sanford interview.
8   *Remarks Presented in Eulogy of William Kerr Scott, Late a Senator from North Carolina* (Washington, DC: Government Printing Office, 1958).
9   Sanford interview.
10 Ibid.
11 *Remarks Presented in Eulogy of William Kerr Scott.*
12 Simmons Fencers, "Kerr Scott: Man of Surprise, Controversy," *News & Observer*, 4 January 1953.
13 Ibid.
14 Jim Chaney, "Umstead and Olive Tangle over Tactics of Campaign," *News & Observer*, 28 May 1952.
15 Woodrow Price, "State's Delegates to Go Unpledged; Rebuffed, Governor 'Takes Back Seat,'" *News & Observer*, 23 May 1952.
16 "Under the Dome," *News & Observer*, 30 May 1952.
17 Terry Sanford, interview with authors, 20 December 1995.
18 "National Guard: Local Unit Shows No White Feather," *Fayetteville Observer*, 2 August 1950.
19 Terry Sanford Papers, Southern Historical Collection, University of North Carolina, Chapel Hill.
20 Sanford interview, 20 December 1995.
21 Ibid.
22 Ibid.
23 Corbitt, *Addresses and Papers of Governor Kerr Scott*, 327.
24 David Leroy Corbitt, ed., *Public Addresses, Letters, and Papers of William Bradley Umstead, Governor of North Carolina 1953–54* (Raleigh: Council of State, 1957), 3.
25 Howard White, "It's 'Private Citizen' Scott Now," *News & Observer*, 9 January 1953.
26 Corbitt, *Addresses and Papers of Governor Kerr Scott*, ix.
27 Corbitt, *Public Addresses, Letters, and Papers of William Bradley Umstead*, vii.
28 "Governor's Heart Attack 'Mild,' Out of Action at Least 2 Weeks," *News & Observer*, 13 January 1953.

29 Luther Hodges, *Businessman in the State House: Six Years as Governor of North Carolina* (Chapel Hill: University of North Carolina Press, 1962), 18.

30 A. G. "Pete" Ivey, *Luther H. Hodges: Practical Idealist* (Minneapolis: T. S. Denison & Co., 1968), 132.

31 Ibid., 122.

32 Hodges, *Businessman in the State House*, 21.

33 Ed Rankin Jr., interview with authors, 7 December 1993.

34 Woodrow Price, "Battle Joined on Road Plan, Effort Futile," *News & Observer*, 12 February 1953.

35 Henry Hall Wilson Jr., unpublished manuscript, private collection.

36 Ibid.

37 Terry Sanford, unpublished manuscript, Terry Sanford Papers, Duke University Archives.

38 Woodrow Price, "Alton Lennon, Wilmington, Appointed as U.S. Senator," *News & Observer*, 11 July 1953.

39 Gayle Lane Fitzgerald, *Remembering a Champion* (Raleigh, NC: Edwards & Broughton, 1988), 94.

40 Sanford, unpublished manuscript.

41 Sanford interview, 20 December 1995.

42 *Remarks Presented in Eulogy of William Kerr Scott.*

43 Terry Sanford, interview with authors, 22 April 1997.

44 Ibid.

45 Scrapbook, Terry Sanford Papers, Southern Historical Collection, University of North Carolina, Chapel Hill.

46 Tom Wicker, *Facing the Lions* (New York: Viking, 1973), 160.

47 Robert W. Scott, interview with authors, 7 May 1998. Scott said that his father miscalculated the number of people who would take him up on the offer and spent far more money than he had anticipated buying bull calves to pay off the winners.

48 Ibid.

49 "Let Tax Folks Scan Taxes, Scott Asks in Radio Speech," *News & Observer*, 7 May 1954.

50 Sanford interview, 20 December 1995.

51 David Halberstam, *The Fifties* (New York: Villard Books, 1993), 250.

52 "McCarthy Called 'National Shame,' " *News & Observer*, 13 May 1954.

53 Terry Sanford Papers, Southern Historical Collection, University of North Carolina, Chapel Hill.

54 John Egerton, *Speak Now Against the Day: The Generation Before the Civil Rights Movement in the South* (New York: Knopf, 1994), 602.

55 Rankin interview.

56 "City Takes Court Ruling on Segregation Calmly," *Greensboro Daily News*, 18 May 1954.

57 J. W. Seabrook, "Some Observations Concerning the Supreme Court Decision of May 17, 1954," J. W. Seabrook papers, North Carolina A&T State University Archives.

58 "Scott Gives Views on Court Decision," *News & Observer*, 18 May 1954.

59 "Race Issue Brought into Senatorial Campaign," *News & Observer*, 21 May 1954.

60 Rankin interview.

61 United Press, "City Acts to 'De-Segregate,' " *News & Observer*, 20 May 1954.

62 George A. Penny, "Candidate Kerr Scott Enjoys Handshaking Tour of Wake County," *News & Observer*, 20 May 1954.

63 Woodrow Price, "Reference to Court Decision Receives Big Hand; 3000 at Convention," *News & Observer*, 21 May 1954.

64 Sanford interview, 27 January 1993.

65 Woodrow Price, "Alton Lennon Forces Flood State with 'Phony' Race Issue Leaflets," *News & Observer*, 28 May 1954.

66 Jim Chaney, "Lennon Travels to Scott; Sanford Shakes Al's Hand," *News & Observer*, 30 May 1954.

67 "A Blast of Clean Air," *News & Observer*, 31 May 1954.

68 Ibid.

69 "Ministers Praise Decision," *News & Observer*, 26 May 1954.

70 "Umstead Advises Calmness about Segregation Verdict," *News & Observer*, 28 May 1954.

71 Paul R. Clancy, *Just a Country Lawyer: A Biography of Senator Sam Ervin* (Bloomington: Indiana University Press, 1974), 153.

8 A Dangerous Dream

1 Roy Wilder, interview with authors, 19 April 1995.

2 Henry Hall Wilson Jr., unpublished manuscript, private collection.

3 Governor Luther H. Hodges, Thomas J. Pearsall, Paul A. Johnson, Robert E. Giles, E. L. Rankin Jr., *Transcribed Session on History of the Integration Situation in North Carolina, Saturday, 3 September 1960, Governor's Office, State Capitol, Raleigh,* Elizabeth Pearsall Papers, Southern Historical Collection, University of North Carolina, Chapel Hill.

4 Elizabeth Pearsall, interview with Walter Campbell, 25 May 1988, Southern Oral History Program, Southern Historical Collection, University of North Carolina, Chapel Hill.

5 Ibid.

6 Bob Smith, *They Closed Their Schools* (Chapel Hill: University of North Carolina Press, 1965), 85.

7 Hodges et al., *Transcribed Session*.

8 Ibid.

9 Ibid.

10 Ibid.

11 *Brown v Board of Education* (1954), transcript of oral arguments, U.S. Supreme Court Library, Washington, DC.

12 Ibid.

13 Hodges et al., *Transcribed Session*.

14 Ed Rankin Jr., interview with authors, 7 December 1993.

15 Hodges et al., *Transcribed Session*.

16 Associated Press, "Private Schools Urged for N.C.," *News & Observer*, 14 July 1955.

17 Hodges et al., *Transcribed Session*.

18 "NAACP Asks Governor to Oust Beverly Lake," *News & Observer*, 17 July 1955.

19 Rankin interview.

20 Associated Press, "Hodges Does Not Believe Mass Integration Coming," *News & Observer*, 19 July 1955.

21 "Amplifies upon Position Taken in Asheboro Speech," *News & Observer*, 20 July 1955.

22 Harry Golden to John Steinbeck, 19 June 1963, Governor's Papers, Terry Sanford Administration, North Carolina Department of Archives and History, Raleigh.

23 Associated Press, "NAACP Head Raps Lake," *News & Observer*, 6 August 1955.

24 James W. Patton, ed., *Addresses and Papers of Governor Luther Hartwell Hodges* (Raleigh, NC: Council of State, 1960), 1:199.

25 "Southern Leadership at Its Best," *News & Observer*, 9 August 1955.

26 "Hodges Hears from Speech," *News & Observer*, 10 August 1955.

27 Paul Green, "Saddened by Speech," *News & Observer*, 11 August 1955.

28 John R. Larkins, *Patterns of Leadership Among Negroes in North Carolina* (Raleigh: Irving-Swain Press, 1959), 8.

29 William H. Chafe, *Civilities and Civil Rights: Greensboro, North Carolina, and the Black Struggle for Freedom* (New York: Oxford University Press, 1980), 22.

30 James Jackson Kilpatrick, *The Southern Case for School Segregation* (N.p.: Crowell-Collier Press, 1962), 22.

31 Harry Groves, interview with authors, 14 January 1997.

32 Ibid.

33 Hodges et al., *Transcribed Session*.

34 Terry Sanford, interview with authors, 27 December 1995.
35 Terry Sanford Papers, Southern Historical Collection, University of North Carolina, Chapel Hill.
36 Julian Scheer, interview with authors, 10 May 1995.
37 Terry Sanford, interview with authors, 18 August 1993.
38 Sanford interview, 27 December 1995.
39 Terry Sanford Papers, Southern Historical Collection, University of North Carolina, Chapel Hill.
40 Terry Sanford, unpublished manuscript, Terry Sanford Papers, Duke University Archives.
41 Ibid.
42 Terry Sanford, interview with authors, 27 January 1993.
43 "Under the Dome," News & Observer, 6 February 1956.
44 Hugh Morton, personal communication.
45 Terry Sanford, interview with authors, 17 March 1995.
46 Joe P. Crawford to Terry Sanford, 2 June 1956, Terry Sanford Papers, Southern Historical Collection, University of North Carolina, Chapel Hill.
47 John Barlow Martin, The Deep South Says "Never" (New York: Ballantine, 1957), 162.
48 Quoted in ibid., 161.
49 Smith, They Closed, 140.
50 Jim Chaney, "Private School Plan Seen as of Doubtful Legality," News & Observer, 7 February 1956.
51 James C. N. Paul, "Part II. The Decision and Alternatives Open to North Carolina — A Legal Analysis," Popular Government, September 1954, 21.
52 Woodrow Price, "Hodges Tells Home Folks That His Hat Is in Ring," News & Observer, 5 February 1956.
53 Woodrow Price, "Virginians Up in Air over School-Aid Plan," News & Observer, 12 July 1956.
54 Elizabeth Pearsall interview.
55 Hodges et al., Transcribed Session.
56 Dallas Herring, interview with authors, 10 February 1996.
57 Hodges et al., Transcribed Session.
58 Woodrow Price, "State Democrats Endorse Stevenson for President," News & Observer, 18 May 1956.
59 Patton, Addresses and Papers of Governor Hodges, 1:32.
60 William Friday, interview with authors, 8 February 1996.
61 Woodrow Price, "Hypocrisy, Illegality Charged," News & Observer, 25 July 1956.
62 Ibid.
63 Arthur Johnsey, "Plan Put under Attack," Greensboro Daily News, 26 July 1956.
64 Hodges et al., Transcribed Session.
65 Ibid.
66 Jim Chaney, "Pearsall Plan Is Legal, Joyner Tells Assembly," News & Observer, 26 July 1956.
67 Ibid.
68 Burke Davis, "Raleigh Notebook," Greensboro Daily News, 26 July 1956.
69 Jim Chaney, " 'Twas Great Show on TV, but Puzzling," News & Observer, 28 July 1956.
70 Terry Sanford Papers, Southern Historical Collection, University of North Carolina, Chapel Hill.
71 Ibid.
72 Terry Sanford, interview with authors, 18 August 1993.
73 Paid advertisement, News & Observer, 7 September 1956.
74 Terry Sanford Papers, Southern Historical Collection, University of North Carolina, Chapel Hill.
75 Sanford interview, 18 August 1993.

76 Harry Golden, *Only in America* (New York: World Publishing, 1958), 121.

77 Paid advertisement, *News & Observer*, 7 September 1956.

78 "Intolerable Situation," *News & Observer*, 7 September 1956.

79 Patton, *Addresses and Papers of Governor Hodges*, 1:592.

80 Jonathan Daniels, interview with Charles Eagles, 9–11 March 1977, Southern Oral History Program, Southern Historical Collection, University of North Carolina, Chapel Hill.

81 Herring interview, 10 February 1996.

82 Albert N. Link, *A Generosity of Spirit* (Research Triangle Park, NC: Research Triangle Foundation, 1995), 79.

83 Donald R. Lennon and Fred D. Ragan, eds., *Politics, Bar and Bench: A Memoir of U.S. District Judge John Davis Larkins Jr.* (N.p.: Historical Society of Eastern North Carolina, 1980), 46.

84 Associated Press, "Kerr Scott Rests Well in Hospital," *News & Observer*, 13 April 1958.

85 Terry Sanford Papers, Duke University Archives.

86 Charles Clay, "Senator W. Kerr Scott Is Dead," *News & Observer*, 17 April 1958.

87 *William Kerr Scott, Late a Senator from North Carolina* (Washington, DC: GPO, 1958), E748.S387.

88 "Kerr Scott," *News & Observer*, 17 April 1958.

89 "Kerr Scott: Esse Quam Videri," *Greensboro Daily News*, 18 April 1958.

90 *William Kerr Scott, Late a Senator*, E748.S387.

91 Terry Sanford Papers, Duke University Archives.

92 Ben F. Bulla, *Textiles & Politics: The Life of B. Everett Jordan* (Durham, NC: Carolina Academic Press, 1992), 7.

93 "Sharp Differences Found in Comment," *News & Observer*, 20 April 1958.

94 Terry Sanford Papers, Duke University Archives.

95 Sanford interview, 18 August 1993.

96 "Under the Dome," *News & Observer*, 19 April 1958.

9 Breaking in Line

1 Ed Rankin Jr., interview with authors, 27 January 1994.

2 Luther Hodges, "The Southern Point of View," Southern Governors Conference, 23 September 1957, Luther Hodges Papers, Division of Archives and History, Raleigh.

3 Leroy Collins, "Can a Southerner Be Elected President?", Southern Governors Conference, 23 September 1957, Luther Hodges Papers, Division of Archives and History, Raleigh.

4 Helen J. Jacobstein, *The Segregation Factor in the Florida Democratic Gubernatorial Primary 1956* (Gainesville: University of Florida Press, 1972), 56.

5 Ibid., 73.

6 Ibid., 74.

7 Ibid.

8 Ibid.

9 Ibid.

10 Stacy Weaver Jr., interview with authors, 30 January 1997.

11 Terry Sanford, interview with authors, 27 December 1995.

12 James B. L. Rush to Terry Sanford, 27 February 1957, Terry Sanford Papers, Duke University Archives.

13 Harry Golden to Terry Sanford, 26 February 1957, Terry Sanford Papers, Duke University Archives.

14 William B. Cochrane to Terry Sanford, undated memorandum, Terry Sanford Papers, Duke University Archives.

15 Ralph Scott to Terry Sanford, undated memorandum, Terry Sanford Papers, Duke University Archives.

16 Statement prepared for news release, Terry Sanford Papers, Duke University Archives.
17 Terry Sanford, speech prepared for delivery 23 January 1958, Terry Sanford Papers, Duke University Archives.
18 Roy Wilder to Terry Sanford, 30 December 1958, Terry Sanford Papers, Southern Historical Collection.
19 Ibid.
20 Henry Hall Wilson Jr., unpublished manuscript, private collection.
21 Ibid.
22 Ibid.
23 Harry Golden, "We Hate Our Own," *Only in America* (New York: World Publishing, 1958), 232.
24 Wilson, unpublished manuscript.
25 Robert W. Scott to Terry Sanford, 7 October 1959, Terry Sanford Papers, Duke University Archives.
26 Hugh Cannon, interview with authors, 10 August 1993.
27 Ibid.
28 I. Beverly Lake, speech, nd, Terry Sanford Papers, Duke University Archives.
29 Robert W. Scott to Terry Sanford, 29 August 1959, Terry Sanford Papers, Duke University Archives.
30 Reed Sarratt, *The Ordeal of Desegregation* (New York: Harper & Row, 1966), 12.

10 *"Puddles of Poison"*

1 Woodrow Price, "Sanford Promises to End 'Hold-the-Line' Budgets," *News & Observer*, 5 February 1960.
2 Roy Wilder, interview with authors, 19 April 1995.
3 "Sanford Assures Wake Followers," *News & Observer*, 19 February 1960.
4 Terry Sanford, *But What About the People?* (New York: Harper & Row, 1966), 15.
5 Terry Sanford, interview with authors, 22 April 1997.
6 Lou Harris and Associates, Inc., *A Second Survey of the Democratic Primary for Governor in North Carolina*, nd, Terry Sanford Papers, Duke University Archives.
7 Donald R. Lennon and Fred D. Ragan, eds., *Politics, Bar and Bench: A Memoir of U.S. District Judge John Davis Larkins Jr.* (N.p.: Historical Society of Eastern North Carolina, 1980), 53.
8 Ibid., 52.
9 Bob Smith, *They Closed Their Schools* (Chapel Hill: University of North Carolina Press, 1965), 152.
10 Gene Roberts Jr., "Lake Says He Won't Enter Campaign for Governor," *News & Observer*, 11 February 1960.
11 "Under the Dome," *News & Observer*, 13 February 1960.
12 Ibid.
13 Ibid.
14 Sanford interview.
15 Charles Craven and David Cooper, "Student Sitdown Strike Spreads to Stores Here," *News & Observer*, 11 February 1960.
16 Ibid.
17 Gene Roberts Jr., interview with authors, 7 October 1995.
18 Gene Roberts Jr., "Negro Leader Urges Students to Continue Segregation Protest," *News & Observer*, 17 February 1960.
19 Roberts interview.
20 Charles Clay, "Lake to Run; Sounds Segregationist Theme," *News & Observer*, 2 March 1960.
21 Gene Roberts Jr., "Lake Stirring Passions on Desegregation Issue," *News & Observer*, 19 May 1960.

22   United Press International, "Lakes Sees Chaos and Confusion If Restaurants Are Integrated," *News & Observer*, 2 March 1960.

23   Terry Sanford Papers, Southern Historical Collection.

24   Ibid.

25   Ibid.

26   Harris et al., *A Second Survey*.

27   Bert Bennett, interview with authors, 27 October 1993.

28   Ibid.

29   Bert Bennett, interview with authors, 10 September 1997.

30   Hargrove Bowles to Paul Thompson, 20 May 1959, Terry Sanford Papers, Southern Historical Collection.

31   Terry Sanford to Henry Hall Wilson Jr., 28 December 1959, Terry Sanford Papers, Southern Historical Collection.

32   Hugh Cannon, interview with authors, 10 August 1993.

33   Bennett interview, 27 October 1993.

34   R. S. Dickson to Hargrove Bowles, 14 December 1959, Terry Sanford Papers, Southern Historical Collection.

35   Sanford interview.

36   Campaign advertising films, Terry Sanford Papers, Southern Historical Collection.

37   Peggy Warren to Terry Sanford, 20 March 1960, Terry Sanford Papers, Southern Historical Collection.

38   Harris et al., *A Second Survey*.

39   Terry Sanford, scrapbook no. 1, microfilm tape 1, North Carolina State Archives.

40   Charles Craven, "Name Tagging Highlights Gubernatorial News Front," *News & Observer*, 1 May 1960.

41   Associated Press, "Lakes Cites Opposition to Program of NAACP," *News & Observer*, 1 May 1960.

42   Associated Press, "Lakes Says NC 'Soft Spot,' " *News & Observer*, 6 May 1960.

43   Charles Clay, "State Plan Working, Keynoter Tells Party," *News & Observer*, 20 May 1960.

44   Cannon interview.

45   Robert Morgan, interview with authors, 8 February 1995.

46   Ibid.

47   Gene Roberts Jr., "Candidates Hits Sanford Vows," *News & Observer*, 31 May 1960.

48   United Press International, 1 July 1960, Terry Sanford Papers, Southern Historical Collection.

49   Charles Craven, "Sanford Tops 82,000," *News & Observer*, 31 May 1960.

50   Terry Sanford, interview with authors, 27 December 1995.

51   Kim Isaac Eisler, *A Justice for All: William J. Brennan Jr. and the Decisions That Transformed America* (New York: Simon & Schuster, 1993), 154.

52   Terry Sanford, interview with authors, 5 October 1993.

53   Woodrow Price, "Sanford Slaps Back at Racist Campaign of Candidate Lake," *News & Observer*, 1 June 1960.

54   Sanford interview, 5 October 1993.

55   Sanford interview, 27 December 1995.

56   Sanford interview, 22 April 1997.

57   David Cooper, "Sanford Lashes Lake Who Raps Labor Leaders," *News & Observer*, 15 June 1960.

58   Campaign films, Terry Sanford Papers, Southern Historical Collection.

59   Sanford interview, 5 October 1993.

60   Terry Sanford Papers, Southern Historical Collection.

61   Roberts, "Sanford Lashes Lake."

62   Gene Roberts Jr., "Lake, Burney Flail N&O at Lumberton," *News & Observer*, 22 June 1960.

63   Gene Roberts, interview with authors, 10 October 1995.

64 Sanford interview, 5 October 1993.
65 Terry Sanford Papers, Southern Historical Collection.
66 Charles Clay, "Runoff Race for Governor May Draw 500,000 Voters," *News & Observer*, 25 June 1960.
67 David Cooper, "Lake's Camp Sang 'Dixie' in Defeat," *News & Observer*, 26 June 1960.
68 Gene Roberts Jr., "Sanford Quarters Hot, But Who Cared?", *News & Observer*, 26 June 1960.
69 Ibid.
70 I. Beverly Lake, interview with Edward L. Harrelson, 1992, University of North Carolina Law School Oral History Project.
71 "A Free Governor," editorial, *News & Observer*, 26 June 1960.

11   A New Day

1 Memory F. Mitchell, ed., *Messages, Addresses, and Public Papers of Terry Sanford, Governor of North Carolina, 1961–1965* (Raleigh: Council of State, 1966), 3.
2 Terry Sanford, unpublished manuscript, Duke University Archives.
3 Ed Rankin Jr., interview with authors, 27 January 1994.
4 Terry Sanford, interview with authors, 22 April 1997.
5 Terry Sanford, interview with Ann M. Campbell, 27 July 1970, Oral History Collection, John F. Kennedy Library, Boston.
6 Sanford, unpublished manuscript.
7 Sanford interview with Campbell.
8 Terry Sanford, interview with Joe B. Frantz, 15 May 1971, Oral History Collection, Lyndon B. Johnson Library, Austin.
9 Ibid.
10 Julian Scheer, interview with authors, 17 May 1996.
11 Sanford interview with Campbell.
12 Terry Sanford, interview with Brent Glass, 20–21 August 1976, Southern Oral History Program, Southern Historical Collection, University of North Carolina, Chapel Hill.
13 Robert W. Scott, interview with authors, 7 May 1998.
14 Dallas Herring, interview with authors, 10 February 1996.
15 Mitchell, *Messages*, 6.
16 "Spruill Isn't First, but He Gets to Speak," *News & Observer*, 14 April 1961.
17 Terry Sanford, interview with authors, 16 November 1993.
18 Thomas Jackson White, interview with Pamela Dean, May–June 1985, Southern Oral History Program, Southern Historical Collection, University of North Carolina, Chapel Hill.
19 Ibid.
20 Mrs. Moye Jordan to Terry Sanford, 1961, Official Papers of Governor Terry Sanford, North Carolina Department of Archives and History, Raleigh.
21 Sanford interview, 16 November 1993.
22 Ibid.
23 Sanford, unpublished manuscript.
24 Mitchell, *Messages*, 11.
25 Sanford, unpublished manuscript.
26 Terry Sanford, interview with authors, 16 November 1993.
27 Mitchell, *Messages*, 26.
28 "Jay Jenkins," editorial, *Charlotte Observer*, 10 March 1961.
29 Terry Sanford, scrapbook no. 2, Terry Sanford Papers, Division of Archives and History, Raleigh, 77.
30 Sanford interview, 16 November 1993.
31 Sanford, unpublished manuscript.
32 Ibid.

33 Sanford, scrapbook no. 2, 195.
34 Gene Roberts, "What Happened to the Opposition," *News & Observer*, 11 June 1961.
35 Cloyd Philpott to Terry Sanford, 25 May 1961, Official Papers of Governor Terry Sanford, North Carolina Department of Archives and History, Raleigh.
36 Hugh Cannon, interview with authors, 18 October 1993.
37 Roy Parker Jr., "Senate Approves Food Tax; House Okays Spending Bill," *News & Observer*, 9 June 1961.
38 Lynn Nesbit, Association of Afternoon Dailies, 15 June 1961.
39 Roberts, "What Happened."
40 Ibid.
41 Senator Joe Eagles to Terry Sanford, 1961, Official Papers of Governor Terry Sanford, North Carolina Department of Archives and History, Raleigh. C&D refers to Conservation and Development.
42 Sanford, scrapbook no. 2, 700.
43 Sanford interview, 16 November 1993.
44 Hugh Cannon, interview with authors, 15 December 1993.
45 Sanford interview, 16 November 1993.
46 Cannon interview, 15 December 1993.
47 Ibid.
48 Cecil Sanford to Terry Sanford, 3 November 1961, Official Papers of Governor Terry Sanford, North Carolina Department of Archives and History, Raleigh.
49 Tom Lambeth, interview with authors, 30 December 1993.
50 Sanford interview, 16 November 1993.
51 Terry Sanford, journal, book no. 8, Duke University Archives.
52 Mitchell, *Messages*, 150.
53 Terry Sanford Papers, Southern Historical Collection.
54 Taylor Branch, *Parting the Waters* (New York: Simon & Schuster, 1988), 441.
55 Mitchell, *Messages*, 555.
56 Bert Bennett to C. C. Hope, 25 May 1964, Terry Sanford Papers, Southern Historical Collection, University of North Carolina Library, Chapel Hill.
57 "Under the Dome," *News & Observer*, 7 September 1961.
58 Sanford interview, 16 November 1993.
59 Roy Parker Jr., "Gov. Begins State Tour for Schools," *News & Observer*, 1 November 1961.
60 W. D. S., "The Sanford Dip," editorial, *Greensboro Daily News*, 14 December 1961.
61 Cannon interview, 15 December 1993.
62 Sanford, scrapbook no. 2, 742.
63 Lou Harris, *Survey of North Carolina Political Climate*, December 1961, Terry Sanford Papers, Duke University Archives.

12   A Shore Still Dimly Seen

1   Tape recording, Terry Sanford Papers, Southern Historical Collection, University of North Carolina Library, Chapel Hill.
2   Terry Sanford, scrapbook no. 3, Terry Sanford Papers, Division of Archives and History, Raleigh, 176.
3   Terry Sanford, interview with authors, 16 November 1993.
4   Ibid.
5   Ibid.
6   Terry Sanford, unpublished manuscript, Duke University Archives.
7   Ibid.
8   McNeill Smith, interview with authors, 17 April 1996.
9   Terry Sanford, interview with authors, 26 June 1997.
10 A. L. Fletcher, *A History of Ashe County* (Jefferson, NC: Ashe County Research Association, 1963).

11 Tom Ellis, interview with authors, 14 October 1997.

12 Ibid.

13 Hargrove Bowles to Terry Sanford, 21 March 1963, Official Papers of Governor Terry Sanford, North Carolina Department of Archives and History, Raleigh.

14 Clint Newton, interview with authors, 12 July 1995.

15 H. L. Riddle to Terry Sanford, nd, Official Papers of Governor Terry Sanford, North Carolina Department of Archives and History, Raleigh.

16 Hugh Cannon, interview with authors, 15 December 1993.

17 State Highway Patrol reports, 9 June 1961, Official Papers of Governor Terry Sanford, North Carolina Department of Archives and History, Raleigh.

18 John R. Larkins to Governor Terry Sanford, "Report on Anson County and Monroe Race Situation," July 1961, Official Papers of Governor Terry Sanford, North Carolina Department of Archives and History, Raleigh.

19 Hugh Canon to John Seigenthaler, 2 August 1961, Official Papers of Governor Terry Sanford, North Carolina Department of Archives and History, Raleigh.

20 Audiotape, 31 August 1961, press conference, Terry Sanford Papers, Southern Historical Collection, University of North Carolina, Chapel Hill.

21 Sanford interview, 26 June 1997.

22 August Meier and Elliott Rudwick, CORE: A Study in the Civil Rights Movement 1942–1968 (New York: Oxford University Press, 1973), 170.

23 James Farmer, Lay Bare the Heart: An Autobiography of the Civil Rights Movement (New York: Arbor House, 1985), 240.

24 Thomas Pearsall to Terry Sanford, 29 May 1961, Official Papers of Governor Terry Sanford, North Carolina Department of Archives and History, Raleigh.

25 Elizabeth Pearsall, interview with Walter Campbell, 25 May 1988.

26 John Winters, interview with authors, 4 May 1995.

27 Ibid.

28 Ibid.

29 Farmer, Lay Bare the Heart, 242.

30 Sanford, unpublished manuscript.

31 C. R. Roderick to Lawrence O'Brien, nd, Official Papers of Governor Terry Sanford, North Carolina Department of Archives and History, Raleigh.

32 "Terry Sanford, a Young Southern Governor Who Thrives on Breaking the Old Rules of Politics," Look, 19 June 1962.

33 William Shires, Association of Afternoon Dailies, 2 October 1962.

34 Terry Sanford, interview with authors, 18 August 1993.

35 Joe Ross to Terry Sanford, 1 October 1962; C. C. McKinnon to Terry Sanford, 26 September 1962, Official Papers of Governor Terry Sanford, North Carolina Department of Archives and History, Raleigh.

36 James P. Dees to Terry Sanford, 25 and 27 September 1962, Official Papers of Governor Terry Sanford, North Carolina Department of Archives and History, Raleigh.

37 Terry Sanford to James Dees, 27 September 1962, Official Papers of Governor Terry Sanford, North Carolina Department of Archives and History, Raleigh.

38 William L. Clarke Jr. to Terry Sanford, 14 August 1961, Official Papers of Governor Terry Sanford, North Carolina Department of Archives and History, Raleigh.

39 Terry Sanford, interview with authors, 16 November 1993.

40 Sanford, unpublished manuscript.

41 Ibid.

42 Tom Wood, "Raleigh Negroes Issued Challenge," News & Observer, 20 November 1961.

43 Memory F. Mitchell, ed., Messages, Addresses, and Public Papers of Terry Sanford, Governor of North Carolina, 1961–1965 (Raleigh: Council of State, 1966) 277.

44 Terry Sanford, interview with authors, 29 December 1993.

45 David Cooper, "Sanford Puts Record on Line," News & Observer, 21 October 1962.

46 Terry Sanford, scrapbook no. 6, Terry Sanford Papers, Division of Archives and History, Raleigh, 40.

47 Jack Potts to Terry Sanford, nd, Official Papers of Governor Terry Sanford, North Carolina Department of Archives and History, Raleigh.

48 Mitchell, *Messages*, 301.

49 John Ehle, *The Free Men* (New York: Harper & Row, 1965), 57.

13   But What About the People?

1 "Next Governor Will Lead Maryland in New Direction," *Washington Post*, 31 October 1994.

2 Terry Sanford with unknown interviewer, nd, audiotape no. 95, Terry Sanford Papers, Southern Historical Collection, University of North Carolina, Chapel Hill.

3 John Ehle, *The Free Men* (New York: Harper & Row, 1965), 57.

4 Ibid., 58.

5 Ibid.

6 Memory F. Mitchell, ed., *Messages, Addresses, and Public Papers of Terry Sanford, Governor of North Carolina, 1961–1965* (Raleigh: Council of State, 1966), 578.

7 Ehle, *The Free Men*, 61.

8 Editorial, *Los Angeles Times*, 30 January 1963.

9 "A Good Neighbor," *Louisville Courier–Journal*, 30 January 1963.

10 Lewis Dowdy to Terry Sanford, 25 January 1963, Official Papers of Governor Terry Sanford, North Carolina Department of Archives and History, Raleigh.

11 Gene Earl Vinson to Terry Sanford, David Douglas to Terry Sanford, Jacqueline Harrell to Terry Sanford, 24 January 1963, Official Papers of Governor Terry Sanford, North Carolina Department of Archives and History, Raleigh.

12 Joseph Knox, "Caswell Rally Held to Fight Racial Mixing," *Greensboro Daily News*, 4 February 1963.

13 Ibid.

14 Terry Sanford, unpublished manuscript, Duke University Archives.

15 John Ehle, interview with authors, 27 October 1993.

16 Ibid.

17 Ibid.

18 Leslie Banner, *A Passionate Preference: The Story of the North Carolina School of the Arts* (Winston-Salem: North Carolina School of the Arts Foundation, 1987), 20.

19 Ehle interview.

20 Ibid.

21 Terry Sanford, interview with authors, 1 February 1994.

22 Terry Sanford, *But What About the People?* (New York: Harper & Row, 1966), 123.

23 Paul Ylvisaker, interview with Charles T. Morrissey, 27 September and 27 October 1973, Ford Foundation Archives, New York City.

24 John Ehle to Vannevar Bush, 2 December 1962, Official Papers of Governor Terry Sanford, North Carolina Department of Archives and History, Raleigh.

25 Mitchell, *Messages*, 34.

26 Ibid., 292.

27 Dallas Herring, interview with authors, 10 February 1996.

28 William A. Link, *William Friday: Power, Purpose & American Higher Education* (Chapel Hill: University of North Carolina Press, 1995), 166.

29 "Senate OKs Funds for Arts School," *News & Observer*, 18 June 1963.

30 Tom Inman, "Arts School Bill Enacted," *News & Observer*, 22 June 1963.

31 Banner, *A Passionate Preference*, 101.

32 Terry Sanford, interview with Joe B. Frantz, 15 May 1971, Oral History Collection, Lyndon B. Johnson Presidential Library, Austin.

33 Mitchell, *Messages*, 344.
34 David Cooper, "Two States' Rights Bills Die in House," *News & Observer*, 14 June 1963.
35 "Sit-In Issue Raised in Money Committee," *News & Observer*, 20 February 1963.
36 Hugh Cannon, interview with authors, 15 December 1993.
37 Roy Parker Jr., "Marchers' Footsteps Echoed in Assembly," *News & Observer*, 29 June 1963.
38 Terry Sanford, scrapbook no. 7, Official Papers of Governor Terry Sanford, North Carolina Department of Archives and History, Raleigh.
39 Jane Hall, "Governor Urges Tension Calmness," *News & Observer*, 11 May 1963.
40 John Winters, interview with authors, 4 May 1995.
41 Terry Sanford, unpublished manuscript, Duke University Archives.
42 Betsee Sanford, interview with authors, 24 April 1996.
43 Tom Lambeth, interview with authors, 30 December 1993.
44 Bob Lynch and Roy Parker Jr., "Negroes Boo Gov. at Mansion," *News & Observer*, 11 May 1963.
45 Winters interview.
46 Ibid.
47 Terry Sanford, interview with authors, 29 December 1993.
48 William H. Chafe, *Civilities and Civil Rights: Greensboro, North Carolina and the Black Struggle for Freedom* (New York: Oxford University Press, 1980), 133.
49 Sanford interview, 29 December 1993.
50 Ibid.
51 James Farmer, *Lay Bare the Heart: An Autobiography of the Civil Rights Movement* (New York: Arbor House, 1985), 241.
52 Nelson Benton, audio recording of CBS News report, 24 June 1963, Terry Sanford Papers, Southern Historical Collection, University of North Carolina, Chapel Hill.
53 Terry Sanford, press conference, 21 May 1963, audiotape no. 113, Terry Sanford Papers, Southern Historical Collection, University of North Carolina, Chapel Hill.
54 Hugh Cannon, interview with authors, 18 October 1993.
55 Terry Sanford Papers, Southern Historical Collection, University of North Carolina, Chapel Hill.
56 Cannon interview, 18 October 1993.
57 *Viewpoint* no. 636, 21 June 1963, WRAL-TV, Raleigh.
58 *Viewpoint* no. 593, 22 April 1963, WRAL-TV, Raleigh.
59 Sanford interview, 29 December 1993.
60 Mitchell, *Messages*, 597.
61 Roy Parker Jr., "Negro Leaders Reject Plea by Sanford; Plan Protests," *News & Observer*, 26 June 1963.
62 Ibid.
63 Capus Waynick, interview with Bill Finger, 4 February 1974, Southern Oral History Program, Southern Historical Collection, University of North Carolina, Chapel Hill.
64 Ibid.
65 Terry Sanford, interview with authors, 14 March 1994.
66 Sanford, scrapbook no. 7.
67 Terry Sanford, unpublished manuscript, Duke University Archives.
68 James Ross, "Action Urged in Resolving Rights Issue," *Greensboro Daily News*, 6 July 1963.
69 Mitchell, *Messages*, 600.
70 David Gergen, interview with authors, 29 March 1996.
71 Farmer, *Lay Bare the Heart*, 243.
72 Brandt Ayers, "Thurmond Skipped Protocol," *News & Observer*, 28 July 1963.
73 Sanford, scrapbook no. 7.
74 Ibid.
75 Terry Sanford, interview with Ann M. Campbell, 27 July 1970, Oral History Collection, John F. Kennedy Library, Boston.

76 Undated memorandum, Terry Sanford Papers, Duke University Archives.

77 Joel Fleishman to Henry Mayer, nd, Official Papers of Governor Terry Sanford, North Carolina Department of Archives and History, Raleigh; Roy Wilkins statement, Terry Sanford Papers, Duke University Archives.

78 Paul Ylvisaker, Oral History transcript, Ford Foundation Archives, New York City.

79 Ibid.

80 Sanford, *But What About the People?*, 125.

81 Ibid., 129.

82 Ibid., 4.

83 Mitchell, *Messages*, 601.

84 Ibid.

85 George Esser, *An Oral History of the North Carolina Fund*, Southern Historical Collection, University of North Carolina, Chapel Hill, June, 1990.

86 Emily Herring Wilson, *For the People of North Carolina* (Winston-Salem: Z. Smith Reynolds Foundation, 1988), 72.

87 Sanford, *But What About the People?*, 131.

88 Ibid., 136.

89 Wilson, *For the People*, 76.

90 Quoted in David E. Brown, "N.C. Fund Yields Legacy of Progress," *Philanthropy Journal* (May 1994).

91 Terry Sanford, press conference, 20 April 1964, audiotape no. 142, Terry Sanford Papers, Southern Historical Collection, University of North Carolina, Chapel Hill.

92 Martha McKay, interview with authors, 6 March 1996.

93 Terry Sanford, unpublished manuscript, Duke University Archives.

94 Oliver Quayle III to Terry Sanford, 18 April 1961, Official Papers of Governor Terry Sanford, North Carolina Department of Archives and History, Raleigh.

95 Mitchell, *Messages*, 607.

96 Terry Sanford, interview with authors, 1 February 1994.

97 Mitchell, *Messages*, 621.

98 Robert F. Kennedy to Terry Sanford, 10 August 1963; Terry Sanford to Robert F. Kennedy, Official Papers of Governor Terry Sanford, North Carolina Department of Archives and History, Raleigh.

99 Terry Sanford, interview with Brent Glass, 20–21 August 1976, Southern Oral History Program, Southern Historical Collection, University of North Carolina, Chapel Hill.

100 Bert Bennett to Terry Sanford, 13 September 1962, Official Papers of Governor Terry Sanford, North Carolina Department of Archives and History, Raleigh.

101 Roy Parker Jr., "Eastern Carolinians Are Mostly Undecided about Next Gov.," *News & Observer*, 23 July 1963.

102 David Britt to Bert Bennett, 16 January 1963, Official Papers of Governor Terry Sanford, North Carolina Department of Archives and History, Raleigh.

103 Bert Bennett to William Joslin, 20 September 1963, Official Papers of Governor Terry Sanford, North Carolina Department of Archives and History, Raleigh.

104 "Under the Dome," *News & Observer*, 27 July 1963.

105 Sanford interview, 1 February 1994.

106 J. Phillips Carlton, interview with authors, 4 May 1998.

107 Ibid.

108 Terry Sanford, interview with authors.

109 Robert W. Scott, interview with authors, 7 May 1998.

110 James R. Spence, *The Making of a Governor: The Moore-Preyer-Lake Primaries of 1964* (Winston-Salem, NC: J. F. Blair Publishers, 1968), 32.

111 Joel Fleishman to Henry Mayer, nd, Official Papers of Governor Terry Sanford, North Carolina Department of Archives and History, Raleigh.

112 Associated Press, "Negro Leaders Okay Mass Raleigh March," *News & Observer*, 20 September 1963.
113 Terry Sanford to Capus Waynick, 18 August 1983, Official Papers of Governor Terry Sanford, North Carolina Department of Archives and History, Raleigh.
114 Samuel Proctor, interview with authors, 1 May 1996.
115 Ibid.
116 Jesse Jackson to Terry Sanford, 30 October 1963, Terry Sanford Papers, Duke University Archives.
117 *Knocking at the Gate*, North Carolina Intercollegiate Council for Human Rights and North Carolina Film Board, North Carolina Department of Archives and History, Raleigh.
118 Jackson to Sanford, 30 October 1963.
119 Marshall Frady, *Jesse: The Life and Pilgrimage of Jesse Jackson* (New York: Random House, 1996), 183.
120 William Shires, Association of Afternoon Dailies, 15 February 1964.
121 Ehle, *Free Men*, 154.
122 Sanford interview, 1 February 1994.
123 Cannon interview, 15 December 1993.
124 Ibid.
125 Bert Bennett, interview with authors, 10 September 1997.
126 "Jay Jenkins," editorial, *Charlotte Observer*, 5 April 1964.
127 Sanford interview, 1 February 1994.
128 Carlton interview, 4 May 1998.
129 Paid advertisement, *News & Observer*, 26 June 1964.
130 Sanford interview, 1 February 1994.
131 Mitchell, *Messages*, 450.
132 Ehle, *Free Men*, 292.
133 Sanford interview with Glass.
134 Tom Inman, "Ex-Lake Voters Swing the Race," *News & Observer*, 24 June 1964.
135 *Report of Good Neighbor Council to Governor Terry Sanford*, 1 March 1964, Terry Sanford Papers, Duke University Archives.
136 Hargrove Bowles, speech, 3 November 1964, Terry Sanford Papers, Duke University Archives.
137 Terry Sanford, scrapbook no. 8, Official Papers of Governor Terry Sanford, North Carolina Department of Archives and History, Raleigh.
138 Sam Ragan, ed., *The New Day* (Zebulon, NC: Record Publishing Co., 1964), 105.
139 Quoted in *Yale Daily News*, 18 November 1994.
140 Hugh Morton, personal communication with authors.
141 Sanford, scrapbook no. 8.
142 Terry Sanford, private memo to authors, nd.
143 J. T. Gresham Jr. to Terry Sanford, 1 November 1961, Official Papers of Governor Terry Sanford, North Carolina Department of Archives and History, Raleigh.
144 Mitchell, *Messages*, 479.
145 Terry Sanford, "The Case for the New South," *Look*, 15 December 1964.
146 Ibid.

14   New Horizons

1 Hugh Cannon, interview with authors, 25 April 1994.
2 James B. Conant, *My Several Lives: Memoirs of a Social Inventor* (New York: Harper & Row, 1970), 649.
3 Eli Evans, interview with authors, 26 January 1996.
4 Terry Sanford, unpublished manuscript, Duke University Archives.
5 Terry Sanford, interview with authors, 1 February 1994.

6 Terry Sanford, interview with Brent Glass, 20–21 August 1976, Southern Oral History Program, Southern Historical Collection, University of North Carolina, Chapel Hill.

7 Terry Sanford, interview with Joe B. Frantz, 15 May 1971, Oral History Collection, Lyndon B. Johnson Presidential Library, Austin.

8 Paul Popple to Walter Jenkins, 20 August 1964, Presidential Papers, Lyndon B. Johnson Presidential Library, Austin.

9 Marvin Watson to Lyndon B. Johnson, 16 July 1966, Presidential Papers, Lyndon B. Johnson Presidential Library, Austin.

10 Oliver Quayle III, *Survey of North Carolina Politics, November 1967*, Terry Sanford Papers, Southern Historical Collection, University of North Carolina, Chapel Hill.

11 Terry Sanford Papers, Southern Historical Collection, University of North Carolina, Chapel Hill.

12 Ibid.

13 Quayle, *Survey of North Carolina Politics*.

14 Terry Sanford, interview with authors, 9 February 1994.

15 Hugh Cannon, interview with authors, 25 April 1994.

16 Sanford interview, 9 February 1994.

17 Ibid.

18 Ibid.

19 Ibid.

20 Ibid.

21 Tom Wicker, "Another 'Southern Strategy,' " *New York Times*, 25 August 1968.

22 Betsee Sanford, interview with authors, 26 April 1996.

23 Sanford interview, 9 February 1994.

24 Ibid.

25 Ibid.

26 Sam Poole, interview with authors, 15 March 1994.

27 Cannon interview.

28 Sanford interview, 9 February 1994.

29 Pat Black, "Knight Warns Against Campus Revolt," *Duke Chronicle*, 5 February 1969.

30 Douglas M. Knight, *Street of Dreams: The Nature and Legacy of the 1960s* (Durham, NC: Duke University Press, 1989), 135.

31 Ibid., 137.

32 United Press International, "Knight Decries Turmoil," *Duke Chronicle*, 8 May 1969.

33 Mary Semans, interview with authors, 11 September 1995.

34 Sanford interview, 9 February 1994.

35 Terry Sanford to William Benton, 29 April 1968, Terry Sanford Papers, Southern Historical Collection, University of North Carolina, Chapel Hill.

36 Sanford interview, 9 February 1994.

37 Poole interview.

38 Terry Sanford, interview with authors, 15 March 1994.

39 Terry Sanford, Duke journal, 17 March 1970, Duke University Archives.

40 J. Alex McMahon, interview with authors, 11 January 1996.

41 Sanford, Duke journal.

42 Semans interview.

43 Sanford interview, 9 February 1994.

44 Ibid.

45 Sanford, Duke journal.

46 Ibid.

47 Ralph Karpinos, "Sanford Named President," *Duke Chronicle*, 15 December 1969.

48 A. J. Fletcher to Terry Sanford, nd, quoted in Sanford journal, Duke University Archives.

1   Terry Sanford, unpublished manuscript, Terry Sanford Papers, Duke University Archives.
2   Bill Green, interview with authors, 7 March 1995.
3   Terry Sanford, interview with authors, 9 January 1998.
4   Terry Sanford, Duke journal, 2 April 1970, Duke University Archives.
5   "Here to Stay?", editorial, *Duke Chronicle*, 10 March 1970.
6   Tom Drew, interview with authors, 10 May 1995.
7   Quoted in Robert J. Bliwise, "Remembering an Uncommon President," *Duke Magazine* (May–June 1998): special section.
8   Ibid.
9   Terry Sanford, interview with authors, 15 March 1994.
10 Ibid.
11 "Faculty Telegram," *Duke Chronicle*, 8 May 1970.
12 Mike Mooney and Jinx Johnstone, "Rally Begins Second Day of Protest," *Duke Chronicle*, 7 May 1970.
13 Quoted in Bliwise, "Remembering."
14 "Strike," *Duke Chronicle*, 7 May 1970.
15 Sanford interview, 15 March 1994.
16 Sanford, Duke journal, nd.
17 Ibid.
18 Mary Semans, interview with authors, 11 September 1995.
19 Terry Sanford, interview with authors, 10 January 1996.
20 Sanford interview, 15 March 1994.
21 Sanford, Duke journal.
22 "Sanford on Unions, Women, Dorms," *Duke Chronicle*, 9 April 1970.
23 Terry Sanford, inauguration speech, 17 October 1970, Terry Sanford Papers, Duke University Archives.
24 Sanford interview, 15 March 1994.
25 John Nordheimer, "Duke President Viewed as '72 Democratic Hope," *New York Times*, 11 October 1970.
26 Quoted in Bliwise, "Remembering."
27 James F. Cook, *Carl Sanders, Spokesman of the New South* (Macon, GA: Mercer University Press, 1993), 327.
28 Sanford interview, 10 January 1996.
29 Terry Sanford, "A Southern Regional Growth Board," 2 May 1971, Duke University Archives.
30 Jon Nordheimer, "Rally Bids South Fight Urban Ills," *New York Times*, 3 May 1971.
31 Sanford interview, 10 January 1996.
32 Terry Sanford, "A Memo to Mr. Agnew," *New York Times*, 17 November 1970.
33 Nordheimer, "Duke President."
34 Sanford interview, 15 March 1994.
35 Terry Sanford, "Gold Memorandum," Terry Sanford Papers, Duke University Archives.
36 Ibid.
37 J. Alex McMahon, interview with authors, 11 January 1996.
38 Sanford, "Gold Memorandum."
39 Ibid.
40 McMahon interview.
41 Robert W. Scott, interview with authors, 7 May 1998.
42 Tom Lambeth, interview with authors, 30 December 1993.
43 Sanford interview, 15 March 1994.
44 Ibid.

45 Terry Sanford, interview with authors, 20 April 1994.
46 Ferrell Guillory, *New Orleans States-Item*, 6 March 1972.
47 Andy Parker, "Sanford Officially Declares for Presidency," *Duke Chronicle*, 9 March 1972.
48 "President: U.S. or Duke?", *Duke Chronicle*, 10 March 1972.
49 "Enter Mr. Sanford," editorial, *New York Times*, 14 March 1972.
50 Joe Napolitan to John Hoving, 17 April 1972, Terry Sanford Papers, Southern Historical Collection, University of North Carolina, Chapel Hill.
51 Quoted in Stephen Lesher, *George Wallace: American Populist* (Reading, MA: Addison-Wesley, 1994), 470.
52 "Wallace Moves North," *Newsweek*, 1 May 1972; Sanford interview, 20 April 1994.
53 Personal recollection of Howard E. Covington Jr.
54 Polly Paddock, "Terry Labels Wallace Man of Blocked Doors," *Charlotte Observer*, 19 April 1972.
55 Paul Clancy, "Wallace Foes in Alabama Look Lovingly at Sanford," *Charlotte Observer*, 13 April 1972.
56 Terry Sanford, interview with authors, 9 February 1994.
57 Cited in Tom Wicker, "Sanford Squaring Off with Wallace," *News & Observer*, 17 April 1972.
58 Notes, Sanford telethon, Charlotte, 2 May 1972, Terry Sanford Papers, Southern Historical Collection, University of North Carolina, Chapel Hill.
59 Julian Scheer, interview with authors, 10 May 1995.
60 Sam Poole, interview with authors, 13 February 1996.
61 Sanford interview, 9 February 1994.
62 Ibid.
63 Sanford interview, 20 April 1994.
64 Terry Sanford, statement, 10 May 1972, Duke University Archives.
65 Quoted in Joe Doster, "Sanford Is Getting Delegate Attention," *Winston-Salem Journal*, 12 July 1972.
66 Drew interview, 10 May 1995.
67 Scheer interview, 10 May 1995.
68 Julian Scheer to Howard Covington, 23 April 1998, private collection.
69 Quoted in J. A. C. Dunn, *Chapel Hill Newspaper*, July 1972.
70 Ibid; quoted in Robert Sherrill, *Saturday Review*, 17 June 1972.
71 Drew interview, 10 May 1995; Sanford interview, 9 January 1998.
72 James Wooten, *Dasher: The Roots and the Rising of Jimmy Carter* (New York: Summit Books, 1978), 312.
73 Hamilton Jordan to Robert Strauss, 12 June 1973, Terry Sanford Papers, Duke University Archives.
74 Terry Sanford, speech, 4 December 1975, Democratic Charter Commission, Duke University Archives.
75 Anne Newman, "Sanford Announces Presidential Bid," *Duke Chronicle*, 2 June 1975.
76 Julian Scheer to Howard Covington, private collection.
77 Lesher, *George Wallace*, 494.
78 Newman, "Sanford Announces."
79 Jon Buchan, "Sanford Tuning In on S.C.," *Charlotte Observer*, 8 June 1975.
80 Sanford interview, 10 January 1996.
81 Joel Fleishman, interview with authors, 22 March 1996.
82 Sanford interview, 20 April 1994.
83 Bob Kolin, "Sanford Calls for Boldness," *Duke Chronicle*, 30 June 1975.
84 Willis Whichard, interview with authors, 24 August 1998.
85 Jules Witcover, *Marathon: The Pursuit of the Presidency, 1972–1976* (New York: Viking, 1977), 149.
86 Bill Green to Terry Sanford, nd, Terry Sanford Papers, Duke University Archives.

87 Quoted in Christopher Colford, "Sanford Is Hospitalized," *Duke Chronicle*, 13 January 1976.
88 Sanford interview, 10 January 1996.
89 Sam Poole, interview with authors, 13 February 1996.
90 Terry Sanford, statement, 26 January 1976, Duke University Archives.
91 Eric Severied, CBS News, 27 January 1976.

16 *"Outrageous Ambitions"*

1 Terry Sanford, interview with authors, 9 January 1998.
2 Terry Sanford, interview with authors, 10 January 1996.
3 J. Alex McMahon, interview with authors, 11 January 1996.
4 Keith Brodie and Leslie Banner, *Keeping an Open Door: Passages in a University Presidency* (Durham, NC: Duke University Press, 1996), 8.
5 McMahon interview.
6 J. B. Fuqua, interview with authors, 13 February 1998.
7 Terry Sanford, Duke journal, Duke University Archives.
8 Sanford interview, 10 January 1996.
9 Robert J. Bliwise, "Go to the Head of the Class," *Duke Magazine*, November–December 1997.
10 Joel Fleishman, interview with authors, 22 March 1996.
11 Terry Sanford, *A Danger of Democracy: The Presidential Nominating Process* (Boulder, CO: Westview, 1981), 100.
12 Ibid., 101.
13 McMahon interview.
14 Terry Sanford to Duke University Board of Trustees Executive Committee, 8 August 1981, Terry Sanford Papers, Duke University Archives.
15 Associated Press, "Nixon Studious at Duke," *Greensboro Daily News*, 18 August 1981.
16 Sanford, Duke journal.
17 Terry Sanford to Charles Rhyne, 27 March 1973, Terry Sanford Papers, Duke University Archives.
18 Terry Sanford to Richard Nixon, 21 May 1973, Terry Sanford Papers, Duke University Archives.
19 David N. Parker to Terry Sanford, 30 May 1973, Terry Sanford Papers, Duke University Archives.
20 Sanford to Duke University Board of Trustees Executive Committee.
21 Quoted in "The Nixon Library: Opening the Door to Debate," *Duke Alumni Register* 68, no. 1 (September–October 1981).
22 Sanford interview, 10 January 1996.
23 Edwin Cady to Terry Sanford, 15 August 1981, Terry Sanford Papers, Duke University Archives.
24 Sanford interview, 10 January 1996.
25 James David Barber, "Duke Not Place for Nixon Library," *Duke Chronicle*, 8 September 1981.
26 Quoted in Erica Johnson, "Trustee Panel Okays Plan," *Duke Chronicle*, 8 September 1981.
27 Quoted in "An Account of Faculty Opposition to the Nixon Library Proposal," *Duke Alumni Register* 68, no. 1 (September–October 1981).
28 McMahon interview.
29 Charles Tanford to Trustees of Duke University, 16 September 1981, Terry Sanford Papers, Duke University Archives.
30 Quoted in Joyce Leviton, "North Carolina's Terry Sanford Goes Dukes Up to Get a Nixon Library," *People*, 28 September 1981.
31 Bill Green, interview with authors, 7 March 1996.

32   "An Account of Faculty Opposition."
33   Terry Sanford, notes of Research Triangle Park meeting, 19 September 1998, Duke University Archives.
34   Ibid.
35   Ibid.
36   Ibid.
37   Sanford interview, 10 January 1996.
38   Terry Sanford, "On Doing the Right Thing," speech delivered to Academic Council, Duke University, 15 December 1983, Terry Sanford Papers, Duke University Archives.
39   Sanford interview, 10 January 1996.
40   "An Honor Code Now?", Duke Chronicle, 1 September 1978.
41   Terry Sanford, "An Avuncular Letter," Terry Sanford Papers, Duke University Archives.
42   Terry Sanford, speech to Duke faculty, 25 October 1984, Terry Sanford Papers, Duke University Archives.
43   Quoted in Bill Arthur, "From Crisis to Consensus," Duke Magazine, May–June 1985.
44   Paul Gaffney, "Building the University," Duke Chronicle, 19 April 1985.
45   Quoted in Duke Magazine, May–June 1985.
46   Brodie and Banner, Keeping an Open Door, 37.
47   Tom Lambeth, speech, Sanford tribute dinner, 2 May 1985, Terry Sanford Papers, Duke University Archives.
48   Townsend Davis, "Architect Chosen for Community," Duke Chronicle, 28 September 1984.
49   "Sanford to Remain Busy," Duke Chronicle, 26 July 1984.
50   Sanford interview, 10 January 1996.
51   Ed Farrell, "Sanford Stays On as President Emeritus," Duke Chronicle, 4 July 1985.
52   Ken Eudy and Tim Funk, "Sanford Drops Out of U.S. Senate Race Two Weeks after Launching Candidacy," Charlotte Observer, 25 September 1985.
53   Sanford interview, 10 January 1996.
54   William A. Link, William Friday: Power, Purpose & American Higher Education (Chapel Hill: University of North Carolina Press, 1995), 372.
55   Sanford interview, 10 January 1996.
56   Ken Eudy, "Sanford Plans Political Comeback," Charlotte Observer, 14 September 1985.
57   Eudy and Funk, "Sanford Dropping Out."
58   "Faircloth Decides to Avoid Rigors of U.S. Senate Race," Charlotte Observer, 17 October 1985.
59   Tom Drew, private communication with authors, 27 April 1998.
60   Sam Poole, interview with authors, 13 February 1996.
61   Robert W. Scott, interview with authors, 7 May 1998.
62   Tim Funk, "Ex-Gov. Terry Sanford to Enter Senate Race," Charlotte Observer, 12 January 1986.
63   J. B. Pritzker, interview with authors, 11 October 1995.
64   Ibid.
65   Elizabeth Leland, "Democratic Challengers Far Behind," Charlotte Observer, 7 May 1986.
66   "The Primaries: Reaffirming Good Traditions," editorial, Charlotte Observer, 8 May 1986.
67   Tim Funk, "Sanford Faces Food Tax Issue Head-On," Charlotte Observer, 16 October 1986.
68   The Communication Company to Terry Sanford, 4 October 1986, Terry Sanford Papers, Duke University Archives.
69   Sanford interview, 10 January 1996.
70   Quoted in Bill Arthur, "Key Voters Saw Sanford as Better Leader, Analysts Say," Charlotte Observer, 21 November 1986.
71   Pritzker interview.
72   Bill Arthur, "Sanford Dissects His Win: Because I Got More Votes," Charlotte Observer, 6 November 1986.
73   "Sanford Beats Odds with Dignified Race," editorial, Durham Herald, 5 November 1986;

Jack Claiborne, "Sanford, Helms State's Contradictory Politics Rooted in Historic Dichotomy," *Charlotte Observer*, 8 November 1986.

74 Quoted in Bill Arthur, "Key Voters Saw Sanford as Better Leader, Analysts Say," *Charlotte Observer*, 21 November 1986.

75 Ibid.

17 Never Look Back

1 Howard Covington, *Uncommon Giving: A. J. Fletcher and a North Carolina Legacy* (Raleigh, NC: A. J. Fletcher Foundation, 1999).

2 Tom Ellis, interview with authors, 17 August 1998.

3 Terry Sanford, interview with authors, 10 December 1997.

4 J. Phillips Carlton, interview with authors, 27 April 1998.

5 Terry Sanford, interview with authors, 18 March 1998.

6 Terry Sanford, interview with authors, 24 March 1998.

7 Terry Sanford, journal, Duke University Archives.

8 Quoted in David Morrison, " 'Varmint Dinner' Fare Looks Foul to Invitees," *Atlanta Constitution*, 4 April 1980.

9 Sanford journal.

10 Jennifer Hillman, interview with authors, 21 November 1997.

11 Sanford interview, 10 December 1997.

12 Jim Martin, quoted in Danny Lineberry, "GOP Whacks 'Turnaround,' " *Durham Herald*, 3 April 1987; "Was Sanford Confused?", editorial, *Durham Herald*, 13 April 1987; Doug Marlette, cartoon, *Charlotte Observer*, 5 May 1997.

13 Sanford interview, 10 December 1997.

14 Ibid.

15 Ibid.

16 Bill Green, interview with authors, 7 March 1996.

17 Sonia Picado, interview with authors, 9 February 1998.

18 Arthur Levitt Jr., interview with authors, 12 February 1998.

19 Sanford journal.

20 Ibid.

21 Speech, Sanford journal.

22 Picado speech, Sanford journal.

23 Arthur Levitt Jr. and Sonia Picado, *The Report of the International Commission for Central American Recovery and Development: Poverty, Conflict and Hope* (Durham, NC: Duke University Press, 1989), 81.

24 William Ascher, "Summary of Work of ICCARD," *Congressional Record*, U.S. Senate, 14 May 1991.

25 Ferrel Guillory, "Central America a Magnet to Tar Heel Senators," *News & Observer*, 14 April 1989.

26 Sanford interview, 10 December 1997.

27 Picado interview.

28 Levitt interview.

29 Bob Dole to Terry Sanford, 11 July 1989, Terry Sanford Papers, Special Collections Library, Duke University; John F. Kerry to Terry Sanford, 15 May 1990, Terry Sanford Papers, Special Collections Library, Duke University.

30 Sanford interview, 10 December 1997.

31 Sanford journal.

32 Bill Green, interview with authors, 8 December 1997.

33 Terry Sanford, unpublished manuscript, Duke University Archives.

34 Sanford interview, 24 March 1998.

35 Terry Sanford, *Congressional Record*, 1 October 1987.

36 "Sen. Helms Has a Tough Day During Committee Meeting," *News & Observer*, 15 September 1988.

37 Recorded in Sanford journal.

38 David Broder, editorial, *Washington Post*, 24 March 1990.

39 Marshall Frady, *Jesse: The Life and Pilgrimage of Jesse Jackson* (New York: Random House, 1996), 181.

18 A North Carolina Regular

1 Terry Sanford, journal, Duke University Archives.

2 Ibid.

3 Ellis Gibbs Arnall, *What the People Want* (New York: Lippincott, 1947), 45.

4 Owen Ullman and Ellen Warren, "Bush Backs Flag Amendment 100 Percent," *Charlotte Observer*, 26 July 1989.

5 Sanford journal.

6 Ibid.

7 U.S. Senate, *Congressional Record*, 101st Cong., 1st session, 17 October 1989.

8 Ibid.

9 Mark Gruenberg, "Sanford Marches to National Drumbeat," *Chapel Hill Newspaper*, 29 November 1988.

10 Sanford journal.

11 Terry Sanford to William J. Armfield IV, 28 September 1989, Terry Sanford Papers, Duke University Archives.

12 Willis Whichard, interview with authors, 24 August 1998.

13 Sanford journal.

14 Paula Levine, interview with authors, 26 April 1998.

15 Ibid.

16 Sanford journal.

17 Ibid.

18 Ibid.

19 Matthew Davis, "Sanford: Bar Attack This Year," *Charlotte Observer*, 5 January 1991.

20 U.S. Senate, *Congressional Record*, 101st Congress, 11 January 1991.

21 Sanford journal.

22 John Monk, "Sanford Still Confident Despite Polls, Criticism," *Charlotte Observer*, 25 February 1991.

23 "Confidential Draft," Terry Sanford Papers, Duke University Archives.

24 Sanford journal.

25 Jim Morrill, "Faircloth Enters Race for Senate, Sanford's First GOP Challenger Is Ex-Ally," *Charlotte Observer*, 19 April 1991.

26 Ibid.

27 Robert W. Scott, interview with authors, 7 May 1998.

28 Terry Sanford Jr., interview with authors, 26 February 1996.

29 Jim Morrill, "Sanford Tests Home Waters after War Vote," *Charlotte Observer*, 26 March 1991.

30 Tony Brown, "You Are Heroes, You Are Home: First Flights Bring Troops to Fort Bragg," *Charlotte Observer*, 9 March 1991.

31 Bruce Henderson, "Kuwait Evacuees Living in U.S. on Borrowed Time," *Charlotte Observer*, 3 September 1991.

32 Terry Sanford, interview with William Ascher, William Chafe, and Ole Holsti, 24 January 1995, Living History Program, Special Collections, Perkins Library, Duke University.

33 Tom Webb, "Four of Keating Five Get Scolding," *Charlotte Observer*, 28 February 1991.

34 Ibid.

35 Phil Kuntz, "Can Terry Sanford Play the Tough Guy?", *Congressional Quarterly*, 21 July 1991.

36 Sam Poole, interview with authors, 13 February 1996.
37 Terry Sanford, interview with authors, 10 December 1997.
38 Sanford journal.
39 "Tar Heel of the Week," *News & Observer*, 6 January 1963.
40 Jim Morrill and John Monk, "GOP's Faircloth Coasts by Myrick," *Charlotte Observer*, 6 May 1992.
41 Bill Adams to John Monk, 27 July 1992, Terry Sanford Papers, Duke University Archives.
42 Campaign memos, Terry Sanford Papers, Duke University Archives.
43 Bill Krueger, "Sanford Selling Democratic Tonic," *News & Observer*, 15 August 1992.
44 Brigid McMenamin, "Senators for Sale," *Forbes*, 2 June 1997.
45 Gregg Trevor and Jim Morrill, "Sanford to Have Surgery to Replace Heart Valve Today," *Charlotte Observer*, 9 October 1992.
46 Sanford interview, 10 December 1997.
47 "Sanford," *Durham Herald-Sun*, 9 October 1992.
48 Sanford interview, 10 December 1997.
49 Quoted in Jim Morrill, "Sanford Leaves Hospital," *Charlotte Observer*, 23 October 1992.
50 Sanford interview, 10 December 1997.
51 Jim Morrill, "Senate Race Focuses on Issues and Health," *Charlotte Observer*, 29 October 1992.
52 Ibid.
53 Tom Drew, personal communication with authors.
54 Jim Morrill and John Monk, "Faircloth Beats Sanford for Senate," *Charlotte Observer*, 4 November 1992.
55 Sanford Jr. interview.

Epilogue: The Eternal Boy Scout

1   Hugh Morton to Howard Covington, personal communication.
2   Quoted in Catherine Clabby, "Terry Sanford Puts Flesh on the Bone," *News & Observer*, 3 October 1994.
3   Edwin Yoder, "Terry Sanford Passed This Way," *Washington Post*, 12 February 1996.
4   Terry Sanford, *Outlive Your Enemies: Grow Old Gracefully* (New York: Nova Science Publishers, 1996), 94.
5   Ibid., 189.
6   John Ruemmler, interview with authors, 30 April 1998.
7   Terry Sanford to John Hope Franklin Jr., 14 June 1996, Terry Sanford Papers, Duke University Archives.
8   Tom Lambeth, interview with authors, 30 December 1993.
9   Rob Christensen, "Fighting for His Life, Sanford Reflects on It," *News & Observer*, 22 February 1998.
10 Terry Sanford, unpublished notes, Terry Sanford Papers, Duke University Archives.
11 "Sanford Remains Positive Despite Tough Battle Ahead," *News & Record*, 13 February 1998.
12 Taylor Batten, "Of All the People He Met in the World, He Remembered Me," *Charlotte Observer*, 23 April 1998.
13 These and subsequent quotations are in Terry Sanford Papers, Duke University Archives.

Bibliography

Manuscript Collections

CHAPEL HILL, NORTH CAROLINA
Southern Historical Collection, Terry Sanford Papers

DURHAM, NORTH CAROLINA
Duke University Archives, Terry Sanford Papers
Duke University, Perkins Library Special Collections, Terry Sanford Papers

RALEIGH, NORTH CAROLINA
North Carolina Division of Archives and History; Official Papers of Governor W. Kerr Scott;
    Official Papers of Governor William B. Umstead; Official Papers of Governor Luther H.
    Hodges; Official Papers of Governor Terry Sanford

WASHINGTON, D.C.
National Archives, Unit Records of the 517th Parachute Regiment Combat Team

Interviews

BY AUTHORS
Ascher, William, April 23, 1998
Autry, George, October 2, 1995
Bennett, Bert, October 27, 1993; September 10, 1997
Beyle, Thad, September 6, 1996
Bubas, Vic, September 17, 1996
Bowles, Erskine, May 27, 1998
Boyle, William, April 18, 1996
Cannon, Hugh, August 10, October 16, and December 15, 1993; April 25, 1994
Carlton, J. Phillips, April 27, 1998
Cochrane, William McWhorter, May 17, 1995
Cooper, David, December 24, 1993
Cramer, Ted, October 25, 1993
DeVries, Walter, September 22, 1995
Drew, Tom, May 10, 1996
Ehle, John, October 27, 1993
Ellis, Thomas, October 14, 1997

Evans, Eli, January 26, 1996
Fleishman, Joel, March 22, 1996
Farris, Ray, July 10, 1995
Fraser, Donald, April 16, 1996
Freidlein, Ken, June 7 and October 10, 1996
Friday, William F., February 8, 1996; April 1, 1998
Fuqua, J. B., February 13, 1998
Garrison, William, May 7, 1996
Gergen, David, March 29, 1996
Graham, Jim, February 22, 1995
Green, William, March 17, 1995; December 8, 1997
Griffith, William, May 11, 1995
Groves, Harry, January 14, 1997
Herring, Dallas, February 10, 1996
Hillman, Jennifer, November 21, 1997
Hoving, John H. F., January 30, 1995
Huestis, Charles, March 30, 1993
Jenkins, Jay, October 18, 1993
Lambeth, Thomas, December 30, 1993; May 3, 1995
Levitt Jr., Arthur, February 12, 1998
Martin, Joe, March 15, 1995
Marsinko, John T., August 8, 1996
McCachren, William, April 11, 1995
McCormick, John, March 15, 1998
McCoy, Donald, November 17, 1993
McCoy, R. F., May 14, 1995
McKay, Martha C., March 6, 1996
McLean, Thomas, October 15, 1998
McMahon, Alex, January 11 and May 2, 1996
McNair, John L., January 5, 1996
McNair, Robert, June 8, 1996
McQueen, Wilma, December 19, 1995
Moore, John Henry, December 18, 1995
Morgan, Robert, February 8, 1995
Morton, Hugh, March 23, 1995
Newton, Clint, July 12, 1995
Parker, Roy Jr., April 23, 1996
Picado, Sonia, February 9, 1998
Phillips, J. Dickson, April 25, 1995; March 8, 1998
Poole, Sam, March 15, 1994; February 13 and June 19, 1996
Pritzker, J. B., October 11, 1995
Proctor, Samuel, May 1, 1996
Ragan, Sam, November 17, 1993
Rankin, Edward, December 7, 1993; January 27, 1994
Reese, Matthew A., January 17, 1996
Roberts, Gene, October 7, 1995
Rose, Charles III, January 17, 1996
Rose, Mary Glenn, August 15, 1996
Sanders, John, April 8, 1996
Sanford, Betsee, April 24, 1996
Sanford, Margaret Rose, September 7, 1995
Sanford, Mary, June 24, 1995
Sanford, Terry, January 14 and 27, August 18, October 5, November 16, December 29, 1993;

February 1 and 9, March 15, April 20, 1994; March 17 and May 14, 1995; April 22, May 26, December 10, 1997; January 9 and 24, February 26, March 18 and 24, 1998

Sanford, Terry Jr., February 26, 1996

Scheer, Julian, May 10, 1995

Scott, Robert W., May 7, 1998

Semans, James H., January 15, 1994; September 11, 1995

Semans, Mary, January 15, 1994; September 11, 1995

Smith, McNeill, April 17, 1996

Simpson, George, September 8, 1997

Staton, William, April 24, 1995

Swem, Dean L., May 22, 1995

Tindall, George, October 6, 1993

Thigpen, Richard, May 10, 1996

Vick, Marsha, August 18, 1998

Weaver, Stacy Jr., January 30, 1997

Whichard, Willis, August 24, 1998

Wilder, Roy, April 19, 1995

Wilhelm, Helen, June 24, 1995

Winters, John, May 4, 1995

Zaytoun, Joseph, June 23, 1998

Zaytoun, Thelma, June 23, 1998

DUKE UNIVERSITY PERKINS LIBRARY, SPECIAL COLLECTIONS
Sanford, Terry, January 24, 1995 (interview by William H. Chafe, Ole Holsti, William Ascher)

JOHN F. KENNEDY PRESIDENTIAL LIBRARY, BOSTON, MASSACHUSETTS
Brawley, H. W., December 19, 1964 (interview by Samuel C. Brightman)
Cohen, Wilbur J. Cohen, December 8, 1968 (interview by David McComb)
Dalton, John, June 28, 1967 (interview by Larry J. Hackman)
Dragon, Ed, March 26, 1976 (interview by William Hartigan)
Gravel, Camille Gravel, May 23, 1967 (interview by John Stewart)
Hodges, Luther H., March 19, 1974
Marshall, Burke Marshall, June 13, 1964 (interview with Anthony Lewis)
McGill, Ralph, January 6, 1966 (interview by Charles T. Morrissey)
Reese, Matthew A., October 24, 1964 (interview by William L. Long)
Sanders, Carl, May 22, 1967 (interview by John F. Stewart)
Sorenson, Theodore C., May 3, 1964 (interview with Carl Kaysen)
Sanford, Terry, July 27, 1970 (interview by Ann M. Campbell)

LYNDON BAINES JOHNSON PRESIDENTIAL LIBRARY, AUSTIN, TEXAS
Sanford, Terry, May 15, 1971 (interview by Joe B. Frantz)

SOUTHERN ORAL HISTORY PROGRAM, UNC-CHAPEL HILL LIBRARY
Ashmore, Harry, June 16, 1990 (interview by John Egerton)
Collins, Leroy, April 13, 1990 (interview by John Egerton)
Dabney, Virginius, March 5, 1990 (interview by John Egerton)
Daniels, Jonathan, March 22, 1972 (interview by Daniel Singal); March 9 and 11, 1977 (interviews by Charles Eagles)
Esser, George, June–August 1990 (interview by Fran Weaver)
Finlator, W. W., April 19, 1985 (interview by Jay Jenkins)
Fleishman, Joel, February 8, 1974 (interview by Walter DeVries and Jack Bass)
Graham, Frank P., June 10, 1962 (interview by Jonathan Daniels); June 10, 1962 (interview by Hank Patterson, James Wallace, and Joel Fleishman); June 11, 1962 (interview by Terry

Sanford); June 12, 1962 (interview by William Friday); June 12, 1962 (interview by Warren Ashby); June 9, 1972 (interview by Charles Jones, Anne Queen, and Stuart Willis)

Goodman, Raymond, June 14, 1989 (interview by B. Kalk)

Heard, Alexander, July 17, 1991 (interview by John Egerton)

Herring, Dallas, February 14, 1987 (interview by Jay Jenkins)

Jones, Graham, December 12, 1973 (interview by Walter DeVries and Jack Bass)

Lake, I. Beverly, September 8, 1987 (interview by Charles Dunn); March 31, 1992 (interview by Edward L. Harrelson)

McKay, Martha, November 20, 1974 (interview by Jack Bass); June 13, 1989 (interview by Kathryn Nasstrom)

McKissick, Floyd, December 6, 1973 (interview by Walter DeVries and Jack Bass)

Pearsall, Elizabeth, May 25, 1988 (interview by Walter Campbell)

Rankin, Ed, August 19–20, 1987 (interview by Jay Jenkins)

Sanford, Terry, August 20–21, 1976, December 16 and 18, 1986 (interviews by Brent Glass)

Scott, Ralph, April 22, 1974 (interview by Bill Finger and Jacqueline Hall)

Queen, Ann, April 30, 1976 (interview by J. Herzenberg)

White, Thomas J., May–June, 1985 (interview by Pamela Dean)

Newspapers

Charlotte Observer
Duke Chronicle
Durham Herald-Sun
Fayetteville Observer
Greensboro Daily News
Laurinburg Exchange
New York Times
News and Observer
Raleigh Times
Washington Post

Published Sources

Ambrose, Stephen E. *Citizen Soldier*. New York: Simon and Schuster, 1997.

Archer, Clark L., ed. *Paratroopers' Odyssey: A History of the 517th Parachute Combat Team*. Hudson, FL: 517th Parachute Combat Team Association, 1985.

Arnall, Ellis Gibbs. *The Shore Dimly Seen*. New York: Lippincott, 1946.

————, *What the People Want*. New York: Lippincott, 1947.

Ayers, Edward L. *The Promise of the New South: Life After Reconstruction*. New York: Oxford University Press, 1992.

Ayers, H. Brandt, and Thomas H. Naylor, eds. *You Can't Eat Magnolias*. New York: McGraw-Hill, 1972.

Badger, Anthony J. *North Carolina and the New Deal*. Raleigh: North Carolina Department of Cultural Resources, 1981.

Banner, Leslie. *A Passionate Preference: The Story of the North Carolina School of the Arts*. Winston-Salem: North Carolina School of the Arts Foundation, 1987.

Bass, Jack, and Walter DeVries. *The Transformation of Southern Politics: Social Change and Political Consequences Since 1945*. Athens: University of Georgia Press, 1976.

Bell, John L. Jr. *Hard Times: Beginnings of the Great Depression in North Carolina 1929–1933*. Raleigh: North Carolina Department of Cultural Resources, Division of Archives and History, 1982.

Black, Earl, and Merle Black. *Politics and Society in the South*. Cambridge, MA: Harvard University Press, 1987.

Branch, Taylor. *Parting The Waters: America in the King Years, 1954–63*. New York: Simon & Schuster, 1988.

Brodie, Keith, and Leslie Banner. *Keeping an Open Door: Passages in a University Presidency*. Durham, NC: Duke University Press, 1996.

Bulla, Ben F. *Textiles & Politics: The Life of B. Everett Jordan*. Durham, NC: Carolina Academic Press, 1992.

Cash, W. J. *The Mind of the South*. New York: Knopf, 1941.

Chafe, William H. *Civilities and Civil Rights: Greensboro, North Carolina, and the Black Struggle for Freedom*. New York: Oxford University Press, 1980.

Clancy, Paul R. *Just a Country Lawyer: A Biography of Senator Sam Ervin*. Bloomington: Indiana University Press, 1974.

Clay, James W., Douglas M. Orr, and Alfred W. Stuart. *North Carolina Atlas: Portrait of a Changing Southern State*. Chapel Hill: University of North Carolina Press, 1975.

Coates, Albert. *Bridging the Gap Between Government in Books and Government in Action*. Chapel Hill, NC: Professor Emeritus Fund, 1974.

———, *What the University of North Carolina Meant to Me*. Richmond, VA: William Byrd Press, 1969.

Cohodas, Nadine. *Strom Thurmond and the Politics of Southern Change*. New York: Simon & Schuster, 1993.

Cook, James F. *Carl Sanders, Spokesman of the New South*. Macon, GA: Mercer University Press, 1993.

Conant, James B. *My Several Lives: Memoirs of a Social Inventor*. New York: Harper & Row, 1970.

Corbitt, David Leroy, ed. *Public Addresses, Letters, and Papers of William Bradley Umstead, Governor of North Carolina 1953–54*. Raleigh, NC: Council of State, 1957.

———. *Addresses and Papers of Governor Kerr Scott*. Raleigh: North Carolina Department of Archives and History, 1953.

Covington, Howard. *Uncommon Giving: A. J. Fletcher and a North Carolina Legacy*. Raleigh, NC: A. J. Fletcher Foundation, 1999.

Crow, Jeffrey J., Paul D. Escott, and Flora Hatley Jr. *A History of African Americans in North Carolina*. Raleigh: North Carolina Division of Archives and History, 1992.

Daniels, Jonathan. *A Southerner Discovers the South*. New York: Macmillan, 1938.

———. *The End of Innocence*. New York: Lippincott, 1954.

———. *The Time Between the Wars*. Garden City, NY: Doubleday & Company, 1966.

———. *Tar Heels: A Portrait of North Carolina*. New York: Dodd, Mead & Company, 1947.

Daniels, Josephus. *Editor in Politics*. Chapel Hill: University of North Carolina Press, 1941.

Durden, Robert F. *The Dukes of Durham, 1865–1929*. Durham, NC: Duke University Press, 1975.

Egerton, John. *Shades of Gray: Dispatches from the Modern South*. Baton Rouge: Louisiana State University Press, 1991.

———. *Speak Now Against the Day: The Generation Before the Civil Rights Movement in the South*. New York: Knopf, 1994.

Ehle, John. *Dr. Frank: Life with Frank Porter Graham*. Chapel Hill, NC: Franklin Street Books, 1993.

———. *The Free Men*. New York: Harper & Row, 1965.

Eisler, Kim Isaac. *A Justice for All: William J. Brennan Jr. and the Decisions That Transformed America*. New York: Simon & Schuster, 1993.

Esser, George. *An Oral History of the North Carolina Fund*. Southern Historical Collection. University of North Carolina, Chapel Hill.

Eure, Thad. *North Carolina Manual, 1961*. Raleigh: North Carolina Secretary of State's Office, 1926.

Evans, Eli. *The Lonely Days Were Sundays: Reflections of a Jewish Southerner*. Jackson: University Press of Mississippi, 1993.

Farmer, James. *Lay Bare the Heart: An Autobiography of the Civil Rights Movement*. New York: Arbor House, 1985.

Fitzgerald, Gayle Lane. *Remembering a Champion*. Raleigh, NC: Edwards & Broughton, 1988.

Fletcher, A. L. *A History of Ashe County*. Jefferson, NC: Ashe County Research Association, 1963.

Frady, Marshall. *Jesse: The Life and Pilgrimage of Jesse Jackson*. New York: Random House, 1996.

Franklin, John Hope. *Reconstruction After the Civil War*. Chicago: University of Chicago Press, 1961.

Furgurson, Ernest B. *Hard Right: The Rise of Jesse Helms*. New York: Norton, 1986.

Goings, Kenneth W. *The NAACP Comes of Age: The Defeat of Judge John J. Parker*. Bloomington: Indiana University Press, 1990.

Golden, Harry. *For 2¢ Plain*. New York: World Publishing, 1959.

———. *Only in America*. New York: World Publishing, 1958.

Gunther, John. *Inside U.S.A.* New York: Harper & Brothers, 1947.

Halberstam, David. *The Fifties*. New York: Villard Books, 1993.

Hays, Brooks. *A Southern Moderate Speaks*. Chapel Hill: University of North Carolina Press, 1959.

Hobbs, Samuel Huntington Jr. *North Carolina: Economic and Social*. Chapel Hill: University of North Carolina Press, 1930.

Hobson, Fred, ed. *South-Watching: Selected Essays by Gerald W. Johnson*. Chapel Hill: University of North Carolina Press, 1983.

Hodges, Luther. *Businessman in the State House: Six Years as Governor of North Carolina*. Chapel Hill: University of North Carolina Press, 1962.

Ivey, A. G. "Pete." *Luther H. Hodges: Practical Idealist*. Minneapolis: T. S. Denison & Co., 1968.

Huneycutt, James E., and Ida C. Huneycutt. *History of Richmond County*. Raleigh, NC: Edwards & Broughton, 1976.

Jacobstein, Helen J. *The Segregation Factor in the Florida Democratic Gubernatorial Primary 1956*. Gainesville: University of Florida Press, 1972.

Kilpatrick, James Jackson. *The Southern Case for School Segregation*. N.p.: Crowell-Collier Press, 1962.

Knight, Douglas M. *Street of Dreams: The Nature and Legacy of the 1960s*. Durham, NC: Duke University Press, 1989.

Larkins, John R. *Patterns of Leadership Among Negroes in North Carolina*. Raleigh, NC: Irving-Swain Press, 1959.

Lemmon, Sarah McCulloh. *North Carolina's Role in World War II*. Raleigh: North Carolina Department of Cultural Resources, 1964.

Lennon, Donald R. and Fred D. Ragan, eds. *Politics, Bar and Bench: A Memoir of U.S. District Judge John Davis Larkins Jr.* N.p.: Historical Society of Eastern North Carolina, 1980.

Lesher, Stephen. *George Wallace: American Populist*. Reading, MA: Addison-Wesley, 1994.

Levitt, Arthur Jr., and Sonia Picado. *The Report of the International Commission for Central American Recovery and Development: Poverty, Conflict and Hope*. Durham, NC: Duke University Press, 1989.

Link, Albert N. *A Generosity of Spirit: The Early History of the Research Triangle Park*. Research Triangle Park, NC: Research Triangle Foundation, 1995.

Link, William A. *William Friday: Power, Purpose & American Higher Education*. Chapel Hill: University of North Carolina Press, 1995.

Luebke, Paul. *Tar Heel Politics: Myths and Realities*. Chapel Hill: University of North Carolina Press, 1990.

MacDonald, Charles B. *A Time for Trumpets: The Untold Story of the Battle of the Bulge*. New York: Morrow, 1984.

Martin, John Bartlow. *The Deep South Says "Never."* New York: Ballantine, 1957.

McCullough, David. *Truman*. New York: Simon & Schuster, 1992.

Meier, August, and Elliott Rudwick. *CORE: A Study in the Civil Rights Movement 1942–1968*. New York: Oxford University Press, 1973.

Mitchell, Memory F., ed. *Messages, Addresses and Public Papers of Terry Sanford, Governor of North Carolina, 1961–1965*. Raleigh: Council of State, 1966.

Morris, Willie, ed. *The South Today: 100 Years After Appomattox*. New York: Harper & Row, 1961.

Parramore, Thomas C. *Express Lanes and Country Roads: The Way We Lived in North Carolina, 1920–1970*. Chapel Hill: University of North Carolina Press, 1983.

Patterson, James T. *Grand Expectations: The United States, 1945–1974*. New York: Oxford University Press, 1996.

Patton, James W., ed. *Addresses and Papers of Governor Luther Hartwell Hodges*. Raleigh, NC: Council of State, 1960.

Pleasants, Julian M., and Augustus M. Burns III. *Frank Porter Graham and the 1950 Senate Race in North Carolina*. Chapel Hill: University of North Carolina Press, 1990.

Powell, William S. *The North Carolina Gazetteer: A Dictionary of Tar Heel Places*. Chapel Hill: University of North Carolina Press, 1968.

Ragan, Sam, ed. *The New Day*. Zebulon, NC: Record Publishing Co., 1964.

Roberts, Bruce, and Nancy Roberts. *The Governor*. Charlotte, NC: McNally and Loftin, 1972.

Sanford, Terry. *A Danger of Democracy: The Presidential Nominating Process*. Boulder, CO: Westview, 1981.

———. *But What About the People?* New York: Harper & Row, 1966.

———, *Outlive Your Enemies: Grow Old Gracefully*. New York: Nova Science Publishers, 1996.

———, *Storm Over the States*. New York: McGraw-Hill, 1967.

Sarratt, Reed. *The Ordeal of Desegregation*. New York: Harper & Row, 1966.

Schlesinger, Arthur M. Jr. *A Thousand Days: John F. Kennedy in the White House*. New York: Houghton Mifflin, 1965.

Schram, Martin. *Running for President 1976: The Carter Campaign*. New York: Stein and Day, 1977.

Semans, James H. *Siena: Six Summers of Music*. N.p.: Author, 1973.

Seymour, Robert. *Whites Only: A Pastor's Retrospective on Signs of the New South*. Valley Forge, PA: Judson Press, 1991.

Sharpe, Bill. *A New Geography of North Carolina*. Raleigh, NC: Sharpe Publishing, 1965.

Siegel, Frederick F. *Troubled Journey: From Pearl Harbor to Ronald Reagan*. New York: Hill and Wang, 1984.

Smith, Bob. *They Closed Their Schools*. Chapel Hill: University of North Carolina Press, 1965.

Snider, William D. *Helms and Hunt: The North Carolina Senate Race 1984*. Chapel Hill: University of North Carolina Press, 1985.

———. *Light on the Hill: A History of the University of North Carolina at Chapel Hill*. Chapel Hill: University of North Carolina Press, 1992.

Spence, James R. *The Making of a Governor: The Moore-Preyer-Lake Primaries of 1964*. Winston-Salem, NC: J. F. Blair Publishers, 1968.

U.S. Senate. *William Kerr Scott, Late a Senator from North Carolina*. Washington, DC: GPO, 1958.

Vandiver, Frank E., ed. *The Idea of the South: Pursuit of a Central Theme*. Chicago: University of Chicago Press, 1964.

Vickers, James, Thomas Scism, and Dixon Qualls. *Chapel Hill: An Illustrated History*. Chapel Hill, NC: Barclay Publishers, 1985.

White, Theodore H. *The Making of the President, 1960*. New York: Atheneum, 1961.

———. *The Making of the President, 1968*. New York: Atheneum, 1969.

———. *The Making of the President, 1972*. New York: Atheneum, 1973.

Wicker, Tom. *Facing the Lions*. New York: Viking, 1973.

Wilhoit, Francis M. *The Politics of Massive Resistance*. New York: George Braziller, 1973.

Wilson, Emily Herring. *For the People of North Carolina*. Winston-Salem: Z. Smith Reynolds Foundation, 1988.

Witcover, Jules. *Marathon: The Pursuit of the Presidency, 1972–1976*. New York: Viking, 1977.

Wooten, James. *Dasher: The Roots and the Rising of Jimmy Carter*. New York: Summit Books, 1978.

Zopf, Paul E. Jr. *North Carolina: A Demographic Profile*. Chapel Hill: The Population Center, 1967.

Index

Gardner, O. Max, 166, 209; conscripts Frank Porter Graham to be president of university, 29; gubernatorial campaign of 1928, 12; influence on Terry Sanford, 32–33, 244; initiatives during Depression, 16; Shelby dynasty, 95, 134
Gardner, O. Max Jr., 102–103, 105, 208–209
Garrett, Nathan, 332
Garrison, Bill, 384, 397
Gary, Kays, 164, 371
Gastonia Gazette, 255
Gavin, Robert, 239, 270
Geneen, Harold, 420
Gergen, David, 324–325
Gill, Edwin, 198, 262, 265, 305, 355
Gilmore, Voit, 40, 183–184
Glease, J. H. R., 138
Glendening, Parris, 294
Glenn, Buddy, 89
Glenn, James K., 263
Glenn, John, 492
Glover, Alice, 490
Golden Corral restaurant chain, 437
Golden, Harry, 113, 155, 173, 175, 193, 196
Goldsboro *News Argus*, 261
Goldwater, Barry, 358
Goodman, Larry, 430
Gordon, Eugene, 101, 103
Gore, Albert, 196
Gore, Al Jr., 468
Governor's School, 301–302, 304–305, 333
Grabarek, R. Wensell, 316, 323
Grace, Daddy, 233
Grady, Henry, 178
Graham, Edward Kidder, 27, 28
Graham, Frank Porter, 40, 56, 94, 126, 145, 147, 181, 312, 392; appointed to U.S. Senate, 101; becomes president of university, 28–29; campaign for U.S. Senate, 102–109, 110, 117, 126, 448; and Capus Waynick, 322; influence on Terry Sanford, 38, 108, 158, 204, 226–227, 244, 287, 326, 349, 381, 484; opposition to Graham presidency, 30–31; politics of, 28–29; postwar UNC president, 85–91, 95; proponent of student government, 31, 47; and Senate race of 1954, 128, 129, 130; Southern Conference on Human Welfare, 90
Gramm–Rudman–Hollings deficit-reduction law, 467
Grandfather Mountain, 491
Graves, Rupert D., 67
Gray, Garland, 148
Gray Areas Programs, 303
Green, Bill, 379, 406, 413, 422, 430, 455, 408, 501
Green, Paul, 157
Greensboro Daily News, 182, 193, 205, 255, 270, 297
Greensboro Record, 205
Grieder, William, 414
Grier, Joe, 98
Griffith, Andy, 372, 392
Groves, Harry, 159–160
Guillory, Ferrel, 460
Gulf War, 483–490

Hackley, Lloyd ("Vic"), 491
Hall, Elmer, 384
Hall, Sam J., 90
Hamilton, Luther, 260
Hammocks Beach State Park, 277
Hamner, Clay, 437
Hanks, Nancy, 369
Harrell, Jacqueline, 298
Harriman, Averill, 195
Harrington, Anthony, 404
Harrington, James, 451
Harris, Fred, 363, 412
Harris, Lou, 205, 215, 219, 234, 272
Harvard University, 294, 421
Harvey, Brantley, 412
Hatcher, Tom, 93
Hatfield, Mark, 450
Hawfields Presbyterian Church, 181
Hawkins, Reginald, 319, 406
Haynie, Hugh, 193
Hay Street Methodist Church, 191
HeadStart, 331
Heald, Henry, 302–303, 328, 371
Heard, Alexander, 33, 40
Heflin, Howell, 496
Hefner, Bill, 439
Helms, Jesse, 107, 115, 126, 319, 409, 438, 445, 447, 465, 472, 483, 509
Henderson, Archibald, 28
Henderson, David, 101
Herbin, Sarah, 345
Herndon, George B., 213
Herring, Dallas, 169, 246–247, 308, 355
Hewlett, Addison, 198
Hickman, Harrison, 445, 489, 491
Higbee, Edward, 304
High Point Enterprise, 96
Hill, Anita, 496

Howard E. Covington Jr. is a writer and former journalist.
During his years as a reporter for the *Charlotte Observer* his
work won many honors including the newspaper's Pulitzer
Prize for Public Service in 1981. His previous books include
Belk: A Century of Retail Leadership, *Linville: A Mountain Home
for 100 Years*, and *Uncommon Giving: A. J. Fletcher and a North
Carolina Legacy*. Marion A. Ellis is a freelance writer who was
also a member of the Pulitzer Prize-winning team at the
Charlotte Observer. He is the author of a number of books,
including *Working Together: The Sheltons of North Carolina* and
The Meaning of Honor: The Life of Frank H. Kenan. In addition,
Covington and Ellis are coauthors of *NationsBank: Changing
the Face of Retail Banking*.

Library of Congress Cataloging-in-Publication Data
Covington, Howard E., Jr.
Terry Sanford : politics, progress, and outrageous ambitions /
Howard E. Covington, Jr. and Marion Ellis.
p.   cm.
Includes bibliographical references and index.
ISBN 0-8223-2356-7 (cloth : alk. paper)
1. Sanford, Terry, 1917–1998.   2. Governors—North Carolina
Biography.   3. North Carolina—Politics and government—
1951-   4. College presidents—North Carolina Biography.
5. Duke University Biography.   6. Legislators—United States
Biography.   7. United States. Congress. Senate Biography.
I. Ellis, Marion A.   II. Title.
F260.42.S26C68   1999
975.6′043′092—dc21   99-26289   [B]   CIP